Essential Papers on
the Psychology of Aging

ESSENTIAL PAPERS IN PSYCHOANALYSIS
General Editor: Leo Goldberger

Essential Papers on Borderline Disorders / Edited by Michael H. Stone, M.D.

Essential Papers on Object Relations / Edited by Peter Buckley, M.D.

Essential Papers on Narcissism / Edited by Andrew P. Morrison, M.D.

Essential Papers on Depression / Edited by James C. Coyne

Essential Papers on Psychosis / Edited by Peter Buckley, M.D.

Essential Papers on Countertransference / Edited by Benjamin Wolstein

Essential Papers on Character Neurosis and Treatment / Edited by Ruth F. Lax

Essential Papers on the Psychology of Women / Edited by Claudia Zanardi

Essential Papers on Transference / Edited by Aaron H. Esman, M.D.

Essential Papers on Dreams / Edited by Melvin R. Lansky, M.D.

Essential Papers on Literature and Psychoanalysis / Edited by Emanuel Berman

Essential Papers on Object Loss / Edited by Rita V. Frankiel

Essential Papers on Masochism / Edited by Margaret Ann Fitzpatrick Hanly

Essential Papers on Short-Term Dynamic Therapy / Edited by James E. Groves, M.D.

Essential Papers on Suicide / Edited by John T. Maltsberger, M.D. and Mark J. Goldblatt, M.D.

Essential Papers on Obsessive-Compulsive Disorder / Edited by Dan J. Stein, M.B., and Michael H. Stone, M.D.

Essential Papers on Addiction / Edited by Daniel L. Yalisove

Essential Papers on the Psychology of Aging / Edited by M. Powell Lawton and Timothy J. Salthouse

Essential Papers on
the Psychology of Aging

Edited by

M. Powell Lawton

and

Timothy A. Salthouse

NEW YORK UNIVERSITY PRESS
New York and London

NEW YORK UNIVERSITY PRESS
New York and London

Library of Congress Cataloging-in-Publication Data
Essential papers on the psychology of aging / edited by M. Powell
Lawton and Timothy A. Salthouse.
p.   cm. —(Essential papers in psychoanalysis)
includes bibliographical references and index.
ISBN 0-8147-5125-3 (hardcover : alk. paper). —ISBN 0-8147-5126-1
(pbk. : alk. paper)
1. Adulthood—Psychological aspects.   2. Aging—Psychological
aspects.   3. Maturation (Psychology)   I. Lawton, M. Powell
(Mortimer Powell), 1923–   . II. Salthouse, Timothy A.
III. Series.
BF724.5E88   1998   98-1220
155.67—dc21   CIP

New York University Press books are printed on acid-free paper,
and their binding materials are chosen for strength and durability.

Manufactured in the United States of America

10   9   8   7   6   5   4   3   2   1

Contents

Introduction

M. Powell Lawton and Timothy A. Salthouse

This volume deals with the period of development that begins with young adulthood and ends with old age and death. When New York University Press raised the possibility of a volume of this type, both of us were immediately enthusiastic about the project because of a shared belief that the most important articles in the psychology of aging should be made available in a more accessible form.

Our first and most important task was to identify publications that might be considered classics in the field of the psychology of aging. Because we did not want to rely exclusively on our own biases for this determination, we solicited nominations of major or "classic" articles from approximately fifty prominent researchers working in the field of psychology and aging. Nearly everyone to whom we wrote responded with several suggestions, and we are very grateful to them for helping us select what we believe are among the most influential articles in our field.

Although much of the material treats the full period of human development in theory, childhood and adolescence are not included in the selections except as they are assumed as part of the life span. This collection deals basically with modern gerontology. Prescientific and historical attempts to shed light on adult development, we suggest, belong in a work dealing explicitly with the history of gerontology. Therefore, the development of academic psychology after World War I provides a rough beginning point. Because the literature in the field has expanded so rapidly, a considerable number of the selections date from the last twenty-five years, although others date back to as early as 1920.

We tried to cover the psychology of adult development and aging in as representative a manner as possible. Although we included theoretical writings and overviews of substantive areas, we saw it as most important to feature empirical research reports that have been influential in setting new directions for theory and research. We feel that the logical progression of the process of scientific inquiry is best portrayed by including such seminal research reports, even if the concepts and methods used in some of them have been superseded by later advances.

Nonetheless, it must be recognized that this decision to focus on individual research reports excluded many genuine classics, especially noteworthy chapters from books whose influence on the growth of gerontology was major. In particular, we recommend the pace-setting *Handbook of Aging and the Individual* (Birren, 1959) and the later product of the American Psychological Association's first Task Force on Aging, organized by Carl Eisdorfer (Eisdorfer & Lawton, 1973). A model of multidisciplinary research for all time was the National Institute of Mental Health's *Human Aging* (Birren et al., 1963).

Unfortunately, in order to keep the volume to a manageable size, we had to make a number of very difficult choices because there were many more candidates than could be accommodated in the available space. In making our choices, we tried to emphasize integrative and innovative articles. Furthermore, as was often the case, when there were several candidates by the same author, we attempted to select those that were most representative of the individual's contributions. The majority of selections are from peer-reviewed journals, but a few chapters from edited books are also included.

Although the elegance of the scientific method is apt to be displayed best in laboratory research directed toward basic psychological issues, the contributions of psychological inquiry to the solution of problems associated with human aging have also been major. Therefore, we felt it important to include applied and clinical research as well as more basic research.

We have arranged the selections in four thematic parts: Theory, Basic Psychological Processes, Social Psychology and Personality, and Clinical and Applied Issues. Each part has a brief introduction intended to place the selections in a broader context.

We hope readers will find this collection valuable. We believe its contents are among the most influential articles on the psychology of aging.

REFERENCES

Birren, J. E. (Ed.) (1959). Handbook of aging and the individual. *Chicago: University of Chicago Press.*

Birren, J. E., Butler, R. N., Greenhouse, S. W., Sokoloff, L. & Yarrow, M. (1963). Human aging. *Public Health Service Publication No. 986. Washington, D.C.: National Institute of Mental Health.*

Eisdorfer, C. & Lawton, M. P. (Eds.) (1973). The psychology of adult development and aging. *Washington, D.C.: American Psychological Association.*

PART 1

Theory

Introduction

Timothy A. Salthouse and M. Powell Lawton

Only five chapters are included in the first part. Nevertheless, we believe that each of these selections has been extremely influential in changing the way researchers think about psychological aging, as well as the way they investigate it.

James E. Birren was one of the first experimentally oriented researchers to consider seriously the possibility of a broad and integrative perspective on psychological aging. Selecting which of his many publications, beginning in the late 1940s, best represents his perspective was difficult. We ultimately chose the 1970 *American Psychologist* article because it summarizes a substantial portion of his research and reflects his joint emphasis on synthesis and analysis. It is also a very rich source of hypotheses and preliminary data relevant to a number of contemporary issues, such as the universality of cognitive decline, the role of speed in age-cognition relations, and the role of experience in optimizing an individual's level of competence.

A number of writers have pointed out that development is not simply attributable to endogeneous or maturational changes within the organism (e.g., Dewey, 1939; Kuhlen, 1940). K. Warner Schaie was the first to outline systematically a methodological approach to allow different types of influences to be distinguished. Although relatively few studies have been conducted employing the sequential designs advocated by Schaie, virtually all researchers in psychological gerontology now recognize that factors external to the individual also need to be considered as influences on development. This seminal article therefore had a major impact not only in introducing a new perspective on development, but also in inspiring later generations of researchers to think more carefully about the meaning of development at all stages of the life span.

The disengagement theory of Elaine Cumming and William E. Henry represented a true alloy of sociology and psychology. Their 1961 book *Growing Old* is a well-written and complete statement of the view that the aging period of life represents a mutual withdrawal of society and older person, one which fosters a pathway to both self-enhancement and preparation for death. Cumming and Henry were very clear that the pattern of disengagement was both normative and positive, and that failure to disengage, by either society or the person, led to stress and psychological ill health. The brief summary by Henry presented in this volume sketches the main features of the theory, together with some reflections on its impact a few years after it was advanced. Their original book should definitely be read as the only full treatment of the richness of the theory, however. Disengagement theory has often been characterized as "discredited." As of 1997, this is an overstatement. A more tempered view is represented in the thoughtful rejoinder to disengagement theory provided by the originators' colleagues, Robert J. Havighurst, Bernice L. Neugarten, and Sheldon S. Tobin. They clearly do not discredit the theory at all. They simply put it in its place as a creative analysis of social psychological domains that describes some people in some situations extraordinarily well. We can agree with Havighurst and colleagues by questioning the universality of disengagement while still respecting the many strengths of that theory.

One of the most influential contemporary researchers in the psychology of aging is Paul B. Baltes. He has had a large impact particularly in his efforts to encompass both child development and aging or adult development into a single life-span perspective. His contribution to this volume illustrates his holistic approach to studying cognition, motivation, and personality, which stands in contrast to the isolated manner in which these topics are usually investigated. This selection also summarizes several of the theoretical distinctions introduced by Baltes and his colleagues that have been valuable in clarifying—and in some sense, redirecting—thinking in the field (e.g., different conceptualizations of cohort, classification of types of developmental influences, the notions of plasticity and testing-the-limits). It is probably still too early to determine whether the life-span perspective will become the dominant paradigm in developmental psychology, but a large number of contemporary researchers agree with many of the "propositions" described in this chapter as assumptions of the life-span perspective.

REFERENCES

Cumming, E. & Henry, W. E. (1961). Growing old: The process of disengagement. New York: Basic Books.

Dewey, J. (1939). Introduction. In E. V. Cowdry (Ed.), Problems of aging. Baltimore: Williams and Wilkins.

Kuhlen, R. G. (1940). Social change: A neglected factor in psychological studies of the life span. School and Society, 52, 14–16.

1. Toward an Experimental Psychology of Aging

James E. Birren

Wɪᴛʜ ᴛʜᴇ ᴘᴀssᴀɢᴇ of time the human organism is changed as a result of biological, psychological, and social influences. Some of these influences are amenable to experimentation, but most are not as yet. The psychologist often must resort to descriptive studies to gain clues about the basis of some of the most profound changes we undergo as individuals and as members of a species. While studies of identical twins as children have become part of the literature of psychology, more recently studies of one-egg twins over the age of 65 have been reported. Similarities are observed in the psychological and biological changes in one-egg twins late in life. Photographs of such twins taken throughout their life span indicate remarkable persistence of resemblance while also showing the transformations of aging (Kallmann & Jarvik, 1959). In a similar way, one can see in the pictures evidence of differences in dress which represents cultural change. One also has the impression that within the range of cultural change, the individuals have selected age-appropriate dress. Were one able to hear samples of the speech of these individuals corresponding to the various phases of the life span pictured, their word choices would very likely reflect contemporary culture and age-appropriate word choice since our word choices reflect the idioms and colloquialisms of the periods through which we live and suggest to our listeners how old we are. The studies of identical twins by Kallmann and Jarvik, and their subsequent follow-up, indicate that there are inherited characteristics of likely length of life, cause of death, and persistence of twin resemblances in measured intellect. Beyond the involvement of our academic egos in the question of whether there is late life change in intellectual function, there is clearly a broad range of problems of considerable scientific importance.

These thoughts suggest a developmental psychology that would partition the variance over the life span as being due to our common heredity as living substance, what we share with other mammals and primates, our special heredity as a species, our unique heredity as individuals within the species,

Reprinted by permission from *American Psychologist* 25 (1970): 124–35. Copyright © 1970 by the American Psychological Association.

cultural differences, generational differences, and even the accumulation of experience in a unique period of history such as a war, a depression, or a golden age.

The title of this chapter is meant to imply the desirability of an experimental psychology of aging as a goal toward which we can work. An experimental psychology of aging would attempt to reproduce the changes in individuals associated with chronological age by manipulation of the independent variables. If, for example, one entertains the major hypothesis that a particular intellectual ability changes with age in adults because of disuse, then one can attempt to raise the level of the ability by increasing its use in selected adults. Two aspects of the disuse hypothesis should be tested, one being that diminished function is associated with disuse, and the other is that the diminished function resulting from lack of use *is* or *is not* reversible. By analogy, diminished physiological function may be associated with undernutrition in the adult, however a dietary deficiency of many years' duration may have consequences that are not simply reversible by reestablishing an adequate diet. Irreversible deficit states in humans are not easily studied.

Several reasons are pertinent to the suggestion that the development of an experimental psychology of aging will be a slow process. One is not privileged to experiment with many of the characteristics of the human environment, particularly with those that may result in permanent or relatively permanent effects. The value we place on the integrity of an individual human life does not allow us to manipulate many relevant aspects of the environment, and to study a relationship one must resort, as we have in child development, to naturally occurring experiments and using analogues in animal experiments.

There seems to be no intrinsic reason why lawful generalizations are not as easily obtained from the study of aging as of early life phenomena, except for the practical fact of the span of time involved. This, however, defines the second of two reasons why an experimental psychology of aging will be slow to develop, that is, the great length of time involved, and closely related difficulty and cost of establishing suitable study populations.

The college sophomore, a particularly favored subject for study by the academic psychologist, has perhaps lived only one-quarter of his life at the time he is studied. An individual who has survived to age 20 could, quite likely, reach the age of 80. Having lived only one-quarter of his life span by age 20, the subject may not yet have had sufficient time to demonstrate latent genetic influences or defects, deficits resulting from maternal disease and diet during pregnancy, childhood diseases and diet, let alone the effects of child-rearing practices and the different learning socializing effects on adults of ethnic and peer groups. Late life outcomes of early life influences are very important and very difficult to study.

One of the characteristic animals for laboratory investigations is the white rat, usually studied at about the age of three to nine months. Someone interested in late life outcomes of early experience using the rat would have to wait over two years for the animal to achieve a ripe old age. One is also faced with the additional expense of maintaining the animals for the life span. Any attempt to study what appear to be important influences, including pathology, over the life span necessarily requires establishing a life-span control group. Only a few investigators are able to subsidize the cost of life-span experiments in animals. A new animal resource has been created in the life-span colony of beagles maintained at the Colorado State University. The initial problem for research was to determine the effects of radiation on mammals, and the beagle was selected. Since some of the effects of radiation do not appear early, it is necessary to maintain the dogs over long periods of the life span. One can only judge deviance in early development and in aging by having a clearly established reference population studied over the life span.

While practical reasons slow dramatic progress, the science seems to be moving toward an experimental psychology of aging or, more properly, toward a comprehensive developmental psychology that embraces the entire life span.

SOME LONGITUDINAL DATA ON INTELLECTUAL FUNCTIONS

Many observers have noted that investigators tend to study readily available captive populations, often in institutions. This is often true of school children and indeed of older adults as well. In 1963, my colleagues and I studied a small number of community residents—men all over the age of 65—in an effort to get an estimate of the capacities of older independently living individuals. In the study there were 47 men all over the age of 65, average age 72 years. The survivors were measured again five years later, and again six years later (Birren, 1968). Of considerable interest to me is the strange distribution of change in these men with time. Differences in scores on such standardized tests as the Raven Progressive Matrices and the Wechsler Adult Intelligence Scale show some aged individuals as having slight or no decrements while still others show dramatic declines in scores. While the sample is not large, the nonnormality in the distribution of change beginning to be reported on older adults is provocative of a tentative hypothesis. That is, that change in intelligence in late life, as measured by conventional techniques, is not normally distributed. It may show little or no change in some healthy men in the seventh, eighth, and ninth decades of life, while concurrently individuals, possibly comprising a subpopulation suffering erosion of health, may show dramatic decline related to their likelihood of survival.

If changes in measured intelligence are part of a process of primary biological aging, every individual would be expected to show some change during the second half of life. The fact that some individuals beyond the age of 70 show large changes and others show none at all suggests that the terminal or near terminal phases of the life span can be accompanied by unique and relatively rapid or precipitous changes in individuals when their health fails. The importance of this is one of establishing our concept of ourselves in old age. There is the possibility that the psychological norm for the species is one of little change in intellectual functions in the years after 65, given good health. Chronic diseases of later life, particularly those involving cardiovascular disease and cerebral insufficiency, can, of course, result in an appreciable number of the population showing marked decline in intellectual function with age, but such need not be accepted as the norm for the species. Thus one of the implications of the study on the elderly men was that some of the higher cognitive processes measured by standard intelligence tests were more related to the health status of the individual than to chronological age. In contrast to intellectual measurements, however, the slowness observed in perceptual and motor tasks seems more intimately associated with chronological age than with health status. The role of speed and timing in cognitive processes of the older adult is far from explained (Birren, 1964, chap. 5). One may, in fact, reverse the usual equation and regard slowness of behavior as the independent variable that sets limits for the older adult in such processes as memory, perception, and problem solving (Birren, Riegel & Morrison, 1962).

AGE DIFFERENCES IN RESPONSE TIME TO VISUAL TASKS

One of my long-standing interests in research has been that of explaining the slowness of behavior seen in adults after middle age. In this regard, I will point out some implications of the relations of response time, and task difficulty, in young and elderly subjects. In one of the earliest experiments that

Botwinick and I (1965) conducted on this topic, we varied the difference between two lines, requiring a judgment as to which was the shortest. In 1906, Henmon reported an elegant experiment in which he found that the time required to make a judgment as to which of two lines was the shorter varied with the amount of the difference between the two lines. Our study was an attempt to test the hypothesis that the increased response time shown by older adults lies in the difficulty of perceiving the stimulus to which they are to respond. If this were so, older adults should show a relatively greater increase in speed of judgment as stimuli are made easier to judge. In the experiment, subjects were required to simply say right or left, indicating the side of the smaller of two lines presented tachistoscopically. The variable line differed from the standard by 1–50%. The work confirmed the report of Henmon for young subjects but found a displaced curve for older adults.

It can be seen from Figure 1.1 that the judgments of older subjects slow down more when the difference between the two line lengths is less than 15%. Beyond 15% the difference in response time is roughly a constant. These data can be related to the question of whether the older subjects *want* more time or *need* more time to make perceptual judgments. The data would seem to answer yes to both parts of the question in the sense that when the perceptual judgments become difficult, in this case less than 15% difference in line length, elderly adult subjects would appear to require more time to respond. On the other hand, above a 15% difference there is no systematic variation. In this range, the data may suggest that older individuals want more time to respond.

The basic condition of the experiment was such as to present the lines to be judged for two seconds. This is longer than the subjects required to respond, thus the subjects had ample time to view the stimulus before responding. A subsequent experiment (Botwinick, Brinley & Robbin, 1958) not only used a two-second exposure but also a shorter exposure time of .15 seconds, which is less time than it takes even the fastest subject to respond.

Under the shortened exposure time, both young and elderly subjects speeded up their responses. However, the largest reductions in time were for the older group for the most difficult discriminations. It is worthwhile to note that under the two-second exposure time, both elderly and young subjects maintained the same percentage of accuracy. The median accuracy for both groups was 100% correct judgment for 2% or greater difference in line length, and at 1% difference the accuracy diminished to 88% accuracy. However, when the exposure time was reduced to .15 seconds, the median accuracy for the elderly subjects dropped to 62% for the 1% line length

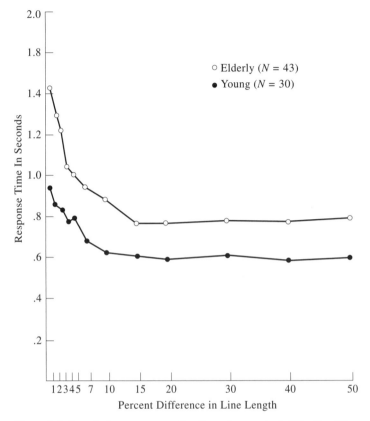

Figure 1.1. Speed of response as a function of perceptual difficulty. (The ordinate represents the vocal response time in judging pairs of lines. The abscissa represents the percentage of difference in the two line lengths being judged as to which was the shorter, "right" or "left." The line graph connects the successive mean values for the two age groups of subjects: young = 19 to 36 years; elderly = 61 to 91 years. From Birren and Botwinick, 1955.)

difference and 88% for the young subjects (elderly subjects, 65–79 years; young subjects, 18–35 years; N was 24 and 36, respectively).

These data clearly indicate that both elderly and young subjects are not at their limit of response time at a two-second exposure time, even maintaining a very high criterion of accuracy. When the duration of the stimulus is reduced to .15 seconds, both young and elderly subjects reduced their accuracy of response. The experiment did indicate that even for difficult discriminations, a considerable decrease in time to make the judgments could be brought about by reducing the exposure duration, and that this decrease does not seem to take place at a greater relative expense of accuracy. This suggests that the evidence lies on the side of the older person taking more time but not requiring more time to make difficult judgments. The effect of a brief stimulus may be to somehow drive or induce a state of need to respond more quickly than the usual self-pacing of the subject. It should be noted, however, that the elderly "driven" subject at short exposures does not respond as quickly as young subjects at long exposures. The age difference in response time was about two-tenths of a second for a two-second exposure. Under the conditions of short exposures the age difference in time to respond was reduced to .15 seconds. Considering the major results of this study the data would seem to lie outside the range of explanations offered by the perceptual difficulty hypothesis or the cautiousness hypothesis as to why older subjects are slow in their judgments.

The conditions of the two previous experiments led Rabbitt and Birren to conduct another experiment on the same topic, but using a broader range of conditions. Also, the decision was made to use circles of varying diameter as stimuli, believing that they would provide a more uniformly judged stimulus than line lengths. A broader range of exposure intervals (from .05 to 2.0 seconds) was used than in the previous experiments, and the exposure interval was randomized together with the percentage difference in stimuli. The experiment of Botwinick et al. (1958) first exposed all stimulus cards at two seconds and then followed it with the second study in which the same subjects judged the stimuli at exposure of .15 seconds. Furthermore, in the analysis of the data, we analyzed separately the times to respond for correct and incorrect judgments. As in the previous experiments, both young and old subjects are slow in their judgments when the percentage difference in the two stimuli was small. Figure 1.2 shows the rise in response time as a function of percentage difference in circle diameters. These data have also been analyzed with respect to the means of the minimum and maximum response times for old and young subjects (see Figure 1.3). If one examines the data with respect to response times of correct or incorrect judgments, the aged appear to be slower in their response times when they are making errors.

One of the important conditions varied systematically was the exposure time. Exposure time was varied randomly from the two seconds in the earliest experiments down to one-twentieth of a second. Figure 1.4 shows that there was not a very dramatic following of response time in relation to the exposure duration. This lack of relationship held for both the correct and incorrect responses for both young and elderly subjects. The results of the experiment

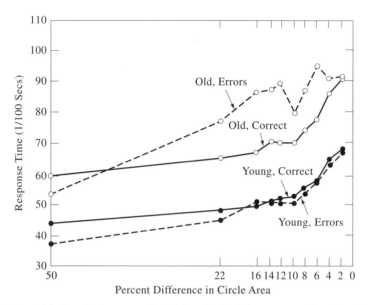

Figure 1.2. Speed of response in judging circle differences as a function of percentage of difference in circle area. (Circles were presented tachisto-scopically, and the subject was required to say "right" or "left" according to the side of the smaller circle. Response times are given in means of correct and incorrect judgments. Young subjects, 20, were between 17 and 29 years. Old subjects, 13, were over 60 years. Older subjects made sig-nificantly more errors; however they commit fewer errors than young sub-jects for easy discriminations and more errors for difficult discriminations. From J. E. Birren and P. M. A. Rabbit, Speed of perceptual judgment as a function of age, exposure interval and difficulty. Unpublished manuscript.)

differ from those obtained by Botwinick et al. (1958), in which they found a relationship between two exposure intervals of two seconds and .15 sec-onds, when the subjects were run through a long series at each level. To me this implies that the subjects could develop a set to respond quickly, given brief exposures, and maintain it over a long series of judgments (see Brinley, 1965). That is, there is a "driving effect" of a short stimulus on both young and elderly subjects, but only if one has a sufficient number of short stimuli so as to develop an expectation. In explaining why older subjects tend to be slow in response, one may invoke a set explanation, or a forcing of response by short duration stimuli, but only if there is a sufficiently large number of stimuli so the subject can develop an expectation. In general one must return

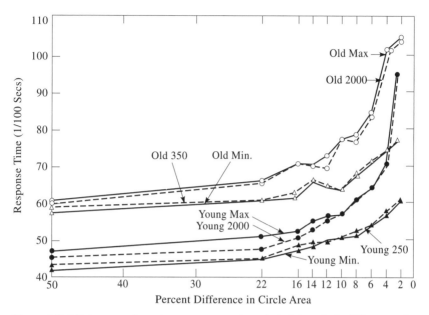

Figure 1.3. Minimum and maximum response times in judging circle differences for young and old subjects. (Also plotted are the exposure time data for both groups at 2000 milliseconds and young at 250 milliseconds and old at 350 milliseconds. "Optimal" exposure duration is shorter for young than for old. From J. E. Birren and P. M. A. Rabbitt, Speed of perceptual judgment as a function of age, exposure interval and difficulty. Unpublished manuscript.)

either to the explanation of the slowness in terms of perceptual difficulty of input, or a generalized slowing yet beyond our concepts or explanation.

In young subjects there is clearly no evidence that the exposure time is influencing their correctness of response or modifying in any important way their speed of judgment. With old subjects one sees a slight tendency for errors to occur for somewhat slow responses to short exposure times. Their correct responses are not faster to short exposure times. Considering the total phenomena of the slowness of judgments in older subjects, I would submit that only a small portion of the variance has been explained by the concept of a cautious reaction to perceptual difficulty or to the driving effects of stimulus duration. In brief, then, the major variance to be accounted for in the slowness of responses of older subjects remains to be explained.

It is quite possible to conceive of experiments that would attempt to partition the large and important age variance neurophysiologically, that is, to

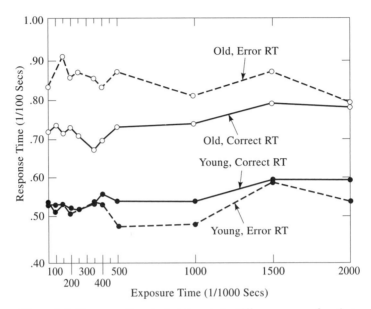

Figure 1.4. Response time in judging circle differences as a function of exposure interval. (Data are given separately for speed of correct and incorrect judgments. Each subject made a total of 1,100 discriminations presented in balanced order for difficulty and exposure interval. From J. E. Birren and P. M. A. Rabbitt, Speed of perceptual judgment as a function of age, exposure interval and difficulty. Unpublished manuscript.)

attempt to find out where in the nervous system the additional time is required in the older subjects (see Hicks & Birren, 1970). However, there are still some useful experiments to be done at the phenomenal level, using psychological variables. Craik (1969) has suggested that older subjects demand a high degree of sensory information before committing themselves to a response. This would appear to be a variation of the cautiousness hypothesis. Using a signal detection theory approach, Craik thought that the judgment criterion would become relatively higher for the older subjects as they were allowed additional time. In the present experiment, additional time in a sense was allowed them by the wide range of stimulus durations. They did not exercise the option, however, of taking more time to make judgments when given long duration stimuli. While the cautiousness of older persons may be slowing their responses, it is not an adequate explanation to account for the majority of the time required in the responses of older subjects in these experiments.

Subsequent to the previous experiment, I adapted the approach of varying the stimulus difficulty to a card-sorting task that students could use in a laboratory demonstration (Birren & Phillips, n.d.). That is, decks of cards, like playing cards, were printed that had on them two circles of varying diameters. Subjects were asked to sort the decks of cards according to the side of the card on which the smaller of two circles appeared. Each card bore a standard circle and a variable smaller circle that might appear on the left-hand or the right-hand side. As a further test of the hypothesis of cautiousness in elderly subjects (in explaining the age difference in response difference time), there was included a deck of cards on which the two circles were of equal diameter.

In the card-sorting experiment, subjects were given decks consisting of 20 cards each. For any given deck of 20 cards the difference between the two circles was constant, although the side of the smaller circle was varied randomly on the left or right. The decks of cards were randomized with respect to size, so that there was no regular progression for differences in the size of the differences of the circles being judged. However, as indicated, included in this random order of decks was a deck in which there was no objective difference in circle size. This was presented to the subjects with no indication

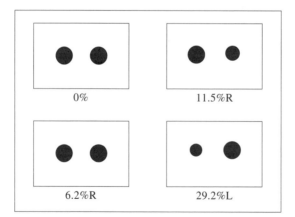

Figure 1.5. Illustration of cards sorted by subjects according to the side of the smaller circle. (Cards were approximately 2 ¼ × 3 ⅜ inches. Beneath each card is given the percentage of difference in circle diameters. From J. E. Birren and S. L. Phillips. Age differences in card sorting as a function of stimulus difficulty. Unpublished manuscript.)

that it was departing from the expectation that there was a real difference to be judged. The cautiousness hypothesis would lead one to expect older subjects to become very slow in the judgment of which side was the smaller circle, when, in fact, there was no difference between the circles, that is, a card of maximum stimulus difficulty or stimulus ambiguity. Surprisingly enough, the inclusion of the card with circles of no difference did not present any problem of resistance on the part of the subjects. That is, they accepted it as part of the sequence and sorted them, although occasionally with remarks that these were indeed very difficult to judge. In fact, when I was being tested by a student demonstrator, I found that I would sort the pack of zero difference with the feeling that, indeed, there were some differences, when I knew one of the decks had no difference. If one looks at the card of equal circle size (Figure 1.5), subjectively one has the impression of spontaneous variations in the size of the circles.

As one looks at a card, the circles seem to possess differences, and one, in sorting through a series of cards, will find that the circles of no difference will show left to right variations in a smaller circle. This is, perhaps, but

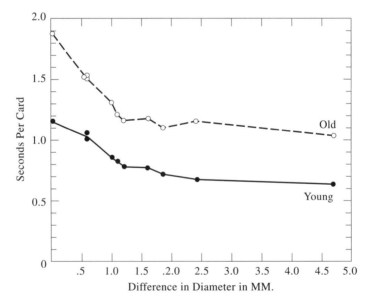

Figure 1.6. Mean card-sorting time for young and old subjects as a function of the difference in circle diameters. (Multiple points plotted at 0.5 millimeter difference are repeated values for these decks. From J. E. Birren and S. L. Phillips. Age differences in card sorting as a function of stimulus difficulty. Unpublished manuscript.)

another demonstration that perception is a dynamic process. If indeed, older subjects have a great need or desire for reducing stimulus ambiguity, they should reject such cards by lengthening markedly their response times. Figure 1.6, however, shows that the average sorting time per card, while it varies with the differences in diameter, shows no marked rise when the card of zero difference is sorted. It is as though the performance is in continuity with the determinants of judgments elsewhere in the sorting tasks. One might, of course, maintain the position that while older subjects are more cautious in their judgments, such an experiment is a trivial test since the consequences of judgments are unimportant. But if so, it still qualifies the extent to which cautiousness in making judgments is a general tendency on the part of the older adult.

ACTIVATION AND NEURAL NOISE

The general tendency for older adults to be slow in their responses can be attacked through a test of two alternative hypotheses. One is that it takes longer for signals to be discriminated because the older nervous system is noisy (Crossman & Szafran, 1956). Alternatively the older nervous system may be in a less activated state so that any stimulus yields a slower response. Essentially the neural noise hypothesis holds that with age the nervous system becomes increasingly noisy, such that the signal to be discriminated must be discriminated against a higher background noise. The reduction of the signal-to-noise ratio thus means that longer time is taken, for example, for perception of input information. The picture is one of a constantly active nervous system into which signals arrive to be discriminated against a level of background neural activity. Random firing of neurons would constitute a limiting factor in all signal recognition. Contributing to an increase in noise with age might be a hyperirritability of cells, and also prolonged aftereffects on brain cells following stimulation. Aftereffects of previous stimulation would constitute noise for subsequent stimulation or signals. Another hypothesis which attempts to explain the slowness of discrimination and response, which I favor, does not emphasize that the signal is competing with a higher background noise level, but rather that the signal itself is weak due to a less excitable nervous system. An attempt was made recently in our laboratory at the University of Southern California to test the two hypotheses. The doctoral dissertation of Dwight Jeffrey (1969) involved the performance of old and young adult subjects on a visual discrimination task. The response was a rapid movement of a finger. Control conditions were the ambient light and

noise level of the building. The experimental conditions were those of increased muscular tension or auditory white noise. Under one experimental
condition, the subject held a constant 20% of his maximum weight in his left
hand while making responses with his right hand. Under the other condition,
a 75-decibel white noise was presented to the earphones of the subject while
he performed the task. The experimental conditions were thought to result in
slower performance of elderly subjects if the neural noise hypothesis was
true. That is, tension and auditory white noise should result in greater slowness on the part of the older adult. In contrast, the activation hypothesis would
predict that the performance of the older subject would improve under conditions of muscular tension and white noise. Neither of the hypotheses was
supported by the results. Instead, the almost classical results were obtained
that older subjects are significantly slower in discrimination tasks than young
subjects, and that the time difference between the two age groups grows with
increasingly complex discrimination tasks (Jeffrey, 1969).

NEW RESEARCH AREAS

The hypotheses tested by Dwight Jeffrey may also be examined by lowering
ambient stimulation. That is, old and young subjects can be placed in environments where the visual and auditory stimulation is reduced. The neural
noise hypothesis suggests that older adults will improve their performance
relatively more when ambient stimulation is reduced. The activation hypothesis, on the other hand, would hold that older subjects will slow down relatively more under conditions of reduced ambient stimulation. There is, of
course, the possibility that the kind of relative sensory deprivation or activation one is attempting to study in older adults is not readily reversible in
hours but may require days to shift.

Other approaches to research on the slowness of behavior with age can
also be undertaken, using recordings of the latencies of evoked potentials in
response to visual or auditory signals. Such latencies could help to indicate
something of the cortical timing involved in the older nervous system. Where
one finds significant differences with age in the latencies of such potentials,
one could explore more directly the effects of chronic or short-term stimulation.

The laboratory rat is still a useful experimental animal with which to study
some problems of aging. Some time ago it was established that the old rat
also showed a slowness in responses with advancing age. Such slowness was
not reversible with practice although susceptibility to fatigue was (Kay &

Birren, 1958). For the more physiologically minded, it is possible with such animals to implant electrodes in a further effort to partition the slowness or the additional time required by the older nervous system.

At the human level, considerable important experimental work remains to be done. Following the lead of Rabbitt, for example, there is more to be learned about the conditions of slowness of older adults when irrelevant information is introduced into the stimulus and when errors are made (Rabbitt & Birren, 1967). A question to be answered is whether the older subject is more distractible to irrelevant information because he cannot maintain vigilance to an assigned task, or whether some other factor accounts for the fact that older subjects may find difficulty in responding to increasing amounts of information in a stimulus display.

The scientific importance of this line of experimentation lies in its contribution to our understanding of the nature of the altered functioning of the nervous system with age. A practical outcome of the experimentation lies in its potential for indicating the conditions of optimum learning for the older adult and for the optimum utilization of stored experience. I have not commented here about some of the subjective aspects of performance and the reasons why older adults change in their life contentment and goals that may bear on their performance. Such have been, and can be, the topics for objective study eventually leading to experimental testing of alternative hypotheses.

The widespread evidence of slowness of behavior with advancing age will no doubt continue to be studied as a dependent variable in relation to other things we can manipulate. On the other hand, slowness of behavior with age, since it appears somewhat independently of disease and a wide range of environmental circumstances, may be used as an independent variable in studying other processes. If, with age, there is a change in the speed with which the central nervous system can mediate responses, it would, in fact, limit not only the speed with which information could be acquired from the environment, but also the speed of retrieval of relevant stored memories, and the likelihood of combining these effectively in new perceptions, novel hypotheses, and complex motor responses. Several studies of adult intelligence have shown that vocabulary scores tend to rise with adult age. Concurrently, however, speed of performance on a decoding task declines with age. This suggests the rather common sense hypothesis that with age one's experience grows, but the speed of manipulation of this experience declines. An important hypothesis should be tested that with advancing age, over the adult years, one enlarges one's unit of information by concept formation. Thus, by grouping past experience under new abstractions, one's previous "bits" can become "chunks," if you like—so that while one grows older, one may process fewer units of information per unit time, but the "chunks" become larger, and thereby effectiveness in an environment may stay the same if not improve. Some exploratory data obtained from interviews with middle-aged men and women would seem to fit this tentative hypothesis and may lead to more designed experimental investigations (Birren, 1969). Subjects between the ages of 30 and 60 years were interviewed around the significant areas of their current life, family, career, health, participation in organizations and clubs, and relations to time. The number of interviews varied from subject to subject from one to six interviews, with the interviews varying in length from one and a half to two hours. Commonplace were reports of reduced energy for carrying out all the tasks associated with being middle aged. One of the important qualities of the interviews was the evidence that the subjects had evolved goals that extended over much of their life span and had evolved various strategies in relation to achieving these goals. Preliminary analysis of the interviews led to the isolation of statements that had the properties of strategies. Subjects appeared to be aware of the fact that when they were younger, they reacted differently to situations and people. The changes imply to me a greater level of abstraction with age. Apparently competent individuals project ahead a tentative plan for action over a several year period, and in relation to these plans use various broad strategies and individual tactics to advance toward their goals. Interestingly enough, despite the opinions of contemporary young adults, middle-aged adults view themselves as increasingly allowing others to behave autonomously, delegating responsibility, and having a direct approach. It is most interesting, although tangential to the present line of thought, that the middle-aged adult is acutely aware of the extent to which he needs others, including the young, and how much of his time is given to planning to raise individuals to positions of authority, responsibility, and autonomy.

While middle-aged and older adults seem to be increasingly aware of the limitations of their performance, and frequently in their energy and health, they do seem to be increasingly effective in their careers by virtue of the abstractions and strategies they form. While in one sense they are processing less information in the same situations than they did when they were younger, they also appear to deal with more significant information, since they are looking for crucial issues according to the abstractions they have formed. By grouping their experiences, the information load placed on the aging adult may be therefore less than on the young adult.

Study of the cognitive strategies used by older persons may be a very promising line of research particularly if one can isolate the strategies used by productive, competent adults. It is possible that such strategies and related tactics could be transmitted verbally. It is, however, questionable whether abstract strategies derived through experience can be transmitted effectively to younger adults without their having at least some of the intervening experience that led to the formation of the strategies. The concept of evolving cognitive strategies and tactics over the adult life span is, at minimum, a useful addendum to qualifying the results of our measuring instruments that purport to measure intelligence in the adult. The level of component capacities may be less critical in the adult than are the strategies that the individual uses in the deployment of these capacities. For example, interviews with physicians and lawyers reveal a strategy of protecting themselves from cognitive overload or affective overload by not becoming as involved with clients as they did in the earlier years of their practice. This again suggests that the older professional is reducing the total information while concentrating on more crucial information.

A question many of us would like to answer at this stage is whether man's effectiveness for decision changes over the life span. We do not know very much about the conditions that give rise to optimum development and maintenance of man's capacity for making the decisions in a complex and changing society. Guilford (1969) reviewed the relations of decision making to age and discussed the various types of decisions that face individuals. Altered perception and capacity of the aging nervous system for dealing with the wide range of input of information and complexities may influence the type of decisions reached. Any particular hypothesis should be tempered by recognition of the point of departure of the investigator, that is, whether he is analyzing perception, intellectual processes, learning and memory, psychomotor skills, or the evaluation of brain deficits. One can place side by side contemporary hypotheses regarding behavioral changes associated with aging as being due to changes in set, disuse, interference of previous learning, retrieval mechanisms, increased neural noise, brain damage, reduced activation, psychosocial disengagement; to some extent these and other hypotheses may be all partially correct, since they tend to apply only to the function of a subsystem of the organism (Birren & Hess, 1968; Heron & Chown, 1967; McFarland, 1969; Welford, 1969).

EPILOGUE

This article began with the title "Toward an Experimental Psychology of Aging." To some extent, the title contains an exhortation much like the admonition to "sin less," or "why can't a woman be more like a man?" I did this to suggest that we should strive against difficulties to manipulate the variables we think cause the major effects we identify with aging. While in the scientific domain I lean toward the encouragement of an experimental science of aging, I also am aware of the fact that many of the psychological regularities or transformations in humans as they age may not be amenable to experimental study. We can, with some profit, take example from a nonexperimental science and note its progress—that of astronomy. Descriptive astronomy for many centuries gathered information about the motions and periodicities of astronomic bodies. Subsequently physical astronomy developed with a concern with the causes or explanations of these regularities. It proposed explanations and laws subject to empirical study. It is interesting to note, however, that the verification of such laws did not involve experimental science. A parallel set of explanations to those of physical astronomy about the causes of the regularities observed in astronomy was that of astrology. Further, a demoniac interpretation of events of the human life span would stand like the relation of astrology to physical astronomy. A descriptive psychology of aging could lead to a demonology, and fads, or it could lead to the development of natural science. In order for the psychology of aging to be part of natural science, it need not always be experimental at this relatively early stage of its progress. Naturally occurring order and regularity can be observed prior to attempts to manipulate experimentally. While striving toward an experimental psychology of aging, we should not rush ahead so quickly that we find ourselves having worked elegantly on the trivial. We need not be faced with the dilemma of either working elegantly on the trivial, or inelegantly on great issues. Rather, it would seem we should encourage a descriptive and analytical psychology of aging while striving toward experimental control of the major causes of aging.

There are many sequences and rhythms to the psychological elements of the human life span to be studied. Pursuit of the understanding of the elements of human life span has, in my opinion, three values: cultural, scientific, and practical.

REFERENCES

Birren, J. E. The psychology of aging. *Englewood Cliffs, N.J.: Prentice-Hall, 1964.*

Birren, J. E. *Increments and decrements in the intellectual status of the aged.* Psychiatric Research Reports, *1968, 23, 207–214.*

Birren, J. E. *Age and decision strategies. In A. T. Welford & J. E. Birren (Eds.),* Decision making and age. *Basel: S. Karger, 1969.*

Birren, J. E. & Botwinick, J. *Speed of response as a function of perceptual difficulty and age.* Journal of Gerontology, *1955, 10, 433–436.*

Birren, J. E. & Hess, R. D. *(Eds.) Influences of biological, psychological and social deprivations upon learning and performance. Chap. 2. In,* Perspectives on human deprivation. *United States Department of Health, Education and Welfare. Washington, D.C.: Government Printing Office, 1968.*

Birren, J. E. & Phillips, S. L. *Age differences in card sorting as a function of stimulus difficulty. Unpublished manuscript, n.d.*

Birren, J. E., Riegel, K. D. & Morrison, D. F. *Age differences in response speed as a function of controlled variations of stimulus conditions: Evidence of a general speed factor.* Gerontologia, *1962, 6, 1–18*

Botwinick, J. & Birren, J. E. *A follow-up study of card-sorting performance in elderly men.* Journal of Gerontology, *1965, 20, 208–210.*

Botwinick, J., Brinley, J. F. & Robbin, J. S. *The interaction effects of perceptual difficulty and stimulus exposure time on age differences in speed and accuracy of response.* Gerontologia, *1958, 2, 1–10.*

Brinley, J. F. *Cognitive sets, speed, and accuracy of performance in the elderly. In A. T. Welford & J. E. Birren (Eds.),* Behavior, aging, and the nervous system. *Springfield, Ill.: Charles C Thomas, 1965.*

Craik, F. I. M. *Applications of signal detection to studies of aging. In A. T. Welford & J. E. Birren (Eds.),* Decision making and age. *Basel: S. Karger, 1969.*

Crossman, E. R. F. W. & Szafran, J. *Changes with age in the speed of information intake and discrimination.* Experientia Supplementum, *1956, 4, 128–135.*

Guilford, J. P. *Intellectual aspects of decision making. In A. T. Welford & J. E. Birren (Eds.),* Decision making and age. *Basel: S. Karger, 1969.*

Henmon, V. A. C. *The time of perception as a measure of differences in sensation.* Arch. Psychol., *1906, 14.*

Heron, A. & Chown, S. M. Age and function. *London: J. & A. Churchill, 1967.*

Hicks, L. H. & Birren, J. E. *Aging, brain damage, and psychomotor slowing.* Psychological Bulletin, *1970, 74, 377–396.*

Jeffrey, D. W. *Age differences in serial reaction time as a function of stimulus complexity under conditions of noise and muscular tension. Unpublished doctoral dissertation, University of Southern California, 1969.*

Kallmann, F. J. & Jarvik, L. F. *Individual differences in constitution and genetic background. In J. E. Birren (Ed.),* Handbook of aging and the individual. *Chicago: University of Chicago Press, 1959.*

Kay, H. & Birren, J. E. *Swimming speed of the albino rat.* Journal of Gerontology, *1958, 13, 378–385.*

McFarland, R. A. *The sensory and perceptual processes in aging*. In K. W. Schaie *(Ed.)*, Theory and methods of research on aging. *Morgantown: West Virginia University, 1969.*

Rabbitt, P. M. A. & Birren, J. E. *Age and responses to sequences of repetitive and interruptive signals*. Journal of Gerontology, *1967, 22, 143–150.*

Riegel, K. F. & Birren, J. E. *Age differences in associative behavior*. Journal of Gerontology, *1965, 20, 125–130.*

Welford, A. T. *Age and skill: Motor, intellectual and social*. In A. T. Welford & J. E. Birren *(Eds.)*, Decision making and age. *Basel: S. Karger, 1969.*

2. A General Model for the Study of Developmental Problems

K. Warner Schaie

I‌T IS THE PURPOSE of this paper to examine various research designs in developmental psychology with a view to resolving some of the contradictory findings reported in studies employing different designs for the investigation of aging effects. In the course of this examination it is proposed to identify certain inherent inadequacies of the conventional longitudinal and cross-sectional approaches. It will be shown that these methods are merely special cases of a general model for research on behavior changes over time. The underlying assumptions of this model will be explicated and several new and more powerful research strategies will be developed.

Kessen (1960), in his excellent discussion of research designs for developmental problems, suggested that the investigation of simple age functions is naive and proposed that most meaningful designs involve either the interaction of age and environmental changes or the analysis of age functions in special populations. Only in passing did he mention the even more typical case where aging interacts simultaneously with differences in population and environment. Special cases may, of course, be derived where one or the other dimension is ignored. While such analyses may be useful and perhaps often present the only available practical approaches, their limitation must be noted and their relation to the general model well understood.[1]

Kessen proposed that in any developmental problem age-function relationships can be established by cross-sectional study in instances where it is possible to segregate subpopulations across the age range being investigated. He also suggested, however, that studies of variables showing small but reliable changes, the analysis of sequences and of rates of change, and the follow-up of early behaviors which are not found in the repertory of older organisms will usually require the longitudinal approach. It will be shown that such distinctions do *not* apply to the general case and that their appli-

Reprinted by permission from *Psychological Bulletin* 64, no. 2 (1965): 92–107. Copyright © 1965 by the American Psychological Association.

cation to special cases has often been the result of misunderstood assumptions.

What then are the attributes of a general developmental model from which both cross-sectional and longitudinal methods can be derived and from which their relationship can be clarified? A beginning may be made with Kessen's formulation that "a characteristic is said to be developmental if it can be related to age in an orderly or lawful way." Proceeding further, Kessen's most general definition of a response in a developmental model will be accepted. In this context he specified that a response may be seen as being a function of age, special population, and environment. Such a formulation will be made even more general, however, by recasting its content in terms which will be found more fruitful for further analysis.

The component of "age" will, of course, remain the central ingredient, but it will be more precisely defined to mean the age of the organism at the time of occurrence of the response to be measured. Even more precisely, age will refer to the number of time units elapsed between the birth (entrance into the environment) of the organism and the point in time at which the response is recorded.

The component of "special population" will be replaced by the term "cohort." This term will imply the total population of organisms born at the same point or interval in time. Restrictions as to the nature of the population and the latitude in defining the interval in time designated as being common to a given cohort will, of course, be introduced by the special assumptions appropriate to the problem to be investigated.

The term "environment" will be replaced by the concept of *time of measurement*. In a most general sense the investigator is not really concerned with describing the nature of the total environment but rather with indexing the total environmental impact as occurring at a given temporal point. Such an index of the state of the environment is clearly provided by indicating the time of measurement (see Kuhlen, 1940).

Our general developmental model will now hold that a response is a function of the age of the organism, the cohort to which the organism belongs, and the time at which measurement occurs. It will shortly be seen that these three components are by no means independent. Their confounding, in fact, dictates the methods available for their separate and joint analysis.

Consider next the temporal boundaries of the general developmental model. If the human life-span is assumed to be bounded by a 100-year limit, one can specify the total time required to measure all cohorts at all ages. The time required is simply twice the absolute life-span of the populations under

Table 2.1. Ages of 20-Year Cohorts at 20-Year Intervals for Cohorts Available to an Investigator in 1960

Time of birth	Age										
1860	0	20	40	60	80	100	—	—	—	—	—
1880	—	0	20	40	60	80	100	—	—	—	—
1900	—	—	0	20	40	60	80	100	—	—	—
1920	—	—	—	0	20	40	60	80	100	—	—
1940	—	—	—	—	0	20	40	60	80	100	—
1960	—	—	—	—	—	0	20	40	60	80	100
Time of measurement	1860	1880	1900	1920	1940	1960	1980	2000	2020	2040	2060

study. Table 2.1 gives an example, where cohorts have 20-year intervals and measurements are taken also at 20-year intervals, for a total developmental study of a population existing in 1960. It will be seen that this model permits, over its total 200-year span, several independent longitudinal studies but only one cross-sectional study which includes members of all cohorts under investigation. Note that only half the model can be studied unless retrospective measures are available, or unless a future study is planned to begin with the cohort born at the first time of measurement.

Although the complete model can be studied with short-lived organisms, it will generally be most interesting to work with all the cohorts available at any given point of measurement. A general developmental model will therefore be described which will hold for that part of the complete life-span of the population which we wish to investigate. To give this model general applicability it is required that each age level be investigated for each cohort and at each time of measurement within the confines of the model.

GENERAL DEVELOPMENTAL MODEL

An example of a complete model is depicted in Table 2.2, which gives the ages of cohorts studied over the age range from 5 to 9 years, measured at annual intervals. In general, if the intervals at which a given characteristic is to be measured are called times of measurement (T), then $2T - 1$ cohorts with interval latitude equal to the time interval will be required for a study of the complete model.

Let us assume for the moment that the characteristics to be investigated

Table 2.2. Ages of Cohorts Measured at Five Ages with Annual Measurement Intervals

Time of birth	Ages								
1951	9	—	—	—	—	—	—	—	—
1952	8	9	—	—	—	—	—	—	—
1953	7	8	9	—	—	—	—	—	—
1954	6_e	7	8	9	—	—	—	—	—
1955	5_f	6_g	7	8	9	—	—	—	—
1956	—	5_h	6_i	7_k	8	9	—	—	—
1957	—	—	5_j	6_l	7	8	9	—	—
1958	—	—	—	5_a	6_b	7	8	9	—
1959	—	—	—	—	5_c	6_d	7	8	9
Time of measurement	1960	1961	1962	1963	1964	1965	1966	1967	1968

may be found only at the times of measurement and for the cohorts (Cs) listed in Table 2.2. Let us also assume that scores for an independent random sample of each of the cohorts are available at each of the measurement times. Let us further assume that all groups have had equal amounts of practice on the characteristic to be measured. One of the striking features of Table 2.2 is the fact that it is impossible to measure all cohorts at all ages or to obtain measures for all ages at each time of measurement. The model can, however, be sectioned horizontally (as indicated by the line in Table 2.2) to obtain a subset containing measures at all ages for all cohorts. Similarly, by vertical sectioning a subset can be obtained for which all ages are measured at all times of measurement. This means that age is always confounded with either differences between cohorts or with differences between times of measurements. In the general model, it is possible to estimate age changes confounded in either manner, depending upon the question we are interested in, or, as will be shown, one can obtain estimates of net age differences whenever certain assumptions are tenable.

Examining Table 2.2, it can readily be seen that differences in mean scores between columns in the vertically sectioned subset will represent differences in time of measurement, that is, differences due to commonly experienced environmental variables or changes in cultural context. Likewise, the differences in row means in the horizontally sectioned subset will represent differences between cohorts; that is, the effect of different life experiences previous to the time of measurement or genetic changes from one cohort to the next. For each subset it is possible also to compare means for the diagonals. Differences between means here involve age differences, which are controlled for time of measurement but confounded with cohort differences in the vertical subset, and controlled for cohort differences but confounded with time of measurement differences in the horizontal subset.

A clearer understanding of the implications of the model may be obtained by deriving the various methods therefrom for the study of developmental change. These include the conventional cross-sectional and longitudinal approaches as well as a third, frequently overlooked but equally important, method which will be identified as the time-lag method.

Relation of the General Model to Conventional Designs

Each of the first five columns in Table 2.2 represents an example of the conventional *cross-sectional* method. The hypothesis to be investigated simply asks whether there are differences in a given characteristic for samples drawn from different cohorts (i.e., born at different times) but measured at the same time. This is an important question, particularly for the student of individual differences. Age differences in behavior at a given point in time may require differential procedures regardless of the antecedent conditions responsible for these differences. It must be recognized, however, that age differences in the cross-sectional design are inextricably confounded with cohort differences and that it is therefore unreasonable to expect that the difference between Cohorts i and j at Time k will have anything to do with the difference between the mean score of Cohort i at Time k and its mean score at Time l. The fact that the temporal interval in years of birth between Cohorts i and j is identical to the temporal interval between Times k and l for Cohort i is quite coincidental and irrelevant. It is conceivable that the difference in means between a group of 5-and 10-year-olds could be representative of the difference between the mean for the 5-year-olds at age 5 and the mean at age 10 if there were no shifts in the environment and content of our culture. But man's environment does change, and projections over time based on cross-sectional studies are therefore fraught with great hazard.[2]

Let us next look at the last five rows in Table 2.2. These rows represent the most general case of the *longitudinal* method, that is, independent random samples of the same cohort drawn at successive times of measurement representing different ages.[3] The hypothesis to be investigated here asks whether there are differences in a given characteristic for samples from the same cohort measured at different times. This question is concerned with the effect of age differences within the same population and must be asked whenever one is concerned with predicting age differences in behavior over time. Longitudinal age differences, however, are obviously confounded with time differences. In cross-sectional studies, great risks are taken if one attempts to generalize age differences from one time of measurement to another. In the longitudinal design, it is for the same reasons equally risky to generalize age differences over time from one cohort to another. Personality theorists interested in developmental problems have traditionally been willing to take this risk, typically in the special case where the same sample is measured repeatedly. It will be shown, however, that such risk is a needless one which can be avoided by more efficient designs.

A third method of developmental analysis is suggested also by the general model. It is not generally recognized but should be of particular interest to the social psychologist. This is the method of *time-lag* illustrated by the diagonals in Table 2.2. The hypothesis here is concerned with asking whether there are differences in a given characteristic for samples of equal age but drawn from different cohorts measured at different times. This is a research design which should be used whenever the investigator is interested in the effect of cultural change upon the performance of individuals of similar age. Again, this effect cannot be measured directly due to its confounding with cohort differences.

Methods for Separating Sources of Developmental Change

It will now be shown that the general model may be used to generate model which make it possible, given certain assumptions, to separate the three sources of developmental change. Several definitions will be required for this purpose:

1. Cohort difference (Cd) = the net effect of differences between a younger cohort, C_i, and an older cohort, C_j, for random samples of subjects controlled for the effect of age and time of measurement; that is, net changes between generations.
2. Time difference (Td) = the net effect of differences between an earlier time of measurement, T_k, and a later time of measurement, T_l, for random samples of subjects, controlled for the effect of age and cohorts; that is, net changes within the environment.
3. Age difference (Ad) = the net effect of maturational change (over

time) from a younger age, A_m, to an older age, A_n, between random samples of subjects controlled for the effect of cohorts and times of measurement; that is, net age changes within the organism.

Next, let us define the three methods of measuring change over time, which we have deduced from the general model, as consisting of the following additive components: (*a*) Cross-sectional difference (CSd) = age differences plus cohort differences (CSd = Ad + Cd; (*b*) Longitudinal difference (LOd) = age differences plus time differences (LOd = Ad + Td); (*c*) Time-lag difference (TLd) = time differences plus cohort differences (TLd = Td + Cd). Transposing and changing signs, it can be shown that:

$$Ad = CSd - Cd, \qquad [1]$$

$$Cd = TLd - Td, \qquad [2]$$

$$Td = LOd - Ad. \qquad [3]$$

It can also be shown by substitution that the following relationships will hold; Substituting Formula 3 into Formula 2, and Formula 2 into Formula 1 will yield

$$Ad = CSd - [TLd - (LOd - Ad)]. \qquad [4]$$

Removing parentheses, collecting terms, and solving for *age difference*, it is then found that

$$Ad = \frac{CSd - TLd + LOd}{2}. \qquad [5]$$

Similarly, substituting Formula 1 into Formula 3, and Formula 3 into Formula 2, we obtain

$$Cd = TLd - [LOd - (CSd - Cd)]. \qquad [6]$$

Again removing parentheses, collecting terms, and solving for *cohort difference*, it is found that

$$Cd = \frac{TLd - LOd + CSd}{2}. \qquad [7]$$

Finally, substituting Formula 2 into Formula 1, and Formula 1 into Formula 3, it may be found that

$$Td = LOd - [CSd - (TLd - Td)].$$ [8]

Solving Formula 8 for *time difference*, it is then shown that

$$Td = \frac{LOd - CSd + TLd}{2}.$$ [9]

Unfortunately, it is not possible to compute these net effects for the general model as a whole, since equal representation cannot be obtained for all parameters. As indicated above, one can either measure all cohorts at all possible measurement times with unequal representation of ages, or one can measure all cohorts at all ages with unequal representation of measurement dates; or lastly, all ages can be measured at all measurement times with unequal representation of cohorts. This restriction is not severe, however, since it is in most cases virtually impossible to obtain successive independent random samples over the life span of all cohorts in a given population.

While it is impossible to separate the sources of variance associated with developmental change for the total model, such unconfounding can readily be effected for any set of samples for which independent estimates of each of the three developmental components are available. With respect to age and cohort differences this will be true for any subset or subsets containing a minimum of two cohorts; independent random samples from which are measured at two ages. It can also be accomplished with respect to age and time differences for subsets with a minimum of two ages; independent random samples of cohorts representing these ages being measured at two times. Moreover, unconfounding can be effected with respect to time and cohort differences for subsets consisting of at least two cohorts which are measured at least twice.

The minimal subset which can be subjected to complete analysis is indicated in the group which is enclosed by a triangle in Table 2.2, since it includes all the minimal combinations specified above. Depending on the generalization intended, it will therefore usually be most economical either to measure at least two cohorts many times or to measure many cohorts at least twice. If a third cohort or measurement occasion is added, moreover, further checks on one's assumptions become possible.

To summarize, the above considerations show clearly that it becomes possible to unconfound the sources of developmental change as soon as one begins to analyze simultaneously two or more behavior sequences. In view of the obvious advantage of obtaining unconfounded measures of age changes, it follows that sequential strategies should be preferred to the conventional longitudinal and cross-sectional methods in most instances. Appropriate sequential strategies will next be discussed in detail; first, for the case of independent samples, and then for the special case of repeated measurements.

COHORT-SEQUENTIAL METHOD

Whenever the subset of samples to be examined contains measures for all cohorts measured at all ages, it may be concluded that it is the investigator's intention to generalize over cohort differences. Such a design samples cohort differences at many times within the life span of the cohorts. This design will be referred to as the *cohort-sequential* method since longitudinal sequences for two or more cohorts are examined simultaneously. The cohort-sequential method permits inferences as to age changes at all points of the age range covered and, also, inferences about cohort differences at all ages. The two bottom rows of Table 2.2 are an example of a typical cohort-sequential design.

The entries in Table 2.2 which have been labeled *a, b, c,* and *d* represent the minimum case for this type of analysis. The questions which can be answered in the illustrative minimum case are as follows:

What is the net age change over one time unit (year) at age 5 (as sampled by Cohorts 1958 and 1959)?

Substituting the appropriate cell labels from Table 2.2 into Formula 5, it may be shown that

$$\text{Ad} = \frac{(c-b)-(c-a)+(c-d)}{2} = \frac{a-b+c-d}{2}.$$

Or, in general, what is the net age change from age m to age n as sampled for cohorts i and j?

$$\text{Ad}_{\text{CS}} = \frac{C_i A_m - C_i A_n + C_j A_m - C_j A_n}{2} \qquad [10]$$

The estimate of the net age difference is obtained by averaging age differences for two successive cohorts measured over successive time intervals.

What is the net cohort difference on a given variable between Cohorts 1958 and 1959 (as sampled at ages 5 and 6)?

Substituting into Formula 7, it will be shown that

$$Cd = \frac{(c-a)-(c-d)+(c-b)}{2} = \frac{c+d-a-b}{2}.$$

Or, in general, what is the net cohort difference between Cohorts i and j, sampled at ages m and n?

$$Cd_{cs} = \frac{C_j A_m + C_j A_n - C_i A_m - C_i A_n}{2} \qquad [11]$$

This estimate averages cohort differences at two ages measured over two successive time intervals.

What is the interaction between age and cohort differences (attributable to and confounded with time of measurement differences)?

Substituting into Formula 9, it is found that

$$Td = \frac{(c-d)-(c-b)+(c-a)}{2} = \frac{b+c-a-d}{2}.$$

Or, in general, what is the average net change per time unit for Cohort i at age m and Cohort j at age n?

$$Td_{cs} = \frac{C_i A_n + C_j A_m - C_i A_n - C_j A_m}{2} \qquad [12]$$

This estimate averages cohort differences irrespective of, and controlling for age level in order to obtain a time difference. It is necessarily confounded as it is impossible to measure two different cohorts of the same age at the same time of measurement.

The analysis of variance may be used to provide a test of significance of the net differences in the cohort-sequential design. Table 2.3 illustrates the re-

Table 2.3. Analysis of Variance for the Cohort-Sequential Model

Source of variation	Degrees of freedom
Between cohorts (C)	$C-1$
Between ages (A)	$A-1$
Cohort $\times$ age interaction	$(C-1)(A-1)$
Error	$N^a-(C)(A)$
Total variation	$N-1$

[a] Number of observations.

lationships described above in the analysis of variance context. It may be noted that increasing the number of successive times of measurement for all cohorts will extend the age range for which cohort differences can be evaluated, while increasing the number of sequences would augment the number of cohorts over which age differences can be generalized.

The cohort-sequential design is clearly the method of choice when a test of the generalizability of constructs over different generations (cohorts) is required. It will be noted that this design controls for cohort differences which might be attributable to genetic changes at all ages and that the cohort differences are controlled for age differences. But it is not possible in this design to identify an unconfounded time difference component. This means that *the cohort-sequential method will yield unambiguous results only when the assumption is met that changes in the variable under study are unrelated to cultural change.*[4] This assumption is rarely met except in the study of physical attributes or in investigations involving infrahuman organisms. Even when this assumption is met, it is as difficult to obtain an ample coverage of the life span of the organism in this variant as in the single-cohort or repeated measurement longitudinal design. Moreover, it will be seen that the cohort-sequential method will provide no more accurate estimates of age differences than do the more efficient alternative procedures.

TIME-SEQUENTIAL METHOD

The first alternative procedure to be advocated is called the *time-sequential* method and applies whenever the subset of samples under examination contains measures of all ages at all times of measurement. The time-sequential method permits inferences as to age differences at all points of the age range covered, as well as inferences about time differences (or cultural shifts) at all ages. The first two columns of Table 2.2 give an example of a typical time-sequential design.

The entries in Table 2.2 which are labeled e, f, g, and h represent the minimum case for time-sequential analysis. The propositions which can be evaluated for the illustrative case are as follows:

What is the net age change over one time unit (year) at age 5 (as sampled at Measurement Times 1960 and 1961)?

Substituting the cell identifiers from Table 2 into Formula 5, it is found that

$$Ad = \frac{(f-e)-(f-h)+(f-g)}{2} = \frac{f+h-e-g}{2}.$$

Or, in general, the net age change from age m to age n as sampled at Times k and l is given by

$$Ad_{TS} = \frac{T_k A_m + T_l A_m - T_k A_n - T_l A_n}{2}. \qquad [13]$$

The estimate of age differences is obtained by averaging age differences at two successive times of measurement for two successive cohort pairs.

What is the net time-lag (cultural shift) for one time unit (year) at Time 1960 (as sampled at ages 5 and 6)?

Substituting into Formula 9, it will be shown that

$$Td = \frac{(f-g)-(f-e)+(f-h)}{2} = \frac{e+f-g-h}{2}.$$

Or, in general, the net time-lag difference from Time k to Time l as sampled at ages m and n is

$$Td_{TS} = \frac{T_k A_n + T_k A_m - T_l A_n - T_l A_m}{2}. \qquad [14]$$

This estimate averages the time lag differences at two ages for two successive pairs of cohorts.

What is the interaction between age and time-lag differences (attributable to and confounded with cohort differences)?

Substituting into Formula 7, it is found that

$$Cd = \frac{(f-h)-(f-g)+(f-e)}{2} = \frac{f+g-e-h}{2}.$$

Or, in general, the average net difference between cohorts measured at Time k for age m and Time l for age n is

$$Cd_{cs} = \frac{T_kA_m+T_lAn-T_kA_n-T_lA_m}{2}. \tag{15}$$

This estimate averages age differences for successive times of measurement to obtain a cohort difference. It is confounded, as it is impossible to obtain members of the same cohort who retain the same age at two different times of measurement.

The analysis of variance is again the appropriate technique for the evaluation of differences in the time-sequential design. Table 2.4 gives the analysis of variance design for the time-sequential model. In this design, adding to the number of ages measured at each time of measurement will extend the age range for which time-lag differences can be evaluated. Increasing the number of times of measurement would serve to augment the degrees of freedom available for evaluating overall time-lag differences.

Two measurements of every cohort will suffice to permit the evaluation of time-lag at all ages of interest to the investigator. It would seem, therefore, that this method should be favored whenever generalizability of a construct over time is at issue. Note that the time-sequential model controls age differences for cultural shift and time-lag differences for the effect of age. It is impossible, however, to identify an unconfounded cohort difference component. This means that the *time-sequential method will yield unambiguous results only when the assumption is met that change in the variable under study is unrelated to genetic or cohort-specific environmental changes.*[5] This assumption is a hazardous one only when physical attributes are involved or when behaviors are studied which are thought to be affected by gross environmental crises such as wars or severe depressions. The assumption would seem to be quite tenable for many variables in the areas of ability, personality,

Table 2.4. Analysis of Variance for the Time-Sequential Model

Source of variation	Degrees of freedom
Between times (T)	$T-1$
Between ages (A)	$A-1$
Time $\times$ age interaction	$(T-1)(A-1)$
Error	$N-(T)(A)$
Total variation	$N-1$

learning, interests, and, in fact, in most matters of concern to the developmental psychologist.

If neither of the assumptions underlying the time-sequential or cohort-sequential model can be met, then recourse must be taken to a third sequential model.

CROSS-SEQUENTIAL METHOD

The cross-sequential method may be applied whenever a subset of samples contains measures of all cohorts at all times of measurement. The cross-sequential method permits inferences as to time-lag differences at all points of the time range covered as well as to cohort differences at all times of measurement. Any rectangular area of Table 2.2 may be subjected to cross-sequential analysis.

The entries of Table 2.2 which are labeled *i, j, k,* and *l* represent the minimum subset for cross-sequential analysis. The propositions which can be evaluated for the illustrative case are as follows:

What is the net cohort difference on a given variable between Cohorts 1956 and 1957 (as sampled at Measurement Times 1962 and 1963)?

Substituting in Formula 7, it is found that

$$\text{Cd} = \frac{(i-l)-(i-k)+(i-j)}{2} = \frac{i+k-j-l}{2}.$$

Or, in general, the net cohort difference between Cohorts *i* and *j* sampled at Times *k* and *l* is

$$Cd_{xs} = \frac{C_iT_k + C_iT_l - C_jT_k - C_jT_l}{2}. \qquad [16]$$

This estimate averages cohort differences at two times of measurement over two successive age slices.

What is the net time-lag (cultural shift) for one time unit (year) at Time 1962 (as sampled for Cohorts 1956 and 1957)?

Substituting into Formula 9, it is found that

$$Td = \frac{(i-k)-(i-j)+(i-l)}{2} = \frac{i+j-k-l}{2}.$$

Or, in general, the net time difference between Times k and l sampled for Cohorts i and j is

$$Td_{xs} = \frac{C_iT_k + C_jT_k - C_sT_l - C_jT_l}{2}. \qquad [17]$$

This estimate averages time differences for two cohorts over two successive age slices.

What is the interaction between cohort and time-lag differences (attributable to and confounded with age differences)?

Substituting into Formula 5, it is found that

$$Ad = \frac{(i-j)-(i-l)+(i-k)}{2} = \frac{i+l-j-k}{2}.$$

Or, in general, the average net age increment per age unit for Cohort i at Time k and for Cohort j at time l is

$$Ad_{xs} = \frac{C_sT_k + C_jT_l - C_jT_k - C_sT_l}{2}. \qquad [18]$$

The analysis of variance design for the cross-sequential model is given in Table 2.5. Adding to the number of cohorts in this design will increase the range over which time differences can be generalized, while augmenting the

Table 2.5. Analysis of Variance for the Cross-Sequential Model

Source of variation	Degrees of freedom
Between cohorts (C)	$C-1$
Between times (T)	$T-1$
Cohort $\times$ time interaction	$(C-1)(T-1)$
Error	$N-(C)(T)$
Total variation	$N-1$

number of times of measurement will permit generalization over time for the cohort differences. Adding both rows and columns will in addition increase the generalizability of the cohort-time interaction.

The cross-sequential model controls time differences for changes over generations and cohort differences for cultural shift. No unconfounded age difference component is available in this model, and consequently it follows that *time-lag methods will yield unambiguous results only when the assumption is met that change in the variable under study is unrelated to age changes.* This assumption may be tenable for many characteristics which remain stable over substantial portions of the organism's life span. It is not usually supportable in developmental studies of childhood but may frequently apply to investigations involving behavior change over time in adults. It should be noted that the cross-sequential model can be applied to any research design employing either the cohort or time-sequential methods by simply adding one more sample as indicated in the upper triangle in Table 2.2.

Empirical Checks for the Assumptions for the Sequential Models

Numerous research situations will arise where there is no independent evidence as to the tenability of the assumptions required for unambiguous inferences from the sequential strategies. From the known relations between the components of developmental change, it will now be possible to point to a number of empirical checks of the assumptions. It will also be possible to identify the consequences of known violations of assumptions, since their result will not be random confounding but will lead to combinations of components which may be of inherent interest. The check of assumptions will generally require conducting analyses for two of the models. This requirement is unreasonable for a combination of the cohort-sequential and time-sequential procedures but, as was pointed out, involves only little extra effort for a combination of either with the cross-sequential strategy. Let us now examine each of the eight possible empirical situations.

Response is unrelated to developmental change. This situation may be detected by any of the three strategies and will obtain when both main effects and the interaction are nonsignificant. Since some developmental change is known to operate in almost any variable, there is danger in accepting the null hypothesis. Even where no differences are found in an analysis via two models, one should be cautious in generalizing from such findings unless large samples have been used. Such a lack of relationship will most likely be found only for limited age, time, or cohort spans.

Response is a simple function of age: $R = f(A)$. If this situation is true, Ad estimates from the cohort-and time-sequential models will be equivalent. The Cd term in the cohort-sequential and the Td term in the time sequentials will be zero. Both Cd and Td terms in the cross-sequential model will be alternate estimates of age change and will equal each other. No interaction can be significant in this instance. Such a finding would mean that there are no genetic or cultural differences, a circumstance most likely to be found in well-controlled animal studies involving acquired behaviors. In human subjects, this outcome implies that the behavior studied varies as a function of a stable maturational sequence.

Response is a simple function of cohort differences: $R = f(C)$. Here the Cd estimates from the cohort-and cross-sequential models will be equivalent. The Ad term in the cohort-sequential and the Td term in the cross-sequential procedures will be zero. Both Ad and Td terms in the time-sequential model will be alternate estimates of cohort differences and will equal each other. Again, no interaction can be significant. These results would mean that there are no cultural or age changes but that response differences must be attributed solely to variation among generations. This situation will arise rarely, except where true genetic changes in physical attributes may be observed.

Response is a simple function of time differences: $R = f(T)$. In this case the Td estimates from the time-and cross-sequential procedures will be equivalent. The Ad term in the time-sequential and the Cd term in the cross-sequential model will be zero. Both Ad and Cd terms in the cohort-sequential model become alternate estimates of time differences which will equal each other. No interaction can be significant in this case. This model implies that there are no age or genetic differences and that response differences must be attributed to time or cultural changes. A situation of this type will probably prevail for behaviors which ordinarily remain stable once they are acquired but which may be modified due to environmental changes. Word usages, attitude patterns, occupational choices, modes of dress, etc., may fit this model.

Response is a function of age and cohort differences: $R = f(A,C)$. If both age and cohort differences are present, the Ad term from the time-sequential model will be significantly larger than the Ad term from the cohort-sequential model. This must be so because the latter is the net Ad estimate, while the former is inflated by cohort differences. Similarly, the Cd term in the cross-sequential model will be significantly larger than the Cd term in the cohort-sequential model. The cohort-sequential Cd term is, of course, the proper Cd estimate in this case. The Td term in the time-sequential model will here actually provide an alternate estimate of net cohort differences, and the Td term in the cross-sequential model is the alternate estimate of net age differences. The interaction term in the cohort-sequential model, if significant, implies differential age changes for different cohorts. The interactions for the other models are confounded and not interpretable. Most motor skills and perceptual variables which have maturational sequences and show some genetic shift, but which are unrelated to cultural change, will fit this paradigm.

Response is a function of age and time differences: $R = f(A,T)$. If developmental change is due to both age and time differences, then the Ad term from the cohort-sequential model must be significantly larger than the Ad term from the time-sequential model. The latter is the true Ad estimate, while the former is inflated by confounding with time differences. Furthermore, the Td term from the cross-sequential model will be significantly larger than the Td term from the time-sequential model. The former is inflated by confounding with age differences and the latter is the net Td estimate. The Cd estimate in the cohort-sequential model in this case provides an alternate estimate of time differences and the Cd estimate in the cross-sequential model estimates the net age differences. The interaction term in the time-sequential model, if significant, may be interpreted to mean differential age changes at different time intervals. The interactions for the other models are again confounded and consequently not interpretable. Most acquired behaviors with maturational sequences will fit this paradigm provided they are unrelated to genetic changes.

Response is a function of cohort and time differences: R = f(C,T). This paradigm is perhaps the most important one for the student of adult age changes, as maturational sequences have often been imputed by researchers where careful analysis would have shown cohort and time differences but no maturational change whatsoever. In this situation the Cd term from the cross-sequential model will be true Cd estimate, and it will be significantly smaller than the Cd term from the cohort-sequential model. The latter represents the cohort differences plus time differences. Also, the Td term from the cross-sequential model will be significantly smaller than the Td term from the time-sequential model. The former is the net Td estimate, while the latter again represents the cohort difference inflated by time differences. The Ad term from the cohort-sequential model yields an alternate estimate of time differences and the Ad term from the time-sequential model represents net cohort differences. The interaction term in the cross-sequential model, if significant, may be interpreted as differential time differences for different cohorts. The interactions for the other models are again not interpretable. This paradigm will fit many adult behaviors which persist through the individual's life span once they are established at maturity, but which show differences due to genetic and cultural factors. Some of the mental abilities, many personality variables, and certain physical characteristics which are modified by nutritional and other environmental intervenors will probably be found to show this pattern upon proper analysis.

Response is a function of age, cohort and time differences: R = f(A,C,T). The last alternative will probably be found in the total life-span study, or at least in studies involving childhood and adolescence of the kind of variables which in adults will fit the R = f(C,T) paradigm. It will, of course, also apply to the limited number of variables with maturational sequences which show both cultural and genetic changes. In this situation, the Ad term from the cohort-sequential model will be inflated by time differences and the Ad term from the time-sequential model will be inflated by cohort differences. Similarly, in the cross-sequential model both the Td and Cd terms will be inflated by age differences. The Cd term in the cohort-sequential model and the Td term in the time-sequential model both represent cohort differences plus time differences. The interaction in the cohort-sequential model implies differential age changes for different cohorts, and the interaction in the time-sequential model represents different age changes at different times. The cross-sequential interaction, if significant, again represents differential cohort changes at different time periods. It should be noted that the confounded Ad

+ Cd and Ad + Td terms accurately represent what are conventionally described as cross-sectional and longitudinal age changes.

The nature of the general developmental model as explained previously does not permit complete unconfounding under these circumstances unless additional assumptions about the form of the age gradients are introduced. The investigator who is interested in the determination of net time or cohort differences, however, can always obtain such information by analyzing the age range or age ranges at which little or no maturational change occurs. Practically all organisms show such periods for most variables of interest. Similarly, if two or more successive cohorts can be found which show no genetic change, it then becomes possible to get net Ad and Td estimates. If two or more measurement times are found for which there is little or no cultural shift, then it is also possible to obtain net Ad and Cd estimates.

Table 2.6 presents a summary of the meaning of the various difference components for each of the above-described paradigms. Inspection of this table shows that the investigator without prior information on the paradigm best fitting his data will be most likely to obtain information on net age differences by use of the cross-sequential method. The best bet for obtaining net cohort differences will be found in the time-sequential method, and coverage for most contingencies in finding net time-lag differences will be obtained by using the cohort-sequential method.

Decision Rules

From the above paradigms, it now becomes possible to generate logical decision rules for the evaluation of empirical data which will permit inferences as to the proper meaning of any developmental changes found in such data. The reader must, however, be cautioned that use of the proposed decision rules is conditional upon the tenability of our assumptions about the slope of the developmental gradients. The scheme presented in Table 2.6 assumes that all differences are unidirectional and positive; that is, an incremental progression exists from a younger to an older age, from an earlier to a later measurement time, and from a younger to an older generation. The scheme will still work if all gradients are negative, but difficulties arise when one of the developmental components differs in slope. Appropriate modification of the schema and the resulting decision rules will therefore be required whenever any of the components of developmental change departs from the assumptions of unidirectionality and/or linearity.[6]

Decision rules will now be given for data which are analyzed by both the

Table 2.6. Interpretation of Difference Components Obtained by the Analysis of Variance for the Sequential Models under the Different Assumptions

Paradigm	Cohort-sequential model			Cross-sequential model			Time-sequential model		
	Age diff.	Cohort diff.	Ad × Cd interact.	Cohort diff.	Time-lag diff.	Cd × Td interact.	Time-lag diff.	Age diff.	Td × Ad interact.
R = f(A)	Ad	—	—	Ad	Ad	—	—	Ad	—
R = f(C)	—	Cd	—	Cd	—	—	Cd	Cd	—
R = f(T)	Td	Td	—	—	Td	—	Td	—	—
R = f(A,C)	Ad	Cd	Ad × Cd	Ad + Cd	Ad	—	Cd	Ad + Cd	—
R = f(A,T)	Ad + Td	Td	—	Ad	Ad + Td	—	Td	Ad	Td × Ad
R = f(C,T)	Td	Cd + Td	—	Cd	Td	Cd × Td	Cd + Td	Cd	—
R = f(A,C,T)	Ad + Td	Cd + Td	Ad × Cd	Ad + Cd	Ad + Td	Cd × Td	Cd + Td	Ad + Cd	Td × Ad

NOTE: The age-difference column for the cohort-sequential model holds true also for the conventional longitudinal method, while the age-difference column for the time-sequential model applies to the conventional cross-sectional method. All differences are assumed to be unidirectional.

cross-sequential and time-sequential methods and also for data which are analyzed by both cross-sequential and cohort-sequential methods. It is assumed that few investigators will have occasion to analyze a set of data by both cohort-sequential and time-sequential methods, but similar decision rules for this case can readily be derived from Table 2.6 if needed.

Decision rules for the TS-XS analyses are as follows:

1. If $Td_{ts} \simeq 0$; then $R = f(A)$; if not, and
2. if $Td_{xs} \simeq 0$; then $R = f(C)$; if not, and
3. if $Cd_{xs} \simeq 0$; then $R = f(T)$; if not, and
4. if $Td_{ts} + Td_{xs} - Ad_{ts} \simeq 0$; then $R = f(A, C)$; if not, and
5. if $Td_{ts} + Cd_{xs} - Td_{xs} \simeq 0$; then $R = f(A,T)$; if not, and
6. if $Td_{xs} + Ad_{ts} - Td_{ts} \simeq 0$; then $R = f(C,T)$; if not, then $R = f(A, C, T)$.

Decision rules for the CS-XS analyses are as follows:

1. If $Cd_{cs} \simeq 0$; then $R = f(A)$; if not, and
2. if $Ad_{cs} \simeq 0$; then $R = f(C)$; if not, and
3. if $Cd_{xs} \simeq 0$; then $R = f(T)$; if not, and
4. if $Cd_{cs} + Td_{xs} - Cd_{xs} \simeq 0$; then $R = f(A, C)$; if not, and
5. if $Cd_{cs} + Cd_{xs} - Ad_{cs} \simeq 0$; then $R = f(A, T)$; if not, and
6. if $Ad_{cs} + Cd_{xs} - Cd_{cs} \simeq 0$; then $R = f(C, T)$; if not, then $R = f(A, C, T)$.

Empirical estimates will, of course, be subject to sampling fluctuations and the definition for zero will have to be subject to the level of confidence specified for a given experiment.[7]

REPEATED MEASUREMENT DESIGNS

Whenever experimental error is large or where differences between experimental conditions, though significant and stable, are expected to be small, variability may be reduced markedly by use of the matched group design. The conventional longitudinal method is essentially an application of such a design. It will now be shown how the matched group design can be applied to the sequential strategies and models discussed above. Before going into such detail, it will be useful to consider some of the general problems of matched group designs in developmental studies.

In a repeated measurement design the investigator obtains measures on the same sample of subjects at different times. Such repetition poses no problems where physical attributes are involved, but complications arise whenever variables are studied which are amenable to practice or where the testing procedure affects the behavior to be measured. Instead of comparing independently derived groups of subjects and being limited thereby statements of the difference between group means, the repeated measurement design permits comparing each observation of a subject's behavior with some earlier or later measurements. In theory, therefore, it should be possible to detect small but reliable changes because the matching procedure will result in more sensitive estimates of such changes. Unless adequate controls are provided, and these are for practical and understandable reasons usually lacking in developmental studies, the small but significant changes may simply be a function of practice or other artifacts.

It is not difficult to draw new random samples from a carefully defined population over long periods of time. In contrast, it is virtually impossible to maintain a single sample in its entirety over any length of time. Unfortunately, sampling attrition is not random but is often related to the very variables being studied. Unless it can be shown that the reduced sample for which repeated measurements are available is substantially similar to the original sample, it is, of course, not possible to generalize even for the single cohort sampled. No such evidence is readily available for most of the various longitudinal studies reported in the literature.

Attention should further be called to the fact that for an equal number of observations the degrees of freedom available for the error term used to test mean differences will always be less for the replicated than for independently derived measurements. The gain in sensitivity must, therefore, exceed the loss caused by testing a smaller number of individuals before the repeated measurement design will pay off. The repeated measurement design will always be inferior to the independent sample design in evaluating cohort differences, since such differences must of necessity involve the comparison of independent samples.

Tables 2.7 and 2.8 give the analysis of variance designs for the cohort- and cross-sequential models with repeated measurements. A time-sequential model is not available for the repeated measurement case, since repeated measurements would not be available for the first and last cohort represented in each subset (see Table 2.2 and the discussion of the general model). It will be noted that the significance of cohort differences in both cohort-and cross-sequential models will be tested by an error term based on the residual variation between subjects which in the cohort-sequential model will have $N - (N/A) - C(A - 1)$ fewer degrees of freedom than in an independent sample design based on the same number of observations. Similarly, the error

Table 2.7. Analysis of Variance for the Cohort-Sequential Model with Repeated Measurements

Source of variation	Degrees of freedom
Between subjects	$\dfrac{N}{A} - 1$
Between cohorts	$C-1$
Residual between subjects	$\dfrac{N}{A} - C$
Within subjects	$N - \dfrac{N}{A}$
Between ages	$A-1$
Cohort × age interaction	$(C-1)(A-1)$
Residual within subjects	$N - \left(\dfrac{N}{A}\right) - C(A-1)$
Total variation	$N-1$

term to be used for testing the significance of cohort differences in the cross-sequential model will have $N - (N/T) - C(T - 1)$ fewer degrees of freedom in the repeated measurement than in the independent sampling design.

The age difference and age-by-cohort-interaction terms in the cohort-sequential repeated measurement design will be confounded both with time

Table 2.8. Analysis of Variance for the Cross-Sequential Model with Repeated Measurements

Source of variation	Degrees of freedom
Between subjects	$\dfrac{N}{T} - 1$
Between cohorts	$C - 1$
Residual between subjects	$\dfrac{N}{T} - C$
Within subjects	$N - \dfrac{N}{T}$
Between times	$T - 1$
Cohort × time interaction	$(C - 1)(T - 1)$
Residual within subjects	$N - \left(\dfrac{N}{T}\right) - C(T - 1)$
Total variation	$N - 1$

differences and practice effects. The error term available to test these differences is based on the residual variance within subjects. This error term will have $N - (N/A)$ fewer degrees of freedom than the comparable error term in an independent sample design with the same number of observations. Similarly, in the cross-sequential repeated measurement design, the time-difference and cohort-time interactions will be confounded with age differences and practice effects. The error term available to test these differences will have $N - (N/T)$ fewer degrees of freedom than the comparable independent sample design.

It follows from the above discussion that the repeated measurement designs will become efficient only where measures have high reliability or where measures are taken at many ages or many times. Furthermore, it is impossible to separate age differences from practice effects in the cohort-sequential model, and it is impossible to separate time differences from practice effects in the cross-sequential model. The precise meaning of the confounded differences under various assumptions may be obtained from Table 2.6 by adding practice effect to each of the entries in the age difference column for the cohort-sequential and in the time-lag difference column for the cross-sequential model. These relationships in the case of the repeated measurement designs will hold only if independent sets of samples are used for the cohort-and cross-sequential analyses. Overlapping will, furthermore, add the practice effect to all Td and all Cd terms in the cohort difference column for the cohort-sequential model.[8]

MEASURING THE EFFECT OF PRACTICE

A direct estimate of the effect of practice as a component of developmental change may be obtained from the repeated measurement designs if, and only if, age is not significantly involved in the cohort-sequential design, or if time is not significantly involved in the cross-sequential design. The effect of practice is confounded with the other components of change whenever a more complex set of assumptions is required. This is unfortunate since it is often important to identify the extent to which a behavior has been altered by the measuring operation or to insure that a gain in scores cannot be explained simply by the increased familiarity of the subjects with the measuring instrument. An independent estimate of practice effects may be obtained under all assumptions, however, if the investigator is willing to employ conjointly repeated measurement and independent random sampling designs.

The procedure to be advocated requires that independent samples be drawn

Table 2.9. Analysis of Variance for the Cross-Sectional Study of Practice Effects

Source of variation	Degrees of freedom
Between ages + cohorts (AC)	AC − 1
Levels of practice (P)	P − 1
Age + cohort × practice interaction	(AC − 1) (P − 1)
Error	N − (AC) (P)
Total variation	N − 1

which are to be compared with the second or subsequent measurements for the repeated measurement group. The investigator must obtain a random sample from the same cohort which differs from the latter group only in the characteristic that it has been measured one time less than the repeated measurement group. The analysis of variance design for the study of practice effects is shown in Table 2.9.

It will be noticed that the proposed design has the usual cross-sectional approach deficiency in that age and cohort differences are confounded and in that the interaction is therefore uninterpretable unless it is known from independent sources that the effect of either age or cohort differences is zero. A far more complex design will be required to remedy this difficulty and is feasible only if an opportunity for at least three measurements exists. In this case, it will also be necessary to obtain a repeated measurement on the random sample first tested on the second occasion. Furthermore, a new random sample must be drawn on the third occasion which differs from both the first and second repeated measurement samples only on the characteristic of having been measured once less than the other groups. Groups may then be split in random halves and appropriate assignment to the different levels of practice made. The analyses for such a design will be similar to the ones given in Tables 2.3, 2.4, and 2.5 except for the addition of a main effect for practice, and the simple and triple interaction between practice and the other components of developmental change. Such a design is quite efficient in the case of the time-and cross-sequential methods. It faces the usual sampling attrition problems in the cohort-sequential approach which for human subjects is, in any event, best limited to short-term studies.

CONCLUSIONS

The results of our analysis suggest that the conventional longitudinal and cross-sectional methods for the study of developmental problems can lead to comparable results only when there are no genetic or cultural changes in response to the variable studied. Such circumstances, however, are rare among the areas of interest to the developmental psychologist. Research strategies are required, therefore, which will permit the unconfounding of the components of developmental change. Consideration of a general model has permitted the development of sequential strategies which permit such unconfounding, and it has furthermore been shown that the conventional methods are simply incomplete special cases of these sequential models. The hazards of the repeated measurement designs have been explored, and alternate methods have been suggested for the study of practice effects.

It must now be argued that the cohort-sequential method (and the conventional longitudinal method as a special case thereof) is basically inefficient. Study of Table 2.6, moreover, will show that the most interesting information available from longitudinal study can equally well be obtained by a combination of the time-and cross-sequential approaches. It is suggested, therefore, that the most efficient design for a developmental study consists of the following scheme:

1. Draw a random sample from each cohort over the age range to be investigated, and measure at Time k (Score A).
2. Get a second measurement on all subjects tested at Time k at Time l (Score B).
3. Draw a new random sample from each cohort in the range tested at Time k plus one cohort below that range, and test at Time l (Score C).

The following comparisons may now be made: (a) Cross-sequential model (Scores A and C), (b) Time-sequential model (Scores A and C), (c) Cross-sequential model with repeated measurements (Scores A and B), (d) Cross-sectional model, controlling for effect of practice (Scores B and C).

Almost all questions of interest to the developmental researcher can be handled by this strategy, which should yield interpretable results in practically all empirical situations.[9] Sampling attrition in the repeated measurement part of the study should be fairly limited over a single time interval. Also, if desired, the new random sample obtained at Time l will provide the base for a second repeated measurement study, and any cohort or cohort sequence can, of course, be followed further if a conventional longitudinal study is to be pursued.

It is hoped that this chapter has clarified the relations between the different types of basic experimental designs in developmental psychology. A next logical step should be in the direction of reexamining some of the studies in the developmental and attitude survey literature with the hope that puzzling inconsistencies can now be resolved or identified as artifacts of improperly understood experimental designs.[10]

NOTES

1. Horst (1963, pp. 106–107) discussed in passing the need for a "trapezoid" model which would provide a mathematical basis for our presentation. No such model, however, has been worked out at this date.

2. Sampling problems pose additional issues which must be dealt with as soon as one proceeds beyond the general case. An extended discussion of sampling problems and their management for the cross-sectional method has been given elsewhere (Schaie, 1959).

3. It should be noted that the conventional longitudinal method is simply a special case involving the repeated measurement of the same sample from a given cohort. The advantages and liabilities of the repeated measurement case will be considered in a later section of this paper.

4. The conventional longitudinal method as a special case of the cohort-sequential method is encumbered by the same restrictive assumption.

5. The assumptions given for the time-sequential model also apply to the conventional cross-sectional method.

6. Nine basic types of slopes may be recognized. These are: zero, positive, negative, concave, convex, positive asymptotic, negative asymptotic accelerating, and decelerating. As a result there are as many as 729 different models when the slopes of the three components are jointly considered. In certain non-linear designs, moreover, confounding may not be complete. It is unlikely that there are empirical data which fit each of the possible models. Also, empirical data might equally well fit several of these models. A more detailed analysis of this problem goes beyond the scope of this paper and will be attempted elsewhere.

7. The decisions will be based on a comparison of the mean squares obtained from the analyses of variance as detailed in Tables 3–5 and 7–9.

8. Bell (1953) presents an overlapped design which confounds the information separated in this chapter by use of the repeated measurement design for the cohort- and cross-sequential models.

9. The proposed research strategy has been applied to the study of developmental changes in adult cognitive behavior (Schaie & Strother, 1964a; 1964b).

10. Examples of studies containing data which could readily be examined via the proposed models may be found in Shuttleworth (1939) and in Hyman and Sheatsley (1964).

REFERENCES

Bell, R. Q. *Convergence: An accelerated longitudinal approach.* Child Development, *1953, 24, 145–152.*

Horst, P. Multivariate models for evaluating change. In C. W. Harris (Ed.), Problems in measuring change. *Madison: University of Wisconsin Press, 1963.*

Hyman, H. H. & Sheatsley, P. B. Attitudes toward desegregation. Scientific American, *1964, 211, 16–23.*

Kessen, W. Research design in the study of developmental problems. In P. Mussen (Ed.), Handbook of research methods in child development. *New York: Wiley, 1960.*

Kuhlen, R. G. Social change: A neglected factor in psychological studies of the life span. School and Society, *1940, 52, 14–16.*

Schaie, K. W. Cross-sectional methods in the study of psychological aspects of aging. Journal of Gerontology, *1959, 14, 208–215.*

Schaie, K. W. & Strother, C. R. A. A cross-sequential study of age changes in cognitive behavior. Paper read at Midwestern Psychological Association, St. Louis, April–May 1964. (a)

Schaie, K. W. & Strother, C. R. The effect of time and cohort differences on the interpretation of age changes in cognitive behavior. American Psychologist, *1964, 19, (Abstract) 546. (b)*

Shuttleworth, F. K. The physical and mental growth of girls and boys age six to nineteen in relation to age at maximum growth. Monographs of the Society for Research in Child Development, *1939, No. 4.*

3. Engagement and Disengagement
Toward a Theory of Adult Development

William E. Henry

DISENGAGEMENT: CONCEPTS AND DATA

In an age of anxiety, detachment seems an inappropriate art, and activity a solution. But wisdom and perspective—so commonly, though conceivably erroneously, attributed to the elders—require a base in leisure. By the term *leisure* I do not mean the common American association to *recreation*, that is, the *utilization* of leisure in particular activities. I refer, rather, to the root definitions of leisure as given in *Webster's New International Dictionary*, definition 2, "freedom or opportunity afforded by exemption from occupation or business" and, particularly, to definition 3, "time at one's command, free from engagement." The crucial ideas here are contained in definition 3, and they suggest two important concepts. The first, "time at one's command," I take to mean that the individual is able to structure time *as he chooses*, or can *ignore time altogether*, since it is he who commands it, rather than time that commands him. The second idea, "free from engagement," implies a possible logic for that kind of choice, that is, that the individual is *free from the sense of being engaged* by various outer events or objects. Thus when the individual is not bound, i.e., not engaged with events and objects, time alters its relationship to the individual, and the individual alters his view of the importance of being engaged. Objects become less vital and time loses its ability to command.

A conviction that time is important and engagement with persons and objects necessary constitutes a firm basis for the maximal involvement with outer world events characteristic of middle-age (and possibly middle-class) life. The raising and training of families, the accumulation of personal property, the commitment to social and occupational mobility are in no fundamental personal sense inevitable. They may be *necessary* for the society, as mechanisms of inducting the young and as means of getting the world's work

---

Reprinted from R. Kastenbaum, ed., *Contributions to the psychobiology of aging* (New York: Springer Publishing Company, 1965), 19–35.

done. And they are perfectly *natural*, in the sense that they are, in most societies, common or modal events. But to become functional for the individual, they require the commitment of engagement. Once the individual to some degree *commits* himself to such values, the activities and objects related to their attainment constitute the interactive scene of early and middle adult life.

But for some adults such interactive values and activities become impossible, and for some possible but meaningless, except insofar as these persons come to invest energy and belief in the outer events and objects characteristic of the adult life scene in their society. This investment is the process intervening between individuals and social actions. It includes intertwining and probably inseparable elements of *commitment to time, and cathexes to objects, persons, and events*. This process, including the commitment of energy and the assumption that time can command, constitutes the necessary basic condition for the engagement in social activities at certain life periods. It is the dissolution, or perhaps only the reassignment, of the energies involved in this process that constitutes the basic condition for the disengagement of later life.

In the report of Elaine Cumming and myself in the book *Growing Old* (1961), based upon data from the Kansas City Studies, we emphasized the concept of *disengagement* as useful in accounting for the reduction in life activities and in ego energy found in most, but not all, older persons. It was our proposal that this was a process both social and psychological and, as such, to be explained as much by psychological events indigenous to the individual as by societal reactions relating to the older persons' inclusion in, or exclusion from, the work and social life of the society.

In the report of Havighurst and his colleagues, given at the Sweden Conference and based upon additional material but from a somewhat depleted sample of these cases, the disengagement process is further examined and the relations of disengagement, activity-maintenance and life satisfaction are more intimately studied (Havighurst, Neugarten & Tobin, 1963). A crucial part of these more detailed findings deals with the fact that the fate, in old age, of the cathexes of an earlier age, appears to depend upon the character of the personality coping mechanisms. While it is clear that varying life circumstances, social and biological, influence the psychic choices made, the manner of resolution and the techniques of coping begin to emerge as crucial differentiating factors. It is in this sense that *styles* of aging are composed of differing patterns of role activity and by differing patterns of relation to self. When Havighurst, Neugarten, and Tobin comment that the individual, regardless of the nature of his social life, does not *disengage from self*, they have made a most important statement. The nature of that self then becomes the crucial variable. A similar conclusion would appear to be implied by Williams and Wirths (1963a) when they make productive differentiations in *lifestyle* by utilizing the essentially *self*-relevant categorizing variables of autonomous-dependent and persistent-precarious.

Disengagement theory, as initially phrased, proposes in rough outline a severing of ties between a person and others in his society, a reduction in available ego energy, and a change in the quality of those ties remaining. It proposes that the changing quality of remaining ties may stem from "an altered basis in the person for the reception and initiation of social events" (Cumming & Henry, 1961, p. 107). We have suggested that this changed basis in the person resides essentially in a realignment of the relation of inner events to outer events in such a manner that the former take on an increasing centrality, that interiority becomes increasingly important. It is consonant with this that normatively governed considerations and hierarchally structured social relations should be less prominent. The proposal of the increased role of inner events in the reception and initiation of social events also permits the observation, variously made in other contexts, that the older person becomes increasingly "like himself," that, as Havighurst, Neugarten, and Tobin comment, he remains engaged with self. If these are reasonable observations, then they are so to the extent that new adjustments to changing norms become less common. The individual thus does not become more like the social scene, changed or unaltered as it may be. He becomes more like his own inner events, the sameness and continuity of which now have every opportunity to be maximized. This would presumably still be true even if, as appears commonly to be the case, general available ego energy declines. The issue here is on what basis personal or social events are judged, what social activities mean for the individual, regardless of whether these events and activities are many or few.

If overt work activity, or any social engagement, has meaning for the individual, that meaning probably is best described through relation to personality concepts, to social interaction values, or both. The personality coping mechanisms seen by Havighurst, Neugarten, and Tobin as crucial in accounting for many of their findings, would seem to me to constitute evidence for an "altered basis in the person for the reception and initiation of social events," of which I have spoken. In other words, these findings considerably advance and modify this aspect of disengagement theory, by giving us a more specific image of the nature of the inner events characteristic of the elderly.

That these various personality coping mechanisms are accompanied by differing life patterns and by a differing sense of life satisfaction would seem to suggest that they do indeed serve as a screen through which outer events are seen and judged.

In a broad sense, a work task for a 10-year-old may take its essential meaning from the affect relationship to the father it may embody. A work task for the 30-year-old male may serve to prove his instrumentality and his independence of that same father. For the 45-year-old it may serve also to demonstrate his social stability, his responsibility, and his care for his family. And for a 64-year-old (assuming retirement at 65) work may be related to efforts to prove to himself he is worthy of continuing work, or become merely a marking of time—something he must do while he waits for retirement.

If the meaning of work does indeed alter with age and social circumstance in some such manner as this, then we would add, for the post–64-year-old, a further stage. This stage would be one in which there occurs a change from the dominance of *instrumentality* to that of *socio-emotionality*. It is in this sense that the suggested increased centrality of self-oriented interiority comes into play and that rewards for activity become dominantly judged in terms of their gain for self, rather than for the gain they might engender for that individual in the work or social scene.

Persons of advanced age who maintain high activity, in contrast to the common pattern of reduction in activity and ego energy, are cases of special interest. Conceivably they are, and always have been, biological specimens of great vigor. Conceivably they are persons, both uncommon and special, whose personal and social circumstances have never presented them with the choice of disengagement and who find the continuance of high activity meaningful and satisfying. But this latter statement is more a re-statement of the fact that such persons exist than an explanation of them.

In our statement of disengagement theory, we said that the loss of certain central roles will result in a loss of morale *"unless different roles, appropriate to the disengaged state, are available."* (Cumming & Henry, 1961, p. 215). On the face of it, these are persons who have found some alternative roles. They are persons for whom the term "re-engagement" or "re-organizers" of roles may indeed be fitting. The emphasis in these terms (re-engagement, re-organizer) upon a dis-engaged period followed by a re-engagement cannot be clarified from our present Kansas City analysis. Neither is it clear whether (rather than dis-engage and then re-establish contact) these people have merely re-grouped or re-organized their life activities into a new but still high activity pattern. Certainly either or both would be possible. But regardless of these possibilities, another issue suggested by disengagement theory requires resolution. In our statement quoted above, it is noted that different roles, appropriate to the disengaged state, may be adopted. The question now becomes whether or not the activities of the older period for these high activity persons are "appropriate to the disengaged state," and, further, what the more precise meaning of this somewhat ambiguous concept is. First, let us agree that some persons may well maintain high activity, with good morale, where those activities are indistinguishable from the clearly instrumental roles of middle-aged life. There are those among the Kansas City group who fit that pattern. It may be that the Reichard-Livson-Peterson (1962) *Mature* men fit that pattern. However, while these authors appear to identify only their *Rocking Chair* type with the notion of disengagement, it should be noted that their reports of the *Mature* men include a great deal of socio-emotionality, sensuality, direct expression of enjoyment in low-activity—while clearly maintaining interest in some activity, hobbies, and other part-time substitutive instrumentality.

In fact, their quotation from one of their mature men, presented in evidence of his active interest as an "enthusiastic breeder of chinchillas" (p. 119), strongly suggests some of the properties of the disengaged, post-64 age state and a rather uncommonly sensual one at that. The full quotation given is:

I saw one of the most beautiful chinchilla herds: I didn't know they existed. This fellow had been in it eight years. And he has the most beautiful animals. I could just sit there and watch them all day. And I was glad I went down to see him. It gives me something to work for.

It is of course inappropriate to imply without fuller material, that this man is in any particular stage of disengagement, Reichard and her co-authors addressed themselves only peripherally to issues of disengagement, and there is little question that their *Mature* group is a meaningful one in its own terms.

The chinchilla breeder, however, in this quotation, strongly suggests that his ego energy has been displaced from active instrumentality and that the still active work involved in chinchilla raising serves him quite differently. Its meaning is not instrumentality in the usual sense, but rather an occasion for unassertive emotional experience and for sensuous, even voyeuristic, observation. Such an orientation, of course, in no way denies the possibility of active work with his chinchillas or even that he may not achieve some instrumental results—in the actual sale of the animals, for example. The basic issue is one of the meaning of the activity to the individual.

Cumming and Henry have also given illustrations in which overt impulse enjoyment seems to play a crucial role. It is indeed our impression that in some instances the release from normatively governed demands, the dropping of "socially expected instrumental tasks," as Williams and Wirths note, tends to be accompanied by a kind of sense of release in which such pleasurable sensuous elements are often prominent. This sense of release is perhaps behind many of the so-called eccentricities of the aged, in which, at least in an affluent society, both the aged and their younger contemporaries seem to take pleasure.

FOCUS UPON INTERIORITY

But this form of expressiveness in disengagement may not be the most common, nor may it be even possible in some cultural contexts. *The basic issue is the resurgence of focus upon interiority and the release from the sense of import formerly attributed to outer world events.* It may well be that the factors determining the specific form of reactions at this point reside in the life style characteristic of the individual's life to that time, and in the characteristic coping mechanisms of the personality. For many Americans, leisure and freedom from occupation have commonly meant the opportunity to play, that is, to be active in non-work contexts, to "enjoy" oneself (on the assumption that one could not in work), to be amused (on the grounds that work was serious). It may be for this reason that "going fishing" is such a satisfactory symbolic, if not actual, activity as an expression of release from work. For many it is a classical form of enjoyment without occupation.

But for others the contemplation of philosophies or of nature may have constituted the definition of the higher, non-obligatory life, that life for which the individual previously was led to believe he had no time. These concerns should then become dominant as appropriate to the disengaged state.

Dr. Talmon-Garber, in personal conversation, has noted that many older persons in the Kibbutzim in Israel do not seek expressivity in the more playful manner just suggested but, rather, devote increased proportions of time to reading—largely of the Bible and other philosophic works. In a sense, this activity is a continuation, even an accentuation, of interest in certain values already a dominant part of their previous lives, values appropriate to their cultural setting. I should think that such socially sponsored and non-instrumental activities should also serve well the gains of interiority and self-contemplation. In a religion-oriented society the philosophic values documented in such reading presumably represent values against which the reader's own personal life had been judged in younger days; and a re-examination of them in later life would seem entirely fitting, both as a socially permitted activity and as a re-contemplation of internally-based, ego-relevant ideas. Certainly, also, the fact that neither active instrumentality nor overt social activity are required elements gives such reading a particular appropriateness.

For individuals whose lives have been highly involved with group and organizational participation, and for whom high value has been placed upon instrumentality in that context, one would suppose that their group and organizational scenes would remain prominent among later associations, even though there might be reduction in total amount of interaction. The crucial issue as to whether, despite level of activity, some disengagement had occurred, would reside in the *nature* of the activity at the later age. Disengagement theory would suggest that the activities maintained could be less instrumental, and that the instrumental ones would be the first dropped, with less official attendance perhaps remaining. For these people, the observation of Williams and Wirths that (for our Kansas City sample) television is "the great disengager," is amply relevant. American TV programming permits that the individual older person can, with complete physical and psychic immobility, contemplate and passively re-examine many values inherent in his earlier life and in the social system at large. The virtues, or at least the common attributes, of achievement motivation, of over-determined social engagement, of complex mutually dependent relations, are all fully displayed. Their merits and their relation to self can easily be re-examined with no commitment whatsoever.

Our concern here is with the degree to which specific forms of mid-adult activities and values serve as the significant basis for judging the particular kind of activities crucial for any particular individual in old age. It would seem likely that the activities of mid-age are the key to the particular interactive scenes of old age. This position is consistent with the proposal that men whose mid-adult activities already stressed interiority and socioemotionality (ministers, educators, for example) find the transition into lower instrumentality and higher socio-emotionality an easier one than men for whom the values and habits of interiority have always been minimal. In a broad sense, the values of the society in question—its definition of the good and the bad, of the permitted and non-permitted, of work and play—influence not only the timing of a possible disengagement, but the activities and interests which might serve functionally as appropriate to that period.

It would also seem fitting if specific forms of disengagement were effected by the degree of tenacity with which, during mid-adult life, the individual clung to his society's definition of the good and the proper and, in particular, the degree to which strong superego restraints influenced choices of action. In an important sense, strong superego restraints represent a flight from interiority, a strict guard against the consideration of actions directed by inner impulse and a preference for actions dictated by social convention, whether those of a contemporary scene or those of the remembered past. These persons should strongly resist the possible upsurge of interiority, while participating in societal activities to the degree that the conventions of their society demanded. For these persons, societal permission to disengage becomes crucial. They may find the adoption of an expressive and socio-emotional style difficult and threatening. These would not be the persons reported by Havighurst, Neugarten, and Tobin as high in both social activity and morale. They should rather be those who tended to remain engaged beyond a period of personal satisfaction in those activities, and to be low in morale—low because their fear of interiority permits them to envision no dignified alternative to the social modes of their mid-adult life style.

ENGAGEMENT AND INVOLVEMENT AS DEVELOPMENTAL EVENTS

Earlier in this chapter, I called attention to the possibility, and I believe it to be a fact, that *en*gagement and the derivation of a sense of commitment are in themselves developmental events. In at least some formulations the schizophrenic is the individual who, at an early age, and presumably through uniquely traumatic circumstances, has never developed the sense of involvement characteristic of most persons. The more common developmental pattern, of course, is the one in which psychic and material gains are the clear-cut rewards, and subsequently the motives, for a demonstrable degree of interest or investment in significant persons in the immediate environment. This process of developing reciprocal involvements is presumably facilitated by firm identifications with these figures and comes to diffuse to include actually and symbolically related persons and events. With increased ego differentiation and the development of autonomy in ego and in other spheres, there probably occurs a fairly stable level of involvement—one to some degree reflective of the past experiences of the individual. It would seem logical to assume that this level of involvement would become greater at some times than at others. For one thing, it perhaps increases at points of new interest— e.g., at adolescence, and at periods of early development of work competence

and of establishment of a family. These are points at which a fairly generalized sense of the import of all commitments becomes more acute. One could
probably maintain that some increase in the level of involvement occurs at
the time of each of what Havighurst has called the Developmental Tasks.

But in spite of the probability of alterations dictated by special circumstances—and certainly retreat from involvement is also possible—it seems
worthwhile to posit a general personality characteristic residing in this level
of involvement. The issue would be one of the psychic distance or closeness
of the individual to the common objects and events of his environment.
Closeness, in this sense, implies that the individual maintains a high awareness of the presence and the stimulation of others and that he himself experiences some sense of need to respond to that stimulation. Distance
presumes a reduced awareness of such environmental events and a reduced
felt need for response. Phrased somewhat differently, the presumption might
be that individuals equilibrate themselves at some characteristic distance from
others and, other things being equal, tend to maintain that distance. It does
not follow from this notion of level of involvement that either closeness or
distance carries with it any particular state of awareness of one's own inner
states, though some relations of the two may be common for certain ages
and/or for certain persons differing in other personal attributes. Thus, it would
be consistent with this proposal that highly engaged persons in mid-adulthood
would experience high involvement, with closeness to other persons and
events, and that during this period formal attention to inner states declines.
During classic periods of "negativism," that of the 3-year-old American
child, perhaps, and the "selfish" periods of adolescence, one might imagine
a preoccupation with inner states to the exclusion of formal attention to involvement with environmental events. The resulting distance from others
could readily produce these accusations of "selfishness" and "negativism."
It is, of course, also our suggestion that, as Cumming (1960) has said, "the
older people are, the more likely they are to be equilibrated at a quite considerable distance from their fellows and the more preoccupied they are likely
to be with their own inner states."

In this context, engagement and disengagement become a general form of
personality dynamic, and the disengagement of the aged becomes a special
case. Further study may suggest that some of the high or low engaged persons
of older age are so in part because of previous developmental experiences
indicative of particular levels of involvement. This would most likely be true
of those well-known cases of extremely high engagement in old age whose
earlier lives appear to have been similarly characterized. It seems intimated,

also, by the remark of Williams and Wirths (1963b) that "preparation for disengagement" before 65 increases the likelihood of successful aging. While forms of "preparation" may well vary, one such prior event may be either an initially low involvement, or a particularly flexible sense of involvement, permitting ready adaptability to a retreating social scene.

OPEN QUESTIONS

We said earlier that the disengagement of the aged is an intrinsic process and that it is inevitable. I would still be inclined to maintain that both those statements are true. However, its inevitability is by no means clear. There are Kansas City cases in whom signs of disengagement have not appeared at quite advanced ages, in at least one of age 86. There are certainly others in whom high activity is still present, but in which the question of altered personal meaning and the switch to increased dominance of socio-emotionality is not resolved. The question of inevitability, however, is less intriguing than the more refined questions variously phrased by the persons working on these data. The examinations reported by Havighurst, Neugarten, and Tobin revolve around the highly complex interactions of activity, ego energy, and the judged estimates of life satisfaction. From their work, it is apparent that several styles of aging are possible, and that the style itself is no criterion of felt satisfaction. Using a different concept of success and typologies based on a more socially interactive concept of life styles, Williams and Wirths derive similar conclusions, focused somewhat more generally upon estimates of disengagement. From this point of view, disengagement occurs in all life styles, but is clearly subordinate, in its timing and nature, to some properties of those long-standing life styles.

The degree to which disengagement is an intrinsic process seems still an open question, and one related in part to how biologically determined one assumes an intrinsic process to be, and where one places the causality in the various interrelations of social fact, personality, and self-estimate with which we have been dealing. I have earlier suggested that the process is intrinsic in the sense that it represents a personality process of level of involvement, and that that process is clearly a life-long one. The emphasis which Havighurst-Neugarten-Tobin and Reichard-Livson-Peterson place on personality as crucial determiners seems to support that notion—at least to the extent that the personality processes dealt with are presumably not specific to old age, but rather are based in earlier life experiences, and maintain considerable determining power in their interaction with the life events of old age. The possibility that evidences of ego-energy-decline precede evidences of reduction in social activity is similarly suggestive, though here problems of differential perception of actual changes confound the picture. To this point it would seem sound to me to suggest that processes of disengagement, in their complexity and interaction with various life events, are intrinsic in the sense only that social environmental events are not sufficient to predict them, and that they appear clearly related to various personality processes generally understood to be of long duration. They are thus ego processes, having a developmental history, a discoverable course of their own, and a positive power that can influence reaction to external events and choice of response to them.

But there is one further highly complex question which I think none of us working with these data have dealt with directly. That is the question of *intentional outside activation*, its utility in social planning, and its effect upon the aged. There are, of course, some implications for this in the present work. There is a presumption that low activity is good because we find examples of it in persons of good morale; there is a presumption that high activity is good when one finds examples of it in persons with high morale. In this context both the Activity Theory and the Disengagement Theory—acknowledgedly less distinct and separate than their names imply—carry the burden of their titles. But, as I think has been amply shown by the work reported, neither of them is sufficient to account for the facts we now know. And neither deals explicitly with the question of the effects upon the persons of specific plans for increasing or decreasing their activity, or for plans of providing one kind of activity as opposed to another. There are, of course, many personal reports of casual as well as intense professional work. As far as I am aware, these reports lend themselves to either or both general theories. And those that appear most substantially to support the implications of one or the other position have arisen from unsystematic circumstances without controls. I take this to be an open and challenging field of research, in social action and psychotherapeutic management. The present group of reports dealing with disengagement should provide some clues for a more refined experimentation and lead to further study of the interactions of personality and social events, and their meaning for life satisfaction.

REFERENCES

Cumming, E. Social change and the dying process. Read at the 13th Annual Conference on Aging, University of Michigan, Ann Arbor, June, 1960.

Cumming, E. & Henry, W. Growing old. *New York: Basic Books, 1961.*

Havighurst, R. J., Neugarten, B. L. & Tobin, S. S. Disengagement and patterns of aging. Read at International Gerontological Research Seminar, Sweden, August, 1963.

Reichard, S., Livson, F. & Peterson, P. Aging and Personality. *New York: John Wiley, 1962, pp. 119–120.*

Webster's New International Dictionary *(2nd edition), 1959, p. 1414.*

Williams, R. & Wirths, C. Styles of life and successful aging, II. Read at International Gerontological Research Seminar, Sweden, August, 1963 (a).

Williams, R. & Wirths, C. Some reflections on disengagement. Read at the International Congress of Gerontology, Copenhagen, August, 1963 (b).

4. Disengagement and Patterns of Aging

Robert J. Havighurst, Bernice L. Neugarten, and Sheldon S. Tobin

In THE SOCIAL-PSYCHOLOGICAL literature of gerontology there are two general points of view with regard to optimum patterns of aging. Both are based on the observed facts that as people grow older their behavior changes, the activities that characterized them in middle age become curtailed, and the extent of their social interaction decreases. The two theories then diverge.

The first view, one that might be called the "activity" theory, implies that, except for the inevitable changes in biology and in health, older people are the same as middle-aged people, with essentially the same psychological and social needs. In this view, the decreased social interaction that characterizes old age results from the withdrawal by society from the aging person; and the decrease in interaction proceeds against the desires of most aging men and women. The older person who ages optimally is the person who stays active and who manages to resist the shrinkage of his social world. He maintains the activities of middle age as long as possible and then finds substitutes for those activities he is forced to relinquish: substitutes for work when he is forced to retire; substitutes for friends and loved ones whom he loses by death.

In the disengagement theory, on the other hand, as originally described by our colleagues, Cumming and Henry (1961), the decreased social interaction is interpreted as a process characterized by mutuality; one in which both society and the aging person withdraw, with the aging individual acceptant, perhaps even desirous of the decreased interaction. It is suggested that the individual's withdrawal has intrinsic, or developmental, qualities as well as responsive ones; that social withdrawal is accompanied by, or preceded by, increased preoccupation with the self and decreased emotional investment in persons and objects in the environment; and that, in this sense, disengagement is a natural rather than an imposed process. In this view, the older person who has a sense of psychological well-being will usually be the

From Bernice Neugarten, ed., *Middle Age and Aging*, (Chicago: University of Chicago Press, 1968), 161–72. Copyright ©1968 by The University of Chicago Press. Used by permission.

person who has reached a new equilibrium characterized by a greater psychological distance, altered types of relationships, and decreased social interaction with the persons around him.

It is to be noted that, implicitly or explicitly, both theories involve value judgments. In the first, the presumption seems to be that, at least in modern Western societies, it is better to be active than to be inactive; to maintain the patterns characteristic of middle age rather than to move to new patterns of old age. In the second theory, it is presumably better to be in a state of equilibrium than in a state of disequilibrium; and better to acquiesce in what is a "natural," not an imposed, process of change. Furthermore, many investigators, including the present authors, in their concern with issues of "successful" aging, have introduced still another set of values in implying that it is better to be happy than unhappy, and that the aging individual himself rather than an observer is the best judge of his success.

Given the difficulties of value-free observations, the focus in the present report will be upon measures of social and psychological interaction, measures of the individual's satisfaction with life, and the relationships between these measures. In an effort to increase objectivity, a distinction is being drawn between disengagement as a *process*— a process which has both its outer and inner, its social and its psychological manifestations—and disengagement as a *theory of optimum aging.*

Presented first is the evidence concerning the process of disengagement; evidence that underlies the conclusion of the present authors that disengagement is, indeed, an accurate term for describing the social and psychological changes characteristic of aging in modern American society. Presented second are the relationships between measures of disengagement and measures of affect and satisfaction with life; evidence that underlies our conclusions that both the activity theory and the disengagement theory of optimal aging need major modifications; and that neither theory is adequate or sufficiently complex to account for the present findings.

Third we shall propose that personality is the pivotal dimension in the various patterns of aging that have emerged from our data and suggest ways of exploring the area of personality difference.

THE SAMPLES AND THE DATA

In order to study the relations between engagement and life satisfaction, it is necessary to establish reliable measures of engagement; then to measure engagement in persons who represent some definite population group. These steps have now been completed in the Kansas City Study of Adult Life, using two samples of men and women who have been studied over a period of six years.

The first sample, referred to as the panel group, were persons aged 50 to 70 at the time they were first interviewed in 1956. The panel represents a stratified probability sample of middle and working class white persons of this age range residing in the metropolitan area of Kansas City. Excluded were the chronically ill and the physically impaired. The method by which the panel was selected resulted in a group that is biased toward middle class—in other words, a group that is better educated, wealthier, and of higher occupational and residential prestige than is true of the universe of 50 to 70-year-olds.

The second group, referred to as the quasi-panel, were persons aged 70–90 who joined the Kansas City Study two years after field work had begun. This older group was built up on the basis of quota sampling rather than probability sampling. The group consists of middle-and working-class persons, none of them financially deprived and none of them bed-ridden or senile.

While the panel probably has a greater middle-class bias than the quasi-panel, it is likely that the second sample, the older members of the study population, are less representative of their universe than is true of the panel members. Not only are these older persons better off financially, but they are in better health than most 70-to 90-year-olds; thus they represent an advantaged rather than a typical group.

Of the original panel, 62 percent are included in the present study. These persons remained as cooperating respondents at the end of seven rounds of interviews. Of the original quasi-panel, 49 percent remained at the end, after five rounds of interviews. Thus, in addition to the various biases operating in the original selection of the two groups (for instance, 16 percent of those on the initial sample list refused to join the panel), there is an unmeasurable effect on the present study due to sample attrition. Of the attrition, 27 percent has been due to deaths; 12 percent, to geographical moves; and the rest, to refusals to be interviewed at some time during the series of interviews, usually because of reported poor health. There is evidence also that persons who were relatively socially isolated constituted a disproportionate number of the dropouts. (The present sample is that which remains of the one described at greater length in Cumming and Henry [1961]. The population being reported here, by contrast, is approximately 55 percent of the original group, and ac-

Table 4.1. The Study Population: By Sex, Social Class, and Age in 1962

| | Age group | | | | | | |
Social class	54–59	60–64	65–69	70–74	75–79	80–94	Total
Upper middle:							
Men	7	4	4	2	4	1	22
Women	3	2	3	4	7	4	23
Lower middle:							
Men	2	4	3	1	4	4	18
Women	4	6	5	7	6	6	34
Working:							
Men	5	7	5	6	5	4	32
Women	4	6	3	5	8	4	30
Total:							
Men	14	15	12	9	13	9	72
Women	11	14	11	16	21	14	87
	25	29	23	25	34	23	159

cordingly has become increasingly less representative of the universe from which it was drawn.)

A total of 159 men and women serve as the study group for the present report. Table 4.1 shows the distribution by age, sex, and social class in 1962, when the final round of interviews was completed. The upper-middle class is composed of business and professional occupations; the lower-middle includes the lower white-collar occupations and a few skilled manual workers; and the working class represents blue-collar workers who are above the lowest 15 percent of the American population in income. Since many of the sample were retired or widowed, the principal occupation of the subject or spouse at the time of his best job was taken as the major index of social status.

The data consisted of lengthy and repeated interviews covering many aspects of the respondent's life pattern, his attitudes, and his values. Included was information on the daily round of activities and the usual week-end round; on other household members, relatives, friends, and neighbors; on income, work, and retirement; religion; voluntary organizations; estimates of the amount of social interaction as compared with the amount at age 45; attitudes toward old age, illness, death, and immortality; questions about loneliness, boredom, anger; and questions regarding the respondent's role models and his self-image. There were also thematic apperception tests included in some of the interviews. A special long interview was carried out with 88 of the sample by a clinical psychologist.

THE MEASURES OF ENGAGEMENT

It is well to begin with a distinction between *social* engagement and *psychological* engagement. The first refers to the interactions that occur between the aging individual and the persons he meets face to face in the course of everyday living; and refers, therefore, to interactions which would be directly visible to an observer (although they are assessed here on the basis of the respondent's own report).

The second refers to behavior that may not be directly observable, that reflects the extent to which the aging individual is preoccupied with, and/or emotionally invested in, persons and events in the external world. The respondent may or may not be aware of changes in quantity or quality of his psychological involvements.

The two types of engagement are usually, but not always, related. The individual whose work, family, and recreational activities bring him into interaction with a great many people in the course of the day is usually the individual who is highly invested in other persons, objects, and events in the environment; while the individual who is socially withdrawn tends also to be psychologically withdrawn. On the other hand, there are many persons for whom this relationship does not hold true: persons who become relatively isolated but who try unsuccessfully to maintain a high level of social participation; and persons whose work, family, and other social commitments remain high in the face of their own preference for increased privacy and what might be termed a growing indifference to many of the persons around them.

With increasing age, the two types of disengagement might be found to proceed independently of each other. It is a matter of major importance whether or not they do, indeed, occur at different rates; and whether one usually precedes the other. In the activity theory for instance, it is presumed that social disengagement occurs in the absence of psychological disengagement; and to the extent that the older person shows psychological withdrawal it is in response to the changed social climate in which he finds himself. In the disengagement theory, however, it is presumed that psychological disengagement accompanies, or even precedes the social; and that disengagement is, accordingly, a developmental phenomenon, inherent within the individual.

Because the question of order and timing of change along these two dimensions is of such theoretical significance, we have attempted to differentiate measures of social from measures of psychological engagement. If psychological disengagement is shown to precede social, this would provide evidence (though not proof) that we are dealing with a developmental phenomenon.

Social Engagement

Social engagement was measured in two ways. The first, called the *Interaction Index*, is a judgment made by the investigator of the amount of each day R spends in the kind of social interaction with other persons in which the hints, cues, and sanctions which govern and control behavior can be exchanged. Scoring was based on verbatim reports of R's daily round of activities. The score does not relate directly to the variety of roles or the number of people interacted with. An aged man who spends all day at home with his wife may receive as high a score as a person who works at a job with others, who has an active social and recreational life, but who lives alone.

The second approach to social engagement involved a set of three measures, all three related to performance in eleven life-roles: worker, spouse, parent, grandparent, kin-group member, home-maker, friend, neighbor, citizen, club-member, and church-member. The first of these is *Present Role Activity*, a summation of subscores based on ratings of extent and intensity of activity in each of the eleven roles. For example, a man who lives with his wife, but who shares with her few activities other than perfunctory routines such as eating his meals in her company, is rated low in the role of spouse. By contrast, a man who plans and carries out most of his day's activities in the company of his wife is rated high in the role of spouse. A widowed man is scored zero on spouse, thus diminishing his total score on Present Role Activity.

A related measure is that of *Ego-Investment in Present Roles*—the extent to which the individual is ego-involved in his various life-roles. For example, the man who prides himself on being a good husband and who gives evidence of this as he talks about his relationship with his wife, is rated high on investment in the role of spouse. Although ego-investment stands somewhere between social and psychological engagement as we have defined the two, the measure used here correlated .87 with role-activity for this sample. It seemed better, accordingly, to treat it as a measure of social engagement rather than as a measure of psychological engagement.

The third measure is *Change in Role Activity since Age 60* (or, for those under 70, change in the past 10 years.) For example, a man who had fully retired from a full-time job would be rated as having had the maximum negative change in that role. Another man who had become a grandfather

Table 4.2. Age Differences in Interaction Index, Role Behavior, Affect, and Life Satisfaction

					Measures of role-behavior					
Age in 1962	Number		Interaction index		Present role activity		Ego investment in present roles		Changes in role activity since age 60	
	M	F	M	F	M	F	M	F	M	F
54–59	14	11	2.6	2.8	43.7	49.1	34.6	42.0	−1.5‡	−1.3‡
60–64	15	14	2.5	2.8	45.9	42.7	35.3	34.0	−1.0	−2.2
65–69	12	11	2.6	2.7	44.1	47.9†	32.5	37.5	−3.1	−3.4
70–74	9	16	2.4	2.5	44.6	38.4	30.1	29.2	−3.1	−5.8
75–79	13	21	2.2	2.4	42.0	37.3	29.0	28.5	−6.4	−7.3
80–94	9	14	2.0	2.1	28.9	31.5	19.2	27.1	−10.0	−10.5
54–69	41	36	2.6	2.8	44.6	46.5	34.2	37.9	−1.8	−2.2
70–94	31	51	2.2	2.4*	38.9*	36.1**	26.5**	28.4**	−6.6**	−7.7**

* The difference on the measures between the below-70- and over-70-year-olds is significant at the .05 level.
** These differences are significant beyond the .01 level.
† The sharp upward turn in Role Activity for the 65–69 age women is due in part to the fact that this group included an unusually low proportion of widows and never-married women, and therefore had an unusually high proportion of women with positive scores in the "spouse" role.
‡ For this group, the questions referred to change over the past 10 years.

but who spent only a few days a year with his grandchildren would be rated as having a small positive change in that role.

Each *S* was rated on all three of these measures with regard to each of the eleven roles. Two independent judges rated each case, and the ratings were averaged. Reliability of ratings was high. For instance, for all ratings on the first 30 cases, and using consecutive pairs from among 10 judges, there were 50 percent exact agreements, and 95 percent agreements within one step on a five-step scale.

The fact that social disengagement takes place with increasing age is documented in Table 4.2, which shows the relations between age and each of the social interaction measures.

Although there is a statistically reliable decrease on these measures between the under-70 and the over-70 groups, the numbers in each age-group are too small to permit conclusions about changes from one five-year age group to the next. Involved also is the fact that given an almost 50 percent attrition in the total sample over the six years of data gathering, and the fact that the groups are based upon age in 1962 rather than in 1956, the age-groups are by no means to be regarded as equally representative.

For example, the 65-to 69-year-old group that remained in the study in

1962 was different in many ways from the other age groups. It included an unusually low proportion of widows and never-married women (widows and never-married women were 50, 18, and 75 percent, respectively, in the age groups 60–64, 65–69, and 70–74.) There had also been an unusually high attrition rate in this group due to deaths and to geographical moves.

For reasons such as these, the overall age trends, but not the differences between adjacent age-groups, provide the reliable indices of change in Table 4.2 as well as in successive tables. (In the authors' judgment, it is primarily the uncontrollable losses and uneven attrition rates in the subsamples that are reflected in the irregularities in the data shown in the tables.)

Psychological Engagement

Two measures of psychological engagement are reported here, both based on the Thematic Apperception Test, and both reflecting "inner" or covert processes.

Ego energy is the name applied to certain dimensions of ego functions: (1) the ability to integrate wide ranges of stimuli; (2) the readiness to perceive or to deal with complicated, challenging, or conflictful situations; (3) the tendency to perceive or to be concerned with feelings and affects as these play a part in life situations; and (4) the tendency to perceive vigorous and assertive activity in the self and in others.

Methods of measuring these dimensions on the TAT have been reported in an earlier study, where it was suggested that there is an intrinsic decrease of ego energy in the latter part of life (Rosen and Neugarten, 1960). This decrease may be due to aging of the central nervous system; to a welling up of unacceptable impulses in the later years which require the use of ego energy for their repression; and/or to the decline in visual and auditory acuity and in physical energy which may place an added burden on the ego when it must act in complex situations. These latter conditions would interfere with the use of ego energy in meeting the demands of everyday life and thus reduce the amount of ego energy available for dealing with the outer world.

The TAT was given to respondents in the second round of interviews, in 1957; and again, in the seventh round, in 1962. When protocols were analyzed without knowledge of age of respondent or date of testing, the data showed consistent drop in ego energy for each of the age-groups, as shown in Table 4.3. This drop in scores is interpreted as indirect evidence of psychological disengagement.

The second index of psychological engagement relates to what may be

Table 4.3. Change in Ego Energy over a 5-Year Interval

Age in 1962	N	Mean Score in 1957	Mean Score in 1962
55–59	24	16.6	14.6
60–64	28	16.1	14.3
65–69*	16	19.1	18.3
70–76	25	14.2	13.9
Total	93	16.3	15.0**

* The 65–69 group was only a part of the total 65–69 group who were studied in 1957. By 1962 there had been more losses in this group than in others owing to deaths and geographical moves.
** The difference between means for the total group is significant at the .01 level.
NOTE: Because of the small numbers in each age group; and because the subgroups are not equally representative, age differences should not be read from either column 2 or column 3, but from the differences between the two columns — that is, from the test-retest differences.

called *ego-style*, as inferred from TAT stories. Without knowledge of age of respondents, TAT protocols for the 135 people for whom these data were available were grouped into three major categories. The categories differ according to the manner in which the respondent perceives psychological issues represented in the pictures and the manner in which he attempts to resolve or to master those issues (Gutmann, 1964).

The category called *Active* included those stories in which issues are perceived as originating primarily in the external world, and in which the approach is assertive and active. In the *Passive* category there is a tendency to withdraw from active engagement with the external world in favor of more passive positions. Aggression and self-assertion are alien to the ego. The self, rather than the world, is the focus of control. In the *Magical* category, stories often contain misinterpretations and distortions of stimuli so gross as to suggest that primitive motivations are interfering with the respondent's accurate perception of the world. Ego functions have undergone regression, and attempts at resolutions are more often magical than realistic.

When the protocols were decoded for age of respondent, the age distribution of ego-styles that emerged is shown in Table 4.4. The increased frequency of Passive and Magical styles in the older age groups—styles in which the self or the inner impulse life pose more salient issues than do stimuli from the external world—is interpreted as evidence of psychological disengagement.

Table 4.4. Ego-Styles: By Age

Ego-style	Age		
	50–56	57–60	61–70
Active:			
Male	11	7	5
Female	10	9	5
Total*	21	16	10
Passive:			
Male	7	13	11
Female	8	4	11
Total*	15	17	22
Magical:			
Male	6	3	10
Female	2	3	12
Total*	8	6	22

*The distribution of age subtotals is significantly different from chance at the .01 level, by the Chi-Square test.
NOTE: This analysis was carried by David L. Gutmann and has been described in greater detail elsewhere (Gutmann, 1964).

The Relationship between Social and Psychological Disengagement

There is substantial evidence in Tables 4.2, 4.3, and 4.4 for decline in both social and psychological engagement:[1] there is demonstrable change with age in the degree and quality of activity in the various life-roles; and a withdrawal of psychological investment from the external environment.

There is clearer decline in psychological than in social engagement in the 50s, possibly a foreshadowing of the social disengagement that appears in the 60s and 70s. The evidence that the psychological seems to precede the social implies that disengagement may be, in some respects, a developmental phenomenon—a process that has intrinsic, as well as responsive, elements. It is true that the present evidence is insufficient to establish this point. Psychological disengagement might represent an anticipatory response process, rather than a developmental one, a process in which the individual anticipates shrinkage in his social world and undergoes adaptive (or defensive) preparatory maneuvers by withdrawing cathexis from the external world. It appears to us more likely, however, given the nature of our psychological measures, that the disengagement process has at least certain developmental elements. At any rate, this is a testable hypothesis which merits further investigation.[2]

MEASURES OF AFFECT AND SATISFACTION

With this evidence for disengagement as a *process* of aging, we turn next to the relations between measures of engagement on the one hand and measures of affect and life satisfaction on the other hand.

Life Satisfaction

The concept of "life satisfaction" as a measure of psychological well-being has been defined in an earlier publication. Rating scales were devised for five components of life satisfaction: Zest (vs. apathy); Resolution and Fortitude; Congruence between desired and achieved goals; Positive self-concept; and Mood tone (Neugarten et al., 1961). In brief, an individual was regarded as being at the positive end of the continuum of psychological well-being to the extent that he: (A) takes pleasure from whatever the round of activities that constitutes his everyday life; (B) regards his life as meaningful and accepts resolutely that which life has been; (C) feels he has succeeded in achieving his major goals; (D) holds a positive image of self; and (E) maintains happy and optimistic attitudes and mood.

Each of these five components was rated on a five-point scale; and the ratings were summed to obtain an overall rating with a possible range from 5 (low) to 25 (high). In making the Life Satisfaction Ratings, all the interview data on each respondent were utilized. Thus the ratings are based, not on R's direct self report of satisfaction (although some questions of this type were included in the interviews), but on the inferences drawn by the raters from all the information available on R, including his interpersonal relationships and the way in which others reacted toward him.

The ratings were made on seven rounds of interviews covering a period of six years in the lives of the respondents. In every case the ratings of two judges working independently were combined. The coefficient of correlation between ratings of two judges for 177 cases was .78 (becoming .87 when the Spearman-Brown coefficient of attenuation is used). For the 159 cases in the present study, LSR scores ranged from 8.5 to 25, with a mean of 17.8 and a standard deviation of 3.3.

It should be noted that the LSR is not limited to feelings of satisfaction with one's present situation. Two of the five components—Resolution or Fortitude, and Congruence between desired and achieved goals—are based upon a person's attitude toward his life as a whole. R might be depressed or apathetic at the time of the interview and still be given fairly high LSR ratings if he accepts resolutely and positively that which life has been for him and if he feels that he has achieved his personal goals in life.

Affect Regarding Present Role Activity

Another measure of psychological well-being was a rating on affect regarding present level of activity in the life-roles. This rating differed from the LSR in being related only to the respondent's feelings about his present activities. (The correlation coefficient between LSR and Affect-*re*-Present-Role-Activity was .46.) A separate rating was made for each of the life-roles, and the ratings were added to give the total "affect" score. A person who was not working, or who was widowed, or who was not a grandparent, was scored zero in these roles, which lowered his total score. Ratings were based on the seventh interview (1962) with such additional evidence as could be obtained from the earlier interviews. The ratings of two judges were averaged for each case. (These ratings were of the same level of reliability as those of LSR.)

Affect-*re*-Present-Activity was not necessarily correlated with level of activity in a role. For example, a man who was still working but wished to retire was rated average or low with regard to affect *re* role of worker. To take another example, a woman who seldom saw her grandchildren and who was therefore rated low in activity as grandmother would be rated high on effect in the grandmother role if she was content with this state of affairs. Another woman who saw her married daughter every day, but complained that her children neglected her, was rated low in affect for the mother role.

Affect re Change in Role Activity

A third measure, as the name itself implies, relates to change rather than to present activity patterns. This was a rating made by judges on the basis of responses to numerous questions asking about changes in role patterns and how the respondent felt about these changes.

The relation of age to each of these three measures of affect and/or satisfaction are shown in Table 4.5.

RELATIONS BETWEEN ENGAGEMENT AND SATISFACTION

The general question that concerns us first is whether people become more or less content with their level of activity as they grow older. We wanted to

Table 4.5. Age Differences in Affect and in Life Satisfaction

	Number		Life satisfaction rating		Affect *re* present role activity		Affect *re* change in role activity	
Age	M	F	M	F	M	F	M	F
54–59	14	11	17.9	17.8	37.5	42.3	−.37	.33
60–64	15	14	17.2	18.5	38.3	35.4	−.47	−.50
65–69	12	11	19.0	17.2	33.4	35.1	.25	2.30
70–74	9	16	18.9	16.7	38.0	34.5	−1.00	−1.30
75–79	13	21	17.8	18.9	33.1	34.5	.31	−1.05
80–94	9	14	16.9	16.6	27.9	32.4	−5.11	−4.36
54–69	41	36	18.0	17.9	36.6	37.7	−.19	.62
70–94	31	51	17.9	17.6	33.0*	33.9*	−1.64	−2.02*

*The overall age trend, but not the differences between adjacent age-groups, provides the reliable index of decline with age. The differences between the under-70 and over-70 groups are statistically reliable at the .05 level or beyond.

know how the sense of psychological well-being varies in relation to role activity and to change of role activity, as persons move from middle age through old age.

There are two ways of approaching this question. The first is to examine the age trends on the various measures.

Age Trends

For this purpose we need to look again at Tables 4.2 and 4.5. Examination of these two tables shows that there are decreases in role-activity and in ego-investment with age; and at the same time, Affect-*re*-Role-Activity decreases. Furthermore, there is increasingly more negative Affect-*re*-Change as people grow older.

Thus, in general, as activity decreases, the sense of well-being associated with it decreases during the years after 60. Most respondents regret the losses in activity, and increasingly so at the oldest ages.

On the other hand the Life Satisfaction Rating does not decrease appreciably with age. People are generally able to accept a loss in role activity as they move through their 70s. They regret the loss, and regard it with negative affect; yet at the same time, they maintain a positive evaluation of themselves and satisfaction with past and present life as a whole.

Table 4.6. Correlations between Measures of Engagement and Measures of Satisfaction (N=159)

	B	C	D	E	F	G
A Present Role Activity	.87	.73	−.51	.40	.46	.53
B Ego Investment in Present Roles		.79	−.44	.41	.51	.54
C Affect *re* Present Role Activity			−.41	.43	.46	.38
D Change in Role Activity Since Age 60*				−.60	−.27	−.30
E Affect *re* Change in Role Activity					.35	.22
F Life Satisfaction Rating						.43
G Interaction Index						X

*The change in role activity is usually, but not always, a decrease. The more the decrease, the less positive the affect. It is this relationship that is expressed in the negative sign of the correlations.

Correlations between Measures

The second approach to the relations between activity and satisfaction is to consider the statistical intercorrelations between our various measures, as shown in Table 4.6.

The correlation between role-activity and Affect-*re*-Role-Activity is .73 for the total group. This suggests that the usual patterns to be found in this sample are high activity together with positive affect, and low activity together with negative affect. At the same time, given the size of the correlation coefficient, there are persons who show the opposite combinations—persons who are content though they are relatively inactive; and persons who are discontent even though they are relatively active.

Next, the correlation is −.60 between *change* in role activity (change is usually, though not always, in the direction of decrease) and affect regarding the change. In other words, the greater the loss of activity, the greater are the negative feelings attached thereto.

Let us turn next to the correlation between role-activity and LSR. Since LSR reflects the subject's evaluation of himself and his life as a whole, both past and present, it might be expected that this measure would have a lower correlation with present role-activity than do the Affect measures. This proves to be the case, since the correlation between activity and LSR is .46.[3]

Both these approaches to the data—age trends on separate measures, and correlations between measures—thus yield the same general findings: that those older persons who continue the greatest amounts of activity generally have greater psychological well-being than those who have lower levels of activity. At the same time, this relationship is far from consistent, and all four combinations of activity and satisfaction exist—that is, high-high and low-low are the most frequent; but there are also high-low and low-high patterns.

Neither the "activity" theory nor the disengagement theory accounts satisfactorily for this diversity.[4]

Changes with Age in Correlations between Measures

If the decrease of role activity is easily tolerated or even welcomed by people as they grow older—as is implied by the disengagement theory—then the correlation coefficients between role activity, affect, and LSR should become smaller in size with advancing age.

To test this hypothesis, the respondents were divided into two groups, those above 70 and those below 70; and the correlations between measures were computed separately for each group. The two sets of intercorrelations are not reproduced here, but they are very similar, which negates the hypothesis. Furthermore, the correlations between activity, ego-investment, and affect-*re*-activity are even higher for those persons over 70 than for those under 70. This indicates that there is no dropping off of concern regarding activity as people move beyond age 70; and, again, that the hypothesis is not substantiated.

With the varied patterns of activity, affect, and life satisfaction before us, we plan to turn next in our analyses of the Kansas City data to a consideration of the ways in which differences in personality are related to these patterns. Meanwhile to summarize our findings thus far:

1. Our data provide convincing evidence of decline in both social and psychological engagement with increasing age. Disengagement seems to us to be a useful term by which to describe these processes of change.

2. In some ways our data support the activity theory of optimal aging: as level of activity decreases, so also does the individual's feeling of contentment regarding his present activity.

3. At the same time, the data in some ways support the disengagement theory of optimal aging. The relationship between life satisfaction and present activity while positive, is only moderate, thus providing all four combinations of activity and life-satisfaction: high-high and low-low, but also high-low and low-high.

4. We conclude that neither the activity theory nor the disengagement theory of optimal aging is itself sufficient to account for what we regard as

the more inclusive description of these findings: that as men and women move beyond age 70 in a modern, industrialized community like Kansas City, they regret the drop in role activity that occurs in their lives. At the same time, most older persons accept this drop as an inevitable accompaniment of growing old; and they succeed in maintaining a sense of self-worth and a sense of satisfaction with past and present life as a whole. Other older persons are less successful in resolving these conflicting elements—not only do they have strong negative affect regarding losses in activity; but the present losses weigh heavily, and are accompanied by a dissatisfaction with past and present life.

5. There appear to be two sets of values operating simultaneously, if not within the same individual then within the group we have been studying: on the one hand, the desire to stay active in order to maintain a sense of self-worth; on the other hand, the desire to withdraw from social commitments and to pursue a more leisurely and a more contemplative way of life. Neither the activity theory nor the disengagement theory of optimum aging takes sufficient account of this duality in value patterns.[5]

6. The relations between levels of activity and life satisfaction are probably influenced also by personality type, particularly by the extent to which the individual remains able to integrate emotional and rational elements of the personality. It is for this reason, also, that neither the activity nor the disengagement theory is satisfactory, since neither deals, except peripherally, with the issue of personality differences. This topic requires further exploration in these data.

A final comment may be warranted in relating disengagement to patterns of aging. The increased freedom of the aged implied in the disengagement theory lies, perhaps, in the freedom from role obligations; the man who is retired and whose family and community responsibilities are diminished is more free to pursue those activities and those ideas that he regards as important. To one individual this may mean freedom to indulge in material comforts, to indulge passive and succorant needs, and to take on a more hedonistic or carefree life. For another this may mean freedom to pursue what he regards as the important social values and to devote more time to the examination of philosophical and religious concepts. For still another, this may mean freedom to choose the work and community roles that symbolize his sense of worth and to remain highly engaged.

From this perspective, the aging individual may or may not disengage from the pattern of role activities that characterized him in middle age. It is highly doubtful, however, that he ever disengages from the values of the society which he has so long internalized. It is even more doubtful that the aging individual ever disengages from the personality pattern that has so long been the self.

NOTES

1. Although both show a decline with age, there is a relatively low degree of correlation between our measures of psychological and social engagement—that is, the individual who is low on one is not necessarily low on the other. In addition to the fact that psychological disengagement seems to precede social disengagement, there are probably three other factors involved: (1) In many important ways, the individual cannot control nor manipulate the environment in ways to suit his needs. He cannot, for instance, choose to become widowed or to become a grandparent; and in this sense he cannot choose, except within limits, a pattern of life that will yield a high score or a low score on role activity. (2) It is not known how much psychological disengagement may occur before this process manifests itself in social behavior; or, conversely, how much of the quality we have called ego-energy is required to sustain a high level of role activity. Perhaps the psychological changes occurring within this sample are all below the threshold, in this regard. (3) In a larger and more representative sample, one in which relatively disadvantaged as well as advantaged 70-and 80-year-olds were included, it might be expected that psychological and social engagement would show a greater degree of correlation.

2. See the chapter by Gutmann in Part 3 of this book, ''Aging among the Highland Maya.'' Gutmann reports substantially the same findings for Mayan man as for Kansas City man.

3. This correlation obscures sex differences: the correlation for men under 70 is .65 and for women under 70 it is .20. For men over 70 the correlation is .44 and for women over 70 it is .52. The correlation drops with increasing age for men, but goes up for women.

4. In a crossnational study now being completed groups of 70 to 75-year-old retired teachers and retired steelworkers were drawn from each of six cities: Bonn (West Germany), Vienna, Nijmegen (Holland), Milan, Warsaw, and Chicago. In group after group the correlations were positive between social role activity and a measure of psychological well-being similar to the LSR; and for all 300 cases pooled, the correlation turned out to be .45, almost exactly the same correlation as found here in the Kansas City data. Findings from the crossnational study Havighurst et al., 1970.

5. The late Dr. Yonina Talmon-Garber, in discussing these findings with us, suggested that the activity theory and the disengagement theory of optimal aging might themselves reflect historical changes in value patterns. As the American society becomes more leisure-than work-oriented, there may be an effect upon the theories put forth by social scientists regarding the sources of satisfaction with life.

REFERENCES

Cumming, E. & Henry, W. (1961). Growing old. *New York: Basic Books.*

Gutmann, D. (1964). An exploration of ego configurations in middle and later life. In B. L. Neugarten (Ed.) Personality in middle and later life *(pp. 114–148). New York: Atherton.*

Gutmann, D. (1967). Aging among the highland Maya: A comparative study. Journal of Personality and Social Psychology, 7, *28–35. Reprinted as chapter 21 in this volume.*

Havighurst, R. J. Munnichs., J. M. A., Neugarten, B. L. & Thomae, H. (Eds.) (1970). Adjustment to retirement. *Assen, Netherlands: Van Gorcum.*

Neugarten, B. L., Havighurst, R. J. & Tobin, S. S. (1961). The measurement of life satisfaction. Journal of Gerontology, 16, *134–143. Reprinted as chapter 30 in this volume.*

Rosen, J. L. & Neugarten, B. L. (1960). Ego functions in the middle and later years. Journal of Gerontology, 15, *62–67.*

5. Theoretical Propositions of Life-Span Developmental Psychology

On the Dynamics between Growth and Decline

Paul B. Baltes

The STUDY OF LIFE-SPAN development is not a homogeneous field. It comes in two major interrelated modes. The first mode is the extension of developmental studies across the life course without a major effort at the construction of metatheory that emanates from life-span work. The second mode includes the endeavor to explore whether life-span research has specific implications for the general nature of developmental theory. The second approach represents the topic of this article.

Specifically, the purpose of this article is twofold. First, after a brief introduction to the field of life-span developmental psychology, some "prototypical" features of the life-span approach in developmental psychology are presented. Second, these features are illustrated by work in one domain: intellectual development. Although the focus of this paper is on life-span developmental psychology and its theoretical thrust, it is important to recognize at the outset that similar perspectives on developmental theory have been advanced in other quarters developmental scholarship as well (Hetherington & Baltes, 1988, Scarr, 1986). There is, however, a major difference in the "gestalt" in which the features of the theoretical perspective of life-span psychology are organized.

Several, if not most, of the arguments presented here are consistent with earlier publications by the author and others on the field of life-span developmental psychology (Baltes, 1983; Baltes & Reese, 1984; Featherman, 1983; Honzik, 1984; Lerner, 1984; Sherrod & Brim, 1986). This article includes two added emphases. First, it represents an effort to illustrate the implications of the theoretical perspectives associated with life-span work for research in cognitive development. Second, two of the more recent perspectives derived from life-span work are given special attention. The first is that *any* process of development entails an inherent dynamic between gains and losses. According to this belief, no process of development consists only of growth or progression. The second proposition states that the range of plasticity can best be studied with a research strategy called *testing-the-limits*.

WHAT IS LIFE-SPAN DEVELOPMENT?

Life-span developmental psychology involves the study of constancy and change in behavior throughout the life course (ontogenesis), from conception to death.[1] The goal is to obtain knowledge about general principles of life-long development, about interindividual differences and similarities in development, as well as about the degree and conditions of individual plasticity or modifiability of development (Baltes, Reese & Nesselroade, 1977; Lerner, 1984; Thomae, 1979).

It is usually assumed that child development, rather than life-span development, was the subject matter of the initial scholarly pursuits into psychological ontogenesis. Several historical reviews suggest that this generalization is inaccurate (Baltes, 1983; Groffmann, 1970; Reinert, 1979). The major historical precursors of scholarship on the nature of psychological development—by Tetens in 1777, Carus in 1808, Quetelet in 1835—were essentially life-span and not child-centered in approach. Despite these early origins of life-span thinking, however, life-span development has begun to be studied empirically only during the last two decades by researchers following the lead of early twentieth-century psychologists such as Charlotte Bühler (1933), Erik H. Erikson (1959), G. Stanley Hall (1922), H. L. Hollingworth (1927), and Carl G. Jung (1933).

Three events seem particularly relevant to the more recent burgeoning of interest in life-span conceptions: (a) population demographic changes toward a higher percentage of elderly members; (b) the concurrent emergence of gerontology as a field of specialization, with its search for the life-long precursors of aging (Birren & Schaie, 1985); and (c) the ''aging'' of the subjects and researchers of the several classical longitudinal studies on child development begun in the 1920s and 1930s (Migdal, Abeles & Sherrod, 1981; Verdonik & Sherrod, 1984). These events and others have pushed developmental scholarship toward recognizing the entire life span as a scientifically and socially important focus.

Added justification for a life-span view of ontogenesis and important scholarly contributions originate in other disciplines as well. One such impetus for life-span work comes from sociology and anthropology (Bertaux & Kohli, 1984; Brim & Wheeler, 1966; Clausen, 1986; Dannefer, 1984; Elder, 1985; Featherman, 1983; Featherman & Lerner, 1985; Kertzer & Keith, 1983; Neugarten & Datan, 1973; Riley, 1985; Riley, Johnson & Foner, 1972). Especially within sociology, the study of the life course and of the interage and intergenerational fabric of society is enjoying a level of attention comparable with that of the life-span approach in psychology.

Another societal or social raison d'être for the existence of life-span interest is the status of the life course in longstanding images that societies and their members hold about the life span (Philibert, 1968; Sears, 1986). In the humanities, for example, life-span considerations have been shown to be part of everyday views of the structure and function of the human condition for many centuries. The Jewish Talmud, Greek and Roman philosophy (e.g., the writings of Solon and Cicero), literary works such as those of Shakespeare, Goethe, or Schopenhauer, all contain fairly precise images and beliefs about the nature of life-long change and its embeddedness in the age-graded structure of the society. Particularly vivid examples of such social images of the life span come from the arts. During the last centuries, many works of art were produced, reproduced, and modified in most European countries, each using stages, steps, or ladders as a framework for depicting the human life course (Joerissen & Will, 1983; Sears, 1986).

These observations on literature, art history, and social images of the life course suggest that the field of life-span development is by no means an invention of developmental psychologists. Rather, its recent emergence in psychology reflects the perhaps belated effort on the part of psychologists to attend to an aspect of the human condition that is part and parcel of our everyday cultural knowledge systems about living organisms. Such social images suggest that the life course is something akin to a natural. social category of knowledge about ontogenesis and the human condition.

IS LIFE-SPAN DEVELOPMENT A THEORY OR A FIELD OF SPECIALIZATION?

What about the theoretical spectrum represented by life-span developmental psychology? Is it a single theory, a collection of subtheories, or just a theoretical orientation? Initial interest often converges on the immediate search for one overarching and unifying theory such as Erikson's (1959). The current research scene suggests that in the immediate future life-span developmental psychology will not be identified with a single theory. It is above all a subject matter divided into varying scholarly specializations. The most general orientation toward this subject matter is simply to view behavioral development as a life-long process.

Such a lack of theoretical specificity may come as a surprise and be seen as a sign that the life-span perspective is doomed. In fact, the quest for a single, good theory (and the resulting frustration when none is offered) is an occasional challenge laid at the doorsteps of life-span scholars (Kaplan, 1983; Scholnick, 1985; Sears, 1980). Note, however, that the same lack of theoretical specificity applies to other fields of developmental specialization. Infant development, child development, gerontology, are also not theories in themselves, nor should one expect that there would be a single theory in any of these fields. In fact, as long as scholars look for *the* theory of life-span development they are likely to be disappointed.

A FAMILY OF PERSPECTIVES CHARACTERIZES THE LIFE-SPAN APPROACH

Much of life-span research proceeds within the theoretical scenarios of child developmental or aging work. In addition, however, efforts have been made by a fair number of life-span scholars to examine the question of whether life-span research suggests a particular metatheoretical world view (Reese & Overton, 1970) on the nature of development. The theoretical posture proffered by this endeavor is the focus of the remainder of this article.

For many researchers, the life-span orientation entails several prototypical beliefs that, in their weighting and coordination, form a *family of perspectives* that together specify a coherent metatheoretical view on the nature of development. The significance of these beliefs lies not in the individual items but in the pattern. Indeed, none of the individual propositions taken separately is new, which is perhaps one reason why some commentators have argued that life-span work has little new to offer (Kaplan, 1983). Their significance consists instead in the whole complex of perspectives considered as a metatheoretical world view and applied with some degree of radicalism to the study of development.

What is this family of perspectives, which in their coordinated application characterizes the life-span approach? Perhaps no single set of beliefs would qualify in any definite sense. However, the beliefs summarized in Table 5.1 are likely to be shared by many life-span scholars. They can be identified primarily from the writings in psychology on this topic (Baltes & Reese, 1984: Baltes, Reese & Lipsitt, 1980; Lerner, 1984; Sherrod & Brim, 1986), but they are also consistent with sociological work on the life course (Elder, 1985; Featherman, 1983; Riley, 1985).

The family of beliefs will be illustrated below, primarily using the study of intellectual development as the forum for exposition. Because, historically, the period of adulthood was the primary arena of relevant research, that age period receives most coverage. It will also be shown, however, that the meta-theoretical posture may shed new light on intellectual development in younger age groups as well.

EMPIRICAL ILLUSTRATION: RESEARCH ON INTELLECTUAL DEVELOPMENT

The area of intellectual functioning is perhaps the best studied domain of life-span developmental psychology. The discussion and elaboration of the empirical and conceptual bases of the family of perspectives presented here is selective. The intent is not to be comprehensive but to offer examples of areas of research. (Different research findings and agendas—see, for instance, Keating & MacLean, 1987; Perlmutter, 1988; Sternberg, 1988, for other similar efforts—could have been used were it not for the particular preferences of the author.) More detailed information on the topic of life-span intelligence is contained in several recent publications (Baltes, Dittmann-Kohli & Dixon, 1984; Berg & Sternberg, 1985; Denney, 1984; Dixon & Baltes, 1986; Labouvie-Vief, 1985; Perlmutter, 1988; Rybash, Hoyer & Roodin, 1986; Salthouse, 1985).

Intellectual Development Is a Life-Long Process Involving Multidirectionality

The first two of the family of perspectives (see Table 5.1) state that behavior-change processes falling under the general rubric of development can occur at any point in the life course, from conception to death. Moreover, such developmental changes can display distinct trajectories as far as their directionality is concerned.

Life-long development. The notion of life-long development implies two aspects. First, there is the general idea that development extends over the entire life span. Second, there is the added possibility that life-long development may involve processes of change that do not originate at birth but lie in later periods of the life span. Considered as a whole, life-long development is a

Table 5.1. Summary of Family of Theoretical Propositions Characteristic of Life-Span Developmental Psychology

Concepts	Propositions
Life-span development	Ontogenetic development is a life-long process. No age period holds supremacy in regulating the nature of development. During development, and at all stages of the life span, both continuous (cumulative) and discontinuous (innovative) processes are at work.
Multidirectionality	Considerable diversity or pluralism is found in the directionality of changes that constitute ontogenesis, even within the same domain. The direction of change varies by categories of behavior. In addition, during the same developmental periods, some systems of behavior show increases, whereas others evince decreases in level of functioning.
Development as gain/loss	The process of development is not a simple movement toward higher efficacy, such as incremental growth. Rather, throughout life, development always consists of the joint occurrence of gain (growth) and loss (decline).
Plasticity	Much intraindividual plasticity (within-person modifiability) is found in psychological development. Depending on the life conditions and experiences by a given individual, his or her developmental course can take many forms. The key developmental agenda is the search for the range of plasticity and its constraints.
Historical embeddedness	Ontogenetic development can also vary substantially in accordance with historical-cultural conditions. How ontogenetic (age-related) development proceeds is markedly influenced by the kind of sociocultural conditions existing in a given historical period, and by how these evolve over time.
Contextualism as paradigm	Any particular course of individual development can be understood as the outcome of the interactions (dialectics) among three systems of developmental influences: age-graded, history-graded, and nonnormative. The operation of these systems can be characterized in terms of the metatheoretical principles associated with contextualism.
Field of development as multidisciplinary	Psychological development needs to be seen in the interdisciplinary context provided by other disciplines (e.g., anthropology, biology, sociology) concerned with human development. The openness of the life-span perspective to interdisciplinary posture implies that a "purist" psychological view offers but a partial representation of behavioral development from conception to death.

system of diverse change patterns that differ, for example, in terms of timing (onset, duration, termination), direction, and order.

One way to give substance to the notion of life-long development is to think of the kinds of demands and opportunities that individuals face as they move through life. Havighurst's (1972; Oerter, 1986) formulation of the concept of developmental tasks is a useful aid for grasping the notion of a life-long system of demands and opportunities. Developmental tasks involve a series of problems, challenges, or life-adjustment situations that come from biological development, social expectations, and personal action. These problems "change through life and give direction, force, and substance to . . . development" (Havighurst, 1973, p. 11).

Thus, the different developmental curves constitutive of life-long development can be interpreted to reflect different developmental tasks. Some of these developmental tasks—like Havighurst's conception—are strongly correlated with age. However, as will be shown later, such developmental tasks are also constituted from certain historical and nonnormative systems of influence.

Multidimensionality and multidirectionality. The terms *multidimensionality* and *multidirectionality* are among the key concepts used by life-span researchers to describe facets of plurality in the course of development and to promote a concept of development that is not bound by a single criterion of growth in terms of a general increase in size or functional efficacy.

Research on psychometric intelligence illustrates the usefulness of multidimensional and multidirectional conceptions of development. The psychometric theory of fluid-crystallized intelligence proposed by Cattell (1971) and Horn (1970, 1982) serves as an example (Figure 5.1). First, according to this theory, intelligence consists of several subcomponents. Fluid and crystallized intelligence are the two most important clusters of abilities in the theory. The postulate of a system of abilities is an example of multidimensionality. Second, these multiple-ability components are expected to differ in the direction of their development. Fluid intelligence shows a turning point in adulthood (toward decline), whereas crystallized intelligence exhibits the continuation of an incremental function. This is an example of the multidirectionality of development.

Meanwhile, the Cattell-Horn theoretical approach to life-span intellectual development has been supplemented with other conceptions, each also suggesting the possibility of multidimensional and multidirectional change. Berg and Sternberg (1985), for example, have examined the implications of Stern-

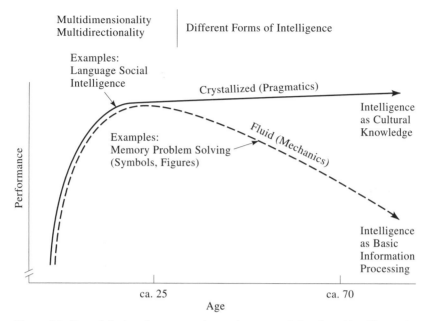

Figure 5.1. One of the best known psychometric structural theories of intelligence is that of Raymond B. Cattell and John L. Horn. (The two main clusters of that theory, fluid and crystallized intelligence, are postulated to display different life-span developmental trajectories.)

berg's triarchic theory of intelligence for the nature of life-long development. They emphasized that the age trajectories for the three postulated components of Sternberg's theory of intelligence (componential, contextual, experiential) are likely to vary in directionality.

Current work on life-span intelligence (Baltes, Dittmann-Kohli & Dixon, 1984; Dixon & Baltes, 1986) has also expanded on the Cattell–Horn model by linking it to ongoing work in cognitive psychology. Two domains of cognitive functioning are distinguished in a dual-process scheme: the "fluid" mechanics and the "crystallized" pragmatics of intelligence. The *mechanics of intelligence* refers to the basic architecture of information processing and problem solving. It deals with the basic cognitive operations and cognitive structures associated with such tasks as perceiving relations and classification. The second domain of the dual-process scheme, the *pragmatics of intelligence*, concerns the context- and knowledge-related application of the mechanics of intelligence. The intent is to subsume under the pragmatics of intelligence (a) fairly general systems of factual and procedural knowledge, such as crystallized intelligence; (b) specialized systems of factual and procedural knowledge, such as occupational expertise; and (c) knowledge about factors of performance, that is, about skills relevant for the activation of intelligence in specific contexts requiring intelligent action. The explicit focus on the pragmatics of intelligence demands (like Sternberg's concern with contextual and experiential components) a forceful consideration of the changing structure and function of knowledge systems across the life span (see also Featherman, 1983; Keating & MacLean, 1987; Labouvie-Vief, 1985; Rybash, Hoyer & Roodin, 1986).

New forms of intelligence in adulthood and old age? What about the question of later-life, "innovative" emergence of new forms of intelligence? It is one thing to argue in principle that new developmental acquisitions can emerge at later points in life with relatively little connection to earlier processes and quite another to demonstrate empirically the existence of such innovative, developmentally late phenomena. A classic example used by life-span researchers to illustrate the developmentally late emergence of a cognitive system is the process of reminiscence and life review (Butler, 1963). The process of reviewing and reconstructing one's life has been argued to be primarily a late-life phenomenon. The phenomenon of autobiographical memory is another example (Strube, 1985).

For the sample case of intelligence, it is an open question whether adulthood and old age bring with them new forms of directionality and intellectual functioning, or whether continuation and quantitative (but not qualitative) variation of past functioning is the gist of the process. On the one hand, there are Flavell's (1970) and Piaget's (1972) cognitive-structuralist accounts, which favor an interpretation of horizontal *décalage* rather than one of further structural evolution or transformation. These authors regard the basic cognitive operations as fixed by early adulthood. What changes afterwards is the content domains to which cognitive structures are applied.

On the other hand, there are very active research programs engaged in the search for qualitatively or structurally new forms of adult intelligence (Commons, Richards Armon, 1984). The work on dialectical and postformal operations by Basseches (1984), Labouvie-Vief (1982, 1985), Kramer (1983), Pascual-Leone (1983), and other related writings (e.g., Keating & MacLean, 1987) are notable examples of this effort. This line of scholarship has been much stimulated (or even launched) by Riegel's work on dialectical psychology and his outline of a possible fifth stage of cognitive development (Riegel, 1973, 1976).

Other work on adult intellectual development proceeds from a neofunctionalist perspective (Beilin, 1983; Dixon & Baltes, 1986) and is informed by work in cognitive psychology. Models of expertise (Glaser, 1984) and knowledge systems (Brown, 1982) guide this approach in which the question of structural stages is of lesser significance. Aside from an interest in the aging of the ''content-free'' mechanics of intelligence (Kliegl & Baltes, 1987), the dominant focus is on changes in systems of factual and procedural knowledge associated with the ''crystallized'' pragmatics of intelligence. The crystallized form of intelligence was highlighted already as an ability cluster exhibiting stability or even positive changes into late adulthood. The concept of crystallized intelligence, however, needs further expansion to cover additional domains of knowledge and to permit consideration of forms of knowledge more typical of the second half of life.

Expertise, a concept currently in vogue in cognitive and developmental psychology (Ericsson, 1985; Glaser, 1984; Hoyer, 1985; Weinert, Schneider & Knopf, 1988), can be used to illustrate this avenue of research. This concept denotes skills and knowledge that are highly developed and practiced. The sciences, chess, or job-related activities (e.g., typing) are often used as substantive domains in which performance in relation to the acquisition and maintenance of expertise is studied. The life course of many individuals most likely offers opportunity for the practice of such forms of expertise. Therefore, one would expect that further growth of intellectual functioning may occur in those domains in which individuals continue to practice and evolve their procedural and factual knowledge (Denny, 1984; Dixon & Baltes, 1986; Hoyer, 1985; Rybash 1986). In other words, expertise in select facets of the pragmatics of intelligence can be maintained, transformed, or even newly acquired in the second half of life if the conditions are such that selective optimization in the associated knowledge system can occur.

Two areas of knowledge have been identified as key candidates for domains in which the pragmatics of intelligence may exhibit positive changes during the second half of life: practical intelligence (Sternberg & Wagner, 1986) and knowledge about the pragmatics of life, such as is evident in research on social intelligence and wisdom (Clayton & Birren, 1980; Dittmann-Kohli & Baltes, 1990; Holliday & Chandler, 1986; Meacham, 1982). Wisdom, in particular, has been identified as a prototypical or exemplar task of the pragmatics of intelligence that may exhibit further advances in adulthood or whose origins may lie primarily in adulthood.

In one approach (Dittmann-Kohli & Baltes, 1990; Dixon & Baltes, 1986; Smith, Dixon & Baltes, n.d. wisdom is defined as an ''expertise in the fundamental pragmatics of life.'' In order to capture wisdom, subjects of different age groups are asked, for example, to elaborate on everyday problems of life planning and life review. The knowledge system displayed in protocols of life planning and life review is scored against a set of criteria derived from the theory of wisdom. First evidence (Smith et al.) suggests, as expected by the theory, that some older adults indeed seem to have available a well-developed system of knowledge about situations involving questions of life planning. For example, when older adults are asked to explore a relatively rare or odd life planning situation involving other older persons, they demonstrate a knowledge system that is more elaborated than that of younger adults.

The study of wisdom is just beginning. Thus, it is still an open question whether the concept of wisdom can be translated into empirical steps resulting in a well-articulated psychological theory of wisdom. We are somewhat optimistic, inasmuch as cognitive psychologists are increasingly studying tasks and reasoning problems that, like the problems to which wisdom is applied, have a high degree of real-life complexity, and whose problem, definition and solution involve uncertainty and relativism in judgment (Dörner, 1983; Neisser, 1982). In the present context, the important point is that research on wisdom is an illustration of the type of knowledge systems that developmental, cognitive researchers are beginning to study as their attention is focused on later periods of life.

Intellectual Development As a Dynamic between Growth (Gain) and Decline (Loss)

The next belief (see Table 5.1) associated with life-span work is the notion that any process of development entails aspects of growth (gain) and decline (loss). This belief is a fairly recent one and its theoretical foundation is not yet fully explored and tested.

The gain/loss argument. The gain/loss view of development emerged primarily for two reasons. The first relates to the task of defining the process of aging in a framework of development. The second reason deals with the fact of multidirectionality described earlier and the ensuing implication of simultaneous, multidirectional change for the characterization of development.

Concerning the issue of the definition of aging versus development: Traditionally in gerontology, there has been a strong push—especially by biologists (Kirkwood, 1985)—to define the essence of aging as decline (i.e., as a unidirectional process of loss in adaptive capacity). Behavioral scientists, because of their findings and expectations of some gains in old age, have had a tendency to reject this unidirectional, decline view of aging. Thus, they wanted to explore whether aging could be considered as part of a framework of development.

How could this integration of aging into the framework of development be achieved in light of the fact that the traditional definition of development was closely linked to growth, whereas that of aging was linked predominantly to decline? The suggestion of life-span researchers was to redefine or expand the concept of development beyond the biological conception of growth or progression. Specifically, the proposal was to expand the concept of development to include not only phenomena of growth (gain), but other directions of change as well (Baltes, 1983). As a result, development was defined as *any* change in the adaptive capacity of an organism, whether positive or negative. In developmental psychology, this proposal was consistent with other trends. Social learning theory, for example, had suggested a similar expansion of the directional nature of ontogenesis (Bandura, 1982).

The second and related reason for the emergence of the theme of gain–loss relations in development is a further elaboration of the notions of multidimensionality and multidirectionality of life-span intelligence. The separate concern for multiple-ability systems associated with multidirectionality was taken one step further to the examination of the relation and perhaps even the dynamic interplay *between* the various subsystems. The question guiding this investigation is whether the occurrence of multidirectional change, concurrently in separate components of the system (e.g., fluid vs. crystallized intelligence), requires a new conception of development itself. One possible avenue is to view development as a gain–loss relation (see also Baltes & Kliegl, 1986; Labouvie-Vief, 1980, 1982; Perlmutter, 1988). According to this view, development at all points of the life course is a joint expression of features of growth (gain) and decline (loss). It is assumed that any developmental progression displays at the same time new adaptive capacity as well as the loss of previously existing capacity. No developmental change during the life course is pure gain.

The view of development as a gain/loss phenomenon, of course, does not imply that throughout life gain and loss exist in equal strength. Systematic age-related changes in the gain/loss proportion are likely to be present. A possible life-span scenario of the dynamic between gains and losses is illustrated in Figure 5.2. Summarizing evidence across a wide spectrum of func-

Life-Span Development:
Gain/Loss Ratios in Adaptive Capacity

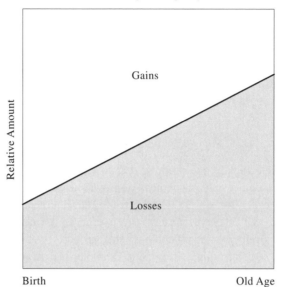

Figure 5.2. One theoretical expectation concerning the average course of gain/loss ratios is a proportional shift
across the life span.

tions, the proposition contained in Figure 5.2 is that the sum total of possible
gains and losses in adaptive capacity shifts proportionally with increasing
age. As a whole, life-span development proceeds within the constraints created by this dynamic.

The concern with an ongoing, developmental dynamic of positive (gains)
and negative (losses) change has spurred new research in life-span work. One
example is the attempt to specify a general process of adaptation that would
represent the life-long nature of development as a gain/loss relation. Some
of this work Baltes, 1987; Baltes, Dittmann-Kohli & Dixon, 1984; Dixon &
Baltes, 1986) has outlined a theoretical framework that is aimed at making
explicit the dynamic relation between gain and loss in development. In Table
5.2, what is described for the case of cognitive aging is perhaps a prototypical
change mechanism of "successful aging"—*selective optimization with compensation.*

The process of selective optimization with compensation has three features, each indicative of a gain/loss relation: (a) continual evolution of spe-

Table 5.2. Selective Optimization with Compensation: A Process Prototypical of Adaptive Life-Span Development of Cognitive Functioning

- A general feature of life-span development is an age-related increase in specialization (selection) of motivational and cognitive resources and skills.
- There are two main features of the aging of cognitive functions:
  (a) The reserve capacity for peak or maximum performances in fluid functioning (mechanics of intelligence) is reduced.
  (b) Some procedural and declarative knowledge systems (pragmatics of intelligence) can continue to evolve and function at peak levels.
- When, and if, limits (thresholds) of capacity are exceeded during the course of aging for a given individual, the following developmental consequences result:
  (a) Increased selection (channeling) and further reduction of the number of high-efficacy domains;
  (b) Development of compensatory and/or substitute mechanisms.

NOTE: This model is adapted from Baltes and Baltes (1980).

cialized forms of adaptation as a general feature of life-span development; (b) adaptation to the conditions of biological and social aging with its increasing limitation of plasticity; and (c) individual selective and compensatory efforts dealing with evolving deficits for the purpose of life mastery and effective aging.

Although the process of selective optimization and associated investments in terms of time, space, and behavior budgeting is assumed to be general and prototypical, its specific manifestation will vary depending on the individual life history. The emergence of compensatory and substitutive cognitive skills will also vary. For example, B. F. Skinner (1983) described in a personal account how and under which conditions he evolved compensatory or substitutive skills in the face of reduced effectiveness in select aspects of intellectual functioning.

Research by Salthouse (1984) on typing skills in old age is one persuasive example of how specialization and compensation interact in older adults to produce a high level of selective efficacy. Older expert typists—although showing less efficient reaction times than young expert typists when confronted with the typing of individual characters—nevertheless display good efficacy. They cope with their loss in reaction time when typing individual letters by developing more extensive forward-processing of letter and word sequences. As a result, older typists use a different combination of component skills than younger typists to produce a comparable level of overall performance.

Relevance of the gain/loss argument for other developmental questions. For historians interested in the study of social change and the idea of progress (Nisbet, 1980), the gain/loss argument is a truism. Few theorists would maintain that all of social change is progress.

What about ontogenesis? The notion that any ontogenetic change entails a dynamic interplay between gain and loss can be found also in biological conceptions such as Waddington's (1975) work on ontogenesis as differentiation and specialization (canalization). Beginning on the cellular level (Cotman, 1985; Lerner, 1984), differentiation clearly implies the loss of alternate courses of cell differentiation. Sociologists, too, have argued that the life course entails a process of specialization in the sense of commitment to and practice in selected domains of life (Featherman, 1983). Such a process of life-course specialization is assumed to imply a loss of alternative options.

Does the consideration of gains and losses as intrinsic to any developmental process have relevance for cognitive development in younger age groups? The fact that progress is not the only feature of age-related cognitive development has been known for quite some time. Weir's (1964) research with children on the developmental progression from maximization to optimization strategies in solving nonperfect probability tasks is a concrete example. This work shows that higher-level cognitive functioning (associated with the so-called optimization strategy) can have its costs when the task in question has no perfect solution. Specifically, when a cognitive task is logically unsolvable because it has no perfect solution, young children can outperform older children and adults. This is so because older children and adults assume the existence of a logically perfect solution and, therefore, engage in a problem-solving behavior that is criterion-inadequate.

One additional example is Ross's (1981) research on the development of judgmental heuristics. Developmentally later or more "mature" heuristics can be less efficient, depending on the problem to be solved. Another case is second-language learning. Although there is disagreement about the sources of this gain/loss phenomenon, the fact seems accepted: The more and more efficient acquisition of a first language is associated with increasing difficulty in learning a second language (Davies, Criper & Howatt, 1984; Kellerman & Smith, 1986).

The gain/loss idea is also contained in the work of Piaget, even though Piagetian theory is likely seen by most as the hallmark of a conception of development that features unidirectional growth. In the study of the age-development of visual illusions, for example, Piaget (1969) described illusions that increase with age and others that decrease with age. When visual illusions increase with age, Piaget ascribed this loss in visual accuracy to advancement in cognitive stage. A related example in Piaget's work (see Chapman, 1988) is what he called the "repression" effect associated with a dynamic between perceptual and cognitive operations. With children of 7 to 8 years of age, Piaget found that their "veridical" perceptual knowledge was repressed by the (in this case, nonveridical) advancement in conceptual schemata. In effect, cognition "repressed" perception. A by-product of cognitive advancement, then, was a loss in veridical judgment involving perception.

It seems worthwhile to explore with greater force the idea that any process of cognitive development entails positive and negative aspects of change in adaptive capacity. In the long run, the treatment of this question is likely to be tied to the topic of adaptive fitness. In other words, as is true for evolutionary theories (as exemplified in the work of Gould and Lewontin [Lerner, 1984]), ontogenesis may not fundamentally be a process of general gain in the sense of a total increase in adaptive efficacy. As specific forms of mind and behavior are "selected" during ontogenesis for activation and growth, some adaptive capacities may actually become reduced. Whether the reduction is manifest would depend (as it true for evolutionary change) on the criterion demands posed by the individual and the environment in subsequent phases of life, or by the experimenter for that matter.

Plasticity of Development

Another belief (Table 5.1) held by many life-span scholars is that there is much plasticity in the course of life-span development. Plasticity refers to within-person variability and designates the potential that individuals have for different forms of behavior or development (Gollin, 1981; Lerner, 1984). Would the same individual develop differently if conditions were different? The question of plasticity is, of course, one that has excited developmental psychologists for a long time (e.g., McGraw's [1985] work in the 1930s on motor development in identical twins). It is of equal interest to current work in developmental biology (e.g., Cotman, 1985) and developmental sociology (Dannefer & Perlmutter, 1986; Featherman & Lerner, 1985).

Cognitive training research with the elderly. Whether it proves to be true, the conclusion that the plasticity of cognitive age differences found in the second half of life is larger than what is known from childhood research has impressed life-span researchers. The salience of the topic of plasticity for researchers in life-span development and the general approach used to study it can be illustrated easily in work on intellectual development during adulthood and old age. Initially, in life-span research the idea of plasticity was promulgated in connection with the question of whether intellectual aging is a simple process of gradual decline (Baltes & Schaie, 1976; Horn & Donaldson, 1976). One of the attractive ways to explore this question was to conduct intervention research.

Since the early 1970s, various research programs have been underway to examine the extent to which the observed aging losses in that cluster of psychometric intelligence evincing most definite decline—fluid intelligence—could be simulated for by performance variation (plasticity) within individuals. For example, elderly people were given practice in solving the type of intelligence problems used to measure fluid intelligence (Baltes & Kliegl, 1986; Willis, 1985). The key research hypothesis was that older persons, on the average, have relatively little test experience and everyday practice in fluid intelligence, but that they possess the reserve—the latent competence—to raise their level of performance on fluid intelligence tasks to that of younger adults.

The cognitive training research conducted with older adults offered strong evidence of sizeable plasticity. After a fairly brief program of cognitive practice, many older adults (age range, 60–80 years) exhibited levels of performance comparable with those observed in many "untreated" younger adults. Such findings have been replicated consistently and in other domains of cognitive functioning (e.g., Denney, 1984; Labouvie-Vief, 1985; Willis, 1985). Meanwhile, the evidence has been extended from cross-sectional to longitudinal age comparisons (Schaie & Willis, 1986).

These studies illustrate the emergence of the strong belief of life-span researchers in sizeable plasticity. Knowledge about plasticity of intelligence was judged to be as important as knowledge about the average course of age development. In order to achieve a comprehensive understanding of a given developmental process, such as intellectual development, one must forcefully advance the study of conditions that produce differences in development and highlight the potential for alternate courses of development. The resulting interpretative posture is that whatever one observes concerning the aging of intelligence is but one of many possible outcomes (Brandtstädter, 1984; Lerner, 1984). Knowing the range and limits of intraindividual functioning, therefore, is a cornerstone of the life-span perspective.

From plasticity to limits of plasticity. Current work on plasticity of life-span intellectual development has added new perspectives beyond those associated with cognitive training research. The focus has changed from demonstration of plasticity toward using research on plasticity as a strategy by which limits and boundaries of development can be identified (Kliegl & Baltes, 1987). This strategy is similar to child research on the "zone" of proximal development in childhood (Brown, 1982; Ferrara, Brown & Campione, 1986).

The resulting focus in the life-span study of plasticity is not on the normal range of intellectual functioning, but on limits of performance. The research strategy chosen to examine different aspects of plasticity and its boundary conditions is known as *testing-the-limits* (Baltes & Kindermann, 1985; Guthke, 1982; Wiedl, 1984). Testing-the-limits involves the systematic application of (a) variations in modes of assessment, (b) methods of intervention aimed at identifying latent reserve capacity, and (c) strategies of identification of the mechanisms involved in growth and decline.

In our research efforts (Baltes, Dittmann-Kohli & Dixon, 1984; Kliegl & Baltes, 1987) intended to determine age-correlated changes in limits of intellectual functioning, three aspects of plasticity are distinguished: (a) baseline performance, (b) baseline reserve capacity, and (c) developmental reserve capacity. *Baseline performance* indicates a person's initial level of performance on a given task, that is, what a person can do in a specified task without intervention or special treatment. *Baseline reserve capacity* denotes the upper range of an individual's performance potential, when, at a given point in time, all available resources are called on to optimize an individual's performance. It is measured by tests of "maximum" performance. When conditions have been added that strengthen an individual's baseline reserve capacity through intervention (or development), we speak of an individual's *developmental reserve capacity*.

Distinguishing between these three aspects of plasticity permits the study not only of plasticity but also of constraints (Keil, 1981) and of what behavior geneticists have called the *norm of reaction* (see Lerner, 1984). Concepts such as constraint and norm of reaction are intended to index those limits— biological and sociocultural—that restrict the formation of a given behavior and its open development. In the long run, assessment of maximum reserve capacity aspires to identify biological boundaries of the plasticity of development. Note, however, that the range and level of maximum reserve capacity is inherently unknowable (see also Keating & MacLean, 1987); it can only be approximated. The possibility always exists that new conditions or agents may be found that produce new levels and forms of intellectual performance on a given task.

The general expectation of testing-the-limits research is to predict developmental differences to be most pronounced, perhaps even approaching the condition of irreversibility (Wohlwill, 1973), near maximum levels of performance. Conversely, age changes are easily masked or modified as long as they are studied within the "normal" range of functioning. Figure 5.3 illustrates how a testing-the-limits strategy is used to obtain information about the range and limits of plasticity during adulthood.

The data presented in Figure 5.3 are based on subjects of different adult age groups who participated in extensive longitudinal intervention studies. In these studies, high levels of cognitive functioning in the use of a mnemonic skill are engineered in the laboratory. Specifically, subjects participated in 30 sessions of training of expert memory for digits and nouns using the Method of Loci (Kliegl, Smith & Baltes, 1986; Smith, Kliegl & Baltes, 1987). The results demonstrate, as expected, the dual nature of results from application of testing-the-limits methodology. On the one hand, sizeable plasticity continues to be evident into old age. The reserve capacity is substantial in all age groups, so that subjects of all ages can learn to remember exceedingly long strings of numerical digits and nouns. On the other hand, pronounced age differences in limits also exist. When subjects are tested under more and more difficult conditions, such as with increased speed of presentation, age differences are magnified. In the present example, the magnification of age

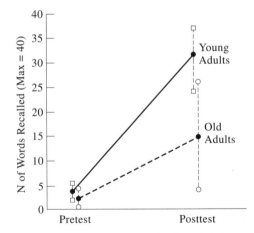

Figure 5.3. Expertise in Method of Loci: Mean and range of recall for 40 words in two subject groups of young and old adults (for data on digit span, see Kliegl, Smith & Baltes, 1986).

differences is of such a degree that, at "limits," IQ-comparable young and older subjects barely overlap in their performance.

With such research on the limits of development, the concern for plasticity has taken a new turn. The task is no longer to focus on the demonstration of plasticity as a sole feature of development. Rather, the search is simultaneously for potential (reserve capacity) and constraints. Testing-the-limits research has a broad range of ramifications. It is not only relevant for the study of intellectual development and aging; its possible usefulness also extends to many other fields of study. Consider the study of behavioral and developmental genetics. A possible view is that the role of genetics in regulating interindividual differences can be best examined when the investigation is focused on limits of performance. Another example is the identification of developmental dysfunctions. Like the stress tests used in biology and medicine (Baltes & Kindermann, 1985; Coper, Jänicke & Schulze, 1986; Fries & Crapo, 1981), psychological tests conducted under conditions of high difficulty or following testing-the-limits-like interventions are likely to be more sensitive to the detection of dysfunctions (such as depression, senile dementia of the Alzheimer type, or reading difficulty) than testing under conditions of the normal range of demand and expertise.

Development Is Codetermined by Multiple Systems of Influence

The fifth and sixth belief systems (historical embeddedness, contextualism) associated with life-span research have expanded the spectrum of influences that are considered determinants of behavioral development. A new taxonomy of influence systems has evolved that entails factors beyond the ones considered in past work on psychological ontogeny.

Ontogenesis and evolution. The perspective of historical embeddedness deals with the relation between individual development (ontogenesis) and evolutionary development (Baltes, 1983; Brent, 1978; Dannefer, 1984; Featherman & Lerner, 1985; Nesselroade & von Eye, 1985; Riegel, 1976). The processes of individual development are governed both by principles of ontogenesis and by factors associated with the concurrent process of biocultural change. Together, ontogenesis and biocultural change constitute the two major systems generating development. As individuals develop, society changes as well.

The role of a changing society in codetermining individual development initially came to the forefront in life-span research on cohort differences (Baltes, 1968; Riley, Johnson & Foner, 1972; Schaie, 1965); later, its significance was amplified because of theoretical issues such as dialectics and contextualism (Lerner, 1984; Lerner & Kauffman, 1985; Riegel, 1976). In research on cohort effects, the age-development of several birth cohorts is studied in a comparative manner. The basic designs are known as cross-sectional and longitudinal sequences. An excellent up-to-date review of design and analysis of cross-sectional and longitudinal sequences is presented by Labouvie and Nesselroade (1985).

Life-span research with sequential methods has been conducted with many age groups, cohorts, and measurement systems (see Baltes, Cornelius & Nesselroade, 1979, and Nesselroade & von Eye, 1985, for review). The empirical story began in the periods of adulthood and old age and subsequently extended into earlier segments of the life span. In adulthood and old age, Schaie (1979, 1983) could show that much of the variance contained in cross-sectional studies of age differences in adult intelligence is associated with historical cohort factors rather than age factors.

In adolescence, Nesselroade and Baltes (1974) obtained data that showed that the level and direction of change in adolescent personality development was as much influenced by the historical context (in this case surrounding the Vietnam War) as by age-associated factors. Elder's (1974; Elder & Liker, 1982) work on the life-span development of children and adolescents stemming from the period of the Great Depression offered clear evidence of the impact of historical factors associated with childhood on adult personality.

With respect to infancy, Porges (1976) argued that much of the controversy about conditionability of neonates may be due to historical changes in prenatal and postnatal care. Since then, the possible impact of cohort variation has been explored in a variety of other areas related to infant and child development, including the structure and function of family systems such as the changing characteristics of fatherhood (Parke & Tinsley, 1984).

In the present context, Schaie's 28-year cohort-sequential study on adult intelligence is particularly relevant. In Schaie's (1979, 1983) data, the historical embedding of intellectual development is paramount. Intelligence does not only change with age. It also changes with history or cohort time. Consider, for instance, 50-or 60-year-olds. Cohort differences between these two age levels can be as large as longitudinal aging changes within the same subjects (Schaie, 1983). In Figure 5.4, such cohort-related changes in same-age individuals are illustrated for a larger range of birth cohorts based on

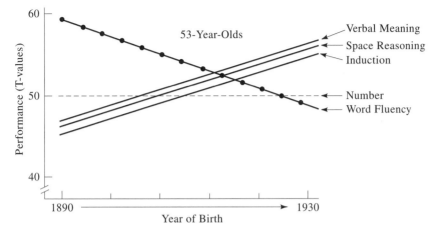

Figure 5.4. Historical, cohort changes in intellectual performance concern level of functioning as well as directionality. (The simplified trends represent the average performance of 53-year-olds from different birth cohorts on five measures of primary mental abilities, as estimated by Schaie [1979] on the basis of time-lag comparisons.)

Schaie's (1983) work. For one age group—53-year-olds—levels of performance are estimated and plotted in a simplified manner separately for the five primary mental abilities studied (number, reasoning, space, verbal meaning, and word fluency). Three of the five abilities show positive historical change; one is cohort-invariant; the fifth evinces negative change with historical time. Changes in intelligence, then, are multidirectional not only with chronological age but also with historical time.

Cohort effects of the magnitude reported in studies of adult intelligence are novel in psychological research. Therefore, it is not surprising that classical psychological theory has little to offer when it comes to interpreting the substantive meaning and origin of such cohort effects (see, however, Dannefer, 1984; Featherman & Lerner, 1985; Riley, 1985). The fields of cultural anthropology, historical sociology, and historical medicine may prove to be more relevant.

Three clusters of influences appear to be primarily involved as origins of cohort effects in life-span development of intelligence: education, health, and work. Successive generations, for example, exhibit, on the average, more formal education and other kinds of education-related experiences, such as those associated with the introduction of television or computers. The work life of recent generations may also entail, on the average, a stronger and differential focus on cognitively oriented labor. Furthermore, historical changes have occurred in health care, including, for example, the better treatment of hypertension, a factor implicated in lowered intellectual functioning among the elderly. Together, these examples indicate that many facets of the texture of everyday life exhibit sociocultural change possibly related to the level and rate of intellectual functioning. At present, however, the factors responsible for the cohort changes observed in intellectual aging have not yet been specified.

In summary then, results from cohort-sequential research on intelligence during adulthood and old age suggest much variability in the level and course of intellectual aging. Part of the nature of the reported findings is that they cannot be generalized to other cultural settings and historical epochs. But this feature of research on the aging of intelligence is at the very core of the argument: Depending on the prevailing cultural conditions, the level and course of intellectual aging can vary markedly. Any single cohort-specific observation does not tell the final story on the nature of intellectual aging.

Are cohort differences and biocultural change always relevant for the study of psychological development? Most likely they are not. Cohort differences are more likely to be a concern for those aspects of development that are not stabilized in the process of genetic and cultural evolution. Thus, it is not surprising that in developed countries, because of the high degree of biocultural stabilization in early life, cohort variation in cognitive development during childhood is relatively small and primarily involves differences in rate (Kendler, 1979; Reese, 1974).

Because cohort differences can have rather different empirical and theoretical significance, Baltes, Cornelius, and Nesselroade (1979) have distinguished among several ways in which cohort variation can be treated in developmental psychology (e.g., as error, historical disturbance, quantitative variation in frequency and rate, or as a theoretical/dialectical process). On the basis of this theoretical analysis of cohort effects, it is recommended that researchers examine carefully which logical status they are prepared to assign to cohort effects. Such a decision will influence the way cohort-sequential research is designed and ensuing data are analyzed.

Other contextual factors and contextualism. In life-span work, the argument for the historical embeddedness of human development was joined by another facet of embeddedness involving additional classes of contextual influences. Historically, the emerging focus on life events (Bandura, 1982; Brim & Ryff, 1980; Dohrenwend & Dohrenwend, 1974; Filipp, 1981; Hultsch & Plemons, 1979) was the initial forum for dialogue about such additional contextual factors and their role in human development. It was proposed that the course of adult development is not only dependent on age-correlated factors of socialization. Rather, ''significant'' live events—with rather distinct patterns of individual occurrence and sequencing—were identified as important regulators of the nature of change during adulthood.

An additional reaction to the evidence on cohort effects and the role of other contextual factors was metatheoretical. Following the lead of Riegel (1973, 1976) and the concurrent emergence of interest in Marxist and Hegelian thought (Datan & Reese, 1977), life-span psychologists began to proffer a metatheoretical view of development that was inherently dialectical and contextual (Dixon, 1986; Featherman & Lerner, 1985; Labouvie-Vief & Chandler, 1978; Lerner & Kauffman, 1985). In its radical form (Gergen, 1980), the metatheoretical argument was that ontogeny, in principle, is not universal. Rather, the nature of psychological ontogeny is always newly created for any given birth cohort or cultural setting.

Meanwhile, this radical view has given way to more moderate but also more refined positions (Dannefer, 1984; Featherman & Lerner, 1985, Lerner & Kauffman, 1985). Note, however, that the metatheoretical argument associated with contextualism in life-span developmental psychology is not necessarily synonymous—on a theoretical level—with the general advancement of an ecological approach evident in other developmental scholarship. Bronfenbrenner (1977) surely emphasized context. His conceptualization of context, however, does not explicitly follow the metatheoretical principles of contextualism. The metatheoretical guidelines of contextualism, for instance, suggest a general conception of development, which Lerner and Kauffman (1985) have called dynamic and probabilistic interactionism. That a focus on the same notion (such as the role of context) does not imply an identical metatheoretical treatment is illustrated in the exchange between Kendler (1986) and Lerner and Kauffman (1986).

A taxonomy of influences. The preceding discussion of interindividual variability and cohort effects and other contextual factors points toward a search for a new conception of developmental influences. The strategy chosen by life-span researchers is to argue that pluralism and complexity in the descriptive form of development is paralleled by a certain pluralism and complexity in the causal scheme of developmental factors and mechanisms.

For the heuristic purpose of organizing the multitude and complexity of developmental influences, a trifactor model has been proposed (Baltes, Cornelius & Nesselroade, 1979, Baltes, Reese & Lipsitt, 1980). In this model, three categories of influences, which developing individuals need to deal with (i.e., process, react to, act on) as their lives progress, are identified: *age-graded* influences, *history-graded* influences, and *nonnormative* influences. These three influences operate throughout the life course, their effects accumulate with time, and, as a dynamic package, they are responsible for how lives develop.

Age-graded influences are identical to what most child psychologists and gerontologists have considered the major source of influence on development. They are defined as those biological and environmental determinants that (a) have a fairly strong relation with chronological age and are therefore fairly predictable in their temporal sequence (onset, duration), and (b) are, for the most part, similar in their direction among individuals. Biological maturation and age-graded socialization events are examples of age-graded influences.

History-graded infuences also involve both biological and environmental determinants. These influences, however, are associated with historical time (Elder, 1985; McCluskey & Reese, 1984; Neugarten & Datan, 1973; Riley, Johnson & Foner, 1972) and define the larger evolutionary, biocultural context in which individuals develop. Two types of history-graded influences are likely to exist: those that evince long-term change functions (e.g., toward modernity), and others that are more time or period-specific (e.g., war).

Nonnormative influences also include both biological and environmental determinants (Bandura, 1982; Callahan & McCluskey, 1983; Filipp, 1981). Their major characteristic is that their occurrence, patterning, and sequencing are not applicable to many individuals, nor are they clearly tied to a dimension of developmental time, whether ontogenetic or historical. Nonnormative influences do not follow a general and predictable course.

The trifactor model is easily misunderstood in two respects. First, it may be seen as static. The intent, rather, is to emphasize temporal dynamics (the systems themselves are not historically invariant) and the notion that codeveloping individuals (such as grandparents, parents, and children; Tinsley & Parke, 1984) participate in different segments of the streams of influences. Second, the model may suggest that its focus is more on "normative," average regularities in development than interindividual differentiation. It is important to note, therefore, that systematic interindividual differences exist within each of the categories. In an exchange with Dannefer (1984), for example, Baltes and Nesselroade (1984) emphasized that macrostructural processes of stratification (related to sex, social class, ethnicity, etc.) are associated with clear-cut patterns of individual differences within the stream of age-graded, history-graded, and nonnormative influences.

Some of the influences identified in life-span models, particularly the age-graded ones, result in interindividual similarity in the direction of development. They are the basic components of those classic ontogenetic theories that have been associated with physical maturation and age-graded socialization, such as Piaget's theory of cognitive development, or Freud's theory of psychosexual development. The second category of influences, those that are history-graded, compounds the variability of human development through the impact of historical changes on the course of life-span development. The third category of influences, the nonnormative, renders the individuality or idiosyncracy of behavioral development most apparent.

In summary then, life-span researchers focus on complex and pluralist explanations of behavioral development. From the recognition of the historical embeddedness of development and the finding of sizeable individual variability in the nature of aging, they have joined other developmental researchers in the recognition of contextual factors and the unique combination of influences that shape a given life course. Some life-span researchers (e.g., Dixon, 1986; Lerner & Kauffman, 1985) have gone beyond the identification of the important role of contextual factors and pushed forcefully in the direction of elevating at least a version of the paradigm of contextualism as the primary metatheoretical avenue for understanding the nature of human development.

Child Intellectual Development in Life-Span Perspective

Concern for the family of perspectives advanced by life-span researchers (as expressed, for instance, in the following concepts: multidimensionality, multidirectionality, gain/loss dynamic, plasticity, and contextualism) has not been as strong on the part of cognitive-developmental researchers concerned with earlier segments of the life span. Aside from the possibility that this evaluation is wrong (Scarr, 1986), there may be a good reason. The data suggest that, in the early phases of the life span, cognitive change toward an increasingly "mature" organism occurs with much regularity. In contrast to the overall regularity surrounding the earlier portion of the life span (McCall, 1979), adulthood and old age are characterized by more openness, variability, and plasticity.

One possible interpretation of this difference between findings on childhood and adulthood locates the origins for this difference in the macrocontext surrounding human development. In adulthood and old age, biological and cultural stabilization is less apparent. The biocultural dynamics shaping adulthood and old age are of fairly recent origin and fluctuate in a manner that permits a fair degree of change and active control by the developing individual (Dixon & Baltes, 1986). Conversely, in childhood, biological and societal conditions have converged to form a relatively more solid fabric of influences that generates regularity.

This possible life-span difference in the relative degree of stability of developmental influences has led Baltes Reese & Lipsitt (1980) to consider the existence of a general profile of the varying, relative importance of the three types of influences (age-graded, history-graded, nonnormative) through the life course. The argument advanced suggested that, on the average, age-graded influences may be the most pronounced in childhood. This is perhaps the reason why developmental psychologists interested in infancy and childhood have focused in their research and theory foremost on developmental conceptions that entail age-graded changes, factors, and mechanisms. History-graded and nonnormative factors, on the other hand, may gain in prominence as individuals move beyond childhood.

On Multidisciplinary Conceptions of Development

The multitude of influences forming a framework for the origins and directionality of life-span development and its variations also makes explicit why life-span researchers believe so strongly that any single-discipline account of behavioral development is incomplete. The sources of and the mechanisms associated with age-graded, history-graded, and nonnormative influences do not lie within the scientific province of a single discipline such as psychology. History-graded influences, for example, are difficult to approach with psychological concepts and methodology.

An in-depth articulation of the conceptual nature of multidisciplinary connections in the study of life-span development is beyond the scope of this article (see Featherman, 1983). A minimum understanding of other disciplines is mandatory for a number of reasons. First, a multidisciplinary perspective helps one to appreciate the incompleteness of any discipline's theory of behavioral development. Psychologists, for example, study vocational interests and career development; sociologists and economists, however, are ready to point out that these phenomena are influenced by social stratification and the conditions of the labor market. Similarly, psychologists investigate parent–child relationships, but family sociologists point to the important role of historical changes in defining family structure and functioning, including aspects of household structure and fertility patterns.

Second, interdisciplinary work is more than the mere recognition of the incompleteness of one's own discipline and the strength of other disciplines. The quest is also for interdisciplinary efforts in the sense of integration of knowledge, as opposed to the separatist differentiation of disciplinary knowledge bases. The life-span perspective offers a unique opportunity as a forum for transdisciplinary integrative efforts. Elder's (1974; Elder & Liker, 1982) work on the relation between conditions of history (e.g., economic depression) and personality development is an example, as is Featherman and Lerner's (1985) recent effort to link sociological with psychological perspectives in arriving at a new conception of development.

RETROSPECT AND PROSPECT

Life-span developmental psychology is presented not as a theory, but as a theoretical perspective. As a perspective, the life-span view coordinates a number of substantive, theoretical, and methodological principles about the nature of behavioral development. Although none of these principles is new, the variation in the strength of the beliefs and the kind of emphasis and coordination contributes uniqueness and novelty.

Essays on historical and theoretical developments in developmental psychology are bound to be somewhat egocentric, topic-centric, and data-centric, to name but a few of the possible centrisms. The field of developmental psychology is more complex and rich than is expressed in this article, where the life-span approach was occasionally juxtaposed with putative theoretical emphases in other fields of developmental specialization. In this respect, the present article surely is an oversimplification.

Having taken the avenue of summarizing what is innovative and possibly useful about the metatheoretical beliefs of life-span developmental psychology, the following observations are offered, both as self-protective disclaimer and as an effort toward achieving better communication between life-span scholars and other developmentalists. Not unlike the gain/loss argument advanced as characteristic of any process of development, the family of beliefs presented here as prototypical of life-span developmental psychology has its dangers and costs. First, there is the question of scientific imperialism. In this sense, life-span scholars are occasionally regarded as holding the opinion that nothing but a life-span view is acceptable (Kaplan, 1983; Sears, 1980). To conclude that the theoretical propositions on the nature of development advanced here have been invented by life-span scholars or to proffer life-span developmental psychology as the royal road of developmental psychology or as the superior approach would be inappropriate. Life-span developmental psychology is but one of the many specializations in developmental scholarship.

Second, there is the issue of theoretical overload. The contributions to metatheory and metamethodology offered by life-span developmental researchers are important. What metatheoretical discourse can achieve, however, is limited. For example, enlarging and opening up the concept of development has its costs, especially if one or the other of the family of perspectives is taken to its extreme (Baltes, 1983; Lerner, 1984; Montada, 1979). As for plasticity, for a few years the emerging position on intellectual aging was one of complete openness, rather than plasticity within a set of constraints. Similarly, the issue of cohort effects was occasionally taken to a posture of full-blown dialectics or historicism, as if there were no regularity to development at all (for a critical evaluation, see Montada, 1979; Scholnick, 1985). Third, life-span researchers disproportionately emphasize adulthood rather than childhood, yet no strong psychology of life-span development can exist without solid research on earlier phases of life.

Such criticisms, putting life-span developmental psychology and life-span developmentalists into jeopardy, are serious. One approach to these dangers is to call for more intellectual modesty and more communication between the different quarters of developmental research (see also Hetherington, Lerner & Perlmutter, 1988). If we achieve such communication without unnecessary irritation, the future of the life-span approach is likely to be productive. Otherwise, life-span developmental psychology will be not only an edifice without a foundation, but also a network of scholars without partners.

NOTE

1. In this article, the terms *life span* and *life course* are used interchangeably. Since the origin of the West Virginia Conference Series (Goulet & Baltes, 1970), psychologists tend to prefer *life span* (see, however, Bühler, 1933), whereas sociologists lean toward the use of the term *life course*.

REFERENCES

Baltes, M. M. (1987). *Erfolgreiches Altern als Ausdruck von Verhaltenskompetenz und Umweltqualität [Successful aging as a function of behavioral competence and environmental quality]. In C. Niemitz (Ed.),* Der Mensch im Zusammenspiel von Anlage und Umwelt *(pp. 353–376). Frankfurt, Germany: Suhrkamp.*

Baltes, M. M. & Kindermann, T. (1985). *Die Bedeutung der Plastizität für die klinische Beurteilung des Leistungsverhaltens im Alter [The significance of plasticity in the clinical assessment of aging]. In D. Bente, H. Coper & S. Kanowski (Eds.),* Hirnorganische Psychosyndrome im Alter: Vol. 2. Methoden zur Objektivierung pharmakother-apeutischer Wirkung *(pp. 171–184). Berlin: Springer Verlag.*

Baltes, P. B. (1968). *Longitudinal and cross-sectional sequences in the study of age and generation effects.* Human Development, 11 *145–171.*

Baltes, P. B. (1983). *Life-span developmental psychology: Observations on history and theory revisited. In R. M. Lerner (Ed.),* Developmental psychology: Historical and philosophical perspectives *(pp. 79–111). Hillsdale, NJ: Erlbaum.*

Baltes, P. B. & Baltes, M. M. (1980). *Plasticity and variability in psychological aging: Methodological and theoretical issues. In G. Gurski (Ed.),* Determining the effects of aging on the central nervous system *(pp. 41–60). Berlin: Schering.*

Baltes, P. B., Cornelius, S. W. & Nesselroade, J. R. (1979). *Cohort effects in developmental psychology. In J. R. Nesselroade & P. B. Baltes (Eds.),* Longitudinal research in the study of behavior and development *(pp. 61–87). New York: Academic Press.*

Baltes, P. B., Dittmann-Kohli, F. & Dixon, R. A. (1984). *New perspectives on the development of intelligence in adulthood: Toward a dual-process conception and a model of selective optimization with compensation. In P. B. Baltes & O. G. Brim, Jr. (Eds.),* Life-span development and behavior *(Vol. 6, pp. 33–76). New York: Academic Press.*

Baltes, P. B. & Kliegl, R. (1986). *On the dynamics between growth and decline in the aging of intelligence and memory. In K. Poeck, H. J. Freund & H. Gänshirt (Eds.),* Neurology *(pp. 1–17). Heidelberg, West Germany: Springer Verlag.*

Baltes, P. B. & Nesselroade, J. R. (1984). *Paradigm lost and paradigm regained: Critique of Dannefer's portrayal of life-span developmental psychology.* American Sociological Review, 49, *841–847.*

Baltes, P. B. & Reese, H. W. (1984). *The life-span perspective in developmental psychology. In M. H. Bornstein & M. E. Lamb (Eds.),* Developmental psychology: An advanced textbook *(pp. 493–531). Hillsdale, NJ: Erlbaum.*

Baltes, P. B., Reese, H. W. & Lipsitt, L. P. (1980). *Life-span developmental psychology.* Annual Review of Psychology, 31, *65–110.*

Baltes, P. B., Reese, H. W. & Nesselroade, J. R. (1977). *Life-span developmental psychology: Introduction to research methods. Monterey, CA: Brooks Cole.*

Baltes, P. B. & Schaie, K. W. (1976). *On the plasticity of intelligence in adulthood and old age: Where Horn and Donaldson fail.* American Psychologist, 31, *720–725.*

Bandura, A. (1982). *The psychology of chance encounters and life paths.* American Psychologist, 37, *747–755.*

Basseches, M. (1984). *Dialectical thinking and adult development. Norwood, NJ: Ablex.*

Beilin, H. (1983). *The new functionalism and Piaget's program. In E. K. Scholnick (Ed.),* New trends in conceptual representation. *Hillsdale, NJ: Erlbaum.*

Berg, C. A. & Sternberg, R. J. (1985). *A triarchic theory of intellectual development during adulthood.* Developmental Review, 5, *334–370.*

Bertaux, D. & Kohli, M. (1984). The life story approach: A continental view. Annual Review of Sociology, 10, 215–237.

Birren, J. E. & Schaie, K. W. (1985). Handbook of the psychology of aging (2nd ed.). New York: Van Nostrand Reinhold.

Brandtstädter, J. (1984). Personal and social control over development: Some implications of an action perspective in life-span developmental psychology. In P. B. Baltes & O. G. Brim, Jr. (Eds.), Life-span development and behavior (Vol. 6, pp. 1–32). New York: Academic Press.

Brent, S. B. (1978). Individual specialization, collective adaptation, and rate of environmental change. Human Development, 21, 21–23.

Brim, O. G., Jr. & Ryff, C. D. (1980). On the properties of life events. In P. B. Baltes & O. G. Brim, Jr. (Eds.), Life-span development and behavior (Vol. 3, pp. 368–388). New York: Academic Press.

Brim, O. G., Jr. & Wheeler, S. (1966). Socialization after childhood: Two essays. New York: Wiley.

Bronfenbrenner, U. (1977). Toward an experimental ecology of human development. American Psychologist, 32, 513–532.

Brown, A. L. (1982). Learning and development: The problem of compatibility, access, and induction. Human Development, 25, 89–115.

Bühler, C. (1933). Der menschliche Lebenslauf als psychologisches Problem [The human life course as a psychological topic]. Leipzig, East Germany: Hirzel.

Butler, R. N. (1963). The life-review: An interpretation of reminiscence in the aged. Psychiatry, 26, 65–76.

Callahan, E. C. & McCluskey, K. A. (Eds.). (1983). Life-span developmental psychology: Nonnormative life events. New York: Academic Press.

Carus, F. A. (1808). Psychologie. Zweiter Theil: Specialpsychologie [Psychology: Vol. 2. Special Psychology]. Leipzig, East Germany: Barth & Kummer.

Cattell, R. B. (1971). Abilities: Their structure growth, and action. Boston: Houghton Mifflin.

Chapman, M. (1988). Constructive evolution: Origins and development of Piaget's thought. Cambridge, England: Cambridge University Press.

Clausen, J. A. (1985). The life course: A sociological perspective. Englewood Cliffs, NJ: Prentice-Hall.

Clayton, V. P. & Birren, J. E. (1980). The development of wisdom across the life span: A reexamination of an ancient topic. In P. B. Baltes & O. G. Brim, Jr. (Eds.), Life-span development and behavior (Vol. 3, pp. 103–135). New York: Academic Press.

Commons, M. L., Richards, F. A. & Armon, C. (Eds.). (1984). Beyond formal operations: Late adolescent and adult cognitive development. New York: Praeger.

Coper, H., Jänicke, B. & Schulze, G. (1986). Biopsychological research on adaptivity across the life span of animals. In P. B. Baltes, D. L. Featherman & R. M. Lerner (Eds.), Life-span development and behavior (Vol. 7, pp. 207–232). Hillsdale, NJ: Erlbaum.

Cotman, C. W. (Ed.). (1985). Synaptic plasticity. New York: Guilford Press.

Dannefer, D. (1984). Adult development and social theory: A paradigmatic reappraisal. American Sociological Review 49, 100–116.

Dannefer, D. & Perlmutter, M. (1986). Lifelong human development: Toward decomposition of the phenomenon and explication of its dynamics. Unpublished manuscript, University of Michigan, Ann Arbor.

Datan, N. & Reese, H. W. (Eds.). (1977). Life-span developmental psychology: Dialectical perspectives on experimental research. New York: Academic Press.

Davies, A., Criper, C. & Howatt, A. P. R. (Eds.). (1984). Interlanguage. Edinburgh, Scotland: Edinburgh University Press.

Denney, N. W. (1984). A model of cognitive development across the life span. Developmental Review, 4, 171–191.

Dittmann-Kohli, F. & Baltes, P. B. (1990). Toward a neofunctionalist conception of adult intellectual development: Wisdom as a proto-typical case of intellectual growth. In C. Alexander & E. Langer (Eds.), Higher stages in human development: Perspectives on adult growth. New York: Oxford University Press.

Dixon, R. A. (1986). Contextualism and life-span developmental psychology. In R. L. Rosnow & M. Gergoudi (Eds.), Contextualism and understanding in behavioral science (pp. 125–144). New York: Praeger.

Dixon, R. A. & Baltes, P. B. (1986). Toward life-span research on the functions and pragmatics of intelligence. In R. J. Sternberg & R. K. Wagner (Eds.), Practical intelligence: Origins of competence in the everyday world (pp. 203–235). New York: Cambridge University Press.

Dohrenwend, B. S. & Dohrenwend, B. P. (Eds.). (1974). Stressful life events. New York: Wiley.

Dörner, D. (1983). Heuristics and cognition in complex systems. In R. Groner, M. Groner & W. F. Bischof (Eds.). Methods of heuristics. Hillsdale, NJ: Erlbaum.

Elder, G. H., Jr. (1974). Children of the Great Depression. Chicago: University of Chicago Press.

Elder, G. H., Jr. (Ed.). (1985). Life course dynamics. Ithaca, NY: Cornell University Press.

Elder, G. H., Jr. & Liker, J. K. (1982). Hard times in women's lives: Historical influences across forty years. American Journal of Sociology, 88, 241–269.

Ericsson, K. A. (1985). Memory skill. Canadian Journal of Psychology, 39, 188–231.

Erikson, E. H. (1959). Identity and the life cycle. Psychological Issues Monograph 1. New York: International University Press.

Featherman, D. L. (1983). The life-span perspective in social science research. In P. B. Baltes & O. G. Brim, Jr. (Eds.), Life-span development and behavior (Vol. 5, pp. 1–59). New York: Academic Press.

Featherman, D. L. & Lerner, R. M. (1985). Ontogenesis and sociogenesis: Problematics for theory and research about development and socialization across the life span. American Sociological Review, 50, 659–676.

Ferrara, R. A., Brown, A. L. & Campione, J. C. (1986). Children's learning and transfer of inductive reasoning rules: Studies of proximal development. Child Development, 57, 1087–1099.

Filipp, S.-H. (Ed.). (1981). Kritische Lebensereignisse [Critical life events]. Munich, West Germany: Urban & Schwarzenberg.

Flavell, J. H. (1970). Cognitive changes in adulthood. In L. R. Goulet & P. B. Baltes

(Eds.), Life-span developmental psychology: Research and theory *(pp. 247–253). New York: Academic Press.*

Fries, J. F. & Crapo, L. M. (1981). Vitality and aging. *San Francisco, CA: Freeman & Co.*

Gergen, K. J. (1980). *The emerging crisis in life-span developmental theory. In P. B. Baltes & O. G. Brim, Jr. (Eds.),* Life-span development and behavior *(Vol. 3, pp. 32–65). New York: Academic Press.*

Glaser, R. (1984). *Education and thinking: The role of knowledge.* American Psychologist, 39, *93–104.*

Gollin, E. S. (1981). *Development and plasticity. In E. S. Gollin (Ed.),* Developmental plasticity: Behavioral and biological aspects of variations in development *(pp. 231–251). New York: Academic Press.*

Goulet, L. R. & Baltes, P. B. (Eds.). (1970). Life-span developmental psychology: Research and theory. *New York: Academic Press.*

Groffmann, K. I. (1970). *Life-span developmental psychology in Europe. In L. R. Goulet & P. B. Baltes (Eds.),* Life-span developmental psychology: Research and theory *(pp. 54–68). New York: Academic Press.*

Guthke, J. (1982). *The learning test concept. An alternative to the traditional static intelligence test.* The German Journal of Psychology, 6, *306–324.*

Hall, G. S. (1922). Senescence: The last half of life. *New York: Appleton.*

Havighurst, R. J. (1972). Developmental tasks and education *(3rd ed.). New York: McKay. (Original work published 1948)*

Havighurst, R. J. (1973). *History of developmental psychology: Socialization and personality development through the life span. In P. B. Baltes & K. W. Schaie (Eds.),* Life-span developmental psychology: Personality and socialization *(pp. 3–24). New York: Academic Press.*

Hetherington, E. M. & Baltes, P. B. (1988). *Child psychology and life-span development. In E. M. Hetherington, R. M. Lerner & M. Perlmutter (Eds.),* Child development and the life-span perspective. *Hillsdale, NJ: Erlbaum.*

Hetherington, E. M., Lerner, R. M., & Perlmutter, M. A. (Eds.). (1988). Child development and the life-span perspective. *Hillsdale, NJ: Erlbaum.*

Holliday, S. G., & Chandler, M. J. (1986). Wisdom: Explorations in adult competence. *In J. A. Meacham (Ed.),* Contributions to human development *(Vol. 17). Basel, Switzerland: Karger.*

Hollingworth, H. L. (1927). Mental growth and decline: A survey of developmental psychology. *New York: Appleton.*

Honzik, M. P. (1984). *Life-span development.* Annual Review of Psychology, 33, *309–331.*

Horn, J. L. (1970). *Organization of data on life-span development of human abilities. In L. R. Goulet & P. B. Baltes (Eds.),* Life-span developmental psychology: Research and theory *(pp. 423–466). New York: Academic Press.*

Horn, J. L. (1982). *The theory of fluid and crystallized intelligence in relation to concepts of cognitive psychology and aging in adulthood. In F. I. M. Craik & S. E. Trehub (Eds.),* Aging and cognitive processes *(pp. 847–870). New York: Plenum Press.*

Horn, J. L. & Donaldson, G. (1976). On the myth of intellectual decline in adulthood. American Psychologist, 31, 701–719.

Hoyer, W. J. (1985). Aging and the development of expert cognition. In T. M. Schlechter & M. P. Toglia (Eds.), New directions in cognitive science (pp. 69–87). Norwood, NJ: Ablex.

Hultsch, D. F. & Plemons, J. K. (1979). Life events and life-span development. In P. B. Baltes & O. G. Brim, Jr. (Eds.), Life-span development and behavior (Vol. 2, pp. 1–37). New York: Academic Press.

Joerissen, P. & Will, C. (1983). Die Lebenstreppe: Bilder der menschlichen Lebensalter [The steps of life: Art and the human ages]. Cologne, West Germany: Rheinland-Verlag.

Jung, C. G. (1933). Modern man in search of a soul. New York: Harcourt, Brace & World.

Kaplan, B.(1983). A trio of trials. In R. M. Lerner (Ed.), Developmental psychology: Historical and philosophical perspectives (pp. 185–228). Hillsdale, NJ: Erlbaum.

Keating, D. & MacLean, D. (1987). Reconstruction in cognitive development: A poststructuralist agenda. In P. B. Baltes, D. L. Featherman & R. M. Lerner (Eds.), Life-span development and behavior (Vol. 8). Hillsdale, NJ: Erlbaum.

Keil, F. C. (1981). Constraints on knowledge and cognitive development. Psychological Review, 88, 187–227.

Kellerman, E. & Smith, M. S. (1986). Crosslinguistic influence in second language acquisition. Oxford, England: Pergamon Press.

Kendler, T. S. (1979). Cross-sectional research, longitudinal theory, and a discriminative transfer ontogeny. Human Development, 22, 235–254.

Kendler, T. S. (1986). World views and the concept of development: A reply to Lerner and Kauffman. Developmental Review, 6, 80–95.

Kertzer, D. I. & Keith, J. (Eds.). (1983). Age and anthropological theory. Ithaca, NY: Cornell University Press.

Kirkwood, T. B. L. (1985). Comparative and evolutionary aspects of longevity. In C. E. Finch & E. L. Schneider (Eds.), Handbook of the biology of aging (pp. 27–44). New York: Van Nostrand Reinhold.

Kliegl, R. & Baltes, P. B. (1987). Theory-guided analysis of development and aging mechanisms through testing-the-limits and research on expertise. In C. Schooler & K. W. Schaie (Eds.), Cognitive functioning and social structure over the life course (pp. 95–119). Norwood, NJ: Ablex.

Kliegl, R., Smith, J. & Baltes, P. B. (1986). Testing-the-limits, expertise, and memory in adulthood and old age. In F. Klix & H. Hagendorf (Eds.), Human memory and cognitive capabilities: Mechanisms and performances (pp. 395–407). Amsterdam, Netherlands: North Holland.

Kramer, D. A. (1983). Postformal operations? A need for further conceptualization. Human Development, 26, 91–105.

Labouvie, E. W. & Nesselroade, J. R. (1985). Age, period, and cohort analysis and the study of individual development and social change. In J. R. Nesselroade & A. von Eye (Eds.), Developmental and social change: Explanatory analysis (pp. 189–212). New York: Academic Press.

Labouvie-Vief, G. (1980). Beyond formal operations: Uses and limits of pure logic in life-span development. Human Development, 23, 141–161.

Labouvie-Vief, G. (1982). Dynamic development and mature autonomy: A theoretical prologue. Human Development, 25, 161–191.

Labouvie-Vief, G. (1985). Intelligence and cognition. In J. E. Birren & K. W. Schaie (Eds.), Handbook of the psychology of aging (2nd ed., pp. 500–530). New York: Van Nostrand Reinhold.

Labouvie-Vief, G. & Chandler, M. (1978). Cognitive development and life-span developmental theory: Idealistic versus contextual perspectives. In P. B. Baltes (Ed.), Life-span development and behavior (Vol. 1, pp. 181–210). New York: Academic Press.

Lerner, R. M. (1984). On the nature of human plasticity. New York: Cambridge University Press.

Lerner, R. M. & Kauffman, M. B. (1985). The concept of development in contextualism. Developmental Review, 5, 309–333.

Lerner, R. M. & Kauffman, M. B. (1986). On the metatheoretical relativism of analyses of metatheoretical analyses: A critique of Kendler's comments. Developmental Review, 6, 96–106.

McCall, R. B. (1979). The development of intellectual functioning in infancy and the prediction of later IQ. In J. Osofsky (Ed.), Handbook of infant development (pp. 707–741). New York: Wiley.

McCluskey, K. A. & Reese, H. W. (Eds.). (1984). Life-span developmental psychology: Historical and generational effects. New York: Academic Press.

McGraw, M. (1985). Professional and personal blunder in child development research. In J. Osofsky (Ed.), Newsletter of the Society for Research in Child Development, Special Supplement to Winter Newsletter.

Meacham, J. A. (1982). Wisdom and the context of knowledge: Knowing that one doesn't know. In D. Kuhn & J. A. Meacham (Eds.), On the development of developmental psychology (pp. 111–134). Basel, Switzerland: Karger.

Migdal, S., Abeles, R. & Sherrod, L. (1981). An inventory of longitudinal studies of middle and old age. New York: Social Science Research Council.

Montada, L. (1979). Entwicklungspsychologie auf der Suche nach einer Identität [Developmental psychology in search of an identity]. In L. Montada (Ed.), Brennpunkte der Entwicklungspsychologie [Current foci in developmental psychology] (pp. 31–44). Stuttgart, West Germany: Kohlhammer.

Neisser, U. (Ed.). (1982). Memory observed: Remembering in natural contexts. San Francisco, CA: Freeman.

Nesselroade, J. R. & Baltes, P. B. (1974). Adolescent personality development and historical change: 1970–72. Monographs of the Society for Research in Child Development, 39 (1, Serial No. 154).

Nesselroade, J. R. & von Eye, A. (Eds.). (1985). Developmental and social change: Explanatory analysis. New York: Academic Press.

Neugarten, B. L. & Datan, N. (1973). Sociological perspectives on the life cycle. In P. B. Baltes & K. W. Schaie (Eds.), Life-span developmental psychology: Personality and socialization (pp. 53–69). New York: Academic Press.

Nisbet, R. (1980). History of the idea of progress. New York: Basic Books.

Oerter, R. (1986). Developmental task through the life span: A new approach to an old concept. In P. B. Baltes, D. L. Featherman & R. M. Lerner (Eds.), Life-span development and behavior (Vol. 7, pp. 233–269). Hillsdale, NJ: Erlbaum.

Parke, R. D. & Tinsley, B. R. (1984). Fatherhood: Historical and contemporary perspectives. In K. A. McClusky & H. W. Reese (Eds.), Life-span developmental psychology: Historical and generational effects. New York: Academic Press.

Pascual-Leone, J. (1983). Growing into human maturity: Toward a metasubjective theory of adulthood stages. In P. B. Baltes & O. G. Brim, Jr. (Eds.), Life-span development and behavior (Vol. 5, pp. 118–156). New York: Academic Press.

Perlmutter, M. (1988). Cognitive development in life-span perspective: From description of differences to explanation of changes. In E. M. Hetherington, R. M. Lerner & M. Perlmutter (Eds.), Child development in life-span perspective. Hillsdale, NJ: Erlbaum.

Philibert, M. (1968). L'échelle des ages [The ladder of ages]. Paris: Seuil.

Piaget, J. (1969). The mechanisms of perception. London: Routledge & Kegan Paul.

Piaget, J. (1972). Intellectual evolution from adolescence to adulthood. Human Development, 15, 1–12.

Porges, S. W. (1976). Cohort effects and apparent secular trends in infant research. In K. F. Riegel & J. A. Meacham (Eds.), The developing individual in a changing world (Vol. 2, pp. 687–695). Chicago: Aldine.

Quetelet, A. (1835). Sur l'homme et le développement de ses facultés [On man and the development of his faculties]. Paris: Bachelier.

Reese, H. W. (1974). Cohort, age, and imagery in children's paired-associate learning. Child Development, 45, 1176–1178.

Reese, H. W. & Overton, W. F. (1970). Models of development and theories of development. In L. R. Goulet & P. B. Baltes (Eds.), Life-span developmental psychology: Research and theory (pp. 115–145). New York: Academic Press.

Reinert, G. (1979). Prolegomena to a history of life-span developmental psychology. In P. B. Baltes & O. G. Brim, Jr. (Eds.), Life-span development and behavior (Vol. 2, pp. 205–254). New York: Academic Press.

Riegel, K. F. (1973). Dialectical operations: The final period of cognitive development. Human Development, 16, 346–370.

Riegel, K. F. (1976). The dialectics of human development. American Psychologist, 31, 689–700.

Riley, M. W. (1985). Age strata in social systems. In R. H. Binstock & E. Shanas (Eds.), Handbook of aging and the social sciences (Vol. 3, pp. 369 11). New York: Van Nostrand Reinhold.

Riley, M. W., Johnson, M. & Foner, A. (Eds.). (1972). Aging and society: Vol. 3. A sociology of age stratification. New York: Russell Sage.

Ross, L. (1981). The "intuitive scientist" formulation and its development implications. In L. Ross & J. Flavell (Eds.), Social cognitive development (pp. 1–42). New York: Cambridge University Press.

Rybash, J. M., Hoyer, W. & Roodin, P. A. (1986). Adult cognition and aging: Developmental changes in processing, knowing, and thinking. New York: Pergamon Press.

Salthouse, T. A. (1984). Effects of age and skill in typing. Journal of Experimental Psychology: General, 113, 345–371.

Salthouse, T. A. (1985). A theory of cognitive aging. Amsterdam, Netherlands: North Holland.

Scarr, S. (1986). How plastic are we? Contemporary Psychology, 31, 565–567.

Schaie, K. W. (1965). A general model for the study of developmental problems. Psychological Bulletin, 64, 92–107.

Schaie, K. W. (1979). The primary mental abilities in adulthood: An exploration in the development of psychometric intelligence. In P. B. Baltes & O. G. Brim, Jr. (Eds.), Life-span development and behavior (Vol. 3, pp. 67–115). New York: Academic Press.

Schaie, K. W. (Ed.). (1983). Longitudinal studies of adult psychological development. New York: Guilford Press.

Schaie, K. W. & Willis, S. L. (1986). Can adult intellectual decline be reversed? Developmental Psychology, 22, 223–232.

Scholnick, E. K. (1985). Unlimited development. Contemporary Psychology, 30, 314–316.

Sears, R. R. (1980). A new school of life span? Contemporary Psychology, 25, 303–304.

Sears, E. (1986). Ages of man: Medieval interpretations of the life cycle. Princeton, NJ: Princeton University Press.

Sherrod, L. R. & Brim, O. G., Jr. (1986). Retrospective and prospective views of life-course research on human development. In A. B. Sorensen, F. E. Weinert & L. R. Sherrod (Eds.), Human development and the life course: Multidisciplinary perspectives. Hillsdale, NJ: Erlbaum.

Skinner, B. F. (1983). Intellectual self-management in old age. American Psychologist, 38, 239–244.

Smith, J., Dixon, R. A. & Baltes, P. B. (n.d.). Expertise in life planning: A new approach to investigating aspects of wisdom. In M. L. Commons, J. D. Sinnott, F. A. Richards & C. Armon (Eds.), Beyond formal operations II. New York: Praeger.

Smith, J., Kliegl, R. & Baltes, P. B. (1987). Testing-the-limits and the study of age differences in cognitive plasticity: The sample case of expert memory. Manuscript submitted for publication.

Sternberg, R. J. (1988). Lessons from the life span: What theorists of intellectual development among children can learn from their counterparts studying adults. In E. M. Hetherington, R. M. Lerner & M. Perlmutter (Eds.), Child development in life-span perspective. Hillsdale, NJ: Erlbaum.

Sternberg, R. J. & Wagner, R. K. (Eds.). (1986). Practical intelligence: Nature and origins of competence in the everyday world. New York: Cambridge University Press.

Strube, G. (1985). Knowing what's going to happen in life: 2. Biographical knowledge in developmental perspective. Unpublished manuscript, Max Planck Institute for Psychological Research, Munich, West Germany.

Tetens, J. N. (1777). Philosophische Versuche über die menschliche Natur und ihre Entwicklung [Philosophical essays on human nature and its development]. Leipzig, East Germany: Weidmanns Erben und Reich.

Thomae, H. (1979). The concept of development and life-span developmental psychology. In P. B. Baltes & O. G. Brim, Jr. (Eds.), Life-span development and behavior (Vol. 2, pp. 282–312). New York: Academic Press.

Tinsley, B. R. & Parke, R. D. (1984). Grandparents as support and socialization agents. In M. Lewis (Ed.), Beyond the dyad. New York: Plenum.

Verdonik, F. & Sherrod, L. (1984). An inventory of longitudinal research on childhood and adolescence. New York: Social Science Research Council.

Waddington, C. H. (1975). The evolution of an evolutionist. Edinburgh, Scotland: Edinburgh University Press.

Weinert, F. E., Schneider, W. & Knopf, M. (1988). Individual differences in memory development across the life span. In P. B. Baltes, D. L. Featherman & R. M. Lerner (Eds.), Life-span development and behavior (Vol. 9). Hillsdale, NJ: Erlbaum.

Weir, M. W. (1964). Developmental changes in problem-solving strategies. Psychological Review, 71, 473–490.

Wiedl, K. H. (1984). Lerntests: Nur Forschungsmittel und Forschungsgegenstand? [Tests of learning: Only a strategy and topic of research?]. Zeitschrift für Entwicklungspsychologie und Pädagogische Psychologie, 16, 245–281.

Willis, S. L. (1985). Towards an educational psychology of the adult learner. In J. E. Birren & K. W. Schaie (Eds.), Handbook of the psychology of aging (pp. 818–847). New York: Van Nostrand Reinhold.

Wohlwill, J. F. (1973). The study of behavioral development. New York: Academic Press.

PART 2

Basic Psychological Processes

Introduction

Timothy A. Salthouse

Part 2 contains several early articles often overlooked by contemporary researchers, but which contain insightful discussions of many issues that are still the subject of intense debate. The article by Josephine Curtis Foster and Grace A. Taylor is one of the first to describe the phenomenon that the magnitude of cognition-age relationships varies across different types of cognition. Although the sample in their study was clearly not optimal for investigating age-related differences, the article is noteworthy for raising questions about how results of tests administered to adults of different ages should be interpreted, for mentioning the possibility of using different types of reference groups, and for proposing adjustments that might allow more meaningful comparisons across age groups. Harold Ellis Jones and Herbert S. Conrad also note the distinction between different types of cognition, and provide a very thorough (and remarkably current) consideration of alternative interpretations of the age-related decline found in measures of cognitive functioning.

The article by Walter R. Miles is one of the initial reports of what may have been the first major project in the United States focused on the relations between age and various psychological abilities. Miles describes results from tests of reaction time and movement time and speculates that, contrary to some recent suggestions, increased age might be associated with an increase in the potency of inhibitory factors. The interested reader is referred to other major articles describing results from this Stanford Later Maturity Project (Miles & Miles, 1932; Miles, 1931, 1933, 1935). A brief article by Catherine Cox Miles is also included here because, though it is seldom cited, it contains some of the first data relevant to how the relations between age and intelligence are affected by cross-sectional versus longitudinal comparisons, and timed versus untimed test administrations. We recognize that we have omitted several important articles from the period before 1950. For example, due to page limitations the pioneering studies by Jeanne Gilbert (1935, 1941), Floyd Ruch (1934), and Edward L. Thorndike and colleagues (1928) could not be included. However, we did include an excellent study by Keith Sward concerning whether there were age-related declines among people engaged in mentally stimulating occupations. The sample in Sward's study consisted entirely of college professors matched according to academic discipline, and all participants in the project were administered a broad battery of cognitive tests that was more comprehensive than several subsequent studies on this topic that have failed to cite it.

Harvey C. Lehman did an enormous amount of research examining the relation between age and achievement. His most impressive and extensive publication is his book *Age and Achievement* (Lehman, 1953), but the article included here illustrates his approach to the topic and describes some typical results from his analyses. Readers interested in contemporary research on this topic should consult various chapters by Dean K. Simonton (e.g., 1990, 1996).

Two somewhat more recent articles focused on psychometric intelligence are also included here. The article by John L. Horn and Raymond B. Cattell was the first to provide empirical data explicitly collected to investigate the distinction between fluid and crystallized intelligence introduced by Cattell (1943). This categorization of two major types of intelligence, with the former declining and the latter remaining stable across most of the adult years, tends to dominate most contemporary discussions of intellectual abilities in adulthood. More extensive descriptions of this framework can be found in Horn (1982) and Horn and S. M. Hofer (1992). The article by K. Warner Schaie is a brief but informative summary of the very important Seattle Longitudinal Study of adult intelligence. Readers interested in a more extensive report of this project, including a description of how it evolved from a doctoral dissertation investigating a relatively narrow set of intellectual abilities to one of the most comprehensive and impressive studies of adult intellectual development, should consult his recent book (Schaie, 1996).

Memory is probably the topic that is receiving the most attention among contemporary researchers in psychological aging. The article by David Schonfield and Betty-Anne Robertson was one of the first to attempt to distinguish processes with differential sensitivity to aging, in this case recognition and recall. The article by Fergus I. M. Craik and Joan M. McDowd represents a more recent, and more sophisticated, approach to this same problem. Again because of page limitations, we were unable to include additional articles by Craik, who has made numerous contributions to this area, or other memory researchers. The article by Harry P. Bahrick and Lynda K. Hall is one of several Bahrick has published in which processes of very long-term memory were investigated. His research is not primarily focused on old people so much as old memories, but it is nonetheless clearly relevant to the relation between aging and memory. Other reports employing a similar approach to the study of very long-term retention of names and faces of high school classmates, of campus landmarks, and of foreign languages are cited in this article.

Only one study on problem solving is included in this collection because it is still a relatively underinvestigated area in the field of psychology and aging. However, this study by David Arenberg deserves status as a classic not only because of its pioneering use of materials specially modified to deal with concerns of ecological validity, but also because it introduced a task that was subsequently examined in several longitudinal comparisons (e.g., Arenberg, 1982).

Alan T. Welford was a pioneer in the study of human skills, and his book *Ageing and Human Skill* (1958) is still one of the most informative books written on the topic of aging. The article included in this volume summarizes some of concepts he used to discuss age-related limitations. Finally, the articles by Neil Charness and myself report research on relations between age and chess and typing, respectively, among people with different amounts of experience. They represent two attempts to investigate the role that experience plays in moderating or eliminating the negative effects of advancing age on aspects of human performance.

REFERENCES

Arenberg, D. (1982). Changes with age in problem solving. In F. I. M. Craik & S. Trehub (Eds.), Aging and cognitive processes (pp. 221–235). New York: Plenum.

Cattell, R. B. (1943). The measurement of adult intelligence. Psychological Bulletin, 40, 153–193.

Gilbert, J. C. (1935). Memory efficiency in senescence. Archives of Psychology, 27, no. 188 (entire issue).

Gilbert, J. C. (1941). Memory loss in senescence. Journal of Abnormal and Social Psychology, 36, 73–86.

Horn, J. L. (1982). The theory of fluid and crystallized intelligence in relation to concepts of cognitive psychology and aging in adulthood. In F. I. M. Craik & S. Trehub (Eds.), Aging and cognitive processes (pp. 237–278). New York: Plenum.

Horn, J. L. & Hofer, S. M. (1992). Major abilities and development in the adult period. In R. Sternberg & C. A. Berg (Eds.), Intellectual development (pp. 44–99). New York: Cambridge University Press.

Lehman, H. C. (1953). Age and achievement. Princeton, N.J.: Princeton University Press.

Miles, C. C. & Miles, W. R. (1932). The correlation of intelligence scores and chron-

ological age from early to late maturity. American Journal of Psychology, 44, *44–78.*

Miles, W. R. (1931). Correlation of reaction and coordination speed with age in adults. American Journal of Psychology, 43, *377–391.*

Miles, W. R. (1933). Age and human ability. Psychological Review, 40, *99–123.*

Miles, W. R. (1935). Training, practice, and mental longevity. Science, 81, *79–87.*

Ruch, F. L. (1934). The differentiative effects of age upon human learning. Journal of General Psychology, 11, *261–285.*

Schaie, K. W. (1996). Intellectual development in adulthood: The Seattle Longitudinal Study. *New York: Cambridge University Press.*

Simonton, D. K. (1990). Creativity and wisdom in aging. In J. E. Birren & K. W. Schaie (Eds.), Handbook of the psychology of aging *(pp. 320–329). San Diego: Academic Press.*

Simonton, D. K. (1996). Creative expertise: A life-span developmental perspective. In K. A. Ericcson (Ed.), The road to excellence: The acquisition of expert performance *(pp. 227–253). Mahwah, N.J.: Lawrence Erlbaum Associates.*

Thorndike, E. L., Bregman, E. O., Tilton, J. W. & Woodyard, E. (1928). Adult learning. *New York: Macmillan.*

Welford, A. T. (1958). Ageing and human skill. *London: Oxford University Press.*

6. The Applicability of Mental Tests to Persons over Fifty Years of Age

Josephine Curtis Foster and Grace A. Taylor

IN PSYCHOLOGICAL examinations made at the Psychopathic Hospital it has for some time seemed evident to the examiners that the majority of patients over 50 years of age do especially poorly in the tests of memory and in certain allied tests. Casual observation and another study[1] showed further that this deficiency depends relatively little upon type of mental disease and relatively much upon chronological age. The present paper is an account of our attempt to find reasons and numerical expression for the differences among our patients. We have attempted also to check our results by studying the influence of chronological age in the case of normal persons.

CASES USED AND THEIR COMPARABILITY

The following groups of cases have been studied. No foreign-speaking adults and no children of foreign-speaking parents are included in any group.

(*a*) 106 older[2] patients in a large general hospital in Boston (not an insane hospital).

76 per cent of this group are men. So far as our problem is concerned, however, a study of the cases reveals no significant influence of sex upon results.

This hospital charges up to $10 a week where payment is exacted, but admits patients free when their families are unable to pay for treatment. 59 per cent were manual laborers. The average social status of the patients of this group is, therefore, relatively low. 32 per cent of them, for instance, left school before the 5th grade, and 85 per cent of them before the 9th grade.

All of these patients were given the Yerkes-Bridges Point Scale by the second writer. Our original plan was to include also several additional memory tests, but they had to be abandoned. In the first place, many of the patients had too poor eyesight to be given any "visual verbal" tests. But more than this, many of the older persons objected to attempting any memory test. At

Reprinted from *The Journal of Applied Psychology* 4 (1920): 39–58.

the mere hearing of the directions "when I am through reading I want you to tell me as much as you can of what I read" many of this group made such remarks as "Oh, no! I couldn't do that" or "Oh, no! my memory is too poor for that" or "That is child's play, don't try anything like that on me." The true reasons for refusal evidently were the conviction that their memory was poor and a reluctance to display this weakness. In general we found in working with normal older persons a similar reluctance to undertake other "difficult" tests. Some half dozen cases, for example, had to be discarded because the patient refused to attempt any test after the twelfth, that is to say, when the thirteenth was given, they would not attempt it, nor would they attempt any succeeding test. We were therefore forced to be content with giving the Point Scale alone.

(*b*) 315 normal young men between ages 20 and 30. This group is distinctly inferior in social status and education to the above group. 79 per cent were manual laborers. 65 per cent of them left school before reaching the 5th grade, and 96 per cent left before reaching the 9th grade. All of these cases were given the Point Scale (omitting tests 14 and 18) by other examiners, but all scoring was checked by us. Tests 14 and 18 were omitted because the majority of the group had too little schooling to be able to do any of the tests involving sentence construction.

(*c*) 316 normal school children between ages 10 and 19. These cases were from the Cambridge public schools and were tested in obtaining the original norms for the Point Scale.[3] Their average social status is at least as high as that of group (*a*).

(*d*) 136 older persons, patients diagnosed psychotic either at the Psychopathic Hospital or at the Foxboro State Hospital. Their social status is comparable with the patients of group (*a*). It is possibly slightly superior. 60 per cent of the group are men. 27 per cent only were manual laborers. 32 per cent left school before reaching the 5th grade and 75 per cent before reaching the 9th. All were given the Point Scale by examiners of the Psychopathic Hospital.

(*e*) 151 younger persons, patients diagnosed psychotic at the Psychopathic Hospital. 52 per cent of the group are men. 22 per cent only were manual laborers. 17 per cent left before reaching the 9th. There is no reason to suppose that the social status of this group is different from that of the above group (*d*). All were given the Point Scale by examiners at the Psychopathic Hospital.

COMPARISON OF OLDER PSYCHOTIC
AND YOUNGER PSYCHOTIC PERSONS
(GROUPS D AND E)

If we temporarily disregard type of mental disease, we find that the younger group attains on the average a higher score on each test as well as a higher total score. The superiority of the younger patients is, to be sure, most marked in tests 13 (words in three minutes), 14 (three words in one sentence), 16 (drawings from memory), and 18 (dissected sentences), but we cannot be sure how much the results are affected by type of disease and by total score (or mental age).

If, in an attempt to eliminate the influence of total score, we fractionate our cases by total score groups, we find two such score-groups sufficiently large for use—53 to 60 (mental age 10) and 72 to 79 (mental age 13). The data for these groups are given in Table 6.1.

From the results given in Table 6.1, we see that the seven tests in which there is a decided difference in score obtained by the two age-groups (older and younger) are 6, 8, 14, 15, 16, 18, and 19. The younger attain in test 16 (drawings from memory) 343 per cent of the score of the older, in test 18 (dissected sentences) 164 per cent, in test 8 (arrangement of weights) 130 per cent, and in test 14 (three words in one sentence), 133 per cent. In test 6 (repetition of sentences), on the contrary, the corresponding figure is but 72 per cent, in test 15 (comprehension of questions) 90 per cent, and in test 19 (definition of abstract terms) 74 per cent. These percentages must not be taken to mean too much because thus far we have paid no attention to character of disease but have grouped all psychotic cases together indiscriminately. We have, of course, an entirely different proportion of some mental diseases, such as senile dementia and arteriosclerosis, in the two groups. The effect of this factor, therefore, may be cutting across the effect of chronological age.

The effect of type of disease can be eliminated only by considering each disease separately. Unfortunately we have only one diagnosis where our cases are sufficiently numerous to warrant such comparison. That disease is dementia praecox. We tried many groupings of total score and of chronological age in these cases and arrived finally at seven subgroups each of which had the same range of total score but different chronological ages and each of which contained at least 10 cases under each age-group. The number of cases in some of these age-groups was as great as 52. The subgroups are: Score 46–71, age 10–19 and 20–29; Score 46–71, age 10–29 and 30–49; Score 46–

Table 6.1. Average Scores of Older and Younger Psychotic Persons

Total score	53–60		72–79	
Age groups	Older	Younger	Older	Younger
Number of Cases	15	18	7	21
Test 1	3.0	3.0	3.0	3.0
2	3.1	3.2	3.7	4.0
3	3.0	2.9	2.8	3.0
4	3.2	3.2	4.1	4.0
5	2.8	3.9	4.0	3.9
6	3.4	2.3	4.2	3.2
7	6.6	8.0	8.5	8.6
8	.8	1.1	1.5	1.9
9	3.8	4.0	5.0	5.3
10	4.2	4.5	6.4	6.1
11	1.8	2.4	2.7	2.0
12	3.1	3.6	4.0	3.8
13	1.4	1.3	2.2	2.6
14	.8	.9	2.2	3.1
15	5.5	4.3	7.1	7.0
16	.1	.7	.7	1.7
17	2.2	1.4	3.2	3.9
18	.2	1.3	3.1	4.1
19	3.2	2.0	5.1	4.1
20	1.4	2.1	2.8	2.7

71, age 10–39 and 40–69; Score 72–85, age 10–29 and 30–49; Score 72–
100, age 20–29 and 30–39; Score 72–100, age 10–29 and 30–49; and Score
72–100, age 10–39 and 40–69. Score 18–71 gives several groups but is too
great a range for reliable comparisons. The comparison of the first twelve
tests in the scale reveals nothing decisive, for now a younger, and now an
older, group appears to be slightly superior. When, however, we come to the
thirteenth test (words in three minutes) we find that in 5 of the 7 sub-groups
the younger are uniformly better. The younger ages with entire uniformity
give higher scores in tests 14 (three words in one sentence), 16 (drawings
from memory), and in 18 (dissected sentences). Their score is greatest in the
16th test (about 200 per cent of the score of the older persons). The older
ages, on the other hand, are superior in tests 15 (comprehension of questions),
17 (detection of absurdities) and 19 (definition of abstract terms). Their best
performance is in test 17 (about 125 per cent). We have not given the complete data in these cases because it does not seem worth while in view of the
relatively small number of cases in the groups and in view of the fact that
with dementia praecox we may not be dealing with a unity after all.

The general result is that judging from our psychotic cases alone and given equal general intelligence, patients over 50 years of age excel those under 50 in comprehension of questions, detection of absurdities, and definition of abstract terms; while they are inferior to the younger patients in construction of sentences and drawings from memory.

COMPARISON OF OLDER PSYCHOTIC AND OLDER NORMAL PERSONS (GROUPS A AND D)

In the preceding section we have been careful to insist that we have been dealing with results on psychotic patients and that it may not be justifiable to infer from them to normals. The reader may also be tempted to argue that the changes in score which appear with advancing chronological age may be due, not to the influence of age itself, but to the influence of the length of time which a patient has suffered from mental disease. That is to say, it is to be expected that deterioration will continue with the progress of a mental disease. We may have been measuring simply the influence of the course of the disease. If so, the psychotic older persons should differ markedly from normal persons of the same age. The next step, therefore, will be to compare older psychotic persons with their normal contemporaries.

Our groups of psychotic and normal older persons (groups *a* and *d*) are of approximately the same social level, with the former holding the possible advantage. In other regards the two groups are also very similar.

If we consider the groups as a whole and disregard both total score and type of disease, we find that the normal old have a higher average total score than the psychotic old, and that in most cases they have a higher average score on each of the tests. The exceptions are test 13 (words in three minutes) where the averages are the same, and test 14 (three words in one sentence) where the older psychotic patients surpass the older normal persons by one tenth of a point. This result in part answers the question we raised above in regard to the deterioration of the older psychotic persons. The older psychotic persons do show a lower intelligence rating than their normal contemporaries. Since they also have, if anything, a higher social rating, we must conclude that this greater deterioration is due to the progress of mental disease. A question remains, however. Is their greater deterioration a quantitative difference simply, or have the psychotic persons fallen off in certain abilities while retaining others to a normal degree? And further, are our results true for all diseases or merely for their average?

The last question may be answered first and most easily. Our cases include dementia praecox, unclassified paranoid psychosis, syphilitic psychoses, acute alcoholic and deteriorating alcoholic psychoses, manic-depressive insanity and senile dementia. If we consider these diseases separately and compare the results for one with the average attainments of normal older persons, we find that the dementia praecox, senile dementia, and arterio-sclerotic persons differ most from normal persons of their age, while manic-depressive and unclassified paranoid cases differ least. There is no disease, however, which gives results contradictory to our earlier figures for the two groups as wholes.

We come now to the question of the particular tests in which these changes are most marked. To reduce the effect of total score, we must once more fractionate our cases accordingly. We then find two groups with sizes sufficiently great for reliable comparison: those with total scores between 53 and 60, and those with total scores between 76 and 79. From the results thus arranged it appears that the low rating of the psychotic cases in some of the tests, at any rate (such as words in three minutes, three words in one sentence, and drawings from memory) is not due to the fact that the patients are psychotic, for normal persons of the same general age, and of the same mental rating, do *even more poorly in these particular tests than do psychotic persons.*

If, then, the particular failures are due not to the disease but to chronological age, we should get the same general results from the consideration of normal cases.

COMPARISON OF OLDER NORMAL AND YOUNGER NORMAL PERSONS (GROUPS A, B, AND C)

The results for our normal older persons are briefly summarized in Table 6.2.

From this table we see that in general the total score falls off with advancing chronological age among normal persons. Of greater importance than the decrease itself, however, is the *manner* of the falling off, that is to say, the particular tests in which lowering of score first appears or in which it appears in greatest degree. In the table, the small number of cases in the highest age-group makes their average scores unreliable. We shall, therefore, confine ourselves to the three younger age-groups. In these three groups it is evident that with advancing chronological age there is a tendency for the scores in each test to fall off. This tendency is most marked in tests 16 (drawings from memory), 18 (dissected sentences), 14 (three words in one sentence), and 13 (words in three minutes). It is least marked; on the other

Table 6.2. Average Point Scale Scores of Older Normal Persons

Chronological age	50–59	60–69	70–79	80–89
Number of cases	55	34	13	4
Test 1	3.0	3.0	3.0	3.0
2	3.8	3.7	3.7	3.0
3	2.9	2.9	2.9	3.0
4	3.8	3.3	3.3	3.5
5	3.8	3.7	3.7	3.3
6	4.1	3.9	3.4	3.0
7	7.8	7.3	7.2	8.0
8	1.8	1.8	1.6	2.0
9	5.5	5.6	5.2	3.0
10	5.9	5.6	5.0	4.0
11	2.6	2.5	2.3	1.8
12	3.7	3.1	3.4	3.3
13	1.6	1.9	.8	1.8
14	1.3	1.0	.7	.5
15	6.7	5.8	5.5	4.8
16	.9	.3	.1	.0
17	3.4	2.9	3.1	2.3
18	2.6	2.3	.7	.5
19	4.4	3.5	2.9	1.5
20	2.3	2.2	1.3	1.0
Total Score	71.9	66.3	59.8	53.3

hand, in the very easy tests (1, 2, 3, and 5, aesthetic comparison, missing parts, comparison of lines and weights, and counting backwards) and in test 17 (absurdities).

When we had reached this point in our investigation, we realized that to make the study complete we needed records of normal persons under 50 years of age of the same general class as our group of older normal persons. It is regrettable that we had not time to continue our work at the General Hospital in which we obtained our older normal cases. We were obliged to use records obtained by other experimenters from other sources. The only records of persons between 30 and 50 years of age which we could easily consult were those of persons so superior intellectually to the cases above considered that they were incomparable. There is, therefore, a gap at ages 30–50 in our Table 6.3, which summarizes the results of all our normal subjects, including school children, young men, and older persons.

No grade could be given to the school-children in test 6 because the form of this test has been changed since they took the examination. Neither could any grade be given the young men in tests 14 and 18 because so many of

Table 6.3. Average Point-Scale Scores for Normal Subjects of Three Age Groups

Total score	Chron. age	Test									
		1	2	3	4	5	6	7	8	9	10
46–52	10–19 (c)	3.0	3.7	2.3	3.4	3.5	?	6.2	.9	4.1	4.6
	20–29 (b)	2.8	3.4	2.9	2.5	3.0	2.4	5.8	1.6	4.7	4.6
	50–84 (a)	2.8	3.6	3.0	3.8	3.2	2.4	6.2	2.0	4.8	5.0
53–60	10–19	3.0	3.7	2.8	3.7	3.8	?	8.2	1.5	4.8	4.8
	20–29	3.0	3.6	2.9	2.9	3.8	2.7	6.5	1.5	5.1	5.0
	50–84	3.0	3.4	2.8	3.3	3.7	3.8	6.6	1.7	4.7	5.1
61–66	10–19	3.0	4.0	3.0	3.9	4.0	?	6.6	1.8	5.1	5.6
	20–29	3.0	3.8	3.0	3.3	3.9	2.9	6.8	1.9	5.4	5.5
	50–84	3.0	3.6	2.8	3.1	3.7	2.8	7.5	1.7	5.2	5.5
67–71	10–19	3.0	4.0	3.0	3.9	4.0	?	6.9	1.6	5.5	5.9
	20–29	3.0	3.7	3.0	3.9	3.9	3.6	6.9	1.9	5.2	5.3
	50–84	3.0	3.7	2.9	3.4	4.0	4.9	7.6	1.7	5.6	5.0
72–75	10–19	3.0	4.0	3.0	3.9	4.0	?	7.2	1.8	5.7	6.2
	20–29	3.0	3.9	3.0	4.2	3.9	4.1	7.1	1.9	5.7	6.2
	50–84	3.0	3.6	3.0	3.8	4.0	5.0	7.5	1.5	5.9	5.6
76–79	10–19	3.0	4.0	3.0	3.9	4.0	?	7.4	1.7	5.8	5.6
	20–29	3.0	3.9	3.0	3.0	3.9	4.5	7.4	2.0	5.6	6.1
	50–84	3.0	3.8	3.0	3.6	4.0	5.6	8.2	2.0	5.4	5.2
80–82	10–19	3.0	4.0	3.0	4.3	4.0	?	7.3	1.9	5.9	6.3
	20–29	3.0	4.0	3.0	4.3	4.0	4.1	7.8	2.0	5.8	6.5
	50–84	3.0	3.8	2.9	3.8	4.0	4.8	8.5	1.5	5.8	6.3
83–100	10–19	3.0	4.0	3.0	4.6	4.0	?	7.9	1.8	5.8	6.9
	20–29	3.0	3.9	3.0	4.7	4.0	4.9	8.0	1.9	5.4	6.8
	50–84	3.0	4.0	3.0	4.3	4.0	4.5	8.1	2.0	6.0	7.1
	Average for the above eight groups										
46–100	10–19	3.0	3.9	2.9	4.0	3.9	?	7.2	1.6	5.3	5.8
	20–29	3.0	3.8	3.0	3.6	3.8	3.7	7.0	1.8	5.4	5.8
	50–84	3.0	3.7	2.9	3.6	3.8	4.2	7.5	1.8	5.4	5.6

this group were illiterate that these tests were omitted. For this group (*d*), therefore, the groups of total scores in the left hand column should read 46–50; 51–56; 57–61; 62–65; 66–68; 69–71; 72–74; and 75–90. In the last section of the table we have given the averages of the eight total-score groups. This, to be sure, is an "average of averages." Even so, however, it is more significant than would be an average of the original scores. In the first place, we could not use the simple average of scores obtained on each test by each of our age-groups because there were so many more high scores among the younger that they would have appeared to too great an advantage. We, therefore, divided our cases in groups by total score attained. The averages for these groups may then be treated as if they had been "corrected" and as if there were an equal number in each total score group, and our "average

11	12	13	14	15	16	17	18	19	20	No. of cases
1.6	2.3	1.7	1.2	2.6	1.0	.9	.1	.2	.9	45
1.8	3.4	.9	?	4.4	1.0	1.6	?	.9	1.1	40
2.6	2.8	.4	.0	3.4	.0	.0	.0	2.4	.2	5
1.8	2.9	2.0	1.9	3.2	1.2	1.5	1.4	.7	1.2	61
1.9	3.1	2.2	?	4.8	1.2	2.0	?	1.9	1.0	64
2.4	3.4	.7	.0	4.4	.0	1.9	.1	2.9	.8	9
2.2	3.2	2.6	2.7	3.8	1.7	1.7	1.9	1.5	1.6	39
2.5	3.3	1.7	?	5.2	1.5	2.0	?	2.3	1.1	60
2.8	3.6	.8	1.1	5.1	.2	2.3	1.3	3.5	1.2	13
2.3	3.4	2.8	2.8	4.5	2.1	2.1	2.6	2.3	2.3	31
2.4	3.5	1.9	?	5.7	2.3	2.7	?	3.1	1.5	42
2.6	3.6	2.0	.7	6.0	.7	3.6	1.3	2.3	2.0	7
2.6	3.5	2.6	3.6	5.1	1.7	3.6	3.2	3.0	2.4	21
2.6	3.7	2.2	?	6.1	1.6	3.2		3.0	1.8	27
2.6	3.9	2.3	1.2	6.6	.3	3.5	2.0	3.0	2.5	8
2.5	3.7	3.3	3.6	5.3	2.5	3.2	3.5	3.3	2.8	31
2.0	3.5	2.4	?	7.1	1.8	3.6	?	4.1	2.1	34
3.0	4.0	1.6	1.5	6.8	.6	4.4	4.0	4.4	1.8	5
2.5	3.6	3.4	3.8	7.1	2.3	3.9	3.8	3.5	3.2	19
2.3	3.9	2.8	?	6.6	2.5	4.0	?	4.1	2.6	26
2.5	3.7	1.9	2.7	7.8	.3	4.3	3.1	4.8	2.8	13
2.6	3.9	3.8	3.8	7.0	3.2	4.0	5.1	4.8	3.9	69
2.7	3.9	3.1	?	6.9	3.2	4.4	?	4.6	3.9	22
2.8	3.7	2.5	2.8	7.9	2.1	4.8	4.9	5.8	4.6	17
2.3	3.3	2.8	2.9	4.8	2.0	2.6	2.7	2.4	2.3	316
2.3	3.5	2.2	?	5.9	1.9	2.9	?	3.0	1.9	315
2.7	3.6	1.5	1.3	5.8	.5	3.1	2.1	3.6	2.0	77

of averages'' is, then, the average score attained on each test by each age-group, supposing the distribution of total scores for the age-groups to be the same.

From Table 6.3 it appears that tests 1 (aesthetic comparison), 3 (comparison of lines and weights), 5 (counting backwards), 7 (description of pictures), 9 (comparison of terms), and 20 (analogies) show little or no regular change with advancing chronological age. Tests 2 (missing parts), 4 (memory span for digits), 6 (memory span for sentences), and 10 (definition of concrete terms) show a slight tendency toward decrease with advancing age. Tests 8 (comparison of weights), 11 (line suggestion), and 12 (copying square and diamond) show a slight tendency for the score to increase with advancing years. The other tests show decided tendencies. Tests 13 (words in three minutes), 14 (three words in one sentence), 16 (drawings from memory), and 18 (dissected sentences), all show a marked falling-off in score as the chronological age increases. This is most marked in test 16 (drawings from memory). On the other hand, the remaining tests, 15 (comprehension of questions), 17 (absurdities), and 19 (definition of abstract terms), show an increase in score with increased age. From the results we may conclude that the improvement in the ability to comprehend questions comes fairly early, since our young men are so far superior to the school children and are practically the same as the older persons. The improvement in absurdities and definitions of abstract terms, on the other hand, seems fairly regular. The falling-off in giving words in three minutes seems regular, but in drawings from memory, the score does not show any decided decrease until late, that is, the young men differ but little from the school children, while the older persons are decidedly inferior to the young men. Here again we regret that the lack of sufficient data on persons between 30 and 50 prevents us from more than guessing at the points at which the various abilities show changes.

The main conclusion to be drawn from our work thus far is that whether we study psychotic or normal persons with approximately the same total score, the younger persons tend to excel the older in giving words in three minutes, in building sentences and in drawing from memory; while the older excel the younger in comprehending questions, in detecting absurdities, and in defining abstract terms. Our results were so consistent throughout that we next turned to the literature to see if experimenters who were looking for something else had results which agreed at all with ours.

RESULTS FROM PREVIOUSLY PUBLISHED WORK

In our paper on "Significant Responses in Certain Memory Tests" (referred to in note 1), in which we consider only Psychopathic Hospital cases, some of whom were diagnosed as "not insane," we find no uniform changes with increasing chronological age in the score of memory span for digits. We do find, however, a decided tendency for the score of drawings from memory thus to decrease. The point at which this decrease begins differed for the different mental diseases, but in all it begins before age 50. A similar decrease is found in the scores of memory for short paragraphs.

Our results in general are also confirmed by a study of the contributions of two other writers. Both of these are reports of Binet examinations (one, the Goddard, 1911, and the other, the Stanford revision). The differences in

Table 6.4. Percentage of Wender's Cases Passing Tests Similar to Point-Scale Tests

Binet 1911 test	Corresponding point-scale test	Percentage passing
VI, 5	1	87
VII, 3	2	37
VIII, 5; X, 3; XII, 1	4	65
VIII, 2	5	67
VII, 2; XV, 1	7	67
IX, 5	8	13
VIII, 1	9	83
VI, 2; IX, 2	10	70
XII, 4	11	17
VII, 4	12	67
XI, 3	13	23
X, 5; XI, 2	14	27
X, 4	15	57
X, 2	16	7
XI, 1	17	33
XI, 5	18	27
XII, 2	19	83

grading and in the tests themselves make a rough comparison the only one possible.

An article by Wender[4] gives much valuable material, though his conclusion on the basis of his selected cases that his data furnish proof for the necessity of a revision of the scale appears unjustified. His Table II shows the tests passed by 30 cases of senile dementia or arterio-sclerosis, with an average chronological age of 74 and an average mental age of 9.4. From it we have calculated the percentage of the cases which passed each test which corresponds to a test on the Point Scale. The results of such calculation are given in Table 6.4.

The most striking points about Table 6.4 are that test 19 (a 12-year Binet test) should have been passed by 83 per cent of a group whose average mental age was only 9.4 and that test 16 (a 10-year test) should have been passed by only 7 per cent of the same group. Tests 2 and 8 (missing parts and arrangement of weights) also give a low average when we consider the age level to which they presumably belong. Test 8 was one of the tests in which our younger psychotic patients were superior to the older psychotic patients. Test 2 was found to change very little until we reached the 80–89 group of our normal older persons. But, other than this, our results do not seem to uphold Wender's findings for tests 2 and 8. The successes in Wender's group

Table 6.5. Percentage of Knollin's Cases Passing Tests at Different Mental Ages

Stanford revision test	Percentage passing at mental ages								Corresponding point-scale test
	10	11	12	13	14	15	16	18	
IX, 2		70	79						8
X, 6		40	60	56	60				13
IX, 5	30	67	75	96					14
X, 5	70	85	98	100	100				15
X, 3	41	52	67	70	73				16
X, 2	50	60	82	81					17
XII, 4		0	27	54	63				18
XII, 2		50	90	83	97				19

are more striking than the failures. We have already mentioned the remarkable performance in test 19 (definition of abstract terms). Tests 15 and 17 (comprehension of questions and absurdities) also give very high percentages. Test 15, a 10-year test, is passed by 57 per cent of the cases; and test 17, an 11-year test, by 33 per cent. These three tests, it will be remembered, were the three which we found to be particularly easy for the older persons, and we may say, therefore, that Wender's work supports our results in so far as the two have anything in common.

The second contribution mentioned is in Terman's statistical account of the bases of the Stanford revision.[5] From this account we have taken the results on Knollin's unemployed men (hoboes), chronological ages 21–60, but chiefly 25–40, mental ages 10–18. The results are summarized in Table 6.5.

The blank spaces in Table 6.5 seem to mean that if the table were completed, there would be zeros in the blanks to the left of the figures given and hundreds to the right. It is, of course, impossible to determine what these subjects might have done on the other comparable tests of the Point Scale because the arrangement of the Stanford is such that they were not given.[6] Test 18 (dissected sentences) is very difficult for the Knollin group. Although it is a 12-year test, only 27 per cent pass at age, and only 63 per cent of cases with a mental age of 14 pass. Likewise test 16 (drawings from memory) is difficult, for although a 10-year test, only 41 per cent of those with mental age 10 pass it, and only 73 per cent of mental age 14 pass. Test 14, again (three words in one sentence), is done but poorly. On the other hand, test 15 (comprehension of questions), gives percentages which are normal for its place in the scale and test 17 (absurdities) is not far behind. Test 19 (definition of abstract terms) is evidently done better than we should expect from school children. We have, then, roughly, though not as decidedly as for Wender's older cases, the conclusion that tests 14, 16, 18, and probably 13 (three words in one sentence, drawings from memory, dissected sentences, and words in three minutes) are difficult for hoboes of chronological ages between 25 and 40, and that test 19 (definition of abstract terms) is easy for them. Furthermore, if we compare these cases with those for Williams' juvenile delinquents,[7] ages mostly 14 to 21, we find that the hoboes do much better than the delinquents in test 19 (definition of abstract terms), and that the delinquents far excel the hoboes in tests 13, 16, and 18 (words in three minutes, drawings from memory, and dissected sentences). The same tendency holds true if we compare them with still younger cases. The only comparison possible between the business men and the High School pupils[8] is on tests 18 and 19 (dissected sentences and definition of abstract terms). Test 19 is passed by 1 per cent more pupils than business men, but in test 18 this percentage rises to 10, showing that test 18, at least, is harder for business men. That is to say, the falling off in ability to put together dissected sentences has begun already in middle-aged business men. In the comparison of abstract terms (a Stanford test which is similar to the Point Scale definition of abstract terms) 13 per cent more business men pass than do pupils. We find again then that younger persons consistently excel older in certain tests and are inferior to them in others.

The results of other investigators, therefore, although obtained for quite different purposes, agree almost absolutely with our findings as to the influence of chronological age.

PROBABLE REASONS FOR THE DIFFERENCES BETWEEN OLDER AND YOUNGER PERSONS

The above data show with reasonable certainty that there are decided changes in the distribution of abilities (as shown by the Point Scale) as persons get older. These changes appear whether we compare the insane or the normal, whether we lump all our cases together or fractionate them by particular disease, whether we compare the very old with the very young, or whether we compare the middle-aged with young adults. The only condition which must be observed is this one: that only those whose total score, or general level of intelligence, is approximately the same may be reliably compared. If we do not make this restriction, the young will be found to excel in each test as well as in the total score.

The next question is: Why do we find this change in ability as persons get older? It is evident, of course, that as a person grows older he loses some of the abilities he had as a child or young adult. We are all familiar with aged persons who fail to remember what happened yesterday, but who expect their grandchildren to recall, as they themselves do, events which happened many years ago. We say commonly that old people have poor recent, but good remote memory, but we seldom inquire into their abilities outside the field of memory.

In the present paper we have tried to determine more exactly the abilities and disabilities of the old and to estimate roughly, at least, the age at which changes are most marked. It is to be supposed that a defect in memory which is clearly present in a person of 80 must have been coming on for some time.

We have found that in the abilities which are tested in the Point Scale the old persons have deteriorated much more in some than in others. The reasons for the individual losses we conceive to be three. In the first place, there is some actual loss in ability. This is shown particularly in the drawings from memory. From our practical acquaintance with aged persons we are forced to conclude that they are actually unable to recall certain recent impressions. In the second place, there is a lack of practice in certain kinds of performance. Such, for example, we take to be the case in the construction of sentences. There seems to be a possibility that, given sufficient incentive and sufficient practice in this test, an older person may equal the performance of his juniors. The difficulty is that the common incentives such as praise, approval, etc., which are so effective with children, are of little avail with the old. We come now upon the third point which is probably the key of the whole problem. The younger subjects are almost invariably more alert and interested. Their experience is such that they fit more naturally into the test situation. They appear more adaptable than the older ones. Moreover, the tests in which they excel are those which most resemble "stunts" or "puzzles" and which, therefore, require not only willingness, but also a rapid adjustment of the subject. If we consider the tests in which the older subjects are superior we find them to be the ones which are more like the problems which arise in the daily life of adults and which could be answered best by persons who had had the accumulated experience of years.

There seems, therefore, to be such a decided break between the older and the younger persons that it is not fair by the former to grade them by an examination intended primarily for adolescents. The whole question of the applicability or fairness of any such examination to older subjects therefore depends on the purpose for which it is given.

The purposes of examinations of persons over 50 seem to us to be two: first, the determination of the degree of deterioration or aberration present; second, the determination of the presence of feeble-mindedness. In both cases there are two possible standards of comparison, namely their supposed former ability (or that of average normal young person) and the average ability of their contemporaries. It is without doubt interesting to note that a person who once had a mental age of 18 has now one of only 10. It is, however, of much greater importance to know whether the average person of the same present chronological age and of the same former mental age has deteriorated to the same degree. If the patient's deterioration is the same in amount and kind as that of his normal contemporary, then we cannot lay that deterioration to the presence of mental disease or to initial feeble-mindedness. Moreover, if the history of an old person convinces us that he has always been of a low grade mentally it is often desirable to know the maximum mental age which the patient ever attained. Our best guess here would be based on those tests in which the normal contemporary has not shown deterioration.

In most work with psychological examinations we have the constant difficulty that many non-psychological persons (and, alas! some psychologists) take our results as too simple. They read the mental age, without taking any notice of the comments of the examiner. If the mental age is less than 12 they glibly diagnose the patient feeble-minded. In order to circumvent such hasty diagnosticians and in order to give a mental age which shall more exactly express the ability of the subject before the influences of old age became marked, we have calculated some allowances which should be made in the case of persons over 50 years of age.

SUGGESTED SCORE CORRECTIONS
FOR OLD AGE

Already at this hospital we had been in the habit of making allowance for the omission of certain tests and we now applied the same method to a scheme for discounting the effect of advancing years. Perhaps it will be as well to give the history of the previous work, so that the present calculations will not seem too fanciful. To be sure, the plan we are about to present has obvious faults and we can claim for it no more than fairly satisfactory results. We give it here in the hope that the idea will lead some others to similar work and will in the end result in an accurate and theoretically correct table.

The first problem of the kind which arose was the question of how to grade patients who were totally deaf and who, therefore, could not be given

Table 6.6. Corrections for Point-Scale Norms When Certain Tests Are Omitted

When 4 and 6 are omitted (deafness)		When 14 and 18 are omitted (education)		When 1, 2, 3 (a), 7, 11 12, 16, and 18 are omitted (total blindness)	
For scores:	Add:	For scores:	Add:	For scores:	Add:
13–25	5	18–51	0	7–13	11
26–60	6	52–58	2	14–15	15
61–78	7	59–62	4	16–21	16
79	8	63–69	6	22–28	17
80–91	9	70–74	8	29–34	18
		75–77	9	35–39	21
		78–90	10	40–42	24
				43–48	27
				49–50	29
				51–52	30
				53	32
				54	33
				55–66	34

tests 4 and 6 (auditory memory span for digits and sentences). Our procedure at first was to add the scores with these tests omitted, call that the minimum mental age, then add to that the highest score obtainable on the two omitted tests, call that the maximum mental age, and then say that the true mental age lay somewhere between those two limits. This was fairly satisfactory, but we thought it possible to get a more accurate statement. This we computed from our table of scores for each test which were to be expected for different ranges of total score.[9] From the table we calculated the amount of credit to be expected on tests 4 and 6 for each of the ranges of total score. We then constructed a table giving the amount that should be added for each total score obtained when the two tests were omitted. We later made similar tables of corrections for omission of tests 14 and 18 (lack of education) and for tests 1, 2, 3(a), 7, 11, 12, 16, and 18 (total blindness). The corrections for lack of education were adopted by the Division of Psychology in the Surgeon General's Office for use in the examination of illiterates. The corrections are given in Table 6.6.

With these tables as models, we proceeded to make a similar table to correct for advanced chronological age. We have found throughout, as we have said, that the older subjects are almost without exception poorer in tests 13, 14, 16, and 18 than younger persons attaining the same total score. We have therefore supposed that these tests should be omitted in giving the ex-

Table 6.7. Corrections for
Point-Scale Norms to be
Used with Older Subjects

When tests 13, 14, 16 and 18 are omitted (advanced chronological age)	
For scores:	Add:
18–36	0
37–43	1
44–48	3
49–53	5
54–55	9
56–58	12
59–61	13
62–66	15
67–69	17
70–82	18

amination to old people and have calculated the corrections for such omission. We do not mean that the tests should actually be omitted. On the contrary, if a person of over 50 years of age obtains a high score on the four tests, it is evident that he has not begun to lose certain abilities which many of his contemporaries have lost. In other words, in our opinion failure on tests 13, 14, 16, and 18 on the Point Scale means little or nothing if the subject is advanced in years, while success on those tests may be very significant. The corrections which we offer tentatively for this group of advanced ages are given in Table 6.7.

At first thought it may appear that if we correct for failures which seem to be due to advanced age alone, we should also correct for successes which are apparently due to the same cause. Perhaps we should. If the idea were carried to its logical extreme we would be correcting for every test except 1 and 20, the only ones in which the average score for young and old is identical. Such a procedure would, of course, be meaningless, and would amount to giving a mental age on the basis of two tests alone. Somewhere, then, we must draw the line between no correction and total correction. We considered at first correcting for those tests in which one age gave an average score which was 120 per cent of the score obtained by the other age. This limit, however, would make us correct for 8 tests, in five of which the younger and in three of which the older were superior. Eight seemed such a large percentage of the total number (20) of tests that we were afraid we were again basing mental age on too few tests. If the limit were raised to 200 per cent, we would be correcting for only three tests, 13, 14, and 16. Test 18 which came next on the list with the younger excelling the older by 136 per cent, was later included because the test is one which many of the older subjects dislike, and which they often cannot see to read. The actual limit used was, therefore, 136 per cent.

CONCLUSIONS

1. There are certain definite changes in the distribution of scores on the Point Scale as the chronological age of the subject increases.

2. These changes are evident in both normal and psychotic persons.

3. There are three probable reasons for the changes: loss of ability, lack of practice, and absence of alertness or of interest in the older subjects.

4. The mental condition of a subject over 50 years of age will be much more accurately presented if two mental ages are given: one which compares him with his own adolescent ability (or with that of normal young persons), and one which compares him with his normal contemporaries.

5. A mental age which compares a subject with his normal contemporaries may be calculated from our Table 6.7.

NOTES

1. To be published shortly by J. C. Foster under the title "Significant Responses in Certain Memory Tests."

2. Older, in this paper, is taken to mean 50 or more years of age. Younger is to be understood similarly as less than 50 years of age.

3. See Yerkes, Bridges, and Hardwick, *A Point Scale for Measuring Mental Ability*, 1915, Chap. 4.

4. "The Applicability of Binet-Simon Tests in Psychoses of the Senium." *N.Y. Medical Journal*, March 6, 1915.

5. Terman and others, *"The Stanford Revision and Extension of the Binet Simon Scale for Measuring Intelligence,"* 1917, p. 163 ff.

6. The above seems to the writers a strong argument for the use of scales of the type of the Point Scale in all cases where there is a probability of wide "scatter." In year scales there is far greater chance of passing over some defect or peculiarity simply because it is not expected at the chronological or mental age of the subject.

7. Terman and others, *op. cit.,* p. 170 ff.

8. *Op. cit.* p. 171 ff.

9. This table was published with some printer's errors, (later corrected) in the *Journal of Abnormal Psychology*, XIII, 1918, p. 77.

7. The Growth and Decline of Intelligence

A Study of a Homogeneous Group between the Ages of Ten and Sixty

Harold Ellis Jones and Herbert S. Conrad

THE PROBLEM AND THE SAMPLE

The Problem and the Test Instrument

In 1921 the Army psychologists suggested that ''the intelligence of the principal sample of the white draft . . . is about 13 years'' (32, p. 785). Probably no other passage in the 890-page report of the Army psychologists aroused greater surprise, indignation, criticism, and controversy. Psychologists (18, 26, 27) at once attempted to fix ''the mental age of adults''—some arguing for the conventional 16-year level originally sponsored by Terman, others favoring the 13- or 14-year level suggested by the Army investigations, and still others urging that intelligence continues to develop as far as, if not beyond, the age of 19. A distinction, however, needs to be made between the peak of development, and the ''mental age of adults.'' The latter phrase is as a matter of fact no more justifiable than would be the expression ''the mental age of children.'' In both cases (with possibly rare exceptions) the mental age changes significantly with the progress of the years: among the children there is growth; among the adults decline.

For several reasons, the most satisfactory method of measuring the decline of intelligence among adults requires measurement of the rise of intelligence among comparable groups of children. The younger subjects supply valid regional norms by which to evaluate the decline observed among the adults. The present monograph undertakes principally to study the growth and decline of intelligence in rural New England, as indicated by 1,191 examinations with the Army Alpha intelligence test (Forms 5 and 7).[1] Subsidiary problems also receiving attention are the relation of variability to age, the

From *Genetic Psychology Monographs* 13, no. 3 (1933): 229–95. Published by Heldref Publications, 1319 Eighteenth Street, N.W., Washington, D.C. 20036–1802. Copyright © 1933 by Clark University. Reprinted by permission of the Helen Dwight Reid Educational Foundation.

form of the developmental curve, regional differences, sex differences, and the problem of differential growth and decline according to intelligence level.

A number of reasons prompted the choice of the Alpha, in preference to other standardized tests. The Alpha was carefully prepared, with perhaps more attention to empirical checks, than any other test appropriate for use among adults (32). The Alpha is better adapted for use over a wide range of intelligence than either the Thurstone or the Otis tests—in which the constant shift of tasks tends to create undesirable difficulties of comprehension, especially under conditions of group administration. The fact that the Alpha test had been administered to nearly 2,000,000 men in the Army and had the sanction of the United States Government (32) was sometimes a favorable talking-point in approaching adults who were asked to cooperate in the survey. Finally, the Alpha test had probably enjoyed wider use than any other group test, thus permitting broader comparisons with results obtained by other investigators.

We should be remiss if we did not point out certain defects of the Army Alpha. Outstandingly, we may question whether tests of the nature of general information (such as Alpha Subtests 4 and 8)[2] should be included in a battery to be used in groups of different ages (1); on the other hand, the growth curves for such tests provide interesting comparisons with the curves from the other Alpha subtests. We could wish that the Alpha contained at least one or two tests in which speed is less at a premium; the factor of speed will be separately considered, in the interpretation of results.

Some readers will consider that our understanding of the term "intelligence" requires discussion. Briefly, the aspects of intelligence in which we are chiefly interested consist in the ability to cope with comparatively new problem situations. The problem situations are assumed to be intellectual (involving symbols and relationships), rather than social or emotional; and to be "new" in the sense that previous knowledge or training is of relatively small importance in determining individual differences. We recognize that the diversity of the "previous knowledge or training" of adults makes the measurement of adult intelligence especially hazardous. It may be that the Alpha score of an *individual* adult is only questionably valid as an indication of his intelligence; yet the *average* score of a *group* of adults living in a relatively homogeneous milieu (such as rural New England) may be assumed to possess sufficient validity for serious scientific use. We should *a priori* consider that Tests 1, 3, 5, 6, and 7 of the Alpha[3] best fulfill the requirements of our definition of "intelligence"; and the performance of groups of persons on this battery of subtests may perhaps be considered the best index (obtainable from Alpha) of the growth and decline of "intelligence."

Method of Administration and Description of the Sample

The present report is derived from a community survey conducted in 19 villages of Massachusetts, New Hampshire, and Vermont. In selecting the specific villages as loci for the study, weight was given to the following considerations:

1. The population examined should be relatively homogeneous in economic status and in educational opportunity. Environmental variables should approach a minimum, to the extent that this may occur under non-experimental conditions.

2. The population should be entirely native-born of native-born stock, in order to reduce factors of language handicap and of differential group traditions.

3. The population should be relatively stationary within a limited district, in order that later additional surveys can be made if desired. A stable group has the further advantage that its earlier genealogy and the present family relationships can be more readily traced than in a group comprising many transients.

The district finally chosen for the survey included a block of nine counties in central and north central New England. These were selected as offering representative rural conditions for the states of Massachusetts, New Hampshire, and Vermont. In the 193 townships (under 2,500 population) of these counties, 19 villages were utilized for the purposes of the survey; they were considered, with their adjacent farming areas, to provide a fair sample of the total rural population of the nine counties. The representatives of these villages appears to be attested by all of the social and economic criteria which have been applied (13).[4]

To develop community cooperation and insure reasonable completeness of sampling, a carefully elaborated administrative technique was employed. This technique involved the use of a free motion-picture show (3) and supplementary house-to-house (or farm-to-farm) testing. Briefly summarized, our sampling and testing procedures included the following steps:

A study of the community with reference to the general educational level, participation in church and club activities, and the local customs and preferences concerning entertainment. The communities were sufficiently similar in these respects, so that the experience derived in the first few villages was of value in determining the later policies of the investigation.

Introduction of the project to local groups. An approach was made to several of the best-known citizens in each community, including usually the minister, and the leading town officials and business men. The first contact was usually made on a social basis, and no more explanation was given than was necessary to elicit their initial interest and approval.

Determination of a meeting place for group testing. In villages possessing a motion-picture hall (where commercial silent films were shown once a week) arrangements were made with the local exhibitor for rental of the hall and projection service. In the smaller villages the town hall or parish hall was used; in these communities a portable (De Vry) 35-mm. projector gave good service. Where electric lines were not available, the necessary current was obtained from a Westinghouse generator. This was belted to a pulley on an extension of an automobile crankshaft; by means of a field rheostat a satisfactorily constant current of 110 volts could be maintained.

Announcement of the first meeting. The following modes of advertising were employed: oral announcements in church, at preceding motion-picture exhibitions, and at meetings of the Grange and other local societies; newspaper notices; placards posted in the village and along country roads; free tickets of invitation, circulated by local canvassers. It was not always necessary to employ all of these methods in a single community; but in each case steps were taken to insure a wide and adequately early announcement—the aim being to reach every family in the community, so that a minimum of special selection would occur. The specific inducement to attend was in each instance a free program of motion pictures, consisting of short subjects and a main feature. In choosing the programs to be employed, over fifty reels of films were inspected in previews, and a further selection was made during the early part of the field work on the basis of an objective study of rural preferences (14).

The programs were successful in appealing to rural groups. The attendance consisted not merely of villagers living near the halls, but also of farmers from remote districts. The latter brought their families, and also gave conveyance, in overloaded cars, to neighbors who lacked their own means of transportation. Our small halls were, as a rule, well filled by an amiably curious throng of from 60 to 150 farmers and villagers; in these thrifty New England communities a free show proved a dependable means of gaining popular interest and support.

The group testing. In the earlier period of the survey, the Alpha test was administered at the end of the main feature of the motion picture show, and before the final reels of short subjects. While monitors passed out pencils and lapboards and Alpha blanks (Forms 5 and 7 being given to alternate persons in order to prevent copying), the examiner gave a brief talk designed to stimulate the interest of the audience and to motivate them by appeals appropriate to the specific group. In the later (and principal) portion of the group testing, where somewhat less time was devoted to the development of community rapport, the method was adopted of giving a motion-picture test took several forms, depending on the particular program used (12); but in each case the test was planned with a view to maintaining the interest and cooperation of the audience and to providing some experience in group measurement. The Alpha was usually administered in the intermission of a second show, scheduled a week or so later.

Generally, then, the Army Alpha was given at the second meeting in a community. The audience had been prepared both for the motion-picture and the Alpha tests through the preliminary advertising, which stated that brief and interesting ''questionnaires'' would be distributed. Cooperation was usually excellent. A previous report concerning the motion-picture tests has stated that

under the age of 40, adequate effort was obtained from over 95 per cent. Above the age of 40, a small, increasing number pleaded exemption, usually because of difficulty in reading. . . . This excuse, whether bona fide or not, doubtless operated to give a very slightly superior selection of cases in the upper age ranges. . . . While an occasional octogenarian filled in our blanks and made a reputable score, it was evident that individuals above 60 or 65, even with corrected vision, were not usually equal to taking a group test, and no systematic attempt was made to collect records beyond the age of 60 (12, p. 228).

The Alpha tests came in smaller type than the (especially printed) motion-picture tests; perhaps for this reason the selection of cases at the upper ages seemed more severe for Alpha than for the motion-picture tests. This selection was compensated for, however, by supplementary home testing.

After the initial period of the survey, the method was adopted of concealing the heading on the Army Alpha by pasting a printed slip across the top of each Alpha blank. This slip contained spaces for the subject to record his sex, age, schooling, and occupation. In place of the intelligence-test caption, a title was given which, together with oral explanations, was designed to motivate an interest in the tests as measures of practical judgment, information, and speed of reading and understanding (2).

Supplementary testing. One of the primary aims of the general survey was the collection of intelligence-test data on entire families. In a given family, it frequently happened that some members were unable to attend our meetings, due to home duties, conflicting engagements, illness, or lack of interest. Sometimes an entire family would be in attendance, but one member would fail to participate because of the lack of reading glasses, the necessity of caring for a younger child, or (rarely) because of a tendency to non-cooperation.

In conditions even slightly unfavorable, no urging was employed at the time, but the family was marked for a later home visit and test. In many communities an attempt was made to test every family containing two parents and two or more children, whether or not they had representatives at the group meetings. In other communities a family census was drawn up from the town records, and a random sample was made of two-child families.[5] In the home or individual tests a technique was used similar to that employed in the group measurements, except that of course the motion-picture entertainment could not be included.

All the records employed in the present study are from native-born individuals coming (with possible rare exceptions) from English-speaking households. About 87% of the total group are primarily of old New England stock, and about 12% of French-Canadian origin, dating back two or more generations in Vermont (13).

Summary

1. The data of the present study consist of Army Alpha intelligence tests of 1,191 subjects between the ages of 10 and 60.

2. The sample is derived from 19 villages in rural Massachusetts, Vermont, and New Hampshire; these villages are considered, with their adjacent farming areas, to provide a fair sample of the rural population of the three states.

3. The testing procedure included the use of group tests in community halls, free exhibits of motion pictures being offered as an inducement for attendance. The sampling was completed by supplementary house-to-house testing.

4. The present study attempts primarily to trace the growth and decline of mental-test ability between the ages of 10 and 60. Subsidiary problems also receiving attention are the relation of variability to age, the form of the developmental curve, regional differences, sex differences, and the problem of differential growth and decline according to intelligence level.

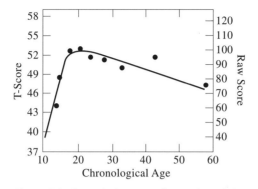

Figure 7.1. Smoothed curve of growth and decline of Army Alpha Test scores of total rural New England sample. Original data (average of mean and median) in small circles.

THE GROWTH AND DECLINE OF INTELLIGENCE

Table 7.1 gives the distribution of scores of each age group in the total Alpha test. The growth and decline of Alpha scores is shown graphically in Figure 7.1, which presents a smoothed curve based on the average of the mean and median performance of each age group. The curve has been drawn in terms of T-scores (21), with the raw score equivalents listed on the right-hand side of the graph.

The chief characteristics of the curve may be summarized as involving a linear growth to about 16 years, with a negative acceleration beyond 16 to a peak between the ages of 18 and 21. A decline follows, which is much more gradual than the curve of growth, but which by the age of 55 involves a recession to the 14-year level. It may be noted that the form of the adolescent growth curve agrees closely with that reported by Lufkin for the Army Alpha in rural schools (20), and also with Teagarden's curve for the juvenile population of Mooseheart (26). To the age of 15 there is also close agreement in actual scores, but between 16 and 20 the Lufkin and Teagarden medians run slightly higher, probably due to some degree of selection at these upper ages. It should be observed that the method of community sampling employed in the present study was designed to avoid those selective effects which must inevitably occur in a survey such as Lufkin's, limited to the public schools. The decline of intelligence scores beyond early maturity is

Table 7.1. Correlation between Chronological Age and Army Alpha Test Scores

Score	10	11	12	13	14	15	16	17	18	19–21	22–24	25–29	30–34	35–39	40–44	45–49	50–54	55–59	Total
200–										2									2
190–								1			1	1	1						4
180–							1			2					1				4
170–								2		6		2	3	3	4		1	1	22
160–						1	1			2	2	1	2	2		3	2	2	18
150–						5	4	2		4	3	4	2	1	4	1	2	2	34
140–				2	4	3		1		5		4	5	4	6	5	1	1	41
130–				2	4	6	1	3		1	3	1	9	7	7	3	2	1	50
120–			1	1	3	6	6	1		6	4	1	7	8	5	1	7		57
110–		2	2	4	2	8	5	6		6	4	8	7	6	6	5	3	1	75
100–		2	1	4	4	6	3	2	1	3	3	6	5	5	5	3	3	2	58
90–	3		2	3	5	9	5	4	5	9	3	12	2	7	9	4	3	2	87
80–		2	8	7	13	8	10	7	3	5	2	10	11	11	10	7	2	5	121
70–	1	2	7	9	1	8	5	3	3	10	6	12	12	5	5	5	4	2	100
60–	5	11	5	6	9	6	5	4	8	7	3	6	8	5	7	8	5	5	113
50–	2	11	10	14	7	3	5	4	1	11	2	9	8	9	8	11	6	2	123
40–	8	3	9	9	4	3	4	2	5	1	4	3	7	6	5	3	6	2	84
30–	4	8	16	5	3	3	4	4	1	6	3	3	6	8	3	4	7	6	94
20–	7	11	4	6	2	2	3		1	1	1	1	5	7	3	2	3		59
10–	2	1	1	5		1				1	2	5	3	6	4	2			33
0–9	2	4		1		1					1	1			1			1	12
Total	34	55	65	71	56	61	75	50	46	87	44	88	106	96	97	68	59	33	1191

NOTE: The class interval containing the mean score for each age group has been heavily boxed.

similar to results previously reported for a variety of motor, sensory, perceptual, and learning functions (7; 24; 29, pp. 106, 133–136).

Perhaps the chief interest in the present material lies in the possibility of comparing the growth curve with the curve of decline, for a population regarded as homogeneous. Considerable attention should, therefore, be given to the validity of our sampling at various age levels. We should analyze the data with these questions in view: To what extent is the decline in intelligence affected by sampling changes at successive ages? Can it be shown that the decline is due to a progressively poorer sampling, rather than to a bona-fide decrement in human abilities? Later sections will consider other problems bearing on the significance of the developmental curves; these problems include a study of sex differences; a study of the Alpha subtests, with a consideration of the validity of total Alpha score as a measure of intelligence; and a comparison of growth and decline in different intelligence groups.

Three methods are possible for testing the homogeneity of sampling:

1. A comparison of cases tested in halls with those obtained as a result of home canvassing.
2. A comparison of groups of communities in terms of completeness of sampling.
3. A comparison of adolescents and adults from the same family groups, with samples of less homogeneous origin.

Figure 7.4 presents curves for the 911 individuals tested in community groups, and for the 280 individuals tested in homes. The hall sample tends to be drawn more largely from village residents and from agricultural families living near villages. Observation of the actual sampling procedure has convinced the writers that the incentives employed in bringing subjects together in groups were (to a slight degree) progressively less effective for individuals of lower intelligence in the upper ages. In other words, while a fairly representative sample was obtained in adolescence and early maturity, in later maturity the group-tested sample tended to be drawn more largely from homes of superior social and educational status. The effect of this is to maintain the curve of decline more nearly on a plateau; in the home-tested cases, on the other hand, a very accelerated decline is to be observed, because one of the functions of the home tests was to add cases which had been missed in the halls, and thus to correct the incompleteness of the hall sampling. The curve for the total sample falls between the curves for the group-tested and the home-tested cases, and doubtless presents a truer picture than either of these.

However, in view of the preponderance of hall-tested cases, it may be suspected that the curve for the total sample in Figure 7.1 is held up to a somewhat slower decline than would be the case if selective factors were balanced by a more comprehensive home testing. This possibility can be

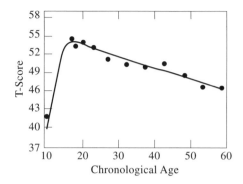

Figure 7.2. Growth and decline of ability in the abbreviated Army Alpha Test (tests 4 and 8 omitted) for total rural New England sample.

investigated by comparing communities which were very intensively tested with those in which the sampling (for reasons of time) was less thorough. In these terms, three divisions of the total sample may be recognized: 14 communities which were "extensively sampled" (Group A), 5 communities which were "intensively sampled" (Group B), and a subgroup of the latter consisting of 3 communities which were "most intensively sampled" (Group B_1). In Leverett Village and East Leverett, approximately 90% of the entire population between the ages of 10 and 60 were tested. Illness, absence from town, and a very few cases of non-cooperation, accounted for the cases not tested. In Gaysville an equally comprehensive program was not attempted, but in addition to the hall tests records were obtained by a home canvass from every family containing two or more children. The five communities of Group B include a fair range of the characteristics of the total sample: Gaysville is primarily an agricultural community, sparsely settled over a wide area; Dana is a small compact rural village, also chiefly agricultural; Leverett and East Leverett are small villages with both industrial (a box factory) and agricultural interests; the remaining town, Bethel, is one of the largest in our sample and contains a large proportion of nonagricultural workers. Each of these communities, moreover, is matched by one or more communities in the remaining group of towns (Group A), having a similar size, location, and occupational distribution. The curves for these three subsamples, given in Figure 7.3, indicate that the less complete or more questionable the subsample, the less rapid the decline of Alpha scores beyond the peak. It seems likely, therefore, that the curve in Figure 7.1 for the total sample must be

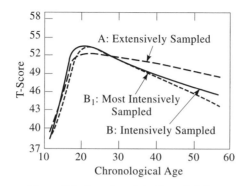

Figure 7.3. Growth and decline of ability in the Army Alpha test for Group A (extensive sampling), Group B (intensive sampling), and Group B₁ (most intensive sampling).

accepted as a conservative or *minimum* estimate of the decline of adult intelligence beyond the age of, say, 20.[6]

Further evidence in support of this view may be obtained from Figure 7.5, which gives curves for three types of cases: (1) In the "complete-family group" both parents of a family and one or more children of these parents were tested by the Alpha; the only children omitted were those too young to be tested by the Alpha, and an insignificantly small number who were out of town. (2) In the "partial-family group" are included either two or more siblings of a family, or one parent and his or her child or children. (3) In the

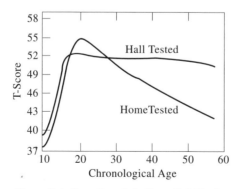

Figure 7.4. Growth and decline of ability in the Army Alpha Test for hall-Tested and home-Tested cases.

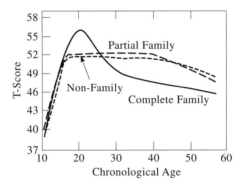

Figure 7.5. Growth and decline of ability in the Army Alpha Test for three groups: "Complete-Family," "Partial-Family," and "Non-Family" (see text).

"non-family" group are included all those cases not already classified in the two preceding groups, viz., single siblings, one or more adults in a family with no child tested, or unmarried persons without a sibling or parent tested.

Figure 7.5 shows that the curve for the complete-family group, like that for the home-tested group, drops more rapidly and to lower values than the curve for the total sample. Homogeneity of sampling in the complete-family group seems indubitable, since the falling portion of the curve is based on measurements of the parents of children in the rising part.[7] It is interesting and important to note that selective migration of brighter adults into the cities can have had little or no effect upon the curve for the complete-family group.[8] Within the limits of the number of cases involved, then, the accelerated drop in the complete-family curve appears thoroughly authentic. It may be noted that only about half of the complete-family group were home-tested.

We may conclude that for reasons of sampling Figure 7.1 must be interpreted as offering a conservative picture of the age decline in intelligence-test scores.

But there are other reasons which point in the same direction. In the first place, correction for zero scores would lower the curve at both of its extremes. These zero scores are not uniformly distributed through the various age groups, being more heavily concentrated at the lower and upper ends of the age range. Inasmuch as a zero score probably denotes a less-than-zero ability (in terms of equal units), correction for this factor would to some extent decrease the measures of central tendency, especially for the younger and older members of our sample. Correction for zero scores, in other words,

Table 7.2. Intelligence of Children of Parents in the "Complete-Family" Group

CA of parent	No. of children[a]	CA of children		Alpha scores of children	
		Mean	Median	Mean	Median
25–29	5	12.9	11.8	51.0	52.5
30–34	31	12.7	12.5	56.9	60.7
35–39	74	14.4	13.9	66.0	56.4
40–44	77	15.6	15.2	78.9	79.4
45–49	68	17.2	16.9	86.5	80.0
50–54	77	17.6	17.1	104.9	101.3
55–59	12	26.4	27.0	105.0	105.0

[a] Each child is recorded twice, once for each of its parents (except in the rare instances where one of the parents, being aged 60 or over, has been excluded from our sample). As the regression may indicate, the correlation between children's and parents' CA is not high, being .44 for the complete-family group (and .50 for the partial-family group, not shown in the table above). The correlation is markedly heteroscedastic; i.e., the age range of children of older parents is much greater than the age range of children of younger parents.

would to a slight degree emphasize both the rise and the decline in the intelligence curves.

Of more fundamental importance in interpreting the significance of Alpha scores, however, is the fact that a proper allowance for the advantage of age and experience in two of the Alpha subtests (Tests 4 and 8) would lower the curve for adults (and raise the curve for the younger ages). Tests of native intelligence assume that the subjects have all enjoyed equal familiarity with the experience variables affecting test score. In the case of information tests (such as Tests 4 and 8)[9] administered over a wide age range, this assumption is manifestly and provedly invalid (1). Particular attention is called, therefore, to Figure 7.2, which presents the curve of growth and decline of the modified Army Alpha test (Tests 4 and 8 deleted). It is suggested that this curve is more acceptable than the curve of Figure 7.1 as a picture of the development of native intelligence with age. In this, the recession by age 55 has reached nearly the 13-year level, as compared with the 14-year level reached at age 55 in Figure 7.1.

Upon examination of the developmental curves for the individual subtests (Figure 7.6, and Table 7.3), one is impressed by the great variation. In some tests, the adolescents are superior to most of the adults; in other tests, the adults, on the average, surpass the adolescents. In some tests, the peak of development is reached around 18 years; in others, a slight rise continues well into advanced maturity. In some tests, decline is fairly precipitous; in others, decline is negligible. This variation can hardly be completely explained on the basis of present knowledge. Certainly no simple "verbal fac-

Table 7.3. *Statistical Constants (Mean, Median, and S.D. of Raw Scores) of Total Sample*

Age group	Total alpha			Abbreviated alpha[a]			Alpha subtest no.								
							1			2			3		
	Mean	Med	S.D.	Mean	Med.	S.D.	Mean	Med.	S.D.	Mean	Med.	S.D.	Mean	Med.	S.D.
10	44.4	42.5	23.5	33.1	32.1	16.1	3.7	3.8	1.9	5.0	4.6	3.0	4.2	4.0	2.5
11	46.8	50.5	23.4	33.5	32.9	15.6	4.7	4.9	2.2	5.4	5.4	2.2	3.9	4.0	2.3
12	56.7	52.5	23.4	40.2	40.3	16.0	5.2	5.8	2.4	6.4	6.6	2.6	5.2	5.1	2.3
13	60.5	57.5	27.0	43.6	42.5	18.4	5.5	6.0	2.3	6.8	7.4	2.9	5.9	5.9	2.7
14	75.7	80.8	28.3	53.1	54.0	17.8	5.8	6.5	2.4	7.1	7.4	2.3	7.5	7.2	3.2
15	85.7	85.6	32.3	60.3	59.4	21.3	6.9	7.4	2.4	8.8	8.8	2.5	8.7	8.5	3.3
16	93.5	91.0	39.0	63.4	63.8	25.3	6.8	7.5	2.5	9.4	9.6	3.3	8.4	8.5	3.7
17	96.6	92.5	38.0	66.0	67.1	23.8	7.1	7.5	2.4	9.1	9.1	2.9	9.2	8.7	4.1
18	97.0	92.0	41.6	63.6	59.2	24.7	7.2	7.6	2.3	9.6	9.5	2.6	9.7	9.8	3.6
19–21	100.7	92.8	45.5	65.1	63.5	27.4	7.2	7.8	2.3	9.7	9.0	3.3	9.1	8.6	3.9
22–24	91.8	90.0	41.6	61.0	60.8	25.1	6.8	7.3	2.1	9.6	8.9	2.9	8.9	9.0	4.1
25–29	90.5	87.0	38.6	55.8	52.0	23.5	5.9	6.1	2.5	9.4	8.9	3.4	8.4	8.1	3.5
30–34	87.0	80.9	44.0	54.9	49.4	26.3	6.0	6.8	2.8	9.1	9.0	3.6	8.5	8.3	4.0
35–39	85.1	84.0	42.5	52.2	50.5	23.9	5.5	5.8	2.7	8.6	8.6	3.4	7.4	7.7	3.3
40–44	92.2	90.6	44.7	54.2	50.4	26.9	6.2	6.7	3.0	9.1	9.2	4.1	8.2	8.0	3.7
45–49	80.7	74.0	39.3	49.0	46.3	23.9	5.7	6.3	2.4	8.6	8.2	3.1	6.8	6.8	3.1
50–54	81.3	71.3	43.1	47.2	40.6	27.1	5.9	6.3	2.3	8.5	8.4	4.3	7.3	7.3	3.7
55–59	78.6	72.5	40.1	45.5	41.3	21.6	6.0	6.3	2.3	9.0	8.5	3.6	7.2	7.1	3.4

Alpha subset no.

Age group	4			5			6			7			8		
	Mean	Med.	S.D.	Mean	Med.	S.D.	Mean	Med.	S.D.	Mean	Med.	S.D.	Mean	Med.	S.D.
10	5.1	4.4	4.7	6.2	6.2	3.7	4.9	4.9	2.9	9.7	9.6	7.1	8.1	8.1	5.5
11	5.4	5.3	5.0	6.6	7.3	4.2	5.2	5.4	3.3	8.5	7.7	7.3	8.3	7.5	6.1
12	6.3	5.5	5.0	8.4	9.1	4.2	5.9	5.7	3.0	11.0	10.5	6.5	10.9	10.4	6.5
13	7.5	6.9	5.9	9.4	9.6	4.7	6.3	6.3	3.4	12.2	11.3	7.6	11.7	11.0	6.6
14	10.3	11.0	6.7	10.1	10.9	4.7	7.7	7.9	3.2	16.1	14.2	8.7	14.2	12.9	7.5
15	11.6	11.4	7.7	12.5	12.4	5.0	7.1	7.8	3.9	18.3	18.2	10.3	16.3	15.5	8.0
16	13.4	14.2	8.6	12.6	12.5	6.1	8.1	8.1	4.0	20.4	22.3	10.8	18.8	18.0	9.0
17	13.4	12.8	8.3	12.7	12.6	5.2	9.0	9.1	4.1	21.0	21.3	10.9	18.9	17.9	9.3
18	14.3	12.5	9.5	12.4	12.8	6.1	8.5	8.9	4.2	18.3	17.5	11.8	19.7	19.8	9.5
19–21	16.2	13.7	10.7	13.3	12.9	6.7	8.3	8.5	4.6	19.5	19.7	12.3	20.3	19.2	9.5
22–24	13.5	12.3	9.8	12.8	13.3	5.9	8.3	8.0	4.4	16.4	13.0	12.0	18.0	18.0	9.7
25–29	14.1	13.6	9.2	12.1	12.0	5.7	7.6	8.0	4.0	14.1	11.7	9.7	20.8	21.1	9.1
30–34	14.0	13.0	10.7	11.3	11.5	6.5	7.7	8.3	3.9	14.2	11.6	11.2	20.1	19.7	10.1
35–39	14.3	13.8	10.8	11.6	12.0	6.8	6.9	7.3	4.1	12.1	10.1	9.2	20.0	21.1	9.8
40–44	16.4	16.2	10.6	11.8	12.0	7.0	7.7	8.1	4.4	12.6	8.9	10.8	21.4	22.2	9.8
45–49	13.7	14.3	9.8	10.5	11.1	5.9	6.6	6.6	4.0	11.5	9.8	9.7	18.5	18.5	9.4
50–54	14.5	15.0	11.2	10.9	10.7	7.0	6.9	7.7	4.4	10.8	6.8	10.5	21.0	21.4	9.9
55–59	13.9	14.5	10.8	10.9	10.8	6.1	6.0	5.3	4.6	8.6	7.6	7.3	20.0	19.8	9.7

[a] Total Alpha *minus* Subtests 4 and 8.

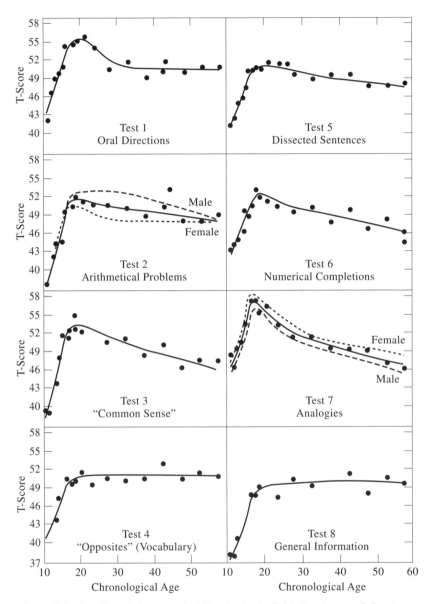

Figure 7.6. Growth and decline of ability in the individual subtests of the Army Alpha.

Males; – – – – – – – ;   females – – – – ;   total ——————

Note: The T-score values for each test are given at the left; chronological age is given at the bottom; original data for total group are plotted as small circles.

tor'' can explain the results. A previous study of the individual items of the Stanford-Binet, administered in the same communities as the Alpha, led to the emphasis of the differential influence of rather specific environmental factors (17); our interpretation of the sustained rise in Tests 4 and 8 may be considered in accord with this environmental hypothesis. There is no evidence in Figure 7.6 to support Thorndike's suggestion (29, p. 158) that the linguistic and arithmetical items impose a special handicap upon adults long out of school. Of special interest is the observation that the tests showing the most rapid decline are Tests 7 (analogies), 3 (''common sense''), and 6 (numerical completions). These tests may perhaps be considered, at least on *a priori* grounds, to be the best in the Alpha for the measurement of basic intelligence, i.e., to be the most free from the influence of environmental variables, and from the accumulative effects of differential experience. Our results here confirm Thorndike's conclusion that age exerts its most adverse influence upon native capacity or ''sheer modifiability'' (29, p. 106).

The utility of the distinction between basic intelligence and acquired abilities is emphasized by the changes, with age, in the proportional contribution of each subtest to total Alpha score (Figure 7.7).[10] Between the ages of 50 and 60, about 40% of total Alpha score is derived from two tests—Tests 4 and 8; at age 10, these tests contribute only 25%. As represented in mental tests, then, the effective intellectual power of the adult, much more than that

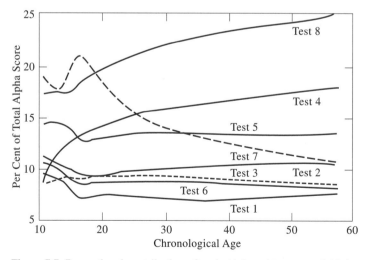

Figure 7.7. Proportional contribution of each Alpha subtest to total Alpha score at each age.

of the 10-year-old, is evidently derived from accumulated stocks of information. One may ponder as to what can be done to give the elderly adult the advantage, not only of experience and training, but also of undiminished native talent. Here is a problem which may well occupy the best energies of future investigators in the field of human biology.

A number of additional factors deserve to be considered as having a possible influence upon the developmental curves.

1. It is possible that older persons are less readily motivated, that they adopt a conservative policy with reference to their resources, refusing to expend their energy unless it is necessary, or obviously and importantly useful to do so. With reference to this hypothesis it would be possible to cite evidence from our field observations which suggest that age was of little importance in determining incentive. It must be remembered that the whole present research was planned precisely with respect to the problem of rapport and cooperation, and that records were made of all cases showing resistance or apparent weak interest. Among those who took the tests, older subjects appeared, on the average, to be as earnest as younger ones in working for a good score. Evidence of greater weight, however, may be found in the curve of decline for the home-tested cases (Figure 7.4). It was among these cases that conditions affecting motivation were undoubtedly best controlled and best adapted to the individual. An examination of the means, standard deviations, and percentage of zero scores among home-tested as compared with the hall-tested cases yields nothing to show that the age decline in intelligence-test score is a function of differential motivation.

2. Older persons may be handicapped by failing eyesight. If this were an important factor, we should expect to find a more rapid decline in the hall-tested than in the home-tested cases, for with the latter it was possible to obtain lighting conditions best adapted to individual needs. We should expect to find little or no decline in Test 1, which is given with oral directions and involves a minimum of reading. And we should expect to find that tests requiring similar tasks with respect to reading (such as Tests 7 and 8, or Tests 3 and 4) would exhibit similar curves of decline. None of these expectations has been met. From this, it is not contended that visual abilities (even when corrected with glasses) remain unaffected by age; but merely that (within the age range of our sample) we find no evidence of any significant effect of eyesight upon average Alpha score.

3. Older persons may be handicapped by an increased difficulty in hearing oral instructions. If this were an important factor, we should expect the decline with age to be especially rapid in Test 1 (which involves oral instruc-

tions);[11] and we also should expect the home-tested adults to show some advantage from a procedure in which extreme care was taken to note and adapt to possible sensory difficulties. The same considerations apply here as in the preceding section, and our conclusion is again negative with reference to the importance of increasing sensory handicap, in determining the results of the present study.

4. Adults may be handicapped by the remoteness of the period of formal schooling. Probably the subtest most closely related to schooling is Test 2 (arithmetic). In this test the rate of decline, far from being rapid, is, as a matter of fact, relatively slow. Willoughby (31) has obtained a similar result with an arithmetic test. It may be noted that improvement in the various subtests persists for a period of four or five years after 15 or 16, when most of our subjects complete their schooling. Within the age range of the present sample, then, remoteness of schooling fails to explain the decline of intelligence-test score with age.

5. Adults may be handicapped by disuse of the functions tested in the various subtests of the Alpha. The maintenance of high test scores by adults in Tests 4 and 8 (vocabulary and information) lends some possible support to this theory. But we must not forget the proper distinction between tests of basic intelligence or capacity, and tests of information or ability (1). Intelligence tests include the latter only in the attempt to measure the former; and we have already pointed out the limitations of information tests for the measurement of intelligence over a wide age range. Opposed to the theory of disuse is the fact of decline in Subtest 1 (directions) and Subtest 3 (common sense) of the Alpha; and Price's finding of a regular decline with age in tests of perceptual ability (23).

6. It has been suggested that adults work less rapidly than adolescents, and that this penalizes the adults because the Alpha is primarily a ''speed,'' rather than a ''power'' test. Requirements of speed may handicap the older adults in various ways, from the mere mechanics of managing a pencil to habits of rapid reading, or to attitudes favoring rapid performance. This problem arose in an earlier study of the growth curve of performance for a series of tests of learning and recall [Motion-Picture Tests A, B, and C (12)]. In these tests, the factor of speed was analyzed by comparing scores for the earlier part of each test, which every one had time to complete when working at his own rate, with scores for the total test worked within a time limit. The elimination of the speed factor did not alter the form of the developmental curve. This result is of peculiar significance when it is remembered that the Alpha and the motion-picture tests show a fairly high correlation with each

other and yield much the same type of developmental curve (3). The cause of this general correspondence between the curtailed motion-picture tests (administered without time restrictions) and the Alpha (administered with strict time limits) seems to lie in the fact that Alpha is not essentially a "speed" test, and the fact that adults do not, as sometimes supposed, work more accurately than adolescents. We cannot here assemble the evidence which indicates that Alpha measures "power" as well as "speed"; it will be sufficient to point out that in samples of adults as well as children (32, pp. 333, 634), the Army Alpha correlates fairly highly with the Stanford-Binet; and this latter can hardly be termed a test merely of "speed."

If the inferiority of the older individuals, which is especially apparent in Test 7, is due chiefly to factors producing retardation in speed, the old would be expected to drop faster in "items attempted" than in "items correct."[12] The diminution in scores would then be due, not to a loss of mental "power," but merely to a slower rate of work. A significant comparison can be made between items attempted on Tests 7 and 8. These maintain practically the same level (there are a total of 40 items in each test) up to the age of 20. Beyond this age, the "attempts" show a decline in Test 7 but not in Test 8—indicating that the cause of the decline lies in the intellectual difficulty of the task and not in factors associated with speed of reading or in the motivation of rapid work. In Test 8, the ratio of "items correct" to "items attempted" increases slightly but consistently after adolescence; this result— quite contrary to that found for Test 7—is evidently due to the accumulation of relevant definite information rather than to an improvement in auto-criticism or in habits of intellectual work. Our results appear to support Thorndike's conclusion that "the older manifest little more caution and care in intellectual operations than the young adults or adolescents" (29, p. 174).

7. Allied to the fallacious "speed-accuracy" theory, is the suggestion that adults make low scores principally through their failure to comprehend directions promptly. If this were an important factor, we should expect to find an excessively rapid decline in Test 1, which depends on oral instructions, and Test 6, which has unusual and complicated instructions. We should expect to find that tests with instructions of similar difficulty, such as Tests 4 and 5, would exhibit similar curves of decline. We should expect that when two tests show dissimilar decline (as in Tests 3 and 5) the more rapid decrement would be associated with more difficult instructions. Such expectations are not, however, borne out by the facts. Probably one reason making this factor of minimal importance, is that particular care was always taken,

through every legitimate means, to secure the best possible attention and comprehension of the directions to every subtest. While the subjects read the directions, they were at the same time spoken by the Examiner loudly, clearly, and rather slowly, with deliberate and well-practiced pauses and inflections. The administrative conditions were good; they were, in fact, best for that group showing the most rapid decline (Figure 7.4). We are almost tempted to suggest that the comparatively small number of individuals who may have been penalized by their failure to understand the directions promptly deserved to be so penalized.

It must be recognized that some of the considerations listed in the last few pages furnish better material for further research than for final conclusions. Even with a conservative attitude on these points, however, it seems difficult to escape the conclusion that the basic intelligence of the older generation is, on the average, poorer than that of the younger. Whatever the advantage of age may be, it does not seem to lie in inherent, basic capacity.

With reference to individual cases, it is of course ill-advised to make any sweeping application of our average results. As Thorndike has remarked in his discussion of the data of the present sample of adults, "individual differences amongst those of the same age . . . enormously outweigh differences between ages" (29, p. 159). It is also probably true that some individuals, through good fortune of endowment or circumstance or care, are able for many years to forestall the decline which ordinarily takes place with the passage of years. We must recognize that the high standard deviations of Table 7.3 indicate that individual differences are the rule and not the exception. Without attempting, then, to minimize the importance of considering each person by himself, we may still speculate whether the developmental curves in Figures 7.1 to 7.7 do not point to important social problems. In the management of educational, industrial, and political affairs, the accumulation of power in the hands of seniors may be assumed to be socially desirable only (1) if later maturity brings with it an accumulation of information or social skills or other favorable factors which compensate for a declining mental power as measured by our tests; or (2) if the decline in mental power is greatly delayed in the case of the very superior.

Summary

1. On the basis of 1,191 examinations of unselected rural New England subjects, developmental curves are presented of the growth and decline of ability in the Army Alpha intelligence test. The chief characteristics of the devel-

opmental curve for the total Alpha test may be summarized as involving a linear growth to about 16 years, with a negative acceleration beyond 16, to a peak between the ages of 18 and 21. A decline follows, which is much more gradual than the curve of growth, but which by the age of 55 involves a recession to the 14-year level. The developmental curves for the individual subtests of the Alpha display important differences among themselves. In some tests, the adolescents are superior to most of the adults; in others, the adults, on the average, surpass the adolescents. In some tests, the peak of development is reached around 18 years; in others, a slight rise continues well into advanced maturity. In some tests, the decline beyond the maximum is fairly precipitous; in others, it is practically negligible. This variation in the developmental curves of the individual subtests can hardly be completely explained on the basis of present knowledge. Certainly no simple ''verbal factor'' nor schooling factor can explain the results. It is noteworthy that the tests of information (Test 4, opposites or vocabulary, and Test 8, general information) fail to exhibit a post-adolescent decline. Decline is most rapid in Subtests 7 (analogies), 3 (''common sense''), and 6 (numerical completions). These tests may perhaps be considered, at least on *a priori* grounds, to be the best in the Alpha for the measurement of basic intelligence or intellectual capacity.

2. The decline of ability beyond the age of 21 is not due to errors of sampling. In fact, the post-adolescent decline is especially marked in the developmental curve for the group of towns most intensively sampled; and also in the curve for the ''complete-family'' group, in which homogeneity of sampling from age to age seems specifically assured.

3. The decline of adult ability beyond the age of 21 is not due to faulty administration of the Alpha. Examinations administered in the homes of the subjects, under conditions closely approximating those of individual testing, lead to the same conclusion as in the case of group tests.

4. The decline of ability in the total Alpha test, and the peculiarities of the developmental curves for the individual subtests, cannot be successfully explained by failure of motivation, remoteness of schooling, lack of understanding of directions, disproportion in attention to accuracy versus speed, lack of practice in the test functions, failing hearing, or failing eyesight.

5. From the point of view of measuring basic or native intelligence, the information tests of the Alpha (Test 4 and 8) present an unfair advantage to those in the upper age brackets. Exclusion of Subtests 4 and 8 from the Alpha gives a picture of comparatively more rapid growth among the adolescents and more rapid decline among the adults.

6. In the sixth decade of life, about 40% of total Alpha score is derived from two tests (Test 4 and Test 8); at age 10, these tests contribute only 25%. As represented in mental tests, then, the effective intellectual power of the adult, much more than that of the 10-year-old, is evidently derived from accumulated stocks of information.

7. Any sweeping application of our average results to individual adults would be ill-advised. Within the age range of the adults in the present sample, individual differences among those of the same age outweigh differences between the ages.

8. The curves for the growth and decline of mental-test abilities are regarded as pointing to important social problems.

NOTES

1. Results from three other tests have been separately reported (12).

2. Test 4 ("opposites") is virtually a vocabulary test; Test 8 measures "general information."

3. These are the oral directions, the "common sense," the disarranged sentences, the numerical completions, and the analogies tests, respectively.

4. Details as to the representativeness of the towns selected, in such important characteristics as population, racial origin, occupational distribution, literacy, education, and rate of emigration, may be found in Jones. (3).

5. Due to the absence of a differential birth-rate in our rural New England communities (5), this selection has not introduced any bias of sampling.

6. Differential mortality is an additional possible factor in this connection. It seems reasonable to suppose that within a given rural population, as within an urban, intelligence is more or less correlated with the occupational and hygienic conditions which make for longer life. Hence, age curves for intelligence, unless derived by cumulative testing of the same individuals, will at the upper ages decline too slowly, because of survivorship selection.

7. If dull parents bear a larger number of offspring than bright, or bear the same number of children within a shorter time, then the rising limb of our intelligence curves is, in a sense, unduly weighted with dullness. Keeping in mind the virtual absence of a differential birth-rate in the communities investigated (5), and, moreover, the imperfect correlation between parental and filial intelligence (13), we may doubt if either of these factors operates significantly. It is probable that the rising portion of the curve is weighted with first-born rather than last-born children (in view of the fact that many families, at the time of testing, were not yet completed). But it has been shown that, at least for these communities, and probably quite generally, there is no relation between birth order of offspring and intelligence (11; 15). It is on *a priori* grounds extremely doubtful if a differential death-rate is the cause of the drop in intelligence-test score during maturity; indeed, a differential death-rate if present, would more likely operate to prevent a decline (see note 6). Finally, it might be

suggested that in the curve for the complete-family group the rising and the falling limbs of the curve are not comparable, due to the regression of offspring to the mean of the race. This suggestion, if it is valid, assumes that the intelligence of rural New England is significantly inferior (or superior) to that of the mean of the race—an assumption which we are by no means prepared to admit. Moreover, significant regression is probably not to the mean of the race, but to the mean of comparatively recent ancestry. For our rural New England group, it may be questioned if the mean of recent ancestry differs sufficiently from the mean of the present generation of parents to make the regression of offspring a factor of importance in the present study.

8. If the decline in intelligence within our sample of adults were due simply to the continuous emigration of brighter parents, we should expect the children of older parents to be progressively inferior in brightness to the children of younger parents. A comparison of Table 7.2 with Table 7.3 fails to indicate any such inferiority. Selective migration, then, is not the cause of the drop in the intelligence curve for the complete-family group; it is even less likely the cause of the (slower) decline in the total sample.

9. Test 4 ("opposites") is virtually a vocabulary test; Test 8 measures "general information."

10. The percentage contribution of a given test at a given age is obtained by dividing the raw score equivalent of the smoothed T-score for the test at the given age, by the sum of the raw score equivalents of the smoothed T-scores of all the subtests at the given age. It is to be observed that we are analyzing central tendency, and not variance; the customary techniques for the analysis of variance (9) have therefore been deliberately disregarded.

11. In interpreting the curve for Test 1 (Figure 7.6) it is well to observe that the proportion of adults tested at home remains fairly constant from age to age—being 30% between the ages of 22 and 39; and 32% between the ages of 40 and 59.

12. We are indebted to Dr. Daniel Harris for statistical work in the investigation of this problem.

REFERENCES

1. Conrad, H. S. *General-information, intelligence, and the decline of intelligence.* J. Appl. Psychol., *1930*, 14, *592–599.*

2. Conrad, H. S. & Jones, H. E. *Psychological studies of motion pictures: III. Fidelity of report as a measure of adult intelligence.* Univ. Calif. Publ. Psychol., *1929, 3, 245–276.*

3. ———. *Psychological studies of motion pictures: IV. The technique of mental-test surveys among adults.* Univ. Calif. Publ. Psychol., *1929, 3, 277–284.*

4. ———. *Psychological studies of motion pictures: V. Adolescent and adult sex differences in immediate and delayed recall.* J. Soc. Psychol., *1931, 2, 433–459.*

5. ———. *A field study of the differential birth rate.* J. Amer. Statis. Asso., *1932, 27, 153–159.*

6. *Conrad, H. S., Jones, H. E. & Hsiao, H. H. Sex differences in mental growth and decline.* J. Educ. Psychol. *(in press).*

7. *Ehinger, G. Âge et declin des aptitudes.* Arch. de psychol., *1927, 20, 318–323.*

8. *Ezekiel, M. Methods of correlation analysis. New York: Wiley, 1930. Pp. vii, 427.*

9. *Fisher, R. A. Statistical methods for research workers. London: Oliver & Boyd, 1930. Pp. xi, 269.*

10. *Garrett, H. E. Statistics in psychology and education. New York: Longmans, Green, 1926. P. 320.*

11. *Hsiao, H. H. The status of the first-born with special reference to intelligence.* Genet. Psychol. Monog., *1931, 9, 1–118.*

12. *Jones, H. E., Conrad, H. S. & Horn, A. Psychological studies of motion pictures: II. Observation and recall as a function of age.* Univ. Calif. Publ. Psychol., *1928, 3, 225–243.*

13. *Jones, H. E. A first study of parent-child resemblance in intelligence.* 27th Yrbk. Nat. Soc. Stud. Educ., *1928, Pt. 1, 61–72.*

14. *Jones, H. E. & Conrad, H. S. Rural preferences in motion pictures.* J. Soc. Psychol., *1930 1, 419–423.*

15. *Jones, H. E. & Hsiao, H. H. A preliminary study of intelligence as a function of birth order.* J. Genet. Psychol., *1928, 35, 428–433.*

16. *Jones, H. E. The pattern of abilities among adult and juvenile defectives.* Univ. Calif. Publ. Psychol., *1931, 5, 47–61.*

17. *Jones, H. E., Conrad, H. S. & Blanchard, M. B. Environmental handicap in mental test performance.* Univ. Calif. Publ. Psychol., *1932, 5, 63–99.*

18. *Keen, A. M. Growth curves and IQ's as determined by testing large families.* School & Soc., *1930, 32 737–742.*

19. *Kelley, T. L. Statistical method. New York: Macmillan, 1924. Pp. xi, 390.*

20. *Lufkin, H. M. Report of the use of the Army Alpha test in rural schools.* School & Soc., *1921, 13, 27–30.*

21. *McCall, W. M. How to measure in education. New York: Macmillan, 1922. P. 416.*

22. *Miles, C. C. & Miles, W. R. The correlation of intelligence scores and chronological age from early to late maturity.* Amer. J. Psychol., *1932, 44, 44–78.*

23. *Price, B. The perceptual ability of persons over fifty years of age.* M. A. thesis, Stanford University, 1931.

24. *Ruger, H. A. & Stoessiger, B. On the growth curves of certain characters in man (males).* Ann. Eug., *1927, 2, 76–110.*

25. *Scarborough, J. B. The invalidity of a commonly used method for computing a certain probable error.* Proc. Nat. Acad. Sci., *1929, 15, 665–668.*

26. *Teagarden, F. M. A study of the upper limits of the development of intelligence.* Teach. Coll. Contrib. Educ., *1924, No. 156. Pp. vi, 112.*

27. *Thorndike, E. L. On the improvement in intelligence scores from thirteen to nineteen.* J. Educ. Psychol., *1926, 17, 73–76.*

28. *Thorndike, E. L., et al. The measurement of intelligence. New York: Teach. Coll., 1926. Pp. xxiv, 616.*

29. ———. *Adult learning. New York: Macmillan, 1928. Pp. x, 335.*

30. *Thurstone, L. L. The absolute zero in intelligence measurement.* Psychol. Rev., *1928, 35, 175–197.*

31. *Willoughby, R. R. Family similarities in mental test abilities.* Genet. Psychol. Monog., *1927, 4, 239–277.*

32. *Yerkes, R. M. (Ed.). Psychological examining in the United States Army.* Mem. Nat. Acad. Sci., *1921, 15. Pp. vi, 890.*

33. *Yule, G. U. An introduction to the theory of statistics. (7th ed.) London: Griffin, 1924. Pp. xv, 424.*

8. Measures of Certain Human Abilities throughout the Life Span

Walter R. Miles

CHILDREN, YOUTHS and adults of college age have been psychologically measured and studied a great deal. Men and women in middle age and especially those in later maturity have largely escaped such investigation; they were not readily available in our laboratories and because of the strong interest that workers have had in the early period of development few have attempted to obtain their cooperation. Now we are beginning to realize that so long as we lack scientific data on the actual changes in human abilities throughout the life span, just so long will we continue merely to guess about the important problem of individual ability and efficiency in maturity and to rate ourselves and others chiefly in terms of chronological age. The importance of the study of later maturity whether in connection with industrial conservation or institutional administration is very obvious. To many, especially eager younger persons, Osler's joke is not a joke. But still we have very little actual knowledge of the facts.[1]

In the study briefly reported in this paper the later age groups were not only included but an effort was made to investigate certain of their abilities with special completeness and in direct comparison with younger groups studied under the same external conditions. The actual research supported by a grant from the Carnegie Corporation was conducted at Stanford University in 1930. Psychological measurements were made on 863 persons; 335 males and 528 females, in age range from 6 to 95 years with as nearly equal numbers in the adult decades as could be secured. About half of these people were 50 years of age or older. Specially outfitted and attractive laboratory rooms, easy of access to those to be examined, were established in two small California cities. Subjects were secured for experiment and measurement through the cooperation and solicitation of lodges, church clubs, etc. For the most part the individuals studied belonged to the upper social strata. No one received personal remuneration. An individual who came to the special lab-

Reprinted from the *Proceedings of the National Academy of Sciences* 17 (1931): 627–33. Copyright © 1931 by W. R. Miles.

oratory for the two-hour series of tests was credited to the organization that sent him and that organization received payment at a rate proportionate to the individual's age. It was thus possible in part to overcome the difficulty of securing older people and every person who came had in addition to curiosity an altruistic and generous motive. Cooperation was excellent. The total two-hour session was broken into four half-hour periods with suitable rest intervals interspersed. The basic abilities: manual motility, reaction speed, visual perception span, judgment of size, judgment of position, code-message substitution, mental and motor learning, immediate memory, ability to overcome memory blocking, and rapid reasoning capacity were tested and measured. Several investigators took part in the research.

The present report is concerned with results from one of the thirty-minute divisions. The two functions studied in this part of the schedule are manual motility and reaction speed. Results for the male subjects only are included in this paper. Apparatus and techniques were so arranged for the measurement of coordination and dexterity that the situations and requirements might seem as natural as possible. The immediate effects of practice were reduced to a minimum.

MANUAL MOTILITY

1. The examination of motility, in manual reach and grasp, was made for each hand separately. The procedure was as follows: Starting from the clock key (the electric clock was in front and in full view of the subject) the subject reached 6 inches to one side, grasped a round pencil 3 inches long which was standing in a vertical hole 1½ inches deep and thrust the pencil into another such opening 1½ inches farther away, then returned his hand to the key, thus stopping the clock. In this performance test the subject took his own speed measurement. The clock started when he let go the key and began to reach; it was stopped when he completed the act and returned to the key. Table 8.1 gives summary results arranged by decades for this apparently simple, but in fact complex, and basic coordination. The total population examined included 331 males; the numbers per age decade are shown. The average score in seconds is the average for the two hands. The average deviation in seconds and the coefficient of variability in per cent are also included. From the table it is apparent that the test in question can be completed by men in their 20s on the average in 1.18 seconds and practically as fast by boys in the late teens, aged 15–19 years. Younger and older ages show

Table 8.1. Coordination in Manual Reach and Grasp. (Decade Scores for Both Hands Combined; Population, 331, Males)

Decades	No. cases	Average score, sec.	Average dev. sec.	c. v. %
80s	13	1.86	0.37	19.9
70s	39	1.53	0.16	10.2
60s	52	1.39	0.16	11.2
50s	58	1.30	0.15	11.5
40s	39	1.24	0.10	8.5
30s	40	1.23	0.12	9.4
20s	42	1.18	0.11	9.3
15–19	21	1.19	0.06	5.1
10–14	17	1.37	0.10	7.2
6–9	10	1.53	0.16	10.3

less speed. The deceleration from the 5th to the 8th decade is regular. But, as far as indicated by the sample, individuals in their 80s are only 50 or 60 per cent slower than the 20-year group. Individual differences are somewhat larger in the later decades. The bottom curve in Figure 8.1 gives the same series of results graphically in terms of semi-decades, thus indicating the degree of regularity in the performance curve in its relation to age. The slope of this curve indicates a rather rapid improvement in coordination ability from 8 to 18, only a slight change from then until age 50, followed by a decline, quite definite, but I think surprisingly small. Of the 52 men who were 70 years of age or older, the fastest third average at 1.35 seconds, a speed of performance which, as indicated by the short vertical arrows on the curve, is equal to the average ability of 60-year-olds and, at the younger end, of 14-year-olds.[2]

The results for three other manual motility measures are also charted in Figure 8.1. These are digital extension-flexion speed, and rotary motility for dominant and subordinate hand separately.

2. The extension-flexion measure was made on the forefinger of the dominant hand. The person lifted his finger from the clock key and brought it down again as quickly as possible. This activity was most efficiently executed by the 25–29-year group who required just less than a tenth of a second. Men 65 to 80 required more than two-tenths and those over 80 three-tenths second. Just as in the period of early development there is a steady increase in ability in this function, so it appears to decline rather steadily from the age of best performance onward. But the averages do not tell the whole story.

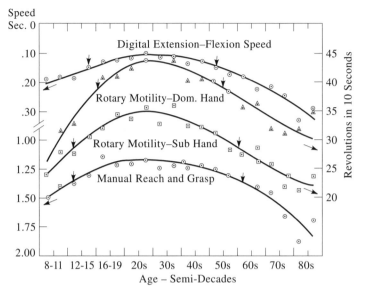

Figure 8.1. Changes in manual motility with age.

In the older ages there is great individual variation exhibited by the fact that the best third of the men over 70 have an average which is better than the 50-year-old mean and equals the 14–15-year level.

3. Rotary motility was measured for each hand by means of a small hand drill mechanism fitted with a revolution counter and supported for easy action. The crank handle of this device when revolved described a circle 5 inches in diameter. The load was minimal and the position favorable. Men 25–39 years of age, the best performers of this function, were able to revolve the dominant hand around this 5-inch circle approximately 44 times in ten seconds, but with the subordinate hand they executed about ten revolutions less. The two curves indicate the increasing difference between dominant and subordinate hands with increasing age up to early adulthood and the maintenance of a rather constant difference throughout middle life and later maturity.

REACTION SPEED

Results for three reaction speed measures are charted in Figure 8.2. These psychological tasks can be briefly described.

1. The curve at the top represents what has been called pursuit reaction.

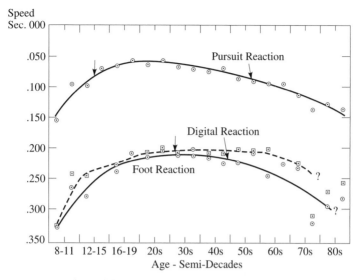

Figure 8.2. Changes in reaction time with age.

The subject repeatedly tried to stop the moving index of an electric clock at a certain zero-point position on the dial. The speed was one revolution in one-half second, and each time he watched the index make one or more revolutions before pressing the key. The average displacement error (sometimes the index was stopped too early, sometimes too late) is recorded here as the reaction score, and the smaller this time value the more accuracy is exhibited in this anticipatory reaction response. Ability in this function increases from ages 8 to 18. Thereafter we find but little change until age 30 after which the average displacement error becomes progressively larger, doubling in size by age 80. However, the best third of the older (above 70) group score better than the average 50-year-old man.

2. In the digital reaction test the subject lifted his finger (forefinger of dominant hand) as soon as possible after hearing the buzzing of the electric clock which was started by the experimenter some time (a variable interval) after a warning verbal signal. Lifting the finger stopped the clock. This simple reaction when unpractised requires about two tenths second for men in their 20s. It seems highly significant that there is retention of this ability into the 6th decade and only slight loss in the 70s and 80s.

3. The foot reaction was of similar nature but here, of course, the key was on the floor and the manipulation was almost identical with that of releasing the gas pedal of an automobile. When the clock was started the

Table 8.2. Correlations of Motor Ability Scores with Age

Function	Eta both sexes	Product-moments (r) coefficient-males			
		20–95	30–95	40–95	50–95
No. cases	866	288	246	206	167
1. Digital extension-flexion speed	0.604	0.599 ± 0.03	0.574 ± 0.03	0.514 ± 0.03	0.457 ± 0.04
No. cases	858	283	241	201	162
2. Manual reach and grasp (both hands)	0.625	0.535 ± 0.03	0.527 ± 0.03	0.541 ± 0.03	0.526 ± 0.04
No. cases	866	285	243	203	164
3. Manual rotary motility, dom. hand	0.462	0.499 ± 0.03	0.498 ± 0.03	0.422 ± 0.04	0.386 ± 0.05
No. cases	868	288	246	206	167
4. Pursuit reaction (anticipatory)	0.534	0.565 ± 0.03	0.519 ± 0.03	0.467 ± 0.04	0.365 ± 0.05
No. cases	469	195	153	115	80
5. Digital reaction (non-anticipatory)	0.518	0.283 ± 0.04	0.311 ± 0.04	0.345 ± 0.06	0.454 ± 0.06
No. cases	469	195	153	115	80
6. Foot reaction (non-anticipatory)	0.464	0.454 ± 0.04	0.425 ± 0.05	0.331 ± 0.06	0.402 ± 0.06
No. cases	439	187	148	110	76
7. Code: letter substitution	0.675	0.537 ± 0.04	0.623 ± 0.04	0.654 ± 0.04	0.407 ± 0.06

subject responded to this auditory signal by lifting the forepart of the foot, using the heel as fulcrum. These results show slightly longer reaction times than are found in responding by lifting the finger and also show a more regular change with increasing age. The results in the semi-decades beyond 70 were too irregular properly to lend themselves to curve fitting.

Some of the correlations of our motility and reaction scores with age are exhibited in Table 8.2. The functions are named in the left-hand column as in the charts. The number of cases used for each correlation is included. In the second column the raw eta coefficients have been entered. These are for both men and women considered as one group and express the relationship of our curvilinear score diagrams with age throughout the entire age span. In this table these values range from 0.46 to 0.67. The other columns present the product movements (r) coefficients for score with age for males considered in four different age groupings: 20–95, 30–95, 40–95, and 50–95 years. All of these correlation coefficients are statistically significant. All of them agree in indicating score decrement with age in the functions tested. But none of them is so large as to show age alone dictating the score. The score variance in these basic human abilities appears to depend as much or more on the sum total of other factors as it does on chronological age.

That particular age grouping which shows the definitely highest correlation coefficient (r) for a given measure indicates thereby the beginning decade in which decrement starts. Digital extension-flexion speed gives the highest correlation in the age range 20 to 95 indicating that there is some decrease in speed between 20 and 30, similarly for pursuit reaction, while with digital reaction the highest correlation is for the age grouping 50 to 95 years. Thus the different measures show different turning points.

Many representative functions need to be surveyed in respect to their changes during man's life span before we can hope to achieve a thorough understanding of ourselves. But scientific theories are always in order. Are the decrements found in the basic motor functions here presented due to neuromuscular deterioration, to less adequate visual and other sensory control, to disuse, to lack of motivation, or to something decidedly different from these? Our experimental conditions were set to provide motivation (I think we were successful); the tasks were selected from among, or closely related to, the *well*-used, and the demands on vision and hearing were slight. You will have noted that when the measure included only the movement, decrement was larger than when the measurement included also the strictly cortical elements of comprehension, selection and readiness for response plus a brief movement. This general distinction may be made between the motility measures and the reaction tests. It is well known that cortical function is economical of energy and that motor function is spendthrift. A possible theory then for the slower and more difficult action in the old is that neural conservation mechanisms are built up or become more potent, with increasing lifetime. A particular decrement according to this theory would not be chiefly chargeable to a defect in the mechanism but to a positive check on it—a neural governor device protective of the mechanism. The weight of years may be in large part neural inhibition-interference to action. This is perhaps the core, or the basic behavior element, in the caution and proverbial good judgment of the old. Surely the self-depreciation and inferiority attitudes exhibited by the majority of older people in reference to action are scarcely warranted from our data. Decrement appears more in feeling than it exists in fact.

NOTES

1. In 1928 this lack of scientific information was drawn to the attention of various research groups in the United States by Professor Lewis M. Terman and the writer.

We prepared a statement, circulated it privately and sought support for investigations. The Carnegie Corporation of New York made a grant to Stanford University to aid such studies. The present paper reports a part of the work thus made possible.

2. In figures 8.1 and 8.2 the short arrows indicate in each instance the average value for the best one-third of the group 70 years old or older.

9. Influence of Speed and Age on Intelligence Scores of Adults

Catharine Cox Miles

The gradual rise of intelligence test scores from the earliest testable age to a maximum somewhere in the teens is well established. High positive correlation between these test scores and chronological age in populations of normal children and youths is regularly expected. Little information relating age and intelligence test scores has, however, been available for the period of adulthood, although many intelligence tests furnish so-called "adult norms" on the basis of which ratings of mature individuals are to be made. Investigators of adult abilities who have used intelligence tests have been struck by an apparent decline of test scores after early maturity. On the basis of the largest collection of such data, in the U.S. Army investigations under Professor Yerkes' chairmanship, the investigators hesitated to posit an age-score decline. Rather it was suggested that the phenomenon might be accounted for by factors of differential selection and not by age as such. We are now able to present new data on this problem. Results obtained in the Stanford Later Maturity Study (directed by W. R. Miles), from giving the Otis S-A Higher Examination Form A as a 15-minute speed test (Miles, 1931) to about 2000 persons of whom more than 250 are 70 years of age or older, show correlations between age and score of approximately −.50 for adults between ages 20 and 95 at each of three educational levels.

Four questions are to be considered relative to these data: (a) The first is the question whether the trend observed in one population persists in others. It is answered in the affirmative by comparing four sizable populations.[1] The normal decline in scoring ability from the third to the ninth decade is in each of the four about 3.3 mental-age years of 25 IQ points on Otis' scale. The "average" individual who probably registers about half-way between our grade-school and high-school levels loses in scoring capacity from the third to the ninth decade at a rate of 6 to 7 mental-age months per decade. (b) The

From *Journal of Genetic Psychology* 10 (1934): 208–10. Published by Heldref Publications, 1319 Eighteenth Street, N. W., Washington, D.C. 20036–1802. Copyright © 1934. Reprinted with the permission of the Helen Dwight Reid Educational Foundation.

Table 9.1.

Score decline in standard score units	Age periods			
	25–49 (41 cases)	50–59 (51 cases)	60–69 (55 cases)	70–89 (43 cases)
Expected	−.40	−.60	−.70	−1.20
Obtained	−.46	−.49	−.84	−1.42

second question concerns the probability that similar score decrement will be found if the same individuals are tested at regular decade intervals from their early to late maturity. Results from a retest in 1932 of 190 persons first tested in 1930 shows approximately the same decline for a two-year period in each of four age segments, as is given by the age-score curve based on the large population of differing individuals (Table 9.1). The group of 190 persons is made up of 135 who returned voluntarily in the second experiment because of interest and 55 others who came because of our special and urgent request for the return of members of the 1930 population. Comparison of the scores of the 135 persons shows somewhat differing results from the above averages for the 190 (Table 9.2). Perhaps a practice effect not evident in the first comparison is registered here. In spite of this, the age influence seems to be progressively present.

(*c*) The third question concerns the factor of speed. Is the age decrement largely due to speed decrement? When Form B of the same Otis Self-Administering Examination series was given *without time limit* to 433 adults who had also taken the 15-minute Form A, age decrement was still found to occur, but the rate of decline from early to late maturity was not identical. In terms of standard scores the average decrement from decade to decade for A is .27 standard score units; for B, .24. In neither case does decline appear

Table 9.2.

Score decline in standard score units	Age periods		
	25–59 (63 cases)	60–69 (44 cases)	70–89 (28 cases)
Expected	− .50	− .70	−1.20
Obtained	+1.75	+1.64	−1.03

significantly before the fifth decade. From early maturity (20s, 30s, 40s) to later maturity (60s), the decline is .76 in standard score units for A, .46 for B; but from later maturity (60s) to old age (80s) it is .87 for A, .98 for B. We may say then that in early and middle maturity speed declines, on the average, rather faster than power, whereas in late maturity the decline of power is relatively more apparent.

(*d*) The fourth question concerns the extent to which the intelligence scores of adults register the intelligence of adults. The items contained in the tests in question make different psychological demands for their solution. It appears that where recognition rather than recall or the organization of new materials is required the decrement is not so great. This has been shown by a comparison of the item-by-item decrement in the Otis test. Further, in connection with quite another investigation, a study of sex differences conducted by Professor Lewis M. Terman and myself and as yet unpublished, I have scored the item-information test, there given without time limit, for 30 people in each decade from the 20s to the 70s. Here recognition rather than recall is required and no problems involving new materials are presented for reorganization. With these conditions the scores rise definitely to a peak in the 40s and 50s to fall again to the early maturity level in the 70s.

Recognition of the speed-energy factor is, I hope, a first step toward the development of a new type of intelligence test standardized on the middle decades rather than on childhood and youth. Scores on this test must correlate for any decade group with the scores now available, but the serial means will show a development curve of a different sort from youth through early to late maturity. A test in which the speed factor is as far as possible eliminated and in which the experiential elements are registered for mature adults as adequately as they appear to be now for children and very young adults will, I expect, show not a curve of early decrement but a rise in score from decade to decade until somewhere in the late maturity period.

The practical value of our results measuring age-score decrement from early to late maturity is in the means which these norms furnish for rating older and younger persons on a single scale of comparison, that is, in terms of percentile rank or standard score within each decade. The curve for any given individual who takes the test under satisfactory conditions can be plotted and an estimate of his maximum rating in early maturity obtained. Of course, such a procedure is crude and has a wide margin of error, but, even so, it is considerably more accurate than any other mental-rating technique at present available for adults. A test score based on performance on two test-forms, preferably one with and one without time limit, has a fairly high validity. For studies of inheritance, comparisons of parents with children, and for individual clinical use, the decade percentiles offer a means of direct ability comparison between old and young. The present discussion has been based on intelligence score results on tests standardized for young people. Some suggestions as to the larger question of the status of intelligence in maturity have emerged from a consideration of these results.

NOTE

1. For a comparison of the first two of these, see Miles and Miles, 1932.

REFERENCES

Miles, C. C. *The Otis S-A as a fifteen-minute intelligence test.* Person. J., *1931,* 10, *246–249.*

Miles, C. C. & Miles, W. R. *The correlation of intelligence scores and chronological age from early to late maturity.* Amer. J. Psychol., *1932,* 44, *44–78.*

10. Age and Mental Ability in Superior Men

Keith Sward

Notwithstanding the lengthening list of titles upon "old age" the normal psychology of the later decades of life is still fragmentary, confused, and to a large extent conjectural. Medical studies adjacent to this field offer, when taken all together, little more than a rough clinical sketch of "senility." Careful psychometric researches upon late maturity are meager. Their results and their limitations may be generally summarized as follows. (1) Performance upon mental tests does frequently indicate a reduction with advancing years; though certain abilities, notably the linguistic resources of the organism, resist the passage of time better than others. (2) Large individual differences are found, as in all other age groups. (3) The causes for observed changes in performance during late maturity are little known. This defect is due in part to the imperfect and inadequate control, during these years, of the conditions of observation and of inference. Especially defective has been the control of selection and sampling of the individuals studied. Moreover, motivation under test and the inevitable changes in experience, interest, outlook and facility in accomplishment, which the mere passage of years brings at any period of life, have not been sufficiently regarded and allowed for. Every existing psychometric study, including the present one, has used a cross-section method of approach. The crucial investigations of the future will employ genetic methods, following up the same individuals throughout the last third of life.

The present investigation has limited itself to individuals of high intelligence and wide academic experience. Although it primarily depends upon a direct comparison of older and younger men within this range, it has tried to improve upon the usual control of essential conditions, notably in the selection and matching of individuals in comparable groups, and in a more careful control of motivation.

Reprinted from *American Journal of Psychology* 58 (1945): 443–79. Copyright © 1945, 1973 by the Board of Trustees of the University of Illinois. Used with permission of the University of Illinois Press.

THE SUBJECTS

The men in our two primary groups were members of two university faculties resident upon the Pacific Coast. Every man in the older group who was identified with the physical or the biological sciences is listed in the 1927 edition of *American Men of Science*. One of our two universities is ranked in that work among ten educational institutions in the United States which lead in anatomy, anthropology, astronomy, botany, mathematics and psychology. The other institution is equally distinguished, as judged by the eminence of its science faculty in geology, pathology and psychology.

Three criteria for admission to the elder and the younger groups were imposed.

1. Age-range. Sixty years or above was set as the minimal age for admission to the later-maturity group. Younger men were drawn, with a few exceptions, from the decade twenty-five to thirty-five.

2. Professional field. The age-groups were matched by professional occupation; e.g., an older chemist was paired with a younger man in the physical sciences. This matching procedure insured some degree of comparability upon grounds of professional specialization.

3. Academic rank. For the younger men the rank of instructor or above was required. The full professorial status was imposed, with two exceptions, for admission to the older group. One hundred older men, active and retired, and one hundred twenty-three younger men satisfied the several requirements at the two institutions. The next step was to secure the cooperation of a fair proportion of this potential population.

SAMPLING

Formal approval of the research was first obtained from the president's office in each university. The later-maturity men were then canvassed. Then for each older man who agreed to serve as subject (*S*) a match was found by selecting serially from an alphabetical list the name of a younger faculty man in the same general field of specialization. The age-range of the participating older men is 60–79 years, with a mean of 66.2, a median of 64.6, and a standard deviation (S.D.) of 5.37. The age-range of the younger *S*s is 21–42 years, with a mean of 31.4, a median of 31.4, and an S.D. of 4.65.

Forty-five *S*s were tested in each group. To obtain this number the investigator had to approach 64 older and 59 younger men. Thus from those who were asked to participate ca. 76 per cent of the resident faculty consented.

Table 10.1. Reasons Given by Non-Participating Subjects for Failure to Serve

	Old	Young
Illness	15	2
Non-residence	21	1
Refusals based on principle		
Fear of the test situation	5	0
"Too busy"	7	7
Hostile attitude towards psychology	7	4
Total	55	14
Mean age of the senescents who served as S		66.2
Mean age of the senescents who did not participate		65.9

The reasons given for non-cooperation are listed in Table 10.1. Among the older faculty the factor of non-residence from May to August is the most important. Next in order of frequency in this group come illness and invalidism.

Several qualitative age-differences are noteworthy among those who declined to serve. (1) Five of the older men showed unmistakable signs of fearing the test-situation. No younger man exhibited such a feeling. An emotionally-toned rejection of the investigator's request was conveyed by such expressions, as "No, I just can't go through with it!" or "I'm afraid of failure—just the introspective experience!" (2) The argument of being "too busy" to participate showed a certain relation to age which Table 10.1 fails to reveal. Fairly definite "anxiety states" seemed to characterize the seven older men who gave this reason for their declination. These potential Ss declared, "I'm overworked, a year behind now. I just can't squander time," or "Time seems more precious and shorter than it used to. Things don't get done. It's breaking my back," and the like. The younger men who refused on the same grounds—of being pressed for time—were more matter of fact. Their feelings were less in evidence. (3) Among the non-cooperating, the old were seemingly readier than the young to give vent to feelings of hostility towards psychology in general and mental tests in particular. In such instances the older man was wont to stay something like, "I'm not a guinea pig or a rat in a maze!" or "These tests are schemes to trick people"; or "Bright men are never heard from. It's the plodders who get there." One non-cooperating older man took the pains to advise the investigator by letter, "You are taking advantage of the faculty. This is a plan to milk the faculty and scoop off the cream. You'll decide when men ought to retire and get out of their professions."

The fact of non-cooperation is unrelated to exact age *within* either of the test-groups. The older men who were approached without success are hardly distinguishable in mean age from the participating Ss. Something like 17 per cent of the resident faculty between sixty and eighty-six years of age had to be eliminated because of health. Of the sub-classes who could not or would not participate, the ill are slightly older by some two to four years. Among the young, neither age nor academic rank is related to the fact of non-participation.

One person was lost in each group after the testing began. An older S (age seventy-two) devoted forty-two minutes to one of the more difficult tests without achieving a single solution. He then withdrew from the experiment altogether, saying that the tests took "too much time." Yet he asked the investigator on two later occasions to "drop around some time and talk about psychology." Some five hours were subsequently devoted to this purpose, with circumspect efforts to enlist cooperation, but without success. One younger man withdrew of his own volition and in disgust after spending one hour and achieving average success on the same test. He couched his intent to withdraw in terms of "overwork" and "nervous strain." He too subsequently invited the investigator to "come over some evening and discuss mental tests."

COMPARABILITY OF OLD AND YOUNG

The methods of equating initial capacity in the two test-groups are far from adequate. But so far as they go, these measures suggest comparability. At least the old and the young are alike in social-economic origins and in collegiate scholarship. Moreover, the doctoral degree, which is somewhat more common among the younger men, is no index to test performance. Finally, insofar as the investigator's results constitute a fair measure of that fact, the groups drawn from the two neighboring universities are more or less homogeneous in make-up. We give five terms of this comparison.

1. Similar social-economic status. Parental occupations were classified according to the Goodenough seven-point scale.[1] In this case, however, the fathers of the old are compared with the grandfathers of the young, since in the matter of age the experimental groups are at least a full generation apart.

Both groups come preponderantly from the upper social strata and in about the same proportion, although here the advantage is slightly in favor of the old. The upper half of this scale contributes 14 per cent more of the old than of the young, and farming and skilled labor produce some 14 per cent more

Table 10.2. Comparison of Older Men Who Hold Doctorate in Philosophy (Ph.D.) with Those Lacking the Degree

	I Ph.D.-group (N=20)			II Non-Ph.D. group (N=20)			Per cent of II at or above the median of I
	Mean	Median	S.D.	Mean	Median	S.D.	
Ingenuity	5.65	5.67	2.39	5.15	5.67	2.31	49.9
Artificial Language[a]	31.36	25.20	15.44	26.96	27.00	8.68	55.8
Synonyms and Antonyms	47.95	51.25	11.70	48.55	49.75	5.64	40.0
Symbol-Digit[a]	57.61	54.49	10.92	58.87	59.90	12.63	58.8
No. Series	7.75	9.00	6.25	8.45	10.20	4.18	55.0
Word Meanings	218.00	220.00	63.00	215.00	210.00	61.20	40.0
Analogies	20.70	20.50	3.44	21.80	23.00	2.62	75.0
Arithmetic	7.30	8.50	3.02	8.15	8.75	2.06	55.0
Total score[b]	362.60	378.00	42.86	381.20	380.80	43.43	57.9
Age (yrs)	66.30	64.66	4.78	67.00	64.00	5.96	

[a] N-19 for calculations in each row
[b] See note 13.

of the young. Very possibly this slight "superiority" of the old is understated inasmuch as the members of the younger group were unable to recall the occupations of ten grandparents. Lack of information on this point may connote a fairly low, or at least undistinguished, mark in the world. Thus at least in their social origins the inferiority of the young may be greater than the figures indicate.

2. Comparable college scholarship. Only 25 of the older men and 37 of the younger were eligible for election to honor societies during the college career. Of this number, about the same proportion are "honors" men—72 per cent of the old and 67.6 per cent of the young. To the extent that college grades can be said to measure capacity, again the older and younger *S*s appear comparable.

3. Higher degrees. The old and the young are similar once more in make-up, as gauged by the incidence of advanced degrees. Twenty of the "senescent"[2] and 26 of the younger academic men are holders of the doctoral degree in philosophy. This particular similarity is not offered as proof of comparability, however, inasmuch as possession of the degree is not *ipso facto* any index of ability—at least within the populations here considered. In Table 10.2 it will be seen that non-doctors in the older group outscored the holders of the degree in five of the eight tests in the total battery (see below) as well as in total scores.[3] It may be said for the senescent, therefore,

Table 10.3. Comparison of Younger Men with Doctorate and the Master's Degree

	I Ph.D.-group (N=26)			II M.A.-group (N=17)			Per cent of I at or above the median of II
	Mean	Median	S.D.	Mean	Median	S.D.	
Ingenuity	7.54	8.00	2.02	7.29	8.25	2.09	48.1
Artificial Language	51.52	52.00	14.72	48.24	47.50	10.56	57.7
Synonyms and Antonyms	39.64	43.00	12.06	39.04	43.75	12.93	44.2
Symbol-Digit	80.14	82.00	9.12	73.78	73.50	9.69	82.7
No. Series	12.42	14.00	3.37	12.35	12.50	3.11	57.7
Word Meanings	137.00	220.00	70.80	251.20	227.60	61.60	48.5
Analogies	24.19	25.33	2.97	24.47	25.25	2.95	51.9
Arithmetic	9.69	10.67	2.13	10.00	11.13	2.28	35.5
Total Score[a]	429.70	431.00	27.06	425.90	434.70	17.06	42.3
Age (yrs)	32.92	31.76	4.24	30.30	29.80	5.08	

[a] See note 13.

that the acquisition of this degree was a matter of preference or opportunity rather than of ability—as measured in this case by an exacting mental test. In fact, eight of the older faculty members who hold only the baccalaureate degree surpass the "doctoral" members in their age-group by a slight margin on three-fourths of the tests. Nor is there any evidence of the fact that possession of this degree is any cue to 'ability' *within* the younger age-group (see Table 10.3).

4. Homogeneity of the two university populations. Insofar as one can judge the matter internally—on the basis of the investigator's test-scores—the two sets of older men are of comparable mental stature. Six of the nine inter-university differences for the senescent (see Table 10.4), are certainly within the limits of chance, and the direction of the difference is not consistent. Six comparisons favor one institution: three point in the opposite direction. But, interestingly enough, the slight suggestion of superiority on the part of University B favors the institution which outranks the other in having a larger number of eminent scientists on its faculty.[4]

The younger men, thus considered, are somewhat less homogeneous, and in this case the advantage lies with Institution A (see Table 10.5). The younger group at University A excel those at B on every test but one; although only in four instances are the differences large enough to be significant. This superiority is seemingly unrelated to age and the incidence of higher degrees or to the field of interest or specialization.[5]

5. Selection and academic rank. All but two members of the older group

Table 10.4. Scores of Older Men Selected from Two Pacific Coast Universities

| | University A (N=24) | | | University B (N=21) | | | Per cent of A at or above the median of B |
	Mean	Median	S.D.	Mean	Median	S.D.	
Ingenuity	6.08	5.89	2.16	5.05	5.63	2.18	59.7
Artificial Language	26.80[a]	24.28[a]	9.40[a]	32.00[b]	29.00[b]	15.48[b]	25.0
Synonyms and Antonyms	48.37	49.00	6.84	49.21	51.10	7.02	38.3
Symbol-Digit	56.77[a]	53.89[a]	10.47[a]	59.80[b]	61.00[b]	11.43[b]	34.8
No. Series	8.38	8.50	4.54	8.57	10.30	4.98	42.1
Word Meanings	215.00	213.40	55.80	213.80	210.00	72.20	52.1
Analogies	20.88	21.50	3.41	21.24	22.25	3.18	40.6
Arithmetic	8.29	8.83	2.26	7.38	8.25	2.87	64.6
Total Score[c]	375.40[a]	357.40[a]	37.03[a]	370.50[b]	383.20[b]	51.32[b]	39.1
Age (yrs)	66.75	67.50	5.74	65.78	63.87	4.59	

[a] Figures based on 23 cases.
[b] Figures based on 20 cases.
[c] See note 13.

are "full" professors. Of the two exceptions, one—an assistant professor—excels in every test. The other, an associate professor, is slightly below the mean of his group all along the line. The younger group includes 18 instructors and 27 assistant and associate professors (see Table 10.6). Here, five of the tests show an advantage for the men of higher rank somewhat larger than can be accounted for by chance. An accident of sampling, therefore, may

Table 10.5. Scores of Young Men Selected from Two Pacific Coast Universities

| | University A (N=30) | | | University B (N=15) | | | Per cent of A at or above the median of B |
	Mean	Median	S.D.	Mean	Median	S.D.	
Ingenuity	7.70	8.38	1.85	6.87	7.75	2.16	65.0
Artificial Language	50.00	50.00	12.56	50.93	48.00	14.84	55.0
Synonyms and Antonyms	40.40	43.51	11.28	36.10	42.25	14.73	54.2
Symbol-Digit	74.80	75.25	9.30	82.10	85.75	10.29	15.8
No. Series	12.67	14.33	3.16	12.13	12.75	3.32	55.8
Word Meanings	250.66	236.00	68.00	227.34	210.00	59.80	73.3
Analogies	24.63	25.43	3.07	23.60	24.50	2.36	70.0
Arithmetic	10.37	11.22	1.64	8.87	10.25	2.68	74.2
Total Score[a]	432.80	435.50	25.61	418.70	418.40	13.04	63.3
Age (yrs)	31.60	31.12	4.76	32.60	32.50	4.46	

[a] See note 13.

Table 10.6. Scores of Younger Men Related to Academic Rank

	A. Professorial Group (N=27)			B. Instructor Group (N=18)			Per cent of A at or above the median of B
	Mean	Median	S.D.	Mean	Median	S.D.	
Ingenuity	7.70	8.38	2.03	7.11	8.17	1.92	53.0
Artificial Language	48.60	45.00	13.92	51.56	52.68	12.64	35.8
Synonyms and							
Antonyms	37.18	40.75	14.40	41.68	44.20	6.88	38.5
Symbol-Digit	79.51	79.75	8.76	74.83	75.00	8.31	70.4
No. Series	13.04	14.75	3.11	11.66	12.00	3.22	70.4
Word Meanings	249.20	245.00	71.60	236.00	220.00	56.60	63.0
Analogies	24.85	25.50	2.62	23.44	24.75	3.09	63.9
Arithmetic	10.22	10.94	1.73	9.33	10.50	2.61	64.8
Total Score*	433.10	433.90	31.10	420.60	425.50	9.64	59.3
Age (yrs)	33.00	32.60	3.87	28.94	29.10	4.58	

ᵃ See note 13.

affect the outcome of the study among the young. For were the youthful group confined to professorial staff-members, the test-scorers of the young might be correspondingly higher.

A METHOD OF TESTING SUPERIOR ADULTS

An extensive search of the literature failed to unearth a satisfactorily standardized battery of mental tests for the superior adult. The investigator was therefore compelled to construct his own scale. He compiled five sub-tests from the content of a score or more of published scales.[6] The borrowed items were then supplemented by new materials. The resulting battery was, for the most part, conventional in make-up.

Choice of material was governed by the following points: (1) *Difficulty*. The tests were to be sufficiently exacting to bring out individual differences in the higher ranges of ability. (2) *General suitability or appropriateness*. Special care was taken to eliminate ambiguous or irritating items. The aim was to devise an inherently interesting series which would motivate a group of bright adults. (3) *Variety*. The sub-tests were chosen to explore 'mental ability' from dissimilar angles. (4) *Generalized content*. An attempt was made to avoid content of a specifically informational or ''achievement'' character.[7] (5) *Abstract intellect*. The investigator was concerned with ''bookish'' as against social intelligence. (6) *Age fairness*. An effort was made to avoid any test-content which might by its nature favor one or the other age-group. The battery seems to meet this particular requirement except in those instances where disuse and remoteness from schooling or relevance to present life probably operate to the disadvantage of the older men. (7) The scale was so standardized as to comply with at least minimal demands of reliability and objectivity.

Eight sub-tests were included in the final scale.[8] Each will now be briefly described.

1. *Ingenuity Problems.* Eleven items of the insightful or problem-solving kind. All the problems could be solved without the aid of any technical knowledge and without the use of sophisticated procedures.

2. *Artificial Language.* Forty sentences to be translated from English into a novel code language and vice versa, with a time allowance of eleven minutes.[9]

3. *Synonyms and Antonyms.* Sixty pairs of words, each pair consisting of either synonyms or antonyms. The list was compiled from a standard dictionary. It was made up, in the main, of difficult abstract terms.[10]

4. *Symbol-Digit Substitution.* Taken from Army Beta, Test No. 4 (Yerkes, 1921), as it stands. In this case, however, the key was so reversed that *S* was required to fill in digits instead of symbols. This change was made to anticipate a motor handicap which might have penalized the older men had the latter been required to copy rapidly unfamiliar symbols. The test was given with a two-minute time limit.

5. *Number-Series Completion.* Sixteen series arranged in order of increasing difficulty. *S* was required to grasp the principle of progression within each row and to extend the series by two additional steps.

6. *Word Meanings.* This is the Reference Test from Roback's *Mentality Tests for Superior Adults.* Fifteen commonplace stimulus words were given, with instructions to indicate as many meanings or usages as possible for each word in the list. Roback's directions call for a 15-minute time limit. In the present study no time limit was used.

7. *Analogies.* Complexity was added to a list of thirty analogy items by shifting the 'critical' proposition so that judgment would not invariably concern the fourth term of the series.

8. *Arithmetic Problems.* Twelve relatively difficult arithmetic problems, chosen to stress ''reasoning,'' yet involving nothing more than fundamental computation.

Most of the sub-tests were first tried with a group of 20 to 30 Stanford upperclassmen who had scored within the first decile of the Stanford population on the Thorndike College Entrance Examination. The original series were then modified to yield an adequate range of difficulty, objective scoring, and proper scaling of items in order of difficulty.[11]

The Testing Procedure

In order to perfect his methods of approach, the investigator did preliminary testing with a group of eight older non-faculty men. His method of approaching the faculty group proper was as follows. Individual appointments were made by telephone. The initial interview was given over to a brief exposition of the object and the auspices of the study. Complete anonymity was assured. In order to anticipate any prejudices at the outset, the investigator purposely understated the presumed value of mental tests. Optimal *rapport* was sought throughout the testing experience by indirect methods, chiefly by means of free conversation both before and after each testing session. The time and place of working were arranged to fit the convenience of each *S*. Each test was given individually. The printed directions explained the procedures which each sub-test entailed. Before undertaking any of the longer ''power'' tests, *S* received an oral warning that he would do well to space his time.

The entire battery required some three or four hours to administer. Three separate testing sessions for each *S* were conducted a week apart. Adequate rest-intervals were interpolated between successive tests at any given sitting, for old and young alike. The technique of spreading the tests was thought to be a practical necessity as well as a means of sustaining interest and of minimizing fatigue among the older men. There is every reason to believe that fatigability commonly increases with age. That belief was borne out, to some extent, by the present study. Eleven older men and four of the younger complained of being tired during one or another of the sittings.

The order in which the several tests were presented was arranged arbitrarily. *Ingenuity Problems* was given first because of its more or less intriguing, if difficult, content. *Arithmetic Problems* was placed last in the series as perhaps the least stimulating unit. The two speed-tests were saved for the second and third sittings so that *S* could adjust himself to the testing situation before having to work against time and under pressure.[12] Several *Ss* expressed a preference for a certain test-sequence. In such cases the option was granted. Times were recorded on each of the power-tests and, aside from the caution to space one's efforts over the whole of a difficult period, no limits were imposed on working time. Few members of either group had ever had any previous experience in this situation. Only four younger men and two of the older had taken a mental test on some earlier occasion.

Behavioral Notes

The investigator was present at every session and took full notes under the guise of abstracting a book. Insofar as possible he made a verbatim copy of the remarks which *S* might volunteer while working. Only spontaneous speech having to do with the tests themselves was recorded, and *S* was unaware of the fact that his behavior was under observation.

The procedure worked well, as a rule. The speech data are incomplete, however, for five older and two younger men for reasons beyond the investigator's control. In such instances the *S* under test withdrew into his private study or the investigator was unable to break away conveniently from some member of his family.

Consistency of the Tests

Internal consistency was checked by correlating scores on equivalent halves, on odd and even items, of each test. The correlations are listed in Table 10.7. Five tests give fairly high values, the raw coefficients ranging from .75 to .99. *Ingenuity Problems, Analogies* and *Arithmetic* are obviously imperfect on this score; their coefficients running from .22 to .52; four of the values near .50, one at .41, another at .22. The three "unreliable" tasks were apparently too easy in spite of their long time-requirements. *Analogies* and

Table 10.7. Reliability Coefficients

Measure	Old group (N = 45)		Young group (N = 45)	
	Raw r	Spearman-Brown	Raw r	Spearman-Brown
Ingenuity	.49 ± .08	.66	.41 ± .08	.58
Artificial Language	.93 ± .01[a]	.96	.93 ± .01	.96
Synonyms and Antonyms	.88 ± .02	.94	.92 ± .02	.96
Symbol-Digit	.99 ± .004[a]	.99	.97 ± .01	.98
No. Series	.86 ± .03	.92	.75 ± .04	.86
Word Meanings	.79 ± .04	.88	.76 ± .04	.86
Analogies	.52 ± .07	.68	.22 ± .10	.36
Arithmetic	.50 ± .08	.67	.52 ± .07	.68

[a] Based on 43 cases

Arithmetic were particularly easy for the young. All things considered, however, most of the tests proved to be sufficiently reliable for the purpose of measuring group tendencies. Were they to be administered to an unselected group, the resulting reliability coefficients would very probably approximate .60 or .70 for each of the individual tests, and .90 for the complete battery.

Checks against Outside Criteria

Test scores were checked against two outside criteria: inclusion in *Who's Who in America* (1930–1931) and election to Phi Beta Kappa or Tau Beta Pi. The second of these two devices could not be applied to 20 older men or eight of the younger group who, for reasons beyond their control, had been ineligible for election to either of the undergraduate honor societies. In Tables 10.8 and 10.9 the "honors" men are compared with those who failed to achieve scholastic distinction as undergraduates. Table 10.8 include the scores of three older men who were in college valedictorians, though not elected those who had won undergraduate honors make consistently higher scores than the non-honors group. It is also noteworthy that in this sample of highly selected adults proficiency on a mental test shows some relationship to school success as achieved more than forty years before.

The same trend, though a less marked one, holds for the younger teachers

Table 10.8. Scores of Older Men and Undergraduate Distinction

	College Valedictorians (N = 3)	Members of B.P.K., T.B.P. (N = 18)		Non-Members of P.B.K., T.B.P. (N = 7)		Per cent of P.B.K.s at or above mean of non-P.B.K.s
	Mean	Mean	S.D.	Mean	S.D.	
Ingenuity	6.33	6.11	2.52	5.00	1.85	72.2
Artificial Language	39.33	32.94	13.54	17.71	5.74	100.0
Synonyms and						
Antonyms	49.67	50.11	6.68	46.29	6.79	83.3
Symbol-Digit	69.33	60.94	10.03	50.00	9.23	83.3
No. Series	13.33	8.78	5.12	7.43	4.74	61.1
Word Meanings	238.67	215.72	62.79	189.14	66.90	66.7
Analogies	21.00	22.06	3.57	20.00	1.85	72.2
Arithmetic	9.67	8.11	2.61	7.57	2.20	66.7
Total Score[a]	412.70	386.10	43.87	346.70	19.18	83.3
Age (yrs)	66.33	64.72	3.53	66.86	5.71	

[a] See note 13.

Table 10.9. Scores of Younger Men Related to School Success

	Members of Phi Beta Kappa or Tau Beta Pi (N = 25)		Non-members of P.B.K. or T.B.P. (N = 12)		Per cent of P.B.K. at or above mean of non-P.B.K.
	Mean	S.D.	Mean	S.D.	
Ingenuity	7.60	1.98	6.92	2.24	76.0
Artificial Language	47.40	14.54	54.58	12.59	32.0
Synonyms and Antonyms	38.16	13.72	37.33	13.26	64.0
Symbol-Digit	75.60	8.92	81.00	8.67	28.0
No. Series	12.48	3.07	11.67	3.81	60.0
Word Meanings	245.92	74.66	229.33	45.96	64.0
Analogies	25.20	1.96	22.92	3.93	88.0
Arithmetic	10.28	1.78	8.67	2.86	84.0
Total Score	431.00	24.56	418.40	38.78	64.0
Age (yrs)	32.40	5.31	30.58	3.41	

(see Table 10.9). Honors men excel the non-elected group in three-fourths of the tests.

The older men who are listed in *Who's Who* make higher scores than the non-included group in all but one test (see Table 10.10). The differences in this direction are small but consistent.

The existence of a relationship between test-scores and both adult 'dis-

Table 10.10. Scores of Older Men and Who's Who Distinction

	Listed in *Who's Who*			Omitted from *Who's Who*			Per cent of *Who's Who* Ss at or above mean of non–*Who's Who*
	N	Mean	S.D.	N	Mean	S.D.	
Ingenuity	34	5.79	2.32	11	4.91	2.43	78.8
Artificial Language	32	29.84	12.37	11	23.55	6.97	61.3
Synonyms and Antonyms	34	49.76	5.51	11	39.82	12.23	93.9
Symbol-Digit	32	56.94	11.53	11	58.73	11.18	48.4
No. Series	34	8.59	4.59	11	8.36	4.76	53.1
Word Meanings	34	227.25	34.36	11	192.64	41.86	68.9
Analogies	34	21.38	3.15	11	20.36	3.62	62.5
Arithmetic	34	8.09	2.08	11	7.55	3.38	65.6
Total Score	32	379.80	40.20	11	353.90	43.08	78.1
Age (yrs)	34	66.70	5.65	11	64.82	4.19	

Table 10.11. Test Inter-Correlations of Older Men (Based on Raw Scores)

	Artificial Language	Synonyms and Antonyms	Symbol-Digit	Number Series	Word Meanings	Analo-gies	Arith-metic
Ingenuity	.15 ± .06	.22 ± .10	.46 ± .08	.60 ± .10	.17 ± .06	.37 ± .10	.60 ± .07
Artificial Language		.60 ± .09	.37 ± .10	.13 ± .09	.08 ± .10	.18 ± .08	.18 ± .09
Synonyms and Antonyms			−.07 ± .10	.23 ± .10	.28 ± .09	.33 ± .10	.45 ± .10
Symbol-Digit				.37 ± .06	−.004 ± .10	.13 ± .10	.22 ± .09
Number Series					.17 ± .08	.45 ± .09	.67 ± .10
Word Meanings						.29 ± .10	.15 ± .06
Analogies							.56 ± .10

NOTE: The Pearson product-moment formula was used after applying the usual checks for linearity of regression.

tinction' and the fact of scholastic excellence in the undergraduate years would seem to indicate that the present scale has a fair degree of validity.

Intercorrelation of the Sub-Test

Inasmuch as the test-battery was diversified and the subjects in this case were heterogeneous in make-up, uniformly high intercorrelations were not expected (see Tables 10.11 and 10.12). There is, however, a significant positive correlation between *Artificial Language and Synonyms and Antonyms* (.45 and .60). These two test apparently make somewhat similar verbal demands. *Word Meanings* and *Analogies,* on the other hand, though ostensibly linguistic in character, are quite unrelated to *Artificial Language* and only moderately related to *Synonyms and Antonyms.* The failure of *Analogies* to correlate more highly with the other tests of a linguistic nature is to some extent a function of the inadequacy of this particular test, which is probably too easy, its internal consistency leaving something to be desired. At the same time, one or two of the remaining coefficients which involve *Analogies* are surprisingly high.

Three of the sub-tests seem to constitute a fairly definite numerical or mathematical grouping. The intercorrelations of *Ingenuity, Number Series* and *Arithmetic* are all in the neighborhood of .50. Only one of the six coefficients is below the accepted standard of reliability. That mathematical ability, as judged by scores on *Arithmetic,* carries over strongly to *Ingenuity* and *Number Series* suggests the influence of either specialized training or special ability. Though some of this association is undoubtedly a function of blocking; i.e., the non-mathematical person confronting certain number series or inge-

Table 10.12. Test Inter-Correlations of Younger Men (Based on Raw Scores)

	Artificial Language	Synonyms and Antonyms	Symbol-Digit	Number Series	Word Meanings	Analo-gies	Arith-metic
Ingenuity	$-.28 \pm .09$	$-.26 \pm .10$	$.10 \pm .10$	$.51 \pm .09$	$.18 \pm .08$	$.07 \pm .10$	$.28 \pm .10$
Artificial Language		$.45 \pm .10$	$.26 \pm .10$	$-.28 \pm .09$	$-.19 \pm .10$	$-.51 \pm .10$	$-.11 \pm .10$
Synonyms and Antonyms			$-.20 \pm .10$	$-.23 \pm .10$	$.21 \pm .10$	$.30 \pm .10$	$-.19 \pm .10$
Symbol-Digit				$.004 \pm .08$	$-.17 \pm .09$	$-.10 \pm .10$	$-.29 \pm .10$
Number Series					$.11 \pm .10$	$.24 \pm .09$	$.40 \pm .10$
Word Meanings						$.22 \pm .09$	$-.17 \pm .08$
Analogies							$.06 \pm .09$

N O T E: The inter-correlations are not strictly comparable in the two age-groups in that the old are more heterogeneous on most tests, particularly on *Analogies* and *Arithmetic*, where the correlations for the young are notably lower. The median coefficients for old and young respectively were .26 and .03. Rank orders of correlation-values from high positive to high negative were compared. The rank orders yielded a *rho* of .67, indicating that the general trend of the inter-correlations was about the same in both age-groups, though the individual values are by no means the same from test to test.

nuity problems was frequently impressed and likewise convinced of his limitations at the very outset. Such an individual was prone to exclaim, ''This is too much for me!'' or ''Oh, this is mathematical!''

MOTIVATION

It was the investigator's belief that he succeeded in maintaining *rapport* throughout. The very nature of the study was designed to stimulate the best efforts of the older group. There are, in addition, certain objective proofs of adequate motivation. Five of these evidences call for comment.

1. Scores and time on the various power-tests are correlated negatively for the most part (cf. Table 10.13). Nine of the fourteen coefficients are slightly negative. This fact alone would seem to indicate a willingness to work. On *Synonyms and Antonyms* with the old *Ss* ($-.61$) and on *Arithmetic* with the young ($-.50$) there was a definite tendency for the unsuccessful subject to hold himself to the task longer than a high-scoring person. The test of *Word Meanings,* on the other hand, obviously offers a measure of perseverence, particularly with the young. In this case, time and scores correlate positively in both groups, .21 for the old and .66 for the young. The *Ingenuity Problems,* as well, give a positive correlation between scores and time for older men, a coefficient of .25 which is almost three times the size of its probable error.

Moreover, motivation, in the sense of willingness to perform, seems to

Table 10.13. Correlations between Scores and Time

	Older group (N = 45)		Younger men (N = 45)	
	r	P.E.	r	P.E.
Ingenuity	.25	±.09	−.07	±.10
Synonyms and Antonyms	−.61	±.06	−.14	±.10
No. Series	.11	±.10	−.14	±.10
Word Meanings	.21	±.10	.66	±.06
Analogies	−.28	±.09	.01	±.10
Arithmetic	−.09	±.10	−.50	±.08
All power tests[a]	−.07	±.10	−.14	±.10

[a] The composite scores were sub-totals based on the power-tests alone, excluding the two speed-tests.

bear little or no relationship to *S*'s field of interest. This fact was demonstrated by checking the length of time which the least successful performers—those in the lowest quartile—devoted to the tests that lay outside their field of specialization. In the majority of such cases the low-scorer "stayed with, the test" slightly longer than the average *S* in his age-group. The physicist, e.g., gave himself to the linguistic test and the professor of English held himself to *Arithmetic* or *Number Series* to the point of giving such tests a reasonable trial.

2. The behavioral notes were culled for evidence of non-motivation. The investigator and another psychologist examined these memoranda independently and checked the comments which seemed to show that the taking of any given test was an irritating or unpleasant experience. In this category fell such remarks as, "I get nervous working against time," or "I don't like this one," or "I never was any good at arithmetic." The results of this analysis are as follows. Only a minority of *S*s took occasion to voice their distaste for this or that test. The older men expressed such feelings about twice as often as the young. The older physical scientists were slightly less negative in their reactions than the others in their age-group. (This difference may be explained by the fact that the scale was somewhat loaded with items of a semi-mathematical nature.) The least popular tests with the old were the numerical or mathematical tasks and the speed-tests. The complaints of the young are somewhat similar, with a minority expressing a dislike for *Synonyms and Antonyms*.

This crude index of motivation was then related to test-performance. The success of each *S* who reported disliking a particular task was compared with the mean of his own sub-group—men of his own age and in the same field of specialization. Here the chief results of interest are (a) that an S's expressed distaste for this or that test had little or no effect on the amount of time he was willing to give to its solution, and (b) that high-scoring Ss complained quite as often as the low performers. On three of the tests, however—*Synonyms and Antonyms, Digit-Symbol,* and *Number Series*—the least successful of the older men were, by a slight margin, the more vocal complainers. Even here, the expression of dislike is not clean-cut proof of insufficient motivation; such negative attitudes may be an effect rather than a cause of the poor performance.

3. Ten of the older teachers and two of the younger ones rationalized their performance on at least one test with a "time alibi." These Ss were wont to say, "I suppose I could do it if I just took the time," or "I could get it if I kept working at it." Such comment, however, is not a clear sign of unwillingness to perform. For, in the majority of cases, the time of the person who raised the temporal argument differs very little, if at all, from that of the mean of his age-group.

4. An index of self-depreciation based on the notes of behavior indicated a general concern about the outcome of the testing. The commonness of self-disparagement would suggest that the tests were taken seriously.

5. Some of the most convincing data on motivation are of an anecdotal character. The older Ss particularly seemed to be patently anxious to excel. From this group the investigator was overwhelmed with requests to be tested at some stipulated "efficient" time of day. In cases of poor or questionable success on any given test, an S would profusely apologize. Sixteen older men showed an emotional carry-over from a previous sitting by making such remarks as, "I made a terrible showing last time. Oh, it was awful!" Two determined older professors reported getting out of bed in the middle of the night to solve certain baffling number-series which they had committed to memory the day before. All but a few of these faculty men asked the investigator to let them know, later on, just "where they stood." In fact, for most of the Ss, young or old, this "psychological" experience was anything but casual.

RESULTS

The chief statistical results of the study are summarized in Table 10.14, which uses two methods of expressing the significance of the difference between means; the first, critical ratios (CR_o), which are based on the obtained raw

Table 10.14. Test Scores of Old and Young

Sub-Test	Statistic	Later Maturity (N = 45)	Younger Men (N = 45)	Critical Ratio $D(m_1 - m_2)/\sigma_{diff.}$
Ingenuity Problems	Mean	5.60	7.47	4.07_0
	Median	5.61	8.25	5.19_{00}
	S.D.	2.36	2.00	
	Q_1	4.85	6.85	
	Q_3	7.96	9.47	
Artificial Language[a]	Mean	28.79	49.07	7.24_0
	Median	25.76	49.50	7.37_{00}
	S.D.	12.54	13.77	
	Q_1	20.83	39.84	
	Q_3	33.24	61.50	
Synonyms and Antonyms	Mean	47.47	38.53	3.89_0
	Median	50.17	43.18	3.96_{00}
	S.D.	8.86	12.71	
	Q_1	45.25	29.35	
	Q_3	53.73	49.38	
Symbol-Digit[a]	Mean	57.56	77.24	8.63_0
	Median	58.38	78.10	8.71_{00}
	S.D.	11.38	9.99	
	Q_1	48.04	69.55	
	Q_3	65.83	86.74	
Number Series	Mean	8.47	12.49	4.67_0
	Median	10.06	13.50	4.90_{00}
	S.D.	4.75	3.22	
	Q_1	5.31	10.75	
	Q_3	12.92	15.96	
Word Meanings	Mean	209.80	241.87	2.28_0
	Median	211.00	228.40	2.44_{00}
	S.D.	64.90	68.24	
	Q_1	168.40	200.60	
	Q_3	252.50	279.00	
Analogies	Mean	21.04	24.29	5.00_0
	Median	21.75	25.19	6.63_{00}
	S.D.	3.32	2.89	
	Q_1	18.88	22.75	
	Q_3	24.19	26.95	
Arithmetic Problems	Mean	7.87	9.87	4.00_0
	Median	8.69	10.81	4.88_{00}
	S.D.	2.59	2.15	
	Q_1	6.88	9.81	
	Q_3	10.42	11.88	
Total Score[a]	Mean	373.10	428.10	7.03_0
	Median	378.70	431.90	
	S.D.	45.45	28.69	
	Q_1	353.10	406.90	
	Q_3	398.8	446.90	

[a] N = 43 for older men

Table 10.15. Indices of Overlapping (for Scores)

	Per cent of young men (N = 45) at or above the median of the old	Per cent of old men (N = 45) at or above the median of the young	Per cent of old men (N = 45) who fall below Q_1 of the young
Symbol-Digit[a]	97.2	4.6	81.4
Artificial Language[a]	96.0	9.3	83.5
Ingenuity	85.3	21.1	63.1
Arithmetic	83.6	17.1	64.6
Analogies	83.3	15.7	58.3
Number Series	79.6	22.2	62.2
Word Meanings	64.0	39.8	42.6
Synonyms and Antonyms	22.9	79.6	3.3
Total Score[a]	96.5	8.7	80.0

[a] N = 43 for older men

scores[13] and the second, corrected or *true* critical ratios (CR_{oo}) where $\sigma_{oo} = \sigma_0 \sqrt{r_{11}}$ and for which the calculations employ the Spearman-Brown reliability values and the Tryon formula of 1928. Data on overlapping are given in Table 10.15.

The major conclusions of the study, drawn from the material reported in these two tables, are as follows:

1. The young excel the old in every test but one. The difference between the average performance of the two age-groups is statistically significant throughout, except in the case of *Word Meanings*.

2. On the numerical tests (*Ingenuity, Arithmetic and Number Series*), approximately 80 per cent of the young reach or exceed the median of the old; nearly two-thirds of the older men fall within the lower quartile of the younger group. Probably no single factor explains this apparent decline in arithmetical proficiency in the "senescent" years. The factor of disuse, as subsequent analysis will suggest, can hardly be ignored.

3. *Analogies* likewise favors the younger members of the faculty. Here again, 80 per cent of the young equal or excel the median of the old, and nearly three-fifths of the senescent group do no better than the poorest fourth of the young. (Success on *Analogies* turned out to be a somewhat in-between" ability, correlating about equally with verbal tests on the one hand and arithmetical tests on the other.)

4. The young again surpass elders, but in a much less striking manner, on *Word Meanings*. On this test about 60 per cent of the younger men reach or exceed the median of the old, and 40 per cent of the old fare no better

than the least successful fourth of the young. This superiority in mean performance, however, is not decisive; it is equal in size to less than half a standard deviation unit. *Word Meanings*, given without a time limit, probably lacked any real differentiating power one way or the other. It also seems to have been affected by motivation. And inasmuch as the young spent less time with it than did the older group, the age-difference in this case may be greater than it appears.

5. Insofar as the old fail to measure up to the performance of their younger colleagues, their outstanding inferiority might seem to be one of retardation.[14] More than 95 per cent of the younger men equal or excel the median of the old on the two speed tests, *Artificial Language and Symbol-Digit*. On these two tasks four-fifths of the old score no higher than the lowest fourth of the younger group. The mean of the young on both tests lies about two standard deviations above the mean of the older subjects.

6. The superiority of the young is every bit as striking in total scores. Again, 96 per cent of the younger academicians surpass the median of the old, and 80 per cent of the scores of the older group lie within the lower quartile of the distribution of the young.

7. Only in *Synonyms and Antonyms* are the older men clearly in the lead. Here, in 80 per cent of the cases, the old succeed in reaching or excelling the median of the younger group.[15]

8. Despite the fact that the results, taken as a whole, point very definitely in one direction, the group-differences between old and young are by no means as impressive as *the range of individual difference that obtains within each of the two groups.*[16]

Time-Scores on the Power-Tests

Further evidence that the later decades, considered in intellectual terms, are primarily a period of retardation—in the sense of slowing down—is to be found in the length of time which it took the older subjects to cope with the power-tests. The old are slower throughout. The differences are negligible on the shorter tasks, such as *Synonyms and Antonyms, Word Meanings,* and *Analogies,* but very marked on the longer and more arduous tests. *The Ingenuity Problems* give the largest age-difference. Here the average time for the old, 76.7 minutes, is a third of an hour longer than the mean time for younger men, 56.5 minutes. This difference is equivalent to the size of one-half of the standard deviation for either group. The older men are correspondingly slower on both *Number Series* and *Arithmetic*, requiring on the average

10 minutes longer than the young for the completion of each of these tasks. In the total time which was required to go through the entire battery, the average senescent subject is slower than the young by approximately one hour. In this case the difference between the mean time of the older men, 3 hours and 53 minutes, and the mean of the young, 3 hours and 3 minutes, is equal to the standard deviation for the younger group (49 minutes).

This fact of deliberateness among the old requires interpretation. It is, in some degree at least, a function of sheer perseverence. On the more difficult tasks, *Ingenuity* and *Number Series* particularly, most of the Ss, young and old, revealed certain signs of blocking; all went through more or less lengthy periods of inner trial-and-error, some of which resulted in failure. Inasmuch as our records make no distinction between productive and non-productive activity, the lengthened times of the old may indicate simply that the factors of tenacity and blocking (which may be only varied and persistent trial without solution) played a larger role in this age-group. The results on the speed-tests, however, would suggest that true retardation is certainly one of the differentiating elements. How much weight to assign to each of the two explanatory factors—a genuine slowing down and a difference in motivation on the part of the aged—is open to question.

Six of the older men gave additional evidence of retardation in requiring more than three sittings in order to finish the scale. Three of these men needed four testing sessions; two required five sittings; and one older person was unable to finish until he had met with the investigator seven times in all. These six Ss are somewhat older than the average member of their age-group. Their average age lies about one standard deviation above the median age for the older group taken as a whole.

Here again, the old are characterized by striking individual differences. One exceptionally well and active emeritus professor, aged seventy-two, asked to combine two sets of tests at a single sitting, remarking that he was "used to doing mental work 12 to 14 hours a day, and this is no exception." This subject proved to be one of the quickest workers, as well as one of the highest scorers in either age-group. He was every bit as remarkable in physical state and competence. Twelve months earlier, in his 71st year, he had undertaken a professional assignment which necessitated his traversing on foot literally hundreds of miles of difficult terrain.

Still another high-scoring older subject who was also a man of science with catholic interests and full of zest was to add a unique war-record to an already long list of professional accomplishments. He was to direct an important branch of war research, being advised that, despite his years, no man in the country was better fitted than he for the work to which he was summoned. When he began his labors in Washington, shortly after the attack at Pearl Harbor, he was eighty-two.

Two members of the youthful group had to spread the tests over four separate sittings. Three of the ablest younger men, on the other hand, combined two sessions into one. The double load was requested against the advice of the investigator. One extremely proficient younger *S* took all the tests at a single sitting, under similar circumstances.

Variability of Old and Young

As has been noted, individual differences outweigh age-differences on every test. It remains to be pointed out, however, that later maturity seems to operate in the direction of increasing the range of individual differences. Such a conclusion would appear to follow from an examination of the coefficients of variation listed in Table 10.16, where $V = \dfrac{100 \text{ S.D.}}{\text{Average}}$. These indices of relative variability are 30 to 50 per cent larger for the old than for the young. The young, by contrast with the older men, are less than half as variable on *Number Series*, about two-thirds as variable on *Ingenuity Problems, Artificial Language, Symbol-Digit,* and *Arithmetic,* four-fifths as variable on *Analogies,* and about 90 per cent as variable on *Word Meanings.*

This existence of a greater degree of spread among the old would suggest either that age increases variability, or that the elders whom this investigator happened to test were scattered over a wider range of initial ability to begin

Table 10.16. Coefficients of Variation

	Test Scores		Time Taken	
	Old	Young	Old	Young
Ingenuity	42	26	38	33
Artificial Language	43	28	—	—
Synonyms and Antonyms	18	33	57	44
Symbol-Digit	19	13	—	—
Number Series	56	25	43	43
Word Meanings	31	28	66	33
Analogies	15	12	39	42
Arithmetic	33	21	59	49
Total Time			32	26

with. The evidence on comparability would seem to favor the first interpretation, namely, that advancing age does, in fact, lower one's facility for coping with some "mental tests," and that inasmuch as such a decline affects certain men more than others, older men as a whole do become more variable in the course of time.

In one instance, however, the findings do not support any such generalization. On *Synonyms and Antonyms* the young are almost twice as variable as the older group. At least in the area of word knowledge or vocabulary, therefore, the opposite is true; age *per se* would seem to bring men in divergent fields closer together, diminishing such individual differences as may have existed within this superior older group at age twenty-five or thirty-five.

The old are likewise less homogeneous in the rate at which they worked or in the speed of the processes which they demonstrated in this situation. In the amount of time devoted to the several power-tests, the young are only four-fifths as variable as the older men, except in the case of *Analogies* and *Number Series*.

Results within the Younger and Older Groups

The relationship which obtains between age and test-performance *within* either of the two age-groups is given in Table 10.17. None of any significance may be said to exist within the older group. Here the coefficients of correlation are all in the neighborhood of −.10.

Within the limits of his testing instrument, therefore, the investigator finds

Table 10.17. Correlations between Age and Scores

	Older group (N = 45)		Younger group (N = 45)	
	r	P.E.	r	P.E.
Ingenuity	−.15[a]	±.10	−.18	±.10
Artificial Language	−.02[a]	±.10	.05	±.10
Synonyms and Antonyms	.04[a]	±.10	.32	±.09
Symbol-Digit	−.10[a]	±.10	.02	±.10
Number Series	−.08	±.10	−.20	±.10
Word Meanings	−.37	±.09	.18	±.10
Analogies	−.19	±.10	.06	±.10
Arithmetic	−.12	±.10	−.17	±.10

NOTE: The Pearson product-moment formula was used. Linearity of regression was tested by inspecting scatter diagrams and applying Blakeman's test in doubtful instances.

[a] These figures based on 43 cases.

no evidence of any active process of functional loss between the ages of sixty and eighty. It might be inferred from this fact that such normal "deterioration" as does occur between the age of twenty-five and the onset of later maturity is of a gradual character.

In the younger group, three tests correlate negatively with age, *Ingenuity Problems, Number Series*, and *Arithmetic*. Each of these coefficients is in the neighborhood of −.18 or −.20; each is approximately twice the size of its probable error. It is particularly noteworthy that the young in the decade twenty-five to thirty-five tend to become progressively less adept at coping with numerical or mathematical operations. This loss in mental efficiency is to be explained, in all probability, as a consequence of mere rustiness. The very fact that disuse begins to operate in this area long before there is any question of psychological decline—5 to 15 years from the date of one's graduation from college—establishes a probability that the corresponding deficiencies which show up in later maturity, 40 to 60 years after the completion of the college career, are explained in part at least by the operation of the same factor—namely by a lack of practice.

Conversely, the effect of an increasing use of, or interest in, a particular faculty or of a continuation of the processes of acquisition would seem to account for the fact that among the young, age and word-knowledge (*Synonyms and Antonyms*) go together, correlating .32 ± .09. The same psychological factor would appear to explain the general superiority of the old in vocabulary. Nor would this advantage on the part of the older men seem to derive from the fact that a good many of the members of this group must have had more or less lengthy training in one or more of the classical languages. At least the psychologist seems to have established that any immediate transfer from the study of Latin (as taught to the present generation) to English vocabulary is slight indeed.[17] The investigator's older *S*s could hardly have carried over, therefore, to their present knowledge of the meaning of English words any large benefits from studies of Latin or Greek that were brought to a close 40 or 50 years earlier.

The correlation of .18 between the age of the younger men and their scores on *Word Meanings*, however, is of doubtful significance on non-statistical grounds. The *Word-Meaning* was noticeably affected by motivation: for the young it gives a correlation between scores and time of .66 ± .06. The slight relationship of .18 between age and scores may indicate, therefore, only that the older men within the group aged twenty-five to thirty-five were somewhat more persevering.

As for the relationship which exists between age and the time devoted to this or that test, low positive correlations seem to be the rule for the older group. The significance of the correlation of .37 ± .09 between the age of the "senescent" and total time taken on all the power-tests is, again, obscure. On the one hand, the relationship could mean that within the 20-year span from sixty to eighty the old do "slow down" to a measurable degree. Or it could signify that an older *S*, coming to grips with a series of power-tests, sticks to the job somewhat longer because of critical self-reference or of a desire to make a good showing in the group.

One coefficient stands out in this particular cluster of correlations—the association of .47 ±.08 between the age of the older *S*s and the time devoted to solving *Arithmetic Problems*. This relationship should be laid alongside the correlation between age and *scores* which obtains for the same age-group (an r of −.12). What the discrepancy between the size of the two coefficients means, apparently, is that one's failure to brush up on arithmetical operations between the ages of sixty and eighty does less to impair accuracy than to interfere with one's speed or dexterity in tasks of this character.

Age and time correlate negatively for the younger men in six instances. Only two of these coefficients, however, are as large as their probable errors. A relationship of −.23 ± .10 in the case of *Synonyms and Antonyms* would seem to be accounted for by the fact that certain younger men in the exact sciences did rather poorly in this test but kept grimly working at it.

Analysis of Sub-Groups

To see whether or not "mental decline" might show some degree of specificity, the data were subjected to a more refined analysis. These results are admittedly tentative because of limited sampling. Both young and old were first classified by academic field as follows:

Letters: English and other languages
Biological sciences: Anatomy, biology, botany, and physiology
Physical sciences: Astronomy, chemistry, engineering, geology, mathematics and physics
Social sciences and studies: Economics, history, political science, psychology and sociology.

The mean and median scores and the standard deviations of each of the sub-groups, old and young, are reproduced in Table 10.18.

From a close examination of the data given in this table it will be seen that the field of interest or of professional specialization is a factor to reckon

Table 10.18. Test Scores of Sub-Groups in Various Academic Fields

	Later Maturity Group				Younger Men			
	N	Mean	Median	S.D.	N	Mean	Median	S.D.
Artificial Language								
Biol. Sci.	11	27.64	24.00	12.93	11	51.27	49.00	11.92
Letters	10	30.80	28.68	11.60	12	57.67	62.00	14.83
Phys. Sci.	15	22.83	23.50	7.08	15	46.40	45.00	10.10
Soc. Sci.	7	34.28	31.00	10.00	7	43.43	41.00	12.36
Symbol-Digit								
Biol. Sci.	11	55.95	53.50	11.21	11	80.23	82.75	8.63
Letters	10	54.40	52.00	8.28	12	75.25	73.00	11.10
Phys. Sci.	15	60.90	64.39	12.24	15	78.30	76.75	6.90
Soc. Sci.	7	59.93	62.50	11.50	7	76.21	80.50	12.09
Synonyms and Antonyms								
Biol. Sci.	11	42.59	47.50	12.55	11	39.05	40.75	9.03
Letters	12	51.00	51.25	5.45	12	50.50	50.50	2.74
Phys. Sci.	15	48.30	49.75	7.39	15	31.30	29.89	12.04
Soc. Sci.	7	50.93	52.50	4.07	7	38.50	38.50	10.27
Word Meanings								
Biol. Sci.	11	215.46	216.60	57.90	11	230.91	250.00	50.72
Letters	12	228.34	240.00	71.86	12	225.00	230.00	89.86
Phys. Sci.	15	188.66	190.00	35.38	15	246.00	223.40	63.34
Soc. Sci.	7	244.28	230.00	82.60	7	232.86	215.00	60.88
Analogies								
Biol. Sci.	11	20.27	20.50	3.08	11	23.91	26.50	3.92
Letters	12	20.33	21.00	2.39	12	24.50	25.25	1.61
Phys. Sci.	15	21.47	23.17	3.98	15	25.25	24.92	2.62
Soc. Sci.	7	22.57	23.25	2.67	7	23.43	22.50	2.67
Ingenuity								
Biol. Sci.	11	4.82	5.75	2.69	11	7.27	7.63	1.35
Letters	12	4.83	5.25	1.38	12	6.42	7.00	1.98
Phys. Sci.	15	7.20	7.75	1.73	15	8.40	8.88	1.36
Soc. Sci.	7	4.71	5.25	2.21	7	7.57	9.17	2.38
Number Series								
Biol. Sci.	11	6.91	7.75	4.34	11	12.09	12.50	3.20
Letters	12	7.00	8.50	4.60	12	10.75	11.50	2.98
Phys. Sci.	15	11.47	12.50	3.38	15	13.27	15.83	2.38
Soc. Sci.	7	7.00	5.50	4.96	7	11.57	12.50	3.58
Arithmetic Test								
Biol. Sci.	11	5.45	6.25	2.90	11	10.09	10.70	1.24
Letters	12	8.33	8.75	1.49	12	8.50	10.00	3.18
Phys. Sci.	15	9.40	10.38	1.74	15	10.80	11.17	0.98
Soc. Sci.	7	7.57	8.50	2.32	7	9.86	10.50	1.81
Total Score								
Biol. Sci.	11	346.60	367.10	51.74	11	423.80	428.90	29.48
Letters	10	374.70	381.50	22.80	12	429.20	433.00	27.60
Phys. Sci.	15	389.80	380.80	33.54	15	436.00	439.00	23.00
Soc. Sci.	7	376.90	362.50	42.65	7	416.10	412.10	26.19
Age in Years								
Biol. Sci.	11	66.27	64.08	5.54	11	31.00	30.60	2.70
Letters	12	66.50	64.00	6.01	12	33.83	33.00	5.97
Phys. Sci.	15	67.80	68.34	4.72	15	30.07	31.24	4.25
Soc. Sci.	7	63.43	62.16	4.82	7	34.14	34.50	3.18

with in any effort to interpret either individual differences or age differences on certain of the tests. *Artificial Language*, for one, favors the younger man of letters to a slight degree. By the same token it penalizes the older physical scientist. Otherwise the age differences on this test are fairly uniform regardless of *S*'s field.

No sub-group is consistently at a disadvantage on *Symbol-Digit*. This task, though somewhat numerical in content, is not demonstrably easier for the physical scientist or more trying for the man of letters. Performance on *Analogies* seems to be unrelated to *S*'s field of specialty within either age-group.

Synonyms and Antonyms falls into a clearly different category. This test definitely discriminates against the younger men who are identified with non-literary pursuits, especially against the younger man in the physical group. The older teachers and research men who took this test are very nearly alike in median score irrespective of the field they work in.[18] Age, therefore, would seem to cross professional lines in its effect on word knowledge, raising all older academic men to something near parity. Likewise, the reported inferiority of the young in vocabulary (cf. Table 10.14) is not so much a general characteristic of youth as a ''deficiency'' which is somewhat restricted to the younger man in the fields of physical science. The median of the older exact scientist lies almost two standard deviations above the median of the young in the same field. In this case the mature physicist (whose profession uses a long series of specialized vocabularies) has perhaps overcome an original shortcoming—in his knowledge of the meaning of words in general—because of a subsequent exposure to literary and general cultural topics.

The effects of specialization are best demonstrated by performance on the numerical tests. On *Ingenuity Problems* the superiority of the older physical scientist over other men in his own age-group is as great as the age-difference within any single professional field. More than that, the competence of the exact scientist in this task is little or not at all impaired by age. Much the same situation recurs on *Number Series* in which the physical scientist is at an advantage and the old show little sign of decline.[19] *Arithmetic,* to a lesser extent, follows the same pattern.

Again, an *S* in the physical group, old or young, stands at the top in total score. This superiority must be, to some degree at least, a function of the scale and its heavy reliance on tests of a semi-mathematical character. Here again the resistance to age, which is demonstrated by the older physicists and their kind would seem to rest on the fact that these men are required by the very nature of their work to keep alive by continual practice such habituated patterns.

Table 10.19. Time Records of Sub-Groups on Three Tests

	Later Maturity Group				Younger Men			
	N	Mean	Median	S.D.	N	Mean	Median	S.D.
Ingenuity Problems								
Letters	12	90.42	82.50	28.47	12	61.67	60.00	18.13
Phys. Sci.	15	71.50	68.75	19.08	15	49.84	46.50	16.00
Biol. Sci.	11	69.78	62.50	25.88	11	63.41	57.50	19.98
Soc. Sci.	7	60.36	57.50	18.10	7	58.22	57.50	23.21
Number Series								
Letters	12	58.40	50.00	27.45	12	49.17	50.00	3.25
Phys. Sci.	15	58.16	52.50	24.08	15	36.90	33.15	14.65
Biol. Sci.	11	51.59	51.25	19.75	11	45.23	43.75	14.23
Soc. Sci.	7	46.07	37.50	16.42	7	53.22	57.50	31.67
Arithmetic Problems								
Letters	12	54.59	52.50	23.32	12	35.00	27.50	18.43
Phys. Sci.	15	33.17	31.90	14.01	15	23.17	21.90	4.03
Biol. Sci.	11	43.41	46.25	19.40	11	27.50	28.75	9.54
Soc. Sci.	7	32.50	32.50	17.83	7	36.79	37.50	13.48

Time Records of the Various Sub-Groups

Only three of the tests (*Ingenuity Problems, Number Series, and Arithmetic*) were difficult enough or long enough to yield significant individual differences or group differences of a temporal character. The average time devoted to these tasks is reported in Table 10.19. Here it will be seen that the younger men in the exact sciences are the more rapid workers. Likewise, the older men of letters are particularly slow in *Arithmetic* and *Ingenuity Problems*. Their average time is about one standard deviation above the mean time for all the other senior groups. The young physical scientist is appreciably faster than the older man in the same field on *Number Series*. Here the mean time for the old is approximately 1.5 standard deviations above the average for the younger men. The factor of practice would seem to account, in part at least, for all these variations in speed, both those which are related to age and those which follow from the fact of professional specialization.

NOTES ON BEHAVIOR

In order to interpret certain incidental data on later maturity the verbatim speech records were first turned into typewritten form. These notes are incomplete for five older and two younger Ss because of testing exigencies already noted. For purposes of quantitative treatment, the investigator first arrived at a general index of verbalization by taking the total number of words used in the testing situation.

As for the results, the older S is found to be far more loquacious than the young; he uses on the average over two and one-half times as many words in the act of coping with the scale in the investigator's presence. Ninety-three per cent of the old are more talkative than the median of the younger group, and the mean of the "senescent" lies approximately two standard deviations above the mean for the young. Moreover, verbalization is fairly constant from test to test. It is not entirely a product of chance or of the effect of reactions to some particular test or group of tests. It will be recalled that sittings were held, as a rule, a week apart. The consistency coefficients, ranging from .56 to .95, are high enough to indicate that talkativeness was a somewhat constant trait.

The average number of words used by all Ss during the third testing session (98.3) is lower than the mean for the initial sitting (142.1). This falling off of overt speech is very probably a function of the particular tests which were administered on the final day. These tasks (*Arithmetic, Analogies,* and *Symbol-Digit*) were relatively short and less conducive to blocking.

Within either of the age-groups, it might be noted, volubility shows no relation whatever to age.

Verbalization and Test Scores

The correlation between test scores and this factor of incidental speech is given in Table 10.20. Only two of the coefficients approach significance; i.e. *Number Series* for the old and *Word Meanings* for the young. In the second case the correlation of .64 is probably a function of patience. Scores and time on this test correlate .66 for the young. Hence mere willingness to work may be indicated indirectly by S's volubility.

Among the old it is interesting to note that five of the seven correlations between scores and verbalization, although low, are negative. Of these relationships the highest occurs on *Number Series*, in which success with the test and the number of words used in achieving that success correlate $-.36 \mp .09$. This association would seem to imply some slight relationship between difficulty and 'thinking aloud' with or without emotive disturbance: the low-scoring S tends to be more talkative.

Table 10.20. Correlation between Number of Words Used and Scores

	Older Men (N = 40)		Younger Men (N = 43)	
	r	P.E.	r	P.E.
Ingenuity	.04	±.11	−.02	±.10
Synonyms and Antonyms	−.05	±.11	.05	±.10
Number Series	−.36	±.09	.06	±.10
Word Meanings	.12	±.10	.64	±.06
Analogies	−.003	±.11	.14	±.11
Arithmetic	−.24	±.10	−.16	±.10
Total Score[a]	−.01	±.11	.05	±.10

[a] The composite score was a sub-total based on the power-tests alone

Verbalization and Speed

The relationship between (1) the number of words used and (2) the time required on each of the power tests is reported in Table 10.20. Time and word-usage correlate positively for every power-test in the battery, and more than a third of the coefficients have a statistical significance. Time and success on a test, it will be remembered, are practically unrelated, with one exception in the case of *Word Meanings*. In view of the data presented in this table, therefore, it must be concluded that lengthened times are an index of difficulty and blocking which resulted in turn in verbal trial-and-error that had little demonstrable effect on the outcome and was often emotively colored. In fact, much of this attendant "thinking aloud" was self-disparaging. That fact adds weight to the belief that the association between time and incidental overt speech is a product of difficulty and consequent interference.

Emotively-toned Speech

To get at the possibility of a qualitative age-difference in volubility, the investigator devised an index of self-disparagement. The type written speech-records were first shuffled at random to preclude easy identification of the papers on an age-basis. Two professional psychologists who were not connected with the study then examined these sheets independently and checked every remark or phrase which indicated self-depreciation or an apologetic attitude toward the self-object.[20] A word count was then made for the separate tabulations. The resulting measures of self-depreciation are highly reliable. The separate word-counts correlate .92 ∓ .02 for the old and .86 ∓ .03 for the young. To arrive at a self-disparagement index for each *S*, young or old, the two word-counts were simply averaged.

As for the outcome, self-depreciation, so measured, is fairly closely related to the total amount of verbalization (or to the total number of words used in the testing situation), with coefficients of .83 ∓ .03 for the older men and .75 ∓ .05 for the young. The age difference in this matter of self-disparagement is striking. Ninety-two percent of the old use more self-belittling words than does the average younger *S*. The mean of the old lies some two standard deviations above the average for the younger group. Expressed in tabular form, these results stand as follows:

Age-group	N	Mean	S.D.
Old	40	92.8	97.6
Young	43	27.3	33.4

Within either of the respective age-groups, however, age and self-depreciation correlate quite indifferently. The coefficients in question are −.08 ± .11 for the old and .20 ± .10 for the young.

Several explanations might be advanced to account for the prevalence of this type of verbalization among the senescent.

Greater self-consciousness of older men. The older man was naturally on the defensive in the test-situation and, having more at stake, had a stronger desire to excel. His susceptibility to self-depreciation may have been aggravated, therefore, by (a) his awareness of the age-reference of the study and a fear of being ''shown up''; (b) the popular belief that mental deterioration is inevitable in later years; hence any difficulty with this or that test may have been taken by the older *S* as a symptom of such a decline and (c) the fact that the older man in this connection has more difficulty than the young in believing his own rationalizations. At least time, in this process, lies against him.[21]

Sophistication of the young. The older and younger academic man may react very differently in the presence of a mental test; the old who have less experience with psychology and are less aware of its limitations may be somewhat more naïve on the subject. In that event the investigator's older *S*s may have regarded his mental test as a somewhat mysterious and infallible instrument; these persons, consequently, may have been more inclined to take more seriously the whole endeavor and their own behavior. It is just as possible that the younger men, more accustomed to tests, were more disposed to treat the experience condescendingly, to submit to the experiment and to get it over with.

An indirect effect of age. Taken as a whole, these tests are admittedly more difficult for the older man. To that extent the older *S* compensated for this disadvantage by working longer. He was likewise more subject to occasional failure and blocking. Under such circumstances, his efforts to succeed very naturally gave rise to a larger display of overt trial-and-error and mild self-depreciation.

Limitations of the Study

The investigator's scale is by its very nature only capable of making an exploratory sounding as to the level of mental preservation that exists among able senescent men. More subtle forms of "intelligence" than we presumed to measure might possibly show signs of marked deterioration in old age. One can think of certain attributes, on the other hand—such as maturity of judgment and the powers of generalization based on a broad experience—in which the old may, if reasonably sound, greatly surpass men of younger years. A change for the worse that may eventually be shown to be of far greater moment in the last third of life, might rest upon an emotive change only faintly related to the original level of intelligence—a fading away of drive and interest induced, in part, by a diminution of physical energy and, in part, by all the cultural influences which impel the older person to relax his efforts and his interests.

SUMMARY

A diversified and exacting mental test, which required three or four hours to administer, was devised and given individually to a group of 45 university professors aged sixty to eighty and to a control group of 45 younger academic men of twenty-five to thirty-five years.

The internal evidence of the study seems to indicate that the two age-groups are roughly comparable in initial ability, that the scale is a reasonably valid, if crude, measure of performance, and that the investigator's subjects were adequately motivated in the testing situation.

Insofar as they bear on the subject of later maturity, the major conclusions of the study are ten:

1. The bright and successful "senescent" subjects show few unambiguous signs of any decided psychological "decline."
2. Individual differences are, without exception, far more impressive than age differences.

3. In the scores obtained from six of the eight tests employed, there is a significant difference in favor of the younger men.

4. The "losses" are in large measure, however, a by-product of disuse and an artifact of the particular test employed. The scale used simply does not divorce itself from the effects of learning and experience. As might be expected, therefore, old age acts selectively and most decidedly on those functions which have suffered for want of practice and sustained interest, all depending upon the older man's field of interest and his specialized knowledge and occupation.

5. Conversely, in word-knowledge or general vocabulary—one attribute in which continued practice or learning uniformly operates in favor of the old—the senescent are uniformly superior to the younger middle-aged (25–35 years).

6. Other things equal, age has the effect of impairing the rate far more than the quality or the accuracy of the mental operations here considered.

7. Even so, one can not infer that retardation in the old is the rule for psychological operations at large. For here, at least on the speed-tests used in the present study, the older man may be rusty, but only in a set of specific habits and performances which he has had neither the occasion nor the desire to preserve in active use.

8. Over and above the reported "losses" which are seemingly explained by disuse or by mere lack of exercise, these results may point to some real residual decline in general capability, the bodily aspects of which remain obscure.

9. All these measured changes appear to be exceedingly gradual; none of any significance is detected *between and within* the ages of sixty and eighty years.

10. Taken as a whole this study indicates that, at least within the upper ranges of ability, an impairment of the "higher mental processes" is by no means an invariable concomitant of the years beyond sixty.

NOTES

1. For the original scale, see Goodenough, *The Kuhlman-Binet Tests for Children of Preschool Age*, Univ. of Minn. Press, 1928, Appendix A. A later revision of the scale was used in this study, one which provides for the following Barr-Taussig classes: 1. professional, 2. semi-professional and large business, 3. Trades, clerical and small business, 4. farmers, 5. skilled labor, 6. semi-skilled labor, 7. unskilled labor.

2. Where this ambiguous term is used it connotes nothing beyond age and implies nothing with respect to "senility."

3. Five older men and two younger specialists in engineering are not considered in Tables 10.2 and 10.3 for the reason that the doctoral degree is still relatively uncommon in this field.

4. Cattell's criterion (*American Men of Science*, 1927, 1128; R. B. Cattell, The measurement of adult intelligence, *Psychol. Bull., 40*, 1943, 153–193).

5. The necessity of matching old and young, field by field, accounts for the unequal sampling of the young at the two institutions—there being 30 in the one case and 15 in the other. See J. C. Foster and G. A. Taylor, The applicability of mental tests to persons over fifty years of age, *J. Appl. Psychol., 4*, 1920, 39–58.

6. Chiefly those prepared by W. T. Miller, J. J. B. Morgan, A. A. Roback, L. M. Terman, E. L. Thorndike and L. L. Thurstone.

7. It may be that the attempt to devise a test of "general ability," where one may assume a rough equality in background, in this case for a group of college professors, may restrict in advance the dimensions of the thing one hopes to measure. The more complex and subtle forms of adult intelligence are perhaps specialized and unique— qualitatively different as between the physicist and the professor of romance languages. In any case, one must admit that no existing mental tests, apart from objective achievement in the world of reality, are capable of measuring the higher, more intricate levels of intellectuality. Cf. H. E. Jones and H. S. Conrad, The growth and decline of intelligence, etc., *Genet. Psychol. Monog., 13*, 1933, 223–298.

8. See C. C. Miles and W. R. Miles, The correlation of intelligence scores and chronological age from early to late maturity, *Am. J. Psych., 44*, 1932, 44–78.

9. L. L. Thurstone and T. G. Thurstone, *Psychological Examination for High-School Graduates and College Freshmen*, Amer. Council on Educ., 1929 ed. Cf. E. L. Thorndike, E. O. Bergman, J. W. Tilton and E. Woodyard, *Adult Learning*, 1928.

10. This test and some of the others were made up with the assistance of Dr. Floyd L. Ruch and Dr. Ralph K. White. Cf. R. C. Tryon, Demonstration of the effect of unreliability of measurement on a difference between groups, *J. Compar. Psychol., 8*, 1928, 1–22.

11. The resulting scale was issued from the Stanford University Press. It was printed as a 16-page booklet on high-grade manila bond. The use of $8\frac{1}{2} \times 11$ in. pages insured liberal spacing. Clear, bold-faced type (14 point Antique) provided optimal legibility. Each test was innocently labeled and was prefaced by suitable printed directions. The last two pages of the booklet comprised a questionary which covered such points as social-economic background, school history, and the like.

Published data are available on several of the tests. For *Artificial Language* the Thurstones report a consistency coefficient of .979 based on split-half correlations (Spearman-Brown formula) for 250 papers. The same test correlates .358 with school success—an average for 21 colleges and universities (L. L. Thurstone and T. G. Thurstone, *op. cit.*). *Symbol-Digit Substitution*, given to large groups of relatively unselected English-speaking whites during the first World War, gave a substantial correlation with several other accepted scales (Army Alpha, .54; Army Beta, .85; Stanford-Binet individual examination, .639).

If the present total battery answers the basic requirements of difficulty and reliability, no new assumption need be made as to precisely *what it tests*. Original data will be presented on internal consistency and on checks against certain outside criteria. Beyond that, however, the tests will be treated at their face value—i.e., only as measures of present efficiency in working arithmetical problems, learning a code, and so on.

12. Two of the older men who had visual handicaps were not given the speed tests. Cf. H. M. Werner, Some psychological tests of the aged, Columbia University, 1927 (dissertation).

13. The score on each sub-test is a summation of the number of items *passed Total scores* are computed as follows: (1) The total score consists of a summation of T-scores on the separate sub-tests. (2) The T-scores are calculated by applying the formula of G. M. Ruch and George D. Stoddard, *Tests and Measurements in High School Instruction,* 1927, 351. (3) Means and sigmas, based on original scores, are derived from the *combined* distributions of young and old on each sub-test. (4) The composite score is based on performance on all eight sub-tests. This combination is favored, rather than a sub-total based on the power-tests alone or a combination including only the more reliable sub-tests, for the following reasons: (a) the investigator thought it best to have the composite score represent an approximately equal sample of verbal, numerical and other elements; and (b) he tried out the matter empirically and found that no other combination of the results produced any truer picture of total performance.

14. The investigator recognizes that he is dealing with an imperfectly standardized scale. His units of measurement on the several sub-tests are, in any exact sense, noncomparable.

15. Since the completion of this investigation, a number of psychologists (Babcock, Wechsler, Claire Wright, *et al.* have used one or another vocabulary test in order to get at the earlier level of intelligence in cases of senility and dementia praecox and certain other states in which the mentality suffers some degree of deterioration. I am indebted to Dr. Terman for the reminder that it was Binet himself who first observed, in 1909, that, in the case of mental decay, language functions are apparently the last to go.

16. Both of the universities from which these subjects are drawn have a compulsory retirement age. Any number of considerations may justify such a provision. Yet, according to the present study, it would seem that academicians, aged sixty to eighty, are anything but all alike in mental acuity or in their state of preservation. The investigator is in no sense, however, looking forward to the day when, to justify his right to tenure, the senescent college professor must repair to the psychological laboratory for an annual certificate of clearance.

17. E. L. Thorndike, The influence of first-year Latin upon range in English vocabulary, *School and Soc.*, 17, 1923, 82–84; E. L. Thorndike and C. J. Ruger, The effect of first-year Latin upon knowledge of English words of Latin derivation, ibid., 18, 1923, 260–270; E. L. Thorndike, The gains made in ability in English by pupils who study Latin and by pupils who do not, *ibid.*, 18, 1923, 690. . . . It should be said, however, that some 75 per cent of the words which went into the *Synonyms and Antonyms* test are of Latin derivation.

18. If these results are explained by the hypothesis that one retains even in old

age what one continues to practice, perhaps the older man of letters should be expected to give a better account of himself on *Synonyms and Antonyms*. The nature of the test may account for his failure to do so. The list of synonyms and antonyms is very general in its make-up. It draws on words which any bright adult might encompass in his vocabulary. Had it included a larger proportion of literary terms, the older man of letters might very well have demonstrated a professional as well as a calendar superiority.

19. Attention is called once more to the important fact that almost nothing is known of the role which blocking and affective disturbance may play in the performance in tests of this character in the case of the older S whose interests are non-mathematical.

20. A key of instructions was prepared in advance in the hope of standardizing these judgments. The major symptoms of self-disparagement were classified as: (1) General statements of inadequacy, e.g., "I'm falling down badly on this, I know," or "I'll be slow at this," (2) Statements of one's ignorance on a particular subject; *e.g.* "I never saw that word before," or "I did something like this once before but it doesn't seem to come to me," and (3) Alibis (such as), "I was always poor in math," or "I could probably do this if I only took more time." By common agreement ahead of time, doubtful or ambiguous statements of this character were ignored.

21. Perhaps a majority of the investigator's older Ss expressed some degree of belief in the doctrine that one's mental faculties must, of necessity, lose some of their sharpness with age. The possibility of confirming such an expectation in one's own case may very well account for the older man's lack of self-confidence in this situation. The younger man, confronted by certain doubts as to his competence on a mental test, would normally project any such uncertainty to the test itself, quickly forgetting the entire experience. The senescent, on the other hand, might be more inclined to ascribe this same difficulty or uncertainty to himself and to the fact of his age.

11. The Creative Production Rates of Present versus Past Generations of Scientists

Harvey C. Lehman

In this study the words "present generation" refer to scientists who were still living at the time when the source book which cited their contributions was published, even though some of the contributors may have died since then. And the words "past generation" refer to scientists born subsequent to the year 1774, and who were known to be deceased at the time when the history which cited their contributions was published. To permit concise expression and to avoid monotonous repetition, the expressions "still-living" and "present generation" will be employed interchangeably hereinafter and similarly the word "deceased" will be employed as a synonym for the expression "past generation."

Although the total performance of the still-living contributors cannot now be fully known because many of them will probably add to their distinguished already-published output, it is true also that while this is occurring other oncoming young workers will also start making their contributions. This raises the question of whether the relative production rates of the several age groups will change appreciably in the years that lie directly ahead.

BACKGROUND

One day in the fall of 1928 I came across a journal article which discussed the prime years of man's life (Nelson, 1928). In it the author vigorously pooh-poohed Robert S. Woodworth's assertion that the period from 20 to 40 is the most favorable one for doing creative work of the highest order (Woodworth, 1921). The author then proceeded to list a number of eminent individuals who did top-notch work up to the age of 80. By selecting some exceptional cases and disregarding all others it is possible, of course, to obtain spurious evidence which will seem to support almost any wishful thinking

From The Journal of Gerontology 17 (1962): 409–417. Reprinted by permission of the Gerontological Society of America.

whatsoever. However, in the aforementioned article the writer obviously was grasping at exceptional cases to prove his *a priori* belief.

A sounder method for study of the correlation between age and achievement would be to canvass authoritative histories of science, noting the dates on which important discoveries have either been made or first reported, and then ascertaining the ages of the various scientists when they first announced their outstanding work. Starting with this assumption, some 25 years later I published my book, *Age and Achievement* (1953).

In that book, I tried to set forth data from authoritative sources which revealed the age levels at which man's most creative work has been done in the sciences and mathematics and also in medicine, music composition, philosophy, various types of literature, paintings in oil, sculpture, practical inventions, and other areas. Because anyone who is still living may yet produce his masterpiece, my book covered mainly dead "greats," and in selecting great achievements for study, to avoid any bias on my part, I employed lists of foremost achievements that had been compiled by experts within each specific field. The findings were presented in the form of tables and graphs, and adequate allowance was always made for the fact that young workers are more numerous than are older ones.

Meanwhile my interest had broadened and before long I was studying not only outstanding creative achievements but also the ages at which champion performances had been exhibited by athletes, chess players, noted orators, and others. Since leaders do not admit of such study because objective data on the quality of their performance is unobtainable, for the following I ascertained merely the ages at which they had occupied their prominent posts, namely, statesmen, college presidents, foreign diplomats, heads of large corporations, and judges on the United States Supreme Court. I also studied the ages at which business men, movie actors, movie actresses, and movie directors were near the top of the earning-power scale, as well as the ages at which annual incomes of $1,000,000.00 or more were received.

I tried similarly to find the ages at which best performances were displayed by the following: makers of the world's rare violins, leading contract bridge players, checker players, rodeo winners, horseshoe pitchers, champion typists, and authors of notable church sermons.

The interested reader can find my collective findings summarized briefly in the final chapter of my book (1953). Since publishing my book I have tried both to supplement by earlier findings and also to find such flaws as I can find in my earlier published results. This study is the first that I have made of the production rates of still-living groups (Table 11.1).

Table 11.1. Average Number of Contributions to Science and Mathematics per Age Interval

Data used in:	15-19	20-24	25-29	30-34	35-39	40-44	45-49	50-54	55-59	60-64	65-69	70-74	75-79	80-84
Fig. 11.1 (138–154–1.12)[a]		.017	.062	.055	.035	.037	.009	.015	.008	.006	.001			
Fig. 11.2 (269–412–1.53)	.007	.029	.078	.077	.058	.043	.019	.013	.016	.023				
Fig. 11.3 (93–187–2.01)		.009	.045	.091	.098	.069	.069	.035	.056	.015				
Fig. 11.4 (76–143–1.88)	.003	.026	.090	.074	.061	.055	.046	.022	.025	.007	.019	.015	.027	
Fig. 11.5 (135–192–1.42)	.001	.007	.025	.070	.066	.051	.032	.028	.019	.016	.039	.015	.015	
Fig. 11.6 Solid line: (2051–3911–1.91)		.005	.043	.077	.083	.068	.053	.041	.025	.014	.009	.003	.001	.002
Fig. 11.6 Broken line: (2374–5128–2.16)		.008	.036	.071	.080	.073	.064	.051	.037	.028	.018	.011	.005	.003

Figs. 11.7 to 11.10, inclusive, were made by employing at each age interval the median percentage value of a group of statistical distributions that were first reduced to percentage values. See text.

Data used in:	15-19	20-24	25-29	30-34	35-39	40-44	45-49	50-54	55-59	60-64	65-69	70-74	75-79	80-84
Fig. 11.7 Solid line	1%	20	82	100	89	64	44	33	24	24	7	1		
Fig. 11.7 Broken line	1	28	79	100	98	76	57	43	29	23	13	8	7	
Fig. 11.8 Solid line		19	88	100	66	53	34	26	20	15	12			
Fig. 11.8 Broken line	2	25	88	100	95	91	78	51	42	31	10	18	7	7
Fig. 11.9 Solid line		23	55	100	93	78	52	42	31	19	10			
Fig. 11.9 Broken line	1	14	53	93	100	85	60	49	46	37	18	15	8	
Fig. 11.10 Solid line		20	79	100	85	67	40	35	27	18	10	15		
Fig. 11.10 Broken line	2	22	77	100	97	84	61	50	37	31	16	14		

NOTE: The peak of each statistical distribution is italized.

[a] The numerals in parenthesis indicate: (1) the number of contributors, (2) the total number of their cited contributions, and (3) the average number of contributions made by each individual contributor.

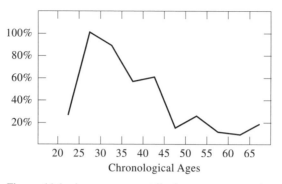

Figure 11.1. Age versus contributions to progress in atomic physics, representing 154 superior contributions by 138 "still-living" contributors (or 1.12 works each).

PROCEDURE

The meaning of the words "creative production rate" is illustrated by Figure 11.1, which presents information regarding chronological age versus contributions to the progress of atomic physics. Data for the construction of this figure were obtained from a book by Wehr and Richards (1960) entitled *Physics of the Atom.* In the appendix of this book the authors have inserted a chronology entitled, The Atomic View of Nature, in which they attempt to pinpoint specific discoveries and other creative accomplishments which have an important bearing on atomic physics.

Because atomic physics is a recent development, to complete their chronology, Wehr and Richards included the contributions of many still-living contributors. Thus, of 345 contributions cited by them, 154 (or 45%) were made by contributors who were still among the living at the time their chronology was published.

Figure 11.1 reveals by 5-year intervals the chronological ages at which 138 contributors, who were alive in 1958, made a total of 154 contributions to atomic physics, or a life-long average of 1.12 contributions per contributor. In study of Figure 11.1, it should be understood that it sets forth the *average* number of contributions per 5-year interval. Adequate allowance is thus made for the larger number of youthful workers. This statement applies to all age curves presented herein.

Although the Wehr-Richards chronology was published in 1960, it includes no contributions made subsequent to 1958. Therefore, in order to obtain sound arithmetical averages, I assumed that each of the then-living contributors died in 1958. That is to say, regardless of when it was published, insofar as my present study is concerned, any book that includes no contributions made subsequent to, let us say, year X, has a terminal year of X.

Employment of the year of publication, 1960, rather than the terminal date of 1958, would have been unsound for my present purpose because such a procedure would have counted as unproductive several years during which production may have occurred but which could not have received due recognition in the Wehr-Richards chronology.

AGES AT WHICH THE MAXIMUM PRODUCTION RATES WERE ATTAINED

Figure 11.1 shows that, for the 5-year interval from 25 to 29, inclusive, the contributors listed in the Wehr-Richards chronology who were still among the living in 1958, but who to suit my present purpose died (statistically) during that year, made a total of 0.0617 contributions. But at ages 60 to 64 the then-living contributors made an average of only 0.00633 contributions. In Figure 11.1 the curve is so drawn as to be only 0.00633/0.0617 as high at 60 to 64 as at 25 to 29. The curve is drawn in this manner in order to show graphically that the average number of contributions per individual was only 0.00633/0.0617 as great at 60 to 64 as it was at 25 to 29.

If, regardless of the number of workers that remained alive, the 60-to 64-year-old workers had contributed at the same average rate as did the 25-to 29-year-old workers, the curve in Figure 11.1 would remain as high at the 60-to 64-year-old age level as it is at the 25-to 29-year-old level. Actually, it exhibits a very noticeable and consistent decrement at the uppermost age levels, thus indicating that the contributors became progressively less productive at those ages.

It is true, of course, that all or almost all of the individuals whose production rate is shown in Figure 11.1 are still living and producing and therefore that Figure 11.1 does not take into account their entire life-work. It is also true, however, that in the years directly ahead, other contributors who were too young to have started making their contributions prior to 1958 will also be producing scientific contributions. Hence, it is not necessarily true that the *relative production rates* of the successive age groups as revealed in Figure 11.1 will change very greatly.

In addition to the Wehr-Richards chronology, age data were obtained from several other source-books. For example, data for the construction of Figure 11.2 were obtained from the second edition of Glasstone's *Sourcebook on*

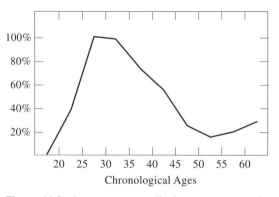

Figure 11.2. Age versus contributions to progress in atomic energy, representing 412 superior contributions by 269 "still-living" contributors (or 1.53 works each).

Atomic Energy, which was published in 1958 with a terminal date of 1957. Of 622 contributions cited by Glasstone, 415 (or 67%) were made by 277 contributors who were still among the living in 1957. Figure 11.2 reveals the production rates for these 277 still-living workers. Like Figure 11.1, the apogee of Figure 11.2 occurs at ages 25 to 29, inclusive, but the production rate shown in Figure 11.2 is almost as great at ages 30 to 34 as it is at ages 25 to 29.

In order to delve more deeply into this problem, several other fields were investigated. Figures 11.3 was obtained by use of data from Waterfield's *A Hundred Years of Astronomy* (1938). The peak production rate for the still-

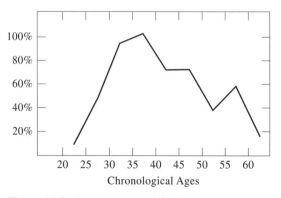

Figure 11.3. Age versus contributions to astronomy, representing 187 superior contributions by 93 "still-living" contributors (or 2.01 works each).

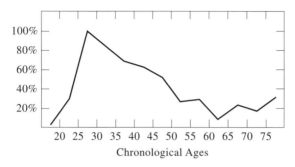

Figure 11.4. Age versus contributions to mathematics, representing 143 superior contributions by 76 "still-living" contributors (or 1.88 works each).

living contributors occurs here at ages 35 to 39, inclusive, and the secondary peak which is to be seen at ages 55 to 59 is probably due to the fact that in this figure so few cases (only 94) are spread over as many as 9 class-intervals. Experience at constructing a great many age curves has led me to believe that secondary peaks are usually the result of chance factors and not likely to be very meaningful.

Figure 11.4 depicts age versus contributions to mathematics made by present-generation workers as listed in Bell's book (1940), *The Development of Mathematics*. In view of what has already been said, detailed comment with reference to this curve seems needless. Figure 11.5 embodies age data obtained from Reed's (1942) history of the plant sciences and is based on 192 contributions made by 135 present-generation contributors, or an average of 1.42 contributions per individual worker.

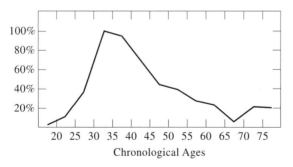

Figure 11.5. Age versus contributions to botany, representing 192 superior contributions by 135 "still-living" contributors (or 1.42 works each).

Because many of the earlier workers were reluctant to publish (Cavendish, Newton, et al.), age data for contributors born prior to about the year 1775 may be less trustworthy than age data for those born more recently. Therefore, in this study I shall present data only for deceased contributors born subsequent to 1774.

Data for both curves of Figure 11.6 were obtained from Kelly's *Encyclopedia of Medical Sources* (1948). Since this present study concerns itself only with creative achievement of the very highest order, rather than with whatever may get itself into print, a studied effort was made to locate sources that contain only the most select, and hence of necessity, small numbers of accomplishments.

Although Kelly's *Encyclopedia* lists almost 10,000 contributions to the progress of medicine, the select nature of his compilation is suggested by the fact that Kelly cites an average of only 1.88 contributions per individual contributor, and it is suggested by the further fact that the contributions cited by Kelly were made by workers from all over the world and throughout recorded history to every aspect of the broad field of medicine. The general nature of Kelly's *Encyclopedia* has been described by a book reviewer (Leikind, 1948) as follows:

Should one wish to read the original description of Babinski's sign, Charcot's disease, or Froelich's syndrome, or use Giemsa's stain, Hitchen's agar, or Pool's meningoscope, this book will provide the exact reference. These are arranged alphabetically by author and include nationality, dates of birth and death, and the discovery or discoveries for which the doctor or scientist is known. The full title (in the original language) and exact citation to journal or book are also given.

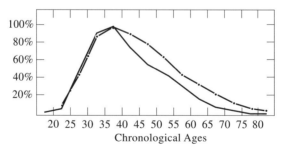

Figure 11.6. Age versus contributions to progress in medicine. *Solid* line, 3911 superior contributions by 2051 "still-living" contributors (an average of 1.91 works each). *Broken* line, 5128 contributions by 2374 deceased contributors born subsequent to 1774 (an average of 2.16 works each).

In Figure 11.6 the broken line sets forth age data for 2,374 deceased contributors born subsequent to 1774, who made 5,128 contributions to medicine. The solid line reveals, on the other hand, comparable information regarding 2,051 contributors who made 3,911 contributions and who were still among the living during the terminal year (1947) of Kelly's *Encyclopedia*.

Notice in Figure 11.6 that, although the maximum production rates for both the still-living and for the deceased workers occur at ages 35 to 39, the production rate for the present generation contributors rises very slightly more abruptly and also wanes somewhat more precipitously than does the production rate for the past generation contributors.

Because the evaluation of scientific findings differs somewhat with the individual who does the evaluating, in the remainder of this study I shall not rely upon the judgment of any one historian but rather upon collective evaluations.

To obtain Figure 11.7, 11 pairs of statistical distributions were made, each member of each pair having been obtained from the same history of chemistry (Berry, 1948, 1954; Farber, 1952; Findlay, 1948; Giua, 1946; Hilditch, 1911; Lieben, 1935; Valentine, 1950; Walden, 1944, 1952; Weeks, 1956). Eleven comparisons of present versus past generations of contributors to chemistry were thus possible. In Figure 11.7 the solid line sets forth, for 11 groups of present generation contributors to chemistry, the median values of their creative production rates per 5-year interval, and the broken line presents comparable information for past generation contributors. The median values were obtained by first converting the statistical distributions into percentage values

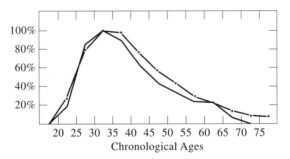

Figure 11.7. Age versus contributions to chemistry. *Solid* line, median values obtained from 11 statistical distributions (percentage values) of age data for "still-living" contributors. *Broken* line, comparable age data for 11 deceased groups born subsequent to 1774.

and the curves of Figure 11.7 were then drawn to show at each age interval the median percentage values of the afore-mentioned statistical distributions.

WHY MEDIAN RATHER THAN MEAN VALUES ARE HERE EMPLOYED

To derive Figure 11.7, median instead of mean values were employed, because, if the mean instead of the median value had been employed for constructing the solid line of Figure 11.7, the historian who was found to cite an average of 4.98 contributions per still-living worker would have had more than four times as much influence in determining the shape of the solid line in Figure 11.7 as would the other historian who cited an average of only 1.21 works per individual contributor. I wished to avoid such an outcome because, as has been shown elsewhere, (Lehman, 1953), when longer (and usually less select) lists of achievements are studied, the maximum production rate is likely to shift to either an older or a younger age level but more often to an older one. But when shorter (and more select) lists are studied the maximum production rate is likely to occur in the thirties.

RESULTS WHEN A CONSENSUS OF OPINION IS EMPLOYED

Notice in Figure 11.7 that: (1) prior to attaining their peaks, the two curves almost coincide, (2) both the present and the past generation contributors to chemistry attained their maximum production rates at ages 30 to 34, and (3) the production rate for present generation contributors (shown by the solid line) falls off slightly more abruptly than does the production rate for past generation contributors.

Figure 11.8 is similar to Figure 11.7 except that Figure 11.8 depicts the production rates for 11 groups of present generation versus 11 groups of past generation contributors to physics. To obtain age data for Figure 11.8, 11 pairs of statistical distributions were first made, each member of each pair having been made with data as found in the same history of physics (Auerbach, 1910, 1923; Crew, 1935; Geiger. 1926; Heathcote, 1953; Hillers & Starke, 1923; Hoppe, 1926; Hull, 1949; Kistner, 1906; Laue, 1950; Wilson, 1950). It will be noted in Figure 11.8 that here too: (1) prior to attaining their maxima, the two curves almost coincide, (2) both curves attain their apogees at ages 30 to 34, and (3) the production rate for the present gener-

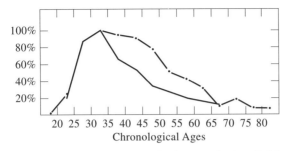

Figure 11.8. Age versus contributions to physics. *Solid* line, median values obtained from 11 statistical distributions (percentage values) of age data for "still-living" contributors. *Broken* line, comparable age data for 11 deceased groups born subsequent to 1774.

ation contributors to physics (shown by the solid line) wanes much more abruptly than does the production rate for past generation contributors.

Figures 11.7 and 11.8 thus exhibit a noticeable difference at the older age levels. Note that, in Figure 11.8 the two curves lie much farther apart during their descent than do the corresponding curves of Figure 11.7. This difference between Figures 11.7 and 11.8 probably results from the fact that the median values used for constructing each of these curves were obtained from as few as 11 statistical distributions, and when median values are obtained from so few statistical distributions, one should not expect to obtain a very high level of precision in one's results. It is questionable that there is any great difference in the production rates of the older still-living contributors to these two fields.

Most of the observations already made with reference to Figures 11.7 and 11.8 apply also to Figure 11.9 which represents data obtained from 15 histories as follows: atomic energy (Glasstone, 1950; Wehr, 1960), astronomy (Doig, 1950; Waterfield, 1938), entomology (Essig, 1931), mathematics (Bell, 1940; Cajori, 1922), medicine (Castiglioni, 1941, 1947; Garrison, 1929; Kelly, 1948), genetics (Cook, 1937), botany (Reed, 1942), psychology (Hulin, 1934) and pathology (Krumbhaar, 1937). Figure 11.9 reveals that, whereas present generation contributors to science and mathematics have attained their maximum production rates at not later than ages 30 to 34, past generation contributors to the same fields have attained theirs not later than 5 years later, namely, at ages 35 to 39.

Figure 11.10 embodies the combined age data employed for the construc-

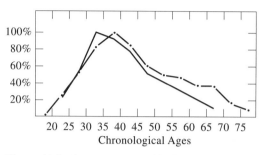

Figure 11.9. Age versus contributions to miscellaneous sciences and mathematics. *Solid* line, median values obtained from 15 statistical distributions (percentage values) of age data for "still-living" contributors. *Broken* line, comparable age data for 15 deceased groups born subsequent to 1774.

tion of Figures 11.7, 11.8, and 11.9; that is to say, data obtained from 11 histories of chemistry, 11 histories of physics, and 15 histories of mathematics and of various other sciences, 37 histories in all. In Figure 11.10 note that: (1) prior to attaining their maximum points, the two curves again almost coincide, (2) both attain their maxima at ages 30 to 34, inclusive, and (3) after attaining its peak the curve which shows the production rates of the present generation workers wanes somewhat more abruptly than does the comparable curve for past generation workers.

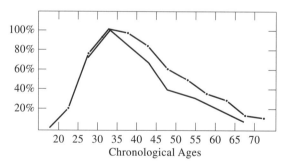

Figure 11.10. Age versus contributions embodied in Figures 11.7, 11.8, and 11.9. *Solid* line, median values obtained from 37 statistical distributions (percentage values) of age data for "still-living" contributors. *Broken* line, comparable data for 37 groups of deceased contributors born subsequent to 1774.

THE SELECT NATURE OF THE CONTRIBUTIONS STUDIED HEREIN

Some appreciation of the highly select nature of the contributions dealt with in the present study may be gleaned from the fact that when the mean number of contributions per contributor was computed for both the still-living and for the deceased groups, the median value (of the arithmetic means) for the 37 still-living groups was only 1.48 and for the 37 deceased groups it was 1.92. This indicates that, from the entire life output of these gifted thinkers, the 37 historians cited and discussed less than two contributions per individual contributor.

Similarly, the median values of the maximum production rates (for any one 5-year interval) was only 0.068 for the still living contributors and only 0.071 for the deceased contributors. Thus, for both the living and for the deceased groups their collective output as cited and discussed in the 37 histories was less than a tenth of a contribution per year. But it should also be borne in mind that at no age level were many of these contributors spending their entire time at research and that few if any of them were engaged even in part-time research during their entire lives.

POTENTIAL VERSUS REALIZED PRODUCTION RATES

Since these curves represent only the production rates that have been realized at successive age levels and not potential production rates, they certainly do not imply that there is a decrement in the *potential* of these gifted individuals that corresponds to the decrements in the curves. Most psychologists believe that few persons ever actually reach the very peak of performance of which they are capable, and, if we can assume that most *individuals* fail to attain their potential peak performance, it is inconceivable that any entire *age group* has ever done so. Since most individuals and *all* age groups are probably content to come to rest at some point below their maximal potential performance, the decrements in these curves probably do not parallel a decrement in the *ability* to achieve at the older age levels.

ASSUMPTIONS UNDERLYING THIS STUDY

In making this study it is not assumed that when a contribution to science is first published any mortal can say precisely just how important that contribution is destined to be, or that the historian of science is able to identify each and every outstanding contribution to his field. It is assumed only that whether or not a contribution to, say chemistry for example, is an important one can best be judged by those who have written our standard histories of chemistry and that, collectively, the historians can, with a fair degree of accuracy and with no bias toward any one age group, make lists of contributions to their fields that possess high merit.

It is assumed also that the present generation chemists whose published findings are now being cited and discussed in our histories of chemistry are our most likely present-day candidates for professional immortality. Granted that, in the days to come, some of the work of present generation contributors (now cited and discussed in histories of chemistry) may be overvalued, and granted also that the work of others whose findings are now ignored by historians will make their future entry into histories of science, it nevertheless seems probable that these changes will occur on a random basis *insofar as the ages of the contributors at time of making their contributions is concerned.* Since it is individual contributions and not the collective work of entire age groups that chroniclers choose for inclusion in their histories of science, it seems probable that at least a rough proportionality will be maintained between the way in which our present-day historians evaluate the production of the successive age groups and the way in which future historians will do so.

THE PROBLEM OF CAUSATION

Although I would be happy to be able to state the specific causes for the age differences in production rates, the mere fact that I have assembled some statistics is no indication that I know any more with reference to the cause-and-effect relationships than does the reader. The causes of such complex behaviors as those I have studied are probably multiple, complex, interrelated, and they doubtless vary from individual to individual. To attack the problem of even the most general causative factors effectively it will be necessary for generations of entire teams of workers from divers fields of endeavor to make cooperative efforts in that direction. Certainly, no one individual, alone and unaided, could hope to accomplish much along that line.

As has been emphasized by Fraser (Anon., 1946), clinical research on aging as an isolated variable is practically impossible at the present time. This results from the fact that there are always many uncontrolled variables to consider. Because in old age pathological conditions are so generally present, in addition to old age itself, and because these pathological conditions are often obscure and illusive, Fraser suggested that it would be better for clinicians to concentrate on studying the pathological conditions themselves rather than to attempt clinical study of the age factor alone. The age factor of itself could hardly be regarded as *causing* anything at all. It is the *concomitants* of advancing age that need to be examined.

Since it is self-evident that further research on creative production and how to make the most of it is greatly needed, here are some not particularly subtle speculations regarding conceivable causes (but unmeasured and perhaps unmeasurable by use of the principle of the single variable) for the rapid rise of the curves in early maturity and their decline after attaining an earlier maximum. With advance in chronological age beyond the early twenties there is likely to be found: a decrement in physical vigor and sensory capacity, more illness, glandular changes, more preoccupation with practical concerns, less favorable conditions for concentration, weakened intellectual curiosity, more mental disorders, and an accumulation of unfavorable habits. For example, some elderly tend to be set in their ways, a poor condition for bold discovery. Moreover, the individual who already has achieved prestige and recognition may try less hard thereafter to achieve further success.

FACTS VERSUS ARTIFACTS

Statistics can be tricky. What they reveal depends on our ability to interpret them. Our problem here is to examine possible reasons for the different decrements in the production rates of the present and the past generations of scientists. To ascertain whether this apparent difference is a genuine or a spurious one, it is first necessary to answer the following questions.

1. Are the contributions of the present and of the past generations of scientists of reasonably equal average merit? As has been shown elsewhere (Lehman, 1953), the production rate for creative contributions of superior average merit tends to wane more rapidly than does the production rate for contributions of lesser average merit. Therefore, really to prove that the decrements at the older ages have changed within recent times, it would first be necessary to make sure that the production rates under consideration are based upon output of equal or nearly equal merit. Needless to say, this would be a difficult if not an impossible undertaking.

If, because of the difficulty of evaluating recent research findings, the historians whose books I studied were more hesitant about citing and discussing the contributions of present generation workers than those of past generation workers, it may well be that the contributions of the present generation contributors that were chosen by the historians for citation are on the average somewhat superior to those that they selected from the total output of the past generation workers. If this is what the historians did, it alone could account for the differential decrements.

2. With the passage of time has there been any significant change as regards the eagerness of scientists to publish their findings? It is asserted in a recent publication (Caplow, 1958) that in many major universities, the evaluation of the faculty member's job performance is based almost exclusively on publication and that, as one result of this, it has become the ambitious academician's goal in many instances to accumulate a long list of published titles as early as is practicable. If this alleged trend be a fact, and if this tendency has influenced our most gifted, as well as our run-of-the-mine scientists, it could have lessened the time lag that inevitably occurs between the making of a scientific discovery and the announcement thereof. This obviously would have produced the more rapid decrement in the age curves for the more recently-born scientists.

3. Is increasingly strong competition responsible for the results reported herein? As is well known, within recent times the contributor to almost every field of science has had a lot more competition for honors in his field than did his predecessors. Therefore, with far more contributions from which to choose, the modern historian of science may perhaps have been able to cite recent contributions that possess somewhat greater average excellence than do the contributions they cited and that were made by past generation workers. That is to say, it is conceivable that my finding reflects no actual change in production rate for contributions of equal merit but merely the fact that the more recent research output has had to measure up to a higher standard of excellence.

SUMMARY AND CONCLUSIONS

From 11 histories of chemistry, 11 histories of physics, and 15 histories of other fields of research, 37 pairs of statistical distributions were made, each member of each pair having been made with data obtained from the same book. Of each of the 37 pairs of distributions one member included age data for the deceased and the other member data for still-living contributors. When, by use of median percentage values, separate age curves were drawn which showed production rates for the chemists, for the physicists, and for the 15 groups of other scientists, the curves for each of these three still-living were found to decline somewhat more abruptly and to terminate earlier than did the curves for the deceased. But for the reasons already mentioned this difference is probably not significant. I speak here not of statistical significance but of *meaningful* significance.

On the whole it seems clear that both past and present generation scientists have produced more than their proportionate share of high-quality research *not later than* at ages 30 to 39 and it is as useless to bemoan this fact as to deny it. It might have been supposed that, as scientific knowledge accumulates, the time when the first important research is done would be pushed to older and older ages. Nevertheless, my data provide no support for that supposition, inasmuch as the curves for the past and for the present generation contributors ascend at almost identical rates.

REFERENCES

Anonymous. Ageing in man and other animals. Nature, *August 24, 1946,* 158, *276–280.*

Auerbach, F. Geschichtstafeln der Physik. Leipzig: Verlag von Johann Ambrosius Barth, 1910.

Auerbach, F. Entwicklungsgeschichte der Modernen Physik. *Berlin: Springer Verlag, 1923.*

Bell, E. T. The development of mathematics. *New York: McGraw-Hill Book Company, 1940.*

Berry, A. J. Modern chemistry: some sketches of its historical development. *Cambridge: Cambridge University Press, 1948.*

Berry, A. J. From classical to modern chemistry. *Cambridge: Cambridge University Press, 1954.*

Cajori, F. A history of mathematics. *New York: Macmillan, 1922.*

Caplow, T., & McGee, R. J. P. The academic marketplace. *New York: Basic Books, 1958.*

Castiglioni, A. A history of medicine. *New York: Alfred A. Knopf, 1941.*

Castiglioni, A. A history of medicine. *New York: Alfred A. Knopf, 1947.*

Cook, R. C. A Chronology of Genetics, in U.S. Department of Agriculture Yearbook of Agriculture, *1937.*

Crew, H. The rise of modern physics. *Baltimore: Williams and Wilkins, 1935.*

Doig, P. A concise history of astronomy. *London: Chapman & Hall, Ltd., 1950.*

Essig, E. O. A history of entomology. *New York: Macmillan, 1931.*

Farber, E. The evolution of chemistry: a history of its ideas, methods, and materials. *New York: Ronald Press, 1952.*

Findlay, A. A hundred years of chemistry. *London: Duckworth, 1948.*

Garrison, F. H. An introduction to the history of medicine. *Philadelphia: W. B. Saunders, 4th ed, 1929.*

Geiger, H. Handbuch der Physik. In 24 Bände. Band I. Geschichte der Physik *von Karl Scheel. Berlin: Springer Verlag, 1926 ff.*

Giua, M. Storia della chemica. *Turin, Italy: Chiantore, 1946.*

Glasstone, S. Sourcebook on atomic energy. *New York: D. van Nostrand, 1st ed, 1950.*

Glasstone, S. Sourcebook on atomic energy. *Princeton, N.J.: D. van Nostrand, 2nd ed, 1958.*

Heathcote, N. H. de V. Nobel Prize Winners in Physics 1901–1950. *New York: Henry Schumann, 1953.*

Hilditch, T. P. A concise history of chemistry. *New York: D. van Nostrand, 1911.*

Hillers, W., & Starke, H. E. Grimsehl Lehrbuch der Physik. In Zwei Bände. Sechste, Vermehrte und verbesserte Auflage. *Berlin: Verlag und Druck von B. G. Teubner, 1923.*

Hoppe, E. Geschichte der Physik. *Braunschweig, Germany: Verlag von Friedr. Vieweg & Sohn, 1926.*

Hulin, W. S. A short history of psychology. *New York: Henry Holt, 1934.*

Hull, G. F. Elementary Modern Physics. *New York: Macmillan, 1949.*

Kelly, E. C. Encyclopedia of medical sources. *Baltimore: Williams and Wilkins, 1948.*

Kistner, A. Geschichte der Physik. *I.* Die Physik bis Newton. *II.* Die Physik von Newton bis zur Gegenwart. *Leipzig: G. J. Göschen'sche Verlagshandlung. 1905.*

Krumbhaar, E. B. Pathology, Vol. XIX *of* Clio Medica: A Series of Primers on the History of Medicine. *New York: Harper & Brothers, 1937.*

Laue, M. von. History of physics. *New York: Academic Press, 1950.*

Lehman, H. C. Age and achievement. *Princeton, N.J.: Princeton University Press, 1953.*

Leikind, M. C. Book review in Science, *1948, 108, p. 544.*

Lieben, F. Geschichte der Physiologischen Chemie. *Leipzig: Deuticke, 1935.*

Nelson, H. The creative years, *Amer. J. Psychol., 1928, 40, 303–311.*

Reed, H. S. A short history of the plant sciences. *Waltham, Mass.: Chronica Botanica Company, 1942.*

Valentine, H. Geschichte der Pharmazie und Chemie in Form von Zeittafeln. *Stuttgart, Germany: Wissenschaftliche Verlagsgesellschaft, Rev. 3rd ed., 1950.*

Walden, P. Drei Jahr Tausende Chemie. *Berlin: Limpert, 1944.*

Walden, P. Chronologische Übersichtstabellen zur Geschichte der Chemie von den ältesten Zeiten bis zur Gegenwart. *Berlin: Springer Verlag, 1952.*

Waterfield, R. L. A hundred years of astronomy. *London: Duckworth, 1938.*

Weeks, M. E. Discovery of the elements, *with a chapter on elements discovered by atomic bombardment, by H. M. Leicester, Ed. Publication of J. Chem. Educ. Easton, Pa., 1956.*

Wehr, M. R., & Richards, J. A. Physics of the atom. *Reading, Mass.: Addison-Wesley, 1960.*

Wilson, W. A hundred years of physics. *London: Duckworth, 1950.*

Woodworth, R. S. Psychology: A study of mental life. *New York: Henry Holt, 1921.*

12. Age Differences in Fluid and Crystallized Intelligence

John L. Horn and Raymond B. Cattell

PURPOSES

This is one of several studies aimed at demonstrating that the theory of fluid and crystallized intelligence (Cattell, 1941, 1950, 1957a, 1963; Horn, 1965a; Horn & Cattell, 1966a, 1966b) provides a useful framework within which to integrate existing knowledge about human abilities. This theory appears to be particularly applicable in the study of relationships between aging in adulthood and changes in intellectual performances.

In a previous study (Horn & Cattell, 1966b) it was shown that when primary mental ability factors (after French, Ekstrom, & Price, 1963) are grouped according to their patterns of loadings on second-order factors (Horn, 1965a; Horn & Cattell, 1966a), then analyses between adult age groupings extending from the "mid-teens" (14–17) to "over forty" (14–61) indicate consistent differences favoring the young on primaries that are relatively pure makers for fluid intelligence (Gf), consistent differences favoring the older adults on primaries which define crystallized intelligence (Gc) most purely and variable age-trend curves for primaries having variance divided roughly equally between Gf and Gc. These results are highly encouraging for the general fluid crystallized theory, but they leave some questions unanswered and they fail to bring out certain details of the relationships between intellectual performance and aging. For example, the question of the influence of educational and sex differences on the results was not answered and the analyses did not clearly show the extent to which the age-trend curves could be altered by statistically controlling the variance measured in general speediness and visualization factors. The present study was designed to help resolve issues of this kind.

From *Acta Psychologica* 26 (1967): 107–29. Copyright © 1967. Reprinted with kind permission of Elsevier Science–NL, Sara Burgerhartstraat 25, 1055 KV Amsterdam, The Netherlands.

THEORETICAL BASIS FOR THIS STUDY

For readers not yet familiar with the most recent expressions of the theory of fluid and crystallized intelligence some outline of this is necessary to put the present investigation in context.

In broad terms the Gf–Gc theory is an attempt to integrate evidence converging from some five kinds of studies of intellectual performance, viz., studies dealing with: (1) the effects of brain damage on abilities, particularly the differential effects associated with early (in development) as compared with late brain damage; (2) the relationships between test scores and opportunities to acquire knowledge; (3) the construction of intelligence tests which will be more nearly fair for all persons regardless of their social class of origin; (4) the factor structure among sets of tests said to measure various aspects of intelligence and; (5) the changes in intellectual performances associated with aging, both in childhood and in adulthood. The principal conclusion deriving from analysis of the evidence in these various areas is that intellectual abilities are organized at a general level into two general intelligence, viz., fluid intelligence and crystallized intelligence. These represent the operation of somewhat different—i.e. independent—influences in development. On the one hand there are those influences which directly affect the physiological structure upon which intellectual processes must be constructed— influences operating through the agencies of heredity and injury: these are most accurately reflected in measures of fluid intelligence. And on the other hand there are those influences which affect physiological structure only indirectly through agencies of learnings, acculturation, etc.: crystallized intelligence is the most direct resultant of individual differences in these influences.

For the reader who prefers concrete, operational definitions of concepts, Table 12.1 gives the actual variables found to define Gf and Gc in a recent and comprehensive study of factor structure among primary mental abilities (Horn, 1965a). Here it can be seen that Gf is defined by tasks such as:

(a) Letter grouping and series from the primary factor I,[1] Inductive reasoning,
(b) Figure classifications, Topology and Matrices from the primary factor CFR, Figural relations,
(c) Common word analogies of CMR, Semantic relations,

Table 12.1. Oblique Structure among a Broad Sample of Primary Mental Ability Factors, after Horn (1965a).

Primary factor symbol and name*		Second-order factors and loading**					
		Gf	Gc	Gv	Gs	C	F
I	Inductive reasoning	50		28			
CFR	Figural relations	46		43			
Ma	Associative memory	32		43			
ISp	Intellectual speed	40				−21	
IL	Intellectual level	51					
R	General reasoning	23	30				
CMR	Semantic relations	33	50				20
Rs	Formal reasoning	34	40				
N	Number facility	24	29		34		
V	Verbal comprehension		69				26
Mk	Mechanical knowledge		48	25			
EMS	Experiential evaluation		43		23		
Fi	Ideational fluency		25		25		42
Fa	Associational fluency		35				60
S	Spatial orientation			50			−20
Vz	Visualization			58			
Cs	Speed of closure	21		36			
Cf	Flexibility of closure			48			
DFT	Figural adaptive flexibility			40			
P	Perceptual speed				48		
Sc	Speed copying				63		
Pf	Productive flexibility		−23		46		
C	Carefulness					60	

* After French, Ekstrom, and Price (1963) and Guilford (1959).
** Factor loadings below .20 and decimal points have been omitted in order to achieve maximum clarity of presentation.

   (d) Nonsense equations and paired associates memory of Ma, Associative memory.

These tasks call for a capacity to perceive relations and educe correlates, as Spearman (1927) defined these functions; they indicate ability to maintain span of immediate awareness; they involve concept formation and attainment, reasoning and abstracting. That is, in general, the tasks which define Gf require intelligence as this concept is usually defined. But it will be noted that the problem materials of these tasks are not such that emphasis in measurement is placed upon individual differences in education or acculturation, broadly conceived. For example, the Letter Series task requires only knowledge of the order of the English alphabet. When used with adults who are products of the American educational system, this knowledge is available to virtually all people tested: the conventional order of listing alphabet characters is about as much over-learned by ditch diggers as by college professors. The figural materials of the Topology test (Cattell, 1957b) on the other hand, are about as novel for college professors as they are for ditch diggers. The problem materials of the tests which define Gf are in these senses relatively culture fair—i.e. about equally novel or equally common for all persons tested in a properly designed study aimed at demonstrating the Gf and Gc functions.

It will be noted that the tasks which define Gc are also of a kind commonly said to indicate intelligence—e.g.,

(a) Vocabulary and general information from the primary factor V, Verbal comprehension,
(b) Syllogistic reasoning and inferences from Rs, Formal reasoning,
(c) Social situations from EMS, Experiential evaluation,
(d) Arithmetic reasoning and destinations from from R, General reasoning,
(e) Ideas and things from Fi, Ideational fluency, etc.

In these tasks, however, the perception of relations, education of correlates, reasoning, etc., required for problem solution must usually be premised on absorption of what can be termed the "collective intelligence of a culture." For example, in an analogy item like this one:

Hippocrates–Galen: Aeschylus–Greece   Euripides   Pericles   Zeno

(modeled on the items of the well known Concept Mastery Test which Terman used in his follow-up studies of the gifted) perception of relations is required for solution, to be sure, but individual differences in reaching solution are also due to awareness of a rather esoteric aspect of Western culture. A person who can solve quite complex problems of the kind which define Gf can easily fail even very simple analogy problems of this sort simply because he lacks information. But perhaps a better example illustrating that Gc is a kind of intelligence and yet distinct from Gf is to be found in the use of what Cattell (1963) has described as "generalized solution instruments" or "aids." The idea of differentiation in the calculus of Newton and Liebnitz is an example of an *aid*. Differentiation enables the person who has mastered it to solve many problems he would otherwise not be able to solve. It thus provides a distinct advantage in problem-solving to the person who has acquired a particular element from the collective intelligence of his culture. And an individual may use this aid, and behave more intelligently by virtue of this use, even when he is incapable of creating the concept of differentiation himself!

Crystallized intelligence indicates the extent to which one has appropriated the collective intelligence of his culture for his own use. In part, of course, this is dependent upon that person's fluid intelligence, for he must have the basic capacity to appropriate that which at one time must have been novel for him. But to a large extent the factors which enable one to come into contact with this culture, and to learn as a result of such contact, are independent of level of fluid intelligence. Not only are the factors which indicate opportunity somewhat independent of Gf, but also many non-intellectual factors of the person himself are thus independent and yet may determine the attainment represented in Gc—factors such as the person's motivations (e.g., what Hayes [1962] has cogently described as "experience producing drives"), his characteristic level of personality integration, his vitality, etc. And since Gc is largely a function of experience, aging throughout life—not only in childhood—will tend to be associated with its increase. Thus it can be seen that Gc, through development, can become quite independent of Gf.

It will be noted that Table 12.1 shows four general factors in addition to Gf and Gc. These, according to our theory, represent functions which are not basically intellectual, as such, but which produce variance on necessarily fallible measures of intelligence.

Gv is a general visualization function producing some variance on all intellectual tasks which involve imaging the way objects may change in appearance as they move in space, maintaining orientation with respect to objects in space, keeping spatial configurations in mind, finding the Gestalt among disparate parts in a visual field, maintaining flexibility concerning other possible structurings of elements in space, etc. It is interesting that many putative tests of intelligence are constructed of spatial materials and thus require visualization. And, of course, we must recognize the importance of vision in the development of intelligence. But in part this emphasis on spatial materials in intelligence tests is fortuitous. As Spearman (1927) pointed out some years ago, there is probably no necessary reason to emphasize use of any particular kind of problem material in measures of intelligence. Many, if not all, of the problems presently phrased, as it were, in spatial symbols might be phrased in auditory symbols. And if this emphasis were present in a set of ability measurements, a general audition factor, analogous to general visualization, would obtrude and produce variance additional to that on the Gf or Gc functions. It's in this sense that Gv is said to account in part for individual differences in measures of intelligence and yet not itself indicate intelligence.

The Gs factor picks up variance from most speeded ability tests and in this sense represents a function determining the rate at which ability problems are solved. This function is largely independent of those indicating the level of complexity one reaches in problem solving, as represented in the Gf and Gc factors. But beyond this, the nature of the Gs function is not clear. It would seem to stem either from a test-taking effortfulness or from a more physiologically-based capacity, but the research which would provide for a clear distinction between these, and possibly other, interpretations has yet to be done. Meanwhile it is recognized as merely a speediness function which produces some variance on intellectual tasks but which is not an essential aspect of the functioning of intelligence, as such.

Carefulness, C, originally defined by Fruchter (1950, 1953), is a dimension of unwillingness to give an incorrect answer to ability-test problems. Here again the essential nature of the function is obscure. Logically, it would appear to be the inverse of the speediness function described above, but in fact the two factors have been quite independent in the research upon which their definition is based (Fruchter, 1953; Horn, 1965a; Howie, 1962). In the present study it is treated primarily as a factor which needs to be statistically controlled because it represents a non-intellectual influence in performances on intelligence tests.

The F function pervades the fluency primary factors. It is perhaps rather surprising that this general dimension should be independent of the general speediness and carefulness factors described above, and yet it was so defined in our previous research. It would appear to involve, principally, a process of quickly bringing concept labels—i.e., mainly words—from a long-term storage unit into immediate awareness. This, in turn, could represent either the size of store of concept labels—something that could be expected to increase with aging—or the degree of short-circuiting of pathways from storage centers to immediate awareness. And, of course, it could represent an interrelation of these two kinds of function. In this study we probably cannot get far toward deciding between these alternative explanations, but because the F factor produces variance on several primaries—particularly those defining Gc—it will be useful to keep track of it, as it were, in covariance analysis.

Now, then, the general theory is that fluid intelligence increases throughout childhood and into young adulthood, but then levels off and eventually declines, whereas crystallized increases thoughout almost the entire period of development, from childhood to late maturity. The reasons for these predictions are numerous and intertwined in a complex manner (see Horn, 1965a, for a fuller treatment), but in general terms they may be summarized as follows:

(1) The neural and other physiological structures upon which intellectual functioning is based mature by growth and increase in complexity until the late teens or early twenties, at which time they reach their full growth and complexity. This maturation is reflected directly in an increase in Gf, for although the development of Gf is a function of learning, the particular learning here involved is mainly dependent upon the adequacy of the physiological structure which supports learning, This maturation is reflected also, though indirectly, in an increase in Gc, because the development of Gc is based in part on the development of Gf and on the same physiological structures which support learning in general.

(2) Injuries to the structures which support intellectual functioning occur throughout life and are irreversible. These injuries are usually so small and few in number during the course of a perceptible time span that they are not noticed, either subjectively by the person himself or by others. Moreover, in childhood the effects of such injuries on intellectual performances are masked by the larger effects resulting from neural growth, learning and other development in this period, But such injuries accumulate nevertheless and have a long-term limiting influence on the development of intelligence. Again, as in the case of maturational influences, this influence is felt most directly in the development of Gf and somewhat more indirectly in the development of Gc. In adulthood, when the masking influences referred to above cease to be potent, the effects of accumulation of neural damage become more evident in intellectual behavior. Hence, because fluid intelligence is most sensitively dependent upon the functioning of the physiological structures which support intellectual behavior, there will tend to be a decline in Gf with aging in adulthood, this reflecting a gradual degeneration of structure due to accumulation of irreversible injuries.

(3) Large injuries to the structures which support intellectual functioning will have occurred more frequently in the population of older people than in the population of younger people. This is likely simply because injury results from exposure in living and older persons would have had more such exposure. It means that, analogous to the accumulation with aging of small injuries within a particular person, there is an accumulation of large injuries

within a sample of people. And because the effects of these larger injuries are also manifested most sensitively in Gf, the mean Gf level for older adults will in general be lower than the mean Gf level for younger adults.

It should be noted at this point that when considered in terms of cross-sectional data (1) and (2) are alternative explanations for the same outcome: a lower Gf mean for older subjects as compared with younger subjects. Comparisons of results from cross-sectional and longitudinal studies can provide a basis for choice between these two or, what is perhaps more reasonable (since both may point to valid phenomena), a basis for estimating the relative potency of the two kinds of influence.

(4) In the human, particularly, but in all organisms to some extent, some learning occurs incidentally, without much effort being expended either on the part of the individual or on the part of those who would educate him. It is this learning which is manifested primarily in Gf, although, as noted, Gc is constructed on top of this learning. But some—perhaps much—learning occurs less incidentally, particularly in the formal agencies for acculturation such as the school. A kind of intensive acculturation can occur and this is likely to be particularly intensive during childhood, when the principal work of the young person is seen to be that of acquiring enough of the knowledge of the culture to be able to maintain it. And since the acquisition resulting from this acculturation is shown mainly in Gc, crystallized intelligence increases at a rapid rate in childhood. But the work of preparing people to maintain a culture is never done; adults learn in their attempts to pass knowledge on to the young; and there are numerous inducements and incentives which encourage adults to acquire more and more of the collective intelligence of their culture. Hence, insofar as various acculturation influences continue to operate throughout adulthood, Gc can increase with aging.

Just as apparent decline in Gf (when seen in the averages provided in cross-sectional studies) can be due either to an accumulation with aging of small decrements in all people, to an age-correlated increase in frequency of large decrements in some people, or to both of these, so, too, an apparent increase with age of Gc can be due either to small increases by all (or most), to large increases by some or to both of these factors.

The principal hypotheses of this study are thus implied. As suggested in our descriptions of factors above, Gv, Gs, C and F were included in the study mainly to provide a basis for statistical control of the potentially distorting influences represented by these factors. However, for reasons similar to those outlined in (1) and (2) above, it was predicted that Gv and possibly Gs and F would decline with age in adulthood, whereas for reasons that are too vague to dignify by specifying them as a hypothesis (but see Horn, 1965a; Horn & Cattell, 1966a), it was thought that C would increase with age.

OPERATIONAL DEFINITION OF CRUCIAL VARIABLES

The factors described in previous sections were estimated by adding together standard scores on several tests. The tests and combinations used are shown in Table 12.2.

Two estimates of each of the two major intelligence factors—Gf and Gc— were obtained, a "pure" measure and an "overall" measure. The "pure" measure was obtained by combining standard scores on the tests which previous analyses (Horn, 1965a) had shown to have substantial loading (i.e., always over .30, usually over .40) on the factor in question (Gf or Gc) and *no loading above .25 on any other factor.* The less "pure" but more general "overall" measure was obtained by summing standard scores on all tests which had loadings above .35 on the factor in question, regardless of the test's loading on other factors.

The reason for this distinction between a "pure" and "overall" estimates of a factor is perhaps more intuitive than rational. In studies of the characteristics of factor scores (Horn, 1964, 1965b; Horn & Miller, 1966) it has seemed that the simple structure concept of a factor is best represented by combining only those variables which fall into one factor alone—and no other—or by very carefully ensuring that extraneous factor influences are cancelled out by combining high-loaded variables having opposite signs in their loadings on extraneous, unwanted factors. The practice of using all variables to estimate a factor, as in the so-called "exact" methods, appears to result in the introduction of "noise"—i.e., random influences—from variables falling in the hyperplane of the factor. The conditions required to achieve the best (in all of several senses) estimate of a factor are difficult to specify and therefore more difficult to impose, but the "pure" estimate obtained here would appear to more nearly achieve the desired end than the so-called "overall" estimate. Actually, our hypothesis was that both kinds of estimate would yield much the same results but that the "pure" estimate would provide a somewhat more accurate description of the predicted age differences.

Estimates of Gv, Gs, C and F were obtained by combining no less than three—and usually more than five—tests having correlations greater than .3 with the factor in question. Two estimates of Gs were obtained. In one, any

Table 12.2. Second-Order Factor Estimates

Factor estimated	Symbol	Test scores combined to obtain estimates
1. "Pure" fluid intelligence	Gf_p	Letter grouping, figure series, topology, matrices, figure classification
2. "Overall" fluid	Gf_o	Gf_p plus number series, Nufferno speed and level, common word analogies, arithmetical reasoning, match arrangements, paired related words, nonsense equations, careful letter series, careful figure classification
3. "Pure" crystallized intelligence	Gc_p	Vocabulary, general information, social situations, abstruse word analogies
4. "Overall" crystallized intelligence	Gc_o	Gc_p plus arithmetical reasoning, common word analogies, mechanical information tool identification, inferences, controlled association, ideas, mixed arithmetic
5. General visualization	Gv	Cards, figures, form boards, match arrangements, street gestalt, designs, backward reading
6. Clerical speed	Gsc	Forward writing, forward printing, unusual writing, matching letters, matching numbers, rapid cancellation
7. General speed (with intellectual components)	Gs	Gsc plus nufferno speed, reading speed
8. General verbal fluency	F	Controlled associations, things round, ideas
9. General carefulness	C	Carefulness on: letter series, figure classification, estimates, dividing, fractions
10. Omnibus intelligence	G	Gf_p, Gc_p, Gv, F, number series, nufferno speed and level, arithmetical reasoning, paired related words, nonsense equations, mechanical information, tool identification, false premises, inferences, mixed arithmetic

test which would be said to involve intelligence to a noteworthy degree was excluded, whereas in the other estimate all tests measuring the Gs function were included.

The reason for the omnibus intelligence measure will be made evident below, after the basic results have been described.

THE SAMPLE

The measurements indicated in Table 12.2 were obtained from a sample of 297 older teenagers and adults drawn from Stateville, Pontiac, and Dwight State Prisons in Illinois, The Illinois Soldiers' and Sailors' Children's School, Canon City State Penitentiary in Colorado, and the Colorado State Employment Office in Denver.[2] All subjects were volunteers. They were offered information about their performances as an inducement for giving their time and doing their best. Of the 297 subjects, 215 were males.

The age range was 14 to 61 years, but there was only one fourteen-year-old, two persons aged 61 and one each aged 56, 55 and 52, the bulk of the sample thus being between 15 and 51. For purposes of analysis the sample was divided into five age categories, viz., (1) "adolescents": 46 subjects 14 to 17 years of age inclusive, (2) "late adolescents": 51 subjects between 18 and 20 years, (3) "young adults": 81 subjects between 21 and 28 years, (4) "adults": 73 subjects between 29 and 39 years, and (5) "mature adults": 46 subjects between 40 and 61 years inclusive. This breakdown was made to provide groups wherein N was large enough to yield stable statistics and with the aim of representing theoretically interesting phases in intellectual development from late childhood into adulthood. Thus, for example, because it is widely held that intellectual development reaches a peak in late adolescence, the sample in the age range from 14 to 20 was divided into the "adolescents" and "late adolescents" groups.

RESULTS

In Table 12.3 results are presented for analyses with the factors and age groupings described in previous sections. The units of measurement for the various factors are arbitrary—i.e., as noted above, test scores were converted to standard score form (made positive, with mean 100 and standard deviation 10) and added with unity nominal weight, so the unit of measurement for a factor depends upon the number of scores combined and their intercorrelations (see Horn, 1964). An asterisk in one of the columns under "covariates" indicates that the particular variable at the head of the column was covaried out. If no asterisk appears in a given row, no covariates were involved and the F-value at the right is for an analysis of variance on the listed means. In some of the analyses on Gf estimates the 14-to 17-year-olds group was omitted. This was done because the mean for this group was lower than the means for the 18–20-and 21-to 28-year-olds groups and, in view of the hypotheses here under consideration, it seemed desirable to avoid (if possible) any implication that this fact was responsible for the significance of the overall F. Depending upon the number of covariates and groups included, the degrees of freedom vary from 3 and 240 to 4 and 292. For these degrees of freedom an F in the neighborhood of 3.38 to 3.87 is significant at the .01 level, one between approximately 3.79 and 4.32 is significant at the .005 level and one

Table 12.3. *Summary of results from analyses of variance and analyses covariance*

Dependent variable	Covariate(s): variable(s) statistically controlled									Means or adjusted means for different age groups						
	Sex	Educ	Gsc	Gs	Gv	C	F	Gfp	Gcp	14–17	18–20	21–28	29–39	40–61	F-Value	η
Gf-Pure										6046	6170	6093	5886	5760	8.91	.33
Gf-Pure											6170	6093	5886	5760	10.66	.34
Gf-Pure	*									6072	6157	6090	5886	5752	9.13	.33
Gf-Pure		*								6172	6182	6091	5848	5682	15.21	.42
Gf-Pure			*							6089	6165	6064	5888	5771	9.41	.33
Gf-Pure				*						6091	6156	6060	5893	5779	9.06	.33
Gf-Pure					*					6170	6095	5998	5886	5887	9.69	.34
Gf-Pure	*	*								6210	6167	6087	5846	5669	16.52	.43
Gf-Pure	*	*									6195	6119	5879	5697	17.39	.42
Gf-Pure	*	*	*							6217	6146	6063	5860	5708	14.37	.41
Gf-Pure	*	*	*								6177	6097	5892	5734	13.87	.38
Gf-Pure	*	*		*						6207	6148	6059	5867	5714	14.11	.40
Gf-Pure	*	*		*							6176	6090	5897	5739	13.76	.38
Gf-Pure	*	*	*		*					6236	6106	6001	5865	5837	14.45	.41
Gf-Pure	*	*	*		*						6140	6037	5901	5870	9.07	.32
Gf-Pure	*	*	*		*	*				6267	6102	6002	5853	5829	17.74	.45
Gf-Pure	*	*	*		*	*					6141	6046	5892	5867	10.87	.34
Gf-Pure	*	*	*		*	*	*			6265	6104	6004	5851	5827	17.78	.45
Gf-Pure	*	*	*		*	*	*				6143	6047	5890	5865	10.85	.34
Gf-Pure	*	*	*		*	*	*		*		6140	6030	5814	5736	26.00	.52
Gf-Pure	*	*	*		*	*	*		*	6327	6187	6081	5867	5793	17.36	.42
Gf-Overall	*									5774	6328	6195	5895	5627	5.54	.27
Gf-Overall	*										6328	6195	5895	5627	5.93	.26
Gf-Overall	*	*								6182	6326	6182	5796	5400	9.80	.34
Gf-Overall	*	*									6394	6258	5875	5472	12.12	.37
Gf-Overall	*	*								6197	6278	6126	5827	5488	7.53	.30
Gf-Overall	*	*									6356	6211	5904	5554	9.13	.32
Gf-Overall	*	*		*						6174	6279	6113	5845	5507	7.34	.35
Gf-Overall	*	*		*							6351	6191	5919	5571	8.90	.31
Gf-Overall	*	*	*		*					6283	6191	5993	5837	5767	4.83	.25
Gf-Overall	*	*	*		*						6277	6084	5922	5839	4.33	.22

*	*	*	*			*	Gf-Overall	6353	6174	5996	5791	5737	8.81	.33
*	*					*	Gf-Overall		6283	6116	5889	5828	6.88	.28
*	*	*				*	Gf-Overall	6344	6190	6009	5779	5725	9.36	.34
*	*	*				*	Gf-Overall		6299	6129	5874	5810	7.96	.30
*	*	*	*		*	*	Gf-Overall	6517	6292	6082	5675	5470	22.25	.49
*	*	*	*		*	*	Gf-Overall		6422	6222	5810	5609	19.02	.44

						*	Gc-Pure	3688	3912	3948	4138	4272	34.16	.56
						*	Gc-Pure	3714	3899	3946	4138	4264	32.45	.55
	*	*	*				Gc-Pure	3787	3922	3947	4108	4211	19.09	.46
	*	*	*		*	*	Gc-Pure	3712	3909	3932	4139	4278	36.43	.58
	*	*	*		*	*	Gc-Pure	3711	3904	3931	4141	4282	37.85	.59
					*	*	Gc-Pure	3824	3907	3944	4107	4199	17.72	.44
			*	*	*	*	Gc-Pure	3826	3898	3933	4112	4215	20.18	.47
			*	*	*	*	Gc-Pure	3822	3998	3931	4116	4219	21.59	.48
				*	*	*	Gc-Pure	3816	3915	3946	4099	4205	19.94	.47
					*	*	Gc-Pure	3832	3912	3945	4093	4202	18.87	.46
					*	*	Gc-Pure	3835	3901	3928	4096	4238	24.04	.50
					*	*	Gc-Pure	3774	3877	3927	4129	4277	32.82	.56

	*				*	*	Gc-Overall	1283	1940	1964	2249	2416	19.49	.46
					*	*	Gc-Overall	1683	1912	1948	2166	2208	5.76	.27
	*	*			*	*	Gc-Overall	1993	1880	1910	2187	2268	7.98	.32
	*	*			*	*	Gc-Overall	1677	1882	1903	2198	2277	9.04	.33
				*	*	*	Gc-Overall	1655	1940	1956	2140	2232	8.70	.33
						*	Gc-Overall	1710	1930	1954	2118	2226	7.29	.30
					*	*	Gc-Overall	1716	1901	1909	2127	2318	11.31	.37
						*	Gc-Overall	1539	1831	1905	2223	2430	25.17	.51

	*				*	*	G Omnibus	0064	1311	1276	1087	0852	5.18	.26
	*				*	*	G Omnibus	0260	1214	1257	1089	0801	3.59	.22
	*				*	*	G Omnibus	0914	1264	1241	0904	0408	3.17	.21
	*				*	*	G Omnibus	0249	0734	0961	1372	1430	14.78	.41
	*			*	*	*	G Omnibus	2003	2023	1857	0873	0013	28.08	.54
					*	*	G Omnibus	0950	1151	1112	0976	0617	1.34	.13
						*	G Omnibus	0896	1158	1089	1013	0647	1.36	.14
		*				*	G Omnibus	1027	0984	0854	0996	1153	0.89	.11
						*	G Omnibus	0975	1069	0923	0932	1089	0.59	.09

Table 12.3. (Continued)

Dependent variable	Covariate(s): variable(s) statistically controlled									Means or adjusted means for different age groups						
	Sex	Educ	Gsc	Gs	Gv	C	F	Gfp	Gcp	14–17	18–20	21–28	29–39	40–61	F-Value	η
G Omnibus	*	*	*		*	*	*			1058	1058	0926	0897	1067	0.75	.10
G Omnibus	*	*	*		*	*	*	*		0525	0846	0913	1188	1405	14.81	.41
G Omnibus	*	*	*		*	*	*		*	1431	1278	1084	0673	0519	15.81	.43
G Omnibus	*	*	*		*	*	*	*	*	0898	1047	1031	0969	0940	1.44	.14
Gv-Visual	*	*								6794	7118	7150	6996	6788	7.77	.30
Gv-Visual		*	*							6953	7099	7142	6967	6701	8.13	.32
Gv-Visual	*	*	*	*						6963	7066	7105	6987	6770	5.48	.26
Gv-Visual		*	*							6948	7071	7102	6996	6773	5.70	.27
Gv-Visual	*	*	*					*		6813	6964	7060	7081	6968	5.58	.27
Gsc-Clerical	*	*								4897	5039	5068	4988	4940	2.27	.17
Gsc-Clerical			*							4978	5059	5068	4958	4883	2.93	.17
Gs-All	*	*								6876	7034	7086	6978	6945	1.95	.16
Gs-All										7007	7058	7085	6934	6858	2.73	.19
C-Careful										4844	5015	5001	5058	5032	3.97	.23
C-Careful	*									4838	5017	5001	5058	5034	4.11	.23
C-Careful		*								4875	5018	5000	5049	5013	2.23	.17
C-Careful	*	*								4869	5020	5001	5049	5015	2.31	.16
F-Fluency	*									2960	2968	2986	3040	3028	1.21	.13
F-Fluency		*								2964	2966	2985	3040	3027	1.17	.13
F-Fluency										3014	2973	2984	3024	2995	0.46	.08

NOTE: Although results in these tables are listed to only 4 places, the calculations (done on a Burroughs 5500 computer) carried 11 or 12 digits throughout. We are grateful to W. H. Eichelberger for help in developing computerprograms and to L. G. Humphreys for guidance on theoretical points of the analyses used here.

between approximately 4.74 and 5.61 is significant at the .001 level.[3] To give some indication not only of the significance of difference between means but also of the degree of association between age and the ability dimensions, the correlation ratios (see Cohen, 1965) have been entered in the column at the far right in Table 12.3. For those who prefer to use these values when thinking about the significance of differences, we may note that with the degrees of freedom here at hand a η above about .20 is significant at the .01 level and one above about .25 is significant at the .001 level. With these boundaries and conditions in mind, let us examine the results of Table 12.3 in detail.

First, as regards fluid ability, notice that the differences favoring the young are significant in all analyses, both those in which the Gf-pure measurements were involved and those which utilized the Gf-overall measurements. These differences remain significant after removal of the linear effects associated with the various covariates and when the grouping for the youngest people has been excluded. Indeed, the data suggest that the influences represented by the covariates tend to obscure the basic relationship showing decline in Gf with aging: when sex and education differences are covaried out in the analyses of Gf-pure measurements, the adjusted means show a clear monotonic negative relationship between aging and ability, and the F-value, indicating significance, increases. The negative relationship and significant F remain when other co-variates are added. Most crucially, perhaps, the relationship remains and the differences continue to be highly significant even when the "pure" estimate of the crystallized function is included as a covariate. Thus, the tenor of these results is clear: when seen in averages for performances of many people at each age level, fluid intelligence declines with age in adulthood and this decline is not ascribable to decline in other functions—notably general speediness and visualization—nor is it due to obtained sampling differences in education and sex.

The findings for crystallized intelligence are no less clear. Here the differences favor the older subjects. These remain significant when variance associated with other factors is partialled in covariance analysis. The correlation ratio drops notably—from .55 to .46—when educational differences are partialled, but even in this case the basic form of the relationship is not altered and the differences between means remain highly significant. And the same can be said when the variance associated with the "pure" estimate of fluid intelligence is removed. Hence again the tenor of the results is clear: on the average, older adults perform better than younger adults in tasks depending primarily on crystallized intelligence, and the differences favoring the older subjects are not ascribable to obtained differences in education, sex, fluency, carefulness, speediness, visualization and fluid intelligence.

The measure referred to as "omnibus intelligence" in Tables 12.2 and 12.3 may be likened to the measure obtained with many popular tests of intelligence, such as the Stanford–Binet, Army Alpha, Otis, Lorge–Thorndike, and Wechsler scales, for in these scales, as here, a single score is obtained by adding together scores on several rather diverse kinds of subtests, each accepted as measuring a valid aspect of intelligence. The logical, empirical justification for this practice is the well-confirmed fact of positive manifold among the intercorrelations for ability tests. But according to the theory presented in this paper, this fact is not sufficient to support the contention (albeit implicit) that a functional unity is represented by the measure thus obtained. Specifically, we argue that the measurements obtained in this manner do *not* represent a functional unity with respect to aging in adulthood. Subtests which intercorrelate positively (and are widely accepted as measuring some aspect of intelligence) may require mainly fluid intelligence—which declines with age in adulthood—mainly crystallized intelligence—which increases with age—or one or the other—i.e., a test may allow for use of alternative mechanisms, either Gf or Gc. And the mixtures of subtests in different omnibus tests vary. Hence, depending upon the mixture of subtests and the Gf–Gc composition of the subtests, a measure of omnibus intelligence may show virtually any relationship between aging and change in intelligence.

The omnibus measure obtained in this study was designed to help illustrate these points. It will be noted that it is based upon a wide range of tests said to involve intelligence in some acceptable sense of this word. In looking at the means for different age groupings for this variable, we are viewing the kind of result obtained in many studies of age changes in general intelligence. It is thus particularly interesting that the results obtained here are consistent with those found in several earlier studies. Thus, for example, if the mean differences are considered before sex and education have been statistically controlled, there is suggestion of a very slight decline in intelligence beginning in the late twenties or early thirties—an interpretation suggested by investigations like those of Barnes (1943), Bayley (1957, 1955), Freeman and Flory (1932), Hunter (1942), and others (see Jones, 1959). But if variance associated with speediness is partialled, the differences for the adjusted means turn out to be *not* significant, an outcome that agrees with Lorge's (1936) early hypothesis and results and with Ghiselli's (1957) more recent findings. And the differences between adjusted means remain insignificant when, additionally, education, general fluency, general visualization, etc., are covaried out. But if the variance of the omnibus measure is forced to reflect more surely the differences in fluid intelligence, by covarying out the component measured with Gc-pure, the differences favoring the young are found to be significant: this outcome agrees with results shown in the Foulds and Raven (1948) and Raven (1948) studies, employing the fluid measurements given by the Matrices subtest, and it agrees with the results found by Corsini and Fassett (1953), Cohen (1957), Riegel (1958), and Wechsler (1944) using the fluid measurements obtained with the so-called "performance" subtests of the Wechsler scales. However, if the component measured by the Gf-pure score is partialled out, thus forcing the variance of the residual to reflect primarily differences in crystallized intelligence, then again the differences between age groupings are found to be significant, but this time the differences favor the older subjects. This finding agrees with results reported in the Bayley and Oden (1955), Bradway and Thompson (1962), and Owens (1953), studies wherein were used Gc-saturated measures like the Concept Mastery, Otis and Stanford–Binet.

The results for the other second-order factors may be dealt with more quickly, since they are not of principal concern in this study.

It is interesting, in view of what is known about the structural bases for visual processes (see Weiss, 1959), that the findings here obtained for general visualization suggest that this function improves through the twenties and declines somewhat thereafter. This relationship needs to be studied more intensively.

The differences shown in the analyses of variance on the carefulness function would appear to reflect mainly influences associated with formal education, for when education is partialled in covariance analyses, the differences for the adjusted means prove to be insignificant. Similarly, no clear aging trends are discernible for the Gs and F factors. These outcomes are consistent with findings from our previous study (Horn & Cattell, 1966b) in which it was found that age differences in speediness, carefulness and fluency related most directly to the residual Gf or Gc variance of the primary factors. But, again, these are matters calling for more intensive study in researches specifically designed to provide for test of the several alternative hypotheses.

DISCUSSION

A particularly noteworthy outcome of this study is that it has shown intelligence to both increase and decrease with age—depending upon the definition of intelligence adopted, fluid or crystallized! This allows us to make sense out of seemingly contradictory results from past research. For whereas several studies have shown that intelligence declines with age in adulthood, others have shown that it increases and still others have shown that it remains more or less constant. But the findings of this study suggest that the apparent contradictions are reflections of the fact that varying mixtures of the fluid and crystallized functions were measured in these earlier investigations. When Gf was prominent, decline was noted; when Gc predominated, increase was found and when the two were nearly evenly mixed (and extraneous factors were controlled), neither increase nor decrease was recorded.

Our results illustrate an essential fallacy implicit in the construction of omnibus measures of intelligence. This fallacy is found in the assumption (perhaps often implicit) that positive manifold among intercorrelations for a set of tests necessarily indicates a functional unity. Here it has been shown that some measures which correlate positively nevertheless have quite different relationships to aging. Just because there is a sense in which various tests can be said to require intelligence, just because these tests are positively intercorrelated, just because older children perform better than younger children on these tests and just because these tests have positive correlations with practical criteria said to involve intelligence, it does not follow that the measure obtained by adding scores from these various tests is valid for the purpose of which it is intended. The resulting omnibus score is analogous to a chemical mixture, whereas it would seem that the more useful scientific measure should be analogous to a chemical compound. To be sure, mixtures are often needed: in practical predictions, for example, where both Gf and Gc are apt to have stable beta weights. But the scientist needs to know the composition of his mixtures in terms of the compounds and elements which go into them. The suggestion from this research is that it is particularly worthwhile to recognize the Gf and Gc compounds in the mixtures provided by omnibus, so-called general intelligence tests, and it is probably useful to remain aware of the fact that these mixtures also usually contain traces of the Gv, Gs, and F and C compounds.

The results and theory presented here are in basic agreement with Humphreys's (1962) and McNemar's (1964) criticisms of the trend in recent years towards proliferation, by factor analytic study, of so-called ''primary mental abilities.'' If only slightly different tasks are used to identify a factor—in the limiting case, merely parallel forms of the same test—then that factor is little more than a swollen specific, not an important factor in scientific discourse. However, our position here obviously does not agree with McNemar's implicit argument that general (omnibus) intelligence is the construct of principal scientific value. The combination of Gf and Gc achieved in omnibus intelligence tests will usually give higher predictions of practical criteria than either Gf or Gc used alone. But an understanding of such predictions, and the ability to change procedures in the light of new circumstances, must be based on awareness of the independent contributions of Gf and Gc, as well as Gv, Gs, F and C. As for the verbal-quantitative distinction which Mc-Nemar favors, our position is that this fits at the level of primary factors, where V, CMR, etc., are distinguished from N and R. Both the verbal and quantitative scores of tests which utilize this breakdown indicate scholastic attainment—and thus acculturation—to a large extent, so both contain primarily Gc variance. Important as this variance is for prediction of academic achievements, exclusive dependence on it is probably shortsighted. Particularly over long periods of time, but not alone in such situations, Gf is apt to account for important parts of the variance on practical criteria.

Finally, we should make it very clear that the reasons for decline in Gf and for increase in Gc are not made clearly evident by our results. It is possible—perhaps even likely—that the decline is due to inevitable and unavoidable processes in the physiology of aging. Elsewhere (Horn, 1965a) we have summarized results from a number of studies showing that differences in central nervous system structure of older and younger persons parallel in some respects the differences in this structure of persons known to have suffered brain damage and persons who apparently have not suffered such damage. It was argued on this basis that there is need to look closely for factors which produce small amounts of brain damage in "normal" aging. An accumulation of such small injuries within all persons could account for the results for Gf in this study. But the observed differences are in averages computed over many individuals at each age level, and such averages need not represent any particular individual. It is possible that only a very few people experience decline in Gf with age, but that the amount of decline for these few is substantial so the average Gf score for older persons can be significantly lower than for younger persons. If a few people suffered large brain damage, for example, this could result. But the decline seen in the averages would not point to any process inherent in aging, per se. The apparent increase with age of Gc can be explained in like manner. Our point is: the results obtained here need to be taken seriously, for they have important practical and theoretical implications, but too much should not be read into them.

NOTES

1. The abbreviations and other labels for ability are those commonly used in the U.S.A. Readers not familiar with this jargon should consult French, Ekstrom, and Price (1963) and Guilford (1959).

2. For aid in securing this sample special thanks are due to Julia Bates, Staff Psychologist at the Illinois Soldiers' and Sailors' Children's School; Arthur V. Huffman, State of Illinois Criminologist; Wilson Meeks, Chairman of the Classification Board at Stateville Prison; Stow E. Syman, Sociologist at Pontiac Prison; Bernard Robinson, Sociologist at Dwight Prison; George Levy, Senior Psychologist at the Colorado State Penitentiary; and David J. Wilson, of the Denver Department of Welfare.

3. That is, the Fs are estimated by linear interpolation in Central F tables such as those provided by Graybill, 1961.

REFERENCES

Anderson, J. E., 1941. *The prediction of terminal intelligence from infant and preschool tests. 39th Yearbook Natl. Soc. Stud. Educ.* 1, 385–403.

Balinsky, B., 1964. *An analysis of the mental factors of various age groups from nine to sixty. Genet. Psychol. Monogr.* 23, 191–234.

Barnes, M. W., 1943. *Gains in the ACE Psychological Examination during the freshman–sophomore years. Sch. and Soc.* 57, 250–252.

Bayley, N., 1955. *On the growth of intelligence. Amer. Psychol.* 10, 805–818.

———. 1957. *Data on the growth of intelligence between 16 and 21 years as measured by the Wechsler-Bellevue scale. J. Genet. Psychol.* 90, 3–15.

Bayley, N., and M. H. Oden, 1955. *The maintenance of intellectual ability in gifted adults. J. Geront.* 10, 91–107.

Bradway, K. P., and E. W. Thompson, 1962. *Intelligence at adulthood. J. Educ. Psychol.* 53, 1–14.

Cattell, R. B., 1941. *Some theoretical issues in adult intelligence testing. Psychol. Bull.* 38, 592.

———, 1950. *Personality. New York: McGraw-Hill.*

———, 1957a. *Personality and motivation structure and measurement. New York: World Book.*

———, 1957b. *The IPAT Culture Fair Intelligence Scales. Champaign, Ill.: Institute for Personality and Ability Testing.*

———, 1963. *Theory of fluid and crystallized intelligence: A critical experiment. J. Educ. Psychol.* 54, 1–22.

Cohen, J., 1957. *The factorial structure of the WAIS between early adulthood and old age. J. Consult. Psychol.* 21, 283–290.

———, 1965. *Some statistical issues in psychological research. In: Handbook of clinical psychology, B. B. Wolman (Ed.). New York: McGraw-Hill, 95–121.*

Corsini, R. J., and K. K. Fassett, 1953. *Intelligence and aging. J. Genet. Psychol.* 83, 249–264.

Ferguson, G. A., 1954. On learning and human ability. J. Canad. Psychol. 8, 95–112.

———, 1956. transfer and the abilities of man. J. Canad. Psychol. 10, 121–131.

Foulds, G. A., and J. C. Raven, 1948. Normal changes in mental abilities of adults as age advances. J. Ment. Sci. 94, 133–142.

Freeman, F. N., and C. D. Flory, 1932. Growth in intellectual ability as measured by repeated tests. Monogr. Soc. Res. Child. Develpm. 2, No. 2.

French, J. W., R. B. Ekstrom, and L. A. Price, 1963. Manual for kit of reference tests for cognitive factors. Princeton, N.J.: Educational Testing Service.

Fruchter, B., 1950. Error scores as a measure of carefulness. J. Educ. Psychol. 41, 279–291.

———, 1953. Differences in factor content of rights and wrongs scores. Psychometrika 18, 257–267.

Ghiselli, E. E., 1957. The relationship between intelligence and age among superior adults. J. Genet. Psychol. 90, 131–42.

Graybill, F. A., 1961. An introduction to linear statistical models. New York: Mc-Graw-Hill.

Guilford, J. P. 1959. Three faces of intellect. Amer. Psychol. 14, 469–479.

Hayes, K. J. 1962. Genes, drives and intellect. Psychol. Repts. 10, 299–342.

Hofstaetter, P. R. 1954. The changing composition of intelligence. J. Genet. Psychol. 85, 159–164.

Horn, J. L., 1963. Equations representing combinations of components in scoring psychological variables. Acta Psychologica 21, 184–217.

———, 1964. A note on the estimation of factor scores. Educ. Psychol. Measmt. 24, 525–527.

———, 1965a. Fluid and crystallized intelligence: A factor analytic study of the structure among primary mental abilities. Ph.D. Thesis, University of Illinois.

———, 1965b. An empirical comparison of methods for estimating factor scores. Educ. Psychol. Measmt. 25, 313–322.

Horn, J. L., and R. B. Cattell, 1966a. Refinement and test of the theory of fluid and crystallized general intelligences. J. Educ. Psychol. 57, 253–270.

———, 1966b. Age differences in primary mental ability factors. J. Gerontol. 21, 210–220.

Horn, J. L., and W. C. Miller, 1966. Evidence on the estimation of factor scores. Educ. Psychol. Measmt. 26, 617–622.

Howie, D., 1962. Speed and accuracy. J. Psychol. 8, 111–119.

Humphreys, L. G., 1960. Investigations of the simplex. Psychometrika 25, 313–323.

———, 1962. The organization of human abilities. Amer. Psychol. 17, 475–483.

Hunter, E. C., 1942. Changes in scores of college students on the American Council Psychological Examination at yearly intervals during the college course. J. Educ. Res. 36, 284–291.

Jones, H. E., 1959. Intelligence and problem-solving. In Birren, J. E. (Ed.), Aging and the individual. Chicago: University of Chicago Press.

Jones, H. E., and H. S. Conrad, 1933. The growth and decline of intelligence. Genet. Psychol. Monogr. 13, 223–298.

Lorge, I., 1936. The influence of the test upon the nature of mental decline as a function of age. J. Educ. Psychol. 27, 100–110.

McNemar, Q., 1964. Lost: Our intelligence? Why? Amer. Psychol. 19, 871–882.

Miles, C. C., 1934. The influence of speed and age on intelligence scores of adults. J. Gen. Psychol. 10, 208–210.

Miles, C. C., and W. R. Miles, 1932. The correlation of intelligence scores and chronological age from early to late maturity. Amer. J. Psychol. 44, 44–78.

Owens, W. A., 1953. Age and mental abilities: A longitudinal study. Genet. Psychol. Monogr. 48, 3–54.

Raven, J. C., 1948. The comparative assessment of intellectual ability. Brit. J. Psychol. 39, 12–19.

Riegel, K. F., 1958. Ergebnisse und Probleme der psychologischen Alternsforschung. Vita Humana 1, 52–64.

Schaie, K. W., F. Rosenthal, and R. M. Perlman, 1953. Differential mental deterioration of factorially "pure" functions in later maturity. J. Geront. 8, 191–196.

Shuey, A. M., 1948. Improvement in scores on the American Council Psychological Examination from freshman to senior year. J. Educ. Psychol. 39, 417–426.

Spearman, C., 1927. The abilities of man. New York: Macmillan.

Wechsler, D., 1944. The measurement of adult intelligence. (3rd ed.) Baltimore: Williams and Wilkins.

Weiss, A. D., 1959. Sensory functions. Aging and the individual. In Birren, J. E. (Ed.), Aging and the individual. Chicago: University of Chicago Press.

Welford, A. T., 1958. Aging and human skill. Oxford: Oxford University Press.

13. The Seattle Longitudinal Studies of Adult Intelligence

K. Warner Schaie

MY PERVADING INTEREST over the years has been to understand the bases for the vast individual variations in the life course of adult intellectual abilities. Most of the relevant work has been done in the context of the Seattle Longitudinal Study (SLS), the first testing of which served as my doctoral dissertation at the University of Washington in 1956 and of which the sixth cycle is currently in progress. This work has been done within the framework of Thurstone's conceptualization of psychometric intelligence. Results of our previous efforts have been widely disseminated in the psychological and gerontological literature, in a comprehensive report through Wave 4 of the study[1] and in various analyses of the data from Waves 5 and 6.[2-4] Here I provide a brief overview.

THE SEATTLE LONGITUDINAL STUDY

Our principal data base consists of over 5,000 subjects on whom cognitive and other collateral data were acquired during our six major testing cycles (1956, 1963, 1970, 1977, 1984, and 1991). In addition, there were four related studies dealing with the effects of life complexity on adult cognitive development, the effects of sampling from an expanded population frame, the "aging" of the test battery, and family similarity in intellectual performance. All of our study participants are or were members of a health maintenance organization (HMO; Group Health Cooperative of Puget Sound) in the Seattle, Washington, metropolitan area, or family members of these individuals. The HMO serves governmental subdivisions and labor unions that attract both blue-and white-collar employees as well as a large, individually recruited membership that includes independent crafts people, people in service occupations, and all levels of professionals. Our samples underrepresent the lowest socioeconomic segment of the population but are quite represen-

From *Current Directions in Psychological Sciences* 2 (1993): 171–75. Copyright © 1993 American Psychological Society. Reprinted with the permission of Cambridge University Press.

tative of at least the upper 75% range of the socioeconomic spectrum. Such broad population representation is rare in most studies of psychological individual difference variables.

As is true in other longitudinal studies, we have encountered non-random subject attrition; subjects who return for retest typically outperform those who do not return. Dropout effects increase in magnitude subsequent to the first retest occasion. They are not systematically related to age, but reasons for drop-out do change across the age span. Attrition effects have been reported for each of our study cycles, and we have proposed corrections for the effects of attrition and other confounds on estimates of cognitive age changes.[5]

Throughout our study, we have assessed the primary mental abilities of verbal meaning, spatial ability, reasoning, number skill, and word fluency, identified by Thurstone as accounting for the major share of individual differences in cognitive abilities in children and adolescents. Although these measures have limitations for school-age populations, they have turned out to be rather useful for the description of normal aging in adults. We have also assessed subjects consistently with rigidity-flexibility measures and an attitude scale of social responsibility.

Limited demographic data were collected during the first three cycles, but since 1974 we have taken a more complete personal data inventory, the Life Complexity Inventory (LCI), which includes topics such as major work circumstances (with homemaking defined as a job), friends and social interactions, daily activities, travel experiences, physical environment, and lifelong educational pursuits. Because of our interest in exploring age changes and differences in factor structure, multiple markers for most abilities were included beginning with the fifth (1984) cycle. The primary abilities of verbal comprehension, spatial orientation, inductive reasoning, numerical computation, and perceptual speed are now measured at the latent-construct level.[6,7] Measures of verbal memory, a criterion measure of real-life tasks (the Basic Skills Test from the Educational Testing Service), and a scale for measuring participants' subjective assessment of ability changes between test cycles have also been added. Health history records have been obtained for subjects followed at least 14 years; each outpatient visit or hospital day is coded by diagnosis, and annual counts of illness incidents and illness episodes are calculated.

BRIEF SUMMARY OF RESULTS FROM THE SLS

Throughout the history of the SLS, an effort now extending over 36 years, we have focused on five major questions, which we have attempted to ask with greater clarity and increasingly sophisticated methodologies at each successive stage of the study.[5] This summary reviews these questions and indicates what we have learned from the SLS to date to answer them.

Does Intelligence Change Uniformly through Adulthood, or Are There Different Life-Course Ability Patterns?

Our studies have shown that in adulthood, there is no uniform pattern of age-related changes across all intellectual abilities. Limiting one's concern to an overall index of intellectual ability (IQ) therefore does not suffice to understand age changes and age differences in intellectual functioning for either individuals or groups. Figure 13.1 shows longitudinal age trends on the five primary mental abilities that have been studied throughout our investigations.[2] Our data provide support for the proposition that active or fluid abilities (those that are primarily genetically determined) tend to decline earlier than passive or crystallized abilities (those that are primarily acquired through cultural mechanisms such as schooling and experience). There are, however, important ability-by-age and ability-by-cohort interactions that complicate matters. Our more recent cross-sectional data suggest that women may decline earlier on fluid abilities than on crystallized abilities, whereas men exhibit the opposite pattern. Fluid abilities begin to decline earlier, but crystallized abilities show steeper decrement than fluid abilities once the late 70s are reached.[1,3,5] Age changes in perceptual speed begin in young adulthood, and group averages show a virtually linear decrement.[8]

Although cohort-related differences in the rate and magnitude of age changes in intelligence remained fairly linear for cohorts entering old age during the first three cycles in our study (until 1970), they have since shown substantial shifts. For example, scores are declining less rapidly now in old age. At the same time, younger groups are scoring lower on tests at the same ages, as we begin to study members of the baby-boom generation. Patterns of socialization unique to a given sex role within a specific historical period may also be major determinants for the pattern of change in abilities. When age changes are decomposed into those due to loss in accuracy and those due to loss in speed, men show greater loss in speed, while women lose more in accuracy.

Cross-sectional analyses of the stability of correlations among the primary mental abilities have recently been conducted over a wide age range. The pattern of factor loadings remains similar across adulthood; however, magnitudes of factor loading do change, indicating that some tests may not mea-

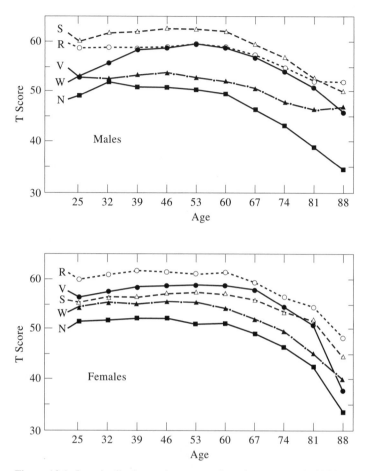

Figure 13.1. Longitudinal age changes on the primary mental abilities, by gender, based on observed changes over 7-year intervals. S = spatial orientation; R = inductive reasoning; W = word fluency; V = verbal meaning; N = number skill. *T* scores are standard scores with mean of 50 and standard deviation of 10. From Schaie.[1] Reprinted by permission.

sure the same ability with equal efficiency at all stages of the life course.[7] Furthermore, the relevance of these findings to everyday behavior has been established by demonstrating substantial relationships between the psychometric abilities and real-life tasks.[9]

At What Age Is There a Reliably Detectable Age Decrement in Ability, and What Is the Magnitude of That Decrement?

Data collected during the first three SLS cycles indicated that average age decrements in psychometric abilities could not be confirmed reliably prior to age 60, but that reliable average decrement is indeed found for all abilities by age 74. More recently, however, we have found small but statistically significant average decrement for some, but not all, cohorts in their 50s. However, even at age 81, fewer than half of all observed individuals showed reliable decrements over the preceding 7 years. Average decrement before age 60 amounts to less than two tenths of a standard deviation, but by age 81, average decrement increases to approximately one standard deviation for most abilities.[1] The magnitude of decrement, however, is significantly reduced when age changes in perceptual speed are removed.[8] Data from the SLS have provided a normative base to determine at what ages declines reach practically significant levels relevant to public policy issues such as mandatory retirement and age discrimination in employment or to determine what proportion of the population can live independently in the community.

What Are the Patterns of Generational Differences, and What Is Their Magnitude?

Controversy remains with regard to the complex assumptions required for the estimation of generational effects. Nevertheless, results from the SLS have demonstrated conclusively the prevalence of substantial generational (cohort) differences in psychometric abilities.[1,3] These cohort trends differ in magnitude and direction by ability and therefore cannot be determined from composite IQ indices. On the one hand, for some abilities, later-born groups have attained successively higher scores at the same ages; that is, positive cohort gradients have been observed for inductive reasoning, verbal meaning, and spatial orientation. On the other hand, number skill peaked with the 1924 birth cohort and has progressively declined thereafter (i.e., has a negative cohort gradient). More recently born cohorts are also at a disadvantage when compared with prior cohorts on word fluency. These findings are similar to those observed for the Scholastic Aptitude Test (SAT) scores. As the baby boomers enter adulthood, their scores continue the negative cohort trends observed in adolescence. From these findings, we conclude that cross-sectional studies used to model age change overestimate age-related decline prior to the 60s for those variables that show positive cohort gradients and underestimate such declines for variables with negative cohort gradients (e.g., for perceptual speed).[8]

The work on generational differences in abilities among unrelated individuals has recently been supplemented by studying family members of our longitudinal-study participants. Most work in developmental behavior genetics has been conducted by means of twin studies and family studies of parents and offspring and nontwin siblings. In the past, family studies employed parents and their young offspring and young sibs; our study is the first effort to explore systematic family similarity through adulthood, and to test for stability of such similarity over time.[4]

Substantial family similarity of an average magnitude of about .25 was found for virtually all mental abilities and measures of flexibility. The similarities were found for parents and their offspring (adult children) and for siblings (brothers and sisters). The two exceptions to this finding were for the attitude measure of social responsibility and for a measure of perceptual speed, neither of which seems to show heritable variance. The magnitude of parent–offspring and sibling similarity differed for different abilities, and the overall similarity was somewhat greater for parent–offspring than for sibling pairs. The sizes of the correlations were also comparable to those found between young adults and their children in other studies.

We examined whether the degree of similarity in ability between parents and their adult children differed for younger and older parents. Because of changes in society, it has been argued that there ought to be a reduction in family similarity for younger as compared with older parent–offspring pairs. The possible reduction in shared environmental influence is thought to be due to increased outside influences in the more recent generation. However, this proposition could be supported only for reasoning and overall IQ, for which the old and middle generations showed somewhat greater similarity with their adult children than the younger generation did. For other abilities, we found stability, and for some abilities (verbal meaning and spatial orientation), an increase in family similarity for more recent generations. Correlations of the performance of offspring or siblings with the subjects who had been in the longitudinal study remained similar over 7, 14, and 21 years, providing additional strong evidence for stability of family similarity over time and age.[4]

What Accounts for Individual Differences in Age-Related Change in Adulthood?

A unique contribution of a longitudinal study such as ours is the investigation of individual differences in antecedent variables that lead to early decrement for some persons and maintenance of high levels of functioning for others well into very advanced age. We have implicated a number of factors that account for individual differences in rate of cognitive change, and some of these factors have been shown to be amenable to experimental intervention. Although controlled experiments are required to confirm the causality of antecedent variables, an understanding of temporal priority provides important clues that then form the basis of subsequent interventions. Variables thus far implicated in reducing the risk of cognitive decline in old age include (a) absence of cardiovascular and other chronic diseases, (b) favorable environment mediated by high socioeconomic status, (c) involvement in a complex and intellectually stimulating environment, (d) flexible personality style at mid-life, (e) high cognitive status of spouse, and (f) maintenance of high levels of perceptual processing speed.

Can Intellectual Decline with Increasing Age Be Reversed by Educational Intervention?

Because longitudinal studies permit tracking individual levels over time, we were able to design interventions that remediate known intellectual decline and reduce the effects of cohort differences in individuals who have remained stable in their own performance over time but who have become disadvantaged compared with younger persons. The cognitive training studies conducted with our longitudinal subjects suggest that observed decline in many community-dwelling older people is likely to be a function of disuse and is often reversible. Indeed, approximately two thirds of our experimental subjects showed significant improvement, and about 40% of those who had declined significantly over 14 years were returned to their predecline level.[10] We have shown also that we did not simply train the test, but rather trained at the ability (latent construct) level, and that the training did not disturb the ability structure. Training gains represent primarily increased accuracy for men, but a mix of improvement in accuracy and speed for women.[10] In our recent follow-up, we have shown that trained subjects remained at a significant advantage over control subjects even after 7 years, and we have replicated the effects of initial training with a new cohort.

Some critics have expressed surprise that our cognitive interventions have been more successful than those in other studies. We believe that this success is related to more careful study design, extensive work in the development of training materials, and more careful outcome assessment than is possible in more limited intervention studies.

SUMMARY

The SLS has charted the course of selected psychometric abilities from young adulthood through old age and has investigated individual differences and differential patterns of change. We not only have been concerned with demonstrating the presence or absence of age-related changes and difference, but have provided data on the magnitude and relative importance of the life-course changes we have been studying. We have been able to identify contextual, health, and personality variables that offer explanations for differential change and that provide a basis for possible interventions. Most recently, we have begun to study age changes and differences in cognitive factor structure, have conducted analyses of the relative effect of speed and accuracy in age decline and training gain, and have investigated the relevance of cognitive training to real-life tasks. Within the context of the SLS, we have also studied cognitive similarity within parent–offspring and sibling pairs, and we have designed cognitive interventions that have been successful in remediating carefully determined declines and in improving the cognitive functions of older persons who have remained stable.

REFERENCES

1. K. W. Schaie, *The Seattle Longitudinal Study: A twenty-one year exploration of psychometric intelligence in adulthood, in* Longitudinal Studies of Adult Psychological Development, *K. W. Schaie, Ed. (Guilford Press, New York, 1983).*
2. K. W. Schaie, *The hazards of cognitive aging, Gerontologist, 29, 484–493 (1989).*
3. K. W. Schaie, *Intellectual development in adulthood, in* Handbook of the Psychology of Aging, *3rd ed., J. E. Birren and K. W. Schaie, Eds. (Academic Press, New York, 1990).*
4. K. W. Schaie, R. Plomin, S. L. Willis, A. Gruber-Baldini, and R. Dutta, *Natural cohorts: Family similarity in adult cognition, in* Psychology and Aging: Nebraska Symposium on Motivation, 1991, *T. Sonderegger, Ed. (University of Nebraska Press, Lincoln, 1992).*
5. K. W. Schaie, *Internal validity threats in studies of adult cognitive development, in* Cognitive Development in Adulthood: Progress in Cognitive Development

Research, *M. L. Howe and C. J. Brainard, Eds. (Springer-Verlag, New York, 1988)*.

6. *K. W. Schaie, R. Dutta, and S. L. Willis, The relationship between rigidity-flexibility and cognitive abilities in adulthood,* Psychology and Aging, 6, *371–383 (1991)*.

7. *K. W. Schaie, S. L. Willis, G. Jay, and H. Chipuer, Structural invariance of cognitive abilities across the adult life span: A cross-sectional study,* Developmental Psychology, 25, *652–662 (1989)*.

8. *K. W. Schaie, Perceptual speed in adulthood: Cross-sectional and longitudinal studies,* Psychology and Aging, *4, 443–453 (1989)*.

9. *S. L. Willis and K. W. Schaie, Practical intelligence in later adulthood, in* Practical Intelligence: Origins of Competence in the Everyday World, *R. J. Sternberg and R. K. Wagner, Eds. (Cambridge University Press, New York, 1986)*.

10. *K. W. Schaie and S. L. Willis, Can intellectual decline in the elderly be reversed?* Developmental Psychology, *22, 223–232 (1986)*.

14. Memory Storage and Aging

David Schonfield and Betty-Anne Robertson

Of LEARNING'S THREE STAGES —acquisition, retention, and remembering (Woodworth, 1938)—it is the last, that of remembering, which is necessarily the dependent variable from which conclusions are drawn concerning the influence of independent variables operating at any of the three stages. If a loss at the remembering stage is demonstrated, it can be interpreted as due to imperfect acquisition, interference in retention, or deficient recollection. When remembering is tested in a situation where acquisition is likely to have been imperfect, or where there are good grounds for assuming interference, there is no need for an additional hypothesis of special impediments operating at the remembering stage itself. The well-established deficits of older subjects in the remembering of a variety of materials have generally been interpreted in just such a manner. Both Jerome (1959) and Welford (1958) in their recent surveys concluded that older people learn more slowly and are perhaps more liable to interference than the young, but that experiments provide no indication of a special incapacity among the aged in the remembering of acquired information or skills.

The evidence that increasing age results in deficiencies in acquisition and retention does not exclude, however, the possibility that there are additional problems for older people at the remembering stage. In fact, the results of several investigations can be interpreted as suggestive of an age-linked impairment in remembering. The well-known difficulty of older groups in the performance of paced tasks (Canestrari, 1963) indicates their need for additional time in retrieving from storage. The proneness of the aged to errors of omission rather than commission (Korchin & Basowitz, 1957) shows a similar difficulty in retrieving from storage. Broadbent and Heron's (1962) demonstration that older subjects show a disproportionate loss in tasks which involve a shift of attention could be considered an example of the difficulty in reinstating a previous memory into the focus of attention. The same ex-

From the *Canadian Journal of Experimental Psychology* 20 (1966): 228–36. Copyright © 1966 by The Division of Life Sciences, University of Toronto, Scarborough Campus. Reprinted by permission.

planation could cover Talland's (1959) experiments with the aged on change of set. These investigations thus point to a particular kind of impairment at the remembering stage. Retrieving from storage would seem to constitute a special difficulty for older groups.

The implication of the previous discussion is that a test of memory which does not require retrieval from storage will show less of a loss with age than a test which involves retrieval. The psychological difference between a voluntary recall method and a recognition method of testing memory seems to fit the distinction between the presence and absence of the requirement of retrieving from storage. As Deese (1963) says, "In recall a subject must produce a set of responses, whereas in recognition the set of responses is produced for him." The prediction would be, therefore, that the aged would have far superior scores on a recognition than on a voluntary recall test, since the act of recognition demands the matching of a stimulus to a stored trace, but does not involve retrieval as such. Of course, recognizing a symbol among a set as the one previously presented almost invariably results in higher scores than requiring a subject to recall a symbol voluntarily. The prediction here is that among older groups the difference between recognition and recall scores will be greater than among younger groups. Further, by comparing the recall scores of both older and younger subjects with their own recognition scores the methodological problem of equating acquisition in different age groups is obviated.

METHOD

Subjects

Ss used in this study were 134 persons aged between 20 and 75 years with a minimum of 20 Ss in each decade between 20 and 60 and over 60 years of age. Approximately half of the Ss were male and half female, but there were more males below 40 and more females over 40 years old. The Ss in the younger age groups were, or had been, attending university. Older age groups consisted of professional people, wives of professionals, and parents or grandparents of university students.

Material

Two lists—A and B—each of 24 monosyllabic or bisyllabic nouns or adjectives constituted the memory tasks. The words were chosen on the basis of frequency on the Thorndike-Lorge count. Each list contained 8 words of high frequency (100 per million), 8 of medium frequency (1 per million). The lists were matched for the number of words beginning with the same letter; thus 4 words beginning with the letter ''b'' were in one list and 4 beginning with ''c'' were in the other. Consecutive words began with different letters.

The two recognition lists consisted of the 24 words from lists A or B each within a group of 4 other words. These additional words were chosen from those given by Palermo and Jenkins (1964) or Russell and Jenkins (1954) as having high (over 100), medium (35–99), low (2–34), and zero association value with the original learning word.

Procedure

The instructions to the S were as follows: ''I am going to show you a list of words one at a time. As soon as the word appears on the screen I want you to say the word aloud once. Try to remember as many words as you can. Do not worry if you forget some of them since no one has remembered all the words.''

The words in a list were presented consecutively on a screen, each for 4 sec., by means of a Kodak Carousel projector. Letters were 2 in. high and the S sat 2 ft. from the screen. Immediately after S had pronounced the last word on the list he was either instructed to say as many of the words as he could recall in any order he wished, or was given the recognition list and told to underline the one word in any group of 5 which he had previously seen on the screen. The recognition and recall tests were untimed.

Ss were tested individually for recognition on one list and recall on the other. Approximately half of the Ss in each group performed the recognition task first, the others the recall task first. Similarly, approximately half the Ss were presented with list A for recognition and with list B for recall, while the remainder had the recognition test on list B and recall test on list A.

In order to provide information on the effect of recall on recognition of the same list and the effect of recognition on the recall of the same list, Ss were given a subsidiary recognition test on list A immediately after their recall of list A. Similarly, after recognition on list A they were given a subsidiary recall test on list A. The same procedure was adopted after recall or recognition of list B.

Table 14.1. Mean Recognition and Recall Scores by List

	Recognition	Recall
List A	$\overline{X} = 19.58$	$\overline{X} = 11.11$
	$\sigma = 2.82$	$\sigma = 3.10$
List B	$\overline{X} = 20.06$	$\overline{X} = 10.80$
	$\sigma = 2.48$	$\sigma = 3.30$
	$t = 1.04$	$t = .55$
	$p > .10$	$p > .10$

RESULTS

Table 14.1 shows the mean recognition scores and voluntary recall scores for lists A and B. It can be seen that the recognition means for the two lists are almost identical, as are the voluntary recall means. The slightly lower recognition score on list A is balanced by the slightly lower voluntary recall score for list B. The differences are obviously due to chance factors and not significant statistically. It can, therefore, be concluded that the attempt to equalize the level of learning difficulty of the two lists was successful.

Table 14.2 compares the mean recognition score when recognition precedes and when it follows voluntary recall on the alternate list; the mean recall scores of subjects tested prior to recognition on the alternate list is also compared to the mean on recall following alternate list recognition. The results show that the two recognition scores are almost identical as are the two recall scores. Neither positive nor negative transfer occurs between the first and second memory tests whether recall or whether recognition comes first. It seems, therefore, justifiable to combine all of the recognition results—

Table 14.2. Mean Recognition and Recall Scores by Order of Presentation

	Recognition	Recall
First	$\overline{X} = 19.87$	$\overline{X} = 11.10$
	$\sigma = 2.57$	$\sigma = 3.55$
Second	$\overline{X} = 19.76$	$\overline{X} = 10.78$
	$\sigma = 2.78$	$\sigma = 3.66$
	$t = .23$	$t = .52$
	$p > .10$	$p > .10$

Table 14.3. Mean Recognition, Recall, and Recognition minus Recall Scores by Age

Age range	N	Recognition	Recall	Recognition minus recall
20–29	36	20.01	13.78	6.42
30–39	23	19.48	12.30	7.17
40–49	32	19.53	10.01	9.47
50–59	21	19.90	9.57	10.24
60 +	22	20.09	7.50	12.59

whether from list A or B and whether recognition precedes or follows recall. This also applies to the combination of all the voluntary recall results.

Table 14.3 gives the mean recognition and voluntary recall scores by age groups. The results show little difference between age groups on recognition scores, but demonstrate a steady decline with age on the voluntary recall scores. The difference between recognition and recall scores shown in the final column has a rho correlation with age groups of $+1.00$. The Pearson product-moment correlation between recognition-minus-recall scores and age is $+.66$, which is significant at beyond the .001 level.

The results of the subsidiary experiment are given in Table 14.4. This table compares recognition scores before and after recall on the *same* list, as well as recall scores before and after recognition on the *same* list. The figures show that recognition is not aided by prior recall on the same list, and, surprisingly, recall may be hindered by recognition on the same list.

Table 14.4. Recognition before and after Recall on the Same List and Recall before and after Recognition on the Same List

	List A	List B
	Recognition	
Before recall	$\overline{X} = 19.58$	$\overline{X} = 20.06$
After recall	$\overline{X} = 19.40$	$\overline{X} = 19.64$
	$t = 0.32$	$t = 0.93$
	$p > 0.10$	$p > 0.10$
	Recall	
Before recognition	$\overline{X} = 11.11$	$\overline{X} = 10.80$
After recognition	$\overline{X} = 9.19$	$\overline{X} = 10.72$
	$t = 2.78$	$t = 0.12$
	$p < 0.01$	$p > 0.10$

DISCUSSION

The prediction that the difference between recognition and recall scores is greater in older than younger subjects is clearly supported by the experimental results. There is no apparent deterioration with age in recognition, whereas on voluntary recall there is a loss of almost 50 per cent between the scores of this group of younger and older people. The subjects performing this experiment were admittedly of superior intelligence level, but there is no obvious reason why the conclusions cannot be generalized to other intelligence levels. There is some evidence (Gilbert, 1935) that differences between age groups of high general ability are less than differences at lower levels. It might, therefore, be expected that recognition scores of those at lower intelligence levels would show some loss, although the relative superiority of recognition compared to recall should be maintained. Gilbert (1935), who included recall and recognition types of tests in her battery, found a greater loss in recall than in recognition, but some loss in both.

It is difficult to envisage how these findings can be explained on the basis of age differences operating at either the acquisition or retention stage of learning. Any such differences in these two stages should manifest themselves to some degree in the recognition scores as much as in the recall scores. The fact that the recognition scores show no loss with age, although surprising, indicates that the results must be explained by factors operating at the time of remembering.

It might be suggested that the 24 words in a list provide a spurious upper limit for recognition scores in the younger groups. Were this true the recognition scores in for the young would not portray their real potential in recognition, while the parallel scores for older groups might show their top capacity. The choice of 24 words in each list was based on a pilot study where no one managed to recognize 24 words. Unfortunately, the maximum recognition score of 24 was reached by 9 of the 134 subjects participating in the present experiment. However, these 9 were evenly distributed among age groups—2 in each decade under 60 and one older than 60 years of age. Consequently, the increase with age in recognition-minus-recall scores cannot be attributed to the inability of the young, as opposed to the old, to reach their ceiling score.

The findings are, therefore, interpreted as supporting the hypothesis that aging causes special difficulties in retrieving memories from storage. Voluntary recall, which involves retrieval, shows a loss with age, whereas recognition, which does not require the retrieval, shows no such deterioration.

It is worth emphasizing that the original prediction was not that recognition would show no loss; it was that recognition scores would not deteriorate to the same extent as recall scores. A repetition of the present experiment which showed some drop in older subjects' recognition scores would not necessarily constitute evidence against the present hypothesis.

The tripartite division of the learning process into acquisition, retention, and remembering might be thought to imply that retrieval is confined to the third stage—that of remembering. However, stages of learning are not paralleled by the psychological mechanisms involved. The acquisition stage of learning normally involves not only an acquisition mechanism, but also a retrieval mechanism. In most learning situations new learning has to be continuously placed in and brought out of storage. A difficulty of older people in retrieving from storage might, therefore, be the main cause of their inefficiency during this so-called acquisition stage. This suggestion is not quite the same as that of other investigators who consider that limitations in immediate memory are the primary cause of learning deficiencies among the aged. The immediate memory span, in fact, shows little if any deterioration with age (Gilbert, 1941; Bromley, 1958). It is, therefore, increased liability of short-term memory to interference which is usually hypothesized as the cause of special age-linked deterioration in acquisition. The suggestion derived from the present experiment is rather more specific and does not involve interference of the usual proactive or retroactive varieties. The special consequences of interference among the aged do not result from information having to be placed in storage, or from effects taking place during storage. It is the problem of reclamation that constitutes the difficulty.

Inglis (1965), on the basis of his experiments with dichotic stimulation, has emphasized another facet of immediate memory as a cause of poorer acquisition among older persons. He and his colleagues (Inglis & Caird, 1963; Inglis & Mackay, 1963) have demonstrated that there is no significant loss with age in the recall of first half-spans but reproduction of the second half-span by older subjects shows progressively greater difficulty. Inglis (1965) interprets his findings as due to an increase in the rate of trace decay as well as increased sensitivity to interference. However, since Broadbent's (1958) distinction between S and P systems is rejected by Inglis, there is no easy explanation for the absence of loss in digits recalled first when similar decay and interference should be operating. According to Inglis's suggested analysis, when 3 digits are presented to each ear, individual digits of the half-span recalled first are held in storage for 3 seconds, while digits recalled last are held for 6 seconds. The greater number of errors in the recall of the final half-span is thus said to be due to the fact that this material is in a holding system for twice as long as material recalled first. By the same argument, however, the first half-span of a 12-digit series presented dichotically should show the same loss as the second half-span of a 6-digit series. But Inglis (1965) emphasized that age differences were found in the second and not in the first half-spans.

In the present experiment the difficulty of the aged in retrieval is detected by a loss or absence of response, but this should not be considered the only way in which such a difficulty might manifest itself. The production of a correct response with a considerably longer latency might be thought of as an alternative manifestation of the difficulty of access to storage. Disproportionate loss of speed, according to the present formulation, should not be expected when there is a prior set for just one response. In such a situation the subject is unlikely to have to retrieve anything from storage, the response being already present at the focus of attention. However, repeated access to storage is required when the subject must execute a series of different responses, and in these cases exaggerated slowness by the aged would be anticipated. The experimental evidence, which shows a relatively small increase with age in simple reaction time (Welford, 1959) but a disproportionate increase in serial and choice reaction times (Singleton, 1955; Goldfarb, 1941), is in accordance with this formulation.

There would appear to be two main strategies which older people utilize in order to overcome their difficulty in retrieval. The first is to prepare for future action by having the necessary information at the focus of attention before the need for it arises. This could be achieved through prior rehearsal. The characteristic care and caution of the aged, observed in many experimental investigations (Welford, 1958), would permit such rehearsal and might be thought of as the organism's attempt to adjust to future retrieval problems. A second strategy employed in endeavouring to reduce the time required for access to storage is to increase the number of stimulus cues which lead to a particular stored item. The tendency of older people to utilize extra cues—visual, auditory, and kinesthetic—has been noticed in a number of investigations (Welford, 1958). The anecdotal evidence that the aged can recall with ease material acquired early in life may be due in part to an accretion of such stimulus cues. If the difficulty in retrieval can be considered as the result of increased "noise" in the aging nervous system (Gregory, 1957), the extra cues serve the function of adding to the signal to noise ratio. Although not specifically concerned with age differences, Miller, Galanter, and Pribram (1960) put forward essentially the same argument. They state that plans for remembering often involve an increase in the number of associations and these serve the function of overcoming the problem of retrieval.

REFERENCES

Broadbent, D. E. Perception and communication. *London, Pergamon, 1958.*

Broadbent, D. E., & Heron, A. *Effects of a subsidiary task on performance involving immediate memory by younger and older men. Brit. J. Psychol.,* 1962, 53, *189–98.*

Bromley, D. B. *Some effects of age on short-term learning and remembering.* J. Gerontol., *1958, 13, 398–406.*

Canestrari, R. E. *Paced and self paced learning in young and elderly adults.* J. Gerontol., *1963, 18, 165–168.*

Deese, J. *Comments on Professor Murdock's paper. In C. N. Cofer & B. S. Musgrave, eds.,* Verbal behavior and learning. *New York, McGraw-Hill, 1963.*

Gilbert, Jeanne G. *Mental efficiency in senescence.* Arch. Psychol., *No. 188, 1935.*
———. *Memory losses in senescence.* J. Abnorm. Soc. Psychol., *1941, 36, 73–86.*

Goldfarb, W. *An investigation of reaction time in older adults and its relationship to certain observed mental test patterns.* Teachers' College Contribution to Education, *No. 831. New York, Columbia Univ., 1941.*

Gregory, R. L. *Increase in "neurological noise" as a factor in ageing. In* Proc. 4th Cong. Internat. Ass. Gerontol. *(Merano), 1957, 1, 314–24.*

Inglis, J. *Immediate memory, age and brain function. In A. T. Welford & J. E.*
Birren, eds., Behavior, aging and the nervous system. *Illinois, Thomas, 1965.*

Inglis, J., & Caird, W. K. *Age differences in successive responses to simultaneous stimulation.* Canad. J. Psychol., *1963, 17, 98–105.*

Inglis, J., & Mackay, H. A. *The effects of age on a short-term auditory storage process. Paper read at the* Sixth International Congress of Gerontology, *Copenhagen, 1963.*

Jerome, E. *Age and learning—experimental studies. In J. E. Birren, ed.,* Hand-book of aging and the individual. *Chicago, University Chicago Press, 1959.*

Korchin, S. J., & Basowitz, H. *Age differences in verbal learning.* J. Abnorm. Soc. Psychol., *1957, 54, 64–69.*

Miller, G. A., Galanter, T., & Pribram, K. H. *Plans and the structure of behavior. New York, Henry Holt, 1960.*

Palermo, D. S., & Jenkins, J. J. *Word association norms grade school through college. Minneapolis, University Minnesota Press, 1964.*

Russell, W. A., & Jenkins, J. J. *The complete Minnesota norms for responses to 100 words from the Kent-Rosanoff word association test. Studies on the role of language behavior.* Tech. Rep. No. 11, *August, 1954. Minneapolis, University Minnesota Press.*

Singleton, W. T. *Age and performance timing on simple skills. In R. E. Turnbridge, ed.,* Old age in the modern world. *London, Livingstone, 1955.*

Talland, G. A. Age and the effect of anticipatory set on accuracy of perception. J. Gerontol., *1959,* 14, *202–7.*

Welford, A. T. Aging and human skill. *London, Oxford University Press, 1958.*

———*Psychomotor performance. In J. E. Birren, ed.,* Handbook of aging and the individual. *Chicago, University Chicago Press, 1959.*

Woodworth, R. S. Experimental psychology. *New York, Henry Holt, 1938.*

15. Age Differences in Recall and Recognition

Fergus I. M. Craik and Joan M. McDowd

THE LITERATURE ON AGE differences in human memory includes a large number of studies comparing the performance of young and old adults on tests of recall and recognition memory. The results of these studies have consistently shown an age decrement in recall performance (see Botwinick, 1978; Burke & Light, 1981; and Craik, 1977; for reviews), but they have been mixed with regard to recognition memory performance. Some studies have shown a significant age decrement in recognition (e.g., Erber, 1974; Gordon & Clark, 1974; White & Cunningham, 1982), whereas other studies have shown no such decrement (e.g., Schonfield & Robertson, 1966). However, the generalization can be made that age decrements are relatively smaller in tests of recognition memory than in tests of recall (Botwinick & Storandt, 1980; Craik, 1977; Schonfield & Robertson, 1966).

This conclusion conceals two difficult methodological issues, however. The first is that younger and older people may adopt different guessing strategies in tests of recognition memory; the clear implication is that some bias-free measure of recognition, such as d', should be used (White & Cunningham, 1982). The second problem concerns the validity of comparing recall and recognition scores. Are the scales really comparable? For example, does a 20 % difference in recall performance mean the same thing as a 20% difference in recognition memory performance? This second problem is clearly compounded by the first. How is it possible to compare age differences in percent recalled with age differences in recognition memory measured by d'?

Arenberg (1985) has recently proposed an ingenious solution to this dilemma. He bypassed the problem of a common metric for the two retrieval tests by calculating the regression of recall on recognition for each age group separately, and then comparing the slopes of the regression lines for the different age groups. Arenberg used the mean number of words recalled from

Reprinted by permission from *The Journal of Experimental Psychology: Learning, Memory and Cognition* 13, no. 3 (1987): 474–79. Copyright © 1987 by the American Psychological Association.

word lists as the measure of recall performance, and A' (a nonparametric measure of sensitivity based on signal detection theory) as the measure of recognition memory. The argument is that if older people perform relatively poorly on recall tests compared with recognition tests, the slope of recall on recognition should be flatter for them. That is, for a given increment in recognition memory, older people should show a smaller increment in recall performance than that shown by younger subjects. In fact, Arenberg demonstrated that the slope of recall on recognition declined fairly systematically decade by decade from subjects in their 20s to people in their 70s and 80s. The conclusion that aging affects recall performance more than it affects recognition performance thus rests on a firmer base. Some questions still surround Arenberg's suggested method, however, and the problem of comparing the two retrieval tasks will be raised again in the Results section of the present article.

Most researchers have attributed the differential age decrements in recall and recognition to the different retrieval demands of the two tasks (Arenberg, 1973; Burke & Light, 1981; Craik, 1977; Schonfield & Robertson, 1966). It has been suggested that recall involves more effortful processing than does recognition, and that older people are relatively penalized when such processing is required (Hasher & Zacks, 1979). In a variant of this position, Craik (1983) suggested that various retrieval tasks could be ordered with respect to the amount of "self-initiated processing" involved, that recall requires more self-initiated processing than recognition, and that older people are less able than their young counterparts to carry out such operations. That is, in a recognition test much of the empirical information is re-presented to the participant; appropriate mental operations are therefore driven largely by the external stimuli associated with the task itself. In recall, by comparison, very few retrieval cues are provided and the participant must necessarily initiate appropriate mental operations in a more effortful manner. Craik's suggestion was that older people are relatively unimpaired on tasks involving either "automatic" processing (Hasher & Zacks, 1979) or a large degree of environmental support but show an age-related decrement in performance on tasks (like free recall) in which these features are absent. In turn, the greater impairment of self-initiated processing shown by older people may result from a reduction in available processing resources with increasing age (Craik, 1983; Craik & Byrd, 1982; Rabinowitz, Craik & Ackerman, 1982).

However, there is an alternative account of the differential age-related losses in recall and recognition. It is well established that age decrements in performance are typically greater with more difficult or complex tasks (Cerella, Poon & Williams, 1980; Welford, 1958), therefore the greater drop with age on recall tasks may simply reflect the fact that recall is usually a more difficult task than recognition. For example, Botwinick (1978) suggested that "perhaps it is not retrieval at all which accounts for the disparity among the age patterns (in recall and recognition), but simply the relative difficulty of the two tasks" (p. 342). Similarly, Salthouse (1982) has written that "at the present time it simply is not possible to determine whether older adults are at a greater disadvantage in recall tasks than in recognition tasks because the former have a greater retrieval component than the latter, or because the former is more difficult than the latter" (p. 142).

But are these two accounts necessarily different? If recall requires a greater involvement of effortful, self-initiated processes than does recognition, presumably recall will appear to be the more "difficult" task, both phenomenologically and in terms of performance level. Rather than attempting to evaluate the relative merits of the "retrieval type" and "task difficulties" hypotheses, it may be more useful to establish further empirical relations to illuminate the problem, and that is the purpose of the present study. Specifically, one way of assessing the relative difficulty (in the sense of resource requirements) of recall and recognition tests is to compare their effects on a secondary task performed simultaneously with the retrieval task. If recall requires more resources than recognition, this difference should be apparent as a greater decrement in the secondary task when recall is the primary task than when recognition is the primary task. If older people have a smaller pool of processing resources, as was hypothesized by Craik and his colleagues, it should also follow that they should show a greater decrement in secondary task performance than their younger counterparts in such a study. This result was reported by Macht and Buschke (1983).

Putting these various arguments and findings together, we should find that if younger and older people perform recall and recognition tasks in the secondary task paradigm, (a) older participants should exhibit greater losses in secondary task performance than the younger participants (Macht & Buschke, 1983), (b) all participants should show greater losses with recall than with recognition, but (c) older people should suffer differentially greater losses than their younger counterparts on recall as opposed to recognition tasks. That is, there should be an interaction between age and type of retrieval task in secondary task costs.

METHOD

In outline, subjects performed a continuous reaction time (RT) task either alone or while simultaneously retrieving words in tests of recognition or of cued recall. The continuous RT task carried out alone gave a baseline level of performance against which to measure the cost of performing the retrieval tasks. The continuous RT task (here termed the secondary task) was a four-choice task in which one of four classes of alphanumeric characters was shown visually, and the subject then pressed the corresponding response key as rapidly as possible. A correct response caused the next visual character to be displayed immediately. The primary task, under dual-task conditions, consisted of either cued recall or recognition memory. In all cases, lists of 12 words were first presented visually to be learned by subjects under conditions of full attention; a descriptive phrase was presented along with each word. In the cued-recall task, the phrases were re-presented auditorily as cues; in the recognition task, the words themselves were re-presented auditorily, along with distractor words. It should be stressed that the continuous RT task was performed concurrently during retrieval only; the words and phrases for the memory tasks were presented alone in the encoding phase.

An attempt was made to equate performance levels in the cued-recall and recognition tasks; this was accomplished by giving the cued-recall tests immediately following each list and delaying the recognition test until all lists had been presented and the recall tests performed. At a superficial level of analysis, task difficulty was approximately equated between recall and recognition by this means, although it must be conceded that difficulty is only loosely related to performance level. At a more practical level, the method ensured that floor and ceiling effects were avoided for both recall and recognition.

It is important to note that Macht and Buschke (1983) found no differences in memory performance between single-task-control and dual-task conditions for either older or younger adults, which indicated that older adults are able to protect primary task performance even when required to perform a secondary task and, thus, that inferences made from the secondary task method are appropriate for both younger and older adults.

Subjects

The younger participants were 15 Erindale college undergraduates who participated for course credit or for money. Mean age in the younger group was

20.7 years. The older participants were 15 men and women recruited from an existing subject pool of university alumni and volunteers from local senior citizens' centers. These older subjects were all living at home and came into the laboratory to be tested; for the most part they were retired middle-income people living in comfortable circumstances. Mean age for the older group was 72.8 years. All participants were reported to be in good health and had no uncorrected vision or hearing problems. The Mill Hill Vocabulary test was administered to both younger and older participants as a measure of verbal ability; mean scores were 14.2 and 15.9 for younger and older, respectively. This difference was significant by t test, t (28)= 2.45, $p < .05$. The younger people had completed an average of 15.1 years ($SD = 1.0$ years) of formal education, and the older group had completed 12.2 years on average ($SD = 3.1$ years). This difference was also statistically reliable, $t(28) = 3.47$, $p < .01$. Interestingly, the older group had therefore been exposed to less formal education but had higher vocabulary scores.

Materials

The to-be-remembered items in the present experiment were phrases and target words of the following sort: *A body of water—pond*. Sixty of these items were taken from those used by Craik and Tulving (1975), and an additional 84 were created by the experimenters with the requirement that the target word would not be the first thing to come to mind given the cue phrase. This assured that testing for memory of these items would be a test of episodic and not semantic memory.

The total of 144 items was broken into 12 lists of 12 phrase–word items and presented visually one item at a time on a computer screen at a rate of 1 item/5 s. The first two lists were considered to be practice and the remaining 10, target lists. Of the 10 target lists, 5 were tested by immediate cued recall and 5 were tested by delayed recognition. That is, 60 words served as targets for cued recall and 60 different words served as targets for recognition. The recognition test also used 60 completely new words as distractors; the 120 words (60 targets plus 60 distractors) were broken up into 10 lists of 12 words, with half of the words old and half of the words new in each list. The makeup of the recognition lists was randomly determined so that those items appearing together in the original presentation lists did not necessarily appear in the same block of recognition items. Recall and recognition tests were prerecorded and presented auditorily over headphones. For the recall test, the original cue phrases were recorded at a rate of 1 phrase/5 s, and the subject's task was to respond aloud with the corresponding target word in each case. For the recognition test, 10 blocks of 12 single words were recorded at a rate of 1 word/5 s and the subject's task was to respond "yes" or "no," depending on whether a given word had been in the presentation lists.

Secondary task. The task to be performed concurrently with the retrieval tests was a four-choice reaction time task with a computer-generated display. The display was a single alphanumeric character, presented in the center of the computer screen. The four-choice decision was whether this character was a vowel or consonant if it was a letter, or an odd or even digit if it was a number. In front of the participant was a keyboard with four keys labeled, from left to right, *vowel, consonant, odd digit, even digit*; the task was to classify the character and press the appropriate key as quickly as possible. Each display remained on the screen until a correct response was made, at which time the screen cleared and a new display was presented. An equal number of characters were presented in each of the four classification categories, and order of presentation was random with the restriction that the same item was never presented more than twice in a row. If an incorrect key press was made by the participant, the same display was repeated until the correct response was made, and a cumulative RT was recorded. Display presentation and recording of RT's were accomplished with the use of a PDP-11 computer. The measure of performance was simply the average RT throughout the retrieval interval.

Retrieval tasks. In the cued-recall task, the descriptive phrases from the preceding list were presented auditorily over headphones at a rate of 1 phrase/5 s and in a different random order from the order of original presentation. The participant's task was to respond vocally with the word corresponding to each phrase during the 5-s interval. While they were recalling, they were also responding to the visual RT task. In the case of the recognition task, participants were presented with lists of single words; half of the words were target words and half were distractors, randomly mixed. The words were presented auditorily, over headphones, at a 5-s rate. The task was simply to respond "yes" or "no" depending on whether the word had been on any of the presented lists. Again, participants performed the visual RT task concurrently with the auditorily presented memory task. Participants' responses to the memory probes were recorded by the experimenter. Because both the recognition and the cued-recall tasks were presented in blocks of 12 items, each block lasted approximately 1 min.

Procedure

All subjects were tested individually, starting with the visual RT task. The nature of the task was explained and each subject was given a minimum of five blocks of 15 trials each as practice. Subjects continued to practice until they produced two consecutive blocks with mean RTs that differed by less than 100 ms. Once this was accomplished, the memory task was explained and participants were informed that they would perform the RT task while trying to remember the list items.

Subjects were initially given one practice block with each of the retrieval tasks (cued recall and recognition) in combination with the RT task. In each case the subject first learned a list of 12 phrase–word items under conditions of undivided attention, and then performed the memory test for those items under dual-task conditions. At test, participants were instructed to consider the memory task to be the primary task and to perform the secondary task as quickly as they could without disrupting memory performance. After the 2 practice lists, participants proceeded through the rest of the lists and tests. Half of the lists, randomly chosen, were tested by cued recall and these tests took place immediately after presentation of the list. The recognition tests on the remaining 5 lists were administered after the participant had studied all 10 lists and completed all recall tests.

Midway through the memory tests and again after all tests had been completed, participants were required to perform another block of the RT task by itself. Baseline measures of performance for each participant on the RT task performed alone were calculated from three blocks: the last practice block before the memory task, a block following the recall tests, and a block following the recognition tests.

RESULTS

Figure 15.1 (left panel) shows the mean proportions of correct responses on the cued-recall task and mean recognition scores (hits—false alarms) for the two age groups. The figure shows that cued recall yielded somewhat higher levels of performance than did recognition in this case. Nevertheless, older participants did less well than the younger group on recall, whereas they performed slightly better than the younger participants in recognition. An Age × Test Type analysis of variance (ANOVA) on the accuracy data showed no significant main effect of age, $F < 1.0$, but a significant effect of test type, $F(1, 28) = 29.57$, $p < .001$, $MS_e = .011$, which indicated that recall perfor-

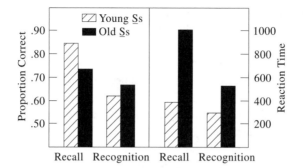

Figure 15.1. Left panel: Cued recall scores (proportion correct) and recognition scores (hits minus false alarms) as a function of age; right panel: RT costs (in milliseconds; mean dual-task RT minus mean baseline RT as a function of age and retrieval task.

mance was significantly higher than recognition performance, and a significant Age × Test Type interaction, $F(1, 28) = 8.07$, $p < .01$, $MS_e = .011$, indicating that the older participants performed less well, relative to the younger group, on recall than on recognition. Subsequent Scheffe tests revealed no reliable age difference on the recognition task, but they did reveal a reliable age decrement ($p<.01$) on recall. Table 15.1 shows the recognition results in greater detail; there were no reliable age differences (all $ts < 1.0$) in either hit rates, false alarm rates, or in d' scores.

Although these results are in line with those of many previous studies, their interpretation is still subject to the difficulties discussed in the introduction: the desirability of taking some bias-free measure (such as d') for recognition, and the consequent difficulty of comparing recall and recognition measures. In order to explore the applicability of Arenberg's (1985) proposal to the present data, d' scores were calculated for each subject; as is shown in Table 15.1 the means were 1.99 and 2.14 for younger and older subjects, respectively. The regressions of recall (measured as proportion correct) on

Table 15.1. Recognition Scores for Younger and Older Subject

Subjects	Hit rate (H)	False alarm rate (FA)	H–FA	d'
Younger	.76	.14	.62	1.99
Older	.80	.13	.67	2.14

NOTE: Age differences were not statistically reliable for any measure.

recognition (measured as d') were then calculated for both age groups. The respective equations were, for the younger group, recall = 0.08 (d') + 0.68, and for the older group, recall = 0.08 (d') + 0.56. Product-moment correlations between the proportions recalled and d' were 0.61 and 0.51 for the younger and older groups respectively; the percentages of variance accounted for by the linear equation were 37% and 26%, respectively. Note that (contrary to Arenberg's findings) there was no age-related difference in regression slopes in the present case.

Although Arenberg (1985) argued that the slope of the regression line for a particular age group can be interpreted as a measure of the relative effectiveness of recall compared with recognition for that group, his logic is perhaps open to question. Arenberg's argument is that "the slope of recall on recognition is dependent on the probability of recalling a recognized item, i.e., the more likely that a recognized item would be recalled, the steeper the slope. Therefore the recall/recognition slope should be steeper for the young than for the old" (p. 2). However, this argument assumes systematic age-related differences in the varying relation between recall and recognition *within* each age group. Specifically, the argument assumes that the differences in recall performance between "good recognizers" and "poor recognizers" will be greater for younger than for older groups. As far as we can see, there is no compelling reason to accept this assumption. On the contrary, from all that is known about the greater sensitivity of recall to cognitive impairment it might be assumed that the decrement in recall performance from good to poor recognizers might be greater for older subjects.

The resolution of this problem is an empirical matter. For the moment we suggest that a modification of Arenberg's idea may yield the required information. The question is, Do older people perform relatively less well than their younger counterparts on recall than on recognition tests? One way of answering the question is to ascertain whether for a given common value of recognition performance (measured say by d'), the older group performs less well than the younger group on recall. Rather than taking either the slopes or the intercepts of the regressions of recall on recognition as the measure of relative efficiency, we suggest carrying out an analysis of covariance (AN-COVA) to establish whether there are significant age differences in recall (measured as proportion correct) when recognition scores (measured as d') are taken as the covariate. This procedure statistically equates recognition performance, measured appropriately, and assesses age differences in recall performance given equivalent recognition performance. An ANCOVA on the present data, taking recall as the dependent measure, yielded adjusted

Table 15.2. Mean Reaction Times and Standard Deviations (in Milliseconds) for Younger and Older Subjects in Baseline (Continuous RT Task Alone) and Dual-Task Conditions

| | Baseline | | | | | | Dual task | | | |
| | Initial | | Postrecall | | Final | | Recall | | Recognition | |
Subjects	RT	SD	RT	SD	RT	SD	RT	SD	RT	SD
Younger	823	159	658	145	585	157	1,135	319	945	319
Older	1,244	218	1,010	221	920	288	2,140	859	1,573	444

mean recall scores of 0.86 and 0.73 for the younger and older groups, respectively; this age difference was highly reliable, $F(1, 27) = 14.78$, $p < .001$, $MS_e = .01$. Therefore, it may be concluded that the older group performed relatively less well than their younger counterparts on cued recall than on recognition memory.

With respect to secondary task performance, a baseline measure was first calculated for each participant performing the visual RT task alone. Three measures of baseline performance were obtained in the course of the experimental session: initial baseline, postrecall baseline, and final baseline (see Table 15.2). For each subject, baseline for the recall task was taken to be the mean of the initial and postrecall single task trials; baseline for the recognition task was taken to be the mean of the postrecall and final single-task trials. By this procedure, the two components of each baseline measure preceded and followed the corresponding retrieval task. Difference scores were then calculated by subtracting these baseline RT scores from the RTs produced while performing the recall and recognition tasks under dual-task conditions (Table 14.2). These difference scores can be interpreted as representing the "cost" of performing each retrieval task.

Figure 15.1 (right panel) shows the mean difference scores for each test type and age group. The figure shows substantially greater costs for the older group, especially in the case of recall. An Age × Test Type ANCOVA carried out on the difference scores revealed a significant main effect of age, $F(1, 28) = 9.43$, $p < .005$, $MS_e = 291.79$, which indicated that primary task performance costs were greater for the older than for the younger subjects; a significant main effect of test type, $F(1, 28) = 14.41$, $p < .001$, $MS_e = 83.98$, which indicated that secondary task performance was significantly more inhibited during the recall task during the recognition task; and a sig-

*Table 15.3. Relative Divided Attention Costs
as a Function of Age and Retrieval Task*

Subjects	Recall	Recognition
Younger	.53	.45
Older	.86	.52

nificant Age × Test Type interaction, $F(1, 28) = 5.99$, $p < .02$, $MS_e = 83.98$, which indicated that the greater cost of performing recall relative to recognition was more pronounced for the older subjects than for the younger. Subsequent Scheffe tests ($p < .05$) revealed no difference in secondary task costs for the younger group between recall and recognition; the difference between the two retrieval tasks was significant in the case of older adults, however.

In addition to these analyses, difference scores from the secondary task were also calculated as a proportion of single task RT levels. This procedure takes into account the age-related differences in the choice RT task performed by itself. A calculation (dual RT—single RT/single RT) was therefore performed for each participant on recall and recognition to yield measures of relative divided-attention (DA) costs (Somberg & Salthouse, 1982). These values are shown in Table 15.3. Relative DA costs were greater for the older group than for the younger group, and somewhat greater for recall than for recognition. An Age × Test Type ANCOVA on the data yielded a marginally significant effect of age, $F(1, 28) = 2.94$, $p < .10$, $MS_e = .21$, a reliable effect of test type, $F(1, 28) = 11.73$, $p; < .01$, $MS_e = .05$, which showed processing costs to be greater for recall than for recognition, and a significant Age × Test Type interaction, $F(1, 28) = 4.67$, $p < .05$, $MS_e = .05$, which indicated that age differences in performance costs were greater for recall than for recognition tests, even when these costs were calculated as a proportion of single-task performance levels.

DISCUSSION

The present experiment has illustrated a number of points concerning age differences in recall and recognition. First, performance on the concurrent RT task confirmed Macht and Buschke's (1983) finding of an age-related decrement in secondary task performance in a dual-task situation. More important, cued recall was more disruptive to secondary task performance than was recognition memory, and this effect was greatly amplified in the older group. We conclude that recall tasks demand more processing resources than do recognition tasks and that because older people have a smaller pool of processing resources at their disposal, they are disproportionately penalized. In the present results at least, the older group performed significantly less well than their younger counterparts both on the RT task performed concurrently with recall, and on the recall task itself.

Second, when recognition scores were expressed as d' values and recall was expressed as proportion correct, an ANCOVA showed a significant age decrement in recall, with d' scores taken as the covariate. That is, when recognition performance was statistically equated between the age groups, an age decrement was found for cued recall. We interpret this result as showing that older people perform relatively less well than younger controls on tasks of recall compared with tasks of recognition, even when recognition performance is measured appropriately by d' scores. The ANCOVA method provides an answer to workers such as White and Cunningham (1982) who have urged researchers to resolve the ambiguities surrounding the relations among recall, recognition, and aging.

Third, does the finding of relatively greater age losses in recall than in recognition fit the general scheme that older people perform relatively poorly on any difficult task (Botwinick, 1978; Salthouse, 1982)? At one level of description the present results do fit that scheme. The recall task was more disruptive to the concurrent continuous RT task than was the recognition task and the effect was enhanced in older subjects. In a sense then, recall was more "difficult" than recognition and this was especially true for the older group. But "difficulty" is an unsatisfactory concept because it involves and possibly confuses different levels of analysis: phenomenological feelings of difficulty, the mental effort required to perform the task satisfactorily, and the resulting performance level. We therefore prefer to interpret the results from the present study as showing that recall tasks require more self-initiated activity or more processing resources than do recognition tasks, and that older people are therefore at more of a disadvantage when recall is involved.

This account is in line with Hasher and Zack's (1979) suggestion that older people are differentially penalized as tasks become less automatic and more effortful. It is also in line with Craik's (1983) notion that memory retrieval tasks may be ordered from those (like free recall) requiring a great deal of self-initiated activity to those (like recognition and priming tasks) requiring little or none, and that age decrements are a function of the degree of self-initiated activity required (see also Light & Singh, in press). Finally, the present results are also compatible with the notion that processing resources decline with advancing age (Craik, 1983; Craik & Byrd, 1982) and that the different patterns of age-related decrements associated with different memory tasks may be attributed to this underlying concomitant of the aging process.

REFERENCES

Arenberg, D. (1973). Cognition and aging: Verbal learning, memory and problem solving. In C. Eisdorfer & M. P. Lawton (Eds.), The psychology of adult development and aging (pp. 74–97). Washington, DC: American Psychological Association.

Arenberg, D. (1985). The problem of comparing recall and recognition in young and old adults. Manuscript submitted for publication.

Botwinick, J. (1978). Aging and behavior (2nd Ed.). New York: Springer-Verlag.

Botwinick, J. & Storandt, M. (1980). Recall and recognition of old information in relation to age and sex. Journal of Gerontology, 35, 70–76.

Burke, D. M. & Light, L. L. (1981). Memory and aging: The role of retrieval processes. Psychological Bulletin, 90, 513–546.

Cerella, J., Poon, L. W. & Williams, D. M. (1980). Age and the complexity hypothesis. In L. W. Poon (Ed.), Aging in the nineteen-eighties: Psychological issues (pp. 332–340). Washington, DC: American Psychological Association.

Craik, F. I. M. (1977). Age differences in human memory. In J. E. Birren & K. W. Schaie (Eds.), Handbook of the psychology of aging (pp. 384–420). New York: Van Nostrand Reinhold.

Craik, F. I. M. (1983). On the transfer of information from temporary to permanent memory. Philosophical Transactions of the Royal Society, London, Series B, 302, 341–359.

Craik, F. I. M. & Byrd, M. (1982). Aging and cognitive deficits: The role of attentional resources. In F. I. M. Craik & S. Trehub (Eds.), Aging and cognitive processes (pp. 191–211). New York: Plenum Press.

Craik, F. I. M. & Tulving, E. (1975). Depth of processing and the retention of words in episodic memory. Journal of Experimental Psychology: General, 104, 268–294.

Erber, J. T. (1974). Age differences in recognition memory. Journal of Gerontology, 29, 177–181.

Gordon, S. K. & Clark, W. C. (1974). Application of signal detection theory to prose recall and recognition in elderly and young adults. Journal of Gerontology, 29, 64–72.

Hasher, L. & Zacks, R. T. (1979). Automatic and effortful processes in memory. Journal of Experimental Psychology: General, 108, 356–388.

Light, L. L. & Singh, A. (In press). Implicit and explicit memory in young and older adults. Journal of Experimental Psychology: Learning, Memory, and Cognition.

Macht, M. L. & Buschke, H. (1983). Age differences in cognitive effort in recall. Journal of Gerontology, 38, 695–700.

Rabinowitz, J. C., Craik, F. I. M. & Ackerman, B. P. (1982). *A processing resource account of age differences in recall.* Canadian Journal of Psychology, 36, *325–344.*

Salthouse, T. A. (1982). Adult cognition: An experimental psychology of human aging. *New York: Springer-Verlag.*

Schonfield, D. & Robertson, B. A. (1966). *Memory storage and aging.* Canadian Journal of Psychology, 20, *228–236.*

Somberg, B. L. & Salthouse, T. A. (1982). *Divided attention abilities in young and old adults.* Journal of Experimental Psychology: Human Perception and Performance, 8, *651–663.*

Welford, A. T. (1958). Ageing and human skill. *London: Methuen Press.*

White, N. & Cunningham, W. R. (1982). *What is the evidence for retrieval problems in the elderly?* Experimental Aging Research, 8, *169–171.*

16. Lifetime Maintenance of High School Mathematics Content

Harry P. Bahrick and Lynda K. Hall

THIS RESEARCH EXPLORES life span retention of content acquired in high school mathematics courses by 1,726 individuals. The investigation also illustrates the use of multiple regression techniques to examine individual-difference variables in life span memory.

BACKGROUND

The present study is the fourth in a series concerned with maintenance of knowledge throughout the life span. The previous investigations (Bahrick, 1983a, 1984; Bahrick, Bahrick & Wittlinger, 1975) identified basic issues for research concerned with maintenance of knowledge that are summarized here because they provide background and focus for the current investigation.

Most knowledge remains accessible only if it is periodically rehearsed or used. Some aspects of knowledge appear to be so well learned, however, that access is maintained for decades or for the entire life span without further rehearsals. Thus, the rules of simple arithmetic, the meanings of common words in one's native language, and so on, may never be forgotten even in the absence of further rehearsals. Such permanent storage is difficult to document because most overlearned knowledge continues to be in frequent use. However, our prior findings document life span retention in the absence of rehearsals for the recognition of names and faces of high school classmates learned incidentally (Bahrick, Bahrick & Wittlinger, 1975) and for a portion of the more formal knowledge acquired in foreign language classes (Bahrick, 1984). The content in these investigations was acquired over several years. In contrast, similar material acquired over shorter time periods exhibits the continuous loss functions traditionally reported for episodic content (Bahrick, 1983b; Squire, 1989). Our goal in the present research was to explore the conditions of acquisition and the types of content of high school mathematics courses that facilitate enduring knowledge.

Cross-sectional investigations using multiple regression analysis have made it possible to study life span retention of naturalistically acquired semantic memory content. In such investigations, retention of content is tested for a large number of individuals who vary in the time elapsed since the content was acquired. Information regarding the length of the retention interval, the degree of original knowledge, and the amount and type of rehearsals during the retention interval are obtained from various sources, including archival records and questionnaires administered to the participants. These data are used as predictor variables and the regression analysis yields equations that predict performance on the memory test. If the retention interval is used as one of the predictor variables, evaluating the regression equation for successive time intervals yields predicted retention functions. The magnitude of the multiple correlation indicates how adequately the function accounts for the observed memory data.

We investigated life span retention of the content of high school algebra and plane geometry for the following reasons: (a) to obtain general retention functions for this content as normative information, (b) to determine the effect of a variety of individual-difference variables (pertaining to constitutional factors or to conditions of acquisition or rehearsal) on the rate of performance decline over a half century, and (c) to establish differential rates of loss for various aspects of content. Differential loss rates associated with either individual-difference variables or content variables have pedagogical implications for the identification of relative strengths and weaknesses in curricula, and relevant findings may provide a basis for increasing the effectiveness of education.

METHOD

Test Development

The major obstacles to assessing memory for our target content were changes in curriculum, emphasis, or terminology in the teaching of high school mathematics courses during the 50-year period from 1937 to 1986. To focus on aspects of content that had not changed, we used textbooks and standardized examinations that spanned the 50-year period, such as the *New York State Regents Examinations.* We examined geometry examinations from the years 1945, 1955, and 1985, and algebra examinations from the years 1945, 1955,

1968, 1984, and 1985. Anticipating that a pilot analysis would show some test items to be faulty or insensitive, we selected or constructed more items than we ultimately expected to use. The preliminary version of our test had an approximately equal number of questions in recognition (multiple choice) and recall format. In addition, we included items that were intended to assess memory for (a) specific, detailed facts, or terminology; (b) knowledge of general principles; and (c) application of a principle to a new situation.

Pilot Testing

We conducted pilot testing to determine reliability, to establish the overall difficulty at a level that avoided floor and ceiling effects, and to identify items sensitive to all levels of knowledge. The tests were also composed without excessively redundant items and at a length that could be completed by most subjects within 90 min.

The preliminary versions contained 112 questions for geometry and 108 questions for algebra (19 of which pertained to content acquired in a second high school algebra course taken by most students, and 89 of which pertained to the content of a first algebra course). Ninety-two participants completed the algebra pilot test, and 103 completed the geometry test. The pilot subjects varied widely in age; they were Ohio Wesleyan University faculty or students, local junior and senior high school students, or they were affiliated with area churches or senior citizens centers. Test items were selected on the basis of the pilot data analysis so as to achieve the objectives mentioned above. The pilot analysis did not examine differences in performance decline for individual test items because we wanted to avoid selecting questions that would bias the degree of retention of content. Odd–even reliability coefficients corrected by the Spearman Brown formula indicated a reliability of .93 for the final geometry test and .94 for the algebra test.

Recruiting and Testing

On the final version of the test, questions were arranged in order of increasing difficulty, and no limits were imposed on test time because we were interested in assessing retention of content, rather than retrieval or processing speed. Most subjects completed the test within 90 min, but some subjects required more time (four percent of the algebra subjects and one percent of the geometry subjects required two hours or more).

We used two versions of the questionnaire: a long version for most participants and an abbreviated version for high school students that omitted questions pertaining to college courses. The questionnaire assessed the degree of original learning, relevant rehearsal activities, the length of the retention interval, and attitudes toward mathematics courses. To assess the influence of rehearsals during the retention interval, we inquired about both vocational and avocational reexposure to the target content and about the duration and recency of each activity. The categorization of these data and their conversion into scales for multiple regression analysis are discussed below.

Participants. A total of 1,050 participants took the algebra test; 946 took the geometry test (270 of which took both tests, usually on different days).

Two control groups were also included in each subject pool. These participants had never taken a course in algebra or geometry, respectively. The student controls were tested during the spring term and were scheduled to enroll in their first algebra or geometry course during the fall. Adult control subjects ranged in age from 19 to 84; their educational level approximated that of our other participants.

Various methods were used for recruiting. Persons between 16 and 30 were recruited primarily at local Ohio high schools and on the campuses of Ohio Wesleyan University and the Ohio State University. Older participants were recruited from Ohio Wesleyan University alumni or from the membership of local churches and service organizations.

Testing. We administered the tests to individuals and to groups of up to 200 participants. The testing occurred in our laboratory, in laboratory space provided by the Ohio State University, in local high school classrooms, and in space provided by churches. Testing occurred from the spring of 1986 through the fall of 1987.

Scoring. Information provided by participants regarding the dates mathematics courses were taken, type of courses taken, grades received, and Scholastic Aptitude Test (SAT) or American College Test (ACT) scores were verified for 661 subjects (38% of the total sample) by examining records from the registrar's offices at Ohio Wesleyan University and the Ohio State University and from the Educational Testing Service. When discrepancies were found between reported and verified data, the verified data were used. Comparison of reported and verified data yielded error rates similar to those reported in a previous investigation (Bahrick, 1984). These errors provide information

*Table 16.1. Distribution of Subjects across the
Retention Interval*

Years since acquisition	Algebra subjects ($n = 927$)	Geometry subjects ($n = 860$)
0	177	127
0.1–1.0	175	88
1.1–2.0	93	68
2.1–5.0	119	188
5.1–10.0	51	110
10.1–25.0	87	93
25.1–40.0	130	104
40.1–55.0	73	52
55.1–74.0	22	30

NOTE: In addition to these subjects, there were 110 student controls and 13 adult controls who took the algebra test (for a total of 1,050) and 61 student controls and 25 adult controls who took the geometry test (for a total of 946).

concerning the accuracy of long-term autobiographical memory; however, we shall forego a more detailed discussion of such errors here because autobiographical memory is not the focus of this article.

The retention interval was specified differently for the algebra and geometry analyses. Because follow-up courses in mathematics usually review and build on the content of preceding courses, the decision as to whether a follow-up course (e.g., a second course in algebra) constitutes part of acquisition or should be considered a rehearsal activity during the retention interval is arbitrary. We considered subsequent algebra courses as part of acquisition because results showed that these courses enhanced rather than just maintained knowledge of the content of the first course. For algebra, the retention interval began with completion of the last algebra course, regardless of whether that course was taken in high school or in college. In contrast, geometry courses taken after the plane geometry course did not generally enhance test performance. Only a course in solid geometry taken by some of the older participants seems to have enhanced test performance. Accordingly, the retention interval for geometry began at the time of completion of the plane geometry course. The effects of subsequent mathematics courses on retention of content covered in the first course are among the most important findings of this investigation, and we shall discuss these effects in detail below. Table 16.1 gives a breakdown of the number of individuals tested as a function of the length of the retention interval.

Rehearsal activities were rated on a three-point scale based on our estimate

Table 16.2. Distribution of Reported Level of Rehearsal as a Function of Highest Level of Math Taken

Highest level of math	Level of rehearsal					
	0	1	2	3	4	5
	Algebra					
Below calculus	445	135	51	9	10	1
Calculus	102	41	5	2	3	3
Above calculus	18	6	4	0	1	4
Total	565	182	60	11	14	8
	Geometry					
Below calculus	417	111	39	4	7	4
Calculus	92	39	6	4	0	5
Above calculus	16	6	2	1	3	3
Total	525	156	47	9	10	12

of the degree of relevance to the content of high school algebra or geometry. Examples of activities rated as highly relevant are tutoring students in algebra or geometry and helping children with relevant homework. Examples of activities rated intermediate in relevance are tutoring students in chemistry or working mathematics puzzles. An example of an activity rated low in relevance is arithmetic computation such as that used in balancing a checkbook. Occupations were rated on an analogous three-point scale. Examples of occupations rated high, medium, and low in relevance are high school math teacher, chemist, and nurse, respectively.

Two rehearsal variables were calculated, one reflecting amount and relevance of rehearsal, the second, recency of relevant rehearsal. For the first variable, we estimated total rehearsal time only for highly relevant activities by multiplying the period during which the activity was reported by the estimated number of hours per week devoted to that activity. The total time estimate was then divided by the participant's retention interval to obtain an estimate of the amount of rehearsal per year of retention. We then derived an ordinal scale of rehearsal. Those who reported no rehearsals were assigned zero on the scale; those who reported only activities or occupations of low or intermediate relevance were assigned a 1: those who reported highly relevant activities were assigned a 2 if they engaged in these activities 5 or fewer hours per year, a 3 for 6 to 100 hours per year, and a 4 for more than 100

Table 16.3. Predictor Variables Included in the Hierarchical Regression Analyses

Type of variable	Algebra	Geometry	Description
Retention interval	ATIME	GTIME	Natural logarithm (retention interval + 1)
	ATIMES	GTIMES	[Natural logarithm (retention interval + 1)]^2
	ATIMEC	GTIMEC	[Natural logarithm (retention interval + 1)]^3
Opportunity to attend college		AGEGRP	0 for high school students; 1 for older subjects
Original learning	ALGNUM		# of algebra courses
		GEONUM	# of geometry courses
	HSMNUM	HSMNUM	# of high school math courses
		HSGNUM	# of high school geometry courses
	CANUM		# of college algebra courses
	CMNUM	CMNUM	# of college math courses
	RELNUM	RELNUM	# of college-level related courses
	MALEV	MALEV	Highest level of math completed
	GRADE		Average algebra grade
		GRADE	Plane geometry grade
Second-order original learning	ALGNUMS		(ALGNUM)^2
		GEONUMS	(GEONUM)^2
	HSMNUMS	HSMNUMS	(HSMNUM)^2
		HAGNUMS	(HSGNUM)^2
	CANUMS		(CANUM)^2
	CMNUMS	CMNUMS	(CMNUM)^2
	RELNUMS	RELNUMS	(RELNUM)^2
	MALEVS	MALEVS	(MALEV)^2
	GRADES	GRADES	(GRADE)^2
Rehearsal	RSCALE	RSCALE	Overall level of rehearsal
	RTIME		Natural logarithm (# years since last rehearsal) divided by ATIME
		RTIME	Natural logarithm (# years since last rehearsal) divided by GTIME
Gender	GENDER	GENDER	

hours per year. Those whose profession involved the continuous performance of highly relevant activities were assigned a 5. The distribution of subjects' reported levels of rehearsal as a function of the highest level of math taken is given in Table 16.2. The table shows that the great majority of participants at all levels of mathematics training reported no relevant rehearsals.

The second rehearsal scale was based on the recency of highly relevant rehearsal activities. The time elapsed since the most recent reported rehearsal date was expressed as a fraction of the total retention interval of the participant.

Table 16.4. Interaction Variables Included in the Hierarchical Regression Analyses

Type of interaction	Algebra	Geometry
Retention interval–original learning	ALGNUM × ATIME	GEONUM × GTIME
	HSMNUM × ATIME	HSMNUM × GTIME
	CANUM × ATIME	HSGNUM × GTIME
	CMNUM × ATIME	CMNUM × GTIME
	RELNUM × ATIME	RELNUM × GTIME
	MALEV × ATIME	MALEV × GTIME
	GRADE × ATIME	GRADE × GTIME
Retention interval–amount of rehearsal	RSCALE × ATIME	RSCALE × GTIME
	RTIME × ATIME	RTIME × GTIME
Retention interval–gender	GENDER × ATIME	GENDER × GTIME

NOTE: See Table 16.3 for meanings of variable acronyms.

Additional variables. Our previous findings (Bahrick, 1984) showed that quadratic terms for several predictor variables improved the predictive power of the regression analysis, but higher order terms beyond the second power did not. We therefore entered quadratic terms in the regression equation for all predictor variables except for gender and except for the two variables reflecting rehearsals. Regarding the retention interval, previous data (Bahrick, 1984) showed that performance declined rapidly during the first few years, then the decline diminished or halted, and finally, the decline resumed approximately 30 years after acquisition. To accommodate such a function, we also entered a cubic term for the retention interval.

Finally, we added interaction variables for every predictor variable, with the first-order variable defining the retention interval. The hierarchical sets of all variables used in our analyses are presented in Tables 16.3 and 16.4, including those directly measured and those added, for the algebra and geometry analyses, respectively.

As indicated in the tables, the first step in the analysis included the three terms that represent the retention interval, and the outcome reveals test performance as a function of time. In the algebra analysis, we then added the variables associated with the degree of original learning of algebra. These specify the number of various categories of mathematics courses each participant had taken in high school and college, the highest level of mathematical training the participant had reached, and the average grade received in algebra courses.

Next, we assessed the impact of seven more groups of variables. First, we entered the quadratic terms for each of the original learning variables to determine contributions of nonlinear relationships. Second, to enhance the parsimony of the model, we removed quadratic terms from the previous step that did not significantly reduce errors in prediction. Third, the two variables based on rehearsals during the retention interval were added, and fourth, the gender of the participants was entered. In Steps 7 to 9, we evaluated the contribution of the interactions of the retention interval with the original learning variables, rehearsal variables, and gender. These last three steps identify variables that significantly affect the rate at which test performance declines during the retention interval.

RESULTS AND DISCUSSION

Regression Analysis for the Retention of Algebra 1 Content

Tables 16.5 and 16.6 show the results of the hierarchical regression analysis of performance on material from the first algebra course. The retention interval alone yields a multiple R of .39, and a multiple correlation of .81 is achieved after the final step. The validity of predicting retention of algebra content exceeds the validity attained in our previous investigations of life span memory, probably because extensive pilot testing assured an appropriate length and difficulty level of the test, and perhaps because knowledge of algebra can be assessed with higher reliability. The validity of prediction is at least as high as the *reliability* (i.e., self-consistency) of most dependent variables used in laboratory investigations of learning and memory (Bahrick, 1977; Rose & Fernandes, 1977; Schlosberg, 1928). A separate regression analysis—based on only five predictors, including standardized test scores

Table 16.5. Results from the Hierarchical Regression Analysis of Performance on Items from the First Algebra Course

Step	R	F to test change	df	p
1. Retention interval	.393	50.65	3, 831	.001
2. Original learning	.779	136.05	7, 824	.001
3. Quadratic learning	.783	2.33	5, 819	.05
4. (Nonsignificant quadratic learning terms removed)				
5. Rehearsal	.788	9.53	2, 820	.001
6. Gender	.791	10.23	1, 819	.002
7. Learning × Retention	.811	11.26	7, 812	.001
8. Rehearsal × Retention	.812	1.08	2, 810	—
9. Gender × Retention	.814	9.66	1, 809	.01

Table 16.6. Regression Weights from Final Step of Algebra 1 Hierarchical Analysis

Variable	Regression coefficient	Standardized regression coefficient	t	p
ATIME	.187	.013	.04	—
ATIMES	−1.058	−.282	−.60	—
ATIMEC	−.023	−.023	−.07	—
ALGNUM	9.525	.216	3.94	.001
HSMNUM	4.825	.111	2.05	.05
CANUM	−4.922	−.097	−1.80	.08
CMNUM	.852	.033	.41	—
RELNUM	1.103	.041	.41	—
MALEV	14.360	.451	2.78	.01
GRADE	9.181	.351	10.61	.001
RELNUMS	.874	.061	.72	—
MALEVS	−3.356	−.397	−2.54	.05
RSCALE	2.174	.104	2.43	.05
RTIME	−.348	−.003	−.07	—
GENDER	.392	.009	.29	—
ALGNUM × ATIME	−2.046	−.245	−2.06	.05
HSMNUM × ATIME	.899	.109	.93	—
CANUM × ATIME	1.090	.045	.92	—
CMNUM × ATIME	1.751	.166	1.89	.06
RELNUM × ATIME	.528	.056	.84	—
MALEV × ATIME	2.688	.330	2.78	.01
GRADE × ATIME	−1.134	−.258	−2.75	.01
RSCALE × ATIME	−.446	−.058	−1.24	—
RTIME × ATIME	−.315	−.021	−.16	—
GENDER × ATIME	−2.001	−.120	−3.11	.01
Constant	−6.751		−.99	—

(SAT or ACT scores), math level, retention interval, grade, and number or college math courses—yields a multiple correlation of .82.

Of particular interest are the variables that have statistically significant interactions with the retention interval (Steps 7 to 9 in the regression program) because the interactions identify those variables that affect the *rate* of performance decline. To illustrate these interactions, we plotted predicted test scores for individuals who varied in regard to retention interval and other critical variables. We first examined the effect of variables that specify the degree of original knowledge of the target content.

Effect of number and level of mathematics courses taken. Figure 16.1 shows predicted retention functions for groups of participants who differ in regard to the number and level of mathematics courses taken. The functions were generated by evaluating the regression equation using the regression weights

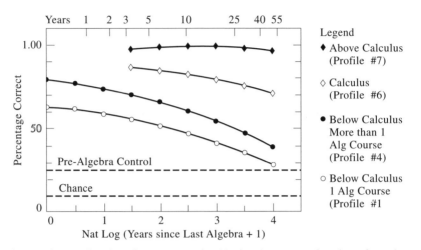

Figure 16.1. Predicted performance on the Algebra 1 test as a function of number and highest level of math courses taken. (A complete list of predictor values for each profile is included in Table 16.7).

in Table 16.6 for increments of .5 of the retention interval. Level and number of mathematics courses are varied as indicated in the figure legend, and other variables are held constant for all profiles at the values specified in Table 16.7 (e.g., rehearsals during the entire retention interval are set at zero).

To increase the number of possible profiles, we collapsed the scales for several variables. For example, the variable of number of college math courses taken was condensed to the three categories of 0, 1 to 2, and 3 or more courses. The reported regression analysis used these condensed scale variables, and the condensation produced only minimal changes in the analysis. The first 2 years of the retention function for individuals trained at or above the level of calculus are omitted, because it generally takes 2 years after completion of the last algebra course to complete courses at the higher levels.

Although it would also be instructive to examine the effects of level and number of mathematics courses independently of each other, these variables are naturally confounded so that participants who took higher level mathematics courses generally took more courses as well. Because all four profiles in Figure 16.1 evaluate the regression equation for individuals who earned a grade of A in algebra, knowledge of content at the time the first algebra course was completed is controlled. Nevertheless, performance at the beginning of the retention interval differs markedly across the groups. These dif-

Table 16.7 Predictor Values in Profiles Used to Illustrate Retention of Algebra and Geometry

Algebra profile	Predictor variable						
	HSMNUM	ALGNUM	CMNUM	RELNUM	GRADE	MATHLEV	GENDER
1	1–2	1	0	0	A	Below	M
2	3+	2+	0	0	C	Below	M
3	3+	2+	0	0	B	Below	M
4	3+	2+	0	0	A	Below	M
5	3+	2+	0	0	A	Below	F
6	3+	2+	1–2	1–2	A	Calculus	M
7	3+	2+	3+	3+	A	Above	M

Geometry profile	Predictor variable						
	HSGNUM	GEONUM	CMNUM	RELNUM	GRADE	MATHLEV	GENDER
1	1	1	0	0	C	Below	M
2	1	1	0	0	B	Below	M
3	1	1	0	0	A	Below	M
4	1	1	1–2	0	A	Below	M
5	1	1	1–2	0	A	Calculus	M
6	1	1	3–4	0	A	Above	M
7	2	2	3–4	0	A	Above	M

NOTE: For all profiles, RSCALE = 0; RTIME = 1. For all algebra profiles, CANUM = 0. For all geometry profiles, HSMNUM = 3+. Gender: M = male; F = female. Below = below calculus; Above = above calculus. See Table 16.3 for meanings of acronyms used in profiles.

ferences reflect additional knowledge of Algebra 1 content acquired in subsequent algebra courses, and our decision to include subsequent algebra courses in the acquisition period rather than the retention interval is based on this finding.

The functions in Figure 16.1 reveal different rates of performance decline, but the differences are somewhat difficult to interpret because they apply to diverse performance levels at the beginning of the retention interval. We therefore replotted the data in Figure 16.2 to reveal the proportion of the original score lost over time. For this purpose, each value in Figure 16.1 is represented in Figure 16.2 by converting the raw score into a chance-adjusted proportion of the score at the beginning of the retention interval and subtracting this proportion from unity. For those with mathematical training at or above the level of calculus, the score at the beginning of the retention interval was estimated at the level of the first data point; these estimates are likely to be fairly accurate, because the functions exhibit very little slope.

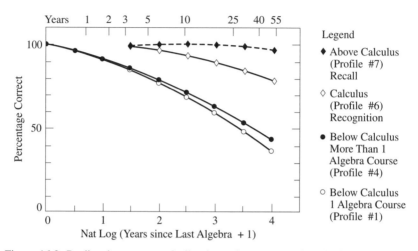

Figure 16.2. Predicted percentage decline in performance on the Algebra 1 test as a function of number and highest level of math courses taken.

Figure 16.2 shows that decline in algebra test performance is strongly affected by taking subsequent courses in mathematics. Those who take no further algebra courses reduce their original score to the control group level during the retention interval. *Those who have taken three or more college mathematics courses with the highest level course above calculus show minimal losses during the course of more than 50 years even though they report no rehearsal activities during that period.* The retention functions of participants with intermediate degrees of mathematical training follow an orderly hierarchy between these extremes.

Effect of average algebra grade. The interaction between retention interval and a second original learning variable, average grade received in algebra courses, was also examined by evaluating the regression equation separately for participants who received grades of A, B, and C. The predicted scores are shown in Figure 16.3. (Further subject characteristics are specified in Table 16.7; none of the participants profiled had taken math courses at or above the level of calculus). The data in Figure 16.3 indicate that grades reflect substantial differences of original knowledge and that they continue to have a substantial effect on performance throughout the 50-year interval; however, compared with number of courses taken, they have a relatively small effect on the *rate* of loss.

Effect of gender. Gender was included as a dummy variable in the regression analysis, with men assigned a score of 0 and women assigned a score of 1.

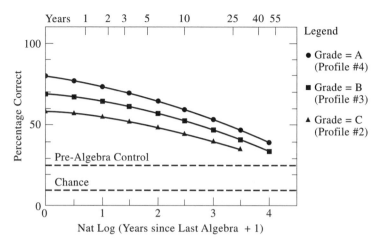

Figure 16.3 Predicted performance on the Algebra 1 test as a function of average algebra grade.

Figure 16.4 shows the rate of loss for men and women. (Other subject characteristics are detailed in Table 16.7). Both profiles represent individuals who had taken no math at or above the level of calculus and who had received an average grade of A in algebra. As shown in the figure, no gender differences in performance exist at the conclusion of the last algebra course, but over time the performance of women declines more than that of men. No-

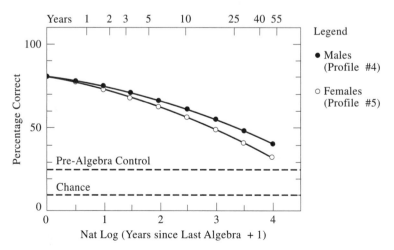

Figure 16.4. Predicted performance on the Algebra 1 test as a function of gender.

tably, this interaction accounts for significant variation in test performance above the total variation accounted for by all other variables included in the analysis. Thus, the result cannot be explained by differences between men and women in number or level of math courses taken or in grades received. Rehearsal conditions were controlled (set at zero) to the extent that they are reflected by our two rehearsal scales. However, any gender differences in rehearsal that are not reflected by our scales because of inaccurate reporting or insensitivity of our scales could affect the data and bring about gender differences in the rate of loss.

Effect of standardized test scores. Of all variables, standardized test scores (i.e., SAT or equivalent ACT scores) had the highest correlation with the retention scores ($r = .65$). We did not include this variable in our analysis program because standardized test scores were not available for two thirds of the participants. More important, the scores were not available for most individuals who had taken algebra courses more than 30 years ago or for individuals who were still in high school. As a result, it was not possible to establish interactions for this variable with the full retention interval (i.e., to determine the influence of standardized test scores on algebra test performance 30 years or more after acquisition).

We conducted a hierarchical regression analysis with only those 284 individuals for whom standardized scores were available. The addition of standardized scores increased the final multiple correlation to .85, but did not yield a statistically significant interaction between standardized scores and the retention interval, indicating that the scores per se do not significantly affect the rate of loss. A major conclusion from these results is the relative independence of effects on test performance from effects on the rate of performance decline. Grades in courses and standardized test scores are the best predictors of test performance, but their influence on the rate of loss is trivial. Variables that have major effects on the rate of loss are not those directly reflecting aptitude or achievement; rather, they reflect the much more manipulable curricular and educational variables concerned with the amount and distribution of practice.

Retention as a function of item characteristics. The preceding analyses have focused on retention of the entire content of Algebra 1 as a function of individual-difference variables. We shall now examine differential retention for various types of content (i.e., for individual test items or groups of items).

The dependent variable in this analysis is the amount of loss observed for each individual test item or for a particular group of items. We obtained an index of performance decline for each item by subtracting the proportion of correct responses to the item given by individuals tested at the end of the retention interval from the proportion of correct responses by individuals tested at the beginning of the retention interval. The difference between these proportions was then expressed as a fraction of the proportion of correct responses at the beginning of the interval. Thus, an item passed by 80% of individuals tested at the beginning of the interval and by 20% of those tested at the end of the interval would receive the following retention index:

$$(.8 - .2)/.8 = .75$$

The validity of the index is limited by possible cohort effects differentiating individuals tested at the beginning of the interval from those tested at the end of the interval.

The following independent variables were established for each test item: (a) the initial difficulty level of the item, (b) student control group performance, and (c) adult control group performance. Item format (recall vs. recognition) and item content (specific term, principle, or application of a principle) also served as predictor variables. Results from a hierarchical analysis are presented in Tables 16.8 and 16.9. The analysis yielded a final multiple correlation of .71, and the two control group scores were the best predictors.

The high predictive contribution associated with student control performance documents the benefits of an extended acquisition period previously observed in the analysis of individual differences. Some of the material taught in algebra courses was also covered in earlier, pre-algebra courses, and high performance by student control subjects identifies such content. This content

Table 16.8. Results for the Hierarchical Regression Analysis of Individual Algebra 1 Items

Step	R	F to test change	df	p
1. Initial difficulty	.084	.53	1, 74	—
2. Control group performance	.689	32.06	2, 72	.001
3. Item format	.705	3.26	1, 71	.08
4. Item content	.713	.72	2, 69	—

Table 16.9. Regression Weights from the Final Step of Hierarchical Analysis of Individual Algebra 1 Items

Variable	Regression coefficient	Standardized regression coefficient	t	p
PTO	.276	.244	2.23	.05
PCA	−.618	−.345	−3.11	.01
PCS	−.659	−.516	−4.55	.001
Format	8.258	.172	1.71	—
TYPE 1	.156	.002	.02	—
TYPE 2	−5.160	−.107	−.98	—
Constant	70.382		7.99	.001

NOTE: PTO = percentage of subjects passing item at time zero: PCA = percentage of adult control group passing the item: PCA = percentage of student control group passing the item. TYPE 1 is a dummy variable that differentiates specific terms from other items. TYPE 2 is a dummy variable that differentiates applications from other items.

is relearned in the algebra course, and the combination of relearning and extending the acquisition period reduces forgetting of the content over the subsequent 50 years.

The adult control performance identifies content acquired outside of formal training in algebra. The acquisition of such content may be based on pre-algebra courses, avocational pursuits, logical analysis not directly based on formal mathematical training, and so on, and such activities may occur at any time during the acquisition period or during the extended retention interval. This type of content is less likely to be forgotten because relevant activities during the retention interval constitute rehearsals.

The following question exemplifies content that yielded little performance decline over the 50-year period:

Two numbers are in the ratio of 1:3 and their sum is 24.

Find the smaller of the two numbers. Of the student control group, 30% passed this item. The following question exemplifies content that yielded large performance decrement over 50 years:

$$\text{Factor: } X^2 - 5X - 24.$$

One percent of the student control group passed this item.

In the final two steps of the hierarchical regression analysis, we added the variables related to item category (i.e., item format and item content). The addition of these variables did not yield a statistically significant increase in the amount of variance accounted for beyond that accounted for by difficulty

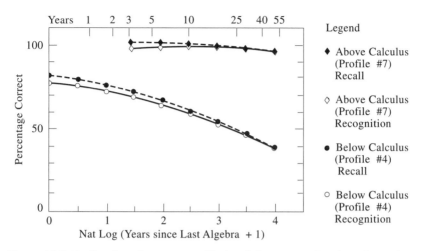

Figure 16.5. Predicted performance on Algebra 1 items as a function of question format and highest level of math courses taken.

level and control group performance. Interrater agreement in classifying items into the three content categories was low, and the unreliability of classification may at least partly account for the failure of this variable to yield differential amounts of forgetting.

The results indicate no statistically significant difference in the amount of performance decline for questions presented in recognition versus recall format, and this finding contrasts with much of the experimental literature. The contrasting results can be explained by the better control over degree of overlearning relative to the performance criterion achieved in the present investigation. Items in recall and recognition format were selected to be approximately equally difficult and to avoid ceiling effects at the beginning of the retention interval. The present findings are reliable because they are based on a very large n, a large number of items varying in difficulty level, and a very long retention interval. Figure 16.5 shows retention functions for all items tested in recognition format versus all items tested in recall format, adjusted for the total number of items tested in each format.

Regression Analysis for the Retention of Algebra 2 Content

Fifteen questions on the algebra test pertained to material covered only in a second course in algebra, and these questions were excluded from all the preceding analyses. We performed a separate multiple regression analysis

Table 16.10. Results from the Hierarchical Regression Analysis of Performance on Items from the Second Algebra Course

Step	R	F to test change	df	p
1. Retention interval	.279	15.69	3, 555	.001
2. Original learning	.749	100.83	6, 549	.001
3. Quadratic learning	.750	.75	4, 545	—
4. (Nonsignificant quadratic learning terms removed)				
5. Rehearsal	.753	3.95	2, 547	.05
6. Gender	.764	21.28	1, 546	.001
7. Learning × Retention	.779	5.49	6, 540	.001
8. Rehearsal × Retention	.780	1.12	2, 538	—
9. Gender × Retention	.783	4.96	1, 537	.05

based only on these items. The steps in this analysis paralleled the analysis previously described for the content of Algebra 1. The program yielded a final multiple correlation of .78, and the original learning variables and gender had a substantial impact on the rate of performance decline (i.e., they had a statistically significant interaction with the retention interval). Results from this analysis are presented in Tables 16.10 and 16.11. Figure 16.6 shows the predicted decline in performance for participants trained at various levels. The characteristics of those profiled in Figure 16.6 are given in Table 16.7. The profiles in Figure 6 support the major conclusions derived from the analysis of the Algebra 1 content. Additional courses are associated with dramatic reductions in performance decline on Algebra 2 content over the course of the next 50 years. The retention losses sustained by individuals with additional training are slightly larger than the losses sustained for the content of Algebra 1 for those with a comparable level of training. This difference may reflect the fact that the content of Algebra 1 receives the benefit of additional rehearsals and relearning during the second algebra course, whereas the content of the second algebra course lacks this benefit. Profiles depicting the effects of grades and of gender yielded results comparable to those obtained for the Algebra 1 content.

Regression Analysis for the Retention of Geometry Content

We performed the same hierarchical analysis on the geometry data as on the algebra data. However, because the retention interval for geometry content began with completion of the plane geometry course, a course usually taken

*Table 16.11. Regression Weights from Final Step of Algebra 2
Hierarchical Analysis*

Variable	Regression coefficient	Standardized regression coefficient	t	p
ATIME	3.339	.883	2.43	.05
ATIMES	−1.568	−1.652	−2.68	.01
ATIMEC	.258	1.033	2.56	.05
HSMNUM	3.306	.197	4.41	.001
CANUM	−2.360	−.221	−3.29	.01
CMNUM	1.249	.211	2.30	.05
RELNUM	.992	.163	2.20	.05
MALEV	1.287	.189	2.17	.05
GRADE	2.374	.379	7.91	.001
RSCALE	.337	.072	1.13	—
RTIME	1.605	.073	1.06	—
GENDER	−.516	−.052	−1.12	—
HSMNUM × ATIME	−.705	−.361	−2.10	.05
CANUM × ATIME	.574	.118	1.84	.07
CMNUM × ATIME	−.070	−.030	−.27	—
RELNUM × ATIME	−.009	−.004	−.05	—
MALEV × ATIME	.517	.285	2.04	.05
GRADE × ATIME	−.294	−.274	−2.04	.05
RSCALE × ATIME	−.038	−.024	−.34	—
RTIME × ATIME	−.838	−.223	−1.38	—
GENDER × ATIME	−.486	−.114	−2.23	.05
Constant	−9.330		−4.12	.001

NOTE: See Table 16.3 for meanings of variable acronyms.

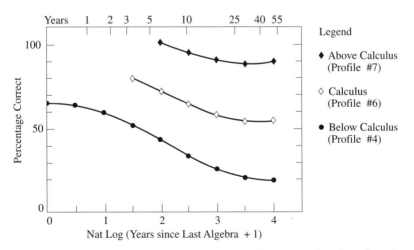

Figure 16.6. Predicted performance on the Algebra 2 test as a function of number
and highest level of math courses taken.

Table 16.12. Results from the Hierarchical Regression Analysis of Performance on Geometry Items

Step	R	F to test change	df	p
1. Retention interval	.168	7.98	3,824	.001
2. College opportunity	.212	14.44	1,823	.001
3. Original learning	.645	74.41	7,816	.001
4. Quadratic learning	.651	2.14	5,811	.06
5. (Nonsignificant quadratic learning terms removed)				
6. Rehearsal	.658	8.31	2,812	.001
7. Gender	.661	5.94	1,811	.02
8. Learning × Retention	.690	9.92	6,805	.001
9. Rehearsal × Retention	.691	.82	2,803	—
10. Gender × Retention	.691	.87	1,802	—

during the sophomore year of high school, participants tested during the first 2 years of the retention interval had no opportunity to take college-level mathematics courses and no retention profiles reflecting the influence of the relevant variables are drawn for the first 2 years of the retention interval.

Results of the analysis are shown in Tables 16.12 and 16.13. Overall, the steps of the regression analysis yielded findings comparable to those obtained for the algebra data. However, two differences are noteworthy: (a) The retention interval accounts for only 2% of variation in performance. (b) The final step of the hierarchical analysis yields a multiple R of .69, which is considerably lower than the validity of prediction achieved for the algebra data. Possible reasons for these differences are discussed below.

Effect of number and level of mathematics courses taken. Figure 16.7 shows predicted retention functions for the geometry content for participants who differ in level of additional math courses taken. Table 16.7 presents the level at which other conditions were held constant for profiled groups of participants.

Test performance immediately after completing higher mathematics courses does not exceed the performance of individuals who received the same grade in geometry and are tested immediately after completing the plane geometry course. The only exception is found with those older participants who took a second high school course in solid geometry and who are represented in the group that completed courses above the level of calculus. The upward trend of that profile during the last 20 years of the retention interval is an artifact that represents the influence of the solid geometry course taken

Table 16.13. Regression Weights from Final Step of Geometry
Hierarchical Analysis

Variable	Regression coefficient	Standardized regression coefficient	t	p
GTIME	−8.419	−.653	−1.91	.06
GTIMES	.379	.121	.20	—
GTIMEC	.192	.242	.60	—
AGEGRP	2.503	.074	1.13	—
GEONUM	.281	.008	.11	—
HSMNUM	1.927	.047	1.21	—
HSGNUM	−.105	−.002	−.05	—
CMNUM	−3.020	−.150	−.88	—
RELNUM	9.051	.143	1.54	—
MALEV	4.461	.186	1.54	—
GRADE	22.417	1.058	3.90	.001
CMNUMS	−1.705	−.166	−1.44	—
GRADES	−1.742	−.507	−1.89	.06
RSCALE	2.273	.142	2.15	.05
RTIME	−2.024	−.027	−.40	—
GENDER	−.797	−.024	−.52	—
GEONUM × GTIME	.822	.106	1.00	—
HSGNUM × GTIME	1.008	.288	3.61	.001
CMNUM × GTIME	2.476	.330	2.67	.01
RELNUM × GTIME	−2.054	−.096	−.99	—
MALEV × GTIME	1.164	.178	1.06	—
GRADE × GTIME	−2.119	−.595	−4.52	.001
RSCALE × GTIME	−.273	−.051	−.75	—
RTIME × GTIME	1.141	.091	.57	—
GENDER × GTIME	−.650	−.046	−.93	—
Constant	−5.649		−.51	—

NOTE: See Table 16.3 for meanings of variable acronyms.

primarily by participants trained during the 1940s and 1950s. Because the solid geometry course has rarely been offered in high school during the last 30 years, it is not possible to establish the immediate effect of the course on plane geometry test performance from the present data. The fact that test performance 30 years later is higher than performance of those who just completed the plane geometry course with the same grade strongly supports an enhancement effect. All participants represented in the above-calculus profile took two geometry courses in high school, but the content of the second geometry course changed over time from solid to analytic geometry. Such cohort effects complicate the analysis of ecological memory data, and the confounding of content of differential predictive value decreases variance accounted for in the regression program and accounts for the apparent rise

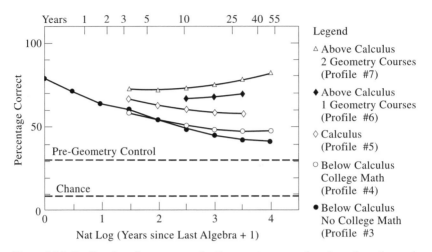

Figure 16.7. Predicted performance on the Geometry test as a function of number and highest level of math courses taken.

of the geometry retention curve. However, the profiles represented in Figure 16.7 confirm the earlier conclusion regarding the influence of additional mathematics courses on retention of content acquired in the first course. With original course grade a constant, those who take additional mathematics

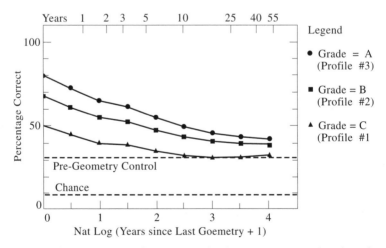

Figure 16.8. Predicted performance on the Geometry test as a function of plane geometry grade.

courses have smaller declines in test performance on the content of the first course over a 50-year period.

Effect of plane geometry grade. Figure 16.8 shows the effect of the plane geometry grade on predicted performance. Those profiled differ in regard to grade; other characteristics are held constant at levels specified in Table 16.7. Participants with higher grades perform better than those with lower grades. Figure 16.8 shows that this advantage diminishes over time, but differences in performance decline are minor, and a floor effect imposed by superior retention of content acquired in pre-geometry training contributes to the attenuation. As observed for algebra content, grades have a large and durable effect on test performance, but in comparison with the effect associated with math level, the magnitude of the effect on rate of loss is minor.

Forgetting as a function of item characteristics. The results of analyses performed on retention of the individual geometry questions paralleled those obtained for the algebra content. The predictor variables, dependent variable, and steps in the regression program were the same as those previously described.

The conclusions yielded by the geometry content analysis are very similar to those reported for the algebra content. The last step of the analysis yielded a multiple correlation of .58, with difficulty level of each item and performance of the adult control group attaining statistically significant regression weights in the final equation. Of these two variables, difficulty level contributes less to predictive power, and performance of the adult control group contributes most. As in the analysis of Algebra 1 content, neither content nor format of items significantly affect the rate of loss.

Comparing Retention of Algebra and Geometry Content

A comparison of the profiles in Figures 16.1 and 16.7 suggests that retention of algebra and geometry test content may differ in several ways. Losses during the first two years appear to be more pronounced for geometry. Individuals profiled for this period have taken only a single geometry course and no college-level mathematics courses. However, the overall decline in performance is smaller for geometry content (the retention interval variables yield a multiple correlation of .39 with Algebra 1 test scores and of .17 with geometry test scores). Diminished declines of geometry performance may be based on higher average degrees of learning achieved in the plane geometry course, and the difference may also reflect greater parsimony and therefore better integration of that content. These interpretations are conjectural because there are no scales for comparing algebra and geometry content in regard to the relevant dimensions.

To some extent, diminished performance decline for geometry content is an artifact of the lower predictability of geometry test scores (R = .69 vs. R = .81). The lower predictability of geometry test scores in turn reflects the greater autonomy of that content from other high-school or college mathematics courses. The reliability of the two tests is comparable (.98 for algebra and .95 for geometry), and the correlation between grade in plane geometry and geometry test performance is actually slightly higher than the comparable correlation between Algebra 1 grade and Algebra 1 test performance (r = .48 vs. r = .41). However, the most important other predictors (e.g., the number of additional mathematics courses, the grades in these courses, and the highest level of mathematics courses taken) correlate more with algebra than with geometry performance, yielding a higher overall predictability in algebra performance, Thus, the greater autonomy of the geometry content yields a lower multiple correlation, which in turn is associated with more regression of predicted scores, and hence with less divergent profiles for participants with varying backgrounds in mathematics. Thus, although the evidence shows that algebra test scores decline more than geometry test scores for most individuals, the magnitude of the difference and the causes for the difference remain conjectural.

Toward a Theory of Maintenance of Knowledge

Results of the present investigation, together with the earlier findings, permit some general conclusions about conditions that yield enduring knowledge. Individual-difference variables that reflect talent and achievement (e.g., SAT scores and grades) predict acquisition levels and retention test performance, but they have relatively minor effects on the rate of decline of performance over time. Clearly the most important predictors of the rate of performance loss pertain to the conditions of original exposure or practice. When rehearsals or exposures are extended over several years, performance levels remain stable for half a century without the benefit of further practice. When the same content is acquired over a shorter period, performance tends to decline rapidly and continuously. Thus, 8 years after having taught students in a single semester course, college teachers fail to recognize most of their names and faces (Bahrick, 1983b), but high-school graduates who spent 4 years together with their classmates recognize nearly 90% of the names and faces 35 years after graduation (Bahrick, Bahrick & Wittlinger, 1975). Similarly, 3 years after taking a single semester of Spanish in college, nearly all the Spanish–English recall vocabulary is lost, but those who studied for five semesters still achieve 60% of their original recall score 25 years later. The data for retention of the content of algebra are convincing. When the acquisition period extends over several years, during which the original content is relearned and used in additional mathematics courses, the performance level at the end of training is retained for more than 50 years, even for participants who report no significant additional rehearsal during this long period. In contrast, those whose acquisition period is limited to a single year perform at near-chance levels at the end of the retention interval. Self-selection variables for individuals who continue to take mathematics courses may play a role, but the superior retention of content acquired in pre-algebra classes provides independent evidence for the important benefits associated with extended exposure and relearning. The absence of statistically significant interactions of standardized test scores and grades with the rate of decline indicates that aptitude and achievement play a minor role.

Because the total amount of practice is confounded with distributed practice in most naturalistic learning situations, it is rarely possible to sort out the respective contributions of these important variables. Those who take more mathematics courses also spread their acquisition of content over longer periods of time, and it is difficult to isolate the effect of having taken more mathematics courses from the effect of having training extended over a longer period of time. However, longitudinal, quasi-experimental data (Bahrick & Phelps, 1987) confirm the independent contribution of the spacing effect over and above the total practice effect. This conclusion is also supported by a variety of other evidence (Dempster, 1988).

A third variable, more difficult to assess, is the degree of coherence or inherent organization of the material to be learned. Certainly mathematical content is more coherent and permits greater integration than the vocabulary of a foreign language or the names and faces of various individuals. Integration may extend the life span of semantic memory content and particularly may render content less vulnerable to losses associated with advancing age. The present study shows that such losses are not inevitable. Those who take several mathematics courses in college show no significant decrement in their retention of high school algebra or geometry content during the half-century retention interval, even if they report no rehearsals of content during that time. Lower degrees of integration of content may account for the substantial losses during the sixth and seventh decades of life previously reported for the recognition of names and faces (Bahrick & Wittling 1975) and for Spanish vocabulary (Bahrick, 1984).

Most, but not all, life span memory functions show a substantial decline of performance during the first few years of the retention interval. Such losses reflect the portion of content most recently added (i.e., material not acquired over an extended period of several years). When no content has been recently added (e.g., high school algebra content for those with several college-level mathematics courses), no early retention losses are observed. The same is true for memory of faces and names of high school classmates after 4 years of exposure.

When the degree of acquisition varies within a given content domain, and a portion of the material is recently added, the more recently added knowledge has a shorter life span, and, as a result, the retention function for the entire content shows rapid decline during the first 3–5 years of the retention interval (Bahrick, 1984).

Potential Contributions of Maintenance of Knowledge Research to Education

For more than a century, educational psychologists have focused on contributions of our discipline to the effectiveness of education (see Herbart, 1892). Scholars of learning, from Thorndike to Skinner, have produced findings that are relevant to educational practice, and their impact on education has been considerable. In contrast, it is difficult to point to a major contribution memory scholars have made to education. This failure is particularly disappointing because the value of education is so dependent on the endurance of the changes that education produces. Memory scholarship has obvious potential relevance to education.

The present investigation suggests that retention losses are relatively unaffected by individual-difference variables pertaining to aptitude and achievement and are much more influenced by the more manipulable variables pertaining to the curriculum and the schedule of instruction. Changes that increase the duration of acquisition or exposure and require maintenance and relearning of content during an extended period extend the life span of knowledge. A variety of curricular interventions could produce such changes, and longitudinal, follow-up investigations can establish each intervention's individual effects through manipulative research that limits confounding. Changes from a quarter to a semester schedule while keeping the number of instructional hours constant; cumulative reexaminations at the end of a program of several years: cumulative, capstone review courses at the end of programs: and delayed review examinations over knowledge considered essential for professional certification are all examples of potentially beneficial interventions.

Finally, the development of cognitive theory in this important and neglected domain of memory research depends on the availability of relevant data. By providing a databank that reveals the long-term effects of a large number of predictor variables on retention, cross-sectional investigations contribute information essential to theories of memory applicable to the life span maintenance of knowledge.

REFERENCES

Bahrick, H. P. (1977). Reliability of measurement in investigations of learning and memory. In I. Birnbaum & E. Parker (Eds.), Alcohol and human memory (pp. 59–71). Hillsdale, NJ: Erlbaum.

Bahrick, H. P. (1983a). The cognitive map of a city: 50 years of learning and memory. In G. Bower (Ed.), The psychology of learning and motivation: Advances in research and theory, 17. San Diego, CA: Academic Press.

Bahrick, H. P. (1983b). Memory for people. In J. Harris & P. Morris (Eds.), Everyday memory, actions and absent-mindedness. San Diego, CA: Academic Press.

Bahrick, H. P. (1984). Semantic memory content in permastore: 50 years of memory for Spanish learned in school. Journal of Experimental Psychology: General, 113, 1–29.

Bahrick, H. P., Bahrick, P. O. & Wittlinger, R. P. (1975). Fifty years of memory for names and faces: A cross-sectional approach. Journal of Experimental Psychology: General, 104, 54–75.

Bahrick, H. P. & Phelps, E. (1987). Retention of Spanish vocabulary over eight years. Journal of Experimental Psychology: Learning Memory, and Cognition, 13, 344–349.

Dempster, F. N. (1988). The spacing effect: A case study in the failure to apply the results of psychological research. American Psychologist, 43, 627–634.

Herbart, J. F. (1892). Psychologie als Wissenschaft neu gegrundet auf Erfahrung, Metaphysik und Mathematik [Psychology as science newly founded in experience, metaphysics, and mathematics]. In K. Kehrbach (Ed.), J. F. Herbart's samtliche Werke. (Part I is in Vol. 5, pp. 177–434; Part II is in Vol. 6, pp. 1–340). Langensalze: H. Beyer & Sohne. (Original work published 1824)

Rose, A. M. & Fernandes, K. (1977). An information processing approach to performance assessment: I. Experimental investigation of an information processing performance battery (Tech. Report No. 1). Washington, DC: American Institutes for Research.

Schlosberg, H. (1928). A study of the conditioned patellar reflex. Journal of Experimental Psychology, *11, 468–494.*

Squire, L. R. (1989). On the course of forgetting in very long-term memory. Journal of Experimental Psychology: Learning, Memory, and Cognition, *15, 241–245.*

17. Concept Problem Solving in Young and Old Adults

David Arenberg

DOES ABILITY to solve reasoning problems differ between young and old adults? Is within-problem performance related to age? These are important questions, but few studies of problem solving and age have been published. Studies other than those of concept problem solving have consistently found striking decrements with age (Jerome, 1962; Welford, 1958; Young, 1966), but clear-cut age differences have not been found for number of correct solutions of concept problems (Wetherick, 1964; Wetherick, 1966; Wiersma & Klausmeier, 1965). The data from these latter studies, however, suggest that when groups are not matched on non-verbal intelligence, performance declines with age on concept problems just as on other types of problems.

The study reported here was conducted to explore the relation between age and performance on concept-identification problems when information was presented sequentially to permit analyses of performance within problems. Specifically, the study was designed to answer four questions: (a) Is reasoning performance of men 60 years or older inferior to performance of young men when age groups are not matched for non-verbal intelligence? (b) Is such an age difference found for all concept problems with one-element solutions or only for certain types of such problems? (c) Is negative information preceded by positive information more conducive to errors for old than for young men? (d) Is redundant information more conducive to errors for old than for young men?

MATERIALS AND METHODS

Subjects

Forty-two men were recruited from two non-profit employment services. Half of the Ss were 17 to 22 years old; the other 21 were 60 to 77. The problems

---

From *The Journal of Gerontology* 23 (1968): 279–82. Reprinted with permission of the Gerontological Society of America.

were administered to any *S* who scored 27 or higher (raw score) on the Vocabulary subtest of the Wechsler Adult Intelligence Scale; however, three men in the old group were replaced because they could not understand the instructions for the problem-solving task. Means of the Vocabulary scores were 52.8 for the old and 41.0 for the young; standard deviations were 12.1 for the old and 10.1 for the young.

Procedure

The problems were modeled after those of Bruner, Goodnow, and Austin (1956). Preliminary work with the old Ss, however, dramatically indicated that dimensions of color, form, and number and the entire task were too abstract to be understood. The problems were converted to poisoned-food problems for the present study.

In each problem, nine foods appeared across the top of a work sheet. The same nine foods were listed for all problems. Ss were told that one of the nine foods had been poisoned in each problem, and that the task was to identify the poisoned food. The three foods in each meal were read by the *E* and recorded by the S. In addition, each meal was identified as "lived" or "died," and this information was also recorded. "Lived" indicated that the poisoned food was not included in the meal (negative instance); "died" indicated that the poisoned food was included in the meal (positive instance). After each meal was recorded, Ss were instructed to cross out those foods listed at the top of the sheet which could be eliminated and to write the foods remaining, i.e., possible solutions, adjacent to that meal. All previous information within a problem was available throughout that problem to minimize the memory component of performance. Whenever a solution (only one possible food) was reached, the problem was terminated even if all the meals had not been presented. Table 17.1 the practice problem correctly solved.

After the practice problem (and clarification, if necessary), ten problems were presented in a fixed order. The first five problems were administered in the order shown in Table 17.2; the last five problems were logically identical to the first five and were presented in the order 4, 5, 3, 2, 1. A rest of one to two minutes was given between the fifth and sixth problems.

The sequential method of presenting instances (meals) and the possible solutions identified by the *S* after each presentation provided data to answer the questions about negative information and redundant information. A meal was considered redundant information if the possibly poisoned foods remained unchanged, i.e., if the meal provided no information not already avail-

Table 17.1. Examples of Problems with Their Solutions

	Practice problem	
Meals (Instances)	Lived or died	Possibly poisoned foods
Coffee, Lamb, Peas	Died	Coffee, Lamb, Peas
Coffee, Veal, Peas	Died	Coffee, Peas
Coffee, Lamb, Corn	Lived	Peas
	Problem 5	
Meals	Lived or died	Possibly poisoned foods
Tea, Lamb, Corn	Died	Tea, Lamb, Corn
Coffee, Lamb, Rice	Lived	Tea, Corn
Milk, Beef, Rice	Lived	Tea, Corn
Tea, Beef, Corn	Died	Tea, Corn
Coffee, Veal, Corn	Lived	Tea

NOTE: Meals and designations of "lived" or "died" were provided by the *E*. Possibly poisoned foods were identified by the *S* after each meal.

able from previous meals. A key error was identified for each problem which was not solved correctly. The key error was as defined as the earliest error from which a *S* did not recover, i.e., the earliest error followed by no correct performance. Key errors thus defined are not attributable to preceding errors. Evaluation of within-problem performance was made by identifying the kind of information (positive, negative, positive redundant, or negative redundant) provided by the meal which resulted in each key error. For example, in

Table 17.2. Representations of the Five Types of Problems and Their Orders

Prob. no.	Sequence of instances
1 and 10	$+,+,+$
2 and 9	$+,-$
3 and 8	$-,-,-,-,-$
4 and 6	$+,+,+(R),+$
5 and 7	$+,-,-(R),+(R),-$

NOTES: $+$ = Positive instance (concept included, designated "died"). $-$ = Negative instance (concept not included, designated "lived"). (R) = redundant instance (no new information).

Problem 5 (Table 17.1), if the response to the first meal was correct and to the second was incorrect and all subsequent responses were incorrect, the key error would be on the second meal which was negative. If, however, the first error was on the second meal, the response to the third meal was correct, and the subsequent responses were incorrect, the key error would be on the fourth meal which was positively redundant. It was positive because it was designated "died" meaning the poisoned food was included in the meal; it was redundant because it provided no information that was not already available prior to that meal.

RESULTS

Means and standard deviations for total problems correct and for each set of five problems are shown in Table 17.3. The performance of the young group was superior to that of the old for each set (first set, t = 4.36, P<00.001; second set, t = 3.07, P<0.01) as well as for all ten problems (t = 4.11, P<0.001).

Table 17.4 shows the number of Ss who correctly solved both, only one, or neither problem for each of the five types of problems. For each type, more young men than old solved both problems correctly, and more old than young failed to solve either correctly. χ^2 values were calculated after the "One" and "Neither" frequencies were combined. All hypotheses were directional; therefore, all values of P are one-tailed.

The old group was not more susceptible than the young to errors when negative information was preceded by positive information. In the second and ninth problems, which consisted of positive followed by negative information, the old group committed 15 key errors on the negative instance compared with ten for the young group. Ten old men and eight young men made at least one key error on the negative instance. In the fifth and seventh problems, which consisted of positive, negative, negative redundant, positive re-

Table 17.3. Means and Standard Deviations for Number of Problems Correct

	Mean		Standard deviation	
	Old	Young	Old	Young
Total Correct	4.5	7.6	2.5	2.4
Correct—1st 5	2.2	3.9	1.2	1.3
Correct—2nd 5	2.3	3.7	1.6	1.3

Table 17.4. Performance on the Five Types of Problems

Problem	Age	Number of Ss Correct on			χ^{2*}	$P\dagger$
		Both	One	Neither		
+,+,+	Old	6	10	5	6.09	<0.01
	Young	15	5	1		
+,−	Old	6	7	8	2.43	<0.10
	Young	12	7	2		
−,−,−,−,−	Old	9	6	6	3.56	<0.05
	Young	16	2	3		
+,+,+(R),+	Old	7	4	10	9.88	<0.01
	Young	18	2	1		
+,−,−(R),+(R),−	Old	3	6	12	1.97	<0.10
	Young	8	6	7		

* Values of χ^2 were calculated after the frequencies under "One" and "Neither" were combined.
† All P values are one-tailed.

dundant, and negative instances in that order, key errors committed on the three negative instances numbered 17 for the old group and 19 for the young. Ten old men and 13 young men made at least one key error on a negative instance. In those problems with positive and negative information, there was little evidence that the performance of old Ss was inferior to that of the young on negative instances.

Redundant errors, however, were age-related. The fourth and sixth problems consisted of four positive instances with the third instance redundant. Five key errors were committed on the redundant instance by four Ss in the old group; no such errors were committed by the young (exact $P = 0.05$). The fifth and seventh problems also included redundant instances. These problems consisted of positive, negative, negative redundant, positive redundant, and negative instances in that order. Key errors were committed on the negative redundant instance by three old and three young Ss. However, five old and no young men made key errors on the positive redundant instance (exact $P<0.05$). For the two types of problems with redundant information, nine old men and no young men committed at least one key error on a positive redundant instance (exact $P<0.001$).

DISCUSSION

Apparently matching on non-verbal intelligence is an important factor in studies of age differences in concept problem solving. When Wetherick (1964,

1966) matched age groups in several studies, no age differences resulted for number of problems solved correctly. In another study (Wetherick, 1966, Expt. III), age groups were not matched on non-verbal intelligence, and the mean number of correct solutions did decline somewhat across three age groups, but the data were not evaluated for age trend. Wiersma and Klaus-meier (1965), in a study covering only the age range 20 to 51, found mean errors to increase somewhat across three age groups. No matching was re-ported for their groups. Although their statistical evaluation of errors showed no reliable age effect, the statistical test failed to take into account the direc-tionality of the age hypothesis. In the present study, groups were not matched, and substantial age differences in number of correct solutions resulted. It is interesting to note that the vocabulary means in this study clearly favored the old group. However, nonverbal intelligence measures were available for many of these participants, and the young group was superior to the old on that measure.

It was hypothesized that the old group would commit more key errors than the young when negative information followed positive information. This hypothesis was based upon the expectation that the old would be more likely than the young to continue a previous mode of operation. The results did not confirm this hypothesis. Findings reported in two papers by Wetherick are relevant here. In one study (Wetherick, 1965), instances were classified as positive or negative by the S, and the E confirmed or disconfirmed each classification. One type of error was the misclassification of negative in-stances when the information on which a correct classification should have been based was an earlier negative instance. That type of error was more prevalent in the old group than in the young. In that study, each instance was withdrawn before the next instance was presented; as a result, the memory component of the task was considerably greater than when all instances (or all previous instances) were available throughout a problem. It is not unrea-sonable that negative instances, which are seldom rich in information, are likely to be forgotten or inadequately processed when memory is taxed.

In another study, Wetherick (1966, Expts. I & II) found that errors in which all negative instances were treated as positive were more prevalent in the solutions of old than young groups. Although all the instances were pre-sented together, the labels for identifying positive and negative instances were "Cat. I" and "Cat. II." When these labels were changed to "In" and "Not in" (Expt. II), negative instances were rarely treated as positive by any S, and no age differences resulted. When instances were labeled "Cat. I" or "Cat. II", it was necessary for Ss to remember which designation was positive and which negative. When that memory component was removed, errors resulting from negative instances treated as positive rarely occurred. Apparently, when negative instances are presented in the context of positive instances, age differences in performance do not result unless some additional memory load is imposed by task procedures. The evidence from Wetherick's research and the current study is consistent with this conclusion. It should be noted, however, that old *S*s made more errors than young when all instances were negative, even without an additional memory load, as in the third and eighth problems of the current study. This suggests that the old rely on a focusing "strategy," and, when no positive instance is available to focus upon, misreasoning results.

Redundant information resulted in more key errors for the old than the young; in fact, not one key error was committed on a redundant positive instance by a young *S*. The preponderance of non-redundant information throughout the problems may have established a set to eliminate at least one food after each meal, and the old may have been more prone to eliminate a food when such behavior was contra-indicated as in redundant instances. It is expected that further study using the sequential method will specify other sources of age differences in concept problem solving.

SUMMARY

Performance on five types of concept-identification problems with one-element solutions was compared for two age groups (N = 21 for each group). The performance of the young men (aged 17–22 years) was superior to that of the old (aged 60–77 years) for each type of problem as well as for total problems solved correctly. Information was presented sequentially within each problem to provide a performance after each presentation of information. The old group committed more errors on redundant positive information than the young (in fact, no such errors were committed by the young), but no age difference emerged for performance on negative information preceded by positive information. Although recent studies of concept problem solving in which groups were matched on non-verbal intelligence did not show age differences in number of correct solutions, age differences did result in this study in which age groups were not matched.

REFERENCES

Bruner, J. S., J. J. Goodnow & G. A. Austin. A Study of thinking. *Wiley, New York, 1956.*

Jerome, E. A. *Decay of heuristic processes in the aged.* In: *C. Tibbitts & W. Donahue (Editors),* Social and Psychological Aspects of Aging. *Columbia University Press, New York, 1962, pp. 808–823.*

Welford, A. T. Ageing and human skill. *Oxford University Press, London, 1958, pp. 192–223.*

Wetherick, N. E. *A comparison of the problem-solving ability of young, middle-aged and old subjects.* Gerontologia, 9: *164–178, 1964.*

Wetherick, N. E. *Changing an established concepts; a comparison of the ability of young, middle-aged and old subjects.* Gerontologia, 11: *82–95, 1965.*

Wetherick, N. E. *The inferential basis of concept attainment.* Brit. J. Psychol., 57: *61–69, 1966.*

Wiersma, W. & H. J. Klausmeier. *The effects of age upon speed and concept attainment.* J. Geront., 20: *398–400, 1965.*

Young, M. L. *Problem-solving performance in two age groups.* J. Geront., 21: *505–509. 1966.*

18. Signal, Noise, Performance, and Age

Alan T. Welford

PAST AND PRESENT

Thirty years ago when post-war research into aging began, the belief was deeply entrenched that all changes of human performance with age could be explained as results of changes in the sense organs, muscles, and joints, rather than in the central function of the brain. Perhaps the most significant achievement of research done in the late 1940s and 1950s was to bring recognition that although peripheral factors play their part, the most important trends of performance in middle and old age are of central origin. Indeed, the burden of proof seems now to lie upon those who wish to claim a role for peripheral mechanisms so that, for instance, Weale (1965) had to go to some pains to show that effects of age changes in the eye upon some perceptual functions had been underrated.

By the mid-1960s, it seemed fair to summarize the previous two decades of research in terms of four types of central change: (1) *slowing* of perception and decision; (2) increased *disruption of short-term memory* by any shift of attention during the time the material was being held; (3) difficulty in *searching for* material in *long-term memory*; and (4) difficulty in dealing with certain types of *complexity*. Today these conclusions still hold broadly true, but research during the past 10 years has given us a deeper and more detailed knowledge which has, on the one hand, qualified our understanding and, on the other, made it more precise and confident. The current situation will be considered here first, and then some leads it provides for the future will be addressed. It may be said at once that there is a remarkable convergence of indications from different areas of research that changes with age during adulthood can be plausibly attributed either directly or indirectly to lowering of signal-to-noise ratio in the brain—that is of the strength of signals coming from sense organs to the brain and from one part of the brain to another, as compared with random neural activity ("neural noise"). It is on this conceptual approach, therefore, that the present survey will concentrate. Direct neurological evidence regarding signal strength and neural noise is usually scanty, but heuristic models developed in the general field of psychological research make good sense of otherwise baffling data on age changes.

Slowing of Performance

It was recognized early in the 1950s that the pattern of slowing that comes with age differs with tasks and circumstances, but why it does so was not clear. Now a good deal more can be said about the mechanisms involved. It is not yet possible to put forward a fully integrated theory, but the time for doing so seems not to be far off.

The central mechanisms concerned with sensory-motor performance can be thought of as falling into three parts: the perception of incoming data, the choice of responses to them, and the detailed timing and phasing of action required to carry out the responses chosen. Of these divisions, the third seems to be relatively little affected by age. Thus, the time required to raise a finger when a light or sound signal appears changes hardly at all between the 20s and 60s and only moderately in the 70s (Miles, 1931; Welford, 1958). The same is true for tapping to and fro between two targets with a pencil (Welford, Norris & Shock, 1969). In both cases, the signals are known and decisions about responding action can be made in advance so that speed depends mainly upon the execution of predetermined responses. Somewhat greater slowing of action occurs with grosser movements carried out at maximum speed (Pierson & Montoye, 1958), but the main slowing of sensory-motor performance with age is clearly attributable to processes concerned with the resolution of uncertainty in the perception of signals and choice of responses.

As regards perception, well-known changes in the sense organs make it obvious that the strength of signals from them to the brain falls with age. Crossman and Szafran (1956) and Gregory (1957; 1974, pp. 167–215) have also produced evidence that perception is affected by an increase of neural noise in the brain with age. Vickers, Nettelbeck, and Willson (1972), reanalyzing data by Botwinick, Brinley, and Robbin (1958), have measured this noise. Botwinick et al. recorded times taken to discriminate the longer of two parallel lines exposed for either 0.15 or 2.0 s. With the brief exposures, the increase in response time, as the percentage difference between the lines fell from 20 to 1, was about the same for subjects aged 18 to 35 and 65 to 79 yr; but the older group was less accurate. Vickers et al. proposed a model in which the central effects of the two lines are independently disturbed from moment to moment by neural noise so that at some moments, especially when the objective difference between the lines is small, the central effect of the shorter line may be greater than that of the longer and thus lead to an error. On the basis of the errors made, they were able to calculate that the average standard deviations of the noise were about 0.21 deg of visual angle for the older subjects and about 0.14 deg for the younger. With the longer exposure, the increase of reaction time as the discrimination became finer was greater for both groups, but more so for the older, while the accuracy of both was equal. The calculated noise level was about 0.10 deg for each. Thus, it appeared that when a signal of longer duration was available, subjects accumulated data from it and thereby averaged out some of the noise. By averaging over a longer time, the older were able to attain accuracy equal to that of the younger.

Turning to choice of response, Crossman and Szafran (1956) suggested that increased neural noise accounted for their older subjects' being slower at sorting playing cards. The time taken rose for all age groups from sorting into red/black, to the four suits, and again to the four suits separating court cards from plain. The time was greater for subjects aged 50 to 80 than for those aged 20 to 25 or 25 to 50 by a roughly constant amount at each degree of choice. The increase could not be explained by older subjects' taking longer to handle the cards because the time required to deal them alternately onto two piles rose very little with age. Similar findings were made in a more conventional choice reaction task by Szafran (1966) and in another card-sorting task by Botwinick, Robbin, and Brinley (1960), whose results are shown in Figure 18.1. It can be seen that the main difference between the older and younger subjects is in the intercept rather than the slope relating time to degree of choice.

A mathematical model for choice reaction time recently proposed by Smith (1977; see also Welford, 1976a) suggests why this should be so. An incoming signal is conceived of as being focused progressively more and more with time onto a particular response until a criterion level is reached, whereupon the response is triggered. The model is expressed in the equation:

$$\text{Choice reaction time} = \text{K} \log \left(n \frac{\text{C}}{\text{E}} + 1 \right) \tag{1}$$

where n is the number of equiprobable choices, E is the signal-to-noise ratio of the incoming signal, and C is the criterion level of signal-to-noise ratio at

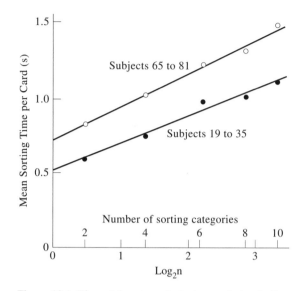

Figure 18.1. Times taken to sort playing cards (excluding practice cards) into 2 to 10 classes by number.

which a response is fired. The constant K varies with the directness with which signals are mapped onto their corresponding responses. The effect of a fall of E with age can be seen if Equation (1) is rewritten:

$$\text{Choice reaction time} = K\left[\log\left(n + \frac{E}{C}\right) + \log C - \log E\right] \quad (2)$$

Log C and Log E are constant whatever the degree of choice, so that if reaction time is plotted against log n, a fall of E will raise the intercept as shown in Figure 18.1, while leaving the slope little changed. The same result could, of course, occur if C rose; in other words, if older subjects adopted higher, more cautious criteria for responding. There is evidence that in some cases they do this (Craik, 1969; Rees & Botwinick, 1971), but the reasons why and the circumstances in which they do so need further study. In at least some cases, apparent caution on the part of older subjects seems to be an indirect effect of decreasing capacity.

One example of this appears in the disproportionate slowing that comes with age in continuous as opposed to discontinuous tasks; that is, in tasks where each response leads immediately to the signal for the next as opposed to those where an appreciable time elapses between the completion of one response and the arrival of the next signal. Ten years ago it seemed reasonable to attribute such disproportionate slowing to aftereffects of signals and responses which acted as noise, blurring the processes dealing with an immediately following signal and response. There was evidence suggesting that these aftereffects lasted longer in older subjects (Welford, 1965). If aftereffects acted in this way, they should cause less disruption when signals and responses are the same as those immediately preceding than when they are different, and it would follow that slowing with age should be less when signals and responses are repetitions of those immediately preceding than when they are not. However, recent experiments have shown the reverse to be true. One experiment compared two-choice reaction times in a discontinuous task in which light signals came 2 s after the completion of a previous response, with times in a similar continuous task in which each signal came immediately on completion of the previous response. Subjects of all ages showed, on average, longer reaction times to repeated signals in the former. In the latter task, the younger subjects (17 to 25) showed shorter average times to repeated signals, but their grandparents (69 to 87) still took longer to respond to repeated signals than to those that were different (Welford, 1977a).

The results can, however, be explained in terms of the single-channel hypothesis (Welford, 1959, 1968, 1977a), as follows:

(1) When a response is either initiated or completed, attention seems to be switched automatically from the response to the feedback for a brief time (150–200 ms, in cases that have been studied). During this time, attention cannot at once be given to any new signal. In other words, monitoring of the previous response delays attention being given to a fresh signal. When a new signal arrives simultaneously with the initiation or completion of the response to a previous signal, it will have to compete for attention with feedback from the response. The winner is likely to be the one that reaches a critical perceptual stage first. It will get immediate attention, while attention to the loser will be delayed.

(2) Where two alternative signals which are clearly different—as they were in this case—are presented one at a time in a random series, the time taken to identify a signal as the same as the one preceding is usually longer than the time required to identify it as different. The likely reason is that while the judgment of "different" is based

on positive evidence, that of "same" is by default of evidence for "different" and can be made only after the "different" judgment has in some sense been rejected (Nickerson, 1969, 1973; Vickers, 1975). Certainly, the signals in the present experiment appeared much more definite when they changed sides than when they reappeared on the same side. Perception of a new signal would, therefore, tend to be slow, and capture of attention by feedback would thus be more likely to occur with repeated signals than with different ones.

(3) The time required to form a visual percept has recently been shown to rise with age (Kline & Szafran, 1975; Walsh, 1976) and it may be supposed that, in consequence, the attention of older subjects is more likely than that of younger subjects to be captured by feedback from the response, especially when signals are repeated.

The point to be noted in these results is that, while increased tendency to monitoring by older people is usually regarded as a sign of caution, it appeared in this case to be due to slowness of perception and was thus an indirect effect of lower signal-to-noise ratio.

Memory

The views that short-term memory is more prone to disruption in older people and that they have difficulty in searching long-term memory have both been seriously questioned during the last few years. Failures of retention and recall that were formerly held to be due to these factors have instead been attributed to failure to place incoming data in store.

In the field of short-term retention, the change of view has resulted largely from theories started by Waugh and Norman (1965). It is now generally held that two types of storage are involved. Of these, the *primary memory* store is capable of holding only about two or three items at any one moment; any futher items fed into it displace items already there. Displaced items are retained only if they are transferred to the *secondary memory* store. The latter appears to have many of the characteristics of long-term memory: for example, if a list of items is given and recalled immediately, it is the items that can be presumed to have been held in secondary memory that may intrude in the recall of another list presented later, while those held in primary memory never seem to do so. The sequence of events envisaged in acquisition and recall is that data are fed into the primary store until it is full, and, then, as further items arrive, the earlier items are either fed into the secondary store or are lost. If, when recall is required, items can be produced in *any* order, the last few presented—presumably held in primary memory—are usually produced first, and very accurately when compared with items presented earlier which presumably have to be recovered from secondary memory. If recall must be in the order of presentation, the advantage for the last few items is lost. Presumably, the recall of earlier items would displace them from primary memory so that they would be retained only if they had been transferred to the secondary store. An experiment by Smith (1975) found that the last two items of a list of eight words presented once were, if recalled first, recalled equally well by subjects aged 20 to 39, 40 to 59, and 60 to 80. However, other items in the list were less well recalled by the older subjects than by the younger, and the same was true for the last two items when not recalled first. It looked, therefore, as if the fall with age was not in primary but in secondary memory.

Smith's results could, on the face of it, imply either that older subjects had difficulty in recovering items from secondary memory or that the items had not been well recorded there. Results of an experiment by Bruning, Holzbauer & Kimberlin (1975) suggest the latter as more likely and also support the indications given by Drachman and Leavitt (1972) that failure by older people to recall is basically due to failure of acquisition during learning. Bruning, Holzbauer & Kimberlin (1975) presented their subjects with four lists of four words, *each once*. Two of the lists were of high imagery words and two of low. One of each pair had to be recalled immediately after presentation, the other after a delay of 20 s. Twenty-four hours later, subjects were asked to recall as many of the 16 words they had seen as they could and were then given the 16 mixed randomly with a further 16 in a recognition test. The results are shown in Table 18.1. The proportion of words recognized correctly was in all cases within the range of the proportions recalled immediately or after 20 s and can reasonably be taken as the proportion that originally entered secondary memory, the remainder having either been recalled immediately from primary memory or lost.

The recognition test also permits a rough calculation of the signal-detection theory parameters d' and β. It was assumed (1) that memory traces of words are likely to be disturbed by neural noise so that the tendency to produce any particular word varies from moment to moment, and (2) that if a word has been presented for memorization, its tendency to be produced is increased. Over a period of time, the momentary tendencies to produce the words in the recognition list that had *not* been presented could thus be envisaged as falling into the distribution shown on the left of Figure 18.2. Those

Table 18.1. Probabilities of Recall and Recognition of Words (Calculated from Data Reported by Bruning, Holzbauer & Kimberlin, 1975)

	Recall at			Recognition at 24 hours				C_N
Age group	0 s	20 s	24 h	False	Correct	d'	β	(see Figure 18.3)
High-Imagery Words								
18–27	0.90	0.83	0.37	0.04	0.83	2.65	3.07	2.98
65–79	0.74	0.46	0.13	0.21	0.51	0.84	1.40	1.96
80–94	0.49	0.20	0.02	0.26	0.49	0.61	1.22	2.91
Low-Imagery Words								
18–27	0.86	0.66	0.21	0.11	0.71	1.80	1.87	2.60
65–79	0.64	0.33	0.03	0.23	0.44	0.62	1.32	2.48
80–94	0.34	0.08	0	0.21	0.33	0.39	1.27	≥2.89[a]

[a] This figure could not be calculated in the same way as the others in the column because none of the 80–94 age group recalled any words at 24 h. It is based on the argument that if 20 subjects were trying to recall 8 words each, their cutoff would have to be at or above the point on the presented words distribution where $p = 1/(20 \times 8)$; i.e., 0.00625. This point is 2.50 standard deviations from the mean of the distribution. Therefore C_N is ≥ 2.50 + d'; i.e., 2.50 + 0.39 = 2.89.

for words that had been presented would fall into the distribution shown on the right. If the distributions overlap, the subject is assumed to set a cutoff point: to treat as having been presented all words whose tendencies at the moment of performing the recognition test fall above this cutoff and to treat as not having been presented all those whose tendencies fall below. Some words presented will thus fail to be recognized, and some not presented will be falsely recognized. Assuming the distributions are normal and of equal variance, calculations of d' can be made in the usual manner as the difference between the means of the two distributions in standard deviation units, and

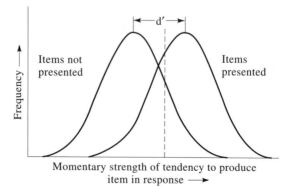

Figure 18.2 A signal detection type model recognition.

of β, as the height at the cutoff point of the ordinate of the right-hand distribution divided by the height at the same point of the ordinate of the left-hand distribution (Parks, 1966).

The two parameters as calculated are shown in the seventh and eighth columns of Table 18.1. It can be seen that both fall dramatically with age. The fall of d', which is a measure of signal-to-noise ratio, implies that the memory traces are relatively weaker in older subjects, either because their strength is less or because the noise in the brain is greater. Which of these alternatives is the case cannot be determined from the present data. The fall of β is quite contrary to the view that older people fail in memory tasks because they adopt very high criteria for response (e.g., Korchin & Basowitz, 1957). Instead, it implies that the older subjects, faced with having to reply on weaker memory traces, lowered their criteria as a means of partial compensation, thereby improving their chance of achieving correct recognitions at the risk of making some false ones.

However, it might still be argued that the poor recall scores 24 h after presentation, especially of the older subjects, were due to high criteria for response. To test this, a quantity C_N was calculated. It was assumed that the proportion of words correctly recalled 24 h after presentation could be represented as a cutoff point on the right-hand distribution of Figure 18.2 which was somewhat higher than that found for the recognition test. Its distance, C_P, from the mean of the right-hand distribution is shown in Figure 18.3. The distance C_N, also shown in Figure 18.3, is the sum of C_P and the d' already calculated from the recognition data. It is the distance of the recall cutoff point from the mean of the distribution for words *not* presented. As shown in the last column of Table 18.1, C_N was remarkably uniform except

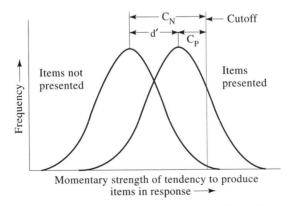

Figure 18.3 A signal detection type model recall.

for a somewhat lower value with high-imagery words among the subjects aged 65 to 79. This discrepancy is perhaps not to be taken very seriously in view of the rather crude assessment of d' and C_N. In any case, it is the opposite of what would be expected if criteria were higher among older subjects. It could be construed as a compensatory tendency similar to that noted for the recognition test. The values of C_N obtained suggest that subjects of all ages set their cutoff for recall at a point high enough to prevent all but a very small proportion of false recalls—on average about 4 per 1000—and that the failure of the older subjects to recall as many items as the younger was not due to their setting their cutoff point higher, but to their memory traces being weaker.

It is not possible here to examine in detail the extent to which this model can cover all the evidence available, but it seems fair to suggest that what have hitherto been regarded as interference effects during presentation appear to be due not to disruption of traces but to the relative failure to transfer material from primary to secondary memory. Interference effects between presentation and recall could be due to the intervening materials deleting primary memory and also effectively adding to the noise, thus broadening the distributions in Figure 18.3. This latter effect would depend upon the extent to which the intervening material found its way into secondary memory and would be likely, therefore, to vary with the precise conditions of different experiments. It is somewhat more difficult to account for the fact that when recall of one-half of the material presented in a short-term memory experiment is called for before the other half, the recall of the second half deteriorates with age more than recall of the first. However, when the subject is told beforehand which half to recall first (e.g., Taub, 1968), he or she seems to *acquire* the first half better than the second (see Welford, 1968, pp. 204–209). When the two halves are presented simultaneously, for example by presenting pairs of items, one to the right ear and one to the left ear (e.g., Inglis & Ankus, 1965), the half recalled first would have the advantage of some items' being able to be recovered from primary memory and would thus show less decline with age.

The traces established in secondary memory by a single presentation of material appear to be weaker in older people but, once established, to remain. Furthermore, although the traces weaken further with time as the fall of recall scores from 0 and 20 s to 24 h shows, they do not do so faster for older than for younger subjects. If it is assumed that the effect of further presentations of the same material is to strengthen the traces and thus increase d', one can account for the indications from several studies that, although older people take more trials to learn to a given extent, once they have done so their retention is little worse than that of younger subjects (e.g., Wimer & Wigdor, 1958).

Complexity

Several choice-reaction studies have been reported in which there is a rise with age not only of intercept, as shown in Figure 18.1, but also of the slope, i.e., K in Equation 1 (for a review, see Welford, 1977b). This occurs typically with cases in which the task of relating signals to responses is not straightforward but involves some kind of intermediate "mental manipulation." Such manipulations fall into two main classes: *spatial transpositions*, as when a signal on the right has to be responded to by pressing a key on the left and vice versa; and *symbolic translations or recodings*, as when signals are digits and responses are the pressing of keys in different spatial positions.

Exactly how these manipulations are effected is not clear. It is known that with long practice they tend to become automatic and seemingly "built into" the subject's system. For example, exposure of the visual forms of digits leads immediately to the corresponding verbal naming in a subject's own language, and the time it takes the subject is virtually independent of the number of different digits that may appear. A response in an unfamiliar language, however, would take longer, and the time required would rise with the number of alternatives that might occur. Until immediacy has been attained, the manipulation seems to involve holding the data from a signal briefly in some kind of memory until a rule of transposition or recoding, also stored, can be applied. It has therefore seemed reasonable in the past to assume that short-term memory is involved and that increased susceptibility of this to interference could account for any fall of performance with age.

However, the adequacy of short-term memory to account for the phenomena associated with incompatibility between signals and responses seems now to be doubtful, not only as regards age changes, but also generally. The storage of data while manipulations are performed can hardly be in primary memory, since, if it were there, there should be no age effect. Yet, the retention seems to be too temporary for it to be a secondary memory that is akin to long-term memory. One is faced with having to postulate either that (1) secondary memory is a third memory system intermediate between primary and long-term; (2) traces in long-term memory take an appreciable time to develop to a durable state; or (3) the memory involved in manipulations between signal and response is different from either primary, secondary, or long-term. The problem is not one for aging studies alone, but is fundamental to the understanding of memory in general. A much greater knowledge of the detailed processes involved in making complex matches between signal and response and, if possible, a metric in which to express them are needed.

Practical Implications

The research results that have been surveyed have a number of fairly obvious implications for the design of work and working environments:

(1) Broadly speaking, they confirm the view developed in the 1950s that the age changes important for most types of work are concerned with perception and decision rather than with the execution of movements and that complexity of relationship between signal and response is more important than degree of choice.

(2) They suggest a need to (a) strengthen signals, not only in the sense of increasing light and sound intensities, but also in designing instruments and other displays; (b) lay out controls so as to convey information without irrelevant detail likely to act as noise; and (c) give clear indications for action. At the same time, as Gregory (1957, 1974) has pointed out, the lowering of signal-to-noise ratio in older people has the surprising implication that they will be less disadvantaged by any external noise than will younger people because external and internal noise can be expected to summate according to a square root law.

(3) Some of the difficulty older people find with tasks requiring speed was formerly thought to be the result of pacing. However, it may be due to the tendency for attention to be concentrated on the monitoring of responses instead of on new signals for action.

(4) Problems of learning and training for older people turn out not to be matters of retention or recovery, but of initial acquisition.

Future Possibilities

Obvious opportunities for future work lie in the application of knowledge already obtained to problems of the employment of middle aged and older people in industry and to the design of accommodation and facilities for the aged. Indications relevant to industry have been outlined by several authors (e.g., Murrell, 1959, 1962; Clay, 1960; Griew, 1964; Welford, 1966), but apart from some important studies of training (Belbin, 1958, 1964; Belbin & Shimmin, 1964; Belbin & Downs, 1966; Belbin, 1965) little has been done so far to put these indications into practice.

As regards fundamental research of practical significance in the human factors field, three areas appear to merit exploration in terms of signal and noise trends with age. All are concerned not so much with capacities or with the demands of tasks as with the strategies employed to relate the one to the other. There have been indications from the late 1940s onward that some characteristic changes of strategy occur with age. They appear often to represent compensatory shifts in the balance between one aspect of performance and another designed either consciously or unconsciously to optimize achievement in the face of changing capacities. It now seems desirable to consider some of these strategies more precisely than they have been heretofore.

Speed and Accuracy

Pew (1969) showed that speed and accuracy of reactions could be related by the equation:

$$\text{Reaction time} = a + b \log\frac{(\text{Probability of Correct Response})}{(\text{Probability of Error})} \tag{3}$$

If so, it is evident that an optimum balance between speed and accuracy will depend on the value of correct responses and the costs of errors and of time. Furthermore, any rise in the probability of error, such as might occur with lowering of signal-to-noise ratio, will mean that optimum achievement will occur with a longer reaction time. One study in which older people, by taking more time, held accuracy constant (Botwinick, Brinley & Robbin, 1958) has already been noted. Some other studies have shown them to take more time and to achieve *greater* accuracy than younger people. In at least one case, the shift toward accuracy appeared to have been carried too far: Craik's (1969) reanalyzing of data by Belbin and Shimmin (1964) showed that poor performance by older subjects at an inspection task could be represented in terms of an unduly high β value which made them reject many items that should have been passed as acceptable. Their average d' value was similar to that of younger subjects, and, with suitable training, their excessive β was reduced so that the performances of the two age groups became equal. Few studies of speed and accuracy in relation to age have hitherto been cast in a form, or reported in enough detail, for these parameters to be calculated. It seems important that future studies should be so designed and reported since, although little can probably be done to prevent a fall of *d'*, β may be capable of modification.

Effort and Stress

A frequent reaction to falling capacity is an increase of effort. In line with this, the first sign of slowing industrial performance on the shop-floor in middle age has been noted as a tendency to work more continuously with fewer or shorter pauses and with various signs of hurrying. The effect is that work is done in a state of chronic stress, leading in the long run to the risk of psychosomatic symptoms. More immediate effects are raised levels of autonomic activity and other indications of increased *arousal*. This is held to result from intensification of the stream of diffuse impulses from the brain stem which render the cells of the cortex more readily fired than they would otherwise be.

The expected effect would be an increase of both signal and noise as shown in Figure 18.4. Both distributions are expanded toward the right in a manner which leaves *d'* little, if at all, changed. But, if the cutoff point remains the same, a fall of β results. The number of correct reactions rises, but so also does the frequency of false positives. In other words, errors of

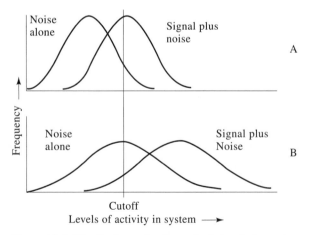

Figure 18.4. Distributions of noise and of signal-plus-noise postulated for lower (A) and higher (B) levels of arousal. (After Welford, 1973.)

omission become fewer, but errors of commission increase (Welford, 1973). Experience of making false positives might lead the subject to raise the cutoff point, but this would probably take a considerable time and would in any case be an ineffective strategy because it would not only reduce false positives but also correct reactions. Until this happened, signs of stress would be detectable as a general over-reactivity combined with enhanced autonomic activity. Very intense arousal might increase noise more than signal either by causing cortical cells to fire instead of merely becoming more sensitive or by causing so much activity that the cortex would be "saturated." In either of these events, over-reactivity would be accompanied by a fall of d', and performance would be likely to deteriorate badly.

Failing capacity means that the right-hand distribution of Figure 18.4 moves toward the left so that d' is reduced. If so, the alternative and more satisfactory strategy would be to lower the cutoff point without increasing arousal level. The optimum cutoff point is given by the equation:

$$\text{Optimum } \beta = \frac{\text{Probability of NO Signal}}{\text{Probability of Signal}}$$

$$\times \frac{\text{Value of Correct NO + Cost of Incorrect YES}}{\text{Value of Correct YES + Cost of Incorrect NO}} \qquad (4)$$

For example, if all costs, benefits, and frequencies are equal, optimum $\beta = 1$, and the optimum cutoff point is at the crossover of the two curves. If the right-hand curve now moves left, the optimum cutoff will also move left. Making the change will result in some increase of false positives but some increase also of correct responses, a compromise which is the best attainable in the circumstances.

Motivation

The basic model shown in Figure 18.4 can be applied to motivation as shown in Figure 18.5 (Welford, 1976b). The tendency to take action in a situation which does not specially call for it but in which it could be taken will, as shown by the left-hand distribution, vary in strength from time to time because of factors such as interest, fatigue, anxiety, and a host of others. Normally the cutoff will be set sufficiently high to prevent action occurring inappropriately except on rare occasions. The effect of a situation specifically calling for action shifts this distribution to the right. The extent of the shift

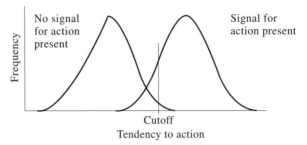

Figure 18.5. The basic signal detection model applied to motivation. (After Welford, 1976b.)

is likely to vary with age because needs change with the years. The effect of any absolute shift will vary with the widths of the distributions; that is, with the amount of the noise in the system. If the distributions are wide, a given absolute shift will produce a smaller change of d' and thus have less motivational effect than if they are narrower.

In recurrent situations, interesting possibilities are implied by Equation 4. The right-hand side of the equation consists of two ratios, both of which seem likely to change with age. First, optimum β is high, and action therefore less likely, when the ratio of no-signal to signal is high; in other words, when calls or opportunities for action are infrequent. One can see that because of this a vicious circle situation could develop for old people; any restriction of activity and any lessening of demand for action will make action even less likely to occur when it is required.

The second ratio is a "payoff matrix." For the present purpose, this ratio may be simplified by considering situations typical of everyday life, where the benefits from inaction are nil and the costs of inaction when action could or should be taken are also nil. The only disadvantage is missing the benefit that would have been gained by taking action. At the same time, the cost of taking positive action is appreciable, although, when it is appropriate, the cost is outweighed by the benefit obtained. The ratio then becomes:

$$\frac{0 + \text{Cost of YES}}{\text{Benefit of Correct YES} + 0}$$

or more directly in terms of motivation:

$$\frac{\text{Cost of Action}}{\text{Benefit of Appropriate Action}} \tag{5}$$

Both costs and benefits are likely to change with age. Any loss of capacity will mean that the cost in terms of effort to be expended in order to attain a given result will rise. At the same time, the achievement in middle age of a well-structured and ordered way of living will mean that the benefits to be gained from many activities will tend to diminish. The overall result in these cases will be an increase of cost-benefit ratio leading to a raising of β and a reduced tendency to take action. On the other hand, some desires, such as those for security, may raise the benefits felt to be obtained from other activities, in which case β for these activities will fall. Overall, therefore, the pattern of activity may change rather than merely diminish with age.

From a human factors standpoint, an important implication of the effect of cost-benefit ratio on motivation lies in the fact that it is almost always more difficult, i.e., "costly," to work out and learn a new procedure than to apply one already known. Thus, any change of working conditions, whether in factories or offices or elsewhere, will tend to produce a temporary rise in cost-benefit ratio unless the change produces a very great improvement in the cost-benefit ratio inherent in the job. Even then, the need to learn new procedures will mean that the full benefits of the change will not be realized immediately. When one takes these facts together with the known cognitive difficulties associated with age, one can understand why changes are often resisted by older people and only accepted under extreme pressure or necessity.

A Concluding Apologetic

Changes with age are many and varied and it is, of course, a gross oversimplification to look at them in terms of signal-to-noise ratio alone. Yet, in aging and in many other areas of human performance, this has already proved to be a powerful unifying concept and heuristic tool, provided it is recognized as operating within a complex system to which many factors of individual capacity, environmental demand, past experience, and future hopes contribute.

In an attempt to grapple with all the factors operating in this system at once, one is likely to be appalled by its complexity. Postulating a few simple principles can help to sort it out. The research and ideas surveyed here suggest that, for this purpose, two concepts are fundamental: first, older people have weaker signals, increased noise, or both in their brains, and second, older people tend to spontaneously adopt strategies which optimize their performance. These concepts appear able not only to unify a great deal of present knowledge about old age, but also to provide a null hypothesis for future research.

REFERENCES

Belbin, E. *Methods of training older workers.* Ergonomics, *1958,* 1, *207–221.*

Belbin, E. *Training the adult worker. D.S.I.R. Problems of progress in industry No. 15. London: H.M.S.O., 1964.*

Belbin, E. & Downs, S. *Teaching paired associates: The problem of age.* Occupational Psychology, *1966,* 40, *67–74.*

Belbin, E. & Shimmin, S. *Training the middle aged for inspection work.* Occupational Psychology, *1964,* 38, *49–57.*

Belbin, R. M. Training methods for older workers. *Paris: O.E.C.D., 1965.*

Botwinick, J., Brinley, J. F. & Robbin, J. S. *The interaction effects of perceptual difficulty and stimulus exposure time on age differences in speed and accuracy of response.* Gerontologia, *1958,* 2, *1–10.*

Botwinick, J., Robbin, J. S. & Brinley, J. F. *Age differences in card-sorting performance in relation to task difficulty, task set, and practice.* Journal of Experimental Psychology, *1960,* 59, *10–18.*

Bruning, R. H., Holzbauer, I. & Kimberlin, C. *Age, word imagery, and delay interval: Effects on short-term and long-term retention.* Journal of Gerontology, *1975,* 30, *312–318.*

Clay, H. M. *The older worker and his job. D.S.I.R. Problems of progress in industry No. 7. London: H.M.S.O., 1960.*

Craik, F. I. M. *Applications of signal detection theory to studies of ageing.* In A. T. Welford & J. E. Birren (Eds.) Decision making and age. *Basel: Karger, 1969.*

Crossman, E. R. F. W. & Szafran, J. *Changes with age in the speed of information intake and discrimination.* Experientia Supplementum, *1956,* 4, *128–135.*

Drachman, D. A. & Leavitt, J. *Memory impairment in the aged: Storage versus retrieval deficit.* Journal of Experimental Psychology, *1972,* 93, *302–308.*

Gregory, R. L. *Increase in "neurological noise" as a factor in ageing.* Proceedings of the 4th Congress of the International Association of Gerontology, *Merano, 1957.*

Gregory, R. L. Concepts and mechanisms of perception. *New York: Charles Scribner's Sons, 1974.*

Griew, S.Job re-design: The application of biological data on ageing to the design of equipment and the organization of work. *Paris: O.E.C.D., 1964.*

Inglis, J. & Ankus, M. N. *Effects of age on short-term storage and serial rote learning.* British Journal of Psychology, *1965,* 56, *183–195.*

Kline, D. W. & Szafran, J. *Age differences in backward monoptic visual noise masking.* Journal of Gerontology, *1975,* 30, *307–311.*

Korchin, S. J. & Basowitz, H. *Age differences in verbal learning.* Journal of Abnormal and Social Psychology, *1957,* 54, *64–69.*

Miles, W. R. *Measures of certain human abilities throughout the life span.* Proceedings of the National Academy of Science, *1931,* 17, *627–633.*

Murrell, K. F. H. *Major problems of industrial gerontology.* Journal of Gerontology, *1959, 14, 216–221.*

Murrell, K. F. H. *Industrial aspects of ageing.* Ergonomics, *1962, 5, 147–153.*

Nickerson, R. S. *"Same"–"Different" response times: A model and a preliminary test.* Acta Psychologica, *1969, 30, 257–275.*

Nickerson, R. S. *The use of binary-classification tasks in the study of human information processing: A tutorial review. In S. Kornblum (Ed.)* Attention and performance IV. *New York: Academic Press, 1973.*

Parks, T. E. *Signal-detectability theory of recognition-memory performance.* Psychological Review, *1966, 73, 44–58.*

Pew, R. W. *The speed-accuracy operating characteristic.* Acta Psychologica. *1969, 30, 16–26.*

Pierson, W. R. & Montoye, H. J. *Movement time, reaction time, and age.* Journal of Gerontology, *1958, 13, 418–421.*

Rees, J. N. & Botwinick, J. *Detection and decision factors in auditory behavior of the elderly.* Journal of Gerontology, *1971, 26, 133–136.*

Smith, A. D. *Aging and interference with memory.* Journal of Gerontology, *1975, 30, 319–325.*

Smith, G. A. *Studies in compatibility and a new model of choice reaction time. In S. Dornic (Ed.)* Attention and performance VI. *Hillsdale, NJ: Lawrence Erlbaum Associates, 1977.*

Szafran, J. *Age, cardiac output and choice reaction time.* Nature, *1966, 209, 836.*

Taub, H. A. *Age differences in memory as a function of rate of presentation, order of report, and stimulus organization.* Journal of Gerontology, *1968, 23, 159–164.*

Vickers, D. *Where Angell feared to tread: Response time and frequency in three-category discrimination. In P. M. A. Rabbitt and S. Dornic (Eds.)* Attention and performance V. *London: Academic Press, 1975.*

Vickers, D., Nettelbeck, T. & Willson, R. J. *Perceptual indices of performance: The measurement of "inspection time" and "noise" in the visual system.* Perception, *1972, 1, 263–295.*

Walsh, D. A. *Age differences in central perceptual processing: A dichoptic backward masking investigation.* Journal of Gerontology, *1976, 31, 178–185.*

Waugh, N. C. & Norman, D. A. *Primary memory.* Psychological Review, *1965, 72, 89–104.*

Weale, R. A. *On the eye. In A. T. Welford & J. E. Birren (Eds.)* Behavior, aging, and the nervous system. *Springfield, IL: Charles C. Thomas, 1965.*

Welford, A. T. *Ageing and human skill. Oxford University Press for the Nuffield Foundation, 1958. (Reprinted by Greenwood Press: Westport, CT, 1973.)*

Welford, A. T. *Performance, biological mechanisms and anism limiting performance in a serial reaction task.* Quarterly Journal of Experimental Psychology, *1959, 11, 193–210.*

Welford, A. T. *Performance, biological mechanisms and age: A theoretical sketch. In A. T. Welford & J. E. Birren (Eds.)* Behavior, aging and the nervous system. *Springfield, IL: Charles C. Thomas, 1965.*

Welford, A. T. *Industrial work suitable for older people: Some British studies.* Gerontologist, *1966, 6, 4–9.*

Welford, A. T. Fundamentals of skill. *London: Methuen, 1968.*

Welford, A. T. *Stress and performance.* Ergonomics, *1973,* 16, *567–580.*

Welford, A. T. Skilled performance: Perceptual and motor skills. *Glenview, IL: Scott Foresman, 1976. (a)*

Welford, A. T. *Motivation, capacity, learning and age.* International Journal of Aging and Human Development, *1976,* 7, *189–199. (b)*

Welford, A. T. *Serial reaction times, continuity of task, single-channel effects and age. In S. Dornic (Ed.)* Attention and performance VI. *Hillsdale, NJ: Lawrence Erlbaum Associates, 1977. (a)*

Welford, A. T. *Motor performance. In J. E. Birren & K. W. Schaie (Eds.)* Handbook of the psychology of aging. *New York: Van Nostrand Reinhold, 1977. (b)*

Welford, A. T., Norris, A. H. & Shock, N. W. *Speed and accuracy of movement and their changes with age.* Acta Psychologica, *1969,* 30, *3–15.*

Wimer, R. E. & Wigdor, B. T. *Age differences in retention of learning.* Journal of Gerontology, *1958,* 13, *291–295.*

19. Aging and Skilled Problem Solving

Neil Charness

Mᴏsᴛ ᴍᴏᴅᴇʟs ᴏғ human problem solving (e.g., Newell & Simon, 1972) are concerned with the performance of adults. The young and the old are often viewed as special cases. As a result, mainstream cognitive research, even when it involves "ecologically valid" (Neisser, 1976) tasks, runs the risk of generating too narrow a theory of performance. Conversely, research on aging seems to have been overly restrictive about investigating "semantically rich" (Simon, 1979) domains, and hence has been accused of lacking external validity (Schaie, 1978).

The purpose of this article is twofold: to suggest a strategy for investigating aging process as they pertain to cognition, and more specifically to examine how problem-solving performance changes over the life span, particularly with respect to the domain of skilled chess playing (Chase & Simon, 1973).

Current research on aging that assesses cognitive changes, particularly memory changes, has produced a wealth of disparate findings (see reviews by Craik, 1977; and Eysenck, 1977), Theoretical debates still continue over whether aging research has demonstrated age-related, as opposed to cohort-related declines (Baltes & Schaie, 1976; Horn & Donaldson, 1976; Horn & Donaldson, 1977). There is also concern expressed whether intelligence tests, paired-associate learning, or word list learning are appropriate tasks to tap aging effects or provide evidence of developmental plasticity (e.g., Scheidt & Schaie, 1978).

If aging is associated with both declines in information-processing ability and the development of compensatory mechanisms, a reasonable expectation is that different mechanisms should underlie equivalent performance in young and old. Thus a more fruitful strategy than hunting for group differences between young and old would be to equate such age groups for molar problem-solving performance and look for differences in component processes (e.g., memory).

Reprinted by permission from *The Journal of Experimental Psychology: General* 110, no. 1 (1981): 21–38. Copyright © 1981 by the American Psychological Association.

If this assumption is correct, aging research should become more concerned with an individual difference approach (see the review by Carroll & Maxwell, 1979). In fact, one of the few unchallenged assertions in gerontology is that individual differences increase with age (Botwinick, 1978).

AGING AS HARDWARE VERSUS SOFTWARE CHANGES

A cornerstone in the approach of understanding individual differences in skilled performers (e.g., Chase & Simon, 1973; Hunt & Love, 1972) is to discern whether invariant processing mechanisms—hardware—or strategies and learning under the control of the performer—software—are responsible for differences. The same approach has been taken successfully in cross-cultural investigations (Wagner, 1978). Such an approach has excellent prospects of bringing some order to the aging area.

The success of many of the aging modification studies, for example, Labouvie-Vief and Gonda (1976) and Plemons, Willis, and Baltes (1978), has been interpreted as evidence against age-related declines being attributable to biological or hardware changes, although Botwinick (1978) has warned correctly that reversibility of deficits need not logically rule out hardware deficits. The fine distinction between hardware and software has blurred even more in the light of successful use of biofeedback to modify age-related alpha rhythm slowing, with consequent decreases in reaction time (Woodruff, cited in Woodruff & Birren, 1975).

Still, a useful heuristic device for considering cognitive aging is to assume that hardware changes may occur with age both in elementary processes (perhaps in speed; Birren, 1974) and in characteristics of structural memory (perhaps in short-term memory capacity). In the absence of suitable software changes (strategies, knowledge structures), there should be observable deficits in performance.

There is considerable evidence that software, in the form of strategy differences, may account for some age-related deficits. Spontaneous use of verbal and visual mediators for paired-associate and list learning decreases with age, as does performance (Hulicka & Grossman, 1967; Rowe & Schnore, 1971). Young and old do not appear to differ in the type of mediator generated when requested (Marshall et al., 1978). Thus studies that instruct the use of mediators usually produce marked improvement in the elderly (Canestrari, 1968; Robertson-Tschabo et al., cited in Botwinick, 1978; Treat & Reese, 1976), but there are exceptions (see Mason & Smith, 1977). Nonetheless, the elderly rarely equal the performance of the young, which suggests that some of the deficit is attributable to hardware. Hardware differences may be responsible for Lyon's (1977) finding that equating strategies reduced but failed to eliminate individual differences in serial recall even among young adults. Nevertheless, the approach of partitioning age-related effects as hardware and software is promising, particularly if a way can be found to quantify proportions of variation attributable to these two sources.

AGE AND PROBLEM SOLVING

Problem solving, although it offers a promising microcosm from which memory can be investigated (e.g., Hitch, 1978; Newell & Simon, 1972), has remained under-investigated with respect to age changes. (See chapters by Botwinick, 1978; and Rabbitt, 1977, for recent reviews.) As in the case of memory, most problem-solving research has been concerned with novel tasks (usually logic and concept formation). The issue of how people with expertise in problem solving respond to aging has been virtually ignored, with some noteworthy exceptions (Elo, 1965; Lehman, 1953; Manniche & Falk, 1957; Zusne, 1976). These investigators, for the most part, examined the performance patterns of the top contributors in various professions from the perspective of assessing when peak performance (e.g., Nobel prize research) was reached (modally at 37). One experimental study by Cjifer (1966), using logic problems, found that older physicians were slightly superior to younger ones. Other experimental investigations of skilled performers, for example, Szafran (1968) and Welford (1973), indicate that the pattern of age-related declines typically found in classical problem-solving tasks seem far less pronounced with expert individuals. Other cases of missing decline, or even improvement with age, have been observed when memory tasks involve comprehension or tap semantic memory (Gardner & Monge, 1977; Perlmutter, 1978; Walsh & Baldwin, 1977; although Cohen, 1979, has found pronounced problems with inference in story comprehension).

The general failure to look at skilled performers operating on tasks in their domain severely handicaps generalizability of the problem-solving studies, particularly with respect to issues such as retirement policy. It can also be argued that certain domains of skilled problem solving offer protection from cohort or generational confounds when using comparatively inexpensive cross-sectional investigations.

Although the debate over the trustworthiness of cross-sectional versus longitudinal versus sequential designs for developmental research has not been settled (see Adam, 1978; Botwinick, 1977; Horn & Donaldson, 1976; and Schaie, 1977), cross-sectional investigations form the overwhelming majority in aging research. The major threat to inference in cross-sectional designs is the cohort or generational confound. When a section is made through chronological age at one point in time, those differing in age also differ in other variables that may correlate with task performance, for example, educational level, health, and current practice in doing similar tasks. The old may be inferior to the young not because their ability has declined but because it was always less well developed. Furthermore, the typical college undergraduate (the usual control) probably has had a great deal more current practice with intentional memorizing than even a well-educated older counterpart. Thus the usual practice of matching old and young on some of these variables (verbal IQ, health, educational level) can never rule out all confounds. Such matching also limits the generalizability of the performance of the older sample, since the sample is almost certainly unrepresentative of the cohort from which it has been drawn.

One problem-solving domain when cohort differences can be minimized is chess. This domain has many attractive properties. Elo (1965, 1978) has developed an interval scale for rating chess players based on chess tournament performance. Rating points are lost or won depending on whether a player wins, draws, or loses, with the amount of gain (or loss), determined by the rating of the opponent. The scale is remarkably valid as a predictor of performance once individuals have built up a pool of rated games.

Although two players may have exactly the same chess rating, and in playing a match reach a drawn result, it is obvious that they may not possess precisely the same knowledge about chess. The rating scale merely guarantees that strengths and weaknesses will balance at the level of molar performance. This property is precisely what is necessary to evaluate how aging might affect problem solving and memory in chess. When one finds equivalently rated old and young players, one might expect to find differences in the component processes underlying that level of skill. The component processes underlying problem solving in chess have been intensively investigated by de Groot (1965, 1966), Newell and Simon (1972), Wagner and Scurrah (1971), and Chase and Simon (1973). Chess is an ancient game that has undergone no significant rule changes in the past century, meaning that there will be few if any generational confoundings related to the time when the game was learned. Chess theory has undergone significant change in the past century, but the mechanism for discovering newer principles of play, search through the game tree, has always been available to players throughout history.

There have been a few investigations into the issues of how aging affects performance in chess (e.g., Buttenweiser, 1936; Lehman, 1953; and Strumilin, cited in Krogius, 1976), but until Elo (1965) generated his rating scale, efforts based on such studies have been suspect. Elo found that there was an inverted U-shaped function relating longitudinal performance of Masters during the 1885–1963 period with their chronological age. The peak tournament performance came at about age 36; however, performances at age 63 equaled that at age 21.

It is quite dangerous to equate performance changes with loss of skill. It is entirely possible that the average level of skill has improved over the past few decades, as has been shown, for instance, for intelligence test components by Schaie (1975) and for age of peak professional contributions in various fields by Lehman (1953). Thus a chess player may in fact maintain or even improve his or her level of skill over the years, yet fail to achieve requisite improved performances simply because he or she is in competition with a new stream of players who start out initially at a higher level of skill than existed in the original pool of competing chess players. It is somewhat counterintuitive, but the more accurate technique for assessing components of skilled performance in chess is a cross-sectional rather than a longitudinal comparison. Given two players of equal strength (rating), yet unequal ages, we can be fairly confident the players possess comparable chess skill. That is, they should score an equal number of points in a match. When a player is examined at two times in his or her career and is found to have the same rating, it is not clear that his or her skill level has remained the same over the years. A 1,600 rating then may be equivalent to a 1,500 rating now.

It is difficult to generalize from the performance of Grandmasters in the Elo study, since they are at least 4–5 standard deviation units above the mean in the rated chess-playing population. Although the issue of whether the aging process treats the more able differently than the less able is unclear, investigations in the area of general intelligence sometimes suggest no differences in decline (e.g., Botwinick, 1977) and sometimes indicate that the more able decline more slowly (Blum & Jarvik, 1974). Furthermore, in these studies there is no taking into account of the age at which "intelligence" is acquired. In chess there does appear to be a relationship between the age when chess was first learned and subsequent performance for those achieving Grandmaster status. Krogius (1976) divided Grandmasters into two groups roughly comparable in ability but differing in starting age. The time to achieve the first Grandmaster level performance was shorter for late starters, $r(38) = -.59$, derived from Krogius's table (p. 241). He also observed that early starters experienced a longer period of optimal results, $r(18) = -.48$. The ranges for starting age and peak period of performance rule out ceiling effects.

In the present study a less extreme range of skill was selected for investigation in the hope of broader generalizability. The amount of variation within age and skill was selected to be roughly comparable. A series of tasks were administered to players to tap both molar problem-solving behavior and some of the component processes thought to underly such problem solving. The tasks involved choosing a move from unfamiliar chess games while thinking out loud, rapid evaluation of end-game positions, and unexpected recall of the initial problems, followed by a forced-choice recognition task.

EXPERIMENT 1

Method

Materials. The positions are shown in Figure 19.1. Three were taken from some 1973 issues of *Chess Life and Review* and one from Fine's *Basic Chess Endings* (1941). They were photographed as slides and were front projected onto a screen. The chessboard subtended a visual angle of approximately 8° × 8°.

Subjects. Thirty-four players provided data. A small fee was provided for participation. Players had all been active in tournaments within the past year and thus had current Chess Federation of Canada (CFC) ratings.[1] Players were male with a rating range from 1,283 to 2,004, with $M = 1,569$ ($SD = 185$), which is somewhat higher than that for the pool of rated Canadian chess players ($M = 1,380$, $SD = 200$). The mean number of hours per week devoted to playing or studying chess was reported as 6.3 ($SD = 5$). The mean age of the sample was 38.7 yr. ($SD = 15.05$), with the range from 16 to 64 yr.; the mean number of years a player had played was 23.2 ($SD = 12.86$), and the mean age when the game was first learned was 15.5 yr. ($SD = 8.56$). Players were selected to vary widely in skill within comparable age levels. Because of the difficulty of filling the planned 3 (age) × 2 (skill level) design, sampling restrictions were relaxed and multiple regression analysis rather than factorial analysis of variance was used.

As seen in Figure 19.2, the attempt to match skill levels and age levels

Position 1

Position 2

Position 3

Position 4

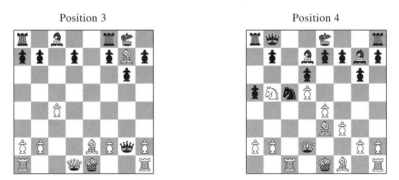

Figure 19.1. Choose-a-move chess positions.

was reasonably successful ($r = .085$). There was no significant relationship between skill level and study time per week ($r = -.004$) nor between age and study time ($r = -.127$). There was a significant relationship between current age and age when chess was first learned ($r = .522$), with current older players being late starters. As expected, there was also a significant correlation between age and number of years of chess ($r = .823$), meaning that current older players had been playing chess for more years than had younger players. There were no other significant correlations among age, skill, study time, starting age, and years of chess playing.

Only two players reported experiencing a serious health problem (stroke, heart attack, severe head injury): one was 64 yr. old and reported a heart attack 10 yr. previously, the other was 22 yr. old and reported having a

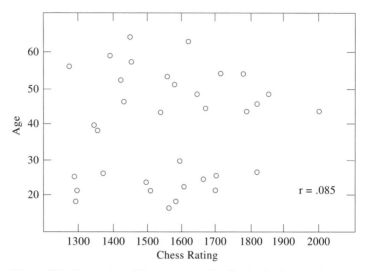

Figure 19.2. Scatterplot of the age-rating distribution in the sample ($r =$ .085).

concussion as a baby. The sample appeared reasonably free of overt illness. All players were screened informally for adequate vision by having them identify chess pieces from a practice slide where a chess piece subtended an angle of approximately $1° \times 1°$. Hearing was considered adequate when players could understand taped instructions.

Procedure. All players filled out a questionnaire asking for age, rating, frequency of play, years of play, and age when chess was learned. As well, players were asked to indicate any serious illnesses or injuries experienced, and whether they had normal vision and hearing.

Tape-recorded instructions outlined the procedure.[2] Players were asked to choose the best move for White while thinking out loud, taking no longer than about 10 min. to do so. If players were silent for very long, the experimenter would prompt them to talk (e.g., "please talk"). Presentation order of the 4 slides was randomized independently for each player. Players' comments were recorded on a cassette recorder with a sensitive lapel microphone.

When the fourth move was announced, the players were introduced to the second task, rapid evaluation. Following the second task, players were asked unexpectedly to recall the four initial problem positions by placing pieces on an empty board. Their recall attempt was videotaped. Following the recall attempt, a recognition task was completed. The 4 problem slides were shown in a randomly ordered set that contained 20 slides from the rapid evaluation task and 6 new slides. Players rated their confidence that each slide presented was a problem slide from 1 to 5: 1 meant that they were certain it was not a problem slide, 3 meant they were uncertain, and 5 indicated certainty that it was a problem slide. Latency to respond was measured with a stopwatch.

Results

Problem Solving. The time to choose a move was recorded to the nearest second. The value of the chosen moves was assessed by an International Master chess player whose FIDE rating[3] at the time was 2,410, slightly more than 2 standard deviations above that of the highest rated player in the study. Moves were rated on a 1–10 scale, with 10 awarded for an immediate winning move (in the Master's judgment) and 1 for a move that immediately loses. The rater reported great difficulty in assigning ratings to nonoptimal moves. In these positions there was only one very good move. This agrees with de Groot (1965), who has argued that for most chess positions there are only one or two good moves, usually just one. The optimal move was rarely chosen by the players, only 17 times out of 136 opportunities.

The two measures[4] were analyzed via multiple regression analysis using the SPSS (Versions 7 and 8) programs (Nie, Hull, Jenkins, Steinbrenner & Bent, 1975). Regression was carried out stepwise,[5] with the first set of predictors entered being CFC (skill level) and age, followed by secondary predictors relevant to the particular analysis. Descriptive statistics for this dependent variable and others are found in Table 19.1 and regression statistics are found in Table 19.2. As can be seen in the tables, the mean time to choose a move correlated positively with skill (24% of the variance accounted) and negatively with age (12% of the variance). The more skilled the player, the longer it took to choose a move; the older the player, the shorter the time taken.

The mean quality of the move was significantly related only to skill level, as seen in Table 19.2. Not surprisingly, the better the player, the better was the selected move, although it must be kept in mind that the best move was rarely selected.

Unexpected Recall. The videotapes were scored for proportion of pieces placed correctly (pieces placed correctly/total pieces in the diagram) and proportion of errors of commission (pieces placed incorrectly/total pieces in the

Table 19.1. Descriptive Statistics for Dependent Variables

Variable	M	SD	Sample size
Age in years	39.00	15.00	34
Chess Federation of Canada rating	1,569.00	185.00	34
Time/problem in seconds	370.00	227.00	34
Problem solution rating	4.30	1.35	34
% pieces placed correctly	68.80	29.50	34
% pieces placed incorrectly	8.20	7.20	34
Number of chunks/position	14.70	4.20	34
Number of pieces/chunk	2.10	.69	34
Median between-chunks latency	4.80	1.28	34
Number of correct chunks/position	9.50	3.20	34
Number of pieces/correct chunk	2.00	.70	34
Confidence rating for target slides	4.80	.41	32
% correct evaluations	56.50	12.20	33
% correct static evaluations	59.70	26.90	30

diagram). Multiple regression analysis, entering the set of predictors of age and skill on the first step and initial study time and either errors of commission or pieces correct yielded the results shown in Table 19.2.

Correct recall was significantly related to both age (37% of the variance) and skill (22%), and time spent problem solving (7%). The older you are, the worse your correct recall score. The more skilled you are, the better your correct recall. The more time spent choosing a move, the better your correct recall.

For errors of commission, the overall equation is significant, but using a conservative test, the only predictor that does account for a significant increment in variance is time (12%), although CFC and age account for between 8% and 10% each. Descriptively, the pattern is the same as for pieces correct. The more skilled, the fewer errors; the older, the more errors; the more time spent choosing a move, the fewer errors.

The failure of older players to recall the positions as accurately as would be expected for their level of skill may be attributable to an encoding and storage problem, a retrieval problem, or some combination of these factors. Previous research has implicated retrieval difficulty as a very important factor (e.g., Schonfield & Robertson, 1966), although there is also evidence for an encoding and storage deficit, for example, Drachman and Leavitt (1972) and Adamowicz (1976). A study by Hultsch (1975) provides evidence that both factors can be operative when categorized lists are recalled. If there is a problem with retrieval, it may be evidenced in failure to access available

Table 19.2. Stepwise Regressions for Dependent Variables

Dependent variable = R^{2b} $R^{2c}=$	V1[a] ΔR^2	+V2 +ΔR^2	+V3 +ΔR^2	+V4 +ΔR^2	+V5	SE
TIME	.633CFC[a]	−5.25AGE	−420			188
	.516	−.348				
	.237*	.120*				
.361[b] .357[c]*						
SOLRATE	.004CFC	−.011AGE	−.011TIME	−1.37		1.12
	.502	−.122	.169			
	.329*	.032	.018			
.318 .380*						
CORR	−1.03AGE	.047CFC	.042TIME	−.197COMM	21.3	17.97
	−.527	.295	.319	−.048		
	.375*	.224*	.074*	.002		
.629 .674*						
COMM	−.003CFC	.051AGE	−.012TIME	−.026CORR	16.51	6.47
	−.064	.107	−.390	−.104		
	.083	.096	.116*	.004		
.201 .298*						
CHNK	−2.40CFC(Z)	1.90AGE(Z)	2.03INTER[d]	.002TIME	13.98	3.21
	−.567	.449	.408	.079		
	.230*	.102*	.158*	.004		
.423 .493*						
PCHNK	.380CFC(Z)	−.359AGE(Z)	−.286INTER	−.0002TIME	2.209	.518
	.553	−.522	−.354	−.077		
	.212*	.165*	.119*	.004		
.431 .500*						
BLAT	−.620CFC(Z)	.246AGE(Z)	.542INTER	−.001TIME	5.119	1.02
	−.483	.191	.359	−.161		
	.286*	.025	.118*	.017		
.368 .445*						
CCHNK	−.008CFC	.048AGE	.008TIME	17.07		2.98
	−.452	.223	.557			
	.026	.001	.199*			
.149 .226*						
PCCHNK	.408CFC(Z)	−.287AGE(Z)	−.269INTER	.0001TIME	1.998	.519
	.579	−.407	−.325	.042		
	.309*	.115*	.098*	.001		
.458 .524*						
TRAT	−.011AGE	.0004CFC	.0003TIME	4.51		.366
	−.417	.167	.164			
	.205*	.063	.017			
.209 .285*						
EVAL	.035CFC	−.043AGE	.332EVALRT	−2.10		10.57
	.528	−.053	.262			
	.238*	.011	.065			
.243 .314*						
STATCORR	.103CFC	−.086AGE	−.859STATIC	−91.32		20.78
	.705	−.048	−.160			
	.440*	.001	.024			
.404 .465*						

NOTE: TIME = solution time/problem; CFC = Chess Federation of Canada Rating; AGE = Age of player in years; SOLRATE = rating of chosen move; CORR = proportion correctly placed pieces/position; COMM = proportion errors of commission/position; CHNK = number of chunks/position; PCHNK = number of pieces/chunk; BLAT = between chunks latency; CCHNK = number of correct chunks/position; PCCHNK = number of pieces/correct chunk; TRAT = confidence rating for target slides; EVAL = % correct evaluations; EVALRT = latency to evaluate a slide; STATCORR = % correct static evaluations; STATIC = number of static evaluations.

[a] Raw score regression weights. Standardized regression weights are in italics.

[b] $R^2 = 1 − (1 − R^2)[(N − 1)/(N − K − 1)]$, an unbiased estimate of the population R^2, with sample size N, and K independent variables.

[c] R^2 is the proportion of variance accounted for by the final equation with K, $N − K − 1$ df. ΔR^2 is the stepwise increment in variance, tested for significance with 1, $N − K − 1$ df. N for each dependent variable appears in Table 19.1.

[d] Interaction term = AGE(Z) × CFC(Z).

*$p < .05$.

information or a slowing down of that process with a subject voluntarily cutting off recall before retrieving all accessible information. One index of retrieval difficulty might be the time taken to begin placing pieces irrespective of whether pieces were encoded correctly initially. Since some players did not attempt recall of all positions, latency to begin recall for those positions was effectively infinite. To circumvent this difficulty, the mean inverse latency to begin a position was computed for all players with unrecalled positions assigned a zero before the mean was computed. Age, CFC, and time (the mean time spent problem solving) were regressed on this measure. There was no significant relationship between inverse latency to begin recall and these predictors, $F(2, 31) = 1.70$. The speed with which information sufficient to activate initial piece placement was accessed did not depend on skill or age.

Recall can also be assessed by segmenting the pattern of piece placements to uncover the chunks into which the position was encoded (Chase & Simon, 1973). Chase and Simon used several criteria for uncovering chunk boundaries—interpiece latency and interpiece relationships. They found that when two successive placements were quick, the number of relations (defense, proximity, color, attack, piece type) among the pieces was high. When pieces were unrelated, the average interpiece latency was quite long, generally greater than 2 sec. Using the 2-sec interpiece latency cutoff, they found good agreement between the imputed chunks for a 5-sec memory task and an immediate perceptual reconstruction task. Similar results have been obtained for the same 2-sec cutoff rule for recall of briefly displayed matrices filled with discs (Bartram, 1978).

Both investigations restricted their subjects to a relatively narrow age range. It may be expected that with increasing age there will be a concurrent increase in retrieval time (e.g., Anders, Fozard & Lillyquist, 1972; Waugh, Thomas & Fozard, 1978). Although there is no evidence for this from the measure of time to begin recall (access any chunk), it is a realistic concern, since it could generate artificial chunk boundaries when the 2-sec cutoff rule is applied. Certainly there is plenty of evidence for a slowing in motor response with age (Welford, 1977), and to place a piece you must first find it at the side of the board, pick it up, and put it down on the correct square.

It was decided to modify the 2-sec rule as follows: Any piece placed within the time frame of 1.5–2.5 sec that had two or more relations (see above) with the preceding piece was considered to be part of the (previous) chunk. If there were fewer than two relations, the piece was assigned to the next chunk. Any piece placed with a latency greater than 2.5 sec was assigned to a new chunk. By dropping .5 sec below 2 sec, we can be conservative about imputing chunk boundaries to young, fast, responders; by extending up to 2.5 sec we can be assured of not penalizing older, slower, responders. At any rate, movement time increases for relatively long movements as a function of age are on the order of about 300 msec at most (e.g., Welford, 1977, p. 455—mean differences between 20–29-yr. old group and 60–69-yr. old group). Furthermore, with people experienced at performing motor tasks, for example, clerks writing digits (LaRiviere & Simonson, 1965), there are no age-related changes evident, so this estimate is probably conservative.

Intercept differences for the Sternberg (1969) memory search task, which are usually interpreted to reflect time to encode the probe and response preparation and execution time, are about the same order of magnitude difference between young and old (about 260 msec; Welford, 1977, p. 394). Assuming additivity for increases with age in mental retrieval and movement time, the 2.5-sec cutoff seems to be a reasonable adjustment.

This segmenting procedure yields a set of chunks that vary in size and a set of within-chunks and between-chunks latencies. Note that all pieces that are placed, irrespective of whether they are correct, enter into this analysis. This includes some cases in which pieces are moved from initial placed positions.

The chunking procedure was applied by Chase and Simon (1973) primarily to recall data following a 5-sec exposure. Recall was presumed to reflect short-term memory processes. Although it is now apparent that 5-sec recall may involve retrieval from long-term memory (Charness, 1976; Frey & Adesman, 1976), it is obvious that the positions being recalled here involve long-term memory and hence may not be as amenable to the same chunking procedure. The same position of 25 pieces could be perfectly reconstructed as 5 chunks with 5 pieces per chunk or as 25 chunks with 1 piece per chunk, given the average problem-solving time of 6 min per position. Conversely, it can be expected that players will encode the position for the problem-solving task in units appropriate to their analysis and will not deal with pieces singly.

The mean number of chunks recalled per position (a different base was adopted for players recalling fewer than four positions) was predicted from age, CFC, and time. An interaction was observed between age and skill, unlike the case for previous dependent variables. Since the interaction term was highly correlated with age ($r = .95$), multi-collinearity problems arose, and the regression programs generated inappropriate beta coefficients (>1). To circumvent this problem, age and CFC were converted to Z scores, then multiplied to yield the interaction term (which yielded $r = -.24$ with age (Z)). As can be seen in Table 19.2, age, skill, and their interaction were significant predictors, accounting jointly for about 42% of the variance (adjusted for shrinkage).

The general pattern indicates that the more skilled the player, the fewer the number of chunks recalled per position, whereas the older the player, the greater the number of chunks recalled per position. The interaction was decomposed by a method suggested by Cohen and Cohen (1975). A family of regression lines was computed from the overall equation by plotting separate equations as a function of high ($Z = 1$), average ($Z = 0$), and low ($Z = -1$) age.[6] This interaction can be interpreted as showing that the sensitivity of chunking to skill level decreases with increasing age.

A complementary pattern is observed in the measure of number of pieces per chunk, as seen in Table 19.2. Again, age, skill, and their interaction account for about 43% of the (corrected) variance. The general picture is that as skill increases, chunk size increases, whereas as age increases, chunk size decreases. When the interaction is analyzed,[7] it can be seen that older players show only a modest increase in chunking efficiency with increasing skill, whereas young players show much greater increases with increasing skill. As would be expected, the two dependent measures of chunk number and chunk size are highly, negatively correlated ($r = -.83$).

The mean median within-chunks and between-chunks latencies were computed for all players. Note that the within-chunks latencies are artificially constrained to be less than 2.5 sec. Nevertheless, it is conceivable that older players would experience some slowing, and this could appear in the within-chunks measure. The between-chunks latencies can involve long time intervals as players struggle to retrieve information that they know is necessary to complete a position. Thus median times were chosen to correct for such long durations.

When within-chunks latency is predicted from age, CFC, and time, there is no significant predictive power, $F(3, 30) = .94$. That is, when players access a chunk, decoding it into component pieces is not related to age, skill, or how long the position (from which the chunk was constructed) was studied. The mean median latency in the sample was 1.1 sec (SD = .37). The integrity of the chunk, once accessed, is maintained despite wide differences in initial encoding ability (skill level) and age. (This replicates and extends the Chase & Simon, 1973, experiment involving long-term memory for games.)

When mean median between-chunks latency is examined, as seen in Table

19.2, there is a significant effect of skill and an Age × Skill interaction. Generally, the better the player, the shorter the time to access the next chunk. As analysis of the interaction demonstrates,[8] this pattern holds only in the lower age ranges, with older players maintaining uniformly long interchunk latencies at all skill levels. The data for younger players provides additional evidence for the Chase and Simon (1973) hypothesis that chunks may be hierarchically organized for better players.

Discussion

A different perspective is obtained with the chunk data compared with the percentage correct recall data. In fact, the correlation between percentage correct recall and chunk size is only .42; recall accuracy correlates −.38 with number of chunks. The most striking finding is the relation between age and chunk size and age and chunk number. Chase and Simon (1973) noted that better players' recall data showed that they stored more pieces in approximately the same number of units. The pattern here was quite similar; better players reconstructed the positions with fewer chunks and more pieces per chunk.

Orthogonal to this pattern was that older players reconstructed the positions with more chunks and fewer pieces per chunk. This peculiar result stands in contradiction to a theory of chess skill that implicates efficient encoding as a determinant of skill. Two players possessing the same rating may vary greatly in chunking pattern if one is young and the other comparatively old, at least for the skill range sampled in this study (1,200–2,000). Note that this is true solely for a measure of long-term retention. It would appear critical to examine a similar sample of age and skill levels for the 5-sec task. There is some indication from another domain that age-correlated effects will be evident for immediate recall. Charness (1979b), using 5-sec recall of a structured bridge hand containing 13 cards, found a significant positive correlation for recall accuracy with skill and a negative correlation with age (accounting for 30% and 28% of variance, respectively, in a stepwise regression). The same recall task with a randomly arranged hand yielded no significant relationships with skill or age.

Note that the inference about encoding is made via recall data. If there is something wrong with the chunking rules, the inference about chunk size may be seriously in error. Remember also that older players do not contribute data that is of equal stability to that provided by younger players. It was therefore decided to reexamine the data for the chunking procedure and apply the analyses only for correct chunks (pieces correctly recalled). This subset of data would exclude guessing (unless successful) and reconstructive activity based on the desire to fill in a logical position in the case of older individuals, who tended to be less successful (see recall scores in Table 19.2, CORR and COMM). The results can be seen in Table 19.2.

Correct chunk data. The total chunk data were partitioned to look at correct chunks only. That is, if a player placed eight chunks of which only three were completely correct, then those three chunks formed the basis for analysis. For some individuals this meant using a very small data base over the four positions. This procedure also penalizes players with large chunks somewhat unduly, since a single large chunk of seven pieces, with only one piece placed incorrectly, is eliminated from the analysis. Thus, conclusions from correct chunk data must be treated cautiously.

The main measures computed were mean number of correct chunks per position recalled (resulting in different denominators for some players who did not recall all four positions), mean number of pieces per correct chunk, mean median within-chunks latency, and the mean median latency between a correct chunk and the next chunk (which could be correct or incorrect). The rules for determining chunk boundaries were the same as those for the total chunk analysis.

As seen in Table 19.2, the only significant predictor of number of correct chunks per position was average time to solve the problems. The more time taken to solve the problem positions, the more correct chunks per position appeared in the recall protocol. That is, people taking longer to solve the problems tended to have the position coded as a larger number of totally correct units—but this does not necessarily mean that their total recall score was higher. The number of chunks and number of correct chunks correlated .52.

As seen in Table 19.2, an identical pattern to that obtained with total chunks is found for correct chunks with respect to number of pieces per chunk (the two measures correlated .88). That is, the more skilled the player, the larger the number of pieces per (correct) chunk, and the older the player, the fewer the number of pieces per (correct) chunk, with the interaction indicating that older players were less affected by increases in skill as far as chunking efficiency was concerned.

There were no significant predictors of either median within-chunks latency or median between-chunks latency.

Recognition. It seems clear that older individuals experience greater difficulty in retrieving information about chess positions when given only the cue to recall them. The recognition task was appended to the recall task to see whether a more sensitive index of retention would clarify the recall results. Some players (both young and old) evidently misunderstood the instructions and rated all previously seen positions (the four problems and the 20 evaluation positions) as 5—certain that the position was a problem position. In the first attempt at analysis, only the responses to target slides were evaluated, and this was done for all players. Any rating of 4 or 5 on a target was credited as a correct recognition. Thus a player could obtain a score of 0–4 on the recognition task. When number of correct recognitions is regressed with age, skill, and solution time, there is no significant prediction, $F(3, 28) = 1.59$. The mean number of hits was 3.66 (SD $= .65$). Virtually every player retained sufficient information to identify targets, even if they could not reconstruct them during recall.

Recall accuracy and recognition are not strongly correlated. Recognition hit score correlates .20 with percentage correct recall (not significant), although this may be due in part to a range restriction for recognition scores. There is a significant positive correlation between recall and rating for targets ($r = .475$); the higher the recall score, the higher the confidence rating for targets in the recognition task. Similarly, the higher the recall, the lower the rating of nontargets ($r = -.383$). Also, the more accurate the recall, the faster the rejection of nontargets ($r = -.494$). There was no correlation between accurate recall and latency to rate a target ($r = .085$).

A plausible interpretation of these results is possible if the recognition task is cast in a signal detection framework. Because targets are so infrequent (4/30 slides), subjects are likely to adopt a conservative criterion for saying yes, or conversely, be rather quick to say no. Latency to respond to nontargets was quick ($M = 5.20$ sec, $SD = 3.1$) compared to latency to respond to targets ($M = 12.2$ sec, $SD = 13.2$).

The simple collapsing of ratings into hits or misses (4, 5 = hit) may fail to provide the most sensitive index of memory. Goldin (1978) has shown that various orienting tasks in an incidental-learning paradigm for chess positions have more pronounced effects on confidence ratings than on recognition accuracy—with shallower processing of chess diagrams leading to lower confidence ratings. Eysenck (1977) and Craik (1977) summarized results that favor the notion that older people tend to process to-be-remembered material in a more shallow fashion. Admittedly, in this experiment all players were supposed to be operating at the same level, a detailed dynamic analysis of the position with the aim of discovering the best move. Nonetheless, older players tended to spend less time on the problem-solving task, although their solutions were equally as good as those of younger players. Thus it was decided to examine the relationship between the mean recognition ratings for targets and three predictors: time spent solving the problems, age, and skill.

As can be seen in Table 19.2, the mean rating of targets was sensitive to age (20% of variance accounted for) with older players showing less confidence in recognizing targets, despite the fact that collapsing 4 and 5 ratings into hits yields no relationship between age and hit rate.

The recognition data indicate that players, regardless of skill level or age, had retained sufficient information to discriminate the problem positions from other recently presented positions, though their confidence levels varied inversely with age, perhaps indicating a more conservative criterion on the part of older players.

EXPERIMENT 2

The second experiment, which served as the interpolated task between problem solving and recall, was designed to tap another important dimension of chess skill, namely, ability to evaluate an end-game position rapidly. (An end-game position contrasts with a middle-game position in that there are usually fewer pieces present and the expected outcome is usually well-defined.)

Method

Materials. Slides were made of 20 diagrams from Fine's (1941) book, *Basic Chess Endings.* Eight were theoretical wins for white, 4 were wins for black, and 8 were draws. The slides were displayed as were the problem slides.

Procedure. Tape-recorded instructions told the subjects to evaluate accurately each position as rapidly as possible into one of three categories: White (the side always on move) wins, the position is drawn, white loses. A slide was terminated when the subject responded. Latency to respond was recorded to the nearest .1 sec. Slide order was randomized independently for each subject.

Results

As can be seen in Table 19.2, the only significant predictor of evaluation accuracy was skill level, accounting for about 24% of the variance in accuracy. Age was not related to accuracy.

Latency to respond was not related to skill, age, or accuracy, $F(3, 29) = 1.57$. The simple correlation of accuracy and latency was .20 (not significant), giving a slight hint of a speed–accuracy trade-off.

It was hoped that the instructions would induce players to respond quickly on the basis of static evaluation[9] of the positions. This was clearly not the case, probably because players within this skill range did not have a very large repertoire of such evaluations. It was decided to break down the data into those cases in which players responded within 10 sec of onset of the diagram, defined as static evaluations, and those in which players responded with a latency greater than 10 sec, defined as dynamic evaluations. Twenty-two players had a majority of over 10-sec responses, 9 players had a majority under 10 sec, and 2 showed an even number of such responses. One was missing data due to equipment failure. In the sample, the mean number of quick responses was 7.4 ($SD = 5.0$), slow responses 12.6 ($SD = 5.0$).

It is possible to examine whether the pattern of responses within these two categories of latency varies as a function of age and skill. The proportion of correct responses within the 10 sec or less and greater than 10 sec latency categories was computed. For some individuals, these proportions are based on a very small number of observations (one, two, or three), and data are missing for a number of players who were either consistently quick or consistently slow. Thus the results must be interpreted cautiously.

Worth examining first is whether the number of quick latencies varies as a function of skill or age. (Recall that the mean latency to respond was not related to skill or age.) The regression equation was not significant, $F(2, 30) < 1$. The number of quick evaluations a player made was not related to age or skill level.

As can be seen in Table 19.2, there is a strong relationship between proportion correct for quick latencies and skill level. The more skilled you are, the higher the proportion of correct quick evaluations. No such relation exists for evaluations that take longer than 10 sec, $F(3, 28) < 1$. Within the constraints of the task, if you cannot decide quickly on an evaluation, you are no more successful at working out an evaluation whether you are highly skilled or less skilled, which for these end-game positions makes some degree of sense. The amount of search necessary to converge on a correct evaluation is probably too great to be completed in under a minute, although the mean performance on long latencies was 55%, which is still better than chance (33%).

Discussion

Knowing the value of end-game positions is very important to a chess player. It is this information that often directly guides decisions about moves in the middle game and sometimes even the opening. Chess games among players of this skill range rarely end in checkmate. Rather, players resign when the position is judged hopelessly lost, or agree to a draw when the position is hopelessly drawn.

Again, there is no significant relationship between age and accuracy of evaluation when the evaluation is speeded. There is a significant relationship to skill. The pattern observed here complements that found for choosing a move.

GENERAL DISCUSSION

When the performance of chess players who vary in age and skill is examined, critical aspects of performance do not relate to the player's age, but only to skill level. This is true for choosing a move and rapidly evaluating an end-game position.

The absence of a relationship between age and performance cannot be attributed to having a sample of extraordinary older people or selection factors critical to continuing to play chess. When memory tasks related to chess are employed, typical deficits are observed with these players. Unexpected recall, a task tapping long-term memory for recent problem-solving activity, shows characteristic negative relationships with age. The recognition task appended to the recall task indicates that the deficits in performance are due primarily to retrieval problems.

More important, for each memory task in which there were negative effects attributable to age, there were positive effects attributable to skill. Age and skill tend to trade-off in memory performance.

As Rabbitt (1977) noted so aptly at the end of his review on age and problem solving (p. 623):

In view of the deterioration of memory and perceptual motor performance with advancing age, the right kind of question may well be not 'why are old people so bad at cognitive tasks,' but rather, 'how, in spite of growing disabilities, do old people preserve such relatively good performance?'

This study echoes that sentiment. Given the retrieval deficits associated with aging in both incidental recall and recognition confidence, why is there no deficit in molar problem-solving performance?

An appealingly simple, yet misleading, explanation for these results can be advanced by drawing on the distinction between *episodic* and *semantic* memory (Tulving, 1972), and suggesting that aging affects the former but not the latter. Yet it is quite clear that choosing a move requires access to both semantic and episodic traces. Phrased in a more neutral fashion, choosing a move in chess requires players to store and retrieve long-term memory information. The specific moves generated during a search episode are generated via accessed long-term memory information (e.g., Newell & Simon's [1972] move productions, an example being capture $\rightarrow$ recapture). Players must also store and access the evaluation for a line of moves in order to choose the move leading to the best outcome. Indeed, they probably must also remember sequences of moves (episodic) to avoid generating them repeatedly.

If older players store and retrieve long-term memory information less efficiently, one would expect more redundant search and probably a longer search episode. Yet, older players took significantly less time to converge on their choice of move. On the other hand, if older players know that they tend to experience retrieval difficulties, it would be adaptive to terminate search as quickly as they do in order to rely more on short-term than on long-term memory. This leaves unanswered the issues of how they still manage to produce equally as good moves as younger players.

Actually, the question might be turned around. Why don't younger players of equivalent skill produce better solutions, given that they take more time to search the problem space? It seems clear that searching a larger number of alternatives leads to improved chess play for computers (Berliner, 1978). The same is true for humans in terms of the quality of play that results from speed chess versus slower tournament play. On the other hand, the absolute amount of time difference as a function of age was relatively small, on the order of a few minutes (5 sec less per year of age, according to the regression equation in Table 19.2) for a 25-yr. age difference. Taking the de Groot (1965) estimate that a new base move is generated about every 2 to 3 min., the extra time would have meant that at most one new base move would have been evaluated by younger players.

Greater selectivity on the part of older players could easily compensate for evaluating one less base move. Thus, one possibility is that the compensatory mechanism for older players involves having more refined move generators or possibly more refined evaluations stored in association with the hypothesized large (but equivalent for a given skill level) repertoire of stored patterns. Another possibility, that older players may have accumulated a larger repertoire of recognizable patterns than comparably skilled younger players, seems to be ruled out by the chunk-size data. The possibility of having more refined evaluations would seem to be ruled out in the analysis of the second experiment in which skill but not age was significantly, positively related to static evaluation accuracy.

An important implication of these results is that chess skill may not be attributable to the same mechanisms at all ages. Even the basic tenet that chess skill is strongly related to efficient encoding (due to a large repertoire of recognizable patterns) may be suspect. The striking results of the chunk analysis showed that age operated inversely to skill with more chunks recalled with fewer pieces per chunk as a function of age, even though the usual Chase and Simon (1973) result was obtained as a function of skill. It is difficult to account for such a result within the framework assumed to underly chess skill, although the crucial test of the encoding hypothesis would necessitate doing an immediate recall task.

In one condition of a study in progress, Charness (1979a) obtained evidence that runs contrary to the encoding-skill hypothesis. A young and an old group with equivalent chess skill recalled six chess positions shown for 4 sec each. The young group correctly recalled a greater proportion of pieces than the equivalently skilled older group (.35 vs. .24, $t(18) = 3.02$). Such a finding contrasts strongly with the work of Chi (1978), who found that children chess players seem to resemble young adult chess players in immediate recall ability.

Some of the limitations as well as strengths of both experiments should be stressed. The term *older players* refers to ages 50–65 yr. The fact that all players were volunteers probably means that any age-related deficits are somewhat underestimated, particularly in view of the self-selection factors that mediate chess tournament participation.

Neither experiment directly addresses the issue of whether skill level declines with age nor takes into account whether the distribution of players to rating level varies with age, although the difficulty of finding rated participants in the upper age ranges suggests that tournament chess is practiced more by the young. On the other hand, the tasks performed by the participants in both studies seem to have good generalizability. It is sobering to note that the only task showing age-related deficits was incidental learning, a task more in the tradition of laboratory research. Also, the finding of no age-related effects for the choose-a-move task is, admittedly, precisely what is to be expected if ratings are valid indicators of chess skill at all ages and if the task is an accurate replica of choosing a move in a tournament game. With only four positions sampled, there is always the risk that the demands of the task environment are transparent to the skill range represented in the sample, but at least for these positions this was not the case. Furthermore, chess ratings are generated on the basis of many hundreds of iterations on choosing a move (the average tournament game lasts about 42 moves), so sampling four exemplars from the choose-a-move task need not lead to as strong a correlation between skill level and solution accuracy as was observed.

The finding of skill-related but not age-related effects for the rapid evaluation task was also somewhat unexpected. There has been some speculation that an important component of skill is static evaluation (Charness, 1977; Newell & Simon, 1972). Initial tests (Winkelman, 1975) using opening game positions showed no significant correlation with chess rating ($r = -.17$), although a more recent test using a 3-min. evaluation period (Holding, 1979) showed stronger players to be more accurate, particularly for end-game positions. In view of the general finding that the elderly do better under self-paced than speeded conditions, it seemed quite likely, a priori, that age-related effects would be found for the evaluation task, but they were not.

Another salient point is that current practice levels in this sample did not correlate with age and represented on the average a relatively modest amount of time per week (less than 1 hr. per day). Comparatively meaningless exercises form the vast majority of experimental tasks for investigating differences between young and old. In most cases early cohorts have probably had far less past and current experience assimilating large bodies of new rote knowledge. This may explain why out-of-practice older individuals are less likely to use mnemonic devices when learning nonsense lists, and why even relatively minor instructional interventions can often produce measurable changes in cognitive performance. The elderly may be "rusty" from disease or disuse, but few studies have explored the latter alternative. At any rate, the confound of lack of current practice with the task is missing from both experiments, which may be more of a strength than a weakness.

CONCLUSION

At the outset, a strategy was suggested for investigating cognitive aging. The idea advanced was to equate different age groups for molar problem-solving performance and to examine whether the component processes differ among the groups. The underlying assumption is that if aging is associated with deficits in hardware or software related to information processing, different mechanisms would mediate equivalent performance in young and old.

This strategy was pursued for problem solving in chess. Players were selected along the continua of age and skill such that the two variables were uncorrelated. Skill was assessed via a chess rating scale. As expected, skill but not age predicted accuracy in a choose-a-move task. Similarly, for rapid evaluation of end-game positions, skill but not age was the significant predictor of performance.

In memory tasks, age and skill jointly determined overall accuracy and chunking efficiency, with age negatively and skill positively associated with performance. The pattern of results suggests that despite decreases in efficiency in encoding and retrieval of information, older players can match the performance of younger players. The compensating mechanism is more efficient search of the problem space, as evidenced by older players taking less time to select an equally good move. This efficiency is probably due to more refined move generation processes. These results argue for a more flexible model of chess skill to describe performance over the life span.

NOTES

1. A new player is provided with a provisional rating via an alternate formula until at least 16 rated games have been played. (See Elo, 1978, for details.)

2. The testing site for players varied to suit their convenience. The main sites were psychology labs at the University of Waterloo and McMaster University, the Toronto Chess Club, the Scarborough Chess Club, and the Willowdale Chess Club.

3. The International Master title is awarded by the Fédération Internationale Des Echecs (FIDE), the international chess federation, based on tournament results in national and international tournaments. Approximately the same rating method is used in Canada by the CFC.

4. Following submission of this article, further analyses have been carried out on the transcribed protocols. They are detailed in Charness (in press).

5. The actual order of entry for the first two variables is determined by whichever variable has the highest correlation with the dependent variable. Entry into the equation is governed by the program requirement that the contribution to explained variance exceed .1%. In all cases the regression was first performed with an Age ×

Skill term forced to enter following age and skill to assess a possible interaction. If a nonsignificant result was obtained with this term in the equation, it was dropped and a simple additive model was assumed. The cases in which an interaction effect was observed are interpreted in the appropriate results section. Because of equipment failure, two subjects were eliminated from consideration since most of their data were missing. Other instances of missing data (where equipment failed or subjects did not respond) were handled by allowing variablewise deletion during regression, and are indicated in the tables where N departs from 34.

6. Rearranging the coefficients in Table 19.2 and assigning the mean solution time yields:

$$\hat{Y} \text{ High} = -.37 \text{ CFC(Z)} + 16.44$$

$$\hat{Y} \text{ Average} = -2.40 \text{ CFC(Z)} + 14.54$$

$$\hat{Y} \text{ Low} = -4.43 \text{ CFC(Z)} + 12.64.$$

7. Plotting a family of equations as a function of age from Table 19.2 as was done before yields:

$$\hat{Y} \text{ High} = .09 \text{ CFC(Z)} + 1.78$$

$$\hat{Y} \text{ Average} = .38 \text{ CFC(Z)} + 2.14$$

$$\hat{Y} \text{ Low} = .65 \text{ CFC(Z)} + 2.49.$$

8. Plotting a family of equations as a function of age from Table 2 yields:

$$\hat{Y} \text{ High} = -.08 \text{ CFC(Z)} + 5.03$$

$$\hat{Y} \text{ Average} = -.62 \text{ CFC(Z)} + 4.79$$

$$\hat{Y} \text{ Low} = -1.16 \text{ CFC(Z)} + 4.54.$$

9. A static evaluation is considered here to be one that is based on recognition. That is, the player does not need to engage in any search through the game tree of move possibilities.

REFERENCES

Adam, J. Sequential strategies and the separation of age, cohort, and time-of-measurement contributions to developmental data. Psychological Bulletin, 1978, 85, 1309–1316.

Adamowicz, J. K. Visual short-term memory and aging. Journal of Gerontology, 1976, 31, 39–46.

Anders, T. R., Fozard, J. L. & Lillyquist, T. D. The effects of age upon retrieval from short-term memory. Developmental Psychology, 1972, 6, 214–217.

Baltes, P. B. & Schaie, K. W. On the plasticity of intelligence in adulthood and old age. American Psychologist, 1976, 31, 720–725.

Bartram, D. J. *Post-iconic visual storage: Chunking in the reproduction of briefly displayed visual patterns.* Cognitive Psychology, *1978, 10,* 324–355.

Berliner, H. A chronology of computer chess and its literature. Artificial Intelligence, *1978,* 10, *201–214.*

Birren, J. E. *Translations in gerontology—from lab to life: Psychophysiology and speed of response.* American Psychologist, *1974, 29, 808–815.*

Blum, J. E. & Jarvik, L. F. *Intellectual performance of octogenarians as a function of education and initial ability.* Human Development, *1974, 17, 364–375.*

Botwinick, J. *Intellectual abilities. In J. E. Birren & K. W. Schaie (Eds.),* Handbook of the psychology of aging. *New York: Van Nostrand Reinhold, 1977.*

Botwinick, J. *Aging and behavior. New York: Springer, 1978.*

Buttenweiser, P. *The relation of age to skill of expert chess players. Unpublished doctoral dissertation, Stanford University, 1936.*

Canestrari, R. E. *Age changes in acquisition. In G. A. Talland (Ed.),* Human aging and behavior. *New York: Academic Press, 1968.*

Carroll, J. B. & Maxwell, S. E. *Individual differences in cognitive abilities.* Annual Review of Psychology, *1979,* 30, *603–640.*

Charness, N. *Memory for chess positions: Resistance to interference.* Journal of Experimental Psychology: Human Learning and Memory, *1976, 2, 641–653.*

Charness, N. *Human chess skill. In P. W. Frey (Ed.),* Chess skill in man and machine. *New York: Springer, 1977.*

Charness, N. *Age-related differences in visual memory. Paper presented at the Canadian Association on Gerontology meeting, Halifax, Nova Scotia, November 1979a.*

Charness, N. *Components of skill in bridge.* Canadian Journal of Psychology, *1979b,* 33, *1–16.*

Charness, N. *Search in chess: Age and skill differences.* Journal of Experimental Psychology: Human Perception and Performance, *in press.*

Chase, W. G. & Simon, H. A. *The mind's eye in chess. In W. G. Chase (Ed.),* Visual information processing. *New York: Academic Press, 1973.*

Chi, M. T. H. *Knowledge structures and memory development. In R. Siegler (Ed.),* Children's thinking: What develops? *Hillsdale, N.J.: Erlbaum, 1978.*

Cjifer, E. *An experiment on some differences in logical thinking between Dutch medical people, under and over the age of 35.* Acta Psychologica, *1966, 25, 159–171.*

Cohen, G. *Language comprehension in old age.* Cognitive Psychology, *1979,* 11, *412–429.*

Cohen, J. & Cohen, P. *Applied multiple regression/correlation analysis for the behavioral sciences. Hillsdale, N.J.: Erlbaum, 1975.*

Craik, F. I. M. *Age differences in human memory. In J. E. Birren & K. W. Schaie (Eds.),* Handbook of the psychology of aging. *New York: Van Nostrand Reinhold, 1977.*

de Groot, A. D. *Thought and choice in chess. The Hague, The Netherlands: Mouton, 1965.*

de Groot, A. D. *Perception and memory versus thought: Some old ideas and recent findings. In B. Kleinmuntz (Ed.),* Problem solving: Research, method and theory. *New York: Wiley, 1966.*

Drachman, D. A. & Leavitt, J. L. Memory impairment in the aged: Storage versus retrieval deficit. Journal of Experimental Psychology, *1972, 93, 302–308.*

Elo, A. E. Age changes in master chess performance. Journal of Gerontology, *1965, 20, 289–299.*

Elo, A. E. The rating of chessplayers past and present. New York: Arco, 1978.

Eysenck, M. W. Human memory: Theory, research and individual differences. Oxford, England: Pergamon Press, 1977.

Fine, R. Basic chess endings. New York: McKay, 1941.

Frey, P. & Adesman, P. Recall-memory for visually presented chess positions. Memory & Cognition, *1976, 4, 541–547.*

Gardner, E. F. & Monge, R. H. Adult age differences in cognitive abilities and educational background. Experimental Aging Research, *1977, 3, 337–383.*

Goldin, S. Effects of orienting tasks on recognition of chess positions. American Journal of Psychology, *1978, 91, 659–671.*

Hitch, G. J. The role of short-term working memory in mental arithmetic. Cognitive Psychology, *1978, 10, 302–323.*

Holding, D. H. Evaluation of chess positions. Simulation & Games, *1979, 10, 207–221.*

Horn, J. L. & Donaldson, G. On the myth of intellectual decline in adulthood. American Psychologist, *1976, 31, 701–719.*

Horn, J. & Donaldson, G. Faith is not enough: A response to the Baltes-Schaie claim that intelligence does not wane. American Psychologist, *1977, 32, 369–373.*

Hulicka, I. M. & Grossman, J. L. Age-group comparisons for the use of mediators in paired-associate learning. Journal of Gerontology, *1967, 22, 46–51.*

Hultsch, D. F. Adult age differences in retrieval: Trace-dependent and cue-dependent forgetting. Developmental Psychology, *1975, 11, 197–201.*

Hunt, F. & Love, T. How good can memory be? In A. W. Melton & E. Martin (Eds.), Coding processes in human memory. *Washington, D.C.: V. H. Winston, 1972.*

Krogius, N. Psychology in chess. New York: RHM Press, 1976.

Labouvie-Vief, G. & Gonda, J. N. Cognitive strategy training and intellectual performance in the elderly. Journal of Gerontology, *1976, 31, 327–332.*

LaRiviere, J. E. & Simonson, E. The effect of age and occupation on speed of writing. Journal of Gerontology, *1965, 20, 415–416.*

Lehman, H. C. Age and achievement. Princeton, N.J.: Princeton University Press, 1953.

Lyon, D. R. Individual differences in immediate serial recall: A matter of mnemonics? Cognitive Psychology, *1977, 9, 403–411.*

Manniche, E. & Falk, G. Age and the Nobel prize. Behavioral Science, *1957, 2, 301–307.*

Marshall, P. H., et al. Age differences in verbal mediation: A structural and functional analysis. Experimental Aging Research, *1978, 4, 175–193.*

Mason, S. E. & Smith, A. D. Imagery in the aged. Experimental Aging Research, *1977, 3, 17–32.*

Neisser, U. Cognition and reality. San Francisco: Freeman, 1976.

Newell, A. & Simon, H. A. Human problem solving. Englewood Cliffs, N.J.: Prentice-Hall, 1972.

Nie, N. H., Hull, C. H., Jenkins, J. G., Steinbrenner, K. & Bent, D. H. SPSS: Statistical package for the social sciences. *New York: McGraw-Hill, 1975.*

Perlmutter, M. What is memory aging the aging of? Developmental Psychology, *1978,* 14, *330–345.*

Plemons, J. L., Willis, S. L. & Baltes, P. B. Modifiability of fluid intelligence in aging: A short-term longitudinal training approach. Journal of Gerontology, *1978,* 33, *224–231.*

Rabbitt, P. Changes in problem-solving ability in old age. In J. E. Birren & K. W. Schaie (Eds.), Handbook of the psychology of aging. *New York: Van Nostrand Reinhold, 1977.*

Rowe, E. J. & Schnore, M. M. Item concreteness and reported strategies in paired-associate learning as a function of age. Journal of Gerontology, *1971,* 26, *470–475.*

Schaie, K. W. Age changes in adult intelligence. In D. S. Woodruff & J. E. Birren (Eds.), Aging: Scientific perspectives and social issues. *New York: Van Nostrand Reinhold, 1975.*

Schaie, K. W. Quasi-experimental research designs in the psychology of aging. In J. E. Birren & K. W. Schaie (Eds.), Handbook of the psychology of aging. *New York: Van Nostrand Reinhold, 1977.*

Schaie, K. W. External validity in the assessment of intellectual performance in adulthood. Journal of Gerontology, *1978,* 33, *695–701.*

Scheidt, R. J. & Schaie, K. W. A taxonomy of situations for an elderly population: Generating situational criteria. Journal of Gerontology, *1978,* 33, *848–857.*

Schonfield, D. & Robertson, B. A. Memory storage and aging. Canadian Journal of Psychology, *1966,* 20, *228–236.*

Simon, H. A. Information processing models of cognition. Annual Review of Psychology, *1979,* 30, *363–396.*

Sternberg, S. Memory scanning: Mental processes revealed by reaction-time experiments. American Scientist, *1969,* 57, *421–457.*

Szafran, J. Psychophysiological studies of aging in pilots. In G. A. Talland (Ed.), Human aging and behavior. *New York: Academic Press, 1968.*

Treat, N. J. & Reese, H. W. Age, pacing, and imagery in paired-associate learning. Developmental Psychology, *1976,* 12, *119–124.*

Tulving, E. Episodic and semantic memory. In E. Tulving & W. Donaldson (Eds.), Organization of memory. *New York: Academic Press, 1972.*

Wagner, D. A. & Scurrah, M. J. Some characteristics of human problem-solving in chess. Cognitive Psychology, *1971,* 2, *454–478.*

Wagner, D. A. Memories of Morocco: The influence of age, schooling, and environment on memory. Cognitive Psychology, *1978,* 10, *1–28.*

Walsh, D. A. & Baldwin, M. Age differences in integrated semantic memory. Developmental Psychology, *1977,* 13, *509–514.*

Waugh, N. C., Thomas, J. C. & Fozard, J. L. Retrieval time from different memory stores. Journal of Gerontology, *1978,* 33, *718–724.*

Welford, A. T. Ageing and human skill. Westport, Conn.: Greenwood Press, 1973. (Originally published by Oxford University Press, London, 1958.)

Welford, A. T. Motor performance. In J. E. Birren & K. W. Schaie (Eds.), Handbook of the psychology of aging. *New York: Van Nostrand Reinhold, 1977.*

Winkelman, J. H. Tests of chess skill. Unpublished manuscript, University of Oregon, 1975.

Woodruff, D. S. & Birren, J. E. (Eds.). Aging: Scientific perspectives and social issues. *New York: Van Nostrand Reinhold, 1975.*

Zusne, L. Age and achievement in psychology. American Psychologist, *1976, 31, 805–807.*

20. Effects of Age and Skill in Typing

Timothy A. Salthouse

ALTHOUGH THERE HAS been considerable research on typing processes, only a small fraction has addressed the question of what skilled typists are doing that less skilled ones are not. The present article focuses on determinants of typing skill by examining correlates of typing proficiency in typists whose net rates (subtracting five characters for each error) ranged from 17 to 104 words per minute (wpm). Variables included in the analysis were selected on the basis of results from earlier studies investigating basic typing phenomena.

SKILL EFFECTS

One of the most dramatic findings from previous research is that the speed of typing is markedly slowed by reducing the number of characters visible in the to-be-typed material. Coover (1923) was apparently the first to report this effect, and it has subsequently been confirmed by Hershman and Hillix (1965), Shaffer (1973, 1976), Shaffer and French (1971), and Shaffer and Hardwick (1970). Shaffer's (1976) results with a single skilled typist are typical. The median interkey interval was 101 ms (approximately 118 gross wpm) for typing with unlimited preview and for typing with 8 characters visible to the right of the to-be-typed character, but was 446 ms (approximately 27 gross wpm) with only 1 character visible prior to each keystroke. Clearly, proficient typing is dependent on the ability to view characters in advance of the one currently being typed. Butsch (1932) and Fuller (1943) reached this same conclusion in an analysis of eye movements recorded while subjects were typing. Butsch (1932) also demonstrated that the span between the character being typed and the character currently being fixated was positively related to typing skill. On the average, typists performing at a rate of 40 wpm had an eye–hand span of 3.96 characters, while 70-wpm typists had an eye–hand span of 5.93 characters. Across 19 typists with typing speeds

Reprinted by permission from *The Journal of Experimental Psychology: General* 13, no. 3 (1984): 345–71. Copyright © 1984 by the American Psychological Association.

from 35 to 100 wpm, the correlation between eye–hand span and typing rate was +.68.

The preceding results, particularly those of Butsch (1932), suggest that one determinant of skilled typing is the ability to process characters in advance of the character whose key is currently being pressed. I examined this possibility by manipulating the number of characters visible in the to-be-typed material and by defining the eye–hand span as the minimum preview window at which typing rate first differs from that of normal typing with unlimited preview. If rate of typing is disrupted, one can infer that the typist normally relies on the viewing of more than the presented number of characters; therefore, the preview at which typing rate is disrupted can serve as an estimate of eye–hand span in normal typing. It is worth noting that the present method probably produces an underestimate of the actual eye–hand span in that the disruption is evident only after the normal span is prevented.

Another well-documented finding is that familiar, meaningful material is typed faster than unfamiliar, nonsense material (e.g., Fendrick, 1937; Hershman & Hillix, 1965; Larochelle, 1983; Olsen & Murray, 1976; Shaffer, 1973, 1976; Shaffer & Hardwick, 1968, 1969a, 1970; Terzuolo & Viviani, 1980; Thomas & Jones, 1970; West & Sabban, 1982). The redundancy of familiar text evidently allows predictable sequences of characters (keystrokes) to be primed in some fashion, thereby facilitating their speed of execution. If a mechanism such as this is responsible for the meaningfulness effect, one may expect typing skill to be related to sensitivity to linguistic redundancy. In other words, fast typists may be fast in part because they are better able to predict and behave appropriately in response to lengthy sequences of characters. I examined this hypothesis by contrasting typing performance on normal text and on text in which the order of characters had been reversed in a letter-by-letter fashion. The reversal preserves the letter frequencies, punctuation, capitalization, and letter groupings of natural language while destroying its meaningfulness. A second manipulation of material meaningfulness was carried out in Study 2 by requiring subjects to type a continuous series of random letters. Although this material shared few structural properties with normal text, it provided a greater range of letter diagram frequencies than was otherwise available.

A result obvious even by casual observation is that all keystrokes are not executed at the same rate. In order to achieve the high rates characteristic of skilled typing, fast typists may be more consistent in their keying speed than less competent typists may be (Gentner, 1982a; Long, Nimmo-Smith & Whitefield, 1983), having somehow managed to reduce the time of what are initially slow keystrokes to nearly the rate of the fastest keystrokes. (Interestingly, however, Harding, 1933, suggested just the opposite and claimed that faster typists exhibit more extreme variation among keystrokes than slower typists.)

There are actually two distinct classes of typing variability (Gentner, 1982a, 1982b), interkeystroke and intrakeystroke, and two plausible sources of the variability, mechanical and experiential. Interkeystroke variability can be easily assessed by means of the interquartile range encompassing the middle 50% of the intervals across all keystrokes. However, in order to determine the consistency of typing the same character, the context in which the character appears should be constant across character repetitions. This was achieved by requiring subjects to type the same sentence 10 times, and then by determining the interquartile range of interkey intervals across the 10 repetitions of the same character. The median of these interquartile ranges across all characters thus served as the measure of intrakeystroke variability.

Mechanical sources of interkeystroke variability include physical constraints such as keyboard location, finger dexterity, and repetition or alternation of finger and hand. For example, Coover (1923), Fox and Stansfield (1964), Gentner (1981, 1982a), Grudin and Larochelle (1982), Kinkead (1975), Lahy (1924), Larochelle (1983), Ostry (1983), Rumelhart and Norman (1982), Shaffer (1976, 1978), and Terzuolo and Viviani (1980) all demonstrated that the interkey interval is about 30–60 ms shorter when the two keystrokes come from opposite hands rather than from the same hand. Kinkead (1975) conducted one of the most complete analyses and reported that keys struck with alternate hands averaged 136 ms; those with the same hand, 168 ms; and those with the same finger, 218 ms. These mechanical factors may extend over sequences of three or more characters (Gentner, 1982b; Gentner, Grudin & Conway, 1980; Rumelhart & Norman, 1982; Shaffer, 1978), and therefore physical constraints could be an important source of variability in interkeystroke timing. The difference between digrams typed with alternate hands and with the same finger is the largest mechanical factor evident in previous studies; thus, skill effects were primarily examined on this variable.

Experiential factors refer to alterations in keying efficiency produced by differential amounts of experience typing specific character sequences. Perhaps the best illustration of this type of influence is the negative relation between interkey interval and frequency of the letter digrams in written language (e.g., Dvorak et al., 1936; Grudin & Larochelle, 1982; Shaffer & Hardwick, 1969b, 1970; Terzuolo & Viviani, 1980). Because the transition time between two keystrokes is inversely related to the frequency of occurrence of the two-letter sequence, it is likely that at least some of the variability across keystrokes is attributable to frequency effects of this type. I investigated skill effects by computing the slope of the function relating digram frequency to interkey interval and then determining whether typing skill is related to the slope parameter, that is, whether faster typists exhibit differential amounts of timing shifts across digrams of varying frequencies than do slower typists.

A second experiential factor that may account for some of the interkeystroke variability is what may be called the *word initiation effect*. If words are stored in memory as integral units, one may expect the latency of the first keystroke in the word to reflect the time required to retrieve the word from memory. Because the magnitude of the word initiation effect may be related to typing skill (Ostry, 1980, 1983), I examined the ratio of the intervals of first keystrokes to all keystrokes in a word for typists of varying levels of skill.

Several investigators also reported that the length of the word being typed is positively related to the latency of either the first or of all keystrokes in the word (e.g., Larochelle, 1983; Ostry, 1980; Shaffer & French, 1971; Shaffer & Hardwick, 1968, 1969b, 1970; Sternberg et al., 1978). I therefore examined the slope of the function relating typing interval to number of characters in words of different lengths in both initial latencies and median interkey intervals.

In addition, I included a number of other variables in the hope that they might contribute to the differentiation of typists of varying skill levels. Among these were assessments of the type and the frequency of errors, and the level of comprehension of the typed material. Because it is possible that typists of varying skill levels exhibit different patterns in the types of errors committed, I contrasted the frequencies of four categories of errors: substitutions, omissions, intrusions, and transpositions. It has also been reported that competent typists detect their error responses immediately, as reflected either in weaker keystrokes on errors (e.g., Rabbitt, 1978; Wells, 1916) or in delayed posterror responses (e.g., Shaffer, 1973, 1975, 1976), and it is conceivable that typing skill is correlated with the ability to accurately monitor finger movements and to immediately detect keying errors (Shaffer & Hardwick, 1969a; West, 1967). Because the delay of posterror responses can be considered a manifestation of error detection, I therefore used the proportion of keystrokes immediately following an error that are slower than the median for all keystrokes as an index of error detectability.

Comprehension of the material being typed was assessed to determine whether some of the efficiency of skilled typists is due to their superior comprehension of the material, thereby allowing potentially greater predictability of forthcoming character sequences. This reasoning is an extension of the argument applied to explain the advantage of typing meaningful material compared with nonsense material—if the mere presence of predictable material is beneficial, then reading and comprehension of the passage should be even more helpful in developing expectations about the content of subsequent material. Because subjects are likely to exhibit considerable variability in comprehension even while merely reading, comprehension was assessed both after typing and after normal reading, with the difference between the two serving as the index of relative typing comprehension.

It should be emphasized that the present analyses do not always provide "pure" assessments of the contribution of each factor. For example, word length is likely to be confounded with word frequency and possibly with digram frequency; digram frequency may be correlated with finger or hand alternation; and so forth. Such confoundings are generally unavoidable when using natural material, and for the present studies, the advantages of such material far outweigh the disadvantages. In the current studies, the primary focus is on individual differences associated with skill and age. Therefore, because all typists received similar kinds of material, the values across individuals can be compared, even if they are not precise with respect to the absolute contribution of each factor considered in isolation.

AGE EFFECTS

A second major goal of the present study was to investigate the effects of adult age on the mechanisms affecting typing skill. The numerous age-related declines in many aspects of cognitive functioning (see Salthouse, 1982a, for a review), and the general tendency for most behavioral activities to become slower with increased age (e.g., Salthouse, in press) lead to the expectation that the rate of typing also should slow down with increased age. In fact, if one extrapolates from the choice reaction time (RT) findings that adults in their 60s require about 100 ms more time per keystroke response than adults in their 20s, typists in their 60s may be expected to type at a rate of only 40 wpm compared with 60 wpm for typists in their 20s. Or expressed differently, 4 hr of continuous typing at a rate of 60 wpm and 5 keystrokes per word yields 72,000 total keystrokes, which at 100 ms extra per keystroke may require the older typist an additional 2 hr to complete. It seems unlikely that differences of this magnitude exist among typists of varying ages, and yet the reasons for this apparent discrepancy from laboratory findings are still not well understood.

One problem with the preceding argument is that typing is much faster than choice RT, and therefore it cannot be based on exactly the same set of processes. Nevertheless, there is considerable agreement among gerontological researchers that many, and perhaps all, perceptual and cognitive processes exhibit age-related declines in speed. Among the processes that appear most relevant to typing, correlations between adult age and rate of performance of +.22 to +.52 have been reported in choice RT tasks (e.g., Borkan & Norris, 1980; Clark, 1960; Dirken, 1972; Jalavisto, 1965; also see Salthouse, in press, for a summary of other similar studies); correlations of +.18 to +.44, in tapping tasks (e.g., Borkan & Norris, 1980; Dirken, 1972; Furukawa et al., 1975; Jalavisto, 1965); and correlations of .42 to .53, in other visual–manual transcription tasks such as the digit–symbol substitution task (see Salthouse, 1982b, for a review). Several studies have reported that one or more of these measures is related to speed of typing (e.g., Ackerson, 1926; Book, 1924; Cleaver & O'Connor, 1982; Flanagan & Fivars, 1964; Flanagan, Fivars & Tuska, 1959; Hayes, 1978; Hayes, Wilson & Schafer, 1977; Leonard & Carpenter, 1964; Muscio & Sowton, 1923; Tuttle, 1923), although there are some contradictory results (e.g., Hansen, 1922). The RT analogy, therefore, still seems relevant, even though the quantitative estimates should not be taken too seriously.

Several years ago, Rabbitt (1977) posed a question with important implications both for the domain of skill and for the applicability of laboratory findings in aging to "real-world" tasks. His question was the following:

In view of the deterioration of memory and perceptual-motor performance with advancing age, the right kind of question may well be not "why are old people so bad at cognitive tasks," but rather, "how, in spite of growing disabilities, do old people preserve such relatively good performance?" (p. 623)

A research strategy introduced by Charness (1981a, 1981b, 1981c) in his studies of the relation between age and components of chess skill represents one approach to answering Rabbitt's question. This strategy can be termed the molar equivalence–molecular decomposition procedure in that it involves the following two steps. First, a sample of individuals is obtained that varies widely on both the skill and age dimensions, but in which the overall correlation between age and skill (molar behavior) is near zero. Next, the effects of age and skill are independently determined in a number of component (molecular) processes thought to be important in developing or maintaining skilled performance.

This strategy of equating age groups on molar performance and then investigating the effects of age on molecular processes is not designed to address the basic issue of whether there are age relations in the overall population in proficiency of the global activity. This normative question is always difficult to answer with small samples, and it is even more complicated with real-life activities because of the problem of differential representativeness of members in various age groups owing to ''selective survival'' of the best-performing individuals in successive age groups.

However, an interesting issue that can be investigated with the molar equivalence–molecular decomposition research strategy is to determine whether age trends similar to those often reported in laboratory studies are evident in the efficiency of (molecular) component processes, despite the equivalence of global (molar) achievement across age groups. Two distinct types of age trends in the component processes are possible. First, the component processes may exhibit age declines typical of those found in many laboratory studies of basic processes, implying that special mechanisms of compensation have been developed for preserving overall performance. This type of outcome would lead to questions about the specific nature of the compensatory mechanisms.

A second possibility is that the years or decades of performance of the molar activity along with its component processes have maintained the efficiency of processes that would have otherwise deteriorated. The potential magnitude of the practice effect with activities that are performed daily is difficult to overestimate, as indicated by a contrast with a recent laboratory experiment. Salthouse and Somberg (1982) had groups of young and old adults perform a variety of perceptual–motor tasks for what seemed to be a long period: 50 hr over approximately 10 weeks. Although performance increased with practice in both groups on all measures that were examined, age differences remained throughout all stages of practice. But now consider the amount of experience that a typist may be expected to receive in the course of normal employment. Fifty hours of typing performance could be completed in less than 2 weeks. The contrast of individual keystrokes is even more dramatic. Subjects in the Salthouse and Somberg (1982) study received 5,000 choice RT trials over the 50 experimental sessions, but a 60-wpm typist would execute that many keystrokes in about 17 min! A rough estimate of the number of keystrokes executed in a year of typing 30 hr per week is 2.7 million. Because increased age is generally positively correlated with increased experience, it is reasonable to expect that if practice can ever prevent the age-related deterioration of perceptual–motor or cognitive efficiency, then effects of such practice would be evident in the components of typing.

The numerous measures included in the present study also provide an ideal environment for investigating the nature of any compensatory mechanisms employed by older typists. Because typists ranged from 19 to 72 years of age, both age and skill level could be considered independent variables in the analyses. Three tests of perceptual–motor efficiency—choice RT, tapping rate, and rate of digit–symbol substitution—were included to investigate the question of maintained or declining component processes, and also to reexamine the relation between these variables and rate of typing.

Two independent studies were conducted, but both involved very similar procedures and hence are described together. The concurrent presentation of the results from the two studies also allows a direct evaluation of the replicability of the major findings.

METHOD

Subjects

Study 1. Thirty-four female typists between 19 and 68 years old participated without monetary compensation in a single session of 1.5 hr. All subjects were electric-typewriter touch typists, but the amount of typing experience over the last 6 months ranged from 0 to 49 hr per week, with a mean of 11.2 hr. The total number of months employed with typing activities required for 10 or more hr per week ranged from 0 to 552 months, with a mean of 113.4 months.

Study 2. Forty typists between 20 and 72 years old, 9 males and 31 females, each received $10 to participate in a single session of 1.5 hr. All were experienced electric-typewriter touch typists with a mean of 13.0 hr of typing per week over the last 6 months, and a range of 0 to 40 hr. The mean number of months employed with at least 10 hr per week of typing activities was 126.9 months, with a range of 0 to 600 months.

Apparatus

All typing was performed on an Apple II+ computer with a Videx Keyboard Enhancer to allow recording and display of both uppercase and lowercase characters. The computer also contained a Mountain Hardware programmable real-time clock that provided temporal measurement to a precision of 10 ms.

Procedure

Study 1. Seven different tasks were performed. Task 1, preceded by several minutes of practice to become familiar with the keyboard and typing in the manner requested, was normal typing from printed copy. The typing was to be performed as rapidly and as accurately as possible, but the (carriage) return key was not to be pressed because the typed copy, which was visible on the display monitor, would automatically wrap around to the next line; no attempt was made to correct errors. The typing selections were Paragraph 2 (for half of the subjects) or paragraph 3 (for the remaining subjects) from Form B of the Nelson–Denny Reading Test. These passages (and similar ones presented later in the session) contained between 1,149 and 1,258 characters, including normal punctuation and capitalization, and were accompanied by four 5-alternative comprehension questions. Subjects were informed that comprehension questions would be asked after typing the passage, but they were encouraged to try to type as normally as possible. A response was required to each comprehension question even if it was only a guess.

In order to provide a basis for evaluating the accuracy of answers to the comprehension questions concerning typed material, Task 2 was to read a similar passage (either Paragraph 6 or 7) from Form B of the Nelson–Denny Reading Test and to answer four 5-alternative comprehension questions about the passage. Subjects indicated when they began and finished reading the passage, so that the reading rate could be timed with a stopwatch.

Task 3 was to type material displayed on a single line of the video monitor and arranged such that each keystroke caused the display to move one space to the left. No visible copy was produced in this task. In successive conditions, the display contained 19, 11, 9, 7, 5, 3, or 1 character of a 60-to 83-characters sentence. The sentences were movie descriptions taken from *TV Guide* magazine and were randomly assigned to preview conditions. One half of the subjects received one order of sentences; the remaining subjects received a different order.

Task 4 consisted of typing sentences in which the sequence of characters had been reversed in a letter-by-letter fashion, beginning with the final period and ending with the capital letter that initiated the first word of the sentence. This material was presented with preview windows of 19 characters and 1 character, using the leftward-moving display described earlier.

Task 5 was a serial choice RT task. Stimuli were uppercase and lowercase versions of the letters L and R, and responses were presses of the leftmost and rightmost keys on the lowest row on the keyboard, Z (for l and L) and/ (for r and R). Subjects were instructed to respond as rapidly and as accurately as possible. Each keystroke caused the immediate display of the next stimulus until a total of 50 randomly arranged stimuli had been presented.

Task 6 was a tapping task in which the subjects, using left and right index fingers, alternately tapped the *f* and *j* keys on the keyboard as rapidly as possible for 15 s. The letters appeared on the video monitor as they were typed, but only speed and not accuracy was stressed in this task.

Finally, Task 7 was to type a standard sentence ("The quick brown fox jumps over the lazy dog.") 10 separate times, always striving for maximum speed and accuracy. The typed material appeared on the display monitor as it was entered by the typist.

Following Task 7, the first five tasks were repeated in the opposite order to provide a counterbalanced sequence. New sentences were presented in the preview conditions, and different paragraphs were presented in the normal typing task (i.e., Nelson–Denny Form B, Paragraph 4 or 8) and reading task (i.e., Nelson–Denny Form B, Paragraph 6 or 7). (No systematic performance differences were observed across the two sets of material; therefore, this control variable is ignored in discussing the results.)

Study 2. Many of the tasks from Study 1 were repeated in Study 2, including the following: (a) normal typing followed by comprehension questions, (b) reading with subsequent comprehension questions, (c) typing normal text with varying number of preview characters, (d) choice RT, and (e) alternate-hand tapping. The initial typing selections were Paragraph 2 (for half of the subjects) and Paragraph 6 (for the remaining subjects) from Form B of the Nelson–Denny Reading Test. The final typing selections were Paragraphs 7 or 5. The reading selections were similarly balanced; the subjects who typed Paragraphs 2 and 7 read Paragraphs 5 and 6, and vice versa. Two *TV Guide* movie description sentences were presented together with preview windows of 11, 9, 7, 5, 3, and 1 character. The length of the material was twice that of Study 1 because only a single test was used with each preview condition. The choice RT and alternate-hand tapping tests were identical to Study 1 except that the tapping test was performed twice instead of only once, and the first choice RT test was preceded by a practice block of 50 trials in an attempt to increase reliability.

New tasks introduced in Study 2 consisted of the following: (a) typing random letters with varying numbers of preview characters, (b) repetitive tapping with only the left index finger on the *f* key, (c) repetitive tapping with only the right index finger on the *j* key, (d) a conventional memory span assessment with randomly selected consonants, and (e) the Digit Symbol Substitution Test from the Wechsler Adult Intelligence Scale.

Six sequences of 120 randomly selected lowercase letters served as the stimulus material in the variable preview task with meaningless material. All subjects were presented preview conditions in the order 1, 3, 5, 7, 9, and 11 characters, but two different pairings of the letter sequences and preview conditions were used, with one half of the subjects receiving each pairing.

In the one-finger tapping tests, the typist simply attempted to tap as rapidly as possible with the appropriate finger for 15 s. The memory span procedure was introduced to investigate a hypothesis about the nature of the eye–hand span (to be discussed later). It involved the 3-s presentation of a random series of consonants with the number of items increased by one after two correct reproductions of the series. A failure to achieve two correct reproductions in five attempts terminated the procedure and the memory span was then identified as one less than the terminal series length, that is, the largest sequence correctly recalled two times.

The order of tasks in Study 2 was as follows: (a) normal typing followed by comprehension questions; (b) reading followed by comprehension questions; (c) normal text with preview windows of 11, 9, 7, 5, 3, and 1 character; (d) choice RT; (e) memory span; (f) alternate-hand tapping; (g) left-hand tapping (right-hand tapping for half the subjects); (h) digit symbol; (i) right-hand tapping (or left-hand tapping for half the subjects); (j) alternate-hand tapping; (k) memory span; (l) choice RT; (m) random letters with preview windows of 1, 3, 5, 7, 9, and 11 characters; (n) reading followed by comprehension questions; and (o) normal typing followed by comprehension questions. In all cases where the same task was presented twice, the mean of the two values was used in all analyses.

RESULTS

Each of the variables is initially considered separately, and the effects of skill level (in net words per minute) and age (in years) are assessed independently by means of correlation and hierarchical multiple regression analyses (see Table 20.1). In none of the hierarchical regression analyses was the Skill × Age interaction significant, and except where noted, the significant main ef-

Table 20.1. Means, Standard Deviations, and Hierarchical Analysis Statistics for All Variables in Studies 1 and 2

Measure	M		SD		MS error		Skill		Age	
	1	2	1	2	1	2	1	2	1	2
Interkeystroke variability	76.76	80.13	35.59	45.37	694.39	1,042.20	28.19*	40.28*	3.11	0.05
Recent experience	11.35	12.95	11.39	10.36	124.35	81.83	2.92	12.95*	1.59	0.09
Relevant employment	96.44	126.85	129.92	161.01	11,430.90	15,650.66	5.46	5.24	12.43*	19.61*
Eye-hand span	3.35	3.45	1.67	1.72	1.72	1.68	13.33*	19.18*	11.02*	5.84
Meaning	1.60	2.01	0.29	0.38	0.08	0.13	2.42	2.76	1.81	2.32
Intrakeystroke variability	32.94	—	13.26	—	85.11	—	34.84*	—	0.27	—
Ratio of slowest: fastest keystroke	1.78	1.73	0.39	0.30	0.14	0.08	1.95	1.30	0.32	1.47
Ratio of one-finger: two-hand digrams	1.48	1.59	0.23	0.26	0.03	0.04	15.48*	25.14*	2.10	0.06
Ratio of digram frequency slope: median interkey interval	0.25	0.27	0.16	0.15	0.02	0.02	0.12	0.05	2.87	1.23
Ratio of first letter latency: median interkey interval of all letters	1.16	1.25	0.18	0.23	0.02	0.05	7.95*	7.58*	3.93	0.00
% substitutions	21.12	22.38	13.71	11.89	189.22	118.44	1.74	4.09	0.83	2.05
% intrusions	36.03	35.93	19.54	13.81	331.59	185.54	0.10	0.17	6.48	4.03
% omissions	34.92	34.53	15.22	16.15	218.68	258.90	2.93	0.79	0.99	0.14
% transpositions	8.03	7.18	6.78	6.85	38.26	37.98	0.06	4.52	9.70*	8.56*
% slow substitutions	74.68	82.05	26.20	23.88	582.47	561.33	0.08	1.21	35.93	19.54
Reading rate	259.06	245.65	68.02	67.27	4,513.53	4,768.14	0.60	0.58	0.71	0.50
Reading comprehension–typing comprehension	11.40	15.40	25.26	26.01	583.73	674.58	5.93	0.06	0.00	2.92
Choice RT	567.35	553.38	62.25	83.27	3,091.60	3,973.47	1.37	8.82*	8.74*	25.94*
Alternate-hand tapping	125.59	125.25	29.04	35.54	566.20	792.27	9.14*	11.48*	7.79*	16.78*
Left-hand tapping	—	169.00	—	26.39	—	341.32	—	10.20*	—	32.00*
Right-hand tapping	—	156.25	—	22.04	—	222.45	—	7.10	—	44.73*
Eye-hand span with random material	—	1.75	—	1.17	—	1.19	—	7.57*	—	0.61
Memory span	—	5.81	—	0.68	—	0.43	—	2.78	—	2.64
Digit symbol	—	62.60	—	14.30	—	102.21	—	21.84*	—	23.46*

NOTE: — = data not applicable.
*$p < .01$.

fects were not altered by varying the order of entry, that is, removing the effects of one variable by entering it before the second variable in the regression equation, and thus only the results when the variable was entered first are reported. Because of the large number of analyses across the two studies, a .01 level of significance was adopted. The statistical results of the regression analyses are summarized in Table 20.1; only the simple correlations are reported in the following text.

Normal Typing

Gross typing speeds in Study 1 ranged from 30.2 wpm to 117.0 wpm with a mean of 61.4 wpm; those in Study 2 ranged from 24.0 wpm to 109.6 wpm, with a mean of 64.4 wpm. However, because the error rate also varied considerably across subjects, a measure of net typing rate was used as the index of skill. Net typing rate in wpm was computed by subtracting five characters (one word) for each error, dividing the net keystrokes by 5 to yield net words, and then dividing this quantity by the number of minutes required to type the entire passage. The mean net wpm across the 34 typists in Study 1 was 54.8, with a range of 17 to 104. The 40 typists in Study 2 averaged 60.0 net wpm, with a range of 23 to 98. Net typing speed was positively, although not always significantly, correlated with recent typing experience (Study 1, $r = .291$; Study 2, $r = .503$) and with the number of months employed with at least 10 hr typing per week (Study 1, $r = .335$; Study 2, $r = .285$). The correlations between recent experience and age were small and were not statistically significant (Study 1, $r = .215$; Study 2, $r = -.041$), but those between total number of months of relevant employment and age were significant and were positive (Study 1, $r = .505$; Study 2, $r = .551$). As expected, because of the way it was computed, net typing speed was highly correlated with median interkey interval (Study 1, $r = -.941$; Study 2, $r = -.897$), and to a lesser extent, with percentage of errors (Study 1, $r = -.581$; Study 2, $r = -.438$). The ranges of these latter two variables across typists in Study 1 were 85–270 ms for median interkey interval, and 0.5–8.3 for percentage of errors. Ranges in Study 2 were 100–340 ms for median interkey interval, and 0.3–8.0 for percentage of errors.

A more detailed method of expressing typing performance is to report the percentage of errors and summary statistics reflecting the intervals between successive keystrokes. Because the interkey intervals are often skewed, I followed the convention of reporting these data in terms of the first (Q1), second (Q2, or median), and third (Q3) quartiles, and the percentage of

Table 20.2. Study 1: Summary Statistics in Typing Conditions

Condition	Correlation[a]	Q1	Q2	Q3	% > 1,000[d]	% errors
Normal typing	.966	148	181	225	1.1	2.4
Repeated sentence	.892[b]	151	183	227	1.4	1.5
Preview: Normal text						
19	.889	148	179	227	2.8	5.3
11	.890	147	183	236	3.1	4.6
9	.901	147	180	231	2.4	3.1
7	.834	152	185	235	2.5	3.7
5	.773	168	205	267	2.7	2.3
3	.646	220	293	425	5.7	6.5
1	.830	554	645	761	13.5	6.4
Preview: Reversed text						
1	.922	602	665	793	15.0	5.8
19	.888	228	285	383	5.3	6.8
Choice RT	.770	510	567	658	8.2	3.7
Tapping	c	110	126	143	0.9	NA

NOTE: Q = quartile. NA = not applicable.
[a] Correlation between medians of 1st and 2nd tests.
[b] Correlation between medians of 1st and 10th tests.
[c] Only one test was administered in this task.
[d] % > 1,000 refers to the percentage of interkey intervals exceeding 1,000 ms.

intervals in excess of 1,000 ms (% > 1,000). The means for each parameter are displayed in Table 20.2 for Study 1 and in Table 20.3 for Study 2.

In Study 1, the typing rates were nearly identical in the normal typing, 19-character preview, and repeated-sentence tasks. Median intervals in the three tasks were also highly correlated (i.e., normal: 19-character preview, r = .948; normal: repetitive sentence, r = .911; 19-character preview: repetitive sentence, r = .906). The convergent estimates from these different procedures and the high reliability of the measurements add credibility to the claim that the present study is assessing the typists' normal levels of typing performance. The nearly equivalent rates in the initial and final normal typing tasks (i.e., 184 ms and 177 ms per keystroke, respectively), which were the first and last performed in the session, and in the 1st and 10th typing of the repeated sentence (i.e., 189 ms and 179 ms per keystroke, respectively), also indicate that fairly stable aspects of typing behavior are being assessed. Study 2 exhibited similar consistency in the measures of normal typing; the initial and final values correlated .961, with means of 172 ms and 173 ms per keystroke, respectively.

Table 20.3. Study 2: Summary Statistics in Typing Conditions

Condition	Q1	Q2	Q3	% > 1000[b]	% errors
Normal typing					
(r = .961)[a]	138	172	219	0.9	1.6
Preview: Normal text					
11	151	190	248	2.6	4.9
9	149	188	250	2.3	5.5
7	153	193	253	2.0	3.6
5	162	206	279	2.4	4.7
3	199	266	411	5.3	6.8
1	604	703	867	18.7	5.7
Preview: Random letters					
11	291	374	516	6.8	5.5
9	291	369	501	6.7	5.0
7	286	362	490	6.5	5.7
5	282	358	488	5.9	5.9
3	317	404	609	9.5	8.3
1	623	677	777	12.9	3.8
Choice RT					
(r = .910)	501	553	639	7.7	4.1
Tapping:					
Two hand					
(r = .899)	108	125	145	0.9	NA
Left hand	159	169	180	1.1	NA
Right hand	146	156	166	1.1	NA

NOTE: *Q*=quartile. NA = not applicable.
  [a]Correlations in the first column relate performance across the two tests with that variable.
  [b]% > 1,000 refers to the percentage of interkey intervals exceeding 1,000 ms.

Age Relations

Figure 20.1 illustrates the relation in Study 1 between typist's age and the median interkey interval in normal typing and choice RT; Figure 20.2 illustrates comparable data from Study 2. Two important points highlight major goals of the present research. The first is the dramatic difference in speed between the typing and choice RT tasks, which ostensibly should involve very similar processes. One goal of the current research is to explain the discrepancy between the temporal performance of these two types of tasks. The second point is that choice RT increases with increased age, whereas typing time remains stable. Linear regression parameters (in ms) were as follows: Study 1, choice RT = 483.3 + 2.02 years, $r = .460$; Study 2, choice RT = 393.4 + 3.74 years, $r = .617$; and Study 1, typing time = 187.8 − 0.17 years, $r = −.057$; Study 2, typing time = 161.0 + 0.25 years, $r = .069$. Typing performance, therefore, appears to be maintained across the

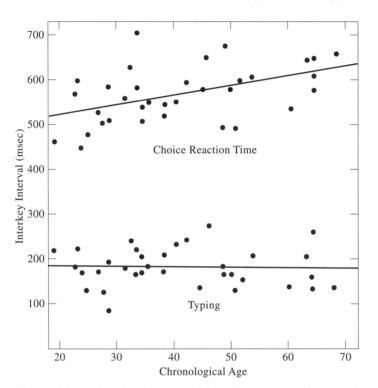

Figure 20.1. Median interkey interval in milliseconds for the normal typing and choice reaction time tasks as a function of typist age in Study 1. (Each point represents a single typist, and the solid lines illustrate the regression equations relating interkey interval to age.)

adult life span in these individuals, whereas "typical" age-related declines are exhibited in choice RT and rate of alternate-hand tapping (i.e., Study 1, tapping time = 91.6 + 0.82 years, r = .398; Study 2, tapping time = 67.8 + 1.34 years, r = .520). Explaining how stability in the molar performance is achieved despite age-related declines in the hypothetical molecular components is the second major goal of the present work.

Preview

Data from the different preview conditions were analyzed in terms of the percentage of errors and the three quartile measures. The median interkey intervals from the fastest and slowest typists in Study 1 are illustrated in Figure 20.3. Both sets of data are typical in that each subject performed at a

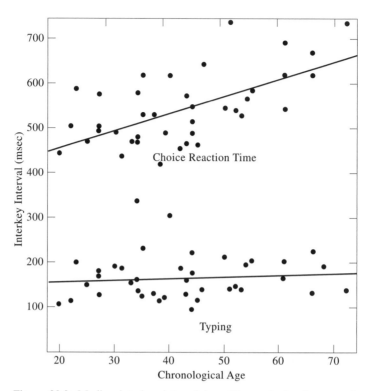

Figure 20.2. Median interkey interval in milliseconds for the normal typing and choice reaction time tasks as a function of typist age in Study 2. (Each point represents a single typist, and the solid lines illustrate the regression equations relating interkey interval to age.)

rate similar to that of normal typing with previews of more than seven characters, but typing rate was much slower with smaller previews.

The eye–hand span in Study 1 was defined as the smallest window at which the first quartile was greater than the second quartile of normal typing. This procedure effectively identified the span as the number of display characters at which 75% of the interkey intervals exceeded the median interval from normal typing. In order to allow direct comparisons across the normal and random-letter material, the eye–hand span in Study 2 was defined as the smallest window at which the first quartile was greater than the smaller of the second quartiles from window sizes 11 or 9. Several alternative operational definitions of the eye–hand span were examined, but they were either highly correlated with the current measures (e.g., span defined as the largest window at which the third quartile first fell below the median of normal

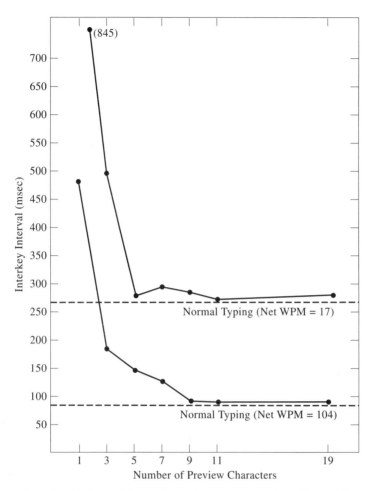

Figure 20.3. Median interkey interval as a function of preview window size for the slowest (net words per minute [WPM] = 17) and fastest (net WPM = 104) typists in Study 1. (The dotted lines indicate the median interkey interval during normal typing with unlimited preview.)

typing) or yielded unstable estimates with a high proportion of discrepancies between ascending (starting from the smallest window) and descending (starting from the largest window) procedures (e.g., span defined as the window at which the interquartile range first exceeded the interquartile range of normal typing).

Both studies were consistent in exhibiting significant positive relations between skill and eye–hand span (Study 1, $r = .500$; Study 2, $r = .527$).

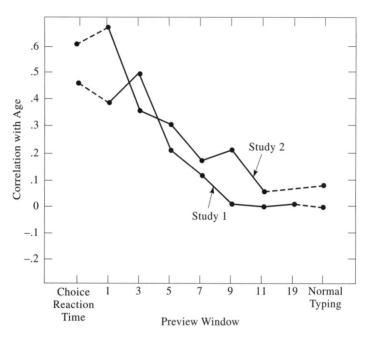

Figure 20.4. Correlation coefficients between interkey interval and typist age across preview window conditions and the choice reaction time and normal typing tasks.

The age effect was significant in Study 1 ($r = .455$) but not in Study 2 ($r = .291$). However, the age variable in Study 2 was significant when entered second in the hierarchical regression model, after controlling for the effects of skill, that is, $F(1, 36) = 8.23$, $p < .01$. Similarly, the correlation between age and eye–hand span after partialing out skill was significant in this study ($r = .406$).

The discovery that the age effects were stronger in Study 2 after controlling for the level of skill prompted a further analysis in which typists below 45 net wpm were excluded. The reasoning was that the fairest test of age relations would be among subjects who were all at least moderately competent typists. Despite the reduction in sample sizes (i.e., to 23 and 33 in Studies 1 and 2, respectively), the age effects on eye–hand span were highly significant, that is, Study 1: $r = .522$, $F(1, 19) = 12.93$; Study 2: $r = .497$, $F(1, 29) = 11.58$, $ps < .01$.

Multiplying the eye–hand span by the median interkey interval during normal typing yields a measure that can be termed the *time span*, in that it reflects the gap between the eye and the hand in units of time. The mean time span across all subjects was 574.7 ms in Study 1 and 550.0 ms in Study 2, with standard deviations of 265.1 ms and 243.3 ms, respectively. The regression parameters relating age to time span were as follows: Study 1, time span = 195.3 + 9.12 years, $r = .487$; and Study 2, time span = 278.48 + 6.34 years, $r = .359$. These values indicate that on the average, typists in their 60s effectively have between 254 and 365 additional ms of preparation time relative to typists in their 20s.

The significant effect of age on the eye–hand span suggests that one mechanism used to compensate for declining perceptual–motor speed with increased age is more extensive anticipation of impending keystrokes. Additional evidence for this interpretation are the correlations between age and median interkey interval across the various preview conditions. Figure 20.4 illustrates these correlations across all preview window sizes and the choice RT and typing tasks. Observe that the correlations systematically decrease as the window size increases, eventually reaching the near-zero correlation of normal typing at a window of nine characters. This pattern indicates that age ceases to be an important predictor of the interkey interval when the typist is able to view simultaneously more than seven characters of the to-be-typed material.

Meaningfulness

Table 20.2 illustrates the interkey interval statistics for 1-and 19-character preview conditions with normal and reversed text. It is obvious that typing efficiency is impaired with reversed text, particularly when the display allows simultaneous examination of many characters. Comparable impairment is evident in the contrast between normal text and random letters illustrated in Table 20.3.

Because the reversed and random-letter texts disrupt the normal ordering of letter sequences, it may be expected that some of the slower performance with meaningless material is attributable to a lower average digram frequency. Analyses conducted on normal typing, typing the reversed text with the 19-character window, and typing the random letters with the 11-character window assessed this possibility. Each letter pair was categorized according to the logarithm of its frequency in written English, as reported by Solso, Barbuto, and Juel (1979), and then the median interkey interval for each category was determined. The means across subjects of these medians are displayed in Figure 20.5, along with histograms confirming the expected difference in digram frequencies between normal and meaningless text. The

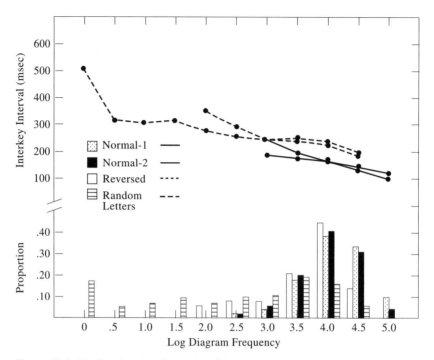

Figure 20.5. Median interkey interval and frequency proportion for normal and re-versed text in Study 1 and normal and random-letter material in Study 2 as a function of log digram frequency.

most important aspect of Figure 20.5 is that the meaningless text is slower than normal text at nearly all digram frequencies. The meaningfulness effect, therefore, cannot be simply attributed to a lower average digram frequency with nonmeaningful material.

A meaningfulness index was established in Study 1 by dividing the median interval of typing reversed text with a 19-character preview by that of typing normal text with a 19-character preview. The index in Study 2 was obtained by dividing the median interval of typing random letters with an 11-character preview by that of typing normal text with an 11-character preview. Neither index was significantly related to skill (Study 1, $r = .267$; Study 2, $r = .257$) or age (Study 1, $r = .230$; Study 2, $r = .236$) in either study.

As noted earlier, the eye–hand span for typing the random-letter material in Study 2 was identified as the smallest window at which the first quartile was greater than the smaller of the second quartiles from window sizes 11 or 9. The mean of this eye–hand span (1.75) was only about half the magnitude of that derived from the same subjects with normal text (3.45). Faster typists had larger eye–hand spans with this meaningless material than did slower typists ($r = .410$), but there was no relation between age and eye–hand span with random letters ($r = .117$).

Intrakeystroke Variability

Temporal analyses of the keystroke intervals in the repetitively typed sentence were conducted after first deleting error responses and responses immediately following errors. The median intervals for each character and the median intrakey interquartile range for the fastest and slowest typists in Study 1 are illustrated in Figure 20.6. An index of intrakey variability was derived by computing the median, across characters, of the interquartile range of the intervals for the same keystroke over the 10 repetitions of the sentence. Faster typists were significantly less variable than slow typists ($r = -.715$), but there was no age relation ($r = -.062$) on this measure of within-keystroke consistency.

Interkeystroke Variability

The remaining analyses of timing variability were based on data from normal copy typing. The first variable was simply the interquartile range of the interkey intervals. Skill was a significant determinant of interkey variability in both studies (Study 1, $r = -.684$; Study 2, $r = -.723$), with faster typists exhibiting lower variability, but the relation between age and interkey variability was not significant in either study (Study 1, $r = -.227$; Study 2, $r = -.024$).

Next, the median interkey interval for each lowercase character with a frequency of more than 10 occurrences in the two normal typing passages was determined. The ratio of the slowest character to that of the fastest character, reflecting the range of timing of separate keystrokes, served as the consistency index for each subject. Neither the skill effect (Study 1, $r = -.239$; Study 2, $r = -.170$) nor age effect (Study 1, $r = -.096$; Study 2, $r = -.181$) was significant with this measure.

Digram Analyses

Although measures for single keystrokes are interesting, it is probably more meaningful to consider at least the immediately preceding keystroke when

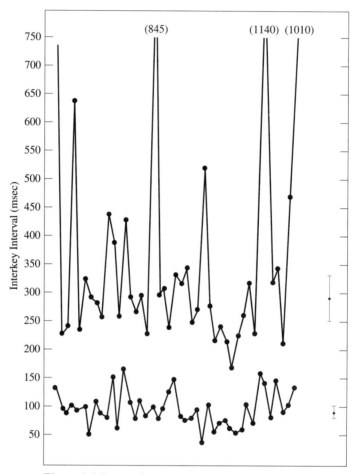

The quick brown fox jumps over the lazy dog.

Figure 20.6. Median interkey interval for the slowest (top) and fastest (bottom) typists in Study 1 across characters in the repetitively typed sentence. (The points and bars at the far right illustrate the overall median interkey interval and interquartile range across all keystrokes in the sentence.)

attempting to partition the variability in interkey intervals. One analysis of this type contrasted the intervals of letter pairs involving the same letter, the same finger but different letters, different fingers on the same hand, and different hands. The means and standard deviations across typists of the quartile statistics for the last interkey interval for these four categories of two-

Table 20.4. Means and Standard Deviations across Typists of Medians and Interquartile Ranges for the Four Digram Categories

| | Median | | | | Interquartile range | | | |
| | Study 1 | | Study 2 | | Study 1 | | Study 2 | |
Category	M	SD	M	SD	M	SD	M	SD
Two hand	155	43	144	46	74	76	64	44
Two finger	194	45	185	51	87	102	70	31
One finger	223	41	221	42	64	60	52	43
Same letter	176	26	168	22	45	69	36	43

NOTE: For medians: Study 1, $F(3, 99) = 98.54$; Study 2, $F(3, 117) = 96.59$, both $ps < .01$. For interquartile ranges: Study 1, $F(3, 99) = 8.25$; Study 2, $F(3, 117) = 17.71$, both $ps < .01$.

letter sequences are illustrated in Table 20.4. Notice that the letter pairs differ significantly across two-hand, two-finger, one-finger, and one-letter pairs in both the median and interquartile range of keystroke intervals.

Both studies revealed significant effects of skill on the ratio of one-finger: two-hand digrams (Study 1, $r = .551$; Study 2, $r = .638$), indicating that faster typists had greater relative differences between one-finger and two-hand digrams than did slower typists. Very similar results were obtained with the ratio of one-finger: two-finger digrams serving as the index of finger overlapping, but this ratio was highly correlated (i.e., Study 1, $r = .648$; Study 2, $r = .656$) with the one-finger: two-hand ratio, and therefore only the latter was included in the analyses. Age was not a significant factor in the ratio of one-finger: two-hand diagrams in either study (Study 1, $r = -.023$; Study 2, $r = .030$).

A second digram analysis was based on the negative relation between digram frequency and interkey interval illustrated in Figure 20.5. The digram frequencies were incorporated into a computer program that computed the regression parameters relating the logarithm of digram frequency to the interval between the appropriate keystrokes. The mean values (in ms) of the parameters across the 34 subjects of Study 1 were as follows: interval = 394 −44 (log digram frequency), $r = -.167$. Values for the 40 subjects of Study 2 were nearly identical: interval = 384 −45 (log digram frequency), $r = -.166$. Although the low correlations indicate that the relation was rather weak, the slope of 44–45 ms/log digram frequency indicates that the interkey interval was shorter with more frequently occurring letter sequences. Analyses on the slope parameter after dividing it by the median interkey interval to convert to a relative score indicated non-significant effects of skill (Study 1, $r = .058$; Study 2, $r = -.035$) and age (Study 1, $r = -.279$; Study 2, $r = .180$).

Word Effects

The mean intervals for initial keystrokes and for the median of all keystrokes in words of one to eight characters are displayed in Figure 20.7. The functions are quite flat, with the slopes across word lengths of three to eight characters averaging 4.4 ms for all interkey intervals and 7.5 ms for initial latencies.

The word initiation effect was quantified by dividing the latency of the initial character in four-letter words by the median interkey interval for all characters in the same four-letter words. Only four-letter words were examined because they were among the most frequent, and other word lengths yielded comparable differences (see Figure 20.7). The skill effect was significant in both studies (Study 1, $r = -.437$; Study 2, $r = -.413$), indicating that faster typists had smaller word initiation effects than did slower

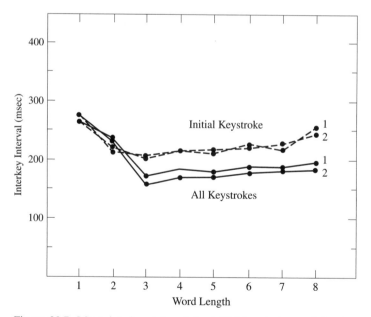

Figure 20.7. Mean interkey interval for initial keystrokes and for the median of all keystrokes in words of one to eight characters in Studies 1 and 2.

typists. The age effect was not significant in either study (Study 1, $r = -.307$; Study 2, $r = .010$).

Errors

Isolated incorrect responses during normal typing were classified into four categories, and the median interkey intervals were determined for the error responses, for the preceding response, and for the first and second responses following the error. (Because of the difficulty of interpretation with series of two or more consecutive errors, which accounted for 55.6% of all errors in Study 1 and 29.5% of all errors in Study 2, only isolated errors were included in these analyses, although all errors were used in the computation of net wpm and the average accuracies that are summarized in Tables 20.2 and 20.3.) In substitution errors, the correct character was replaced with an inappropriate character (e.g., *work* for *word*); in omission errors, a character was deleted (e.g., *wod* for *word*); in intrusion errors, a character was added (e.g., *wored* for *word*); and in transposition errors, a letter sequence was reversed (e.g., *wrod* for *word*). Skill was not a significant predictor of any type of error in either study ($-.296 < r < .306$), but age was negatively correlated (Study 1, $r = -.494$; Study 2, $r = -.422$) with the relative proportion of transposition errors. The correlations between age and the absolute number of transposition errors were $-.332$ and $-.225$ for Studies 1 and 2, respectively. Although both were in the same direction as the proportion results, neither value was statistically significant, indicating that it is not simply the total number of transpositions but their number relative to the total number of errors that exhibits the significant age relation. Correlations between age and the proportions of other types of error were not significant in either study ($-.210 < r < .413$), although there was a tendency in both studies for age to be positively correlated with the proportion of intrusion errors.

Figure 20.8 illustrates the median intervals of keystrokes surrounding single error responses for each type of error. The posterror intervals are difficult to interpret in the case of omission errors because the omitted keystroke might have been too weak to have activated the key, and its interval may thus be incorporated into the interval of the posterror response. The data from intrusion errors are also complicated because many of the intrusions were a consequence of the nearly simultaneous (i.e., latencies less than 20 ms) activation of two keystrokes. The data from substitution and transposition errors are unambiguous, however, and clearly indicate that the responses following er-

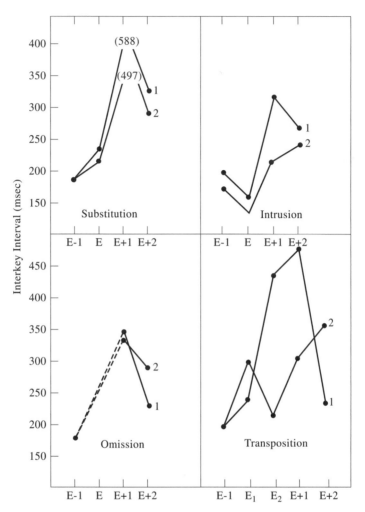

Figure 20.8. Mean interkey interval for keystrokes preceding and following isolated errors (E) in Studies 1 and 2.

rors are much slower than the average response. The percentages of subjects in Study 1 with interkey intervals greater than their median interval for all keystrokes were as follows: 51.5% and 53.6% for keystrokes preceding substitution and transposition errors, respectively, and 87.9% and 96.4% for keystrokes immediately following substitution and transposition errors, respectively. Comparable percentages in Study 2 were 48.7% and 46.7% for keystrokes preceding errors, and 89.7% and 83.3% for keystrokes following errors.

Skill and age analyses were conducted on the percentage of posterror substitution responses greater than the subject's median interval across all keystrokes. The other error categories were not analyzed in this fashion because of the interpretation problems with the omission and intrusion data, and the low frequencies of transposition errors. Neither the skill effect (Study 1, $r = -.045$; Study 2, $r = .175$) nor the age effect (Study 1, $r = -.385$; Study 2, $r = -.192$) was significant in either study.

Typing and Reading Comprehension

Across subjects, mean accuracy on questions assessing comprehension of typed material was 45.6% in Study 1 and 43.7% in Study 2, and that on questions assessing comprehension of similar material that was only read was 57.0% in Study 1 and 59.1% in Study 2. A comprehension differential score was derived for each subject by subtracting typing comprehension from reading comprehension. Neither study exhibited a significant skill effect (Study 1, $r = .406$; Study 2, $r = .038$) or age effect (Study 1, $r = -.007$; Study 2, $r = .273$) on this variable. Reading rate was not related to skill (Study 1, $r = .133$; Study 2, $r = .126$) or age (Study 1, $r = .145$; Study 2, $r = -.116$) in either study.

Choice RTs

The RT data were analyzed in the same fashion as the typing data, and the mean values across all subjects are displayed in Tables 20.2 and 20.3. The skill effect was not significant in Study 1 ($r = -.182$) but was significant in Study 2 ($r = -.360$). Age was positively and significantly related to RT in both studies (Study 1, $r = .460$; Study 2, $r = .617$).

Tapping

Mean values of interkey intervals while tapping with alternate hands are displayed in Tables 20.2 and 20.3. The skill (Study 1, $r = -.431$; Study 2, $r = -.430$) and age (Study 1, $r = .398$; Study 2, $r = .520$) effects were significant in both studies, indicating that faster and younger typists were faster in tapping than slower and older typists. Both left- and right-hand tapping rates in Study 2 exhibited significant age relations (left hand, $r =$

.634; right hand, $r = .725$), with younger typists faster than older typists, but with weaker effects of skill (left hand, $r = -.358$; right hand, $r = -.289$).

Memory Span

No significant effects of skill ($r = .259$) or age ($r = -.253$) were evident on the measure of conventional memory span obtained in Study 2.

Digit Symbol

Younger typists ($r = -.548$) and faster typists ($r = .529$) had significantly higher scores on the Digit Symbol Substitution Test in Study 2 than did older or slower typists.

Predicting Typing Skill

A stepwise multiple regression analysis was conducted to determine the independent sources of variance related to typing skill. A forward selection procedure with a .05 significance level for variable entry was conducted with predictor variables consisting of all variables found to yield significant skill effects in each study. The variables with significant skill relations in Study 1 were as follows: eye–hand span, interkeystroke variability, intrakeystroke variability, ratio of one-finger:two-hand digrams, ratio of first keystrokes: all keystrokes in four-letter words, and alternate-hand tapping time. Four of these variables were found to make significant and independent contributions in the regression equation predicting net typing speed: eye–hand span, intrakeystroke variability, ratio of two-hand: one-finger digrams, and tapping time. The four-variable equation yielded an R^2 of .877, with successive increments of .511 for intrakeystroke variability, .161 for the ratio of two-hand: one-finger digrams, .091 for eye–hand span, and .114 for rate of alternate-hand tapping.

The variables entering into the equation for Study 2 were as follows: eye–hand span with normal text, eye-hand span with random letters, interkeystroke variability, ratio of one-finger: two-hand digrams, ratio of first keystrokes: all keystrokes in four-letter words, choice RT, alternate-hand tapping time, left-hand tapping time, and digit–symbol substitution score. The variables making independent contributions to the prediction of net typing speed, and their respective proportions of variance, were as follows: interkeystroke variability, .523; ratio of one-finger: two-hand digrams, .193; and rate of left-hand tapping, .067. The cumulative R^2 for the three-variable equation was .783. Although the particular variables entering the equation differ somewhat across Studies 1 and 2, this is largely attributable to the existence of variables not available in the other study, for example, intrakeystroke variability in Study 1 but not in Study 2, left-hand tapping in Study 2 but not in Study 1.

Two additional analyses were conducted in which only variables common to the two studies were included, that is, eye–hand span with normal material, interkeystroke variability, ratio of one-finger: two-hand digrams, ratio of first keystrokes: all keystrokes in four-letter words, choice RT, and alternate-hand tapping rate. The cumulative R^2 after four variables (i.e., interkeystroke variability, ratio of one-finger: two-hand digrams, eye–hand span, and alternate-hand tapping rate) was .830 for Study 1 and .772 for Study 2.

DISCUSSION

Before discussing the theoretical implications of the results, it is important to emphasize the close agreement of the data from the two studies. Despite different samples of typist subjects, with different forms of compensation and slightly different experimental procedures, the major results from the two studies were nearly identical. This correspondence is apparent in Figures 20.1, 20.2, 20.4, 20.7, and 20.8, and in all of the tables. Particularly impressive are the very similar patterns of relationships evident in the correlations reported in the preceding text and the summary of means and F ratios in Table 20.1. Given such consistency, there seems little reason to doubt the reliability of the current findings.

General Model of Typing

Two questions motivated the present research: What differentiates skilled typists from less-skilled ones, and how are older adults able to circumvent limitations of slower RT to achieve rapid typing speeds? Many of the current findings are relevant to these issues, but their interpretation requires a general model of typing behavior within which the effects of skill and age can be set. Most of the properties of the model I describe have been suggested by others, and therefore it is best considered a synthesis or a composite view of the activity of typing. Another caveat is that the model clearly does not provide a complete explanation of all aspects of typing, but focuses on the limited set of phenomena established or confirmed in this study.

It is useful to begin a description of the model by distinguishing among four categories of processing. The first is termed *input processes* because there has to be some way for the to-be-typed material to enter the processing system. The extensive experience typists have had with reading makes it likely that the input material is initially segmented into familiar, meaningful units such as words or phrases. The output of the system must eventually consist of discrete keystroke responses, however, and thus a second category of processing consists of *parsing* the large reading units into discrete characters. A third set of processes then *translates* characters into patterns of finger movements and also *monitors* the keystroke actions. The fourth and final category of processes is responsible for the actual *execution* of the finger movements that culminate in overt keystrokes.

A fundamental property of this model is that all of the processing steps are assumed to be capable of simultaneous operation (e.g., Book, 1908; Coover, 1923; Dvorak et al., 1936; Gentner, 1982a; Hershman & Hillix, 1965; Logan, 1983; Norman & Rumelhart, 1983; Olsen & Murray, 1976; Rabbitt, 1978; Rumelhart & Norman, 1982; Shaffer, 1971, 1973, 1976; Shaffer & Hardwick, 1969b). That is, the keystroke for one character may be executed while the immediately following character is being translated to patterns of finger motions, the character after that is being parsed from the input string, and still other characters are being registered and encoded by the input processes. It is this property that is postulated to be responsible for much of the speed of typing compared with serial reaction tasks because the interkey interval is assumed to represent only the time between the final processes of successive keystrokes, rather than the time between the initial and final processes of a single keystroke as in RT tasks. The dramatic reduction in typing speed produced by restricting the number of simultaneously visible characters found in these studies and others (e.g., Coover, 1923; Hershman & Hillix, 1965; Shaffer, 1973, 1976; Shaffer & French, 1971; Shaffer & Hardwick, 1970) is consistent with the parallel execution assumption because curtailing the preview reduces the possibility of overlapping in processing.

In fact, the notion of overlapping processing is so dominant in typing performance that I referred to each processing step as a category or set of processes to allow for the possibility of overlap in the subprocesses within each category. An example of this type of within-categories overlap was described by Gentner, Grudin, and Conway (1980) in their analyses of high-speed films of skilled typing. (Also see Olsen & Murray, 1976, for a similar analysis.) These investigators reported that the average interval between the initiation of a finger movement and its completion was 261 ms, but that the average interval between successive keystrokes was 124 ms. Many cases of two or more fingers simultaneously in motion were also observed, and thus the overlapping of processing has been empirically documented at least within the set of processes responsible for keystroke execution.

Although overlapping of processing is assumed to be extensive, physical constraints imposed by the configuration of fingers and the layout of the keyboard set limits on the degree of overlap in at least the execution processes (e.g., Rumelhart & Norman, 1982). Specifically, overlap of finger movements is least likely when successive keystrokes involve the same finger, increases somewhat when the two characters involve different fingers on the same hand, and is most likely when the digram involves fingers on alternate hands. This is precisely the ordering of interkey intervals found in the current studies and in earlier reports by Dvorak et al. (1936), Gentner (1981, 1982a), Kinkead (1975), Rumelhart and Norman (1982), and Terzuolo and Viviani (1980).

Many experiential effects, such as the negative relation between digram frequency and interkey interval found here and elsewhere (e.g., Dvorak et al., 1936; Grudin & Larochelle, 1982; Terzuolo & Viviani, 1980) are probably due to extensive practice leading to the development of more efficient techniques of overlapping those particular keystrokes. Less frequent digrams have not had the benefit of such extensive practice and thus are still typed without overlapping or with inefficient modes of overlapping.

Other phenomena are not so easily explained by the concept of parallel activity of various processes but seem to be due to other properties of the typing model. For example, the robust effect of material meaningfulness appears to extend beyond the digram level because the reversed and random-letter texts were found to be typed slower than normal text even when the frequency of letter digrams was controlled (see Figure 20.4). Terzuolo and Viviani (1980) also reported that the same digrams were typed faster in meaningful text than in randomly arranged letters, thereby further confirming this observation. A likely candidate for the meaningfulness effect is the parsing process in which the input units are segmented into individual characters (Rumelhart & Norman, 1982; Shaffer, 1976). The decomposition of familiar words and phrases is likely to be facilitated by knowledge of orthographic rules governing the sequencing of letters in English and by the thousands of hours of viewing the intact units in reading. Meaningless material often violates orthographic rules and almost by definition is not as familiar as meaningful material. The meaningfulness effect could also be localized in the input processes, but if so, it is unlikely to extend beyond the level of the word because several investigators found that randomly arranged words are typed about as rapidly as normal text (e.g., Fendrick, 1937; Hershman & Hillix, 1965; Olsen & Murray, 1976; Shaffer, 1973; Shaffer & Hardwick, 1968; Shulansky & Herrmann, 1977; Terzuolo & Viviani, 1980; Thomas & Jones, 1970; West & Sabban, 1982).

The word initiation effect, that is, the tendency for the first keystroke in a word to have a longer interval than other keystrokes in the word (e.g., Larochelle, 1983; Ostry, 1980, 1983; Shaffer & Hardwick, 1970; Terzuolo & Viviani, 1980; Thomas & Jones, 1970), may have its primary origin in the input processes. Words appear to be natural units in reading and therefore are presumed to correspond to the groupings received by the input processes. The parsing mechanism may also play a role in this phenomenon because the transition from space to letter found in the first character of a word is distinctive among primarily letter-to-letter sequences. Translation and execution processes seem unlikely candidates for the slower initial keystrokes in words because the space bar is pressed with the thumb and thus should allow considerable overlapping of subsequent finger movements.

The claim that errors are detected rapidly, often before the following keystroke is completed (e.g., Rabbitt, 1978; Shaffer, 1973, 1975, 1976; Shaffer & Hardwick, 1969a), is supported in the present study by the markedly slower posterror intervals with substitution and transposition errors (see Figure 20.7). This phenomenon seems to necessitate some type of monitoring mechanism at the level of the individual keystrokes but not involving the keystrokes themselves or no error would have resulted. The processes in the model responsible for translating characters to finger movements seem ideally suited for this kind of monitoring. If the feedback received from the completed finger movement does not correspond to the intended signal, a temporary blockage of communication channels may result (e.g., Logan, 1982, 1983) or the next keystroke could simply be inhibited while higher levels of processing become directed to the error.

The remaining general typing phenomenon that constrains the typing model is the eye–hand span. In the procedure followed here, the span is the minimum number of characters of preview necessary to achieve one's normal rate of typing. Because typing rate is slowed when fewer than the span number of characters is presented, the typist must normally be using that many characters in some fashion.

When analyzing a phenomenon such as the eye–hand span, it is important to think of it in both dynamic and functional terms. (See Logan, 1983, for a related discussion of this issue.) The span is dynamic because it is continuously being updated with new items as earlier items are typed, and its apparent function is to ensure an uninterrupted stream of input to later processing steps. These considerations suggest that the most plausible origin for the span is in the requirements of the parsing processes for a steady flow of information from the input processes. Parsing processes do not operate in isolation, however, and it is likely that both translation and execution processes contribute to the driving of the parsing mechanism. A lag or span between the character being parsed and the character whose keystroke is being executed is therefore assumed to arise in response to the need for a continuous flow of information to all subsequent processes.

The origin of the span is assumed to be downstream, that is, later in the processing sequence, because performance is impaired when fewer than the span number of characters is available. A simple mismatch of capacities between early and late processes, with larger capacities in earlier processes, could produce a spanlike buffer, but in this case performance would not suffer with subspan previews. An analogy with a commonplace toilet may help illustrate this distinction between later (demand–deficit) and earlier (supply–surplus) interpretations. The amount of water in the toilet tank can be considered to represent a "span" in that it consists of an accumulation of water in some type of storage system. When the toilet is flushed, nearly all of that water is used, and if the tank was not full, the flushing might be incomplete. Because the performance of the system is impaired by subspan quantities, this is a case in which the span exists to prevent a deficit in response to the demand. Now consider what happens when a blockage forms in the plumbing below the toilet. A flush of the toilet will produce a considerable amount of water filling the toilet bowl, but when it cannot drain adequately, it will create a quantity (span) of water above the blockage. In this case, reducing the amount of water in the toilet bowl will not substantially affect the flow of water in the pipes below the blockage (i.e., performance is not impaired by subspan quantities), and thus the span is produced by a surplus of supply rather than an attempt to minimize deficit to demand.

My interpretation of the eye–hand span in typing is that it is more analogous to the toilet tank rather than the blockage-induced overflowing toilet bowl, or in more scholarly language, it is a span that is driven by demand rather than by surplus of supply. This view leads to several implications concerning the eye–hand span measured here. One implication is that because the span is presumed to arise as a consequence of the rapid and efficient operation of parsing, translation, and execution processes, faster typists would be expected to have greater spans than would slower typists. This prediction is confirmed in the present results.

A second prediction is that the same typists should have smaller eye–hand spans when their rate of typing is slower, as is the case when typing unfamiliar, meaningless material. This hypothesis was confirmed in Study 2 in which the eye–hand span with random letters was substantially smaller than the eye–hand span with normal material. The span is therefore a characteristic of a momentary typing rate and not a fixed attribute of the typist. Fuller (1943) reached a similar conclusion on the basis of examinations of eye movements when typists were asked to type at normal and slow speeds, and when they were typing text in unfamiliar French rather than text in their native English.

A third implication of the current view of the eye–hand span is that it is unlikely to be correlated with conventional measures of memory span. The reason is that conventional estimates of memory span appear to be assessing the static (surplus) capacity of a particular memory structure, and not the dynamic (demand) requirements of later processes for continuous input as in the eye–hand span. The results of the traditional measure of memory span available in Study 2 confirm this prediction; there was no relation ($r = -.124$) between eye–hand span in typing and the conventional memory span for letter sequences. The correlation between the conventional memory span and the eye–hand span with random letter material was also low and nonsignificant ($r = .214$).

To summarize, a general model of typing is proposed with four categories of processing: input, parsing, translation, and execution. There is assumed to be considerable operational overlap or parallel processing among and within each processing category, and this feature is assumed to be responsible for many of the phenomena that have been observed in studies of typing. No single unit of typing can be identified in this model because different processes are presumed to operate with different segments of information, for example, the parser decomposes reading units into single characters, the translator converts character representations into motor patterns and monitors the individual movements, and so forth. Finally, typing performance is degraded by restricting the number of visible characters because the parsing, translation, and execution processes require a steady flow of information in order to obtain maximum efficiency.

Skill Effects

Assuming that typing proceeds in approximately the manner previously described, how do skilled typists differ from less skilled ones? At a purely descriptive level, skilled typists relative to less skilled typists are less variable both across keystrokes and in the execution of the same keystroke across repetitions; they tend to rely on more of the advance copy while typing; they have a smaller relative variation between two-hand and one-finger digrams; they have a smaller relative difference between the timing of initial keystrokes and subsequent keystrokes in words; they have higher rates of alternate-hand tapping; they are faster at manually writing symbols in place of digits; and they may be faster at choice RT.

The stepwise regression analyses were useful in reducing these variables to a minimum set of predictors with independent contributions to the variance in typing performance. Variables not included in these equations can be presumed to share substantial variance with the variables that were included (e.g., the ratio of initial keystrokes:all keystrokes in four-letter words is probably encompassed by the measure of interkeystroke variability). Four such unique predictors were identified as consistent across the two studies: interkeystroke variability, ratio of two-hand:one-finger digrams, eye–hand span, and speed of alternate-hand tapping.

Although both studies exhibited highly significant relations between skill and interkeystroke variability, the stepwise analysis in Study 1 indicated that most of this common variance was attributable to the measure of intrakeystroke variability. That is, once intrakeystroke variability was entered into the regression equation, the interkeystroke variability measure no longer made a significant contribution. The skill effect on the measure of intrakeystroke variability indicates that faster typists are more consistent than slower typists in executing the same keystroke. Because the context was identical across repetitions, mechanical and experiential factors were held constant in this procedure. The greater consistency of skilled typists must therefore be attributed to internal factors such as rhythm, finger coordination, and precision of finger placement. Faster tapping among skilled typists can also be interpreted as evidence that one concomitant of skill is more efficient coordination of elementary finger movements. A somewhat more complex correlate of skill, although still motoric in nature, is the ratio of one-finger:two-hand digrams. Faster typists were found to have larger ratios than slower typists, indicating that they had developed more efficient modes of overlapping two-hand sequences. One-finger letter digrams were also typed faster by skilled typists

(Study 1, $r = -.876$; Study 2, $r = -.826$), but execution processes cannot overlap when the same finger must make two responses in succession, and therefore this variable provides a reasonable baseline for estimating the relative efficiency of two-hand overlapping.

The preceding three variables, although making independent contributions to the prediction of typing speed, can all be classified as primarily motoric, or in Book's (1908) terminology, "habits of manipulation." Their primary locus in the current typing model is therefore in the execution processes, with perhaps some influence on the translation processes. A variable that appears more cognitive in nature, or a habit of control in the words of Book, is the eye–hand span, which was found to be significantly larger in skilled typists than in unskilled ones. According to the interpretation previously proposed, the larger span among skilled typists arises because of a need for higher rates of transmission of information to the parsing, translation, and execution processes. These processes are apparently either more efficient or overlap more extensively among the skilled typists, such that there is a greater demand for information about forthcoming characters.

It is interesting to compare the present interpretation of the skill difference with that proposed by several earlier researchers (e.g., Book, 1908; Dvorak et al., 1936; Swift, 1904). For many years the dominant explanation of skilled typing was that the fastest individuals typed in units of words or phrases, whereas beginners were limited to individual letters. Implicit in this perspective was a top-down view of the eye–hand span in which the acquisition of larger units was assumed to be responsible for the faster rates of typing. By contrast, a bottom-up view of typing is implied from the current perspective because the span is assumed to be a consequence, and not a cause, of the faster rate of typing. The skill relations observed in the motoric variables of same keystroke consistency, tapping speed, and two-hand digram efficiency are also consistent with the view that many of the skill effects arise because of increased efficiency of component processes. Although not pursued at the time, isolated references to a bottom-up interpretation of the eye–hand span can be found in the earlier literature. For example, Coover (1923) stated that, "The telescoping of preparation for sequences of letters leads to word units in copy-getting and in typing" (p. 564), and Butsch (1932) claimed, "It is probable that the eye simply keeps far enough ahead to provide copy for the hand as it is needed, and rapidly enough to prevent retarding the writing" (p. 113).

Age Effects

Three categories of variables are significantly related to the age of the typist: transposition errors, component process variables, and the eye–hand span. Older typists made relatively fewer transposition errors than did younger typists in both studies. This finding may be interpreted as suggesting that with increased age, and consequently experience, there is more precise control over the sequencing of keystrokes. No other evidence is available for this inference, however, and the low incidence of transposition errors among all typists (between 7% and 8% of all errors) should make one cautious about this result.

The discovery that several measures of perceptual–motor efficiency— choice RT, rate of tapping, and digit-symbol substitution rate—were all slower with increased age is consistent with the results of many previous studies in the aging literature (see Salthouse, in press). Assuming that such measures are components of typing, this result provides no evidence that even millions of "trials" of experience can lead to the preservation of basic capacities. However, the samples are too small and variable to consider the present study a strong test of the maintenance-with-practice hypothesis. Nevertheless, the slower performance on these tasks was accompanied by virtually unchanged performance across the adult life span in the rate of typing. Individuals in the current samples could expect to differ by between 80 ms and 150 ms in choice RT between age 20 and age 60, and yet the average interkey interval in typing was found to be nearly identical for 60-year-old typists compared with 20-year-old typists. A dramatic discrepancy therefore clearly exists between the results of traditional laboratory tasks and the performance of the real-life activity of typing.

The existence of a significant relation between age and eye–hand span, independent of the relation between span and skill, suggests a possible mechanism that may allow older typists to compensate for lower perceptual–motor efficiency. Older typists were found to have larger eye–hand spans than did younger typists, and it is conceivable that this larger span is a reflection of more extensive overlapping and anticipation of impending characters developed in order to maintain relatively high speeds of typing in the face of declining basic capacities. That is, the span may be larger because the older typists have adapted to their slower rates of processing by planning further ahead, in effect, scheduling around the bottlenecks in the system as much as possible. The computations of time span, that is, the product of eye–hand span and median interkey interval, indicate that this mechanism may allow typists in their 60s an additional 254 ms to 365 ms of preparation for a given keystroke compared with typists in their 20s.

Although I tend to favor the compensation interpretation of the age–span relation, another interpretation cannot be rejected. This is the notion that the older typists were once much faster and that their larger eye–hand spans are merely a residual consequence of their former degree of skill. In other words, the larger spans of older typists may be a reflection of their previous higher levels of skill, but as the efficiency of component processes and speed of molar performance declined with increased age, the span remained at the length appropriate for the former, more proficient, level of skill. This interpretation does not seem testable without extensive longitudinal investigations, and thus we cannot distinguish between this and the compensation interpretation previously offered.

REFERENCES

Ackerson, L. (1926). A correlational analysis of proficiency in typing. Archives of Psychology (No. 82), 1–73.

Book, W. F. (1908). The psychology of skill. Missoula University of Montana Press.

Book, W. F. (1924). Voluntary motor ability of the world's champion typists. Journal of Applied Psychology, 8, 283–308.

Borkan, G. A. & Norris, A. H. (1980). Assessment of biological age using a profile of physical parameters. Journal of Gerontology, 35, 177–184.

Butsch, R. L. C. (1932). Eye movements and the eye–hand span in typewriting. Journal of Educational Psychology, 23, 104–121.

Charness, N. (1981a). Aging and skilled problem solving. Journal of Experimental Psychology: General, 110, 21–38.

Charness, N. (1981b). Search in chess: Age and skill differences. Journal of Experimental Psychology: Human Perception and Performance, 7, 467–476.

Charness, N. (1981c). Visual short-term memory and aging in chess players. Journal of Gerontology, 36, 615–619.

Clark, J. W. (1960). The aging dimension: A factorial analysis of individual differences with age on psychological and physiological measurements. Journal of Gerontology, 15, 183–187.

Cleaver, T. G. & O'Connor, C. (1982). Prediction of success at typing. Human Factors, 24, 373–376.

Coover, J. E. (1923). A method of teaching typewriting based upon a psychological analysis of expert typing. National Education Association: Addresses and Proceedings, 61, 561–567.

Dirken, J. M. (1972). Functional age of industrial workers. Groningen, Netherlands: Wolters-Noordhof.

Dvorak, A., Merrick, N. L., Dealey, W. L., & Ford, G. C. (1936). Typewriting behavior. New York: American Book.

Fendrick, P. (1937). *Hierarchical skills in typewriting.* Journal of Educational Psychology, 28, *609–620.*

Flanagan, J. C. & Fivars, G. (1964). *The tapping test: A new tool to predict aptitude for typing.* Delta Pi Epsilon, 6, *33–39.*

Flanagan, J. C., Fivars, G. & Tuska, S. A. (1959). *Predicting success in typing and keyboard operation.* Personnel and Guidance Journal, 37, *353–357.*

Fox, J. G. & Stansfield, R. G. (1964). *Digram keying times for typists.* Ergonomics, 7, *317–320.*

Fuller, D. C. (1943). Reading factors in typewriting. *Unpublished doctoral dissertation, Harvard University, Cambridge, MA.*

Furukawa, T., Inoue, M., Kajiya, F., Inada, H., Takasugi, S., Fukui, S., Takeda, H. & Abe, H. (1975). *Assessment of biological age by multiple regression analysis.* Journal of Gerontology, 30, *422–434.*

Gentner, D. R. (1981). Skilled finger movements in typing *(Tech. Rep. No. CHIP 104). San Diego: University of California, Center for Human Information Processing.*

Gentner, D. R. (1982a). The development of typewriting skill *(Tech. Rep. No. CHIP 114). San Diego: University of California, Center for Human Information Processing.*

Gentner, D. R. (1982b). *Evidence against a central control model of timing in typing.* Journal of Experimental Psychology: Human Perception and Performance, 8, *793–810.*

Gentner, D. R., Grudin, J. & Conway, E. (1980). Finger movements in transcription typing *(Tech. Rep. No. 8001). San Diego: University of California, Center for Human Information Processing.*

Grudin, J. T. & Larochelle, S. (1982). Digraph frequency effects in skilled typing *(Tech. Rep. No. CHIP 110). San Diego: University of California, Center for Human Information Processing.*

Hansen, C. F. (1922). *Serial action as a basic measure of motor capacity.* Psychological Monographs, 31, *320–382.*

Harding, D. W. (1933). *Rhythmization and speed of work.* British Journal of Psychology, 23, *262–278.*

Hayes, V. (1978). *Relationship between typewriting rate and responses to individual characters on the typewriter keyboard.* Perceptual and Motor Skills, 46, *1339–1343.*

Hayes, V., Wilson, D. D. & Schafer, R. L. (1977). *Typewriting rate as a function of reaction time.* Perceptual and Motor Skills, 45, *1179–1184.*

Hershman, R. L. & Hillix, W. A. (1965). *Data processing in typing: Typing rate as a function of kind of material and amount exposed.* Human Factors, 7, *483–492.*

Jalavisto, E. (1965). *The role of simple tests measuring speed of performance in the assessment of biological vigour: A factorial study in elderly women. In A. T. Welford & J. E. Birren (Eds.),* Behavior, aging and the nervous system *(pp. 353–365). Springfield, IL: Charles C Thomas.*

Kinkead, R. (1975). *Typing speed, keying rates, and optimal keyboard layouts.* Proceedings of the Human Factors Society, *159–161.*

Lahy, J. M. (1924). Motion study in typewriting (Studies and Reports, Series J, No. 3). Geneva: International Labour Office.

Larochelle, S. (1983). A comparison of skilled and novice performance in discontinuous typing. In W. E. Cooper (Ed.), Cognitive aspects of skilled typewriting (pp. 67–94). New York: Springer-Verlag.

Leonard, J. A. & Carpenter, A. (1964). On the correlation between a serial choice reaction task and subsequent achievement at typewriting. Ergonomics, 7, 197–204.

Logan, G. D. (1982). On the ability to inhibit complex movements: A stop-signal study of typewriting. Journal of Experimental Psychology: Human Perception and Performance, 8, 778–792.

Logan, G. D. (1983). Time, information, and the various spans in typewriting. In W. E. Cooper (Ed.), Cognitive aspects of skilled typewriting (pp. 197–224). New York: Springer-Verlag.

Long, J., Nimmo-Smith, I. & Whitefield, A. (1983). Skilled typing: A characterization based on the distribution of times between responses. In W. E. Cooper (Ed.), Cognitive aspects of skilled typewriting (pp. 145–195). New York: Springer-Verlag.

Muscio, B. & Sowton, S. C. M. (1923). Vocational tests and typewriting. British Journal of Psychology, 13, 344–369.

Norman, D. A. & Rumelhart, D. E. (1983). Studies of typing from the LNR Research Group. In W. E. Cooper (Ed.), Cognitive aspects of skilled typewriting (pp. 45–66). New York: Springer-Verlag.

Olsen, R. A. & Murray, R. A. (1976). Finger motion analysis in typing of texts of varying complexity. Proceedings of the Sixth Congress of the International Ergonomics Association, 446–450.

Ostry, D. J. (1980). Execution-time movement control. In G. E. Stelmach & J. Requin (Eds.), Tutorials in motor behavior (pp. 457–468). Determinants of interkey times in typing. In W. E. Cooper (Ed.), Cognitive aspects of skilled typewriting (pp. 225–246). New York: Springer-Verlag.

Ostry, D. J. (1983) Determinants of interkey times in typing. In W. E. Cooper (Ed.), Cognitive aspects of skilled typewriting (pp. 225–246). New York; Springer-Verlag.

Rabbitt, P. M. A. (1977). Changes in problem-solving ability in old age. In J. E. Birren & K. W. Schaie (Eds.), Handbook of the psychology of aging (pp. 606–625). New York: Van Nostrand Reinhold.

Rabbitt, P. M. A. (1978). Detection of errors by skilled typists. Ergonomics, 21, 945–958.

Rumelhart, D. E. & Norman, D. A. (1982). Simulating a skilled typist: A study of skilled cognitive-motor performance. Cognitive Science, 6, 1–36.

Salthouse, T. A. (1982a). Adult cognition: An experimental psychology of human aging. New York: Springer-Verlag.

Salthouse, T. A. (1982b). Psychomotor indices of physiological age. In M. E. Reff & E. L. Schneider (Eds.), Biological markers of aging (pp. 202–209). Bethesda, MD: U.S. Department of Health and Human Services.

Salthouse, T. A. (in press). Speed of behavior and its implications for cognition. In J. E. Birren & K. W. Schaie (Eds.), Handbook of the psychology of aging (2nd ed.). New York: Van Nostrand Reinhold.

Salthouse, T. A. & Somberg, B. L. (1982). Skilled performance: The effects of adult age and experience on elementary processes. Journal of Experimental Psychology: General, 111, 176–207.

Shaffer, L. H. (1971). Attention in transcription skill. Quarterly Journal of Experimental Psychology, 23, 107–112.

Shaffer, L. H. (1973). Latency mechanisms in transcription. In S. Kornblum (Ed.), Attention and performance IV (pp. 435–446). New York: Academic Press.

Shaffer, L. H. (1975). Control processes in typing. Quarterly Journal of Experimental Psychology, 27, 419–432.

Shaffer, L. H. (1976). Intention and performance. Psychological Review, 83, 375–393.

Shaffer, L. H. (1978). Timing in the motor programming of typing. Quarterly Journal of Experimental Psychology, 30, 333–345.

Shaffer, L. H. & French, A. (1971). Coding factors in transcription. Quarterly Journal of Experimental Psychology, 20, 360–369.

Schaffer, L. H. & Hardwick, J. (1968). Typing performance as a function of text. Quarterly Journal of Experimental Psychology, 20, 360–369.

Shaffer, L. H. & Hardwick, J. (1969a). Errors and error detection in typing. Quarterly Journal of Experimental Psychology, 21, 209–213.

Shaffer, L. H. & Hardwick, J. (1969b). Reading and typing. Quarterly Journal of Experimental Psychology, 21, 381–383.

Shaffer, L. H. & Hardwick, J. (1970). The basis of transcription skill. Journal of Experimental Psychology, 84, 424–440.

Shulansky, J. D. & Herrmann, D. J. (1977). The influence of linguistic structure on typing. Language and Speech, 20, 80–85.

Solso, R. L., Barbuto, P. F. & Juel, C. L. (1979). Bigram and trigram frequencies and versatilities in the English language. Behavior Research Methods & Instrumentation, 11, 475–484.

Sternberg, S., Monsell, S., Knoll, R. L. & Wright, C. E. (1978). The latency and duration of rapid movement sequences: Comparisons of speech and typewriting. In G. Stelmach (Ed.), Information processing in motor control and learning (pp. 118–152). New York: Academic Press.

Swift, E. J. (1904). The acquisition of skill in typewriting: A contribution to the psychology of learning. Psychological Bulletin, 1, 295–305.

Terzuolo, C. A. & Viviani, P. (1980). Determinants and characteristics of motor patterns used for typing. Neuroscience, 5, 1085–1103.

Thomas, E. A. C. & Jones, R. G. (1970). A model for subjective grouping in typewriting. Quarterly Journal of Experimental Psychology, 22, 353–367.

Tuttle, W. W. (1923). The determination of ability for learning typewriting. Journal of Educational Psychology, 14, 177–181.

Wells, F. L. (1916). On the psychomotor mechanisms of typewriting. American Journal of Psychology, 27, 47–70.

West, L. J. (1967). Vision and kinaesthesis in the acquisition of typewriting skill. Journal of Applied Psychology, 51, 161–166.

West, L. J. & Sabban, Y. (1982). Hierarchy of stroking habits at the typewriter. Journal of Applied Psychology, 67, 370–376.

PART 3

Social Psychology and Personality

Introduction

M. Powell Lawton

Bernice Neugarten and her colleagues at the University of Chicago were early explorers in the dynamics of personality. Her early chapters, reprinted in Neugarten (1996), are still worth careful study and are relevant to contemporary research in the social and personality aspects of aging. A representative contribution from this intellectual tradition is the cross-cultural research of Neugarten's student, David Gutmann. We have included here his study of Mayan men, in which he relates the behavioral styles of active mastery, passive mastery, and magical mastery to stages of maturing. His research was accomplished largely by qualitative, clinical methods, an approach rarely found in today's research literature.

Marjorie Fiske (formerly Lowenthal) shares the psychodynamic and social perspectives of the Chicago group. The concept of the confidant as the buffer between a stressed person and a mental health outcome was introduced by Lowenthal and Clayton Haven in the paper included here. This provocative buffering hypothesis and its implied nonlinearity (i.e., one confidant makes a difference in outcome disproportionate to additional close relationships) continue to provide stimulation for contemporary research on social relationships, stress, and mental health.

Concern over the structure and stability of personality has characterized much research over the past two decades. The contributions of Paul T. Costa Jr. and Robert R. McCrae stand out in this respect. The article included here portrays the stability of personality in its ability to predict happiness over a ten-year period. Another of their articles (not included here) documents the longitudinal and cross-sequential stability of traditional personality measures (Costa & McCrae, 1988). The affective aspects of aging were investigated to some extent in these latter studies and in the Chicago studies, but it was not until the renaissance of general psychology's concern with emotion had become firmly established that similar research began in gerontology, stimulated particularly by a theoretical article by Richard Schulz (1982). Included in this volume are two research reports on emotions. Gisela Labouvie-Vief, Marlene De Voe, and Diana Bulka report an investigation of differences in the cognitive complexity with which emotions are described in six age groups. Increased maturity in viewing emotions and in the way inner and outer controls are utilized was seen as age increased from preadolescence to middle adulthood, with minimal difference or slight decrease in complexity in old age. In the arena of social behavior, Laura L. Carstensen's (1993) social selectivity theory formed the basis for Barbara L. Frederickson and Carstensen's research report included in this volume. Their results suggest a revised explanation for the repeated observation that social behaviors decreased with age. Their results suggested that reduced interaction levels were the result, not of a general withdrawal of affect or decrease in social interest, but of greater selectivity in the willingness to invest affect in social relationships in later life.

Contributions to the understanding of the social psychology of later life have been relatively lacking in gerontology. Although issues in social-interactive behavior, social support, and caregiving processes have been investigated by many psychologists, their concepts have tended to develop from the sociological tradition rather than from mainstream social psychological principles. One area that emerged early in gerontology (see, e.g., Tuckman & Lorge, 1952) and has continued to be of interest is that of social cognitions of the aged and the aging process. The article reprinted here is one of a series by Nathan Kogan that set a benchmark for all later research on attitudes associated with aging, and is still frequently cited. An earlier article (Kogan, 1961) reported the development of a psychometrically carefully designed attitude scale that is still frequently used. In the article reprinted here, Kogan demonstrates a persistent question that arises when comparing attitudinal problems across age groups, namely, that an acquiescent response among older cohorts may need to be accounted for. Much age-attitudinal research has followed; a useful review has been offered by Walter Crockett and Mary Hummert (1987).

Another favorite construct has been that of personal control, an area requiring that the researcher account for both the personality characteristic associated with control and the social context in which it occurs. At virtually the same time, two independent reports on the outcomes associated with providing opportunity to control an element of nursing-home life appeared (Langer & Rodin, 1976; Schulz, chapter 27 in this volume). The interventions were designed to counteract the usual institutional environment, which removes much decision-making from the vulnerable elder. Richard Schulz's article is included here, primarily because the event to be controlled was unambiguous—the frequency and duration of friendly visits from college students—as contrasted with the more general and diffuse intervention of Langer and Rodin.

The complexities of the locus of control construct are illustrated well in Margie E. Lachman's study, which first reviewed the literature to locate ambiguities and then reported new research designed to remove some of those ambiguities. Lachman demonstrates the utility of including both multidimensional facets of locus of control and of testing its action in different domains of life (intelligence and health). Another effective use of differentiation among domains, in this case domains within which attributions were made, may also be found in Lachman and Leslie McArthur's (1986) study of attribution in stereotyped attitudes toward elders.

Like the other social sciences, the psychology of adult development and aging was slow to recognize the importance of minority issues in gerontology. Unquestionably the landmark study in this area was the first attempt to study a nationally representative sample of African Americans in this age range, the National Survey of Black Americans. Although the preference in this book has been for articles reporting primary data, the chapter by James S. Jackson, Linda M. Chatters, and Robert Joseph Taylor that concludes their book (Jackson, Chatters & Taylor, 1993) represents an ideal integration of their findings with both broader knowledge about older Americans and with the social issues of the late century. It should be emphasized that there is still a notable lack of research in the intrapsychic aspects of ethnicity, to say nothing of in-depth research of the type reported by Jackson and his colleagues as applied to other minority groups.

REFERENCES

Carstensen, L. L. (1993). Motivation for social contact across the life span: A theory of socioemotional selectivity. In J. E. Jacobs (Ed.), Nebraska symposium on motivation (pp. 209–254). Lincoln: University of Nebraska Press.

Costa, P. T. & McCrae, R. R. (1988). Personality in adulthood: A six-year longitudinal study of self-reports and spouse ratings on the NEO Personality Inventory. Journal of Personality and Social Psychology, 54, 853–863.

Crockett, W. H. & Hummert, M. L. (1987). Perceptions of aging and the elderly. In K. W. Schaie (Ed.), Annual Review of Gerontology and Geriatrics, 7, 217–242.

Jackson, J. S., Chatters, L. M. & Taylor, R. J. (1993). Aging in black America. Newbury Park, CA: Sage.

Kogan, N. L. (1961). Attitudes toward old people: The development of a scale and examination of correlates. Journal of Abnormal and Social Psychology, 62, 616–622.

Lachman, M. E. & McArthur, L. Z. (1986). Adulthood age differences in causal attributions for cognitive, physical, and social performance. Psychology and Aging, 1, 127–132.

Langer, E. & Rodin, J. (1976). The effects of choice and enhanced personal responsibility for the aged. Journal of Personality and Social Psychology, 34, 191–198.

Neugarten, B. L. (1996). The meanings of age. Chicago: University of Chicago Press.

Schulz, R. (1982). Emotionality and aging: A theoretical and empirical analysis. Journal of Gerontology, 37, 42–51.

Tuckman, J. & Lorge, I. (1952). The best years of life: A study in ranking. Journal of Psychology, 34, 137–149.

21. Aging among the Highland Maya

A Comparative Study

David Gutmann

THE STUDY OF TAT responses and other psychological data from middle-aged and aging men resident in the urban United States has led to developmental hypotheses concerning the ego psychology of the aging process (Gutmann, 1964; Neugarten & Gutmann, 1958). Briefly, mature and aging American men seem to move through three major ego states, each representing a distinctive integration of drives, defenses, and self–other definitions. In the first stage, termed *alloplastic mastery*, the emphasis is on control of outer-world affairs, in pursuit of achievement and independence. In the second stage, termed *autoplastic mastery* (or passive mastery), the emphasis is on accommodation to the outer world and on changing the self, rather than the external domain. Thought substitutes for action, and philosophic resignation begins to substitutes for achievement and autonomy drives. In the last stage, termed *omniplastic mastery* (or magical mastery), security and self-esteem are maintained by the regressive defensive strategies of denial and projection, rather than through instrumental action against either the outer world or the self. To a statistically significant degree, younger American men (aged 40–54) are characterized by alloplastic mastery, while older men (55–70) are characterized by autoplastic and omniplastic mastery.

The age differences—from greater to lesser autonomy, from greater to lesser objectivity, etc.—suggested a replication, though in reverse chronological order, of the maturational stages of early life and thereby pointed to possible developmental explanations of the observed age differences. If intrinsic, developmental factors do exercise some influence over the direction of psychological change in later life, their presence could best be demonstrated through data gathered over a variety of cultures, different from the urban United States and from each other in terms of value systems, socioeconomic organization, and especially the social supports provided older men. Should equivalent psychological states be found in age peers across

Reprinted by permission from *Journal of Personality and Social Psychology* 7, no. 1 (1967): 28–35. Copyright © 1967 by the American Psychological Association.

such diverse cultures, the developmental hypothesis would receive strong support.

METHOD

This paper reports results from one such study, a series of intensive interviews carried out with 40 men of the Highland Maya group, preliterate, subsistence-level corn farmers resident in the remote Mexican province of Chiapas. Interviewing was carried out in the Tzeltal-speaking village of Aguacatanango (32 interviews) and in the Tzotzil-speaking town of Zinacantan (8 interviews). Subjects were typical villagers, ranging in age from 30 to 90 (though only 2 men were younger than 35 and only 3 men were over 75). Some subjects spoke the contact language, Spanish, but interviewing generally required the aid of local interpreters, who also recruited subjects. The interviews were given prior to the administration of projective tests, and various approaches were used to insure reliable personality data; for example, no rigid schedule was followed, and the investigator tried to remain sensitive to personal and implicit drifts in the subject's conventional responses—as much as possible he picked up on and tried to amplify the respondent's personal feelings about the facts that he was reporting. Also, in order to clear the air, the investigator invited respondents to interview him, telling them that he would give them the kinds of frank answers that he hoped to get. Areas covered with most subjects included personal history, with special emphasis on important figures and important deaths; views of the future; views of old men's roles; the way in which contentment was gained, lost, and restored; dreams; and the loss and conservation of vitality in later life.

In general, the hypothesis was that dimensions suggested by the mastery typology would accommodate the interview data, and that these dimensions would discriminate age groups in predictable ways. For example, younger men (aged 30–49) should be concerned with their productive and competitive relationship to the outer world, whereas older men (in their 50s and early 60s) should be less involved with production, competition, and future opportunity. It was predicted that these older men, like their American age peers, would handle their concerns in more autoplastic ways, that is, through comparative retrenchment, accommodation, and self-restriction. Finally, the prediction was that the oldest men (in their late 60s and 70s) would define both pleasure and pain in immediate, body-centered, and oral terms; and that they would defend and comfort themselves in irrational ways, through denials and distortions of troubling reality.

In order to avoid halo effects, each question and the data that it elicited was dealt with individually, across interviews. The mastery typology suggested categories for ordering the data, and each response was assigned to that category best representative of the dominant theme that it expressed. The data generated by those questions which discriminated age groups will be reported. Given the open, unstructured nature of the interviewing, each question was not routinely put to each respondent. Accordingly, the respondent *N* varies for each question, and in no case equals the sample *N* of 40.

RESULTS

Psychosexual Regression

The most striking age trend found in these data is towards a passive-dependent and explicitly oral stance among older Highland Maya men. This movement, toward passive-incorporative and away from instrumental orientations, comes out most clearly in replies to questions dealing with pleasure, displeasure, and vitality.

Responses to the question, ''What are the things in your life that give you pleasure?'' were grouped by three major categories: pleasure in productive work, pleasure in maintaining the status quo (''I am happy when I and my family are healthy.''), and pleasure in passive receptivity. Sixty percent of the younger men (aged 30–49) are found in the production-centered category: they are happy tilling their corn fields, selling their goods in the market, fattening animals, and so forth. A few declare themselves dissatisfied with their present work, but not with work per se; they still hope to find employment more productive and less gruelling than their present tillage. By contrast, older men (aged 50–90) visualize contentment in other than achievement and production terms: only 29% of them cite productive work as a source of contentment. For some of the older men (grouped in the status quo category) contentment involves staving off physical threats of one sort or another; they are happy if they are not ill or if they stay out of trouble. But the largest block of oldest men—41%—define contentment in oral, sensual terms and are therefore grouped in the passive-receptive category. For this group happiness comes from something beautiful or when one is visited by friends or relatives, drinks with friends, listens to the music of marimba, or has sufficient food.

Thus, as summarized in Table 26.1, the age shift in terms of contentment, though not statistically significant, is from achievement, from the rewards of

Table 21.1. Age and Thematic Distribution: Responses to Question, "What Makes You Happy?"

Age	Productive work	Maintaining status quo	Passive receptivity
30–49	9[a]	0	4
50–90	6	6	9

NOTE: $N = 34$.

[a] The age distributions of response categories productive work and passive receptivity were compared, using Fisher's exact-probability test. The differences were not significant.

productive work (herds of animals, tiled roofs), to a more custodial "getting by" orientation, and finally to a receptive, oral posture where the next meal or the next bit of affection is the focus of interest.[1]

Responses to the question, "What makes you unhappy?" were accommodated by these categories: interruptions and risks of production, illness, and anaclitic losses. Seventy-nine percent of the younger men are found in the interruptions of production category, and this group clearly visualizes frustration and pain in terms of what might be called a production-competition syndrome: they are bothered if their work does not produce capital or if they lack investment capital (to buy animals and new land), but they also tend to be frightened of the murderous envy generated by the competitive struggle in their society. (Like many preliterate people, the Highland Maya fear ambush and witchcraft from neighbors and relatives envious of their accumulated wealth.)

By contrast, only 12% of the older men are found in the production-competition category; their complaints refer instead to the anaclitic losses category, and 47% of them are found there. Thus, the older men are made unhappy by fairly immediate physical and emotional deprivations: the loss of physical comfort (as in illness), the loss of loved and/or nurturant figures, and the loss of oral supplies ("I am unhappy when there is not enough corn and beans.").

In sum, younger men's discontents refer to a relatively wide sphere of economic and interpersonal activities. They worry about markets and about the competition, envy, and retaliation that result from the striving orientation. For older men, the relevant world seems to have shrunk down to the narrower precincts of the family, the circle of friends, necessary supplies, and their own bodies.[2] It is in these more restricted terms that they define discomfort (see Table 21.2).

Table 21.2. Age and Thematic Distribution: Responses to Question, "What Makes You Unhappy?"

Age	Interruptions and risks of production	Illness	Anaclitic losses
30–49	10[a]	1	0
50–90	2	7	8

NOTE: $N = 28$.

[a] The age distributions of response categories interruptions and risks of production and anaclitic losses were compared, using Fisher's exact-probability test. The differences were significant at the .005 level.

Responses to the question, "When you are unhappy, how do you make yourself happy again?" are more clearly diagnostic of the age shift from productive to passive-receptive interests. In all, three major ways of restoring lost contentment are found: reliance on instrumental action, reliance on omnipotent figures, and reliance on oral supplies. A plurality of the sample, who claimed that they rely on their own actions and resources to restore contentment, fall in the first category: "When I am discontented, I go back to work"; "I take a trip, I look for work"; "I cure myself and so am happy again"; etc. The next largest group of subjects, in the second category, claim to restore contentment through reliance on some powerful external figures: "I burn my candle to the Virgin, so the envy that is around us is pushed away"; "The doctors give me a medicine for it and tell me that I will live for a long time"; "If there were armed soldiers in the village, there would be peace here and so I would be content again"; etc. Finally, many respondents mention food, drink, and medicine as means of restoring contentment and so are found in the third category: "When I have my corn and beans, and my tortilla, I grow happy again"; "Well, a little drink will warm the body and drive away the sadness. One drinks with friends and calls for marimba music"; "The doctor gives me a tonic to make me feel better"; etc.

Seventy-three percent of the younger men and only 29% of the older men are found in the first category, involving instrumental action against the causes of discomfort. Eighteen percent of younger men and 29% of older men are found in the second category, involving reliance on powerful external figures. Nine percent of younger men and 41% of older men are found in the third category, involving restoration of contentment through oral intake. The significant age shift, then, is from reliance on internal or "self" resources to dependence on external sources, in the form of powerful persons or strength-giving foods and tonics (see Table 21.3).

Table 21.3. Age and Thematic Distribution: Responses to Question, "How Do You Restore Contentment?"

Age	Reliance on instrumental action	Reliance on omnipotent figures	Reliance on oral supplies
30–49	8[a]	2	1
50–90	5	5	7

NOTE: $N = 28$.

[a] The age distributions of response categories reliance on action and reliance on oral supplies were compared, using Fisher's exact-probability test. The differences were significant at the .05 level.

The age shift to an explicitly oral orientation also comes out in older men's responses to the linked questions, "Are your forces declining?"; and "Can the forces be restored?" Respondents' beliefs concerning the loss, conservation, and restoration of vitality are grouped under three categories: denial and externalization, irreversible attrition, and oral equivalent. Denial and externalization groups those respondents who either deny that their forces are diminishing or who impute responsibility for such loss to accidental, possibly reversible, processes, such as illness. These men seem to suggest that the loss of forces is not an intrinsic process, with its own scheduling, but is the product of fortuitous events. Sixty-four percent of the younger men and only 21% of the older men are found in this category. The men grouped in the irreversible-process category refer to a natural event, an inevitable concomitant of aging: "The blood gets tired"; "Your strength goes out with your sweat"; etc. These men do not seem to believe that the forces can be restored or the process reversed. Twenty-one percent of the younger men are found here, as against 29% of the older men.

The third group see physical strength and energy as an oral equivalent and imply that the correct foods and medicines will conserve or partly restore the forces that are lost: "We start losing our forces after 40. Only rich men who eat greens and vitamins continue to grow strong and fat after 40." Only 14% of the younger men are found in this group, as opposed to 50% of the older men. Thus, to a statistically significant degree (see Table 21.4), older men see physical energy and well-being as a concrete quality that resides in food or in medicinal tonics. Younger men reluctantly note their declining vigor, but do not concertize vital force into an entity existing apart from the body processes that produce it—an entity that can be put back into the body through the mouth.

The older men's preference for passive-receptive modalities is reflected in

Table 21.4. Age and Thematic Distribution: Subjects' Views concerning the Loss, Conservation, and Restoration of Vital Forces

Age	Denial of loss and/of externalization of cause (e.g., illness)	Irreversible attrition	Oral equivalent (forces maintained or restored by food)
30–49	9[a]	3	2
50–90	3	4	7

NOTE: $N = 28$.
[a] The age distributions of response categories denial of loss and oral equivalent were compared, using Fisher's exact-probability test. The differences were significant at the .05 level.

their dreams. In all, 15 men reported dreams. Seventy-one percent of the dreams reported by older men involved helplessness before external or internal attack; they were dying, etc.: "Sometimes in my dreams they throw me into a canyon or into the water"; "I dream that I will die and that I am sad. I ask, 'Who will support my daughters?' "[3] By contrast, younger men's dreams are generally more benign and suggest that the ego is on top of potentially troublesome issues: in one case a man dreams that he is working; in four cases the dreamer meets a deceased kinsman, recognized in the dream as dead. Such dreams may represent attempts to come to terms with loss: "My mother comes to me and only looks at me without saying anything"; "I dream that my father visits my house, and I tell him that I am content with my family and my work."

Thus, to a significant degree, young men tend to have mastery dreams, while older men tend to have dreams in which they are passive and overwhelmed. The dream, like other forms of fantasy, is the portrait of a wish, and these dreams may convey the older men's unconscious wish to be dominated, much like a child, by powerful external forces.

Table 21.5. Age and Thematic Distribution: Dreams

Age	"Mastery" dreams: Work, acceptance of loss	Passivity: Before death or external attack
30–49	5[a]	1
50–90	2	7

NOTE: $N = 15$.
[a] The age distributions of the two categories were compared, using Fisher's exact-probability test. Differences were significant at the .05 level.

Cognitive Regression

Psychosexual regression towards oral-aggressive and oral-incorporative positions may have consequences for ego process, as well as ego interests. Older men's responses to at least two questions suggest regressive thought and defensive processes, involving the erosion of ego boundaries and heightened cognitive subjectivity.

The subjects' questions reflect their concerns and the terms in which they comprehend the world. Thus, the age-graded trends in thinking are first illustrated by the questions asked by those subjects who interviewed the investigator. These questions could be grouped into two major classes: "objective" or "self-referent." The objective questioners recognized that he came from a different society, and they took him as an informant on work and living conditions in that society. The more subjective, self-referent questioners tried to understand him in terms of their own fears and suspicions: they saw him as someone who might either help or harm them.

To a significant degree, younger men are found in the objective category: they wanted to know about the investigator's work, pay, and training. These younger men were intrigued rather than put off by the fact that he was a foreigner: for them it implied new work styles and new opportunities. By contrast, 50% of the older men (and only 20% of the younger men) group in the more subjective category, in that they tended to ask situation-bound, self-referent questions. They wanted to know why he asked questions, and who would hear his tapes. As a foreigner, he was something of a threat; being different, he was also morally deviant. Thus, some elders stated that he was a loafer because he did not work hard to grow corn. Accordingly, while the younger men tried to understand him in his own terms, the older men to a significant degree saw him as someone to be judged against the values and moral standards by which they judged themselves (see Table 21.6).

The shift in later life towards more referential thinking may influence older men's conceptions of death. Most subjects reported the deaths of friends and family members, and most subjects attributed the death to some cause: illness, physical assault, witchcraft, or other supernatural agency ("Perhaps it is a punishment for my sins."). Explanations concerning supernatural agency, and especially witchcraft, are especially meaningful to 44% of the older respondents: one reports, "My brother was fooling around with a married woman, and her husband put a stick in the road, and he tripped on it and that caused my brother to die." By contrast, even where the deceased had been murdered,

Table 21.6. Age and Thematic Distribution: Questions Asked of Interviewer

Age	Objective questions	Both objective curiosity and self-referent questions	Concrete, self-referent questions
30–49	6[a]	2	3
50–90	5	3	8

NOTE: $N = 27$.

[a] The age distribution of objective questions and concrete, self-referent questions were compared, using Fisher's exact-probability test. Differences were significant at the .05 level.

no younger man claims that witchcraft was involved. Three younger men cite murder as the cause of a death, but in these cases the murder was carried out in a prosaic way, as with a shotgun or machete. In one case, a younger man denies that witchcraft killed his stepfather, even though other people suspected it: "I got home and my stepfather was already dead. Many people were crying, and some were talking about witches, but I knew that the old man drank too much." (See Table 21.7).

The heightened belief in witchcraft suggests a more primitive phrasing of the acquisitive motivations among older men: the younger man's decorous pursuit of land, animals, and tiled roofs via productive labor may become the older man's more directly oral-sadistic readiness to appropriate angrily, to swallow up all good things, and to envy those who possess what he lacks.

There is some Rorschach evidence for this speculation: older men tend to see biting, contending animals and demons in the cards. But the Rorschach taps unconscious processes; these primitive wishes are experienced projec-

Table 21.7. Distribution by Age and Cause: Explanations of Significant Deaths

Age	"Prosaic" and/or impersonal causes (illness, murderous assault)	Supernatural, personally referent causes (envy, witchcraft, retribution for sins, etc.)
30–49	11[a]	0
50–90	11	7

NOTE: $N = 29$.

[a] The age distributions of the two categories were compared, using Fisher's exact-probabilities test. Differences were significant at the .05 level.

tively, as an external threat, a property of the witch who murders out of envy.[4] Possibly, there is a return in later life to more archaic ego states, where the "good" is perceived as "inside," and the "bad" is experienced as alien and "outside."

In any event, the older man's sensitivity to witchcraft points to some primitivization of ego functions: in later life the boundary between self and other, between emotion and the object of emotion, may begin to break down. Phenomena are understood in terms of their relevance for the older observer, and death is the signature of personal malice, envious thoughts, rather than natural, impersonal process.

THREE CASE STUDIES

Three protocols, one from each major age period, are presented to illustrate the ways in which the age-discriminant responses fit together in the individual interview.

Don Hermelindo Aguilar is 46 years old and a life-long resident of Aguacatanango. His opening question concerns the investigator's work: "What is your work—your project? What do you learn from it?" Reviewing family history, he gives a younger man's "objective" explanation of his father's death: his father was killed by a son-in-law in a dispute over some lime trees. The subject misses his father deeply because he now serves in the village government, and, were he alive, his father would advise him about his duties. However, the subject's dreams suggest that he can get along, as a man in his own right, without his father's help: "I dream that my father visits my house. 'How are you?' he says. 'Very well,' I answer. My father says, 'I see that you have work and what to eat. Now I am going to another place for I am already far away from here.' "

Regarding contentment, the subject says, "We always think of our work, where we make our money. We think, 'Is there enough to eat?' We think every day of work, of getting corn and beans."

The subject's problems are met by direct action: "If there's not enough to eat, then we go out and work some more." As for the decline of his "forces," the subject mentions only that he sometimes feels cold and that he has trouble getting out of bed and getting to work in the early morning.

Don Alcadio Gomez is 55 years old. His questions are fairly direct and personal, indicate some suspicion, and do not go much beyond our immediate contact: "Am I 55?" He asks, "Why do you need these talks? What do you need from me? It's easier to talk about one's life if there's a drink to start with.'' Reviewing his life and the significant deaths in it, the subject says that his parents died of fever, but that his three children were killed by witchcraft of envious people. He seems to be trying to fend off any blame for these deaths: ''*We* don't know how it happens, *we* just do our work and try to get something for our families and then somebody might die.'' Discussing the important people in his life, the subject refers mainly to his mother: he had been working in the coffee plantations far from the village but, ''My mother was always crying, so I returned from the *finca* to help her.''

Orally receptive themes pervade his version of contentment: ''I am happy eating, not being sick, and working happily.'' He also mentions the pleasure he gets from drinking and listening to the marimba in the company of his friends. He is made unhappy ''by the death of loved ones,'' and by the threat from unknown enemies: he fears being shot from ambush and is reluctant for this reason to travel on the road. Contentment is restored by work, liquor, and God: ''I put my faith in God's hands. I beg God for relief; what if they kill me, what if I die? It is all in God's hands, and so I feel better, happy with God.'' Predictably, Don Alcadio dreams that a man has come to kill him.

Don Cyrilo Aguilar, aged 66, is a sad and dignified man who asks if there are aged men like himself in the United States and if the investigator plans to help them. He then makes his self-concern more explicit by asking for medicine, for his own pain.

Reporting the death of his children and grandchildren, Don Cyrilo cites witchcraft, explaining that he once led a religious faction that was opposed to other village factions and thus made enemies. He fears imminent death, probably from the same agents, and advises his sons not to fight when he is gone. His gloomy prediction may be based on his father's fate: unlike the younger Don Hermelindo, who recalls the competent role-model parent, Don Cyrilo remembers his father as a victim, thrown into a pot of boiling cane juice by envous co-workers in the sugar plantations.

The subject has a custodial view of contentment: he is happy being without sickness or pain. He is unhappy when he remembers his dead grandchildren, whom he once embraced. Contentment is restored only by passive and incorporative means: ''I stay quiet,'' meaning that he does nothing provocative, and he prays to his favorite saint. When too much troubled by grief, Don Cyrilo drinks for two days, ''until there is no more pain,'' and then returns to work. His dreams alternate between images of death, magical escape, and oral comfort:

I dream that they are cutting meat and that they gave me the meat as a gift. . . . I dream that I run from something. I escape through a crack in the wall. A man tries to catch me, and I can't run. Then, suddenly I fly away. A woman calls me, but I don't want to go to her. . . . I am offered food. They offer me grains of corn. I put it in a pocket and eat it.

Clearly, oral intake is recruited to the service of defensive denial, for Don Cyrilo uses the imagery of his dream to describe the comfort that comes from liquor: "After two days of drinking, I don't feel alive. *It's just like flying.*" Along the same lines he asks, "Are there any medicines to restore the forces?"

In these three representative men we see the benchmarks of allo-, auto-, and omni-plastic mastery. Don Hermelindo, the youngest, is involved in production and in his prestigeful role in the village government; difficulties are handled through work and through emulation of successful men. Don Alcadio, 9 years older, is still involved in competitive, productive striving, but he is also terrified of the more primitive implications of that striving. The oral calculus—"If I have something good, it was taken from him and he will envy me"—begins to order his understanding of events. His world is personalized, full of "envious ones." His solution is to passively put his fate in the hands of the omnipotent *Tata Dios* (Father-God) and to abide by his larger will. Finally, the eldest, Don Cyrilo, fears death on both realistic and superstitious grounds. He falls back on various autoplastic and omniplastic tactics to deny fear and to frustrate the assassin. He avoids provocation ("I stay quiet."). He enlists the help of powerful *Santos*, and he bolsters himself with potent oral allies: liquor gives him wings to fly from death; good food gives temporary pleasure; medicines restore lost forces.

This is an admittedly small sample on which to base generalizations, but there are, overall, some provocative similarities between the United States and Mexican data. The age differences found in the interview data from middle-aged and older Highland Maya men replicate, in a broad thematic sense, age differences found in projective data from a sample of urban American men of similar age composition. Men of both societies seem to move at a similar pace through successive alloplastic, autoplastic, and omniplastic ego stages such that equivalent libidinal, defense, and cognitive shifts are found in both sets of data. These shifts are towards explicitly oral definitions of pleasure and pain, simplistic defensive tactics of denial and projection, and subjectivity of thinking.

Similar shifts have been found in projective materials from the Lowland

Maya of the Yucatan, a group distantly related to and geographically separate from the Highland Maya (Gutmann, 1966).

The sociocultural factors common to these three diverse societies are negligible. Accordingly, the cross-cultural similarities begin to suggest intrinsic developmental influences on the psychology of men in middle and later life.

NOTES

1. Simmons (1945) cites data from a wide range of preliterate cultures in support of the contention, also stated here, that food becomes increasingly important to older people. He proposes that orality among the aged has a completely rational basis, as a strategy for prolonging life: "A dominant interest in old age is to live long, perhaps as long as possible. Therefore, food becomes a matter of increasing concern" (p. 12). However, as suggested here, the increased interest in food is linked to a general passive-receptive posture, which informs many interests and activities of later life besides the preparation and ingestion of food. If this is so, then the transcultural interest in food among the aged has less circumscribed, more irrational roots.

2. It can be argued that the grievances of older men refer to realistic problems— the losses of health, vitality, and intimates necessarily attendant on aging—and not to more intrinsic shifts at the irrational levels of personality. It does not say much about the psychology of older men that they get sick more often than younger men, and that they complain about their ills. However, if all references to illness are left out of the statistical comparison (see Table 21.2), the remaining grievances cited by older men—object loss (death) and oral insupply—reflect the already noted passive-receptive concerns.

Also, the experience of death is not age graded for the Highland Maya: the infant mortality rate is very high, and young men experience death as frequently or more frequently than do older men. Accordingly, older men's emphasis on object loss as a cause of discontent suggests the greater sharpness rather than the greater frequency of this experience for them. In sum, irrational or psychological vulnerability may account for much of the generational difference in the causes of discontent.

3. Robert Butler, a psychoanalyst, has done extensive studies of aging in this country. He reports that the assassin dream is very common among his older American subjects.

4. There are, of course, other possible explanations of this age-graded tendency toward witchcraft explanations: while all villagers believe in witchcraft (and younger men do the dirty work of killing known witches), younger men might be more knowledgeable about the gringo view of death and so feed it back to the investigator. By the same token, the older men may feel freer to speak of these "secret" things, as they no longer compete with the investigator as a peer; for them, confession is not equated with shameful submission. However, younger men mention ordinary murder with about the same frequency that older men mention witchcraft murder. It is not the readiness to discuss murder, but to blame the witch, that distinguishes older men.

REFERENCES

Gutmann, D. *An exploration of ego configurations in middle and later life.* In B. Neugarten (Ed.), Personality in middle and later life. *New York: Atherton, 1964. Pp. 114–148.*

Gutmann, D. *Mayan aging—A comparative TAT study.* Psychiatry, *1966, 29, 246– 259.*

Neugarten, B. & Gutmann, D. *Age-sex roles and personality in middle age: A thematic apperception study.* Psychological Monographs, *1958, 72(17, Whole No. 470).*

Simmons, L. W. *The role of the aged in primitive society. New Haven: Yale University Press, 1945. Chap. 1.*

22. Interaction and Adaptation

Intimacy as a Critical Variable

Marjorie Fiske Lowenthal and Clayton Haven

INTRODUCTION

This paper is a sequel to previous studies in which we noted certain anomalies in the relation between traditional measures of social deprivation, on the one hand, and indicators of morale and psychiatric condition, on the other, in studies of older populations. For example, lifelong isolates tend to have average or better morale and to be no more prone to hospitalization for mental illness in old age than anyone else, but those who have tried and failed to establish social relationships appear particularly vulnerable.[1] Nor, with certain exceptions, do age-linked trauma involving social deprivation, such as widowhood and retirement, precipitate mental illness.[2] While these events do tend to be associated with low morale, they are by no means universally so. Furthermore, a voluntary reduction in social activity, that is, one which is not accounted for by widowhood, retirement or physical impairment, does not necessarily have a deleterious effect on either morale or on professionally appraised mental health status.[3]

In analyzing detailed life histories of a small group of the subjects making up the samples for these studies, we were struck by the fact that the happiest and healthiest among them often seemed to be people who were, or had been, involved in one or more close personal relationships. It therefore appeared that the existence of such a relationship might serve as a buffer against age-linked social losses and thus explain some of these seeming anomalies. The purpose of the present study is to explore this possibility. In doing so, we shall first illustrate how two rather conventional measures of interaction and role status are related to three measures of adaptation which represent different frames of reference. Taking advantage of the panel nature of the data, we shall further document these relationships by analyzing the effect of social gains and losses on adaptation. We shall then show how the presence or absence of a confidant serves as an explanatory variable in the overall trends

From *American Sociological Review* 33 (1968): 20–30.

and deviations noted in the relationships between the more conventional social measures and adaptation. Finally, we shall describe briefly the characteristics of those who do and do not have a confidant, and discuss the
implications of these findings for adult socialization and adaptation.

The Concept of Intimacy

As we explored the literature prior to analyzing our own material on intimacy,
we were struck by the paucity of references to the quality, depth or reciprocity
of personal relationships in social science materials. In their studies of the
relationship between social interaction and adjustment, sociologists traditionally have been concerned with the concepts of isolation and anomie, often
gauged or inferred from low rankings on quantitative indicators of social roles
and contacts; that is, with questions such as how many roles a person fills,
how much of his time is spent in interaction with others, and the relationship
to the subject of persons with whom this interaction takes place. Several of
these studies have established a modest relationship between social isolation
and maladjustment.[4] With a few exceptions noted below, they have not taken
into account the quality or intensity of the individual's relationships with
others.

Psychologists have been concerned with dyadic relationships, including
the parental and the marital, but although there are references in the literature
to Freud's possibly apocryphal mention of the capacity for love as a criterion
of mental health, one finds little research directly related to qualities or behavior reflecting the capacity for intimacy or reciprocity. Nor do the traditional personality tests often tap characteristics relevant to such concepts.
Some research on animal and human infants, however, has explored this
dimension. Harlow and Zimmermann[5] have shown that infant monkeys spend
a great deal more time with a cloth mother surrogate than with a wire surrogate, regardless of which mother provides the milk. They conclude, as have
Spitz and Wolf in their studies of human infants,[6] that the need for love is
instinctual. Ferreira,[7] drawing on his own research and that of Bowlby,[8] concludes that the need for intimacy is "primary and of an instinctual nature . . .
the intimacy need may represent a more basic instinctual force than oral or
even nursing needs."

It is primarily the psychoanalysts and the analytically-oriented psychologists who, largely on the basis of clinical insights, have stressed this capacity
or need, often implying that from its development and fulfillment grow all
other forms of social growth and constructive social action. One of the fun-

damental precepts of Angyal's theory[9] is that "existing in the thought and affection of another really is a very concrete level of existence." He goes on to say that the establishment and maintenance of such a close relationship is "the crux of our existence from the cradle to the grave." Erikson postulates the capacity for intimacy as one of the major developmental tasks of life, ideally to be achieved in the establishment of a close relationship with a person of the opposite sex in late adolescence and early adulthood.[10] While our data support this view, it seems clear that there are other viable forms of intimacy which are not necessarily experienced as substitutes for, or supplements to, a stable heterosexual relationship.

In the light of the general paucity of research on the problem of intimacy, it is not surprising that it has not been systematically explored in relation to older populations. Rosow's important study of friendship patterns under varying age-density conditions[11] does not take the depth of these relationships into account. Arth,[12] in his study of friendships in an aging population, is concerned with "close" friendships, but he does not define closeness. Blau's pioneering study of structural constraints on friendships of the aged[13] documents the importance of prevailing age–sex–marital status patterns in the establishment of friendships, but it does not discuss the quality or intensity of these relationships.

Obviously, this is a delicate area to explore with field research methods, and our own approach was a simple—if not crude—one. The analysis rests largely on responses to the question: "Is there anyone in particular you confide in or talk to about yourself or your problems?" followed by a description of the identity of the confidant. Still, the findings tend not only to confirm the insights of clinicians and the rather sparse observations of other researchers, but also to clarify some of the puzzling deviations we have noted in our own work in regard to the relationship between social measures, on the one hand, and adaptation, on the other.

THE SAMPLE

The sample on which this report is based consists of 280 sample-survivors in a panel study of community-resident aged, interviewed three times at approximately annual intervals. The parent sample included 600 persons aged sixty and older, drawn on a stratified-random basis from 18 census tracts in San Francisco. The sample of 280 remaining at the third round of interviewing is about equally divided in terms of the original stratifying variables of sex, three age levels, and social living arrangements (alone or with others).

As might be expected, the panel differs from elderly San Franciscans (and elderly Americans), as a whole, by including proportionally more of the very elderly, more males, and more persons living alone. Largely because of the oversampling of persons living alone, the proportion of single, widowed, and divorced persons, and of working women, is higher than among elderly Americans in general. Partly because of the higher proportion of working women, their income level was higher than average (44 percent having an income of over $2,000 per year, compared with 25 percent among all older Americans). The proportion of foreign born (34 percent) resembles that for older San Franciscans in general (36 percent), which is considerably more than for all older Americans (18 percent). While some of these sample biases may tend to underplay the frequency of the presence of a confidant, we have no reason to believe that they would influence findings from our major research question, namely the role of the confidant as an intervening variable between social resources and deprivation and adaptation.

Measures of Role, Interaction, and Adaptation

The two conventional social measures to be reported here are number of social roles[14] and level of social interaction.[15] Men tend to rank somewhat lower than women in social interaction in the younger groups, but up through age 74, fewer than 17 percent of either sex rank "low" on this measure (defined as being visited [only] by relatives, contacts only with persons in dwelling, or contacts for essentials only).[16] Isolation increases sharply beginning with age 75, however, and in that phase women are slightly more isolated than men (32 percent compared with 28 percent), possibly because of the higher proportion of widows than of widowers. In general, because they are less likely to be widowed and more likely to be working, men have more roles than women at all age levels, and this discrepancy becomes particularly wide at 75 or older, when 40 percent of the men, compared with only 15 percent of the women, have three or more roles. Among men, a low level of social interaction and a paucity of social roles tend to be related to low socioeconomic status, but this does not hold true for women.

The principal measure of adaptation in this analysis is a satisfaction-depression (or morale) score based on a cluster analysis of answers to 8 questions.[17] For a subsample of 112, we shall also report ratings of psychiatric impairment by three psychiatrists, who, working independently, reviewed the protocols in detail but did not see the subjects.[18] We thus have a subjective indicator of the sense of well-being, and a professional appraisal of mental health status. A third measure, opinion as to whether one is young or old for one's age, is included to round out the adaptation dimension with an indication of what might be called the respondent's opinion as to his relative deprivation—that is, whether he thinks he is better or worse off than his age peers.

As is true for the social indicators, there are age, sex, and class differences in regard to these adaptation measures which we shall have to bear in mind in analyzing the relationship between these two dimensions. Among men, morale deteriorates evenly with advancing age, from somewhat over one-third ''depressed'' among those under 65 to about three-fifths among those 75 or older. The youngest women are more depressed than the youngest men (47 percent depressed), but there is no increase—in fact there is a slight decrease—in depression among the 65–74-year-old women. The oldest women, however, are nearly as depressed as the oldest men. There are no consistent age or sex trends in regard to whether the subject thinks he is young or old for his age—a slight majority of both sexes at all age levels consider themselves young.

Mental health status, as judged by psychiatrists, indicates that if all age groups are combined, men are psychiatrically more robust than women. This is especially true for the oldest group (75 or older), where four-fifths of the men, compared with only two-fifths of the women, are considered unimpaired. The sex difference is reversed, however, in the middle age-range (65–74), where men are judged to be more impaired than women (44 percent, compared with 29 percent rated impaired). While at first glance this discrepancy might be interpreted as a consequence of psychic crises relating to retirement, detailed analysis of a large psychiatrically hospitalized older sample[19] indicates that retirement rarely precipitates psychiatric disorder. But this same analysis does demonstrate clearly that physical deterioration in the elderly is frequently accompanied by psychiatric impairment. The sharp reversal of sex differences in mental health status in the middle age group may, therefore, be associated with the earlier onset of physical impairment among men. The fact that the death rate for men between 65 and 74 is considerably greater than for women may, in turn, on the principle of survival of the fittest, account for the oldest men's (75 or more) again being judged of more robust mental health than women.

In view of the association between physical and mental health in the elderly, and of the association between poor health and low socioeconomic status, it is not surprising that there is also some relationship between low socioeconomic status and psychiatric impairment, though this association is more marked for men than for women. Low morale, on the other hand, is related to low socioeconomic status among both men and women.[20]

Relationship between Social Measures and Adaptation

As Table 22.1 indicates, there is a clear and consistent relationship between social resources and good morale, and between social deprivation and low morale. Low social interaction, in particular, is strongly related to depression. While high ranks on both social measures contribute to the sense of relative privilege (feel young for age), a low rank is not related as consistently to a sense of relative deprivation as it is to poor morale. A high rank on the two social measures is more closely associated with professional ratings of good mental health than with the respondents' with reports on mood and sense of relative advantage or deprivation. A low rank on social measures, however, is not consistently or markedly related to a rating of impairment. In other words, social resources and social deficits appear to influence self-appraisals of mood, comparison of self with others, and professional appraisals of adaptation in different ways. Social roles and high interaction are apparently considered to be indicators of, or associated with, mental health—but their absence is not necessarily construed as indicative of impairment. The pattern of association between the social indicators and morale is just the reverse. Social deficits—at least as indicated by the social interaction measure—are

Table 22.1. Social Indicators and Adaptation

	Social Interaction		Role Status	
	High	Low	High	Low
	%	%	%	%
Psychiatric status				
Unimpaired	73	42	90	61
Impaired	27	58	10	39
Opinon of own age				
Young	65	39	67	57
Not young	35	61	33	43
Morale				
Satisfied	58	15	60	46
Depressed	42	85	40	54

Table 22.2. The Relation between Change in Social Measures and Adaptation

	Social Interaction			Role Status		
	Increased	Decreased	Unchanged	Increased	Decreased	Unchanged
	%	%	%	%	%	%
Psychiatric status						
Unimpaired	(32)[a]	42	30	(11)	(45)	35
Impaired	(68)	58	70	(89)	(55)	65
Opinion of own age						
Young	70	49	63	53	55	63
Not Young	30	51	37	47	45	37
Morale						
Satisfied	47	35	58	50	47	53
Depressed	53	65	42	50	53	47

[a] Percentages are placed in parentheses when the numbers on which they are based are less than 20; the N's for the percentages in parentheses range from 14–19.

more highly correlated with a depressed state than are social resources correlated with a satisfied state. The sense of relative privilege is enhanced by social advantage, but social disadvantage does not necessarily evoke a sense of relative deprivation, at least insofar as this sense is reflected by feeling average or old for one's age.

If we compare these social indicators, as reported at the second follow-up, with those reported at the first follow-up approximately one year earlier, we find that several changes took place (see Table 22.2). These trends were on the order of those noted for other variables used in the panel questionnaire.[21] Social interaction and role status closely resemble each other with respect to change, with 14 and 15 percent, respectively, "improving," and 20 and 21 percent, respectively, "deteriorating." The broad patterns of relationship between change in social resources and the three indicators of adaptation resemble those which emerged in the more static picture shown in Table 22.1. Social losses are related to poor morale, but gains are not related to high morale. Gains are, however, highly correlated with good psychiatric status, though again decrements are not so strongly associated with poor status. Improvements in role and social interaction are related to a sense of relative advantage, as indicated by feeling young for one's age, but losses do not markedly contribute to a sense of relative deprivation (feeling old). This again suggests that a professional's judgment of mental impairment rests on factors other than the absence of indicators of health; an individual's subjective sense of well-being does not automatically result from supplying the role and interaction deficits that often are associated with low morale.

On the other hand, maintaining the status quo in social interaction and role is related to good adaptation, regardless of which indicator of adjustment is used. In fact, on four of the six correlations, stability proves to be more highly associated with good adaptation than does "improvement." At the same time, we note that sizeable proportions of those who suffered social decrements are well-adapted, ranging from one-third to over half, depending on the adaptation measure used. Clearly, our conventional measures alone do not fully explain the relation between the individual's position and behavior in his social milieu, on the one hand, and his adjustment, on the other.

Pursuing our hypothesis with regard to the potential importance of a confidant as a buffer against social losses, we turn to Table 22.3, which shows the current presence or absence of a confidant, and recent losses, gains, or stability in intimate relationships, in conjunction with the three adaptation measures. As the first column shows, the presence of a confidant is positively associated with all three indicators of adjustment. The absence of a confidant is related to low morale. Lack of a present confidant does not, however, have much bearing on the individual's sense of relative deprivation, or on the psychiatric judgments of mental impairment. We suggest, though with the present data we cannot fully document, two possible explanations for these

Table 22.3. The Effect of a Confidant on Adaptation

	Current Presence of Confidant		Change in Confidant Past Year		
	Yes	No	Gained	Lost	Maintained same confidant
	%	%	%	%	%
Psychiatric status					
Unimpaired	69	60	(60)	(56)	80
Impaired	31	40	(40)	(44)	20
Opinion of own age					
Young	60	62	42	49	61
Not young	40	38	58	51	39
Morale					
Satisfied	59	41	44	30	68
Depressed	41	59	56	70	32

findings. First, as we have previously noted,[22] there are some lifelong isolates and near-isolates whose late-life adaptation apparently is not related to social resources. The sense of relative deprivation, at least for older persons, no doubt applies not only to current comparisons with one's peers, but also to comparisons with one's own earlier self. This would contribute to an explanation of the fact that some older people without a confidant are satisfied. They do not miss what they never have had. Our second explanation echoes the old adage that it is better to have loved and lost than never to have loved at all. The psychiatrists, in rating mental health status, may take *capacity* for intimacy into account, as indicated by past relationships such as marriage or parenthood. The respondent, in a more or less "objective" comparison of himself with his peers, may also take these past gratifications into account. However, such recollections may well be less serviceable on the more subjective level of morale and mood.

The right side of the table, showing change and stability in the confidant relationship, dramatically exemplifies the significance of intimacy for the subjective sense of well being: the great majority of those who lost a confidant are depressed, and the great majority of those who maintained one are satisfied. Gaining one helps, but not much, suggesting again the importance of stability, which we have noted in relation to the other social measures. Maintenance of an intimate relationship also is strongly correlated with self–other comparisons and with psychiatrists' judgments, though losses do not show the obverse. This supports our suggestion that evidence of the *capacity* for intimacy may be relevant to these two more objective indicators of adaptation.

The great significance of the confidant from a subjective viewpoint, combined with the fact that sizeable proportions of people who showed decrements in social interaction or social role nevertheless were satisfied, raised the possibility that the maintenance of an intimate relationship may serve as a buffer against the depression that might otherwise result from decrements in social role or interaction, or from the more drastic social losses frequently suffered by older persons, namely widowhood and retirement. To test this hypothesis, we examined the morale of changers on the interaction and role measures in the light of whether they did or did not have a confidant.

The Intimate Relationship As a Buffer against Social Losses

As Table 22.4 shows, it is clear that if you have a confidant, you can decrease your social interaction and run no greater risk of becoming depressed than

Table 22.4. Effect on Morale of Changes in Social Interaction and Role Status, in the Presence and Absence of a Confidant

	Social Interaction			
	Increased		Decreased	
	Has Confidant	No Confidant	Has Confidnat	No Confidant
	%	%	%	%
Morale				
Satisfied	55	(30)	56	13
Depressed	45	(70)	44	87

	Role Status			
	Increased		Decreased	
	Has Confidant	No Confidant	Has Confidant	No Confidant
	%	%	%	%
Morale				
Satisfied	55	(42)	56	(38)
Depressed	45	(58)	44	(62)

if you had increased it. Further, if you have no confidant, you may increase your social activities and yet be far more likely to be depressed than the individual who has a confidant but has lowered his interaction level.[23] Finally, if you have no confidant and retrench in your social life, the odds for depression become overwhelming. The findings are similar, though not so dramatic, in regard to change in social role: if you have a confidant, roles can be decreased with no effect on morale; if you do not have a confidant, you are likely to be depressed whether your roles are increased or decreased (though slightly more so if they are decreased). In other words, the presence of an intimate relationship apparently does serve as a buffer against such decrements as loss of role or reduction of social interaction.

What about the more dramatic "insults" of aging, such as widowhood or retirement? While a few people became widowed or retired during our second follow-up year (and are therefore included among the "decreases" in social role), there were not enough of them to explore fully the impact of these age-linked stresses. We therefore have checked back in the life histories of our subjects and located persons who retired within a seven-year period prior to the second follow-up interview or who became widowed within this period. Though our concern is primarily with social deficits, we added persons who had suffered serious physical illness within two years before the second follow-up contact, since we know that such stresses also influence adaptation.

Table 22.5 indicates that the hypothesis is confirmed in regard to the more traumatic social deprivations. An individual who has been widowed within seven years, and who has a confidant, has even higher morale than a person who remains married but lacks a confidant. In fact, given a confidant, widowhood within such a comparatively long period makes a rather undramatic impact on morale. Among those having confidants, only 10 percent more of the widowed than of the married are depressed, but nearly three-fourths of the widowed who have no confidant are depressed, compared with only about half, among the married, who have no confidant.[24] The story is similar with respect to retirement. The retired with a confidant rank the same in regard to morale as those still working who have no confidant; those both retired and

Table 22.5. *Effect of Confidant on Morale in the Contexts of Widowhood, Retirement and Physical Illness*

	Satisfied	Depressed
	%	%
Widowed within 7 Years		
Has confidant	55	45
No confidant	(27)	(73)
Married		
Has confidant	65	35
No confidant	(47)	(53)
Retired within 7 Years		
Has confidant	50	50
No confidant	(36)	(64)
Not retired		
Has confidant	70	30
No confidant	50	50
Serious physical illness within 2 Years		
Has confidant	(16)	(84)
No confidant	(13)	(87)
No serious illness		
Has confidant	64	36
No confidant	42	58

having no confidant are almost twice as likely to be depressed as to be sat-isfied, whereas among those both working and having a confidant, the ratio is more than reversed.

Although relatively few people (35) developed serious physical illness in the two-year period prior to the second follow-up interview, it is nevertheless amply clear that a confidant does not play a mediating role between this "insult" of aging and adjustment as measured by the depression-satisfaction score. The aged person who is (or has recently been) seriously ill is over-whelmingly depressed, regardless of whether or not he has an intimate relationship. Superficially, one might conclude that this is a logical state of affairs. A social support—such as an intimate relationship—may serve as a mediating, palliative or alleviating factor in the face of social losses, but one should not expect it to cross system boundaries and serve a similar role in the face of physical losses. On the other hand, why doesn't one feel more cheerful, though ill, if one has an intimate on whom to rely for support, or to whom one can pour out complaints? At this point we can only conjecture, but one possible explanation is that serious physical illness is usually accom-panied by an increase in dependence on others, which in turn may set off a conflict in the ill person more disruptive to his intimate relationships than to more casual ones. This may be especially true of dependent persons whose dependency is masked.[25] A second possibility is that the assumption of the sick role may be a response to the failure to fulfill certain developmental tasks. In this event, illness would be vitally necessary as an ego defense, and efforts of intimates directed toward recovery would be resisted.[26] A third possibility is that illness is accompanied by increased apprehension of death. Even in an intimate relationship, it may be easier (and more acceptable) to talk about the grief associated with widowhood or the anxieties or losses associated with retirement than to confess one's fears about the increasing imminence of death.

Characteristics of Persons Having a Confidant; Confidant Identity

In turning to the question of who does, and who does not, maintain an inti-mate relationship, we found sex and marital status differences that were not unexpected, and some discrepancies with respect to age and socioeconomic status that seemed, at first glance, puzzling. Despite the fact that there were about twice as many widows as widowers in this sample, women were more likely to have a confidant than were men (69 percent, compared with 57 percent). (See Table 22.6.) Age trends are irregular. Both persons under 65 and those 75 and older were less likely to have a confidant than the 65 to 74 year olds. Women are more likely than men to have an intimate relationship at all age levels, and the differences between the sexes are especially pronounced in those under 65, where nearly three-fourths of the women and only half the men reported that they have a confidant. These findings tend to support those of Arth[27] and Blau[28] in regard to the social capacities and advantages of women. The married are notably more likely to have a confidant than those who are not; single persons are most deprived on this score, and the widowed fall between. Persons above the median on our socioeconomic measure are considerably more likely to have a confidant than those below it, and the differences are more marked for men than women. Edu-

Table 22.6. Characteristics of Persons Having a Confidant

	Percent with Confidant		
	Men	Women	Total
Sex			
Men			57
Women			69
Age			
60–64	50	72	62
65–74	68	75	72
75+	55	59	57
Marital status			
Single	36	67	46
Married	74	81	77
Separated/Divorced	50	57	54
Widowed	50	65	62
Socioeconomic status			
High	69	77	73
Low	38	56	47
Educational level			
Less than 8 years	51	67	56
8 years	58	62	60
More than 8 years	61	70	67
Occupational level			
Blue colar	48	67	55
White collar	65	69	67
Social interaction			
High	62	72	68
Low	39	50	44
Role status index			
3–5 roles	71	84	76
0–2 roles	45	62	55

cation makes suprisingly little difference for either sex, but occupational differences are marked for men.

As to the identity of the confidant, among the nearly two-thirds of the sample who do have a confidant, the identity of this person is fairly evenly distributed among spouse, child and friend. Siblings or other relatives as confidants are comparatively rare. Among women in general, husbands are least frequently mentioned, while wives are the most important for men. This is not only because women are more likely to be widowed, for if we look only at those who are married, or still married, men at all age levels are more likely to report a spouse than are women. Women are about twice as likely as men to mention a child or another relative, and more likely to name friends.

In view of the frequently noted class differences in social interaction,[29] it does not surprise us that more than half again as many of those above the median on our socioeconomic measure have a confidant than do those below the median. The generally reported wider range of friendship patterns among the higher socioeconomic groups does not prepare us for the class differences in the identity of confidants reported by this older sample, however. More than three times as many of the higher class report a spouse than do those of lower socioeconomic status (28 percent compared with 8 percent). While this tendency holds among both sexes, the discrepancies are most dramatic among men (36 compared with 2 percent). Conversely, more than twice as many of the low socioeconomic group report a friend, and again it is men who account entirely for the discrepancy. Women of higher status are slightly more likely to have a friend as confidant than are women of lower status. Analysis of detailed life history interviews available for a subsample provide some evidence that the lesser importance of the spouse as confidant among the men of the lower socioeconomic group is connected with problems of masculine role and identity, low-status males considering close association with women a sign of male weakness. This he-man theory gains some support in the fact that among men, not having a confidant is more related to blue collar occupational status than it is to little schooling. Men in the blue collar occupations, whether skilled or unskilled, would obviously—at least in the United States—have less opportunity to associate with women than would white collar males.

In these same life history studies, we have noted some examples of ''a regression or escape into intimacy'' with advancing age. That is, people who have maintained both intimate and other types of social relationships may, on retirement, for example, or after the departure of children from the home, withdraw to a situation where a close relationship with the spouse is, in effect, the only social contact. But this is by no means the rule. In general, the more complex the social life, the more likely is there to be an intimate relationship, no doubt, in part, because of the larger pool of social resources from which a confidant may be drawn. Among persons having three or more social roles, for example, three-fourths have a confidant, whereas among those having two or fewer social roles, only slightly more than half have a confidant. Similarly, two-thirds of those on the highest level of social interaction have an intimate relationship, while the majority of those whose interaction is limited to being visited by relatives do not. Such resources, however, are more important for men than for women.

IMPLICATIONS

This study indicates that when two conventional indicators of social role and interaction are used, the significance for adaptation of being socially deprived or advantaged varies in accordance with the degree of subjectivity of the adjustment measure used. Social resources are more related to professional appraisals of good health than to subjective appraisals of high morale; social deprivation, on the other hand, is associated with subjective reports of poor morale, but not with professional assessments of poor mental health. A more objective self-report involving comparisons with others resembles the psychiatrists' judgments; that is, being socially privileged enhances one's evaluation but being socially underprivileged does not deflate it. Regardless of the indicator of adaptation which is examined, however, the deviant cells are sizeable.

To help explain these variations, we went on to show that the maintenance of a stable intimate relationship is more closely associated with good mental health and high morale than is high social interaction or role status, or stability in interaction and role. Similarly, the loss of a confidant has a more deleterious effect on morale, though not on mental health status, than does a reduction in either of the other two social measures. We suggested that while psychiatrists may take the capacity for an intimate relationship into account in their professional judgments, awareness that he has such a potential does not elevate an individual's mood if he has recently lost a confidant. Finally, we have noted that the impact on adjustment of a decrease in social interaction, or a loss of social roles, is considerably softened if the individual has a close personal relationship. In addition, the age-linked losses of widowhood and retirement are also ameliorated by the presence of a confidant, though the assault of physical illness clearly is not.

In view of the apparently critical importance of an intimate relationship, the sex and class differences we have noted in the reporting of the presence or absence of a confidant provoke speculation. In the youngest age group (those between 60 and 64, presumably a period where the pool of potential confidants is greatest), nearly half again as many women as men reported an intimate companion. We are reminded, in this connection, of the observations of psychoanalyst Prescott Thompson in regard to age trends in the significance of interpersonal communication among spouses. In early periods of the adult life span, he suggests, communication problems may well have been obscured by the pressures and distractions of job and children; as the empty nest and retirement phases approach, awareness of deficiencies in this respect may become acute.[30] Significantly, it is the wives who are most likely first to become conscious of the problem, and to be able to talk about it.[31]

There seems little doubt that, to some extent, marital status is an indication of the capacity for intimacy. We have seen that the married are most likely to have a confidant, whether spouse or some other. Among those not married and living with spouse when we interviewed them, widows and widowers were most likely to have a confidant, single persons least, and the divorced and separated fell between. Finally, the class and sex differences we have noted suggest that the lower class men may harbor a concept of virility which discourages the development of types of intimacy other than the purely sexual. Thus, with the waning of sexual potency or the loss of a partner with advanced age, they are left with fewer alternatives for an intimate relationship than are women.

At this stage of our knowledge, we can only wonder whether women's greater sensitivity to close relationships, and, as we have seen, their greater versatility in the choice of objects for such relationships, has any causal connection with their greater adaptability for survival. Not only is the overall death rate higher among men, but among them, and not among women, the suicide rate increases rapidly with age. And despite their greater potentiality for remarriage, it is among men, not women, that widowhood is more likely to trigger mental illness. Conversely, the few instances where retirement precipitates mental disturbance tend to be found among working women rather than men, suggesting that an important source of frustration and conflict may lie precisely in the incapacity, or lack of opportunity, to carry out the special feminine task of developing and sustaining intimate relationships.[32] We are reminded once more of Angyal's guiding thesis,[33] that the maintenance of closeness with another is the center of existence up to the very end of life.

NOTES

1. Marjorie Fiske Lowenthal, "Social Isolation and Mental Illness in Old Age," *American Sociological Review*, 29 (February 1964), pp. 54–70.

2. Marjorie Fiske Lowenthal, "Antecedents of Isolation and Mental Illness in Old Age," *Archives of General Psychiatry*, 12 (March 1965), pp. 245–254.

3. Marjorie Fiske Lowenthal and Deetje Boler, "Voluntary vs. Involuntary Social Withdrawal," *Journal of Gerontology*, 20 (July 1965), pp. 363–371.

4. For a selected review of this literature, see Lowenthal (1964), *op. cit.*

5. Harry F. Harlow and Robert R. Zimmermann, "Affectional Responses in the Infant Monkey," *Science*, 130 (1959), pp. 421–432.

6. Rene A. Spitz and Katherine M. Wolf, "Anaclitic Depression," *Psychoanalytic Study of the Child*, 2, New York: International Universities Press, 1946, pp. 313–342.

7. A. J. Ferreira, "The Intimacy Need in Psychotherapy," *American Journal of Psychoanalysis*, 24 (November 1964), pp. 190–194.

8. John Bowlby, "The Nature of the Child's Tie to His Mother," *International Journal of Psychoanalysis*, 39 (September–October 1958), pp. 350–373.

9. Andras Angyal, *Neurosis and Treatment: A Holistic Theory*, New York: John Wiley and Sons, 1965, p. 19.

10. Erik H. Erikson, "Identity and the Life Cycle," *Psychological Issues*, [Monograph 1], New York: International Universities Press, 1959.

11. Irving Rosow, *Social Integration of the Aged*, New York: Free Press, 1967.

12. Malcolm Arth, "American Culture and the Phenomenon of Friendship in the Aged," in Clark Tibbitts and Wilma Donahue, eds., *Social and Psychological Aspects of Aging*, New York: Columbia University Press, 1962, pp. 529–534.

13. Zena Smith Blau, "Structural Constraints on Friendships in Old Age," *American Sociological Review*, 26 (June 1961), pp. 429–440.

14. Roles include parent, spouse, worker, church-goer and organization member.

15. Ranging from "contributes to goals of organizations" to "contacts for the material essentials of life only." All measures of interaction and adaptation reported here pertain to the second round of follow-up.

16. Only a few of the tables drawn upon for this paper are presented in the text; others are available on request.

17. The distribution of individual cluster scores was dichotomized at the median: persons falling below the median are called "depressed," and persons falling above the median are called "satisfied." Questions pertained to the sense of satisfaction with life, happiness, usefulness, mood and planning.

18. One-third (38 persons) were judged impaired, the majority (30 persons) only mildly so. Seven were rated moderately, and one severely impaired.

19. Marjorie Fiske Lowenthal, Paul L. Berkman, and Associates, *Aging and Mental Disorder in San Francisco: A Social Psychiatric Study*, San Francisco: Jossey-

Bass, Inc., 1967; Alexander Simon, Marjorie Fiske Lowenthal, and Leon J. Epstein, *Crisis and Intervention* (working title), New York: Basic Books, pending.

20. The index of current economic position is based on a combination of monthly rent, annual income, and the Tryon Index of San Francisco census tracts. The Tryon Index, with scores ranging from zero (low) to 10 (high), is based on proportions of persons in professional or managerial occupations, with college education, and self-employed, the proportion of dwelling units with one or fewer persons per room, and the proportion of domestic and service workers. See Robert C. Tryon, *Identification of Social Areas by Cluster Analysis*, Berkeley: University of California Press, 1955. The lowest quartile consists of persons who scored below the median on all three measures (the medians were: income, $2,500; rent, $60; Tryon score, 4.5), and the highest quartile consists of persons who scored above the median on all three socioeconomic measures.

21. Lowenthal and Berkman, *op. cit*

22. Lowenthal (1964), *op. cit.*

23. Parallel analyses of the other two adjustment measures are not included here. The psychiatric ratings are available for only a subsample of 112 (and cells would become too small). The indicator of opinion of own age reflects trends similar, though not so marked, as those shown here, except for increase in role status, where the absence of a confidant does not contribute to a negative opinion.

24. This finding suggests the need for far more detailed questioning on the confidant relationship than we were able to undertake. It may well be that some married persons assumed that the question pertained to confidants other than spouses.

25. Alvin Goldfarb, "Psychodynamics and the Three-Generation Family," in Ethel Shanas and Gordon F. Streib, eds., *Social Structure and the Family: Generational Relations*, Englewood Cliffs, New Jersey: Prentice-Hall, 1965, pp. 10–45.

26. Lowenthal and Berkman, *op. cit.*

27. Arth, *op. cit.*

28. Blau, *op. cit.*

29. *Ibid.*; Rosow, *op. cit.*

30. Prescott W. Thompson and Ronald Chen, "Experiences with Older Psychiatric Patients and Spouses Together in a Residential Treatment Setting," *Bulletin of the Menninger Clinic*, 30 (January 1966), pp. 23–31.

31. Prescott W. Thompson, Personal Communication, 1966.

32. Lowenthal and Berkman, *op. cit.*

33. Angyal, *op. cit.*

23. Influence of Extraversion and Neuroticism on Subjective Well-Being

Happy and Unhappy People

Paul T. Costa Jr. and Robert R. McCrae

N OWHERE IS THE relevance of psychology to human concern more evident than in studies of happiness or subjective well-being. Interest in measuring the quality of life has led researchers (Andrews & Withey, 1976; Bradburn & Caplovitz, 1965; Campbell, Converse & Rodgers, 1976; Cantril, 1965) to conduct national surveys of happiness and to examine the influence of social-structural or demographic variables on perceived well-being. Adaptation-level (AL) theory (Helson, 1964) has been applied to explain individual perceptions of happiness (Brickman & Campbell, 1971; Brickman, Coates & Janoff-Bulman, 1978). As a result of these studies, a number of issues have been clarified and a few unexpected findings replicated. The present article is an attempt to summarize the state of current knowledge on personality and happiness and to offer a model of happiness that clarifies and extends it. Data are provided in support of several parts of the model.

CONCEPTUALIZING AND MEASURING HAPPINESS

Researchers have used a variety of measures that indicate something of the nature and diversity of conceptions of subjective well-being. Gurin, Veroff, and Feld (1960) adopted the most straightforward and intuitive method of assessing happiness: They asked subjects if they were "very happy," "pretty happy," or "not too happy." To obtain a more differentiated estimate of life satisfaction, Campbell, Converse, and Rodgers (1976) required subjects to rate their satisfaction within each of 10 areas of life—job, marriage, family, and so on. Campbell (1976) regarded this strategy as a "cognitive" appraisal of life satisfaction, since it avoided any direct reference to feelings or affects

Reprinted by permission from *Journal of Personality and Social Psychology* 38, no. 4 (1980): 668–78. Copyright © 1980 by the American Psychological Association.

and allowed the subject to assess his or her satisfaction according to his or her own standards and expectations.

Cantril (1965) used a so-called self-anchoring scale, in which individuals defined a "best life" and a "worst life" for themselves, and then rated their present life on this best-to-worst scale. A different approach that has attained considerable use by researchers was developed by Bradburn and his colleagues at the National Opinion Research Center (Bradburn, 1969; Bradburn & Caplovitz, 1965). Instead of asking for cognitive judgments of the adequacy of one's life, he measured feelings or affects. Following the old idea that happiness is the sum of pleasures minus pains, Bradburn developed an Affect Balance Scale by subtracting negative affects (boredom, loneliness, depression) experienced during the past two weeks from positive affects (pride, excitement, pleasure).

Despite the variety of approaches used to this point, the scope and limits of the domain of measures relevant to subjective well-being or happiness have not yet been established. In particular, scales originated in clinical contexts to measure dysphoric affect, hopelessness, or insecurity may measure what we recognize within normal limits to be simple unhappiness. The phrase "psychological well-being" itself carries with it the connotation of mental health and has been so interpreted by many researchers (e.g., Moriwaki, 1974; Robinson, 1969).

This array of alternative operationalizations of happiness would be almost unmanageable were it not for one happy circumstance: The scales all show reasonably high intercorrelations. Bradburn (1969) found that the Negative Affect Scale (NAS), the Positive Affect Scale (PAS), and especially the Affect Balance Scale (ABS) scores correlated significantly with avowals of "very happy," "pretty happy," or "not too happy." Campbell (1976), in a national probability sample, showed that his index containing judgments of life satisfaction in several areas of life correlated highly ($r = .57$) with an index of general affect based on semantic differential ratings of life on such scales as interesting–boring and enjoyable–miserable.

Moriwaki (1974) demonstrated the close kinship of morale scales to the subjective well-being domain when she reported a correlation of .61 between the ABS and the Rosow Morale Scale in a small sample of elderly persons. And in the most comprehensive study of the subject, Andrews and Withey (1976) correlated 68 measures and indices of happiness (including the Gurin, Cantril, and Bradburn scales) in five national probability samples. They concluded that measures "involving a general evaluation of the respondents' life-as-a-whole from an absolute perspective tend to cluster together. . . . Measures that tap life-as-a-whole less generally . . . show positive relationships of varying strength to the core cluster'' (Andrews & Withey, 1976, p. 76).

In marked contrast to the apparent ease of measurement in the domain of subjective well-being are the conceptual enigmas that have emerged in the course of research. The first of these is the meager relation between objective and subjective indicators of happiness or well-being. Common sense suggests that wealth, youth, and social privilege should contribute substantially to happiness, and much research has been devoted to an investigation of this hypothesis. Yet Campbell (1976) reports that only 17% of life satisfaction is predictable from *10* demographic indicators in a national probability sample. Similarly, Andrews and Withey (1976), also using national probability samples, account for only 8% of the variance in life satisfaction using age, family cycle stage, family income, education, race, and sex as predictors, either singly or in combination. An even more dramatic instance of the apparent irrelevance of objective circumstances to subjective well-being is provided by Brickman, Coates, and Janoff-Bulman (1978), who report that lottery winners were no happier than controls on present and estimated future happiness. Paraplegics, although somewhat less happy than controls, did not differ from lottery winners or controls in estimation of future happiness.

The second problem is a paradox that has never been fully explained. In 1969, Bradburn reported that when positive and negative affects are independently measured, the items form two independent clusters. Although *positive* and *negative* carry the strong mathematical suggestion of being opposite, Bradburn's PAS and NAS were not opposite (negatively correlated) but independent, virtually uncorrelated. Despite this, both positive and negative affects were found to be associated with overall estimates of happiness. Using a slight modification of the three Bradburn scales, Lowenthal, Thurner, and Chiriboga (1975) confirmed that positive and negative affect were independent predictors of global happiness. Similarly, Costa and McCrae (1977b) found a median correlation of only −.11 between PAS and NAS across four administrations. Andrews and Withey (1976) also replicated the finding, using both the three Bradburn scales and ''cognitive'' items that required respondents to assess the ''good'' and ''bad'' aspects of their life separately. It is not surprising that pleasant emotions enhance life satisfaction or that unpleasant emotions diminish it, but the repeated observation that the pleasantness and unpleasantness of one's life are uncorrelated is a puzzling phenomenon the explanation for which is of considerable theoretical importance.

PERSONALITY CORRELATES OF
SUBJECTIVE WELL-BEING

Personality descriptions of happy persons generally resemble descriptions of psychological and social adjustment. Smith (1961), for example, lists as correlates of happiness: optimism, warmth, emotional stability, sociability, and self-insight. Wessman and Ricks (1966), in their intensive study of a small sample of Harvard and Radcliffe students, point to large negative correlations with the Minnesota Multiphasic Personality Inventory D scale and the 16 Personality Factor (PF) O or "guilt-prone" scale in justifying their conclusion that characteristically happier people are well-adjusted, high in ego strength, and high in self-esteem, as well as being socially involved.

Wilson (1967), in his studies, found social and family adjustment and self–ideal congruence to be important correlates of happiness and concluded his review of the literature by asserting that "happiness is consistently related to successful involvement with people" (p. 304). At the unhappy pole, a number of investigators have found signs of psychopathology or neuroticism among unhappy people. Veroff, Feld, and Gurin (1962) reported worry, anxiety, and psychosomatic concerns among the correlates of unhappiness, as did Bradburn and Caplovitz (1965). Finally, self-rated health has also recurred as an important predictor of subjective well-being (Palmore & Kivett, 1977; Wolk & Telleen, 1976).

The prominence of the Bradburn scales has begun to encourage investigators to look for personality correlates of positive and negative affect separately, and some revealing trends have begun to emerge. Moriwaki (1974) reported that a nine-item mental health scale was significantly related to NAS but not to PAS. Beiser (1974) found that reports of psychophysiological disorders were associated with a negative affect factor but not with a positive affect factor in his instruments. On the other hand, role planning and social participation were associated with positive but not negative affect factors. Recently, Bradburn (1977) has pointed out a similar trend in his data. He reports that positive affect exclusively is related to social interest, sociability, and activity and that negative affect only is associated with psychosomatic symptoms, anxiety, poor role adjustment, and worries.

These findings suggest a hypothesis that may explain the independence of positive and negative affect and meaningfully organize the body of evidence on personality and happiness. It is hypothesized that one set of dispositions is responsible for positive affect or satisfaction, whereas another, independent set of dispositions influences negative affect or dissatisfaction.

In Study 1 the relation between four measures of happiness and seven personality dispositions hypothesized to be related to positive or negative affect is examined. In Study 2 an attempt is made to clarify and organize the results by testing the original hypothesis using measures of the broader dimensions of extraversion (E) and neuroticism (N). Finally, in Study 3 happiness is predicted from E and N data obtained 10 years previously.

STUDY 1

From the large number of traits with reported associations to subjective well-being, some emerge as more likely to be associated uniquely with one side or the other of the affect balance formula. Some of the specific facets of temperament articulated by Buss and Plomin (1975) fall into this category. Buss and Plomin trace negative affects (particularly fear and anger) to strength of emotional drive, and they speculate that "If there is temperamental input into individual differences in *positive* emotions, it is likely to be activity (for elation) or sociability (for friendliness and warmth)" (p. 57). Some evidence supporting this idea is offered in terms of daily level of mood ratings, and the division of traits agrees generally with Bradburn's (1977) observations. Study 1 tests the hypothesis that the temperamental traits of emotionality, fearfulness, hostility, and impulsivity will be associated with lower levels of happiness and especially with high negative affect, and that temperamental traits of sociability and activity will be associated with higher levels of happiness and, particularly, with positive affect.

Method

Subjects. The data reported were collected as part of a project on smoking and personality conducted in collaboration with the Normative Aging Study, an interdisciplinary longitudinal study of health and aging in men (Bell, Rose & Damon, 1972). Participants, volunteers screened for health and geographical stability, ranged in age from 35 to 85 at the time of this research. The sample consists largely of white veterans, with all but the lowest socioeconomic groups well represented. A subsample of 1,100 men was contacted by mail and was asked to complete a series of four questionnaires mailed at intervals of 3 months in 1976. Response rates were 79%, 82%, 73%, and

54% for the four mailings. Additional information was obtained on a sub-sample of 172 subjects visiting the study center for regular medical examinations during the data collection period. Results are based on all available cases, with specific *ns* given in each table.

Measures. Four measures of happiness were collected. The principal measure was Bradburn's (1969) scales, which yielded scores for PAS, NAS, and the difference of these scores, ABS. The Bradburn measures were obtained at each of the four quarterly mailings. An ABS sum score was calculated by summing the ABS scores over the four administrations.

The Hopelessness Scale (Beck, Weissman, Lester & Trexler, 1974) was given in the third questionnaire mailing. The scale was developed to assess hopelessness or pessimism in clinical populations. In a sample of 294 hospitalized patients, internal consistency was found to be .93. Correlations with clinicians' ratings of hopelessness ranged from .62 to .74. Little evidence of the test's applicability to nonpsychiatric populations has yet been provided.

The Personal Security Inventory (Knutson, 1952) was designed to measure personal security as the subjective evaluation of "success, satisfaction, and surety or confidence" (p. 24) in a number of areas of life. Knutson reports validation studies in which psychiatric patients scored significantly lower than normals; personal security was also found to be positively related to occupational status. A shortened, 16-item form of the Personal Security Inventory was given as part of the fourth mailing.

Those subjects who came to the study for medical examinations during the data collection period were asked to complete the Life Satisfaction Index. For each of nine areas (work, health, money, appearance, self-respect, getting

Table 23.1. Intercorrelations of Happiness Measures

Measure	1	2	3	4
1. ABS sum	—	.64**	.61**	.40**
2. Personal security	524	—	.59**	.32**
3. Hopelessness[a]	529	552	—	.18*
4. Life Satisfaction Index	82	93	135	—

NOTE: *N*s are given below the diagonal. ABS = Affect Balance Scale.
[a] Scale reflected to "hopefulness."
*$p < .50$. **$p < .001$.

along with others, love, sex, and religious faith) subjects rated their satisfaction on a 5-point scale. Internal consistency (coefficient alpha) for the summed score was .84 in our sample of 172.

Scales from the EASI-III Temperament Survey (Emotionality/Activity/Sociability/Impulsivity; Buss & Plomin, 1975) were included in the second mailing. Each scale consists of five items and was developed through factor analysis and rating validation. Two-to three-month test–retest reliabilities averaged .79 in a sample of 32 women; self-reports correlated .51 on the average with spouse ratings in a sample of 137 couples. Scales hypothesized to relate to NAS included general emotionality, fear, anger, and poor inhibition of impulse; scales hypothesized to relate to PAS included sociability, tempo, and vigor.

Analyses. Pearson correlations among the four happiness measures were used to examine evidence for convergent validity. Correlations were then computed between happiness and temperament measures. Finally, correlations between temperaments and the components of ABS were calculated for each of the four time points to examine the hypothesized relations of the measured traits to PAS and NAS over four replications.

Results and Discussion

Correlations between the three Bradburn scales and the alternative happiness measures at four times follow the pattern reported in the literature: PAS and NAS scores are significantly related to happiness measures in 23 of 24 cases, but in every case ABS is more highly correlated with the Beck scale, the Knutson inventory, and the index than either of its components is. Of the Bradburn scales, the ABS thus appears to measure happiness best.

Table 23.1 presents the intercorrelations of the ABS Sum and the three other happiness measures and suggests that different strategies or instruments for measuring subjective well-being produce similar results. All correlations are significant and are generally high enough to suggest convergent validity for the measures. The Life Satisfaction Index appears to be a weaker indicator of happiness in this group, but Campbell's (1976) correlation of .57 between a similar index and a happiness measure strengthens the argument for treating the index as a measure of happiness.

The temperamental correlates of happiness, shown in Table 23.2, are also consistent with the literature. Happiness is positively associated with socia-

Table 23.2. Correlations of Temperament Scales with Happiness Measures

Measure	General emotionality	Fear	Anger	Poor inhibition of impulse	Socia- bility	Tempo	Vigor
ABS sum (529)	−.33***	−.40***	−.21***	−.22***	.32***	.13**	.28***
Hopelessness[a] (757)	−.33***	−.41***	−.19***	−.23***	.25***	.09**	.18***
Personal security (563)	−.25***	−.40***	−.09*	−.16***	.32***	.12**	.28***
Life Satisfaction Index (149)	−.21**	−.32***	−.12	−.15*	.24***	.21**	.32***

NOTE: *n*s are given in parentheses. ABS = Affect Balance Scale.
  [a] Scale reflected to "hopefulness."
  *$p < .05$. **$p < .01$. ***$p < .001$.

bility and activity and negatively associated with emotionality and impulsivity.

All of the 28 correlations are in the predicted direction, and 27 of them are statistically significant. The median correlation is .24, a value that compares favorably with *multiple* correlations of .41 (Campbell, Converse & Rodgers, 1976) or .28 (Andrews & Withey, 1976) reported by survey researchers when demographic characteristics are used to predict life satisfaction.

The hypothesis that the scales of general emotionality, fear, anger, and poor inhibition of impulse influence primarily negative affect, whereas sociability, tempo, and vigor scales will influence primarily positive affect, is tested in Table 23.3.

For three of the temperament scales—general emotionality, anger, and poor inhibition of impulse—it is clear that only the negative side of affect balance is substantially related. In each case, correlations with NAS are higher than with the corresponding ABS score. The pattern for the fear scale is not so clear: At each time, fear is more closely related to NAS than to PAS, but it does show a consistent effect on lowering PAS as well.

Similarly, two of the positive temperament scales—tempo and vigor— are associated with PAS but not with NAS, as predicted. Sociability is more closely related to PAS than to NAS, as predicted, but it also appears to have a consistent effect on NAS.

Thus five of the seven scales appear to influence happiness by their impact on only one side of the affect balance equation. Two others show their primary effect on the hypothesized affect component but also show some influence on the other as well.

Table 23.3. Correlations of Temperament Scales with Bradburn Scales at Four Times

Time	n	General emotionality	Fear	Anger	Poor inhibition of impulse	Sociability	Tempo	Vigor
				Positive Affect Scale				
1	823	−.07**	−.18***	−.00	−.03	.23***	.17***	.23***
2	903	−.06*	−.20***	−.02	−.06*	.24***	.21***	.24***
3	757	−.13***	−.22***	−.02	−.08*	.24***	.14***	.23***
4	566	−.05	−.17***	.00	−.04	.22***	.19***	.29***
				Negative Affect Scale				
1	823	.30***	.26***	.24***	.21***	−.13***	.05	−.06*
2	903	.38***	.34***	.26***	.28***	−.20***	.05	−.06*
3	757	.34***	.28***	.21***	.22***	−.20***	.02	−.06
4	566	.32***	.33***	.20***	.24***	−.13***	.04	−.08*
				Affect Balance Scale				
1	823	−.25***	−.29***	−.17***	−.16***	.24***	.08*	.19***
2	903	−.29***	−.36***	−.18***	−.23***	.29***	.10***	.20***
3	757	−.28***	−.31***	−.14***	−.18***	.28***	.08*	.18***
4	566	−.23***	−.32***	−.12***	−.18***	.23***	.10**	.24***

*p < .05. **p < .01. ***p < .001.

STUDY 2

The hypothesis that some traits influence positive affect and some influence negative affect was generally supported by the results of Study 1. It is possible to take these results one step further by noting that these traits have an internal organization and coherence. To those familiar with factor models of personality, the list of traits provided by Study 1 (and much previous research) begins to take the shape of two established dimensions of personality: extraversion (E) and neuroticism (N). And indeed, factor analyses (Costa & McCrae, in press) showed that the EASI-III scales of general emotionality, fear, anger, and poor inhibition of impulse defined an N factor, whereas sociability, tempo, and vigor formed part of an E factor. It is now possible to propose a model of the relations between personality and happiness. Extraversion, together with its component traits of sociability, tempo, and vigor, predisposes individuals toward positive affect, whereas neuroticism (and hence general emotionality, impulsivity, fear, and anger) predisposes individuals toward negative affect. The simplest test of the model is direct correlation of measures of E and N with happiness measures.

Method

Subjects. Study 2 employed the same sample and procedures as Study 1.

Measures. Two measures of N and E were administered to the subjects by mail, as in Study 1. Cluster analysis of the Cattell Sixteen Personality Factor Questionnaire (16 PF) scales (Costa & McCrae, 1976) had shown an anxiety or N cluster and an E cluster that closely resembled the major second-order factors reported for the 16 PF (Cattell, Eber & Tatsuoka, 1970). Multiple regression was used to identify the 15 items in Form A that best predicted full N and E scores in a sample of 969 men. These 30 items were used as short-form N and E cluster scales and were included in the third mailing. Additionally, the standard Form A of the Eysenck Personality Inventory (EPI: Eysenck & Eysenck, 1964) was included in the fourth mailing. The theoretically independent dimensions of E and N were empirically uncorrelated in the present sample ($r = .00$, $n = 808$ for short-form 16 PF scales; $r = -.02$, $n = 576$ for EPI scales). Evidence of convergent validity is seen in the correlation of .65 ($n = 549$) between the 16 PF and EPI E measures and .68 ($n = 553$) between the two N measures.

Results and Discussion

Table 23.4 shows the Pearson correlations of E and N measures with the Bradburn scales at four times, 3 months apart.

In all eight (Time × Measures) cases, neuroticism or anxiety is more strongly correlated with NAS than with either PAS or ABS. In all eight cases, extraversion is more strongly correlated with PAS than with NAS or, in six of the eight cases, than with ABS.

When E and N measures are correlated with the three alternative operationalizations of happiness—hopelessness, personal security, and the Life Satisfaction Index—11 of the 12 correlations are statistically significant, and all are in the predicted direction. Thus, E and N not only influence the experience of positive or negative affect; they also show consistent correlations with measures of happiness that do not depend on direct reports of affective experience.

Most factorial-based trait systems recognize N and E as the broadest and most pervasive dimensions of personality. Eysenck (Eysenck & Eysenck, 1969) has devoted most of his research to an investigation of these two

Table 23.4. Correlations of 16 PF and EPI Scales with Bradburn Scales at Four Times

Time	16 PF Short-Form scales			EPI Scales		
	N	E	n	N	E	n
			Positive Affect Scale			
1	−.11***	.16***	753	−.11**	.16***	554
2	−.06	.22***	757	−.08**	.21***	559
3	−.16***	.19***	808	−.17***	.17***	549
4	−.10**	.25***	556	−.15***	.27***	575
			Negative Affect Scale			
1	.29***	−.03	753	.35***	−.01	554
2	.41***	−.04	757	.38***	−.01	559
3	.40***	−.13***	808	.39***	−.05	549
4	.34***	−.12**	556	.43***	−.07*	575
			Affect Balance Scale			
1	−.27***	.12***	753	−.31***	.11**	575
2	−.31***	.17***	757	−.32***	.15***	559
3	−.34***	.20***	808	−.34***	.15**	549
4	−.27***	.25***	556	−.39***	.22***	575

NOTE: PF = Cattell Sixteen Personality Factor Questionnaire. EPI = Eysenck Personality Inventory.
  N = neuroticism. E = extraversion.
  *$p < .05$. **$p < .01$. ***$p < .001$.

dimensions directly. Cattell (1973) sees them as second-order traits and has attempted to measure the more molecular, first-order aspects of personality that form them. Guilford (1976) prefers to call the E cluster *social activity* and the N cluster *emotional health*, but the similarity of these schemes is beyond question. The bulk of the literature on the personality correlates of happiness can be summarized by saying that more extraverted and more adjusted people are happier. The characteristics listed somewhat indiscriminately under the heading of "psychological and social adjustment" can now be broken apart into two discrete groups. Under the heading of E come sociability, warmth, involvement with people, social participation, and activity. Under N come such characteristics as ego strength, guilt proneness, anxiety, psychosomatic concerns, and worry. Extraverted traits contribute to one's positive enjoyment or satisfaction in life, although they do not generally appear to reduce the unpleasantness of adverse circumstances. Neurotic traits predispose one to suffer more acutely from one's misfortunes, but they do not necessarily diminish one's joy or pleasures.

STUDY 3

Studies 1 and 2 made the causal assumption that personality influenced happiness or subjective well-being—an interpretation that simple correlations cannot themselves sustain. Although it appears unlikely that temporary states of happiness would substantially alter personality, it is plausible to argue that short-term moods or states may affect responses to personality measures. Perhaps an individual in an upbeat mood will respond like an extravert, whereas the person who is temporarily depressed will score high on neuroticism. The long-term stability of E and N (Costa & McCrae, 1977a, in press; Moss & Susman, in press) argues against this interpretation, but a more direct test is given by an examination of the predictive relations between personality measures and levels of subjective well-being obtained 10 years later. Over this long a time span, any systematic bias introduced by temporary moods or states should be eliminated. Predictive relations between E, N, and happiness would thus strengthen the contemporaneous evidence for the proposed model.

Method

Subjects. Subjects were a subset of those described in Study 1 who had been given the 16 PF between 1965 and 1967. Data were available for 234 men.

Measures. An N and an E cluster score were obtained from analysis of combined A and B forms of the 16 PF (Costa & McCrae, 1976). (These scores formed the criterion in the selection of items for the short-form 16 PF scales described in Study 2.) These clusters resemble the second-order factors reported by Cattell; evidence for their validity and stability is reported elsewhere (Costa & McCrae, 1977a).

Results and Discussion

N cluster scores were significantly related to NAS ($r = .39$, $p < .001$) and to ABS ($r = -.30$, $p < .001$) but not to PAS ($r = -.08$, *ns*). E cluster scores, by contrast, were not related to NAS ($r = .03$, *ns*) but were related to PAS ($r = .23$, $p < .001$) and ABS ($r = .14$ $p < .05$). Knowing an individual's standing on these two personality dimensions allows a prediction of how happy the person will be 10 years later. These data effectively rule out the alternative explanation that associations between happiness and personality result solely from the mediating effect of temporary moods or states. This finding is also impressive as indirect evidence of the enduring effects of these dimensions of personality.

GENERAL DISCUSSION

A Model of Happiness

Figure 23.1 presents a model of happiness that accounts for the correlational data reported here and in the literature.

The personality traits found to be correlates of happiness have been grouped under the headings of E and N. The direct outcomes of these dispositions, according to the model, are positive affect and negative affect, respectively. These two components are subjectively "balanced" by the individual to arrive at a net sense of subjective well-being, which may be measured as morale, life satisfaction, hopefulness, or simply happiness.

Although it has been known for some time that positive and negative affect were independent contributions to global happiness, no one has ever provided a fully satisfactory explanation for this phenomenon. It is clear that there must be two independent sources of variation, two sets of causes operating to produce the two independent effects. In his initial attempt at an explanation, Bradburn looked for objective sources. He suggested that the situations that contribute to positive affect are separate from those that contribute to negative affect. It is easy to find examples that support the plausibility of

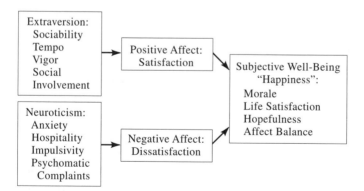

Figure 23.1. A model of personality influences on positive and negative affect on subjective well-being.

this position. Thus, poor health makes one unhappy, but good health is taken for granted, not seen as a source of positive joy. Conversely, a hobby may bring us considerable pleasure, but few of us have hobbies that carry much potential for pain.

Plausible as the objective sources idea is, it rests more on speculation than on fact. Some of the available facts even contradict it. For example, we might expect that when we ask subjects to rate their level of satisfaction with separate parts of their life—job, marriage, money, religion, and so on—there would be little correlation between them, even though all might contribute to overall happiness. Instead, such items tend to intercorrelate substantially in our own data and that of others (e.g., Campbell, Converse & Rodgers, 1976). Regardless of the area of life, people tend to be either satisfied or dissatisfied. The two sources of variation must lie *within* the person, and the dimensions of E and N are prime candidates.

Figure 23.1 calls attention to the separability of satisfaction from dissatisfaction, a phenomenon somewhat foreign to ''common sense'' notions of happiness. We tend to assume that these two components are opposites and that more of one means less of the other. The data show that reality is more complex. The difference between common sense and the model is seen most clearly when the traits of E and N are considered in combination. Low N introverts and high N extraverts may have similar levels of life satisfaction or happiness, but they achieve this result in utterly different ways. The former are seldom depressed but just as seldom elated. The latter are prone to both extremes and reach ''average'' satisfaction only because there is as much satisfaction as dissatisfaction in their lives. In some respects, the two groups are similar, but future studies should also be sensitive to the many differences between individuals who may show the same level of subjective well-being.

Finally, Figure 23.1 points out a need for conceptual clarification of the relation between happiness and mental health. Many researchers consider the Bradburn scales a measure of mental health, and our finding that the ABS is strongly related to two clinically validated scales—the Beck Hopelessness Scale and the Knutson Personal Security Inventory—might reinforce this notion. If these scales were only associated with N, there would be little reason to object to considering them as measures of adjustment, since N is clearly a conceptual correlate of mental illness. But the happiness scales also reflect E, whose conceptual relation to mental health is by no means unequivocal. The use of happiness scales as criteria of adjustment portrays introverts as less mentally healthy than extraverts; scientific researchers should consider whether they wish to so penalize introverts. The independence of E and N argues that introverts are no more prone to anxiety, depression, or anger than are extraverts. Whether they should be considered lower in mental health simply because they show less zest, vigor, or enthusiasm is a thorny question, conceptual rather than empirical in nature. This caution applies particularly to social gerontologists (Lemon, Bengtson & Peterson, 1972; Neugarten, Havighurst & Tobin, 1961) who have used as criteria of adjustment in old-age measures that include "zest" as a component of life satisfaction.

Happiness, Personality, and Adaptation Level

Few would argue against the position that, for normal people, the major determinant of *momentary* happiness is the specific situation in which the individual finds himself or herself. Social slights hurt our feelings, toothaches make us miserable, compliments raise our spirits, eating a good meal leaves us satisfied. The contribution of personality to any one of these feelings is doubtless small. Yet over time, the small but persistent effects of traits emerge as a systematic source of variation in happiness, whereas situational determinants that vary more or less randomly tend to cancel each other out (cf. Epstein, 1977).

On the other hand, the finding that traits predict happiness more successfully than such enduring objective conditions as health, wealth, sex, or race is more problematic. We all believe that we would be happier if we had more vigor, money, or power. Survey research data, however, show that these circumstances have very limited impact on subjective estimates of well-being. Brickman has proposed that adaptation-level theory can account for these facts. Brickman and Campbell (1971) state as the fundamental postulate of AL theory that "the subjective experience of stimulus input is a function not of the absolute level of that input but of the discrepancy between the input and past levels" (p. 287). As applied to happiness, this means that the standards by which people judge the pleasantness or unpleasantness of events or circumstances are not absolute but relative, set and reset by the positive and negative experiences of the individual. According to this view, habituation makes extreme circumstances (like great wealth or great poverty) appear more normal to the individual concerned, who comes to take advantages for granted or learns to live with misfortunes. Additionally, AL theory predicts that in contrast to extreme events, more mundane experiences will be devalued. In this way, highly favorable circumstances deprive the individual of many routine pleasures. Brickman found that lottery winners took less pleasure in such small matters as watching television than did control subjects (although the correlative prediction that paraplegics would take more pleasure in mundane activities was not confirmed).

AL theory can thus be used to explain the small magnitude of the effects of objective circumstances on well-being. As a theory of happiness, however, it fails to account for the large observable individual differences in happiness. Indeed, if happiness were solely the outcome of processes of adaptation, we would expect that all individuals would answer that they were "neutral" on the dimension of happiness. Brickman and Campbell speak gloomily about the "hedonic treadmill" and give the impression that no one can remain happy for long. Yet Gurin reports that 35 % of the population considers itself to be "very happy," and the stability coefficients of well-being measures, which range from .4 to .5 (Andrews & Withey, 1976; Costa & McCrae, 1977b; Palmore & Kivett, 1977), indicate that people tend to stay at the same relative level of happiness over long periods of time. This relative stability in well-being is most easily interpreted as an outcome of the stability of personality dimensions that underlie characteristic levels of happiness.

AL theory predicts that subjective judgments will be a function of the discrepancy of present stimuli from a neutral point determined by past experience. In the case of happiness, it appears that this formulation is insufficient. Constants representing the contributions of E and N must be added to the value predicted by AL theory. People will adapt to changing circumstances, which in the long run will neither add to nor detract from their happiness. But throughout these changes, the absolute advantages of being more extraverted or less neurotic will continue. We may all be on hedonic treadmills, but the treadmills of adjusted extraverts are much happier places to be.

REFERENCES

Andrews, F. M., & Withey, S. B. Social indicators of well-being: Americans' perceptions of life quality. *New York: Plenum, 1976.*

Beck, A. T., Weissman, A., Lester, D. & Trexler, L. The measurement of pessimism: The Hopelessness Scale. Journal of Consulting and Clinical Psychology, *1974, 42, 861–865.*

Beiser, M. Components and correlates of mental well-being. Journal of Health and Social Behavior, *1974, 15, 320–327.*

Bell, B., Rose, C. L. & Damon, A. The normative aging study: An interdisciplinary and longitudinal study of health and aging. Aging and Human Development, *1972, 3, 5–17.*

Bradburn, N. M. The structure of psychological well-being. *Chicago: Aldine, 1969.*

Bradburn, N. The measurement of psychological well-being. *In Jack Ellinson (Chair),* Health goals and health indicators. *Symposium presented at the meeting of the American Association for the Advancement of Science, Denver, 1977.*

Bradburn, N. M. & Caplovitz, D. Reports on happiness : A pilot study of behavior related to mental health. *Chicago: Aldine, 1965.*

Brickman, P. & Campbell, D. T. Hedonic relativism and planning the good society. In M. H. Appley (Ed.), Adaptation level theory: A symposium. *New York: Academic Press, 1971.*

Brickman, P., Coates, D. & Janoff-Bulman, R. Lottery winners and accident victims: Is happiness relative? Journal of Personality and Social Psychology, *1978, 36,* 917–927.

Buss, A. H. & Plomin, R. A temperament theory of personality development. *New York: Wiley, 1975.*

Campbell, A. Subjective measures of well-being. American Psychologist, *1976, 31,* 117–124.

Campbell, A., Converse, P. E. & Rodgers, W. L. The quality of American life: Perceptions, evaluations, and satisfactions. *New York: Russell Sage Foundation, 1976.*

Cantril, H. The pattern of human concerns. *New Brunswick, N.J.: Rutgers University Press, 1965.*

Cattell, R. B. Personality and mood by questionnaire. *San Francisco: Jossey-Bass, 1973.*

Cattell, R. B., Eber, H. W. & Tatsuoka, M. M. The handbook for the Sixteen Personality Factor Questionnaire. *Champaign, Ill.: Institute for Personality and Ability Testing, 1970.*

Costa, P. T., Jr. & McCrae, R. R. Age differences in personality structure: A cluster analytic approach. Journal of Gerontology, *1976, 31, 564–570.*

Costa, P. T., Jr. & McCrae, R. R. Age differences in personality structure revisited: Studies in validity, stability, and change. Aging and Human Development *1977a, 8, 261–275.*

Costa, P. T., Jr. & McCrae, R. R. The relations between smoking motives, personality, and feelings, Progress Report III. *Boston: University of Massachusetts at Boston, 1977b.*

Costa, P. T., Jr. & McCrae, R. R. Still stable after all these years: Personality as a key to some issues in aging. In P. B. Baltes & O. G. Brim, Jr. (Eds.), Life span development and behavior *(Vol. 3). New York: Academic Press, in press.*

Epstein, S. Traits are alive and well. In P. Magnusson & N. S. Endler (Eds.), Personality at the crossroads: Current issues in interactional psychology. *Hillsdale, N.J.: Erlbaum, 1977.*

Eysenck, H. J. & Eysenck, S. B. G. Manual of the Eysenck personality inventory. *San Diego, Calif.: Educational & Industrial Testing Service, 1964.*

Eysenck, H. J. & Eysenck, S. B. G. Personality structure and measurement. *San Diego, Calif.: Robert R. Knapp, 1969.*

Guilford, J. S., Zimmerman, W. S. & Guilford, J. P. The Guilford-Zimmerman temperament survey handbook: Twenty-five years of research and application. *San Diego, Calif.: Educational & Industrial Testing Service, 1976.*

Gurin, G., Veroff, J. & Feld, S. Americans view their mental health. *New York: Basic Books, 1960.*

Helson, H. Adaptation-level theory. *New York: Harper & Row, 1964.*

Knutson, A. Personal security as related to station in life. Psychological Monographs, *1952,* 66 *(4, whole No. 336) pp. 1–31.*

Lemon, B. W., Bengtson, V. L. & Peterson, J. A. An exploration of the activity theory of aging: Activity types and life satisfaction among in-movers to a retirement community. Journal of Gerontology, *1972,* 27, *511–523.*

Lowenthal, M. F., Thurner, M. & Chiriboga, D. Four stages of life. *San Francisco: Jossey-Bass, 1975.*

Moriwaki, S. Y. The affect balance scale: A validity study with aged samples. Journal of Gerontology, *1974,* 29, *73–78.*

Moss, H. A. & Susman, E.J. Constancy and change in personality development. In O. G. Brim, Jr. & J. Kagan (Eds.), Constancy and change in human development. *Cambridge, Mass.: Harvard University Press, in press.*

Neugarten, B. L., Havighurst, R. J. & Tobin, S. S. Measurement of life satisfaction. Journal of Gerontology, *1961,* 16, *134–143.*

Palmore, E. & Kivett, V. Change in life satisfaction: A longitudinal study of persons aged 46–70. Journal of Gerontology *1977,* 32, *311–316.*

Robinson, J. P. Life satisfaction and happiness. In J. P. Robinson & P. R. Shaver (Eds.), Measures of social psychological attitudes, *Ann Arbor, Mich.: Institute for Social Research, 1969.*

Smith, H. C. Personality adjustment. *New York: McGraw-Hill, 1961.*

Veroff, J., Feld. & Gurin, G. Dimensions of subjective adjustment. Journal of Abnormal and Social Psychology, *1962,* 64, *192–205.*

Wessman, A. E. & Ricks, D. F. Mood and personality. *New York: Holt, Rinehart & Winston, 1966.*

Wilson, W. Correlates of avowed happiness. Psychological Bulletin, *1967,* 67, *294–306.*

Wolk, S. & Telleen, S. Psychological and social correlates of life satisfaction as a function of residential constraint. Journal of Gerontology *1976,* 31, *89–98.*

24. Speaking about Feelings

Conceptions of Emotion across the Life Span

Gisela Labouvie-Vief, Marlene De Voe, and Diana Bulka

MUCH RECENT INTEREST has focused on the question of whether adaptive development continues past youth and into mature and late adulthood (e.g., Commons, Richards & Armon, 1984; Labouvie-Vief, 1982; Rybash, Hoyer & Roodin, 1986). Developmental movements in adulthood often have been difficult, however, to demonstrate. Most available theories of development have dealt with early development and depicted how the youth's thinking moves toward an abstract, objective mode of dealing with reality. In contrast, mature adulthood may bring to maturity a mode of thought different from that optimized in youth.

The primary developmental task of early development is acquisitive (Schaie, 1977/1978) and focused on the mastery of symbol systems—the languages, rules, and norms—of culture. In this movement, the direction is "outward": In the process of adaptation to an outer reality, the youth needs to be able to dissociate abstract collective meanings from more concrete and idiosyncratic private ones. In contrast, adulthood has often been said to bring an "inward" turn (see, e.g., Neugarten, 1968): a focus on inner dynamics, on private experience, on the continuity and integrity of autobiographical memories (Erikson, 1978; Jung, 1933; Labouvie-Vief & Hakim-Larson, in press; McAdams, 1985). As Jung (1933) suggested, whereas the theme early development is socialization, that of later development is individuation.

Much recent evidence suggests that this transformation of thought is of extraordinary breadth and encompasses dimensions that are cognitive, intrapersonal, and interpersonal. On the cognitive side, for example, the transition from youth to mature adulthood appears to bring an enhanced understanding of the contextual and reflexive nature of thinking (e.g., Blanchard-Fields, 1986; Commons, Richards & Armon, 1984; Kitchener, 1983; Labouvie-Vief, 1982). As a result, while the youth's thinking is regulated by judgment

Reprinted by permission from *Psychology and Aging* 4, no. 4 (1989): 425–37. Copyright © 1989 by the American Psychological Association.

processes that are understood as outer and objective, the mature adult possesses a richer understanding that thinking emanates from an active self who authors, judges, and monitors (Edelstein & Noam, 1982; Labouvie-Vief & Blanchard-Fields, 1982; Wood, 1983). These advances, in turn, appear to be related to more complex understanding of intra-and interpersonal processes involved in ego mechanisms, coping, and defense (e.g., Haan, 1977; Ihilevich & Gleser, 1986; Labouvie-Vief, Hakim-Larson & Hobart, 1987; Loevinger, 1976; Vaillant, 1977). Thus, much evidence suggests that adulthood brings progressive developmental movements that have significant implications for the ways in which individuals regulate their thinking and behavior.

In the present research, we are concerned with one particular area of self-regulation—how individuals conceptualize their emotional processes. The area of emotional regulation is particularly relevant to study the developmental movements outlined above, because to regulate her or his emotional life the individual relies on a duality of control mechanisms. On one hand, such conceptual processes as interpretation, evaluation, and appraisal bear on the flexibility of processes of emotional modulation; on the other hand, such conceptual processes are constrained by certain species-specific biological response systems (e.g., Buck, 1984; Ekman, 1984; Ekman & Friesen, 1975; Izard & Buechler, 1980; Lazarus & Folkman, 1984; Plutchik, 1984; Tomkins, 1984; Zajonc, 1984). Thus, more complex and abstract ways of representing emotional states are not always adaptive, but also can be characterized by processes of distortion that, if carried into adulthood, can become a source of maladaptation and pathology (e.g., Beck, 1976; Tomkins, 1984).

Our assumption that individuals' conception of their emotion bears on issues of self-regulation is an extension of current cognitive-developmental approaches to the evolution of emotional understanding during the first part of the life span. Following Piaget (1981), many researchers (e.g., Harris, 1983; Harter, 1983; Kegan, 1982; Lewis & Michalson, 1983; Selman, 1980) have assumed that the evolving cognitive system transforms the individual's repertoire in coping with emotions. Even though certain emotion prototypes appear early in the life span and remain quite stable thereafter (Lewis & Rosenblum, 1978), the contexts in which emotions are experienced, the types of emotions experienced, and the rules of how and when to modulate emotional expression all change considerably as the individual matures. Specifically, research with children has indicated that this process consists of several interrelated movements.

First, younger or less mature individuals are typically found to express emotions externally in terms of actions, physical processes, and their concrete social consequences. In contrast, older or more mature individuals come to understand their emotions as inner, cognitive or "mental" processes that are different from their outward expression, and emotions come to be more and more linked with processes that are symbolic and that emanate from one's memories, wishes, and other inner states (Bretherton, Fritz, Zahn-Waxler & Ridgeway, 1986; Harris, 1983; Selman, 1980).

Second, this movement appears to go along with a progressive differentiation of an emotional vocabulary. From early to later childhood this vocabulary changes from terms that are relatively undifferentiated, such as "happy," "sad," or "mad," to ones that are more complex, such as "excited," "joyful," "disappointed," "worried," or "guilty." At the same time, older children are better able to understand that different emotions can coexist (Harter & Buddin, 1987; Shaver, Schwartz, Kirson & O'Conner, 1987).

Third, as children develop a more complex and inner, mental language of emotions, they also are able to regulate their emotions and behavior with a variety of purely inner and mental processes, such as forgetting, wishing, deciding, and redirecting attention (Donaldson & Westerman, 1986; Harris, Olthof & Terwogt, 1981). Similarly, processes of coping and defense also come to be dominated by more complex intellectual and interpretive processes (Ihilevich & Gleser, 1986).

Finally, the types of standards or norms by which the individual references and regulates his or her behavior also become more complex. For the regulation of behavior, the young child depends on identification with concrete reference persons such as parents and, later, peers. By adolescence, a somewhat more autonomous self emerges that is no longer in need of such direct supervision, but that has internalized more abstract, conventional, and collective standards (e.g., Kegan, 1982; Kohlberg, 1969; Saarni, 1984).

Research on adults has demonstrated, however, that these gains still are relative. The use of mental mechanisms often occurs at the expense of acknowledging the organismic reality of emotions, as demonstrated in Vaillant's (1977) finding that the ability of young people to modulate their emotions across time and context was still rigid. Young people were found to engage to a significant extent in such relatively "immature" defense strategies as repression, intellectualization, displacement, and dissociation, while middle-aged adults showed significantly higher use of such mature strategies as altruism, humor, suppression, anticipation, and sublimation. More recently, Labouvie-Vief, Hakim-Larson, and Hobart (1987) reported that from adolescence to later adulthood, there was a significant increase in the defense mechanism of reversal and a significant decrease in the use of the defense and coping mechanisms of projection, turning against the other, escape–avoidance, and distancing. Indeed, an increase in the flexibility of processes of coping and defense is emerging as one of the most stable findings of the literature on coping processes in adulthood (e.g., Cytrynbaum et al., 1980; Folkman, Lazarus, Pimley & Novacek, 1987; Haan, 1977; Hauser, 1976; Ihilevich & Gleser, 1986; Loevinger, 1976; McCrae & Costa, 1984).

These changes in mind–body differentiation and integration are paralleled by ones related to the domain of self, other, and norms. The youth's self and emotional life are not well differentiated from collective conventional standards. Loevinger's theory of ego development (e.g., Loevinger & Wessler, 1978), for example, proposes that early in development, the impulsivity and immediacy of gratification of the child is superordinated by conventional social norms that modulate one's inner subjective life. By adolescence, feelings are expressed through a language that is stereotypical, static, and of low complexity. With maturity and the development of more autonomous standards, a more flexible language evolves that can incorporate conflicts between impulse and norm, self and other, and self and society. Now the individual is able to acknowledge conflicting feelings within self and other. Overall, the language of self-regulation becomes more vivid and specific, and less stereotypical. Mature cognitive–emotional complexity thus is evidenced by a language that is complex, nonstereotypical, and nondualistic; that tolerates intra-and interindividual conflict; and that appreciates the uniqueness of individual experience.

There is conclusive evidence, then, suggesting that the ability to self-regulate emotions develops early in life and may continue to do so thereafter. In line with these various findings, we predicted that developmental movements in emotional understanding would continue into mature adulthood along the dimensions established for earlier phases of the life span. Specifically, we anticipated that this movement would be expressed in the further evolution of four dimensions. First, we expected that the younger or less mature individuals' descriptions of emotion as inner process would rely on a language that is abstracting, conventionalized, and technical rather than being personalized and conveying a vivid sense of inner process. Second, we predicted further changes in the complexity of emotion language in terms of increasing dynamism and use of qualifiers, comparisons, and contrasts. Third, we expected that the younger or less mature individual would be more concerned with the mental repression and containment of emotion, while more mature individuals would be concerned with integrating mental control with more explicit awareness of their feelings, impulses, and unconscious processes. Finally, we also expected that the older and more mature individual would evolve different standards for judging his or her emotional life, relying less on simple conventional standards and evolving ones that are more tolerant of the uniqueness of individual experience in self and other.

These four dimensions formed components of a scheme for levels of emotional understanding applied to a sample of individuals from preadolescence to late life. We hypothesized that maturity of emotional understanding would show significant increases from adolescence to mature and later adulthood. However, in line with our earlier analysis (Labouvie-Vief, Hakim-Larson & Hobart, 1987), we also predicted that emotional maturity and age would show a curvilinear rather than linear relationship later in adulthood, while other variables indicative of cognitive-developmental complexity would continue to show a linear relationship. Thus, we included two measures related to cognitive-developmental complexity, specifically, verbal ability and Loevinger's (Loevinger & Wessler, 1978) measure of ego development.

While we did not expect sex to be significantly related to levels of emotional understanding, we did predict that it would emerge as a significant factor when examining the convergent and discriminant validity of our cognitive-developmental measures. Previous analysis (Labouvie-Vief, Hakim-Larson & Hobart, 1987) showed that similar measures predicted a significant share of the variance in external measures of coping and defense, but that an additional and independent source of variation was due to sex rather than differences in developmental complexity. Thus, we hypothesized that two independent sources of variation would emerge in the current data, one related to developmental complexity and the other to sex.

METHOD

Participants

The sample comprised 72 individuals, ranging in age from 10 to 77, selected from a total sample of 100 individuals. The remaining 28 participants were used for the purpose of developing the coding scheme described below (see Labouvie-Vief, Hakim-Larson, DeVoe & Schoeberlein, 1989). Thus, the data of 72 participants were analyzed for this report.

Participants were volunteers selected from suburban neighborhoods in a major midwestern metropolitan area on the basis of 1980 U.S. census information. The sampling procedure has been described in detail by Labouvie-

Vief, Hakim-Larson, and Hobart (1987). There were six females and six males in each of the following age groups: preadolescent (10–14), adolescent (15–18), young adult (19–29), adult (30–45), middle-aged adult (46–59), and elderly adult (60–77). Eighty-three percent of the participants reported a family income of over $40,000, and of the adults, all but three women were college graduates. Thus, the sample yielded a population positively selected in terms of cultural background and sophistication in responding to the measurements.

Procedure

Participants were assessed in two separate sessions. In the first session, lasting about 2 hr, participants were interviewed about their personal experiences of the four prototypical emotions of anger, fear, sadness, and happiness. All emotions were counterbalanced except for happiness, which was always given last so the participants would not leave the session in a negative mood. During the second session, lasting about 2 ½ to 3 hr, participants completed a battery of measurements, including demographic data and measurements of ego level, verbal ability, coping, and defense.

Emotion interview. In individual sessions, participants were instructed to think about a situation during the last month or so in which they felt particularly angry (sad, fearful, or happy), to picture it and think about it for 1 min, and then to talk about it by giving a spontaneous description of the cause, context, and course of the feeling state. Then, a series of open-ended probe questions were used to determine how participants described and controlled that particular emotion. Only the responses to questions pertaining to the description of emotions were used for the purposes of this study. Specifically, these questions were (a) How did you know you were angry (sad, fearful, or happy)? and (b) How did you feel inside when you felt angry (sad, fearful, or happy)?

Six graduate students served as interviewers. They were randomly assigned to interview an equal number of participants across age groups and sex. Interviewers were trained about how and when to ask participants for elaboration of their responses. All interviews were both audio-and video-taped.

Ego level. To provide an independent assessment of developmental level, participants completed the Sentence Completion Test of ego development by Loevinger and her colleagues (Loevinger & Wessler, 1978). This test consists of separate forms for males and females, each of which is based on 36 sentence stems. Each sentence completion item was scored by one of four trained coders using the procedure outlined for training and coding in the scoring manual. As recommended by Loevinger and Wessler (1978), a Total Protocol Rating (TPR) was assigned to each protocol. This score can be directly interpreted as indicating one of nine levels: (a) impulsive, (b) self-protective, (c) self-protective/conformist, (d) conformist, (e) conformist/conscientious, (f) conscientious, (g) conscientious/autonomous, (h) autonomous, and (i) integrated. Interrater reliability ranged from 67% to 100% exact agreement, with a median of 80%, and 100% agreement within a half step (see Labouvie-Vief, Hakim-Larson & Hobart, 1987, for detailed description).

Ways of coping. To provide a first measure relating to processes of coping and defense, participants completed the Ways of Coping (Revised) questionnaire developed by Lazarus and Folkman (1984). This test asks individuals to provide a brief descriptive statement of a stressful experience. Then, they are asked to endorse 66 statements referring to strategies of coping the researchers identified on the basis of previous research. Possible responses range from 0 to 3. Following Folkman, Lazarus, Dunkel-Schetter, DeLongis, and Gruen (1986), eight scales were computed by summing responses for each scale. These eight scales and sample items of each scale are as follows: confrontive coping (e.g., "Stood my ground and fought for what I wanted"), distancing (e.g., "Didn't let it get to me; refused to think about it too much"), self-control (e.g., "I tried to keep my feelings to myself"), seeking social support (e.g., "Talked to someone to find out more about the situation"), accepting responsibility (e.g., "Realized I brought the problem on myself"), escape-avoidance (e.g., "Wished that the situation would go away or somehow be over"), planful problem solving (e.g., "I knew what had to be done, so I doubled my efforts to make things work"), and positive reappraisal (e.g., "Changed or grew as a person in a good way").

Defense Mechanism Inventory. As a second measure of coping-defense processes, individuals completed an age-appropriate version of Gleser and Ihilevich's (1969) Defense Mechanism Inventory. This test provides 10 hypothetical situations, each followed by four questions and five multiple choice responses asking the individual the most likely and least likely way he or she would react in the given situation. Responses concern actual behavior, fantasy, thoughts, and feelings and comprise five defensive clusters: turning against others, projection, principalization, turning against self, and reversal. Turning against others involves defenses dealing with conflict by attack of an object considered frustrating (e.g., displacement or identification with the aggressor). Projection entails attributing negative intent to an external object without external evidence. Principalization encompasses the defenses of isolation, intellectualization, and rationalization (e.g., conflict is managed by splitting affect from content and repressing affect). Turning against self incorporates conflict resolution through aggressive behavior, fantasy, or affect toward the self. Reversal is a defense in which positive or neutral responses are given rather than the expected negative reaction. Six defense scores were computed following instructions of Gleser and Ihilevich (1969).

Verbal ability. Finally, to provide a general index of verbal ability level, the vocabulary subtest from the Wechsler Adult Intelligence Scale (WAIS) was administered to each participant. As is customary in research on life span changes in cognition (see Botwinick, 1978), nonstandardized scores were used in the analyses, so as not to attenuate age-related variance.

Coding of Levels of Emotional Understanding

In developing a coding scheme, we worked both inductively, by examining the content of the responses, and deductively, by formulating coding criteria along the theoretical rationale outlined previously (see Labouvie-Vief et al., 1989). After the protocols were transcribed, coders examined the interviews and identified several recurrent issues. Specifically, four issues appeared to exhaust the content of participant responses. Issue 1 comprised descriptions of emotions that referred to them as sensorimotor actions and physical processes; such descriptions ranged from ones that were relatively external to ones that were highly internal. Issue 2 concerned psychological labels of emotions; these ranged from ones that were relatively undifferentiated and static to ones that were highly differentiated and dynamic. Issue 3 covered descriptions of emotions not in terms of their felt sense, but in terms of one's effort to mentally regulate them; these descriptions ranged from ones that showed limited flexibility of modulation to ones that were flexible and well integrated. Finally, Issue 4 comprised responses that mentioned individuals' efforts to modulate their emotions vis-à-vis social reference and reciprocity; these responses ranged from ones that showed a relatively low degree of self–other differentiation and high egocentrism to ones that were more differentiated and less egocentric.

These issues were clustered into two major themes. Issues 1 and 2, involving direct characterizations of the felt experience through a variety of state descriptors, constituted the theme of internal state; Issues 3 and 4, involving less direct reference to the emotional state through descriptions of how it was modulated rather than experienced, constituted the theme of modulation.

These two themes and four issues were carried across four levels of emotional understanding. The resulting four levels are described in detail in Tables 24.1 and 24.2. Our conceptualization of these four levels was influenced by Loevinger, and our specific formulation was based on Labouvie-Vief's (1982) four levels of adult self-regulation. At the lowest *presystemic* level, the individual still functions concretely. She or he does not yet master a generalized and internalized conventional language of emotions but describes feeling states in terms of outer actions, externally observable physical processes, and unmodulated impulses. At the *intrasystemic* level, she or he has gained a more systemic understanding of emotional life. This is reflected in a more conventional language of symbols and norms that emphasize impulse control through inner, mental-reflective processes. Emphasis is on stability, certainty, and normative generalization rather than emotional expressivity in self and others. The individual is not yet able, however, to formulate a reflective meta-language of this system, an ability that emerges at the *intersystemic* level. Now the individual elaborates a concept of emotional regulation that tries to integrate the need for mentally oriented modulation with that for emotional expression. Ability to embrace conflict and tension increases, though there still remains a concern with equilibrium and certainty. Finally, for the individual at the *integrated* level openness to feeling and flexibility are at a maximum. The individual now fully accepts emotional conflict and individuality; yet she or he does so on the background of full responsibility and commitment to a value system that transcends the conventional and encompasses more general dimensions of the human condition.

Coding Procedure

For each participant, four verbatim protocols (anger, sadness, fear, and happiness) were transcribed and coded according to the above coding scheme. Two raters independently scored the protocols, with 24 randomly selected protocols double scored. Order of emotions was randomly determined, with sadness scored first, and anger, fear, and happiness next. For the purpose of yielding scores, responses were coded for each of the two themes, internal state and modulation. Consequently, an average across the two themes was

Table 24.1. Levels of Emotional Understanding: Summary and Examples for Internal State

Level	Level summary	Examples
Presystemic	Responses emphasize external, physical, and action-based aspects of emotions or involve simple, undifferentiated psychological labels. Feeling terms lack reference to inner subjective states and processes.	Physical and sensorimotor actions and reactions: "I cried"; "You sweat." Undifferentiated labels: "I was mad"; "I felt hot" (or "cold"); "I was up"; "I was down." Simple qualifiers: "I was very mad."
Intrasystemic	Inner states are described through abstract conventional language. Technical terminology, conventional metaphors, and a generalized rather than personalized language are used. There is simple differentiation of emotions by degrees, category, or introduction of a new emotional label.	Technical language: "Your blood pressure rises." Conventional terminology: "I felt tense"; "I was burning." Simple elaborations and comparisons: "I was not that mad, more helpless"; "It was a verbal anger." Nonvivid and nondynamic metaphors: "I felt empty"; "Things were bottled up."
Intersystemic	Individuals convey a vivid, felt sense of emotions. They communicate feelings through vivid, dynamic metaphors, through bodily sensations that are more personal and internal, and through highly differentiated, complex, and dynamic comparisons.	Complex elaborations and comparisons: "It was not so much the fear itself at the moment, because fear can take a variety of dimensions. It could mean somebody walking up to you with a gun. But fear with him was something far-reaching. It would be fear spread over a longer period of time, not an immediate fear." Vivid and dynamic metaphors: "Everything is like a cyclone going around." "It felt like someone was pulling my insides out and then twisting them."
Integrated	Individuals integrate conventional, objective cultural knowledge with their own unique subjective experience and humanitarian concerns. They are no longer concerned with tension reduction but explore the tension between mental/physical and transform it in ways that permits both objective distancing and empathic engagement.	Mind and body integrated as a functioning unit: "Everything was accelerated, my adrenaline started pumping, my mind started thinking what to do next. I was flashing things through my mind, I'm sure my heartbeat sped up. I did feel fearful." Psychological integration of objective and subjective awareness: "You have sunshine in your heart. During the wedding the candles were glowing. And that's just how I felt. I was glowing too. It was kind of dull outside, but that isn't how I felt. Everybody in the church even felt like they were glowing. It was that kind of feeling."

Table 24.2. Levels of Emotional Understanding: Summary and Examples for Modulation

Level	Level summary	Examples
Presystemic	In the absence of general standards, the individual remains impulsive, unable to tolerate tension, and oriented toward maintaining personal comfort. Emotions are described in terms of egocentric standards and impulsive thoughts or actions.	Unmonitored impulsive mentations: "I just wanted to punch her out"; "I was screaming." Self-comfort should be maintained by others: "How could she do this to me?"
Intrasystemic	Automaticity gives way to control based on the notion of an ideal abstract state. Emotion language is preoccupied with the mental control of emotions or the failure of such control. Emotions and actions are justified by social norms binding for all.	Concern with mental control: "You want to change whatever is making you angry, right away. It's a hard emotion to get off of once you're on it." Knowledge of inner tendencies—static: "I'm an emotional person to begin with. I watch television and the tears start." Use of ideal external state/norm to justify emotion or action: "I was really scared, because I knew if I didn't play good, that they'd tease me about it."
Intersystemic	Control now involves exploration of feelings, thoughts, and impulses. Increased flexibility involves distancing oneself from the situation and thinking of alternative actions. Inner tendencies are more fully acknowledged and used as a check on one's behavior. Increased subjectivity brings acceptance of others' feelings, intentions, and thoughts as separate from oneself.	Distanced self-reflection: "I was so charged up that everything I did was exaggerated." Knowledge of inner tendencies—process: "That's my classic pattern when I get mad. I go through a quiet stage and it normally passes." Use of others as "sounding board": "It feels good to discuss it and actually talk about it and think about it. And in doing so maybe I'll think more about a solution to it."
Integrated	The emotional state is accepted and viewed as an opportunity for the development of self and other. Emotions are defined as energy that can be transformed into outward constructive action or new inner perspective-taking. Subjectivity and individual responsibility are placed within broad social concerns.	Emotions and mental processes linked together: "The feelings stem from inside. Emotionally you feel the loss and intellectually you accept the fact that it's a sad feeling that you have." Transformative definition of emotion: "No constructive way to utilize it at the time until you sort it out later, say well, I can compensate in this area by not doing this or doing more of that." Feelings are related to a larger process or context: "I had a big win at the lottery and then a lot of other problems were put in a minor position. . . . there's no sacrifice to help somebody. . . . So putting a new roof on my mother's house is a selfish reaction on my part."

obtained for each emotion. Scores were rounded to the nearest full or transitional ("half") level. Where the two coders disagreed in level assignment, resolution was achieved by subsequent discussion.

Interrater reliability for qualitative data such as those described here is usually assessed by comparing different methods (see Colby, Kohlberg, Gibbs & Lieberman, 1983; Loevinger & Wessler, 1978). Before resolution, exact agreement between raters was 46% for anger, 71% for sadness, 58% for fear, and 83% for happiness. After eliminating coder disagreements of one-half level, agreement rose to 96% for all emotions. Thus, for each of the emotions, all but one of the disagreements were in the very narrow range of one-half level or less. The intraclass correlations derived from exact agreements were .69, .79, .77, and .99. These reliabilities were judged adequate. Although those for anger appear to approach the lower limits of statistical acceptability, further analyses corroborated that they did produce statistically reliable results.

RESULTS

Analyses of the data were aimed at answering several distinct questions. First, following several preliminary and descriptive analyses, hierarchical multiple regression analyses were performed to determine the linear and quadratic contributions of ego level, verbal ability, and age group to the overall levels of emotional understanding scores. This analysis was followed by examining age and ego level effects for the four separate emotions (anger, sadness, fear, and happiness), using multivariate analyses of variance (MANOVAS) with age group and ego level as the independent variables. Finally, we attempted to further validate our levels of emotional understanding scores by relating them to external measures of coping and defense strategies. Following Labouvie-Vief, Hakim-Larson, and Hobart (1987), a canonical variate analysis was performed, using as independent variables the measures concerned with developmental complexity as well as sex, and as dependent variables the Ways of Coping and Defense Mechanism Inventory scales.

Hierarchical Multiple Regression

Adolescent and adult age groups. Prior to examining the relative importance of the independent variables in predicting emotional maturity, several descriptive statistics were computed. First, group means for the overall emotional maturity scores and for the scores for separate emotions suggested

Table 24.3. Correlations between Levels of Emotional Understanding, Age, Ego Level, and Verbal Ability

Variable	1	2	3	4	5	6	7	8
Level of emotional understanding								
1. Anger	—	.54**	.55**	.53**	.84**	.46**	.45**	.51**
2. Sadness		—	.47**	.40**	.77**	.44**	.55**	.48**
3. Fear			—	.53**	.79**	.28**	.41**	.40**
4. Happiness				—	.77**	.34**	.28**	.50**
5. Overall level					—	.48**	.54**	.60**
Independent variable								
6. Age						—	.47**	.61**
7. Ego level							—	.61**
8. Verbal ability								—

$*p < .01.$ $**p < .001.$

convergent patterns for all dependent measures. Intercorrelations among the emotional maturity measures as well as between the emotional maturity measures and age, ego level, and verbal ability (see Table 24.3) showed that measures of emotional maturity were highly intercorrelated (as would be expected from the high alpha), with a range of $r = .40$ to .55. Table 24.3 further indicates that there was high collinearity among the independent variables of age group, ego level, and verbal ability, with a range of $r = .77$ to .84. Sex, on the other hand, was not correlated with either the dependent variables or the remaining independent variables.

To further rule out interaction effects of sex with any of the remaining independent variables, several multiple regression analyses were performed. These analyses confirmed that sex was insignificant as a main effect, as was the interaction of sex with verbal ability, ego level, or age group. Thus, sex was eliminated in further analyses (with the exception of the canonical variate analysis; see below).

Next, a hierarchical multiple regression was employed to determine the relative contribution of verbal ability, ego level, and age group to overall levels of emotional understanding. Since age was highly correlated with verbal ability and ego level and since it is often associated with a quadratic trend for variables measuring cognitive complexity, the squares of these variables were also entered in the equation. Because we were interested in the linear and quadratic effects of age after verbal ability and ego level were partialed out, we first entered verbal ability and ego level (Step 1). Because no quadratic effect of either variable was expected (and since preliminary analysis

Table 24.4. Hierarchical Multiple Regression of Verbal Ability, Ego Level, and Age Group on the Levels of Emotional Understanding for Adolescents and Adults

Variable	R^2	ΔR^2	Incremental F	β^a
Step 1				
Verbal ability				.283*
Ego level	.40	.40	23.40***	.220
Step 2				
Age group	.44	.04	4.14*	.262*
Step 3				
Age group squared	.49	.05	6.27**	N/A

NOTE: $R = .70$, $F(4,67) = 15.86$, $p < .001$. N/A = not applicable.
^{a} β weights are for simultaneous entry of only linear components.
*$p < .05$. **p .01. ***$p < .001$.

substantiated this expectation), these effects were not included in the equation. Step 2 consisted of entering age group for the linear component of age, and Step 3 consisted of entering age group squared for the quadratic component of age.

Table 24.4 displays the results of the hierarchical analysis for each step. Displayed are the R^2 and changes in R^2 at each step, as well as the incremental F value. The last column displays the standardized beta weights for the simultaneous regression, with only the linear components entered. The quadratic effect of age was omitted to avoid suppressor effects resulting from the high collinearity ($r = .98$) of the linear and quadratic components of age. The multiple R for the total equation was .70, $F(4, 67) = 15.86, p < .001$. Verbal ability and ego level were entered in the first step of the hierarchical analysis and significantly accounted for 40% of the variance in levels of emotional understanding. Age group was entered on the second step and significantly accounted for 4% of the variance. Age group squared was entered on the last step and significantly accounted for an additional 5% of the variance. Thus, the hierarchical analysis indicates that verbal ability and ego level when entered as covariates significantly accounted for 40% of the variance, while age and age squared significantly accounted for 9% of the variance. Further, the beta weights demonstrate that only verbal ability and age group contributed significant linear effects. However, using the squared semipartial correlations for each independent variable, only age group (6%) and age group squared (5%) were found to contribute unique variance.

Adult age groups. One possible reason for the strong linear and quadratic components of age is that our inclusion of two adolescent groups reflects a

Table 24.5. Hierarchical Multiple Regression of Verbal Ability, Ego Level, and Age Group on the Levels of Emotional Understanding for Adults

Variable	R^2	ΔR^2	Incremental F	β^a
Step 1				
Verbal ability				.206
Ego level	.13	.13	3.48*	.272
Step 2				
Age group	.13	.00	0.03	.024
Step 3				
Age group squared	.21	.07	3.83	N/A

NOTE: = .45, $F(4, 43)$ = 2.78, $p < .05$. N/A = not applicable.
 $^a \beta$ weight are for simultaneous entry of only linear components.
 $*p < .05$.

maturational pattern unique to the early part of the life span only. If that hypothesis were true, age might drop out as a significant predictor if only the adult groups are considered, while verbal ability and ego level should then account for significant linear components of variance. To examine that hypothesis, a similar hierarchical regression was performed with just the four adult age groups to determine whether our results were taking advantage of including the two adolescent groups.

Table 24.5 displays the analysis that yielded a multiple R for the total equation of .45, $F(4, 43)$ = 2.78, $p; < .05$. Verbal ability and ego level were entered in the first step, and significantly accounted for 13% of the variance in the levels of emotional understanding for the adult groups. Age group, entered on the second step, and age group squared, entered on the third step, did not significantly account for further variance.

For the total equation, none of the beta weights were significant (although ego level just failed to reach significance, $p < .06$). However, the squared semipartial correlations show that ego level significantly accounted for 8% of the variance for levels of emotional understanding for the adult groups. Verbal ability, age group, and age group squared do not significantly account for unique variance after the other independent variables are entered in the equation.

Multivariate Analysis of Variance

Age. Because age group appeared to be the most important independent variable in the regression analysis for all six age groups, a one-way MANOVA was performed to determine the effect of age group on levels of emotional

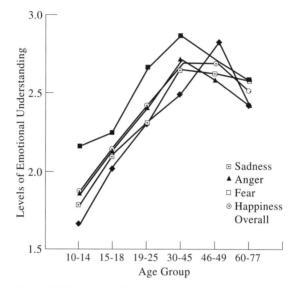

Figure 24.1. Levels of emotional understanding for six age groups.

understanding for anger, sadness, fear, and happiness as the four dependent variables.

With the use of Wilks's criterion, the dependent variables (levels of emotional understanding for anger, sadness, fear, and happiness) were significantly affected by age group, (Wilks's lambda = .43, $F(20,246)$ = 3.04, p < .001. The association was substantial between age group and the dependent variables, π^2 = .57.

To investigate the main effect of age on the individual dependent variables, further univariate analyses were performed. Significant age effects were obtained for all emotions: anger, $F(5, 66)$ = 9.36, p < .001; sadness, $F(5,66)$ = 6.22, p < .001; fear, $F(5, 66)$ = 4.73, p < .001; and happiness, $F(5, 66)$ = 5.20, p < .001. With alpha set at .05, Newman-Keuls post hoc analyses indicated that the patterns of significant differences varied somewhat with emotion. The means for the six age groups are displayed in Figure 24.1. For anger, the means of all the adult groups and the adolescent group were significantly higher than those of the preadolescents, and the means of the middle-aged adults were significantly higher than those of the adolescents and young adults. For sadness, the means of all of the adult groups were significantly higher than those of the preadolescents. For fear, the means of the adult groups, except for the elderly adults, were significantly higher than those of the preadolescents. In addition, the means of the 30–44-year-old adults were significantly higher than those of the adolescents. For happiness, the means of all the adult groups were significantly higher than those of the preadolescents, and the means of the 30–44-year-old adults were also higher than those of the adolescent group. Overall, then, these results demonstrate that positive developmental changes in emotional understanding continue at least until middle adulthood for three of the emotions. Level of emotional understanding appears to level off at an earlier age for sadness than for the other emotions.

Ego level. Since regression analysis suggested that ego level is a significant predictor of emotional understanding among the adult age groups, we performed a second MANOVA using ego level rather than age as the independent variable. There was a significant main effect of ego level, Wilks's lambda=.62, $F(12, 172)=2.84$; $p<.001$. The degree of association, $\pi^2=.38$, was moderately high between ego level and the dependent variables. Figure 24.2 displays the means for levels of emotional understanding for preconformist, conformist, conscientious, and postconscientious levels of ego development.

Further univariate analyses showed significant ego level effects for three emotions: anger, $F(3, 64) = 5.19$, $p < .01$; sadness, $F(3, 64) = 8.71$, $p < .0001$; and fear, $F(3, 64) = 4.96$. $p < .01$. With alpha set at .05, Newman-

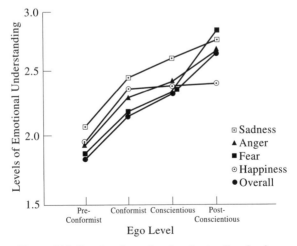

Figure 24.2. Levels of emotional understanding for four ego levels.

Keuls post hoc analyses indicated more differentiation of groups for anger and sadness. Means are displayed in Figure 24.2 For anger, the postconscientious and conscientious groups differ from the conformist and preconformist groups. In addition, the postconscientious means differ from the conformist means. For sadness, the postconscientious and conscientious groups score higher than the preconformist groups. In addition, the postconscientious groups differ from the conformist and the conscientious groups. For fear, the postconscientious, the conscientious, and the conformist groups differ from the preconformist group. Thus, there is little differentiation for level of emotional understanding of fear past the preconformist level of ego development. The level of emotional understanding of anger and sadness continues to rise after the conformist level of ego development.

Canonical Correlation of the Developmental-Sex Variables with the Coping-Defense Variables

To examine the external validity of our levels of emotional understanding, we performed a canonical variate analysis including the measures of coping and defense. This analysis, modeled after Labouvie-Vief, Hakim-Larson, and Hobart (1987) and described in Tabachnick and Fidell (1983), treated the coping–defense measures as the dependent variable set. The variables related to developmental complexity (age, ego level, and verbal ability) formed the predictor variable set. In addition, since the previous analyses suggest that these three developmental variables are highly interrelated with emotional maturity, that variable also was treated as part of the independent variable set. Finally, since our previous research (see Labouvie-Vief, Hakim-Larson Hobart, 1987) showed sex to be a significant independent variable in predicting coping and defense mechanisms, sex also was added to the predictor variable set. Thus, ego level, age group, verbal ability, overall levels of emotional understanding, and sex constituted the developmental-sex set of independent variables: Higher scores indicate higher ego level, verbal ability, levels of emotional understanding, age, and female sex. The subscales of the Defense Mechanism Inventory and the subscales of Lazarus's Ways of Coping constituted the coping-defense set of dependent variables: Larger numbers indicate higher endorsement of the respective coping and defense mechanisms.

Of five possible pairs of linear composites, only the first two canonical correlations were significant (see Table 24.6). The canonical correlation be-

Table 24.6. *Canonical Correlation between Developmental Complexity–Sex and Coping–Defense Mechanisms*

Function	Eigenvalue	%	Canonical R	Wilks's lambda
1	1.10	42.92	.72	.15**
2	0.73	28.35	.65	.39*

*$p < .05$. **$p < .001$.

tween the first pair of linear composites was .72 and accounted for 52% of the variance in that pair. The canonical correlation between the second pair of linear composites was .65, which accounted for 42% of the variance in that pair. The remaining three canonical correlations were not significant. With all five canonical correlations included, Wilks's lambda was .15, $F(65, 250) = 1.94$ $p < .001$, and with the first canonical correlation removed, Wilks's lambda was .30, $F(48, 206) = 1.55$, $p < .05$. Further F tests were not significant. Therefore, the first two canonical correlations accounted for the significant relationships between the two sets of variables. Analyses of the two pairs of canonical variates appear in Table 24.7. Shown in the table are structural correlations between the variables and the two significant canonical variates.

Using a cutoff correlation of .35 for interpretation, the variables relevant to the first canonical variate in the developmental-sex independent variable set were verbal ability and sex, indicating that high verbal ability and being male defined high scores on this variate. In the coping-defense dependent variable set, seeking social support, escape-avoidance, and accepting responsibility were the variables relevant to the first canonical variate. Taken as a pair, the first canonical variates indicate that those who are male or of higher verbal ability tended to use the coping mechanisms of seeking social support, escape-avoidance, and accepting responsibility less than those who are female or of lower verbal ability. This linear composite, which is uncorrelated with the second canonical variate, can be viewed as a feminine response of coping. Taken as a pair, the first canonical variates indicate that men ($M = 5.78$) tend to seek social support less than women ($M = 8.51$), $t(69) = -3.37$ $p < .001$, and men ($M = 4.78$) are less likely to use escape–avoidance than are women ($M = 6.89$), $t(69) = -2.46$, $p < .05$. Although accepting responsibility was correlated with the sex and verbal ability variate, the mean difference between men ($M = 4.25$) and women ($M = 4.31$) was not significant. Since there also are no sex differences on verbal ability (M = 27.64 for women, M = 26.08 for men), $t(70)$ = −.76, ns, accepting responsibility appears to be a function of verbal ability.

The second canonical variate in the developmental–sex independent variable set was composed of overall levels of emotional understanding, age group, verbal ability, and ego level. Thus, this canonical variate formed a developmental dimension on which sex was not relevant. The coping–defense dependent variables relevant to the developmental dimension were the defenses of reversal, turning against the self, turning against others, projection, and the coping strategies of distancing (denial) and escape-avoidance. Taken as a pair, the second canonical variates indicate that those who have higher emotional understanding, are older, have higher verbal ability, and have higher ego levels also tend to use the defenses of reversal and turning against the self more, and turning against others and projection less than those who are not as developmentally mature. More mature individuals on this developmental dimension also are less likely to use the coping strategies of distancing (denial) and escape–avoidance than are less mature individuals. Of the defense and coping strategies, turning against the self is significantly different between women (M = 37.86) and men (M = 33.56), $t(69)$ = 2.91,

Table 24.7. Correlations of Variables with Canonical Variates

Variable	Variate 1	Variate 2
Developmental complexity–sex set		
Age group	.22	.88
Emotional understanding	.22	.79
Verbal ability	.59	.69
Ego level	.18	.53
Sex	−.69	.32
Coping-defense set		
Seeking social support	−.74	.20
Escape-avoidance	−.48	−.40
Accepting responsibility	−.41	−.31
Reversal	−.07	.63
Turning against others	.08	−.55
Projection	.24	−.52
Turning against self	−.32	.48
Distancing	−.32	−.42
Principalization	.03	.22
Planful problem solving	.04	.16
Positive reappraisal	−.32	−.09
Self controlling	−.05	−.02
Confrontive coping	−.34	.02

Table 24.8 Multiple Regression of Verbal Ability, Ego Level, Sex, Age, and Levels of Emotional Understanding on the Standardized Scores of the Second Canonical Variate (Dimension of Maturity of Coping and Defense)

Variable	r	β^{a}	sr^2 (unique variance)
Verbal ability	.43	−.003	.000
Ego level	.35	−.098	.005
Sex	.24	.243*	.056*
Age group	.55	.434**	.087**
Level of emotional understanding	.52	.302*	.051*

NOTE: R^2 = .42*** (unique variability = .21; shared variability = .21); sr^2 = squared semipartial correlation.
   *$p < .05$. **$p < .01$.

$p < .005$. As mentioned above, the endorsement of escape–avoidance is also significantly different between the sexes.

To examine the relationship among the variables defining the independent variables of the developmental dimension (age group, verbal ability, overall levels of emotional understanding, and ego level), canonical variate scores for the second linear composite of the dependent coping and defense variables were computed. These scores were used as the dependent variable in a multiple regression analysis. The multiple correlation was .64, $F(5, 64) = 8.72$, $p < .001$. Regression weights and squared semi-partial correlations are shown in Table 24.8. Variables accounting for unique variance in the dimension of maturity of coping–defense are age (9%), levels of emotional understanding (5%), and sex (6%). Verbal ability and ego level do not significantly account for unique variance on this dimension.

DISCUSSION

In this study, we demonstrated significant differences from preadolescence to late adulthood in how individuals describe their emotions. Using a cognitive-developmental perspective, we found that the older or developmentally more mature individual described her or his emotions in terms of a language that is more oriented toward inner felt sense and that describes states more dynamically as varying across time and context. She or he also reports modulating emotions more flexibly than does the younger or less mature individual and is better able to differentiate the self's state from that of the other and to understand emotional encounters as genuinely reciprocal.

In general, our results indicate that when charted along age as a parameter, and when using overall level of emotional understanding scores, this developmental pattern is curvilinear, appearing to abate in adulthood. However, this curvilinear relationship to age appears to reflect a maturational trend, pronounced especially at the pre-adult levels. Thus, when these age groups are excluded and when ego level and verbal ability are used as independent markers of developmental maturity, the relationship to levels of emotional understanding scores is linear. In addition, these variables explain variance over and beyond that due to age. Thus, these results substantiate our earlier findings (Labouvie-Vief, Hakim-Larson & Hobart, 1987) that development in adulthood is not best indexed by age.

Although levels of emotional understanding scores in adulthood are more strongly related to ego level and verbal ability than to age, interesting age-related patterns did emerge when the emotions were examined separately. On three of the emotions—anger, fear, and happiness—the adults around mid-life (45–59 for anger, 30–44 for fear and happiness) achieved the highest scores. The oldest group, in turn, scored somewhat lower, although it is noteworthy that their response levels and patterns were almost identical to those of young adults.

It is not clear whether the leveling off of complexity of emotional understanding in adulthood reflects a genuine ontogenetic trend. It is possible that this pattern results from cohort differences. For example, patterns of coping and defense would seem to be strongly influenced by sociocultural conditions, and it is possible that the oldest cohorts received more rigid training about how to self-regulate emotions. Hence, what appears as a lack of continued development could reflect enhanced development in more recent cohorts.

With that proviso, the current results further extend our earlier findings that significant cognitive-developmental differences characterize the adult life span. Again, these differences are found to have significant bearing on processes of coping and ego organization. Thus, as in the Labouvie-Vief, Hakim-Larson, and Hobart (1987) study, we find that individuals who score higher on a dimension of developmental complexity show a different pattern of endorsing coping and defense strategies. Specifically, in this study those who describe emotions in a more mature manner are older, have higher verbal ability and higher ego level, and use the defenses of turning against the self and reversal more, while endorsing the defenses of turning against others and projection and the coping strategy of distancing-denial and escape-avoidance to a lesser degree. However, of the variables loading on the developmental complexity dimension, ego level and verbal ability did not contribute any unique variance toward the prediction of coping and defense processes, while age, level of emotional understanding, and sex did. The sex difference, in turn, appeared to result from differences between males and females on the coping–defense variable of turning against the self and escape-avoidance.

The relationship between developmental complexity and coping–defense found in this study is virtually identical to that found in the Labouvie-Vief, Hakim-Larson, and Hobart, (1987) study. In the former study, however, turning against the self achieved a lower correlation (.29) with the developmental dimension, while the correlation for escape–avoidance was higher (−.58). These variations appear to be due to the fact that in the present study, the developmental dimension also was correlated with sex.

That the present findings should replicate our earlier ones is not surprising, since the analysis was based on a subsample of the previous study. Nevertheless, this replication is not merely trivial, since there were significant differences between the two studies in how the developmental dimension was defined. In the first study, that dimension was defined (in declining order of correlation) by age, the complexity with which individuals described stressful encounters, and ego level. In this study, in turn, that dimension was defined (also in declining order of correlation) by age levels of emotional understanding, verbal ability, ego level, and sex. Even though a different pattern of variables served to indicate developmental complexity, however, the relationship between the dimension of developmental complexity and coping and defense was virtually identical. These findings, then, substantiate our earlier ones.

The findings relating to gender are also in agreement with those reported in our earlier study (Labouvie-Vief, Hakim-Larson & Hobart, 1987). In that study, women were found to be more likely than men to use the coping strategies of escape-avoidance and seeking social support, and to turn against the self. Similarly, in the present study, men were less likely to endorse these strategies. These results are consistent with the finding that women are more likely than men to internalize conflict, while men are more likely to externalize (e.g., Cramer, 1979).

While the current findings replicate our earlier ones, the present analysis offers a theoretical refinement and extension in suggesting a more process-oriented account of the specific mechanisms that appear to be responsible for such a strong relationship between developmental complexity and maturity of coping-defense. The coding scheme of levels of emotional understanding reported here is specifically predicated on the assumption that increased efficacy in the self-regulation of emotion is mediated by such cognitive-developmental mechanisms as increasing differentiation and integration of emotion terms, of clearer differentiation of dimensions of inner and outer experience, of higher levels of reflective monitoring of emotional processes, of increasing reliance on self-generated rather than conventional standards, and of greater differentiation of self and other.

It is necessary to point out, however, that the measure developed in the present study is based on how individuals conceptualize and verbalize these processes, rather than on more direct, behavioral measures of self-regulation. Conceptualizations often contain omissions and distortions (see Nisbett & Ross, 1980) of actual behavior, and it would thus be desirable to validate our measure with observational data.[1] Nevertheless, the current levels of emotional understanding are predicated on the psychoanalytic assumption that conceptual simplicity in the narrative of autobiographical events is itself indicative of defensive and distortive processes (see Schafer, 1980; Vaillant, 1977). In the same vein, our measure shows strong and meaningful relationships with other measures of ego organization, coping, and defense.

An important question raised by our data is whether the levels we have defined are indeed unique to processes of emotional understanding. Since verbal ability and ego level enter as strong predictors of levels of emotional understanding, it could be argued that our measure reflects, in the main, individuals' general verbal sophistication rather than a dimension of maturity of emotional understanding per se. This issue can be addressed from at least two perspectives.

On one hand, our data indicate that even though verbal ability is strongly correlated with levels of emotional understanding, it does not eliminate the relationship to other variables related to developmental complexity. Thus, for the adult age groups, ego level is an even stronger predictor of levels of emotional understanding, and these levels are meaningfully related to strategies of coping and defense that also have been associated with more complex cognitive processes (e.g., Ihilevich & Gleser, 1986). Even though levels of emotional understanding share variance with verbal ability, then, they indicate a somewhat separate construct.

On the other hand, a significant relationship of verbal ability to emotional understanding does not render findings about group differences in the latter trivial, since one should not theoretically expect verbal ability to be independent of dimensions of developmental complexity, such as the current levels of emotional understanding or ego development. As Werner (e.g., Werner & Kaplan, 1984) has pointed out, language is a medium through which people are able to represent and conceptualize processes, thereby objectifying these processes and making them more reflective. Thus, it is not surprising that from childhood on, language complexity is a strong predictor of many other competencies, and one should expect a similar relationship to continue into adulthood. Indeed, in that context it is significant to point out that measures such as verbal ability, which are often associated with crystallized intelligence, show a pattern very similar to the pattern of the present study, continuing to increase well into middle adulthood (for review, see Labouvie-Vief, 1985). Nevertheless, it is also important to note that measures such as ego development or levels of emotional understanding are based to a considerable extent on an analysis of the complexity of language use rather than on sheer familiarity with target words (as is true of measures of verbal ability). As suggested by our results, such complexity-based measures may account for even more variance in coping and defense processes than verbal ability per se.

In a somewhat related vein, it is possible that the group differences reported here do not reflect any processes unique to emotional understanding, but rather that they are a reflection of variations in general levels of intelligence or education, of which verbal ability tests are good markers. Again, it is necessary here to raise the possibility that variations in general intelligence should not be independent of the measure used in this study. Since that measure is based on dimensions of cognitive complexity, it should correlate substantially with measures of intelligence. Even though most researchers now propose multiple component interpretations of intelligence (see Sternberg & Powell, 1982), correlations between different components tend to be substantial. However, the exact degree to which our measure reflects a domain-specific competence or converges with other measures of intelligence is not known at the present time. Nor is it known whether our measure reflects, indeed, one single competence rather than several domain-specific ones, since for each emotion, level scores were collapsed across a multitude of criteria.

However, even if our measure were correlated with variations in general intelligence, such a correlation does not render our levels of emotional understanding trivial. Even though from an individual-differences perspective such a correlation might be interpreted as spurious, it takes on a different meaning if one adopts the cognitive-developmental assumption that quantitative variations in intelligence are correlated with profound qualitative differences in patterns of thought (see Kohlberg, 1969; Lerner, 1986) that cannot be reduced to, or predicted by, quantitative differences in intelligence. Thus, our findings offer potential insight into the process related to variations in emotional understanding that could not be gleaned from standard measures of intelligence. Nevertheless, they are in agreement with the well-replicated finding that many measures of intellectual functioning show increases well into middle adulthood (for review, see Labouvie-Vief, 1985).

A somewhat related question is whether levels of emotional understanding may not reflect the effects of education rather than a pattern of development. This question is best addressed by highlighting the concept of "development" that underlies the present research. While many writers have asked whether adaptation in adulthood is developmental (representing a universal patterning of life course processes) or situational, an emerging concept of development is predicated on the assumption that levels of developmental complexity are situationally modulated (for review, see Lerner, 1986). For example, it is well documented that profound changes in self-regulation and self-other differentiation have occurred over historical time (see, e.g., de-Mause, 1974; Elias, 1978). Such changes can be in the direction of greater flexibility of self-regulation at the cultural level, and, further, these changes are likely to filter down to the individual level through processes of education and socialization. Hence, education itself can become a factor that profoundly modulates the process of development—a modulation that affects the biological as well as the psychological level (Woodruff, 1977).

In that context it is significant to note, as well, that we do not claim that the pattern found in the present study is representative for the population at large. Our sampling clearly was not representative, but aimed at maximizing the possibility to include individuals from the more mature levels. Thus, it is likely that in samples less positively selected more individuals would occupy the lower levels. To what degree levels of emotional understanding vary with such sampling conditions must remain a subject for further study.

Despite these various limitations, the present data indicate that a fairly broad conceptual component underlies individuals' self-reported ability to experience and deal with emotions. This finding appears to contradict the claim that variations in coping are primarily due to situational variations rather than a somewhat stable intrapersonal competency (e.g., Lazarus & Folkman, 1984). However, since the measure employed in this study is based on a rationale different from that underlying many other measures of coping, it may complement rather than contradict results obtained by other authors.

Specifically, our coding system differentiates levels of complexity or maturity in strategies for which other instruments merely code absence or presence. In this way, for example, the Ways of Coping questionnaire creates a scale score for seeking social support. In the present study, however, responses scored under the theme of self—other indicated that individuals sought social support for vastly different reasons. Those at the presystemic level primarily attempted to find a more powerful other to intervene for them. Those at the intrasystemic level seemed primarily motivated to find group support that would justify their emotion. Those at the intersystemic and integrated levels, however, were not primarily interested in justifying their emotions, but in "sounding them out" so as to examine their objectivity. Such developmental variance is collapsed in the Ways of Coping questionnaire, and thus situational variance is the primary variance accounted for. Our approach suggests, instead, that measures based on cognitive-developmental considerations may well reveal a broader, competence-based dimension of coping.

In sum, the present results suggest the usefulness of a cognitive-developmental approach for an analysis of emotional and coping processes in adulthood and later life. Although in some sense our findings raise at least as many questions as they have answered, they suggest that research on adult coping processes will receive many payoffs by adopting a life span oriented, cognitive-developmental approach. Thus, we hope that they will help stimulate the future development of a research domain much in need of an orientation that promises both heuristic and theoretical richness (see also Schulz, 1985; Whitbourne, 1985).

NOTE

1. To provide such validation is the aim of other analyses issuing from this research, and preliminary evidence suggests that our levels of emotional understanding predict flexible affective expression as coded by Ekman's (see Ekman & Friesen, 1975) facial action coding system DeVoe, 1988).

REFERENCES

Beck, A. (1976). Cognitive therapy and the emotional disorders. New York: International Universities Press.

Blanchard-Fields, F. (1986). Reasoning on social dilemmas varying in emotional saliency: An adult developmental perspective. Psychology and Aging, 1, 325–333.

Botwinick, J. (1978). Aging and behavior (2nd ed). New York: Springer.

Bretherton, I., Fritz, J., Zahn-Waxler, C. & Ridgeway, D. (1986). Learning to talk about emotion: A functionalist perspective. Child Development, 57, 529–548.

Buck, R. (1984). The communication of emotion. New York: Guilford Press.

Colby, A., Kohlberg, L., Gibbs, J. & Lieberman, M. (1983). A longitudinal study of moral development. Monographs of the Society for Research in Child Development, 49 (2, Serial No. 206).

Commons, M. L., Richards, F. A. & Armon, C. (1984). Beyond formal operations: Late adolescent and cognitive development. *New York: Praeger.*

Cramer, P. (1979). *Defense mechanisms in adolescence.* Developmental Psychology, 15, 476–477.

Cytrynbaum, S., Blum, L., Patrick, R., Stein, J., Wasner, D. & Wilk, C. (1980). *Midlife development: A personality and social system perspective. In L. W. Poon (Ed.),* Aging in the 1980's: Psychological issues *(pp. 463–474). Washington, DC: American Psychological Association.*

deMause, L. (1974). The history of childhood. *New York: Psychohistory Press.*

DeVoe, M. (1988). Smile controllers and qualifiers in adolescence and adulthood. *Unpublished master's thesis, Wayne State University, Detroit, MI.*

Donaldson, S. K. & Westerman, M. A. (1986). *Development of children's understanding of ambivalence and causal theories of emotions.* Developmental Psychology, 22, 655–662.

Edelstein, W. & Noam, G. (1982). *Regulatory structures of the self and 'postformal' stages in adulthood.* Human Development, 25, 407–422.

Ekman, P. (1984). *Expression and the nature of emotion. In K. R. Scherer & P. Ekman (Eds.),* Approaches to emotion *(pp. 319–343). Hillsdale, NJ: Erlbaum.*

Ekman, P. & Friesen, W. (1975). Unmasking the face. *Englewood Cliffs, NJ: Prentice-Hall.*

Elias, N. (1978). The civilizing process: Vol. 1. The history of manners. *New York: Pantheon Books.*

Erikson, E. (1978). Reflections on Dr. Borg's life cycle. In E. Erikson (Ed.), Adulthood *(pp. 1–31). New York: Norton.*

Folkman, S., Lazarus, R. S., Dunkel-Schetter, C., DeLongis, A. & Gruen, R. (1986). *Dynamics of a stressful encounter: Cognitive appraisal, coping, and encounter outcomes.* Journal of Personality and Social Psychology, 50, 992–1003.

Folkman, S., Lazarus, R. S., Pimley, S. & Novacek, J. (1987). *Age differences and stress and copying processes.* Psychology and Aging, 2, 171–184.

Gleser, G. C. & Ihilevich, D. (1969). *An objective instrument for measuring defense mechanisms.* Journal of Consulting and Clinical Psychology, 33, 51–60.

Haan, N. (1977). Coping and defending: Processes of self environment organization. *New York: Academic Press.*

Harris, P. L. (1983). *Children's understanding of the link between situation and emotion.* Journal of Experimental Psychology, 36, 490–509.

Harris, P. L., Olthof, T. & Terwogt, M. (1981). *Children's knowledge of emotions.* Journal of Child Psychology and Psychiatry, 22, 247–261.

Harter, S. (1983). *Developmental perspectives on the self system. In E. M. Hetherington (Ed.),* Handbook of child psychology *(Vol. 4, pp. 275–385). New York: Wiley.*

Harter, S. & Buddin, B. J. (1987). *Children's understanding of the simultaneity of two emotions: A five-stage developmental acquisition sequence.* Developmental Psychology, 23, 388–399.

Hauser, S. T. (1976). *Loevingers's model and measure of ego development: A critical review.* Psychological Bulletin, 83, 928–955.

Ihilevich, D. & Gleser, G. (1986). Defense mechanisms. *Owosso, MI: DMI Associates.*

Izard, C. E. & Buechler, S. (1980). Aspects of consciousness and personality in terms of differential emotions theory. In R. Plutchik & H. Kellerman (Eds.), Emotion: Theory, research, and experience *(Vol. 1, pp. 165–187). New York: Academic Press.*

Jung, C. G. (1933). Modern man in search of a soul. *New York: Harcourt, Brace & World.*

Kegan, R. (1982). The evolving self. *Cambridge: Harvard University Press.*

Kitchener, K. S. (1983). Cognition, metacognition, and epistemic cognition. A three-level model of cognitive processing. Human Development, 26, 222–232.

Kohlberg, L. (1969). Stage and sequence: The cognitive-developmental approach to socialization. In D. A. Goslin (Ed.), Handbook of socialization theory and research *(pp. 347–480). Chicago: Rand McNally.*

Labouvie-Vief, G. (1982). Dynamic development and mature autonomy: A theoretical prologue. Human Development, 25, 161–191.

Labouvie-Vief, G. (1985). Intelligence and cognition. In J. E. Birren & K. W. Schaie (Eds.), Handbook of the psychology of aging *(2nd ed., pp. 500–530). New York: Van Nostrand Reinhold.*

Labouvie-Vief, G. & Blanchard-Fields, F. (1982). Cognitive ageing and psychological growth. Ageing and Society, 2, 183–209.

Labouvie-Vief, G. & Hakim-Larson, J. (in press). Developmental shifts in adult thoughts. In S. Hunter & M. Sundel (Eds.), Midlife myths. *Newbury Park, CA: Sage.*

Labouvie-Vief, G., Hakim-Larson, J., DeVoe, M. & Schoeberlein, S. (1989). The language of self-regulation: A life-span view. Human Development, 32, 279–299.

Labouvie-Vief, G., Hakim-Larson, J. & Hobart, C. (1987). Age, ego level, and the life-span development of coping and defense processes. Psychology and Aging, 2, 286–293.

Lazarus, R. S. & Folkman, S. (1984). Stress, appraisal, and coping. *New York: Springer.*

Lerner, R. M. (1986). Concepts and theories of human development *(2nd ed.). New York: Random House.*

Lewis, M. & Michalson, L. (1983). Children's emotions and moods. *New York: Plenum Press.*

Lewis, M. & Rosenblum, L. A. (Eds.). (1978). The development of affect *(Vol. 1). New York: Plenum Press.*

Loevinger, J. (1976). Ego development. *San Francisco: Jossey-Bass.*

Loevinger, J. & Wessler, R. (1978). Measuring ego development. *San Francisco: Jossey-Bass.*

McAdams, D. (1985). Power, intimacy and the life story. *Homewood, IL: Dorsey.*

McCrae, R. R. & Costa, P. T., Jr. (1984). Emerging lives, enduring dispositions. *Boston: Little Brown.*

Neugarten, B. (1968). The awareness of middle age. In B. Neugarten (Ed.), Middle age and aging *(pp. 93–98). Chicago: University of Chicago Press.*

Nisbett, R. & Ross, L. (1980). Human inference: Strategies and short-comings of social judgment. *Englewood Cliffs, NJ: Prentice-Hall.*

Piaget, J. (1981). Intelligence and affectivity. *Palo Alto, CA: Annual Reviews.*

Plutchik, R. (1984). Emotions: A general psychoevolutionary theory. In K. R. Scherer & P. Ekman (Eds.), Approaches to emotion (pp. 197–219). Hillsdale, NJ: Erlbaum.

Rybash, J., Hoyer, W. J. & Roodin, P. (1986). Adult cognition and aging. New York: Pergamon.

Saarni, C. (1984). An observational study of children's attempts to monitor their expressive behavior. Child Development, 55, 1504–1513.

Schafer, R. (1980). Narrative actions in psychoanalysis. Worchester, MA: Clark University Press.

Schaie, K. W. (1977/1978). Towards a stage theory of adult development. International Journal of Aging and Human Development, 8, 129–138.

Schulz, R. (1985). Emotion and affect. In J. E. Birren & K. W. Schaie (Eds.), Handbook of the psychology of aging (2nd ed., pp. 531–543). New York: Van Nostrand Reinhold.

Selman, R. L. (1980). The growth of interpersonal understanding. New York: Academic Press.

Shaver, P., Schwartz, J., Kirson, D. & O'Conner, C. (1987). Emotion knowledge: Further exploration of a prototype approach. Journal of Personality and Social Psychology, 52, 1062–1086.

Sternberg, R. J. & Powell, J. S. (1982). Theories of intelligence. In R. J. Sternberg (Ed.), Handbook of human intelligence (pp. 975–1005). Cambridge: Cambridge University Press.

Tabachnick, B. G. & Fidell, L. S. (1983). Using multivariate statistics. New York: Harper & Row.

Tomkins, S. S. (1984). Affect theory. In K. R. Scherer & P. Ekman (Eds.), Approaches to emotion (pp. 163–195). Hillsdale, NJ: Erlbaum.

Vaillant, G. E. (1977). Adaptation to life. Boston: Little, Brown.

Werner, H. & Kaplan, B. (1984). Symbol formation. Hillsdale, NJ: Erlbaum.

Whitbourne, S. K. (1985). The psychological construction of the life span. In J. E. Birren & K. W. Schaie (Eds.), Handbook of the psychology of aging (2nd ed., pp. 594–618). New York: Van Nostrand Reinhold.

Wood, P. K. (1983). Inquiring systems and problem structure: Implications for cognitive development. Human Development, 26, 249–265.

Woodruff, D. S. (1977). Can you live to be 100? New York: Chatham Press.

Zajonc, R. B. (1984). The interaction of affect and cognition. In K. R. Scherer & P. Ekman (Eds.), Approaches to emotion (pp. 239–246). Hillsdale, NJ: Erlbaum.

25. Choosing Social Partners

How Old Age and Anticipated Endings Make People More Selective

Barbara L. Fredrickson and Laura L. Carstensen

FROM BIRTH, HUMANS are immediately social. Long before infants can perform basic life functions, such as walking or independent feeding, they engage in complex social interaction, making fine discriminations among the emotional states of their caretakers and responding in kind to these states (Scherer, 1982; Stern, 1985; Tronick, 1982). This readiness for social interaction is so prominent, so reliable, it is considered by most to be innate (Campos & Barrett, 1984).

People maintain social connections with numerous others throughout life. But during the later part of adulthood, rates of social interaction begin to decline. The basic finding that social activity declines in old age is widely accepted, supported by both cross-sectional research (Cumming & Henry, 1961; Gordon & Gaitz, 1976; Youmans, 1962) and longitudinal research (Carstensen, 1989; Field & Minkler, 1988; Palmore, 1981). Yet, the meaning of this reduction remains the most hotly disputed issue in social gerontology (Carstensen, 1987; Palmore, 1981).

Proponents of what has come to be called *activity theory* claim that reductions in social contact reflects barriers to interaction, such as limited mobility associated with health problems and the deaths of friends and loved ones (Maddox, 1963). This perspective has prompted numerous interventions designed to provide the elderly with opportunities for social interaction and even tangible rewards for interaction when higher rates are obtained (Blackman, Howe & Pinkston, 1976; Konarski, Johnson & Whitman, 1980; Quattrochi-Tubin & Jason, 1980). Indeed, the primary aim of applied social gerontology has been to increase rates of social contact. Empirical evidence for the contention that increased social activity improves psychological well-being, however, remains equivocal (Carstensen, 1986; Carstensen & Erickson, 1986).

Reprinted by permission from *Psychology and Aging* 5, no. 3 (1990): 335–47. Copyright © 1989 by the American Psychological Association.

The activity approach works in direct opposition to *disengagement theory*, an alternative explanatory model of declining social activity. Proponents of this theory assert that reductions in interaction reflect a natural process by which older people voluntarily decrease their investment in social contact in a symbolic preparation for death (Cumming & Henry, 1961). From this perspective, interventions aimed at increasing social contacts are inherently ill conceived. Yet, the theory has been criticized for failing to acknowledge the vital involvement in the social world that elderly people do maintain. The presence of intimate friendships and confidants is clearly central to psychological well-being even among the oldest old (Antonucci & Jackson, 1987; Duckitt, 1982, 1983; Erikson, Erikson & Kivnick, 1986; Lowenthal & Haven, 1968). Also, the flattening of affect and emotional withdrawal implicit in disengagement theory are not supported empirically (see Malatesta, 1981).

At a theoretical level, a central question concerns the role that older individuals play in the reduction of social contact: Are reductions imposed on or instigated by the older adult? Carstensen (1987, 1989) has proposed selectivity theory as an alternative to disengagement and activity theories of socioemotional aging. She contends that throughout life, people become more selective in choosing their social partners. Selectivity serves at least two functions: It allows individuals to conserve physical energy, a task that becomes increasingly important with age, and it operates as a mechanism for affect regulation. Because most emotions occur in the context of social relationships, maximizing contact and investment in one's closest relationships and minimizing interaction with less familiar social partners is an adaptive mechanism for affect regulation, particularly in old age. Stated simply, selectivity theory suggests that by reducing levels of social interaction, older people optimize the experience of positive affect and minimize negative affect. Besides positing affect as central to age-related reductions in social interaction, a selectivity view diverges theoretically from previous models of socioemotional aging in that (a) change is assumed to be gradual and to begin early in life, (b) observed reductions in interaction do not include all classes of social partners, and (c) change is not accounted for exclusively by a decrease in the availability of social partners but instead is rooted in the thoughts and preferences of the aging individual.

Although incompatible with both activity and disengagement theories, selectivity theory is congruous with broader models of late-life adaptation—models that view development in terms of gains and losses (P. B. Baltes, 1987) and that view individuals as active in selecting optimal environments (Lawton, 1987). P. B. Baltes and M. M. Baltes described successful aging as a process of selective optimization with compensation: People adapt to losses in circumscribed areas of competence by selecting and concentrating on other domains that are of high priority (M. M. Baltes, 1986; M. M. Baltes & Schmid, 1987; P. B. Baltes, 1987; P. B. Baltes, Dittman-Kohli & Dixon, 1984). Relatedly, Lawton and Nahemow's (1973) press–competence model of aging contends that people experience stress when the demands of a particular environment either exceed or fail to challenge their abilities. Lawton (1987) argued that the field of gerontology has focused primarily on the ''press'' aspect of the model, paying too little attention to individual competencies. In response, he proposed the proactivity hypothesis, which states that individuals play a central role in orchestrating their own environments: ''Far from being pawns, older people engage in active behavior by choosing what is desirable or relevant from all that exists in the 'environment out there.' An even more active level is to create an environment of one's own choice'' (p. 37).

The model of psychological change developed in selectivity theory suggests age-related cognitive changes in an individual's consideration of potential social partners. Specifically, selectivity theory posits that with age and the subsequent demand for increased conservation of energy, the criteria for choosing social partners change. For example, older people may judge novel partners less desirable and familiar partners more desirable because familiar partners lead more reliably to positive (or at least predictable) affect. Also, place in the life cycle may limit future possibilities with novel social partners. For an 80-year-old, for example, developing a long-term friendship with a new acquaintance is extremely unlikely. As such, old age can represent an inevitable social ending, a circumstance that may limit interest in social interaction with unfamiliar people. We contend that the patterns of social activity in old age reflect a general phenomenon associated with perceived social endings. In this view, partner selectivity is a self-regulatory mechanism not specific to old age and death, but instigated by a range of social situations—including geographic relocation, retirements, and graduations—that constrain prospects for future contacts.

EMPIRICAL STRATEGY

We investigated age-related differences in social cognition in an effort to understand age-related differences in social behavior. In Study 1, we assessed judgments of social partners among people aged 14 to 95 years using a card-sort procedure that reduces demand for socially desirable responding. We then used three-way multidimensional scaling to identify the dimensions used to discriminate among the different types of people who might be partners in social interaction. Multidimensional scaling is a mathematical modeling technique that relies on similarity judgments; as such, data reflect subjects' own cognitive distinctions among social partners, rather than their responses to prespecified rating scales. (Readers interested in a thorough exposition of how three-way multidimensional scaling can be used to recover cognitive–social schemata are directed to Rudy & Merluzzi, 1984.) Collecting similarity data has two clear advantages. First, it minimizes investigator contamination at the measurement stage, so it enables investigators to discover rather than impose relevant organizing constructs (Rudy & Merluzzi, 1984; Shepard, 1974). Second, by avoiding leading questions like "Would you like spending social time with your new neighbor?" similarity classification lessens the effects of social desirability and demand characteristics. This makes it an advantageous assessment tool for older adults because clinical experience and research suggest that the elderly can be susceptible to social conformity (Klein, 1972). In Study 1, we hypothesized that (a) common psychological dimensions would emerge across groups and (b) the relative salience of those dimensions would vary with age. Specifically, because we posit that emotion conservation becomes increasingly important with age, we predicted that affective dimensions would be most salient to our oldest subjects.

In Study 2, we investigated whether partner selectivity is responsive to situational constraints, particularly the constraints associated with anticipated social endings. In a within-subject design, we manipulated the salience of social endings and asked people ranging in age from 11 to 92 to choose among familiar and novel social partners. We hypothesized that (a) in general, older people—because of their place in the life cycle—would choose familiar social partners more often than would younger people but (b) younger people would pattern the social choices of the elderly when endings were made salient.

STUDY 1

Method

Subjects

Forty elderly, 20 middle-aged, and 20 adolescent individuals served as voluntary participants in this study. The elderly sample comprised two age-matched groups: 20 home-dwelling community residents (mean age = 80.0;

range = 69–92) and 20 nursing home residents (mean age = 83.4; range = 75–95). The middle-aged sample (mean age = 39.9; range = 35–44) was recruited at Stanford University, and most were university employees. The teen sample (mean age = 16.4; range = 14–19) was recruited from a local private high school in San Francisco. All subjects were offered $10 compensation for their participation in a study of social activity. Given our primary interest in the elderly samples, and the sex composition of the elderly population from which these samples were drawn, we intentionally overincluded female subjects in each sample: Overall, 76% of subjects were female. While none of the teen sample had yet attended college, 100% of the middle-aged, 95% of the community elderly, and 50% of the nursing home samples had had at least some college education.

Because health is inextricably confounded with age, focusing exclusively on very healthy or very infirm old people can lead to gross misconceptions about aging per se. This confound poses a particular challenge in research on normal aging when the objective is to study the psychological aspects of age, not of illness. Moreover, we have argued that a primary motivating force behind selectivity is declining energy reserve, which of course is associated with poor health. In this research, we expected that both healthy and infirm old people would demonstrate partner selectivity but that active subjects would be less likely to show the effect and institutionalized subjects would be more likely. Most of our community elderly sample were recruited at a local senior center. Because senior centers are used by only 15% of the aged population (Stone, 1986), this sample probably represents socially active and healthy old people; nursing home populations represent less active and more infirm old people.

Measures

Written materials. Subjects rated their own physical and mental health, relative to the average person their age, on a 10-point scale ranging from *poor* (1) to *excellent* (10). We assessed perceived social support using three questions reported by Berkman and Syme (1979): (a) "How many close friends do you have?" (b) "How many relatives do you have that you feel close to?" and (c) "How often do you see these people each month?" Finally, we assessed trait sociability and trait shyness using Cheek and Buss's (1981) 11-item Shyness and Sociability Scale. We included these measures to demonstrate similarity among groups along individual difference dimensions that potentially affect social activity.

Table 25.1. List of 18 Potential Social Partners Used in the Card-Sort Task

Item	Description on card
1. A close friend of yours	
2. A recent acquaintance, with whom you seem to have nothing in common	
3. Your doctor	
4. A member of your immediate family	
5. A casual acquaintance of yours	
6. A person whom you know but dislike	
7. An attractive person whom you do not know	
8. A relative, not in your immediate family	
9. A recent acquaintance, with whom you seem to have much in common	
10. A sales representative	
11. A new neighbor	
12. The author of a book you've read	
13. Your sibling	
14. A poet or artist whose work you like	
15. A stranger about your age	
16. A clergy person (e.g., pastor, rabbi, or priest)	
17. A younger relative (e.g., niece, nephew, or cousin)	
18. A person running for a local political position	

Card-sort Tasks. Brief descriptions of 18 potential social partners were printed individually on 4×6 inch index cards. Examples include "a member of your immediate family," "a recent acquaintance with whom you seem to have much in common," and "a sales representative." Descriptions were general so that subjects of all ages could envision each social partner as someone with whom they might interact. For example, descriptions like "a younger relative" were used rather than "your grandchild" to provide consistent stimuli across ages. A complete list of potential social partners is presented in Table 25.1. In addition to the social partner card sort, we compiled two other sorts—one 5-item set of foods and one 18-item set of physical symptoms (adapted from Pennebaker, 1982)—to give subjects a brief example of and a parallel practice trail with the card-sort task.

Procedure

Subjects first provided informed consent and relevant personal information, including self-rated health and perceived social support. Subjects then completed the Shyness and Sociability Scale. Next, following the brief example of the card-sort task with food items, and the practice trail with physical

symptoms, subjects completed the social partner card sort. Verbal instructions
were as follows:

Now I'm going to ask you to do the same kind of sorting task with people instead
of symptoms. And, of course, there will again be many different ways you could
arrange the cards, but we're interested in what particular grouping of people makes
most sense to *you*. Now let me give you a little background to make this task easier
for you. All of these people described on these cards refer to people you know or to
people you might know. I'd like you to imagine that with each of these people, you
have the chance to sit down and talk with him or her—perhaps over coffee or a
snack—for half an hour or so. You will interact with each of these people in a *social*
manner, not a professional or business manner. (For example, one of the cards is
printed with *your doctor*, and for this card you should consider spending time socially
with your doctor, not seeing him or her on an office visit.)

Now, what I'd like you to do is to sort these cards into piles based on how similar
or alike you feel it would be for you to spend some time talking with these people—to
interact socially with them—for this short time. You should put people with whom
such interaction would be alike or similar into the same pile: For example, if you
think that spending time with your sister is very much like spending time with a close
friend, then you'd put those two cards in the same pile. Whereas, those who in some
way would be different for you to interact with should go into a different pile: For
example, a sales representative might go in a different pile than the sister and the
close friend. You can use as many or as few piles as you need to represent your
views—and it is okay to place a person in a pile all their own. Remember, what
we're interested in is your own view of these people as those whom you might interact
with socially, so there is no correct or incorrect sorting arrangement.

Subjects were handed the set of 18 cards in a predetermined random order.
Their task was to arrange the cards such that similar social partners were
sorted into same groups and dissimilar social partners were sorted into different groups. After the card-sort task, subjects were asked open-ended questions about which social partners described on the cards were most preferred,
and which, if any, they currently did not know well but would like to get to
know better.

Results and Discussion

Self-Rated Health, Social Traits, and Social Support

To provide a strong test of our hypotheses, we needed to limit differences
among groups to their cognitive consideration of the social partners represented in the card-sort task. First, we needed to demonstrate that the four
groups were well matched on measures of mental and physical health, per-

Table 25.2. Mean Ratings of Health, Social Traits, and Social Support by Group

Measure	Group			
	Teens	Middle-aged	Community elderly	Nursing home
		Self-rated health		
Mental				
M	6.75	8.00	7.89	7.42
SD	2.00	1.38	2.00	2.39
Physical				
M	7.10[a,b]	7.85[a]	8.11[a]	6.05[b]
SD	1.86	1.56	1.81	2.12
		Social trait		
Sociability				
M	24.90	25.20	25.17	24.58
SD	4.71	5.09	4.34	5.25
Shyness				
M	23.30[a]	20.00[a,b]	16.28[b]	18.47[a,b]
SD	5.13	6.26	7.36	6.15
		Perceived social support		
Close friends				
M	4.60[a]	5.05[a]	8.44[b]	3.80[a]
SD	3.10	2.06	6.53	2.91
Close relatives				
M	3.05	7.15	6.61	4.45
SD	1.90	8.46	6.42	2.72
Frequency of contact				
M	15.90[a]	8.43[b]	13.25[a,b]	5.52[b]
SD	12.30	8.07	11.38	7.12

NOTE: Means with different superscripts, within measures, are significantly different at $p < .05$.

sonality traits relevant to social behavior, and perceived social support. Mean responses by group on these measures are presented in Table 25.2. All post hoc multiple comparisons were computed with Tukey's method ($\alpha = .05$).

Health status. All subjects rated their mental health as better than the average person their age, and groups did not differ on this index, $F(3, 73) = 1.65$, *ns*. Although subjects also rated their physical health as better than average relative to peers, groups differed on this index, $F(3, 74) = 4.71$. $p<.01$. Post hoc pairwise comparisons indicated that the nursing home residents, on average, rated their physical health lower than the community elderly and the middle-aged samples but not significantly lower than the teen sample.

Social traits. Groups did not differ on levels of trait sociability, $F(3, 73)<1$, *ns*, but they did differ on levels of trait shyness, $F(3, 73) = 4.27$, p; $<.01$.

Post hoc pairwise comparisons indicated that teens, on average, rated themselves as shyer than the sample of community elderly. The shyness ratings of the three adult groups did not differ.

Perceived social support. Groups differed in their reported numbers of close friends, $F(3,74) = 5.01$. $p<.01$. Post hoc pairwise comparisons indicated that the community elderly sample reported more close friends than any other sample. The remaining groups did not differ on numbers of close friends they reported. Also, groups did not differ on the number of relatives to whom they felt close, $F(3, 74) = 2.34$, *ns.* Finally, groups differed on the frequencies they reported seeing close friends and relatives each month, $F(3, 74) = 4.40$, $p < .01$. Post hoc pairwise comparisons revealed that the teen sample reported more frequent contact than did the middle-aged and nursing home samples but not significantly more than the community elderly sample.

Overall, although some reliable group differences emerged, the four samples were well matched on the questionnaire assessments. The samples did not differ on self-rated mental health, trait sociability, or number of relatives they felt close to. The differences among the groups were not surprising: Nursing home residents rated themselves as less physically healthy, an expected finding given this relatively frail population; teens were more shy, a finding consistent with shyness research (Cheek, Carpentieri, Smith, Rierdan & Koff, 1986), and the community elderly reported more friends, a finding that probably reflects the recruiting source. It is important to note that the nursing home sample, although frail, did not differ greatly from the other samples: Like the other samples, they reported better than average physical health; they showed comparable levels of trait sociability and trait shyness; they did not differ from the middle-aged and teen samples in mean number of close friends, and they did not differ from the middle-aged or elderly community samples on how often they reported seeing close friends and relatives each month. In short, the questionnaire measures did not clearly distinguish among samples by age or residential status. As such, obvious differences in self-reported health, shyness, sociability, or perceived social support cannot adequately account for differences in the cognitive consideration of social partners.

Overview of Multidimensional Scaling

We recorded the groupings of potential social partners made by each of the 80 subjects as 0–1 incidence matrices, in which 1 indicated that two items had been placed in the same pile (see Rudy & Merluzzi, 1984). We then summed these similarity matrices across the 20 subjects of each group to produce four similarity matrices (i.e., teen, middle-aged, community elderly, and nursing home matrices). Finally, we analyzed these four matrices using three-way multidimensional scaling (MDS). MDS models arrange stimuli in multidimensional space according to perceived similarity so that stimuli that are frequently grouped as similar to one another are proximate, whereas stimuli frequently grouped as different from one another are distant. Once the MDS procedure achieves a stable representation of the data, investigators interpret the dimensions that define the multidimensional space. Three-way MDS models have the added capability of analyzing group or individual differences. Group differences are represented with weights for each group on each dimension of a multidimensional configuration that is common to all subjects.

Scaling Results

Overall stimulus configuration. First, we analyzed the similarity matrices for the four groups with the SINDSCAL algorithm of three-way MDS (Carroll & Wish, 1974), yielding the common three-dimensional configuration represented in Figures 25.1 and 25.2. This solution accounted for 77% of the variance in the similarity data and was considered appropriate because no interpretable relationships resulted from the addition of more dimensions to the solution. In addition, we found no substantive sex differences in card-sort responses.

Dimension 1 is clearly the primary dimension in this scaling solution: It accounted for 46% of the variance in the similarity data. Figures 25.1 and 25.2 each represent Dimension 1 on their horizontal axes. Family members and the close friend cluster to the right in both representations of the stimulus configuration. These social partners shared positive values on Dimension 1 with the poet or artist, the author, and the "acquaintance with whom you seem to have much in common." By contrast, social partners with negative values on Dimension 1 included the "acquaintance with whom you seem to have nothing in common," the disliked person, the sales representative, and the stranger. This pattern of proximities led us to interpret Dimension 1 as *anticipated affect*: It distinguished positive from negative affect in the anticipated social interaction. Dimension 1 cannot simply be an index of familiarity because the presumably unfamiliar poet or artist and author were perceived as similar to the more familiar friends and family. The comment

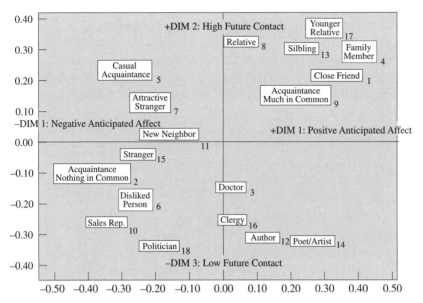

Figure 25.1. Stimulus configuration derived by SINDSCAL for potential social partners for Dimensions 1 and 2. (Subscripts refer to the item numbers of verbatim descriptions presented in Table 25.1)

of 1 elderly subject aided our interpretation of Dimension 1: "I always enjoy meeting famous people."

Dimension 2, represented on the vertical axis of Figure 25.1, accounted for 18% of the variance. Potential social partners with positive values on Dimension 2 included all family members and relatives, as well as the close friend, the much-in-common acquaintance, the casual acquaintance, and the attractive stranger. By contrast, those with negative values on Dimension 2 included the poet or artist, the author, the clergy person, the local politician, and the disliked person. At first glance, Dimension 2 seems to represent degree of formality, particularly because all social partners with occupational titles have low values. Yet, considering that the disliked person and the nothing-in-common acquaintance shared low values with those in occupational roles, the more relevant concept is social distance, rather than role-defined formality per se. In practical terms, social distance translates into low probability of future contact or involvement. So, we interpreted Dimension 2 as the likelihood of subsequent interaction and labeled it *future contact*.

Dimension 3, represented on the vertical axis of Figure 25.2, accounted

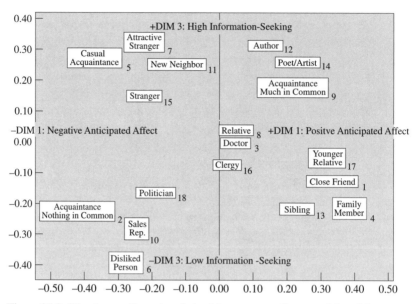

Figure 25.2. Stimulus configuration derived by SINDSCAL for potential social partners for Dimensions 1 and 3. (Subscripts refer to the item numbers of verbatim descriptions presented in Table 25.1.)

for 14% of the variance. Potential social partners with positive values on Dimension 3 included the author, the poet or artist, the new neighbor, the attractive stranger, the much-in-common acquaintance, the casual acquaintance, and the stranger. Those with negative values were a seemingly odd assortment, including family members, the close friend, the disliked person, the sales representative, and the nothing-in-common acquaintance. We interpreted this third dimension as *information seeking*: It represents the degree to which subjects would seek out additional information about the social partners in order to get acquainted. It makes sense that quite familiar social partners (e.g., close friends and family) as well as those individuals clearly not worthwhile (e.g., disliked person and sales representative) would not be queried in the getting-acquainted process to the same degree as novel individuals who are genuinely compelling.

Group Differences. To represent differences among groups, three-way MDS yielded weights for the four groups on the dimensions uncovered in the common stimulus configuration. Weights indicate the salience (or importance) of the three dimensions to each group of subjects and are used to gain insight into each group's distinct cognitive representation of the potential social partners. Figure 25.3 represents the dimension weights for each group. High-dimension weights indicate that the associated dimension is more important to a group, whereas low-dimension weights indicate that a dimension is less important to a group.

The pattern of dimension weights suggests that anticipated affect (Dimension 1, illustrated on the horizontal axes of Figure 25.3) becomes increasingly important with age and infirmity. In particular, nursing home residents tended to consider potential social partners almost exclusively on the basis of anticipated affect, with little regard for possibilities of future contact or information seeking. The importance of future contact (Dimension 2, represented on the vertical axis of Figure 25.3, top) declined with age and infirmity: It was most important to the teen sample and least important to the nursing home sample. This pattern reasonably reflected the ages and life circumstances of the four groups. Finally, information seeking in effort to get acquainted (Dimension 3, represented on the vertical axis of Figure 25.3, bottom) was most important to the middle-aged sample, followed in order by the community elderly and teen samples. The nursing home sample showed almost no interest in information seeking.

The weights represented in Figure 25.3 can be applied to the coordinates of the overall stimulus configuration represented in Figures 25.1 and 25.2 to obtain configurations unique to each group. The scaling solution for the nursing home sample, for example, would be distributed along Dimension 1 in an elliptical fashion. In other words, older, institutionalized subjects judged the potential social partners primarily on the basis of anticipated affect, with little regard for differences in future contact or information seeking.

Verification of Dimension Interpretation

Three-way MDS produces unique dimensions, leaving only the interpretation of those dimensions a task for the investigators. To provide consensual validity for the subjective interpretation of the three scaling dimensions, we asked 111 student raters to evaluate each of the 18 potential social partners on three bipolar scales that directly corresponded to the interpretation of the three-dimensional scaling solution represented in Figures 25.1 and 25.2. Raters were blind to the authors' a priori interpretations of the dimensions that distinguished among the social partners.

On the first bipolar scale (Anticipated Affect), raters indicated how positively they would feel about interacting socially with each potential social partner. On the second bipolar scale (Future Contact), raters judged how

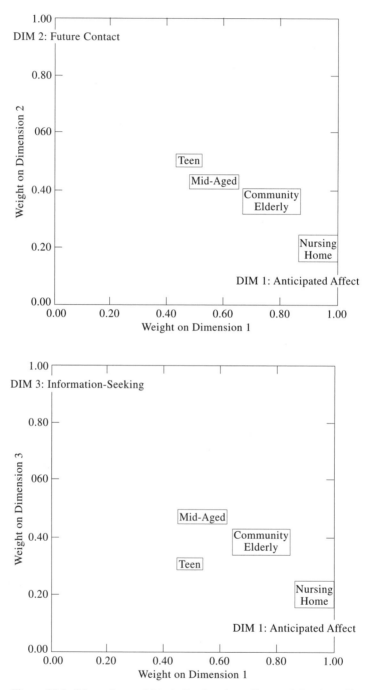

Figure 25.3. Dimension weights indicating the salience of the three dimensions for separate groups. (Top: Weights for Dimensions 1 and 2. Bottom: Weights for Dimensions 1 and 3.)

Table 25.3. Multiple Regression of Bipolar Scale Ratings on Dimensions of Social Partner Scaling Solution

Rating scale	Regression weights (direction cosines): Dimension			R
	1	2	3	
Anticipated Affect	.822	.387	.416	.912*
Future Contact	.464	.884	.047	.940*
Information Seeking	.260	.065	.963	.849*

NOTE: Direction cosines are regression coefficients that have been normalized so that their sum of squares equals 1.00 for every scale.
  $*p < .001$.

likely subsequent interaction with each potential social partner would be. Finally, on the third bipolar scale (Information Seeking), raters indicated the degree to which they might actively seek information about each potential social partner to get acquainted. All ratings were made on 7-point scales.

We averaged the ratings of each potential social partner on each scale over raters. Using multiple linear regression, we then regressed these mean ratings over the potential social partners' coordinates on the three-dimensional MDS solution. The results of this multiple regression are shown in Table 25.3.

Two conditions should be met for a rating scale to provide a good interpretation of a scaling dimension (Kruskal & Wish, 1978): First, the multiple correlation for the rating scale must be significant at $p < .01$, and second, the rating scale must have a high regression weight on that and only that dimension. Our results satisfied both conditions. The last column of Table 25.3 indicates that the multiple correlations of all three bipolar scales were significant at .001, indicating that the mean ratings of each scale were well predicted by the coordinates of the MDS configuration. The optimum dimension weights corresponding to each multiple correlation are shown in the first three columns of Table 25.3. The pattern of these weights strongly confirms the a priori dimension labels: Dimension 1 is best fit by the Anticipated Affect scale; Dimension 2 is best fit by the Future Contact scale; and Dimension 3 is best fit by the Information-Seeking scale.

Results of this validation procedure indicated that the organization of potential social partners uncovered in the scaling analysis can be conceptualized in terms of anticipated affect, future contact, and degree of information seeking. In turn, these findings support our interpretation of group differences in the relative importance of these three dimensions in the cognitive consideration of potential social partners.

Partner Preferences

Selectivity theory predicts that older people will favor familiar social partners and that young and middle-aged people will more often interact with novel partners. Exploring these ideas, we asked our card-sort subjects some final questions regarding their partner preferences. First, we asked them which individuals (among those described on the cards) they would most like to spend their social time with. We divided subject responses into two categories: "familiar partners only" and "novel partners included." Groups differed significantly in their partner preferences, $\chi^2(3, N = 79) = 19.74$, $p<.001$: The majority of the teen sample (75%), half the middle-aged, and half the community elderly samples (i.e., 50% each) included novel social partners among those most preferred; in contrast, only 5% of the nursing home residents favored a novel social partner.

Finally, we asked subjects whether any of the descriptions printed on the cards represented people whom they did not know well but whom they would like to get to know better. Again, groups differed significantly in their responses, $\chi^2(3, N = 75) = 24.88$, $p<.001$: The majority of each age group except the nursing home sample nominated social partners they wanted to get to know better (teen sample, 95%; middle-aged sample, 100%; community elderly, 81%; nursing home sample, 42%). These findings underscore the pattern of increasing social conservation with age and infirmity.

In sum, the card-sort method and MDS analyses of Study 1 uncovered naturally occurring dimensions that organize people's consideration of their potential social partners. The results demonstrate that people at different points in the life cycle differ in their cognitive appraisal of potential social partners. Compared with their younger counterparts, elderly individuals, particularly nursing home residents, give more importance to the affect anticipated in the interaction than to possibilities for future contact or information seeking. This finding is consistent with the predictions of selectivity theory: If emotion conservation is a primary goal, then anticipation of positive versus negative experience in a potential interaction is a necessary precursor to choosing optimal social partners. Also consistent with selectivity theory, we found that nursing home residents showed a strong preference for familiar over novel social partners.

STUDY 2

Yet, what is it about age that makes interaction with novel social partners less compelling? Old age places implicit limits on opportunities for future involvement. That is, place in the life cycle can represent a type of social ending. Intuitively, anticipated endings may be more a function of nearness to death than to chronological age per se. The differences we obtained between our two age-matched elderly samples support this contention; given the fragility of nursing home residents, one could assume that their life expectancy is lower than their community-dwelling peers. Moreover, "the belief that a nursing home is one's final home" (Gubrium, 1975, p. 84) may heighten age-related partner selectivity among nursing home residents. That is, older adults may view the nursing home itself as a symbol of inevitable social endings (see also Rowles, 1979, and Tobin & Lieberman, 1976, for discussions of the meaning of place in late life). We argue that individuals facing social endings may respond cognitively by favoring familiar over novel social partners, which functions to maximize pleasurable social contact in the short run. Yet, unlike the "symbolic preparation for death" discussed by disengagement theorists, we propose that social endings instigate affect regulation via partner selectivity, not affect flattening or unilateral social withdrawal.

Moreover, we do not conceptualize the cognitive responses to anticipated social endings as necessarily caused by, or specific to, age or impending death. Rather, we believe that people at other points of the life cycle will also respond to situations characterized by social endings in much the same way that the elderly respond to their life circumstances. For example, a young college graduate heading for volunteer work in Africa or a single scholar facing the academic job market might also show a preference for familiar over novel social partners. When social endings are salient, individuals may recognize they do not have limitless time in which to develop new social relationships. This awareness, in turn, can trigger partner selectivity; that is, people facing endings may prefer to spend social time with members of their family and longtime friends rather than with new acquaintances. Alternatively, when anticipated endings are not an issue, individuals will more frequently choose novel social partners (e.g., new acquaintances or attractive strangers) perhaps because of compelling possibilities for future involvement.

Although Study 1 illuminated differences in judgments of social partners associated with age and infirmity, several questions arose that prompted further investigation. First, compared with their younger counterparts, do most older people more frequently choose familiar over novel social partners? If so, this would confirm that partner selectivity is indeed related to (but not necessarily *caused by*) age. Second, can we alter the circumstances of younger people so that their social choices pattern those of older people? If we can manipulate the partner preferences of the young by introducing anticipated endings, this would suggest that partner selectivity in the face of social endings is a general phenomenon not unique to age or nearness to death. In Study 2, we explored these ideas in a within-subject design: We asked people across a wide age range to choose their preferred social partners under unspecified and ending conditions.

Method

Subjects

Volunteer subjects were 380 community residents in the San Francisco and Los Angeles areas surveyed by telephone. Telephone numbers were drawn from randomly selected blocks of the alphabet in community telephone directories. Within these blocks a random position on the directory page was identified, and each household in that position on every page was called. A female interviewer greeted individuals who answered the telephone and asked if they could spare a few minutes to answer a few simple questions about how they might spend their leisure time; 70% of those called consented to this request. Subjects ranged in age from 11 to 92 years and were 234 women (mean age = 48.9, SD = 18.2) and 146 men (mean age = 46.6, SD = 18.9).

Procedure

The interviewer first recorded the subject's sex and age, then posed the *unspecified* partner-choice question of Condition 1:

Imagine that you have half an hour of free time, with no pressing commitments. You have decided that you'd like to spend this time with another person. Assuming that the following three people are available to you, which person would you choose to spend that time with?

Social partner options included one familiar social partner ("a member of your immediate family") and two novel social partners ("a recent acquaintance, with whom you seem to have much in common" and "the author of a book you've read''). Order of partner options was varied. We selected these social partners from those in Study 1 with positive affective valences (i.e., high values on Dimension 1) so that each could reasonably be viewed as a desirable partner. After subjects reported their choices, the interviewer posed the *ending* partner-choice question of Condition 2:

Now imagine this new situation: In just a few weeks, you plan to move across the country—by yourself. No members of your family or current social circle will be accompanying you on this cross-country move. Although you are preparing for your big departure, you find that you have half an hour of free time, with no pressing commitments. You have decided that you would like to spend this time with another person. Assuming that the following three people are available to you, which person would you choose to spend that time with?

The social partner options in Condition 2 were the same as in Condition 1, although items were presented in a different random order and varied across subjects. The frame of geographic relocation was not intended to be a strict analogy of old age. Rather, it represents a logically distinct example of a social ending.

Results and Discussion

Because we found no significant sex differences in subject responses, all analyses reported here reflect responses of both sexes combined. We initially screened the data in 5-year cohorts (e.g., under 25, 25–29, 30–34, etc.) and subsequently collapsed them into larger age groupings that preserved clear age-related trends. This screening procedure ultimately resulted in three age groups: young (mean age = 23.2; range = 11–29), middle-aged (mean age = 45.7; range = 30–64), and old (mean age = 72.0; range = 65–92). Sample sizes are presented in Table 25.4.

Age Differences in Partner Choice

As hypothesized, in Condition 1—in which subjects chose a social partner without any modifying conditions—age groups differed in their social partner choices, test-of-association $\chi^2(2, N = 380) = 21.25$, $p<.001$. Table 25.4 lists partner preferences by age group. Only 35% of young subjects chose familiar social partners, an amount no greater than expected by chance selection among the three alternatives, goodness-of-fit $\chi^2(1, N = 75) = 0.06$, *ns*. In contrast, 65% of old subjects chose familiar social partners, significantly more

Table 25.4. Cross-Tabulation of Age Group by Social Partner Choice in Condition 1

| | Social partner choice | | | | | |
| | Familiar | | Novel | | Total | |
Age	%	n	%	n	%	n
Young	35	26	65	49	20	75
Middle-aged	64	132	36	76	55	208
Old	65	63	35	34	25	97
Total	58	221	42	159	100	380

NOTE: Test-of-association $\chi^2(2, N = 380) = 21.25, p < .001$.

than expected by chance, goodness-of-fit χ^2 (1, $N = 97$) = 43.63, $p<.001$. These results are consistent with the age-related differences put forth in selectivity theory.

One initially puzzling finding in Table 25.4 is that the social partner choices of the middle-aged group were nearly identical to those of the old group. Given the relatively young age of this cohort, anticipated social endings do not potently explain their social preferences. An alternative explanation of the middle-aged social choices might lie in immediate-family commitments. That is, people with young families may prefer familiar over novel social partners simply because time constraints dictate frugal allocation of their social energy.

To explore this idea, a subset of the sample ($n = 211$) was asked whether they were caretakers of children living in their home. Not surprisingly, the

Table 25.5. Cross-Tabulation of Social Partner Choices in Condition 1 for Middle-Aged Subjects with and without Children

| | Social partner choice | | | | | |
| | Familiar | | Novel | | Total | |
Family status	%	n	%	n	%	n
No children	42	27	58	37	53	64
Children	79	45	21	12	47	57
Total	60	72	40	49	100	121

NOTE: Test-of-association $\chi^2(1, N = 121) = 15.42, p < .001$.

vast majority responding positively were in the middle-aged group (83%, compared with 12% of the young group and only 6% of the old group). The relationship of family status to partner preference was revealing (see Table 25.5): Having children in the home accounted for the partner choices of the middle-aged sample, test-of-association χ^2 (1, $N = 121$) = 15.42, $p<.001$. That is, among middle-aged subjects' responses to Condition 1, 79% of those who had children chose familiar social partners, significantly more than expected by chance, goodness-of-fit χ^2 (1, $N = 57$) = 53.37, $p<.001$. By contrast, only 42% of those without children selected familiar social partners, not significantly more than expected by chance, goodness-of-fit χ^2 (1, $N = 64$) = 2.26, ns. Figure 25.4 shows a clearer view of partner preferences delineated by age and family status. In general, people in their 30s and older preferred familiar over novel social partners; yet, only people in their 50s

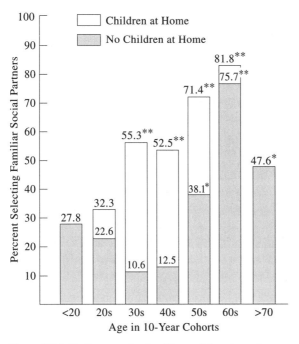

Figure 25.4. Preferences for familiar social partners by age in 10-year cohorts. (Percentages of each cohort without children at home are indicated by darker bars. Asterisks indicate that choice of the familiar social partner is more frequent than expected by chance selection alone: *$p<.05$ and **$p<.10$.)

and older showed a preference for familiar partners beyond that associated with home-dwelling children. In sum, the middle-aged people *without* children acted like the young sample, whereas the middle-aged people *with* children acted like the old sample. The presence of children, however, cannot account for the social partner preferences of the old group.

Responses to Anticipated Social Endings

Can the social circumstances of younger people be manipulated to induce social decisions characteristic of older people? We expected the geographic relocation scenario to make the young group favor familiar social partners, as the old group did under general circumstances. The results presented in Table 25.6 support our hypothesis. Recall that under unspecified conditions (Condition 1), only 35% of the young subjects chose familiar social partners (no more than chance). In contrast, under conditions characterized by social endings (Condition 2), a full 80% of the young subjects chose familiar social partners. This within-subject difference, from 35% to 80%, is significant, χ^2 $(1, N = 75) = 26.27$, $p<.001$ (refer to Glass & Hopkins, 1984, p. 291, on chi-square statistics for paired observations). Although the majorities of both the middle-aged and old groups already preferred familiar social partners, the minorities that did not also exhibited significant increases toward partner selectivity in Condition 2, χ^2 $(1, N = 208) = 47.51$ and χ^2 $(1, N = 97) = 10.52$, respectively. This shows that the heightened salience of anticipated endings inherent in geographic relocation can be influential at any age.

In sum, Study 2 supported our two hypotheses: First, under unspecified circumstances, middle-aged and older people choose familiar social partners more frequently than do younger people. More important, the introduction

Table 25.6. *Cross-Tabulation of Social Partner Choices in Conditions 1 and 2 for Young Subjects*

	Condition 2					
	Familiar		Novel		Total	
Condition 1	%	n	%	n	%	n
Familiar	81	21	19	5	35	26
Novel	80	39	20	10	65	49
Total	80	60	20	15	100	75

NOTE: $\chi^2(1, N = 75) = 26.27$, $p < .001$.

of anticipated social endings induces younger people to mimic the social choices of older people. This supports the notion that social endings comprise a general phenomenon, one that can explain, in part, the increased selectivity in partner choice evidenced by people aware of upcoming social endings.

DISCUSSION

The first study uncovered three dimensions used to discriminate among potential social partners at the cognitive level. The dimension that accounted for most of the variance in subject responses distinguished positive from negative affect in the anticipated social interaction. Other dimensions distinguished among varying possibilities for future interaction and the degree of information seeking likely to transpire. Consistent with selectivity theory, groups differed in the relative importance they placed on these three dimensions: (a) Nursing home residents placed most importance on anticipated affect, followed in order by the community elderly, the middle-aged, and finally, the teens; (b) teens held future contacts as most important, followed in order by the middle-aged, the community elderly, and then the nursing home residents; finally, (c) the middle-aged group was most invested in information seeking to get acquainted, followed in order by the community elderly, the teens, and finally, the nursing home residents. We contend that differences in the cognitive appraisal of potential social partners reflect differences in the social experience and social goals of the different groups. Whereas younger people are most interested in the future prospects of the relationship and opportunities for gaining knowledge, older people, particularly those living in nursing homes, are primarily concerned with the immediate affective rewards and costs of interaction. The finding that nursing home residents do not prefer or seek out novel partners provides clear evidence for this contention.

Old age is not a uniform experience across individuals. Some octogenarians, for example, enjoy relatively good health and are active community members, whereas others are more disabled; still others are confined to long-term-care facilities. We do not claim to have disentangled the effects of age per se, from those of health, disability, or both, particularly because the self-ratings of health that we collected may have underestimated actual health differences among our samples. Moreover, in addition to their being infirm, institutionalized elderly—because they are living in their ''last home''—may conceive social endings as more salient than our community groups. We suggest that such salience also contributes to the high degree of partner selectivity evidenced by our nursing home sample. Future research of this kind would best incorporate more objective measures of physical health and of anticipated social endings to distinguish effects of age from those of disability and perceived limitations of the future. Despite these limitations, this study demonstrates that partner selectivity is evident to some degree in two very different samples of old people, thereby providing support that this phenomenon is indeed associated with age-related factors.

The second study confirmed two hypotheses regarding social partner selection. First, it showed that older people more often choose familiar social partners than do younger people. However, as the post hoc analysis of the effect of having children living at home suggests, factors other than age are also associated with partner selectivity. Second, Study 2 demonstrated that selectivity in partner choice can be manipulated by increasing the salience of social endings. This pattern of results suggests that the social behavior characteristic of the elderly— that is, diminished interest in "fringe" social interaction, coupled with great investment in family—may not be a response unique to age, physical health, or nearness to death but instead may reflect normal self-regulatory responses to constraints in current and expected social circumstances.

We realize that the partner options of Study 2 confounded familial ties with familiarity. As such, we cannot dismiss the possibility that our youngest subjects prefer novel partners because they seek to individuate themselves from their kin. That is, except under unusual circumstances, such as moving away, families may be of low social priority to adolescents and young adults. By contrast, families may assume top social priority for middle-aged and older adults. This alternative way of considering the data suggests unique social priorities associated with youth rather than old age. Yet the proposition that teens consider family members as less desirable social partners is not consistent with the results of Study 1: Teens in that study anticipated positive affect in interactions with family members much as middle-aged adults did. Additional research that differentiates familiar and familial social relationships is necessary to test directly alternative explanations for the pattern of partner choices that we found.

In both studies, the potential for affective gain played a dominant role in older people's selection of social partners. When anticipated affect was either negative or absent, elderly subjects regularly found the prospective social partner to be less appealing. Although affect was also important to our younger subjects, future prospects and information gain also played central roles in their selection processes. Our youngest subjects were predominantly interested in novelty even when negative affect was probable. In illustration, in Study 1, when subjects were asked which of the social partners they would most like to get to know better, 1 adolescent responded: "The people I dislike—I would like to find out what it is about them I dislike." This decision implies foregoing positive affect in favor of information gain. Such affective risk taking was plainly absent among our older subjects, especially the nursing home residents who were, in all likelihood, closest to the end of their lives. The comment of 1 nursing home resident was typical: "I don't have time for any of those [other] people. When I get a few moments to myself, I want to rest." This statement well conveys the proactive conservation that distinguishes selectivity theory from activity theory. The essential difference between selectivity theory and disengagement theory is that selectivity predicts that affective gain from interaction is *more*, not *less*, salient among older people compared with their younger counterparts. Our results indicate that it is precisely within the affective domain that older people evaluate and choose their social partners.

These findings are not compatible with models of social aging based on the tacit assumption that old and young people are psychologically equivalent and that declining rates of social interaction simply reflect limited access to social partners. Rather, we see evidence for developmental changes in socioemotional aging, changes that indeed play a role in the reduction of social interaction. This is not to say that social activity is unimportant in old age. Instead, our findings underscore the fact that social activity is not a monolithic construct and further, that social partners are not uniformly compelling.

Finally, we want to acknowledge that additional age-related factors, factors unrelated to ontogenetic change per se, also influence interaction patterns. Ageist attitudes reflected in some people's behavior, for example, might also influence older people's partner preferences. Such issues clearly deserve further research attention.

When differences between old and young have been observed, the behavior of the old is often assumed to reflect decrement that begs for remediation. We do not intend to minimize the importance of social and physical barriers to social interaction. Rather, we aim to expand our focus to include age-related psychological change at the level of the individual. The old may be more selective in choosing their social partners in an effort to regulate emotion and conserve physical energy. Perhaps also their lifelong accumulation of social experiences have taught them to be better judges of rewarding social relationships. Additionally, perhaps the realization that time is a limited personal resource fundamentally changes older people's social priorities. Presently, little empirical research has been directed toward normative intraindividual change that may contribute to reduced social interaction in late life. As we face a rapidly aging population, it is more essential than ever to understand the meaning and the mechanisms responsible for these reductions. Such investigations will not only inform us about old age but will allow us to know when and how best to intervene.

REFERENCES

Antonucci, T. & Jackson, J. (1987). Social support, interpersonal efficacy, and health: A life course perspective. In L. L. Carstensen & B. A. Edelstein (Eds.), Handbook of clinical gerontology (pp. 291–311). New York: Pergamon Press.

Baltes, M. M. (1986, November). Selective optimization with compensation: The dynamics between independence and dependence. Paper presented at the annual meeting of the Gerontological Society of America, Chicago.

Baltes, M. M. & Schmid, U. (1987). Psychological gerontology. The German Journal of Psychology, 11, 87–123.

Baltes, P. B. (1987). Theoretical propositions of life-span developmental psychology: On the dynamics between growth and decline. Developmental Psychology, 23, 611–626.

Baltes, P. B., Dittman-Kohli, F. & Dixon, R. A. (1984). New perspectives on the development of intelligence in adulthood: Toward a dual-process conception and a model of selective optimization with compensation. In P. B. Baltes & O. G. Brim, Jr. (Eds.), Life-span development and behavior (Vol. 6, pp. 33–76). New York: Academic Press.

Berkman, L. & Syme, S. L. (1979). Social networks, host resistance and mortality: A nine year follow-up study of Alameda County residents. American Journal of Epidemiology, 109, 186–204.

Blackman, D. K., Howe, M. & Pinkston, E. M. (1976). Increasing participation in social interaction of the institutionalized elderly. The Gerontologist, 16, 69–76.

Campos, J. J. & Barrett, K. C. (1984). Toward a new understanding of emotions and their development. In C. E. Izard, J. Kagan, & R. B. Zajonc (Eds.), Emotions, cognition, and behavior (pp. 229–263). Cambridge: Cambridge University Press.

Carroll, J. D. & Wish, M. (1974). Models and methods for three-way multidimensional scaling. In R. C. Atkinson, D. H. Krantz, R. D. Luce & P. Suppes (Eds.), Contemporary developments in mathematical psychology (Vol. 2, pp. 57–105). San Francisco: Freeman.

Carstensen, L. L. (1986). Social support among the elderly: Limitations of behavioral interventions. The Behavior Therapist, 6, 111–113.

Carstensen, L. L. (1987). Age-related changes in social activity. In L. L. Carstensen & B. A. Edelstein (Eds.), Handbook of clinical gerontology (pp. 222–237). New York: Pergamon Press.

Carstensen, L. L. (1989, November). A longitudinal analysis of social and emotional dimensions of interpersonal relationships. *Paper presented at the annual meeting of the Gerontological Society of America, Minneapolis, MN.*

Carstensen, L. L. & Erickson, R. E. (1986). *Enhancing the social environments of elderly nursing home residents: Are high rates of interactions enough?* Journal of Applied Behavior Analysis, 19, *349–355.*

Cheek, J. M. & Buss, A. H. (1981). *Shyness and sociability.* Journal of Personality and Social Psychology, 41, *330–339.*

Cheek, J. M. Carpentieri, A. M. Smith, T. G., Rierdan, J. & Koff, E. (1986). *Adolescent shyness. In W. H. Jones, J. M. Cheek, & S. R. Briggs (Eds.),* Shyness: Perspectives on research and treatment *(pp. 105–115). New York: Plenum Press.*

Cumming, E. & Henry, W. H. (1961). Growing old: The process of disengagement. *New York: Basic Books.*

Duckitt, J. H. (1982). *Social interaction and psychological well-being: A study of elderly persons living in the inner-city area of Pretoria.* Humanitas: Journal for Research in the Human Sciences, 8, *121–129.*

Duckitt, J. H. (1983). *Predictors of subjective well-being in later life: An empirical assessment of theoretical frameworks in social gerontology.* Humanitas: Journal for Research in the Human Sciences, 9, *211–219.*

Erikson, E. H., Erikson, J. M. & Kivnick, H. Q. (1986). Vital involvement in old age: The experience of old age in our time. *New York: Norton.*

Field, D. & Minkler, M. (1988). *Continuity and change in social support between young-old, old-old, and very-old adults.* Journal of Gerontology, 43, *P100–P106.*

Glass, G. V. & Hopkins, K. D. (1984). Statistical methods in education and psychology *(2nd ed.). Englewood Cliffs, NJ: Prentice-Hall.*

Gordon, C. & Gaitz, C. M. (1976). *Leisure and lives. In R. Binstock & E. Shanas (Eds.),* Handbook of aging and the social sciences *(pp. 310–341). New York: Van Nostrand Reinhold.*

Gubrium, J. F. (1975). Living and dying at Murrey Manor. *New York: St. Martin's Press.*

Klein, R. L. (1972). *Age, sex and task difficulty as predictors of social conformity.* Journal of Gerontology, 27, *229–236.*

Konarski, E. Q., Johnson, M. R. & Whitman, T. L. (1980). *A systematic investigation of resident participation in a nursing home's activities program.* Journal of Behavior Therapy and Experimental Psychiatry, 11, *249–257.*

Kruskal, J. B. & Wish, M. (1978). Multidimensional scaling *(Sage University Paper series on Quantitative Applications in the Social Sciences, Series No. 07-011). Beverly Hills, CA: Sage.*

Lawton, M. P. (1987). *Environment and the need satisfaction of the aging. In L. L. Carstensen & B. A. Edelstein (Eds.),* Handbook of clinical gerontology *(pp. 33–40). New York: Pergamon Press.*

Lawton, M. P. & Nahemow, L. (1973). *Ecology and the aging process. In C. Eisdorfer & M. P. Lawton (Eds.),* Psychology of adult development and aging *(pp. 619–674). Washington, DC: American Psychological Association.*

Lowenthal, M. & Haven, C. (1968). *Interaction and adaption: Intimacy as a critical variable. In B. L. Neugarten (Ed.),* Middle age and aging: A reader in social psychology *(pp. 390–400). Chicago: University of Chicago Press.*

Maddox, G. L. (1963). Activity and morale: A longitudinal study of selected elderly subjects. Social Forces, 42, 195–204.

Malatesta, C. Z. (1981). Affective development over the lifespan: Involution or growth? Merrill-Palmer Quarterly, 27, 145–173.

Palmore, E. (1981). Social patterns in normal aging: Findings from the Duke Longitudinal Study. Durham, NC: Duke University Press.

Pennebaker, J. W. (1982). The psychology of physical symptoms. New York: Springer-Verlag.

Quattrochi-Tubin, S. & Jason, L. A. (1980). Enhancing social interactions and activity among the elderly through stimulus control. Journal of Applied Behavior Analysis, 13, 159–169.

Rowles, G. D. (1979). The last new home: Facilitating the older person's adjustment to institutional space. In S. M. Golant (Ed.), Location and environment of the elderly population (pp. 81–94). New York: Wiley.

Rudy, T. E. & Merluzzi, T. V. (1984). Recovering social-cognitive schemata: Descriptions and applications of multidimensional scaling for clinical research. Advances in Cognitive-Behavioral Research and Therapy, 3, 61–102.

Scherer, K. R. (1982). The assessment of vocal expression in infants and children. In C. E. Izard (Ed.), Measuring emotions in infants and children (pp. 127–163). Cambridge: Cambridge University Press.

Shepard, R. N. (1974). Representation of structure in similarity data: Problems and prospects. Psychometrika, 39, 373–421.

Stern, D. N. (1985). The interpersonal world of the infant. New York: Basic Books.

Stone, R. (1986, September 30). Aging in the eighties, age 65 years and over—Use of community services. Advance data from vital and health statistics of the National Center for Health Statistics (PHS No. 124). Washington, DC: U.S. Department of Health and Human Services, Public Health Service.

Tobin, S. S. & Lieberman, M. A. (1976). Last home for the aged. San Francisco: Jossey-Bass.

Tronick, E. Z. (Ed.). (1982). Social interchange in infancy: Affect, cognition, and communication. Baltimore, MD: University Park Press.

Youmans, E. (1962). Leisure time activities of older persons in selected rural and urban areas of Kentucky (Progress Report 115). Lexington, KY: Kentucky Agricultural Experiment Station.

26. Attitudes Toward Old People in an Older Sample

Nathan Kogan

I N A RECENT PAPER (Kogan, 1961), the present author described the development of a scale measuring attitudes toward old people (OP scale). For college samples, a positively and a negatively worded version of the OP scale were significantly correlated in the content direction, and scale reliabilities were generally satisfactory. In addition, significant relationships that could not be attributed to response set effects were found between OP scale scores and other attitudinal and personality variables.

This paper reports results obtained from the administration of the OP scale to a sample of apparently healthy older adults of better-than-average intelligence and education. With college students' responses serving as "baseline" data, OP scale characteristics are examined in the older sample with particular reference to the favorability and variability of the attitude, the internal consistency of the scales, the logical consistency in response to positively and negatively worded versions of the scales, and direction and magnitude of relations with other attitudinal variables.

Specific predictions of differences between the younger and older samples were derived from two general assumptions. First, it was assumed that older people in American society have many of the qualities of a minority group, a point that has been stressed by a number of investigators (Barron, 1953; Drake, 1958; Linden, 1957a, 1957b). If Lewin's (1945) concept of "self-hatred" is applied in the present case, the empirical consequences might well take the form of a greater polarization in the attitude; older people would be more likely than younger respondents to be found at either extreme regarding the issue. Hence, older adults should manifest greater inter-individual variability. Second, it was assumed that there would be a greater "ego involvement" on the part of older people in the content of the OP scale items. As a member of a group that comprised the object of the attitude under study, an older person might be expected to take a closer, more considered look at each OP item than would a younger one. Accordingly, we should expect

From *Journal of Abnormal and Social Psychology* 62, no. 3 (1961): 616–22.

older subjects to exhibit somewhat greater logical consistency in responding to matched positive and negative OP items.

No hypotheses were formulated with respect to differences between younger and older subjects in the favorability level of attitudes toward old people. If older individuals exhibit considerable variability in the extent of acceptance-disparagement of old people as a group, it is difficult to predict whether older subjects should be more or less biased than younger subjects.

Similarly, no hypotheses are advanced respecting the magnitude of relations between OP scale responses and responses to other attitudinal content in the older and younger samples. It will first be necessary to examine the extent to which stylistic response tendencies can account for relations between the variables.

METHOD

Subjects

Older subjects (89 males and 115 females) were obtained from the Age Center of New England, Inc., a nonprofit gerontological research organization in Boston, Massachusetts. These subjects were volunteers, noninstitutionalized, and in apparently good health, whose membership in the organization involved a commitment to participate in a variety of research studies. Chronological ages of the subjects ranged from 54 to 92 for the males, with a mean of 70.8 (SD = 7.3), and from 49 to 86 for the females, with a mean of 69.4 (SD = 7.9).

Approximately 70% of the older subjects held or are now holding professional or managerial positions; most of the remaining 30 % belong to the clerical or skilled craftsman occupational groups. The mean educational level in the sample was 13.7 (SD = 2.8) and 12.9 (SD = 3.1) years of school for males and females, respectively. *Current Population Reports* (Bureau of the Census, 1960), citing years of school completed for the civilian population of the United States in March 1959, reports a median figure of 8.7 for males 55–64 years and 8.2 for males 65 years and over. The corresponding figures for females of those ages are 8.9 and 8.4 years of school, respectively. By contrast, median school years completed is 12.4 for both males and females in the 20–24 age group. Hence, the educational level of the older subjects could well be considered superior to a contemporary college student group. This inference is further supported by intelligence data available on a random subsample of 52 males and 73 females, who were given the vocabulary subtest of Wechsler's (1944) intelligence test for adults. The mean scores for males and females were 34.7 (SD = 4.8) and 33.9 (SD = 5.4), respectively. Both means are slightly larger than those reported by Dana (1957) for college student samples.

Young adult subjects (87 males and 81 females) were obtained from introductory classes in social science at Boston University.[1]

Measuring Instruments

A set of 34 "old people" items, 17 expressing negative sentiments about old people (OP−) and 17 reversed in wording expressing positive sentiments (OP+), were interspersed among statements from other attitude domains yielding a 98-item battery for the older sample and a 72-item battery for the student subjects. Common to both samples, in addition to the OP scales, were 12-item F and reversed F scales and 6-item "religious conventionalism" (RC) and reversed RC scales. The particular items used in the OP and F scales are reported in Kogan (1961). RC items were selected from Levinson (1954) and a set of matched items of opposite sign was constructed (Table 26.1).

The following response categories were provided for all of the items: "strongly disagree," "disagree," "slightly disagree," "slightly agree,"

Table 26.1. Original and Reversed RC Scale Items

1(+).   Every explanation of man and the world is incomplete unless it takes into account God's will.

1(−).   God's will should play no part in explaining man and the world; scientific knowledge is all that is needed.

2(+).   The chief end of man is nothing other than eternal salvation.

2(−).   The promotion of individual personal happiness is the chief end of man.

3(+).   Every person should have complete faith in some supernatural power whose decisions he obeys without question.

3(−).   There is no faith or supernatural power whose commandments one should obey without question.

4(+).   In addition to faith we need help from God in order to resist temptation.

4(−).   Prayer and faith in God don't help very much in resisting temptation.

5(+).   The most important aim of the churches at the present time should be to encourage spiritual worship and a sense of communion with the highest.

5(−).   The most important aim of the churches at the present time should be to encourage man's humanity to man.

6(+).   Life could hardly be worth living without the promise of immortality and life after death.

6(−).   The promise of immortality and life after death is quite unnecessary for a worthwhile and happy life.

"agree," and "strongly agree." These were scored 1, 2, 3, 5, 6, and 7, respectively, with a score of 4 assigned in the few cases where respondents omitted an item.

RESULTS

Mean scale scores for young and old subjects are shown in Table 26.2. While no age differences emerge for the OP− scale, there is a highly significant difference for OP+, with older subjects exhibiting a greater tendency to endorse such items. The latter finding when viewed relative to the direction of the mean differences for OP− would suggest that an acquiescent response set exerted a stronger influence in the older sample.

Such an interpretation, however, is not unequivocally supported by the mean differences observed for the F and RC scales. With regard to authoritarianism items, it is the older men who score significantly higher in authoritarianism on F+, while the older women are significantly lower in authoritarianism on F−. While both sets of differences can be attributed to

Table 26.2. Mean Differences between Young and Old Subjects on OP, F, and RC Scales

Scale	Young Men (N = 87)		Old Men (N = 89)			Young Women (N = 81)		Old Women (N = 115)		
	M	SD	M	SD	t	M	SD	M	SD	t
OP−	55.85	11.73	57.26	11.97	.79	53.78	10.21[b]	55.83	12.61[b]	1.26
	(3.28)[a]		(3.36)			(3.16)		(3.28)		
OP+	64.06	11.10	56.91	9.84	4.52**	64.30	10.73	57.79	11.37	4.08**
	(3.77)		(3.34)			(3.78)		(3.40)		
F+	42.24	8.44[c]	51.84	12.09[c]	6.12**	47.29	9.09[c]	49.31	12.29[c]	1.32
	(3.52)		(4.31)			(3.94)		(4.11)		
F−	46.04	6.33[b]	44.83	8.01[b]	1.11	48.60	6.63	42.84	7.30	5.74**
	(3.84)		(3.74)			(4.05)		(3.57)		
RC+	23.80	8.50	29.45	8.18	4.49**	24.62	7.64	29.96	9.01	4.47**
	(3.96)		(4.91)			(4.10)		(4.99)		
RC−	26.83	6.75	26.90	6.06	.07	25.72	6.00	27.94	5.92	2.57*
	(4.47)		(4.48)			(4.28)		(4.65)		

NOTE: Converted means are shown for the OP+, F−, and RC− scales in order that means for positive and negative scales be comparable, i.e., higher values reflecting more negative attitudes toward old people, more authoritarianism and more religious conventionalism.

[a] Per item means.
[b] Variances differ significantly at .05 level.
[c] Variances differ significantly at .01 level.
* Significant at the .05 level.
** Significant at the .01 level.

a stronger acquiescent response tendency in the older subjects, the fact remains that such tendencies were not of equal strength for original and reversed items. Similar findings may be noted in the domain of religious conventionalism. The older males achieve significantly higher scores on RC+ items, with no difference obtaining for RC−. The older women, on the other hand, manifest more religious conventionalism on both RC+ and RC− items, a finding directly counter to a simple acquiescence interpretation. In sum, it is evident that mean scale differences between samples reflect a combination of set and content, with the relative contribution of set related to the particular content area of a scale.

It will be recalled that we hypothesized greater variability among older subjects in their attitudes toward old people. Only for females on the OP— scale were the variances significantly different in the predicted direction. Variances were significantly different between age groups, however, for both males and females on F+, and for males on F−. This may simply reflect the greater range of education in the older samples (Christie, Havel & Seidenberg, 1958).

Reliability coefficients and intercorrelations between the various scales are shown in Table 26.3. With the exception of the F− scale, reliabilities for the four samples are of moderate to high magnitude. Turning to relationships

Table 26.3. Odd-Even Reliability Coefficients (Spearman-Brown) and Interscale Correlations for Young and Old Subjects

	OP−		OP+		F+		F−		RC+		RC−	
OP−	.83	.79	.60**	−.02	.46**	.46**	.17	−.21*	.30**	.04	.05	−.36**
	.75	.84	.41**	.05	.16	.46**	.04	−.19*	.22*	.24*	.08	−.31**
OP+			.74	.73	.07	−.35**	.11	.34**	.16	−.21*	.13	.31**
			.79	.82	−.30**	−.35**	−.04	.17	.00	−.24*	.17	.10
F+					.61	.80	.48**	.15	.29**	.41**	.04	−.18
					.59	.81	.31**	.23*	.26*	.42**	.03	−.18*
F−							.23	.23	−.02	.04	−.03	.39**
							.25	.28	.08	−.13	.31**	.14
RC+									.86	.82	.76**	.42**
									.71	.90	.65**	.44**
RC−											.71	.63
											.51	.53

NOTE: The four samples of 87 young men (YM), 81 young women (YW), 89 old men (OM), and 115 old women (OW) are arranged in the cells of the table as follows:

YM	OM
YW	OW

*Significant at the .05 level.
**Significant at the .01 level.

between positively and negatively worded versions of the three scales, it should be noted that r's can theoretically range from $+1.00$ (perfect logical consistency) to -1.00 (perfect logical inconsistency). It is apparent that r's are uniformly higher in the content direction for younger subjects. Indeed, with the exception of r's for females on the F$-$ scale, differences between the younger and older samples in positive-negative scale correlations are statistically significant beyond the .05 level or better (two-tailed test).[2] Accordingly, we must abandon the hypothesis that the greater involvement of older subjects in OP item content is reflected in a higher correlation between oppositely worded versions of the OP scale. Particularly puzzling is the fact that the absolute level of r between OP$-$ and OP$+$ for older subjects is less than that observed for F and RC items. Both of the latter would seem to be of less direct relevance to older subjects than are items explicitly referring to various attributes of old people.

Consider next the relations between the OP, F, and RC scales reported in Table 26.3. In every case, significant (positive) r's between scales based on items worded in the same direction become nonsignificant or significant in the set (negative) direction when r's are computed between scales of opposite wording. In sum, it must be concluded that there are no clear content relationships between the three attitudinal domains under study for either young or old adults. An attempt to explain the absence of a relationship between OP and F in younger samples may be found in Kogan (1961).

DISCUSSION

The results reported above generally do not support the hypotheses advanced earlier in the paper. In but one case out of four did older subjects exhibit greater variability in their attitudes toward old people. Correlations between positively and negatively worded versions of the OP scale not only failed to exceed those reported for younger subjects, but actually were of approximately zero magnitude.

Do these results call for a modification of the assumptions from which hypotheses were derived? It will be recalled that the older sample was distinguished from the younger in terms of the presence of tendencies toward disparagement of one's age group and "ego involvement" in the issue at hand. These assumptions appear so very basic in terms of logic and previously reported evidence that one is prompted to look elsewhere in accounting for the unexpected results of the study. It is most likely that the difficulty lies in the nature of the transition from assumption to hypothesis. In particular, does the well-known phenomenon of assimilation of "majority group" values in some "minority group" members necessarily imply greater inter-individual variability for the minority than the majority in responses to "minority group" items? Further, does stronger personal involvement in an issue necessarily imply a heightened awareness of the logical oppositeness of statements regarding that issue?

It is a generally accepted view (Kuhlen, 1959; Riegel, 1959) that the role of the older person in American society is one likely to give rise to feelings of denial and ambivalence regarding one's aging. A number of investigators (Kutner, Fanshel, Togo & Langner, 1956; Phillips, 1957; Tuckman & Lorge, 1954) report that substantial numbers of persons in their sixties and above decline to classify themselves as "elderly" or "old." Given the inexorable physical changes accompanying aging and their social stimulus value, the attitudes of many older persons toward their age peers should be characterized by ambivalence. The operational consequent of such ambivalence may well be an increased intraindividual variability in this attitude domain. The comparability of scale reliabilities for young and old subjects indicates that such differential variability is not manifested within uniformly positive or negative item sets. Rather, it is expressed in the extent to which younger and older subjects are consistent in responding to matched items of reversed wording.

Are we dealing here with anything more than differences in response sets in younger and older persons? There is little doubt in the present data that older subjects are more prone than younger subjects to "set" as opposed to "content" consistency in responding to attitude items. This does not imply, of course, that older individuals make more response errors when filling out written questionnaires. Rather, the phenomenon of acquiescence can probably best be considered an important personality correlate of aging or an aspect of an "old age" syndrome. This view is consistent with recent theory and research regarding response set as a stylistic personality variable in its own right (Couch & Keniston, 1960; Jackson & Messick, 1958). Given the energy loss, passivity and dependency alleged to be associated with old age, one might well expect older individuals to differ from their younger counterparts in willingness to endorse "authoritative" statements. Indeed, Jackson (1959) has recently demonstrated a relationship between response acquiescence and "cognitive energy" level.

The foregoing observations do not, however, account for the fact that the magnitude of the response set effect varied greatly across scales for older subjects and was ordered in a direction contrary to expectations, i.e., least content consistency on the OP scales. This finding suggests that the greater emotional involvement of old people in the attitude domain under consideration may have one of two alternative effects. Either the effect is one of a basic failure to apprehend the logical incompatibility in the paired statements, or, more likely, the feelings and experience of the older person are such that the matched statements may be logical, but not psychological, opposites. In the latter case, the inference is made that the attitude domain is less likely to be unidimensional for an older than a younger subject. More specifically, the older person's ambivalence regarding aging and his direct exposure to individual differences among age peers may be contrasted with the overgeneralized view, positive or negative, that college age subjects are likely to form of a group relatively remote from them in age status.

The older subject confronted with a statement describing "good" qualities of old people, and a matched statement describing the absence of such qualities or opposing "bad" characteristics, may conceive of the former as fitting a particular kind of old people, the latter as appropriate to a different kind. In most cases, of course, the respondent, if not dissociating himself completely from the class of old people, very probably considers himself as the sort of old person described in the positively worded items.

There is some evidence for this interpretation in the OP item statistics[3] for the younger and older subjects. The item yielding the highest absolute mean (most unfavorable response) for older subjects and the greatest mean discrepancy between younger and older subjects (younger subjects more favorable) reads as follows: "If old people expect to be liked, their first step is to try to get rid of their irritating faults." This evidence further serves to clarify the psychological basis for failing to endow old people with "logically" consistent qualities. For, while an older subject may have a generally positive view of old people, a sensitivity to "irritating faults" necessarily results in his agreeing with statements expressing those faults of special annoyance to him. Given, in addition, a stronger disposition to acquiesce in older persons, the observed differences between younger and older subjects assume a meaningful pattern.

The present work may be of relevance to the broader area of minority-majority group relations. It will be acknowledged that the criteria for belonging in the "minority group" of old people are considerably more ambiguous than those for ethnic or religious group membership. Nevertheless, a search for generalities might prove of value.

Prentice (1956) obtained very high correlations in the content direction between positively and negatively worded religious and racial minority items. Would these high correlations be maintained for minority group members responding to matched items of reversed wording whose content concerns the minority in question? Would the magnitude of the correlation reflect the extent of "marginality" (Glaser, 1958) in the group? Of course, it would be necessary in studies of this kind to control for response set effects by including matched positive and negative items from other attitude domains. With response set controlled, it might prove possible to obtain item discrepancy scores for the individual minority group member, which would reflect major areas of ambivalence in one's ethnic or religious identification.

In a more practical vein, do the low OP interscale correlations for older subjects essentially rule out attitudes toward old people as a metric that can be studied in terms of its relations with other variables in older samples? This would appear to be an extreme view. While the OP interscale correlations hovered around zero for the older samples, r's between specific item pairs exhibited considerable variation. For five of the OP item pairs, these r's were statistically significant for both male and female older subjects. There are, in other words, certain aspects of the attitude on which there is more consensus and, correspondingly, less ambivalence among older persons. The addition of other items of this kind and deletion of item pairs correlating nonsignificantly could well raise the interscale r to the levels obtained for younger samples. Alternatively, one might consider dividing the OP scales into unidimensional subscales, each reflecting a particular aspect of the attitude domain. The major focus of the present paper, however, has been one of accounting for differences between older and younger subjects in responses to a common set of items.

SUMMARY

The present paper compares the responses of college students and noninstitutionalized older people of comparable education and intelligence to a set of statements measuring attitudes toward old people (OP scale), authoritarian tendencies (F Scale), and religious conventionalism (RC Scale). For each scale, matched positively and negatively worded items were used. Hypotheses formulated for the OP scales—that older subjects would show greater interindividual variability and higher interscale correlations than younger subjects—were not confirmed. In fact, r's between the OP+ and OP− scales for the older subjects were approximately zero, and significantly less than those obtained for the younger samples. In the older samples, interscale r's for the F and RC scales, while higher in the content direction than the interscale r's for OP, were nevertheless significantly less than the corresponding

r's obtained in the student samples. On the basis of these results (in conjunction with the pattern of young-old mean differences on the scales), it was apparent that older subjects are more disposed than younger individuals toward acquiescent response tendencies.

In accounting for age differences in OP scale results, emphasis was placed upon the ambivalence of the older person regarding his own age status and that of his age peers, with the result that logically incompatible statements were rendered psychologically consistent. By contrast, younger subjects were imputed to have a more consistently negative or positive view of "old people," with the consequence of a closer match between logical and psychological consistency.

NOTES

1. I am grateful to Robert Smart for making subjects available.

2. Two-tailed tests were employed for OP scale comparisons for two reasons. First, a result in the direction opposite to that predicted could not be considered psychologically meaningless given the primitive state of theory in this area. Hence, the present problem does not seem to meet criteria proposed by Kimmel (1957) for the use of one-tailed tests. Second, the difference between the OP interscale r's for young adults and maximum possible r's for older subjects (the product of the square roots of the reliabilities) is considerably less than the difference between the former and the minimum r's possible for older subjects. In other words, it is statistically more difficult for the OP interscale r's of the older subjects to be larger rather than smaller than the corresponding r's for younger subjects.

3. A three-page table giving OP item means, standard deviations, item-sum correlations and matched item pair correlations for the young and old samples has been deposited with the American Documentation Institute. Order Document No. 6766 from ADI Auxiliary Publications Project, Photoduplication Service, Library of Congress; Washington, D.C.

REFERENCES

Barron, M. L. Minority group characteristics of the aged in American society. J. Geront., 1953, 8, 477–482.

Bureau of the Census. Current population reports, population characteristics. (Series P-20, No. 99) Washington, D.C., 1960.

Christie, R., Havel, Joan, & Seidenberg, B. Is the F Scale irreversible? J. Abnorm. Soc. Psychol., 1958, 56, 143–159.

Couch, A., & Keniston, K. Yeasayers and naysayers: Agreeing response set as a personality variable. J. Abnorm. Soc. Psychol., 1960, 60, 151–174.

Dana, R. H. A comparison of four verbal subtests on the Wechsler-Bellevue, Form I, and the WAIS. J. Clin. Psychol., 1957, 13, 70–71.

Drake, J. T. The aged in American society. *New York: Ronald, 1958.*

Glaser, D. *Dynamics of ethnic identification.* Amer. J. Sociol., *1958, 23, 31–40.*

Jackson, D. N. *Cognitive energy level, response acquiescence, and authoritarianism.* J. Soc. Psychol., *1959, 49, 65–69.*

Jackson, D. N., & Messick, S. *J. Content and style in personality assessment.* Psychol. Bull., *1958, 55, 243–252.*

Kimmel, H. D. *Three criteria for the use of one-tailed tests.* Psychol. Bull., *1957, 54, 351–353.*

Kogan, N. *Attitudes toward old people: The development of a scale and an examination of correlates.* J. Abnorm. Soc. Psychol., *1961, 62, 44–54.*

Kuhlen, R. G. *Aging and life adjustment. In J. E. Birren (Ed.),* Handbook of aging and the individual. *Chicago: Univer. Chicago Press, 1959. Pp. 852–879.*

Kutner, B., Fanshel, D., Togo, Alice M., & Langner, T. S. Five hundred over sixty. *New York: Russell Sage Foundation, 1956.*

Levinson, D. J. *The intergroup relations workshop: Its psychological aims and effects.* J. Psychol., *1954, 38, 103–126.*

Lewin, K. Resolving social conflicts. *New York: Harper, 1945.*

Linden, M. E. *Effects of social attitudes on the mental health of the aging.* Geriatrics, *1957, 12, 109–114. (a)*

Linden, M. E. *Relationships between social attitudes toward aging and the delinquencies of youth.* Amer. J. Psychiat., *1957, 114, 444–448. (b)*

Phillips, B. S. *A role theory approach to adjustment in old age.* Amer. Sociol. Rev., *1957, 22, 212–217.*

Prentice, N. M. *The comparability of positive and negative items in scales of ethnic prejudice.* J. Abnorm. Soc. Psychol., *1956, 52, 420–421.*

Riegel, K. F. *Personality theory and aging. In J. E. Birren (Ed.),* Handbook of aging and the individual. *Chicago: University Chicago Press, 1959. Pp. 797–851.*

Tuckman, J., & Lorge, I. *Classification of the self as young, middle aged, or old.* Geriatrics, *1954, 9, 534–536.*

Wechsler, D. The measurement of adult intelligence. *Baltimore: Williams & Wilkins, 1944.*

27. Effects of Control and Predictability on the Physical and Psychological Well-Being of the Institutionalized Aged

Richard Schulz

FROM THE VERY YOUNG to the very old and dying, persons strive to control their environments. More than a decade ago, White (1959) concluded that many of an infant's diverse behaviors are motivated by a biological drive which prompts the organism to find out how to deal effectively with its environment. More recently, the importance of contingency between behavior and outcome for the normal development of organisms has been demonstrated in both humans (Seligman, 1975; Skeels, 1966; Spitz, 1962; Watson, 1970) and animals (Harlow, 1968; Joffe, Rawson & Mulick, cited in Seligman, 1975). Learning deficits as well as the ability to carry on normal social interactions with other organisms are typical results of prolonged experiences of noncontingency.

Although less is known about human development beyond childhood and adolescence, one characteristic of adult development is that most individuals continue to expand their realm of competencies. For example, increased social and financial status enable most individuals continually to enlarge control over the environment as they grow older.

Typically, however, retirement and old age precipitate an abrupt decline in control. Retirement means the loss of one of the most meaningful sources of instrumental control in life, the work role. Closely related is the loss of income, often resulting in further shrinkage of an individual's control as it becomes necessary to curtail activities requiring money. In addition, many individuals at this age experience some deterioration in physical condition, representing a further shrinkage of their sphere of control. Finally, aged individuals suffer the loss of the child-rearing role, which was undoubtedly an important source of competence and environmental control in their younger and middle years.

Reprinted by permission from *Journal of Personality and Social Psychology* 33, no. 5 (1976): 563–73. Copyright © 1976 by the American Psychological Association.

In addition to the role losses associated with retirement, many aged individuals experience further declines in their ability to manipulate and control the environment as a result of institutionalization. Schulz and Aderman (1973) have noted that a patient's adverse reactions to institutionalization are probably mediated by feelings of helplessness, born out of the patient's perception that the institutional demands for passivity represent a real loss in his ability to control the environment. The consequences of such a loss of control usually include withdrawal, depression (Schulz & Aderman, 1974; Streib, 1971), and sometimes early death (Schulz & Aderman, 1973). Experimental studies with animals (for a review, see Seligman, Maier & Solomon, 1971) and humans (Roth & Kubal, 1975) amply demonstrate the negative effects of loss of control. Seligman (1974) attributes motivational, cognitive, and emotional deficits to any prolonged experience with lack of contingency between individuals' behavior and their outcomes. Roth and Kubal (1975) demonstrated that subjects working on an important task who received large amounts of exposure to a noncontingency situation behaved helplessly in a subsequent task situation.

CONTROL AND PREDICTABILITY

Personal control is generally defined as the ability to manipulate some aspect of the environment. In his recent review of the control literature, Averill (1973) distinguishes three types of control—behavioral, cognitive, and decisional—and points out that each type can be beneficial in alleviating the negative effects of a stressor. It is not clear, however, whether the beneficial effects are attributable to control or increased predictability. For example, stimulus regulation, a type of behavioral control where the subject determines either when an aversive stimulus is delivered or who delivers it, is found to be stress reducing only when accompanied by the reduction of uncertainty regarding the threatening event (Averill, 1973). Similarly, the reduction in experienced stress resulting from signaled as opposed to unsignaled shock is readily attributable to the greater predictability of the former.

Thus, control is confounded by predictability in that having control over a stimulus also means that it is predictable. It becomes important to ask, therefore, whether the ability to control adds something over and above the ability to predict.

Experiments designed to answer this question were carried out by Reim, Glass, and Singer (1971) and Geer and Maisel (1972). In the Reim, Glass, and Singer (1971) study, subjects given perceived control over the termination of aversive noise exhibited significantly less autonomic reactivity (vasoconstriction) when compared to subjects in predictable and unpredictable noise conditions. In addition, subjects in the perceived control and predictable noise conditions exhibited significantly better performance than subjects in the unpredictable noise condition on a proofreading task given after the noise experience. There were, however, no differences between the predict and perceived control groups on the proofreading task. In the experiment by Geer and Maisél (1972), one group (control) of subjects could control the termination of aversive photographs of dead bodies, while subjects in the predict group knew when and how long the photographs would be presented but had no control over when the photographs would be terminated. Subjects in the no-control–no-predictability group could neither control nor predict the occurrence of the photographs. The results revealed that subjects with control over the termination of the aversive stimulus exhibited lower galvanic skin response reactivity to the stimulus than those subjects with prediction alone. Results from both of the above studies indicate that control is more than just predictability, although the advantages of control appear to be limited to physiological measures taken in the presence of the stressor. In view of the limited research on this issue and the existence of alternative explanations for the reported findings (see Geer & Maisel, 1972; Seligman, 1975), further research is warranted.

The existing literature on control focuses almost exclusively on the effects of having control over aversive events. Only a few investigators have used positive stimuli such as food or money in the context of a control experiment.

In addition to several studies already cited (Skeels, 1966; Spitz, 1962; Watson, 1970) demonstrating the importance of acquiring control over positive reinforcers for adequate infant development, several additional studies illustrate the importance of control over positive events in mature organisms. In an experiment carried out by Engberg, Hanse, Walker, and Thomas (cited in Seligman, 1975), hungry pigeons who in the past had been contingently reinforced with food were better at subsequent learning tasks than pigeons who had been reinforced noncontingently. Other animal studies have demonstrated that organisms prefer working for positive reinforcers over securing them for free. Carder and Berkowitz (1970), Jensen (1963), and Neuringer (1969) have all reported that rats prefer response-contingent food over response-independent food, suggesting that response-contingent stimulation is probably more positive than the same stimulation when it is response independent.

Using human subjects, Lanzetta and Driscoll (1966) examined the preference for information about a potential outcome as a function of whether it was negative (shock) or positive (monetary reward). Lanzetta and Driscoll found that subjects preferred to have information as opposed to no information about an anticipated event, regardless of potential outcomes. This suggests that information which might be useful in achieving cognitive control is just as desirable when the outcome is positive as when it is negative. With this exception, little is in fact known about how humans react to controlled versus random positive events.

THE PRESENT STUDY

The present study was designed to assess the effects of increased control over and predictability of a positive outcome upon the psychological and physiological well-being of the aged. The intent of this research was twofold. First, viewed form the perspective of the theoretical literature on control, this study was designed to answer some important questions on the effect of having control over positive outcomes. In addition, the study was designed to assess the relative importance of control and predictability in relation to positive events. Second, since this was an experimental field as opposed to correlational study, it was expected that cause and effect statements could be made about the importance of these variables to successful aging.

In order to give some of the aged subjects the opportunity to exert control over a positive event in their environment, it was decided to make a student visitor available to them for a 2-month period. Since institutionalized aged persons are often very lonely (Streib, 1971), being visited by a friendly college student was conceptualized as a significant positive event. Control subjects could exert control over the frequency and duration of visits they received, giving them the opportunity both to regulate and to modify the positive event.

To assess the effects of predictability, a second group of subjects was informed at what time and how long they would be visited but was not given any control over these details. A third group of subjects was visited on a random schedule. They were not given any control over the duration or frequency of visits. This group served as one of two "control" conditions. Finally, a fourth group of subjects served as a baseline comparison group. These individuals were not visited except to collect data. Individuals in predict and random groups were yoked to the control group in order to keep the frequency and duration of visits constant across all three conditions.

Data relevant to level of activity and the physical and psychological status of each subject were collected before and after being visited for a 2-month period. On the basis of existing literature on control, it was predicted that having control and predictability would result in significantly greater positive effects on the physical and psychological status indicators than random visits or no treatment. This prediction was based on the notion that making a significant positive event either predictable or controllable would halt or reverse the process of continued loss of control and therefore have a positive impact on the physical and psychological status of the aged, as well as positively affect their evaluation of the visits. Given that these aged individuals were very lonely to begin with, it was further hypothesized that being visited even on a random basis would be beneficial to the subjects. Finally, since the focus of this research was on the generalized effects of control and predictability, no specific predictions about the advantages of control over predictability were made. On the basis of previous studies with aversive events (Reim, Glass & Singer, 1971), one would not expect to find such differences.

METHOD

Subjects and Setting

Thirty-six retired women and 6 retired men living in a private, church-affiliated retirement home in North Carolina served as subjects for this study. Subjects ranged in age from 67 to 96 years old with a mean age of 81.5. The ability to walk and talk were the two criteria for being included in the study.

Subjects were asked at either a group meeting in the retirement home or individually to participate in a dissertation project which involved charting the "daily activities of aged individuals." Only 1 person refused to participate when asked individually. Subjects were randomly assigned to one of four conditions. Two subjects initially included in the study had to be replaced in order to have 10 subjects per condition. One subject left the home to go on a long vacation and the other became incommunicable because of emotional problems. The latter subject was in the random visitor group, while the former was in the control visitor group.

A resident's regular contact with others in the home was usually limited to two or three close friends living in close proximity. To avoid arousing suspicion and the contamination of the manipulations, an effort was made to exclude individuals from the study who might be in close contact with each other and compare notes about what was happening.

Procedure

After obtaining permission to carry out this study from the directors of the retirement home, the experimenter was invited to attend a "town house" meeting to present his research plan to the residents of the home. Approximately 40 people attended the meeting and 16 of those present expressed some interest in participating in an investigation described to them as an effort to "chart the daily activities of aged individuals." These 16 individuals as well as 27 others were later personally approached by the experimenter. The 27 subjects were chosen on the basis of location within the home such that communication among them would be minimized. In each case, the experimenter, wearing a sports coat and tie, introduced himself as a graduate student interested in studying senior citizens. After approximately 30 minutes of casual conversation, the initial interview began.

Initial Interview

If the subject was still able to read and write, the experimenter left a folder containing three questionnaires with the subject. Before leaving, the experimenter explained each questionnaire in detail. For those individuals too blind to read or too shaky to write, the experimenter administered the questionnaires verbally. A fourth questionnaire, the Wohlford Hope Scale (1966), and some health status questions were administered verbally to all subjects at the initial meeting.

The four questionnaires administered at the interview were entitled "Activities," "My Usual Day," "Future Diary," and the "Wohlford Hope Scale." Answers to six open-ended items on the Activities questionnaire were used to calculate an Activity Index. The index was calculated by adding together the frequency per week of those pursuits requiring active participation. These included number of visits to neighbors in the building, number of visits outside the building, number of times the building was left for activities other than visiting, number of club meetings attended, number of visits to church, and number of phone calls made.

The remaining three printed questionnaires were taken from Schonfield (1973) and have been demonstrated to be useful indicators of successful aging. Briefly, data from the "Usual Day" questionnaire was used to calculate the percentage of waking time the subject spent in active pursuits in a day. The "Future Diary" questionnaire was used to assess the percentage of time devoted to special commitments during the waking hours of the next 7 days (see Schonfield, 1973, for a detailed description of these measurement devices).

In administering the "Wohlford Hope Scale," the experimenter simply asked the subjects to "name 10 things that you have talked about or thought about in the last week or two." After the subject completed this task, the experimenter continued:

I am going to read back to you each of the things you have mentioned. I want you to describe each by giving it certain ratings: past, present, or future. Decide whether at the time you thought about it, the idea or topic referred to something mostly in the past, present, or future. Finally, I want you to give me the actual date or approximate date when the thing occurred or probably will occur. If it occurs over a period of time, give your best estimate of the range of dates.

The following tabulation scale was used to weigh each item either negatively if it occurred in the past or positively if it occurred in the future:

0 = under 2 hours,
1 = 2 hours to 1 week,
2 = 1 week to under 1 month,
3 = 1 month to under 4 months,
4 = 4 months to 1 year,
5 = 1 year to 4 years,
6 = 4 years or over.

A mean score ranging from −6 to +6 was obtained for each subject where the higher the number (the more future-oriented), the greater the level of hope.

In order to assess health status, subjects were asked whether they had any disabilities (e.g., diabetes, arthritis, blindness, etc.), how often they visited the infirmary per week, and how many different types of medication they took each day as well as the quantity of each.

The order in which the questionnaires were administered was the same for all subjects. The Wohlford Hope Scale was first, followed by the Activity, Usual Day, and the Future Diary questionnaires, in that order. The health status questions were last. As soon as all of the initial information was collected, subjects were randomly assigned to one of four experimental conditions and the manipulation phase of the experiment began.

Manipulation Phase

Five undergraduate students (four females and one male) visited the residents at the home. Each visitor was assigned subjects in sets of three, one in each visitation condition, and trained to carry out the manipulations accurately.

Regardless of condition, all visitors made their initial contact with subjects by introducing themselves as Duke undergraduates and as friends of the experimenter. They stated that they were interested in having some firsthand interaction experience with elderly individuals. They added that they were taking a course on aging at Duke and thought it would be a good experience "to get out into the real world and talk to some elderly people." They also remarked that the experimenter had suggested that they "might enjoy having someone to talk to." After delivering these opening statements, the visitors allowed the subject to control the content of the discussions that ensued. The tension typically aroused when two strangers meet usually dissipated very quickly. The three experimental manipulations described below were introduced at the end of the first visit.

Control visitor group. Individuals assigned to this condition had the opportunity to control both the duration (modify) and frequency (regulate) of visits they received. After approximately 45 minutes of the initial meeting had elapsed, the visitor informed the subject that "I don't want to take any more of your time today than you can afford to spare. So if you would like to stop at any time, please tell me." The subject usually responded by saying that it would be all right to spend a few more minutes together. On subsequent visits, the visitor reminded the subject at the beginning of the visit not "to let me stay any longer than you want me to." Shortly before leaving, the visitor said, "I really enjoyed talking to you. My schedule is very open right now. I can come back any time you would like me to. Do you know when would be a good time for me to come back for another visit?" After waiting for a response, the visitor added, "Let me write down my name and phone number for you. If you ever just feel like talking, give me a call and I'll be over." Arrangements for the second meeting were usually made at the first meeting. For subsequent meetings, however, subjects began making arrangements by telephone as well.

Predict visitor group. Individuals assigned to this condition were informed when to expect a visitor but were not given the opportunity to determine when a visitor came or how long he stayed. When arranging the visit with the subject, the visitor first asked, "How are you doing?" and then stated, "I'll be at the home_____. I'll drop by to see you at_____o'clock." Each subject in this group was yoked to a specific individual in the control visitor group such that the amount of visitation was the same in this condition as in the control visitor condition. Since control visitor subjects were always seen first, the visitor knew when to terminate each visit with the yoked predict visitor subject. To make the duration of the visit as predictable as possible, subjects were informed at the beginning of each meeting approximately how long the visit would last. In addition, as soon as the visitor knew when the next visit with the control visitor subject would occur, the yoked predict visitor subject was informed of the time of the next visit either by telephone or in person. In order to hold the visitor's expressed liking for the subject constant across all conditions, each meeting was terminated with the visitor saying, "I really enjoyed talking with you."

Random visitor group. Subjects in this group were also yoked to individuals in the control visitor group such that they were visited just as frequently and for the same length of time as individuals in the control visitor group. They were not, however, given the opportunity to control either when a visitor came or how long he stayed. Nor were they notified when a visitor was coming. Upon arriving at the subject's room, the visitor first asked, "How are you doing?" and then stated, "I decided to drop by and pay you a visit today." Since it was likely that expectancies would be created if the visitor came the same time every week, visits were scattered such that they never occurred on the same day of the week for any 2 consecutive weeks. As was the case with the other visitation conditions, all meetings were terminated with the visitor saying, "I really enjoyed talking to you."

Visitors were instructed to keep their behavior as constant as possible across all conditions. This was accomplished by having the visitor play a relatively passive role when interacting with the subject. Each visitor was asked to keep a diary in which were recorded the number of visits made per week, the length of each visit, and, on a 9-point Likert-type scale, how much they enjoyed each visit. The latter scale was used to assess the quality of interactions from the visitor's point of view.

Postinterview

To assess the effects of the manipulations, the three visitation groups and the no-visit comparison group were interviewed by two experiments approximately 2 months after the initial interview. Experimenter 1, the same individual who carried out the initial interview, administered the same battery of questionnaires used in the first interview. With the exception of the Wohlford Hope Scale, all responses were scored the same way for this set of questionnaires as they were for the first set. In scoring the Wohlford Hope Scale, all references to the visitor were excluded in order to make comparisons between the visitation groups and the no-visit comparison group valid. Difference scores representing pre-to postmanipulation changes were calculated for all measures. Experimenter 1 was blind as to which condition each subject was in.

Experimenter 1 also administered two additional 9-point Likert-type scales to the activities director at the home. The activities director was asked to rate each subject on two scales entitled "Health Status" (the two extremes were labeled "in perfect health" and "extremely ill") and "Zest for Life" (the two extremes were "extremely enthusiastic about life" and "completely hopeless"). The activities director had worked at the home for many years as a nurse before taking on this new position and was as a result personally acquainted with all the participants in the study. However, she knew nothing about the study and was therefore blind as to which condition each subject was in.

Experimenter 2 introduced himself to the subject as a friend of Experimenter 1 who was "helping him collect some information." Experimenter 2 verbally administered three questionnaires entitled "Background Data," "Visitation Questions," and "Tri-Scales."

The Background Data questionnaire consisted of seven questions. Subjects were asked how long they had lived at the home, under what circumstances they had come to the home, how much they liked the home, what percentage of the time they were lonely, percentage of time bored, whether they had lost any close friends or relatives recently, and what kinds of physical problems they had.

The Visitation Questions survey contained 10 items pertaining to the visitor. Several of the items were manipulated checks, while others served as dependent measures. Among the manipulation checks were the following questions: How often were you visited? Did your visitor come the same time every week? Did he/she let you know when he/she was coming? Who decided when the visitor should come? Who determined how long the visitor stayed? How dependable a person do you think the visitor is? Questions pertaining to how well the visitor was liked and how much the visits were enjoyed by the subject served as dependent measures. On a 9-point Likert-type scale ranging from the two extremes "do not like at all" to "like very much," subjects indicated how much they liked the visitor. On an identical scale, subjects were asked to indicate how much they liked the visitor "compared to the person you like most in the world." Subjects also used 9-point scales to indicate how much they enjoyed the visits and how much they enjoyed the visits "compared to what you enjoy doing most."

The final questionnaire, "Tri-Scales," consisted of 10 9-point Likert-type scales tapping such dimensions as happiness, health status, usefulness, etc. In order to give subjects a reference point, the mid-point of the scale was always labeled "Average American." Given this midpoint, subjects were first asked to rate themselves on each of the 10 dimensions as they perceived themselves at present by placing an "X" on the scale. A second rating was obtained to indicate a subject's "best year" on each dimension. This was done by placing a "B" on the scale. Finally, a subject made a third rating by placing an "O" on the scale where they perceived other old people to fall on each dimension. A composite score similar to one used by Schonfield (1973) for each dimension was derived using the formula $3X - B - O$.[1] Experimenter 2 administered all questionnaires verbally and, although he knew whether a subject was visited, he was unaware of the contingencies under which these visits occurred.

RESULTS

Manipulation Checks

Subjects assigned to the visitation groups were visited an average of 1.3 times per week with the mean length of each visit being 50.8, 49.0, and 50.0 minutes for the random, predict, and control groups, respectively. Thus, there were no differences in the frequency or duration of visits among the three visitation groups.

To check on the effectiveness of the control manipulation, all subjects in the visitation groups were asked, "Who decided when the visitor should come?" Nine of 10 control subjects responded that they determined when he came. Two of 8 predict subjects felt they determined the delivery of the positive event, while only 1 of 10 random subjects felt this way. Fisher's exact test showed the differences between the control and the other two visitation groups to be significant (control versus predict, $p < .005$; control versus random, $p < .005$). Answers to the question of who determined how long the visitor stayed, revealed a similar pattern of results. Eight of 10 control subjects felt that they determined the length of visits, while only 2 of 10 predict and 3 of 10 random subjects felt this way. Comparisons between the control group and the other two groups were again significant. The probability level for both comparisons using Fisher's exact test was less than .025.

The effectiveness of the predictability manipulation was assessed by the question, "Did the visitor let you know when he was coming?" As expected, control and predict subjects felt they had been informed, while random sub-jects reported not being informed. Nine of 10 control and 9 of 10 predict subjects reported being informed. None of the random subjects felt this way. Fisher's exact test again revealed highly significant results when comparing control with random ($p < .005$) and predict with random subjects ($p < .005$). It was also expected that the visitor would be perceived as being more de-pendable by the control and predict groups. The mean dependability ratings for the three groups were 6.6 (random), 7.3 (predict), and 8.1 (control), with high scores reflecting higher levels of perceived dependability. The difference between random and predict groups was not significant, while a comparison between predict and control conditions revealed a significant effect, $F(1, 36) = 4.20, p < .05$.

It can be safely concluded from these results that the manipulations had their intended effects. As expected, control subjects felt they controlled both the frequency and duration of visits. Predict subjects reported knowing when visitors would come, and random subjects perceived neither forewarning nor control over the delivery of the reinforcer.

Major Analysis

A total of 15 dependent variables were analyzed such that the effects of the manipulations on health status, psychological status, and activity level could be assessed. The general plan of the analysis was as follows. Initially, three orthogonal comparisons were carried out for all variables. They were as fol-lows: (a) no treatment versus random, to determine the effects of a positive reinforcer per se; (b) predict versus control, to test the effects of control over and above predictability; and finally (c) no treatment plus random versus predict plus control, to determine the effects of experimental treatment rela-tive to the two "control" conditions. A multivariate analysis of variance for each comparison yielded a significant multivariate F only for the comparison of no treatment plus random with predict plus control, multivariate $F(15, 22) = 2.50, p < .025$.

To assess the effectiveness of the random assignment procedure, multi-variate analyses of variance were carried out on all of the pre-measures in-cluding age of subject and length of time at the home. No significant multivariate Fs were found, although there was a marginally significant dif-ference when univariate Fs for age were examined, predict versus control $F(1, 36) = 2.902, p < .097$; random versus no visits $F(1, 36) = 3.247, p < .080$. Subjects in the random visits group tended to be older than subjects in the no-visits group (83.4 and 77.9, respectively) and subjects in the control group tended to be older than subjects in the predict group (85.0 and 79.8, respectively). It can be safely concluded from this analysis that the random assignment procedure was effective.

Health Status Indicators

Five different indicators of health status were used to assess the effects of the experimental manipulations. The comparison of no treatment plus random against predict plus control yielded several significant results. The predict plus control groups were rated as significantly healthier by the activities director at the home than a combination of the no-treatment and random groups, $F(1, 36) = 4.457$, $p < .042$. Analysis of change scores on quantity of medication taken per day revealed a significant effect for the same contrast, $F(1, 36) = 5.953$, $p < .02$. Table 27.1 shows that mean increases in quantity of medication were smaller for the predict plus control groups than the no-treatment plus random groups. A marginally significant difference for the same contrast was found when analyzing the change scores for number of different types of medication taken per day, $F(1, 36) = 3.041$, $p < .09$. The means in Table 27.1 show that, although all groups increase their intake of the number of different types of medication, the increase is smaller for the predict and control groups.

Psychological Status Indicators

Six dependent measures were analyzed to determine the effects of the manipulations on psychological status. Again only the comparison of predict

Table 27.1. Mean Health Status Indicators by Condition

	Condition			
Variable	No treatment	Random	Predict	Control
Health status as assessed by activities director at home[a]	5.10	4.70	6.10	6.90
Triscale composite on health[a]	19.80	20.30	21.20	20.80
Change in number of types of medication used per day[b]	+.70	+.80	+.40	+.40
Change in quantity of medication taken per day[b]	+2.40	+2.40	+.90	+.80
Change in number of trips to the infirmary per week[b]	+.70	+.85	+.30	+.85

[a] The higher the score, the better the perceived health of the individual.
[b] Positive numbers represent increases.

plus control with no treatment plus random yielded statistically significant results for these variables. Relative to the no-treatment plus random groups, the predict plus control groups perceived themselves as significantly happier, $F(1, 36) = 7.134$, $p < .011$, and were judged to have significantly more "zest for life," $F(1, 36) = 8.072$, $p < .007$. Table 27.2 reveals that both no-treatment and random groups evidenced a decline in level of hope, while the predict and control groups showed an increase, $F(1, 36) = 5.467$, $p < .025$. Marginally significant differences for the same comparison were found for the variables, percentage of time lonely, $F(1, 36) = 3.682$, $p < .063$, percentage of time bored, $F(1, 36) = 3.046$, $p < .089$, and usefulness, $F(1, 36) = 4.008$, $p < .053$. The means in Table 27.2 reveal that, for all dependent variables, the predict and control groups were superior in psychological status when compared to the no-treatment and random groups.

Activity Level Indicators

All four indicators of activity level revealed significant differences when comparing predict plus control against no treatment plus random. Predict plus control group subjects evidenced more positive change in the time devoted to active pursuits in a "Usual Day," $F(1, 36) = 4.744$, $p < .036$, in the time devoted to "Future Commitments," $F(1, 36) = 11.71$, $p < .002$, and on the "Activity Index," $F(1, 36) = 10.736$, $p < .002$, than the no-treatment plus random groups. In addition, predict plus control subjects perceived them-

Table 27.2. Mean Psychological Status Indicators by Condition

	Condition			
Variable	No treatment	Random	Predict	Control
"Zest for Life" as rated by activities director at home[a]	4.30	5.00	6.10	7.00
Change in level of hope[b]	−.31	−.07	+.20	+.42
Percentage of time lonely	8.00	11.00	3.00	1.00
Percentage of time bored	7.00	15.50	4.00	4.00
Triscale composite on happiness[c]	19.50	20.90	22.70	23.30
Triscale composite on usefulness[d]	17.40	17.50	18.90	21.60

[a] The higher the score, the greater the individual's perceived zest for life.
[b] Positive numbers represent increases, negative numbers decreases.
[c] The higher the score, the more happy the individual perceives himself to be.
[d] The higher the score, the more useful the individual perceives himself to be.

selves as significantly more active, $F(1, 36) = 6.133$, $p < .018$ than no-treatment and random subjects.

The comparison between random and no-treatment groups revealed one significant univariate F, $F(1, 36) = 5.08$, $p < .03$, for change in "Usual Day" and one marginally significant univariate F, $F(1, 36) = 3.849$, $p < .058$, for change in "Future Commitments." On both measures, the random group was superior to the no-treatment group. However, since the multivariate F for this comparison was not statistically significant, these univariate Fs must be viewed with some caution. It is possible that they are merely chance effects.

Direction of Effects

Since several of the dependent measures were change scores, it is possible to say something about the directional effects of the manipulations. That is, did the manipulations inhibit a progressive decline or did they actually effect improvement? The mean changes for indicators of physical status in Table 27.1 show that all groups increased their intake of drugs and number of trips to the infirmary, but that this increase was smallest for the predict and control groups. Thus, in the case of health status indicators, the manipulations effectively inhibited a progressive physical decline. Mean changes in indicators of psychological status and activity level suggest, however, that the manipulations actually reversed the pattern of progressive decline. Tables 27.2 and 27.3 show that, on the average, predict and control groups evidenced a positive increase, while the no-treatment and random groups showed a slight decrease.

Table 27.3. Mean Activity Level Indicators by Condition

	Condition			
Variable	No treatment	Random	Predict	Control
Change in "Usual Day"[a]	−1.49	+1.31	+1.47	+2.18
Change in "Future Commitments"[a]	−.40	+.05	+.27	+.50
Change in Activity Index[a]	−.60	.00	+1.30	+1.00
Triscale composite on activity[b]	19.40	19.50	22.10	22.30

[a] Positive numbers represent increases, negative numbers decreases.
[b] The higher the score, the more active the individual perceives himself to be.

DISCUSSION

The results of this study demonstrated that predict and control groups were consistently and significantly superior on indicators of physical and psychological status, as well as level of activity. The manipulation of control and predictability had meaningful generalized effects on the well-being of the institutionalized aged subjects of this study. The absence of significant differences between the predict and control groups and between the random and no-treatment groups suggests that the relatively positive outcome of the predict and control groups is attributable to predictability alone. These data paralleled the findings of Reim (1971) who also failed to find generalized advantages of controllability over predictability. No predictability–control differences on proofreading ability, assessed after the noise experiences, were found in their study.

Despite the similarities in results, some important differences between this and previous control studies should be noted. First, both Reim, Glass, and Singer (1971) and Geer and Maisel (1972) used predictable or controllable aversive events (loud noise and photographs of mutilated bodies, respectively), while a positive event was used in the present study. Second, differences between predictability and control found in previous studies were obtained on physiological indicators (vasoconstriction and galvanic response) taken in the presence of the stressor; such measures were unavailable in the present study and it is therefore impossible to know whether such differences existed. The third difference between the present study and previous research is that individuals in this experiment were given control over another human being whereas subjects in previous studies were given control over impersonal physical events. Undoubtedly, the exercise of control in the present study was limited by considerations for how the demands might be perceived, as well as by situational constraints against inappropriate behavior. Experience gained from the present investigation suggests that it would be easier to differentiate predictability from control if the thing to be predicted or controlled were something inanimate such as a food menu or aspects of the physical environment rather than another human being. From an applied perspective, it is important to continue the search for an answer to the predictability–control issue since in most settings it is easier to make an environment predictable than controllable.

It was expected that subjects in the random group would benefit from being visited even though the visits were not predictable. Since being visited was conceptualized as a positive event, it was thought that a visit would be analogous to being pleasantly surprised. Apparently, this was not the case. Random subjects were not significantly or consistently superior to the no-treatment subjects in any category of variables. Several explanations may account for this absence of difference.

First, it is possible that, because of its unpredictability, the quality of the interaction between visitor and random subjects was very inferior, perhaps even aversive, when compared to the quality of interaction occurring in the predict and control conditions. The subjects' ratings of their enjoyment of the visitation experience contradicts this explanation, however. Random subjects reported enjoying the visits just as much as predict and control subjects. The differences between the subjects' enjoyment of the visits and their enjoyment of "their favorite activity" were also not significant across the three conditions. Thus, subjects in the random group apparently enjoyed the visits just as much as subjects in the predict and control groups. It is possible, then, that a positive event has generalized benefits only to the extent that the individual has the opportunity to look forward to it (it is predictable). Extensive correlational and observational research with hospital patients supports the notion that having something positive to look forward to is beneficial to a speedy recovery (Schulz, 1973).

The relevance of these findings to the process of aging is evident. This study demonstrates that the decline in physical and psychological status and level of activity associated with increased age can be inhibited or reversed by making a predictable or controllable significant positive event available to aged individuals. The study further supports the conceptualization that the many negative consequences of aging may be mediated by increased unpredictability and uncontrollability and that, to the extent that aged individuals are able to maintain a predictable and controllable environment, they should experience relatively less physical and psychological deterioration with increasing age.

The idea that the aged should have the opportunity to retain as much autonomy in their lives as possible is not new to gerontologists. Pfeiffer (1973), at a recent conference on alternatives to institutional care for the older Americans, remarked that total care for the aged is just as bad as no care at all. Brody (1973) is at present carrying out some research on alternatives to institutionalization which emphasizes the importance of enabling the aged individual to retain some autonomy in his environment. These gerontologists appear to have reached their conclusions on the basis of intuition, personal experience, and a large body of correlational research. The present investigation supports their points of view and suggests some specific psychological variables which appear to be causally related to successful aging. A qualification is in order here. The population used in this study was of relatively high socioeconomic status and caution is therefore advised before generalizing to all aged individuals. Future research should investigate other populations as well as individual differences within those populations.

Finally, we know little about the process through which control and predictability come to have their effects on the individual. In order to begin to construct a model that would enable us to predict the impact of these variables at any given point in a person's life, we need to collect data on individual differences. It is probable that the kind of life experiences an individual has had contributes greatly to his experiences for a controllable and predictable world and that his response to a particular environment is affected by the degree to which these expectancies are violated.

NOTE

1. The rationale behind this formula was as follows: Assessing an individual's status on each dimension should first be based on where he perceives himself at present (the "X" score). The disparity between "best year" and present state ($B - X$) was subtracted from present state since this represents self-assessed deterioration. When there has been no deterioration ($B - X = O$) the X score is not decreased indicating that the individual is aging successfully (Schonfield, 1973). Self-assessed present superiority over other old people should add to feelings of well-being, while feelings of inferiority should reduce such feelings. Thus, the difference could either be positive or negative. The formula finally arrived at was $X - (B - X) + (X - O) = 3X - B - O$. In order to ensure a minimum score of 1, the constant 16 was added. The possible range of scores was 1 (when $X = 1$, $B = 9$, $O = 9$) to 40 (when $X = 9$, $B = 1$, $O = 1$).

REFERENCES

Averill, J. R. Personal control over aversive stimuli and its relationship to stress. Psychological Bulletin, 1973, 80, 286–303.

Brody, E. Seeking appropriate options for living arrangements. In E. Pfeiffer (Ed.), Alternatives to institutional care for older Americans: Practice and planning. Durham, N.C.: Duke University Center for Study of Aging and Human Development, 1973.

Carder, B., & Berkowitz, K. Rats' preference for earned in comparison with free food. Science, 1970, 167, 1273–1274.

Geer, J. H., & Maisel, E. Evaluating the effects of the prediction-control confound. Journal of Personality and Social Psychology, 1972, 23, 314–319.

Harlow, H. F. *The heterosexual affectional system in monkeys. In W. G. Bennis, E. H. Schein, F. I. Steele, & D. E. Berlew (Eds.),* Interpersonal dynamics. *Homewood, Ill.: Dorsey Press, 1968.*

Jensen, G. D. *Preference for bar pressing over 'free-loading' as a function of the number of rewarded presses.* Journal of Experimental Psychology, *1963, 65, 451–454.*

Lanzetta, J. T., & Driscoll, J. M. *Preference for information about an uncertain but unavoidable outcome.* Journal of Personality and Social Psychology, *1966, 3, 96–102.*

Neuringer, A. J. *Animals respond for food in the presence of free food.* Science, *1969, 166, 399–400.*

Pfeiffer, E. *Introduction to the conference report. In E. Pfeiffer (Ed.),* Alternatives to institutional care for older Americans: Practice and planning. *Durham, N.C.: Duke University Center for Aging and Human Development, 1973.*

Reim, B., Glass, D. C., & Singer, J. E. *Behavioral consequences of exposure to uncontrollable and unpredictable noise.* Journal of Applied Social Psychology, *1971, 1, 44–56.*

Roth, S., & Kubal, L. *Effects of noncontingent reinforcement on tasks of differing importance: Facilitation and learned helplessness.* Journal of Personality and Social Psychology, *1975, 32, 680–691.*

Schonfield, D. *Future commitments and successful aging. I. The random sample.* Journal of Gerontology, *1973, 28, 189–196.*

Schulz, R. *The psychology of death, dying and bereavement. Unpublished manuscript, Duke University, 1973.*

Schulz, R., & Aderman, D. *Effect of residential change on the temporal distance of death of terminal cancer patients.* Omega: Journal of Death and Dying, *1973, 4, 157–162.*

Schulz, R., & Aderman, D. *Clinical research and the stages of dying.* Omega: Journal of Death and Dying, *1974, 5, 137–143.*

Seligman, M. E. P. *Depression and learned helplessness. In R. J. Friedman & M. M. Katz (Eds.),* The psychology of depression: Contemporary theory and research. *New York: Wiley, 1974.*

Seligman, M. E. P. Helplessness. *San Francisco: W. H. Freeman, 1975.*

Seligman, M. E. P., Maier, S. F., & Solomon, R. L. *Unpredictable and uncontrollable aversive events. In F. R. Brush (Ed.),* Aversive conditioning and learning. *New York: Academic Press, 1971.*

Skeels, H. M. *Adult status of children with contrasting early life experiences.* Monograph for Social Research in Child Development, *1966, 31, 3.*

Spitz, R. A. *Hospitalism: An inquiry into the genesis of psychiatric conditions in early childhood. In R. S. Eissler et al. (Eds.),* The psychoanalytic study of the child *(3rd ed., Vol. 1).* New York: International University Press, 1962.

Streib, G. F. *New roles and activities for retirement. In G. L. Maddox (Ed.),* The future of aging and the aged. *Atlanta: SNPA Foundation, 1971.*

Watson, J. S. *Smiling, cooing, and the 'game.' Paper presented at the meeting of the American Psychological Association, Miami Beach, Florida, September 1970.*

White, R. *Motivation reconsidered: The concept of competence.* Psychological Review, *1959, 66, 297–333.*

Wohlford, P. *Extension of personal time, affective states, and expectation of personal death.* Journal of Personality and Social Psychology, *1966,* 3, *559–566.*

28. Locus of Control in Aging Research

A Case for Multidimensional and Domain-Specific Assessment

Margie E. Lachman

Two MAJOR QUESTIONS dominate the literature on locus of control and aging. First, are there age differences or aging-related changes in locus control? Second, what aging-relevant behaviors are related to individual differences in locus of control orientation?

With regard to age differences and changes, the findings have been remarkably inconsistent. The results of 14 investigations are summarized in Table 28.1. Whereas some studies have shown that an internal locus of control decreases in later life (Bradley & Webb, 1976; Brim, 1974; Lao, 1974; Lachman, 1983; Ryckman & Malikioski, 1975; Saltz & Magruder-Habib, 1982; Siegler & Gatz, 1985), an almost equal number have shown increases in internal control with aging (Gatz & Siegler, 1981; Lachman, 1985; Staats, 1974; Strickland & Shaffer, 1971; Wolk & Kurtz, 1975). Still other studies have found that locus of control remains stable throughout adulthood and old age (Andrisani, 1978; Bradley & Webb, 1976; Nehrke, Hulicka & Morganti, 1980; Saltz & Magruder-Habib, 1982). Clarification of the normative patterns of change and stability as well as age differences in personal control during adulthood and old age is called for in order to facilitate explanation and prediction as well as to enable modification and enhancement of later life beliefs in control.

Possible explanations for the discrepant findings include differences across studies in sample composition, study design, and measurement instruments. As to sample differences, it is known that locus of control is related to such factors as educational level and gender, but it is unclear whether patterns of change or age differences vary as a function of these factors. Many of the research reports, however, do not provide information about the relevant demographic characteristics of their subjects. Thus, it is difficult, with existing

Reprinted by permission from *Psychology and Aging* 1, no. 1 (1986): 34–40. Copyright © 1986 by the American Psychological Association.

data, to determine how subject variables might contribute to the diverse results.

As to design, both cross-sectional and longitudinal studies have been conducted, although the majority are cross sectional. The results, however, do not appear to vary systematically by design, as was found to be the case for intelligence (Baltes & Labouvie, 1973). If any consistent pattern can be detected, it is that later life increases in internal control are not found in the longitudinal studies. Cross-sectional studies show increases, decreases, and no differences (stability) in control with age, whereas longitudinal studies show only decreases or stability.

Finally, as to measurement, several varieties of measurement instruments have been identified (Lefcourt, 1981; Paulhus, 1983). One important distinction across locus of control instruments is the number of dimensions. A multidimensional representation acknowledges that there are multiple sources of control such as self, chance, and other people (Levenson, 1974; Paulhus, 1983). These sources of control may operate either in a generalized way (i.e., across all behavioral domains) or within specific domains or spheres of behavior (Paulhus, 1983). In the present study, both generalized and domain-specific versions of multidimensional assessment instruments were employed. The domain-specific scales contain content relevant to health and intellectual behavior. These two behavioral domains were selected for study because they are areas in which changes generally are expected to occur in later life; thus, they should be sensitive to age differences.

Most studies on locus of control and aging have used unidimensional and generalized measures, such as Rotter's (1966) I-E scale. As summarized in Table 28.1, 11 of the 14 studies reviewed used unidimensional scales and 12 used generalized scales. It is suggested here that application of alternative measurement strategies may shed additional light on both aging-related change patterns and aging-relevant correlates of locus of control. The present studies examined the implications of using multidimensional and domain-specific measures for the assessment of locus of control in aging.

Although conceived within a social learning perspective (Rotter, 1966), locus of control has been treated as an individual differences variable that is stable over time and across situations. In the recent assessment literature on locus of control, the lability of control has been acknowledged (Lefcourt, 1981), and multidimensional and domain-specific measurement features have been given a great deal of attention (Endler & Edwards, 1978; Paulhus, 1983; Reid, 1977; Rotter, 1975). The multidimensional nature of locus of control

Table 28.1. Studies of Age Differences in Locus of Control

Study	Age of subjects	Design	Measure and classification	Results
Strickland & Shaffer (1971)	$M = 17$, $M = 45$, $M = 60$	Cross sectional	Rotter, unidimensional generalized	Older subjects more internal
Brim (1974)	20–70+	Cross sectional	Unpublished, unidimensional generalized	Increases in internality to age 50; decreases in internality from age 55–70+
Lao (1974)	15–85	Cross sectional	Rotter, unidimensional generalized	Teenagers less internal than 30-to 60-year-olds; increase in internality through 30s; decrease in internality after 60.
Staats (1974)	5–15, 16–25, 46–60	Cross sectional	Rotter, unidimensional generalized	Older adults more internal than young groups
Ryckman & Malikioski (1975)	20–29, 30–39, 40–49, 50–59, 60–69, 70–79	Cross sectional	Levenson, multidimensional generalized	College students and 70-year-olds less internal than other age groups
Wolk & Kurtz (1975)	60–85	Cross sectional	Rotter, unidimensional generalized	Elderly more internal relative to contemporary college students in other studies.
Bradley & Webb (1976)	13–18, 19–25, 35–50	Cross sectional	LOCITAD, unidimensional domain specific	Young more internal in social and physical domains; no age differences in intellectual domain
Andrisani (1978)	16–26, 48-62	Cross sectional	Rotter (4 items), unidimensional generalized	No differences between young and middle-age groups
Nehrke, Hulicka & Morganti (1980)	50–59, 60–69, 70+	Cross sectional	Rotter, unidimensional generalized	No differences between middle-and old-age groups
Gatz & Siegler (1981)	18–26, 46–54, 63–70	Cross sectional	Jessor, unidimensional generalized	Middle-age and elderly groups more internal than college students

Author	Age range	Design	Scale	Findings
Saltz & Magruder-Habib (1982)	21–88	Cross sectional	Levenson, multidimensional generalized	Young more internal on chance scale than elderly; no differences on internal or powerful others scale
			MHLC, multidimensional, domain specific	Young more internal on powerful others in health domain; no differences on internal or chance
Lachman (1983)	60–89	2-year longitudinal	Levenson, multidimensional generalized	Decrease in internality; high correlational stability
Lachman (1985)	35–69	4-year cross-sequential	ISR personal efficacy, unidimensional generalized	Elderly more internal than middle-age groups; no change over 4 years
Siegler & Gatz (1985)	46–69	6-year longitudinal	Jessor, unidimensional generalized	Decrease in internality over time

NOTE: MHLC = Multidimensional Health Locus of Control; ISR = Institute for Social Research.

has been noted in response to several factor analytic studies of the Rotter scale (e.g., Gurin, Gurin & Morrison, 1978; Levenson, 1974). Levenson (1974) challenged Rotter's conception, in which internal and external control were treated as mutually exclusive. In Levenson's model, internal and external components are orthogonal, and subsequent empirical work has confirmed that correlations between the internal and external dimensions are low. Moreover, Levenson parceled the external dimension into two components. Chance control represents unordered forces such as fate and luck, whereas powerful others represents ordered forces of control associated with powerful people such as government officials.

The multidimensional measurement feature is desirable for aging research because it allows for the possibility of differential change trajectories across dimensions (Gurin & Brim, 1984). For instance, it is possible that with aging one becomes more sensitive to the forces of powerful others and chance, without changing one's sense of internal control. If there is such differential chance, it may be obscured with the use of unidimensional measures.

Domain specificity also has important implications for aging research. It is possible that aging-related changes are more likely to occur within specific domains. As illustrated by the following items from Levenson's scale, generalized scale items either ignore specific domains altogether (e.g., When I get what I want, it's usually because I'm lucky) or they include multiple domains (such as physical or social) in the same scale (e.g., Whether or not I get into a car accident is mostly a matter of luck, how many friends I have depends on how nice a person I am). If there is change in some domains but not in others, or if there is change in specific domains but not in a general sense of control, then generalized scales would not be sensitive to these patterns.

Multidimensional and domain-specific scales also may be advantageous for examining correlates of aging. In previous research it has been demonstrated that correlations between locus of control and intellectual performance in the elderly were more consistent and greater in magnitude with domain-specific measures than with generalized measures (Lachman, Baltes, Nesselroade & Willis, 1982). One question addressed by the present study is whether this pattern would occur in another aging-relevant domain, the health domain. Also, what has not been addressed previously is whether it is advantageous to use domain-specific scales in conjunction with generalized scales for predicting aging-relevant behavior. The multidimensional feature also is relevant in the investigation of predictors or correlates because some dimensions may be better predictors of behavior than others.

The present studies were concerned with sensitivity to age differences as well as with predictability of outcomes, as a function of type of measurement instrument. Multidimensional scales of the generalized and domain-specific varieties were used and compared. In the first study, it was predicted that the elderly would be more external than younger persons on chance and powerful others, but would not be different in internal control. Also, it was predicted that the expected age differences would be greater for control within an aging-relevant domain (intelligence) than for generalized control. The second study served as a replication and an extension of these hypotheses to a second domain (health). A third study was conducted for further examination of the age differences hypotheses, and for consideration of outcome measures for the two domains. It was predicted that domain-specific scales would be better predictors of behavioral outcomes, within their respective domains, than would the generalized scales.

METHOD

Subjects

Three independent samples of young and elderly adults participated in this research. The young adults were college students recruited from introductory psychology classes, and they were given research credit for their participation. The elderly adults were community-residing volunteers from senior citizen organizations, and they were paid a nominal fee for their participation.

To minimize extraneous factors that could contribute to age differences, the elderly were positively selected on educational background compared to national cohort norms. Subjects were Caucasian and from middle-or upper-middle-class backgrounds. All of the subjects reported that they were in moderately good health or better.

In Study 1, the participants were 100 college students (24 men, 76 women) with a mean age of 21 years ($SD = 1$) and 96 elderly adults (17 men, 79 women) with a mean age of 69.22 ($SD = 6.88$, range $= 60–89$), from rural communities in central Pennsylvania. The mean number of years of education for the elderly was 11.85 ($SD = 3.19$).

Participants in Study 2 were 51 college students (26 men, 25 women) with a mean age of 19.45 ($SD = 0.88$) and 48 elderly adults (23 men, 25 women) with a mean age of 71.55 ($SD = 8.53$, range $= 60–87$), from several suburban towns in Massachusetts and Indiana. The mean education for the elderly was 13.79 years ($SD = 2.59$).

Study 3 participants were 37 college students (18 men, 19 women) with a mean age of 19.49 (SD = 1.15) and 48 older adults (27 men, 21 women) with a mean age of 75.13 (SD = 6.03, range = 64–91), from suburban Boston. The elderly group had a mean education of 15.06 years (SD = 2.83).

Measures

The locus of control battery included three self-report, multidimensional instruments: one generalized and two domain specific.

Generalized Scales. Levenson's (1974) locus of control instrument includes three scales: internal (personal efficacy), chance (luck, fate), and powerful others. Each scale contains eight items rated on a 6-point scale (*strongly agree to strongly disagree*), with a scoring range of 0–40.

Domain-specific scales. The domain-specific measures were the Personality in Intellectual (Aging) Contexts (PIC) inventory (Lachman et al., 1982) and the Multidimensional Health Locus of Control (MHLC) scale (Wallston & Wallston, 1981). Both instruments were modeled after the Levenson scales, and contain internal (I), chance (C), and powerful others (P) scales.

The domain-specific scales have moderate levels of convergent validity with their counterpart generalized scales. They reflect their "parent" generalized dimensions on a general conceptual level, whereas their content is more narrowly focused on intellectual behavior and aging (PIC) or health and illness (MHLC). The PIC assesses beliefs and attributions about control over intellectual functioning associated with everyday situations and laboratory tasks, as illustrated in the following sample items: (a) It's up to me to keep my mental faculties from deteriorating (I); (b) I have little control over my mental state (C); and (c) I wouldn't be able to figure out postal rates on a package without the postman's help (P). Each scale contains 12 items rated on a 6-point Likert scale (*strongly agree to strongly disagree*), with a scoring range of 0–60.

The MHLC reflects beliefs about sources of control over the prevention of cure of illness. The following are sample items: (a) If I take care of myself, I can avoid illness (I); (b) No matter what I do, if I am going to get sick, I will get sick (C); and (c) Regarding my health, I can only do what my doctor tells me to do (P). Each scale contains six items rated on a 6-point scale from *strongly agree to strongly disagree*, with a possible scoring range of 0–30.

Outcome measures. In Study 3, subjects also completed outcome measures for intelligence and health. The outcome measures for intelligence were two intellectual ability subtests, the Letter Series test from the Primary Mental Abilities test (Thurstone, 1962), and the Advanced Vocabulary subtest from the French Kit (Ekstrom, French, Harmon & Derman, 1976). These tests were chosen because in earlier research they were shown to have among the most salient factor loadings on two broad intelligence factors, fluid and crystallized abilities, respectively (Baltes, Cornelius, Spiro, Nesselroade & Willis, 1980).

The health outcome measures were two questionnaire items: "Compared to other people my age, I believe my health to be" (1 = *very good* to 6 = *very poor*) and "Approximately how many times have you seen a doctor in the last year?"

Procedure

The Levenson generalized scales and the PIC domain-specific scales were administered in all three studies. The MHLC domain-specific scales were given in Studies 2 and 3, and the intelligence and health outcome measures were given in Study 3.

Subjects were tested in groups of 2 to 10 persons. The college students were tested in a psychology laboratory or a classroom, and the elderly were tested in meeting halls and senior centers. Either a young or a middle-aged woman administered the tests. Instructions were read aloud, and any questions were answered before the group was instructed to begin. The entire group worked simultaneously on the same test.

RESULTS AND DISCUSSION

Several analytic strategies were adopted. To examine age differences between groups, two-tailed *t* tests were used, and the .01 significance level was adopted. All means, standard deviations, and *t* values appear in Table 28.2. The significant effects are reported later. To control for educational differences between age groups, partial correlations were examined. Age was correlated with the locus of control scales, and education was partialed. None of the significant age effects (as shown in Table 28.2 with *t* tests) was affected by partialing education.

To examine the relations of age, sex, and education with locus of control within age groups, Pearson correlations were computed. No significant effects were found within the young group. The significant effects for age, sex, and education within the elderly group are reported later.[1]

Table 28.2. Age Differences in Generalized and Domain-Specific Locus of Control Dimensions

| | Age group | | | | |
| | Young | | Elderly | | |
Dimension	M	SD	M	SD	t-value
		Study 1			
Generalized					
Internal	28.34	5.02	28.55	5.98	0.24
Chance	14.54	6.75	16.66	7.77	2.04
Powerful others	14.27	5.77	15.07	7.58	0.82
Intelligence specific					
Internal	51.41	6.15	46.87	10.30	3.69**
Chance	15.17	6.92	24.88	10.58	7.53**
Powerful others	14.09	7.64	18.96	10.13	3.80**
		Study 2			
Generalized					
Internal	29.10	4.16	27.98	4.95	1.21
Chance	13.22	5.79	15.19	7.49	1.45
Powerful others	13.65	5.17	14.13	6.97	0.38
Intelligence specific					
Internal	53.13	5.38	50.75	7.09	1.88
Chance	12.02	6.85	23.40	11.60	5.90**
Powerful others	9.63	6.97	15.90	12.34	3.09*
Health specific					
Internal	23.00	5.17	20.85	5.95	1.90
Chance	9.92	6.45	11.26	6.25	1.04
Powerful others	8.27	4.62	13.68	6.00	4.96**
		Study 3			
Generalized					
Internal	30.27	4.72	29.00	5.91	1.10
Chance	13.24	5.96	15.71	8.21	1.60
Powerful others	13.03	6.14	13.28	7.52	0.16
Intelligence specific					
Internal	53.41	4.57	51.15	7.15	1.77
Chance	12.89	7.73	22.65	10.75	4.86**
Powerful others	12.62	9.84	14.85	10.15	1.02
Health specific					
Internal	22.11	4.48	20.69	5.43	1.32
Chance	10.89	6.88	11.21	6.30	0.22
Powerful others	7.24	5.34	14.04	6.21	5.42**

$*p < .01.$ $**p < .001.$

Study 1

For Levenson's three generalized scales no significant age-group differences were found. Age differences were significant at the .001 level for all three of the intelligence-specific scales. The elderly were less internal and more external (on both chance and powerful others) than were college students. Within the elderly group, female subjects scored lower than male subjects on the Levenson internal scale, $r = -.26$, $p < .01$, and those with more education were lower on the PIC chance, $r = -.34$, $p < .001$, and powerful others scales, $r = -.34$, $p < .001$.

These results supported the prediction that age differences in internality would be more readily detected with domain-specific measures, in this case in the intelligence domain. The expectation that age differences would be more likely on the external dimensions was not supported, as differences were also found for the internal dimension. A second study was conducted to see if the same pattern could be replicated in the intellectual domain and extended to the health domain.

Study 2

As in the previous study, there were no significant differences on the generalized scales. In contrast, significant age differences were found on several domain-specific scales. For intelligence-specific control there were significant differences for chance and powerful others. The elderly adults were more external than the young on both dimensions. For health-specific control, the elderly were significantly more external on the powerful others dimension.

Within the elderly group, female subjects scored higher than did male subjects on intelligence-specific powerful others, $r = .38$, $p < .01$, and educational level was negatively correlated with the intelligence-specific powerful others scale, $r = -.36$, $p < .01$. Also within the elderly group, age was positively correlated with the PIC chance, $r = .60$, $p < .01$, and powerful others scales, $r = .64$, $r < .01$. This indicates that the younger and older members of the elderly group differed in beliefs about control over intellectual functioning.

Again, the results supported the predictions that age differences would be more salient for control in specific domains than in generalized control. This finding was not only replicated in the intelligence domain; it was also extended to the health domain. Also, as predicted, the significant differences were found only on the external control dimensions and not on the internal dimension. The elderly had more external beliefs in chance for their intellectual functioning and stronger beliefs in the role of powerful others for both their intellectual and health functioning. Elderly female subjects and those with less education had the strongest beliefs in powerful others, with regard to intellectual functioning.

A third study was conducted to examine further the pattern of age differences in generalized and intelligence-specific control, as well as to allow for a replication in the health domain. The third study also enabled a comparison of the effectiveness of generalized versus specific scales for predicting behavioral outcomes.

Study 3

Age differences in locus of control. As predicted, no significant age differences were found for the generalized measures. For the domain-specific measures, the elderly were more external than the young for intelligence-specific chance control and health-specific powerful others control. No significant within-group differences were found.

The results were supportive of the predictions. First, age differences were found for domain-specific measures, but not for generalized measures. Also, in keeping with the results of Study 2 and the prediction that there would be age differences only on the external dimensions, the elderly were more external on chance and powerful others, but they did not differ from the young on the internal dimension. At least for domain-specific assessments, then, the internal dimension was less subject to aging effects.

Locus of control as a predictor. As mentioned earlier, the domain-specific scales have been shown to correlate significantly with their counterpart generalized scales. Convergent validity correlations for the present samples were all statistically significant at the .05 level, and they ranged from .25 to .74, with an average of .43. These correlations lend support to the claim that the domain-specific scales are indicators of locus of control, even though the items tap beliefs in specific areas.

An attractive feature of the domain-specific measures is that they have higher correlations than do their counterpart generalized scales with domain-relevant behavioral outcomes (Lachman, Baltes, Nesselroade & Willis, 1982). What has not been established, however, is the relative advantage of using the domain-specific scales in terms of amount of variance accounted for in the dependent variable. For example, Huebner and Lipsey (1981) found multidimensional domain-specific scales to be superior to multidimensional generalized scales for predicting behavior and attitudes in the domain of environmental activism. Of interest here is whether the domain-specific scales account for significant variance over and above the generalized scales in aging-relevant domains.

Hierarchical regression analysis (Cohen & Cohen, 1983) was used to determine the relative predictive values of generalized versus specific scales. In the first model (Model 1), the three generalized measures were entered as a set on the first step and the three domain-specific scales were entered second. In the second model (Model 2), the sets of variables were entered in reverse order. An incremental F test of the difference in R^2 between the two sets of variables was computed for both models to determine whether the second set of predictors made a significant contribution to the total R^2 (Cohen & Cohen, 1983). For each age group, the two models were tested separately for two dependent variables in each domain, for a total of eight models. The R^2 for the intelligence and health models are presented in Tables 28.3 and 28.4 respectively.

The dependent measures in the intelligence domain were Letter Series and Vocabulary Test performance. As shown in Table 28.3, for college students the order of entry of generalized versus domain-specific scales made no difference. The R^2 increment was not significant for any of the models.

For the elderly, the R^2 increment was significant for the first model for both the Letter Series, $F(3, 41) = 4.18$, $p < .05$, and the Advanced Vocabulary subtests, $F(3, 41) = 5.79$, $p < .01$. In contrast, the R^2 increment was not significant for the second model. These results indicate that the domain-

Table 28.3. Variance Accounted for (R^2) in Hierarchical Regression Analyses for Intelligence Outcomes

	Young		Elderly	
Locus of control dimensions entered	Letter series	Vocabulary	Letter series	Vocabulary
Model 1				
Step 1-generalized	.02	.10	.06	.16
Step 2-specific	.14	.15	.28*	.41**
Model 2				
Step 1-specific	.12	.03	.25	.38
Step 2-generalized	.14	.15	.28	.41

*R^2 increment significant at $p < .05$.
**R^2 increment significant at $p < .01$.

Table 28.4. Variance Accounted for (R^2) in Hierarchical Regression Analyses for Health Outcomes

	Young		Elderly	
Locus of control dimensions entered	Health	Doctor visits	Health	Doctor visits
Model 1				
Step 1-generalized	.19	.25	.04	.02
Step 2-specific	.23	.38	.09	.25*
Model 2				
Step 1-specific	.01	.24	.06	.20
Step 2-generalized	.23*	.38	.09	.25

* R^2 increment significant at $p < .05$.

specific scales accounted for the bulk of the variance and that the generalized measures did not add anything significant beyond the specific measures. In all of the models for the elderly, the best single predictor of intellectual performance was the intelligence-specific powerful others dimension, which is consistent with previous research findings (see Lachman, Baltes, Nesselroade & Willis, 1982). Those elderly who were higher on powerful others control scored lower on Letter Series and Advanced Vocabulary.

The dependent measures in the health domain were self-rated health and number of doctor's visits. In Model 1 for college students, the R^2 increment was not significant for either health or doctor's visits. In Model 2, the R^2 increment was significant for health, $F(3, 30) = 2.92$, $p < .05$, but it was not significant for doctor's visits. Thus, for college students the generalized scales were better predictors of perceived health than were the health-specific scales.

For the elderly, in the first model the increment was significant only for doctor's visits, $F(3, 41) = 4.19$, $p < .05$, indicating that adding the domain-specific measures accounted for additional variance beyond the generalized measures. In the second model, when specific scales were added first, neither R^2 increased significantly. Again, these results indicated the generalized scales did not add any additional variance beyond the domain-specific scales, but that the domain-specific scales accounted for significant variance above and beyond the generalized scales. Similar to the intelligence domain, the best single predictor of health outcomes for the elderly was the health-specific powerful others scale. Those with a stronger belief in powerful others' control over health visited the doctor more frequently.

CONCLUSION

The results of the three studies support the use of multidimensional and do-main-specific assessments of locus of control for aging research. Whereas the use of generalized or unidimensional measures in previous studies has created a body of inconsistent results, the present results show that age differences can be more clearly and consistently defined with domain-specific measures. Similar to past findings with other global personality traits, age differences were not found in the generalized sense of control. In contrast, within the two domains examined (intelligence and health), the elderly were more external than were college students, and these age patterns were not influenced by educational differences. Although the elderly were more external than college students in both domains, it remains to be seen whether there are some domains (e.g., social competence) in which the elderly are more internal than the young.

A number of questions can be raised in response to the results for domain-specific control beliefs. Do the observed age differences reflect accurate perceptions of control or rather stereotypic expectations about control over health and intellectual functioning? What are the sources of individual differences in control beliefs? The focus of future research will be on examining how individual differences in control beliefs both affect and are affected by the aging process.

With regard to multidimensionality, the pattern of results suggests that age differences were more often associated with the external dimensions. Thus, elderly adults, in contrast to young adults, acknowledged the salience of external forces and, yet, maintained strong beliefs in their internal control (personal efficacy). Only in Study 1 were age differences found on the (intelligence-specific) internal dimension. This variation could be due to differences in the characteristics of the Study 1 sample. In this sample women predominated; they were from rural areas, and their educational level was lower. Thus, there was support, although mixed, for the notion that the internal dimension does not show age differences, whereas the external dimensions do. As the elderly confront the increasing likelihood of illness and death, as well as a lack of power in the social, economic, and political spheres, it is likely that their sense of chance and powerful others control would increase (Kuypers & Bengtson, 1973). Internal control (i.e., personal efficacy), on the other hand, is not as likely to be affected, because the aging individual comes to know his or her own capabilities and limitations and, possibly, to compensate for them (Baltes, Dittmann-Kohli & Dixon, 1984).

Of course the present cross-sectional results cannot provide direct evidence of aging-related change or stability, but the results nevertheless highlight the need for studying multidimensional and domain-specific conceptions of control with longitudinal designs.

The use of domain-specific and multidimensional measures was also supported by the data on behavioral predictions. Researchers had previously established that domain-specific measures were more highly correlated with outcome measures, but had not explored the relative contribution of the different types of scales (Lachman, Baltes, Nesselroade & Willis, 1982). The results show that if the goal is to maximize predicted variance within a given behavioral domain, then specific scales alone are better than generalized scales alone. The advantage of using domain-specific measures, however, seems to hold for the elderly but not for the young. This may indicate that locus of control is more differentiated in the elderly. For the young, locus of control may be a generalized phenomenon that is related to behavior in a wide variety of domains, whereas for the elderly, perceived control may vary across domains. As a consequence, the generalized scales are less adequate for predicting behavior in any one domain for the elderly. It is also possible, however, that examination of control beliefs in domains that are more relevant for the young, (e.g., academic achievement, work) would lead to different conclusions. Predictability of outcomes for any age group is likely to be dependent on using control measures that are relevant in the context of interest.

For the elderly, the best predictors of behavioral outcomes were the domain-specific, powerful others scales. High scores on the powerful others dimension indicates the belief that it is necessary to depend on others for assistance. Those elderly subjects who perceived their intellectual and health outcomes as dependent on powerful others showed poorer performance on intelligence tests and visited the doctor more frequently. For the elderly, health locus of control seems to be related to health behaviors (i.e., going to the doctor) rather than to perceived health status.

In future research it will be important to determine the consequences of locus of control beliefs for a wider range of behaviors associated with aging. Also of interest for future research will be whether locus of control in the elderly can be modified or optimized. If locus of control in specific domains can be changed, will this have an effect on behavioral functioning or on a generalized sense of worth? Further attention to the multidimensional and domain-specific aspects of locus of control scales, hopefully, will contribute to increased understanding of aging changes and behavioral outcomes associated with locus of control

NOTE

1. For comparison purposes, multiple regression analysis was used in Studies 2 and 3. Models were tested, both for the combined sample and separately within age groups, with locus of control scales as dependent variables, and age, education, and sex as independent variables. The significant effects obtained using both forward inclusion and forced entry procedures replicated those obtained using univariate correlations.

REFERENCES

Andrisani, P. J. (1978). Work attitudes and labor market experience. New York: Praeger.

Baltes, P. B., Cornelius, S. W., Spiro, A. III, Nesselroade, J. R. & Willis, S. L. (1980). Integration versus differentiation of fluid-crystallized intelligence in old age. Developmental Psychology, 16, 625–635.

Baltes, P. B., Dittmann-Kohli, F. & Dixon, R. A. (1984). New perspectives on the development of intelligence in adulthood: Toward a dual-process conception and a model of selective optimization with compensation. In P. B. Baltes & O. G. Brim (Eds.), Life-span development and behavior (Vol. 6, pp. 33–76). New York: Academic Press.

Baltes, P. B. & Labouvie, G. V. (1973). Adult development of intellectual performance: Description, explanation, modification. In C. Eisdorfer & M. P. Lawton (Eds.), The psychology of adult development and aging (pp. 157–219). Washington, D.C: American Psychological Association.

Bradley, R. H. & Webb, R. (1976). Age-related differences in locus of control orientation in three behavior domains. Human Development, 19, 49–55.

Brim, O. G., Jr. (1974, September). The sense of personal control over one's life. Paper presented at the 82nd annual convention of the American Psychological Association, New Orleans, LA.

Cohen, J. & Cohen, P. (1983). Applied multiple regression/correlation analysis for the behavioral sciences (2nd ed.). Hillsdale, NJ: Erlbaum.

Ekstrom, R., French, J., Harmon, H. & Derman, D. (1976). Manual for kit of factor-referenced tests. Princeton, NJ: Educational Testing Service.

Endler, N. S. & Edwards, J. (1978). Person by treatment interactions in personality research. In L. A. Pervin & M. Lewis (Eds.), Perspectives in in interactional psychology (pp. 141–169). New York: Plenum.

Gatz, M. & Siegler, I. C. (1981, August). Locus of control: A retrospective. Paper presented at the American Psychological Association Meetings, Los Angeles.

Gurin, P., & Brim, O. G., Jr. (1984). Change in self in adulthood: The example of *sense of control. In P. B. Baltes & O. G. Brim, Jr. (Eds.),* Life-span development and behavior *(Vol. 6, pp. 281–334). New York: Academic Press.*

Gurin, P., Gurin, G. & Morrison, B. M. *(1978). Personal and ideological aspects of internal and external control.* Social Psychology, 41, *275–296.*

Huebner, R. B. & Lipsey, M. W. *(1981). The relationship of three measures of locus of control to environmental activism.* Basic and Applied Social Psychology, 2, *45–58.*

Kuypers, J. A. & Bengtson, V. L. *(1973). Social breakdown and competence: A model of normal aging.* Human Development, 16, *181–201.*

Lachman, M. E. *(1983). Perceptions of intellectual aging: Antecedent or consequence of intellectual functioning?* Developmental Psychology, 19, *482–498.*

Lachman, M. E. *(1985). Personal efficacy in middle and old age: Differential and normative patterns of change. In G. H. Elder, Jr. (Ed.),* Life-course dynamics: Trajectories and transitions, 1968–1980. *Ithaca, NY: Cornell University Press.*

Lachman, M. E., Baltes, P. B., Nesselroade, J. R. & Willis, S. L. *(1982). Examination of personality-ability relationships in the elderly: The role of the contextual (interface) assessment mode.* Journal of Research in Personality, 16, *485–501.*

Lao, R. C. *(1974, September).* The development trend of the locus of control. *Paper presented at the meeting of the American Psychological Association, New Orleans, LA.*

Lefcourt, H. M. (Ed.). *(1981).* Research with the locus of control construct: Assessment methods *(Vol. 1). New York: Academic Press.*

Levenson, H. *(1974). Activism and powerful others: Distinctions within the concept of internal-external control.* Journal of Personality Assessment, 38, *377–383.*

Nehrke, M. F., Hulicka, I. H. & Morganti, J. *(1980). Age differences in life satisfaction, locus of control, and self-concept.* International Journal of Aging and Human Development, 11, *25–33.*

Paulhus, D. *(1983). Sphere-specific measures of perceived control.* Journal of Personality and Social Psychology, 44, *1253–1265.*

Reid, D. W. *(1977). Locus of control as an important concept for an interactionist approach to behavior. In D. Magnusson & N. S. Endler (Eds.),* Personality at the crossroads: Current issues in interactional psychology *(pp. 185–191). Hillsdale, NJ:Erlbaum.*

Rotter, J. B. *(1966). Generalized expectancies for internal versus external control of reinforcement.* Psychological Monographs, 80(1, *Whole No. 609).*

Rotter, J. B. *(1975). Some problems and misconceptions related to the construct of internal control of reinforcement.* Journal of Consulting and Clinical Psychology, 43, *56–67.*

Ryckman, R. M. & Malikioski, M. *(1975). Relationship between locus of control and chronological age.* Psychological Reports, 36, *655–658.*

Saltz, C. & Magruder-Habib, K. *(1982, November).* Age as an indicator of depression and locus of control among non-psychiatric inpatients. *Paper presented at the meeting of the Gerontological Society of America, Boston, MA.*

Siegler, I. C. & Gatz, M. *(1985). Age patterns in locus of control. In E. Palmore, E. Busse, G. Maddox, J. Nowlin, & I. Siegler (Eds.),* Normal aging III. *Durham, NC: Duke University Press.*

Staats, S. (1974). Internal versus external locus of control for three age groups. International Journal of Aging and Human Development, 5, *7–10.*

Strickland, B. R. & Shaffer, S. (1971). I-E, I-E, and F. Journal for the Scientific Study of Religion, 10, *366–369.*

Thurstone, T. G. (1962). Primary mental abilities for grades 9–12. Chicago: Science Research Associates.

Wallston, K. A. & Wallston, B. S. (1981). Health locus of control scales. In H. M. Lefcourt (Ed.), Research with the locus of control construct: Assessment methods *(Vol. 1, pp. 189–243). New York: Academic Press.*

Wolk, S. & Kurtz, J. (1975). Positive adjustment and involvement during aging and expectancy for internal control. Journal of Consulting and Clinical Psychology, 43(2), *173–178.*

29 Status and Functioning of Future Cohorts of African-American Elderly
Conclusions and Speculations

James S. Jackson, Linda M. Chatters, and Robert Joseph Taylor

I N OTHER CHAPTERS we have addressed several substantive issues and the deficit in empirical data that has plagued previous research on the status and functioning of African-American elderly. We have placed these empirical findings within a larger theoretical context that views such statuses and functioning within a model of role changes and adaptations over the individual and group life course. In this chapter we would like to highlight and synthesize the major findings and speculate about what coming decades may portend for future cohorts of African-American elderly.

In this chapter we summarize the major findings, examine briefly the general issues of the middle-aged "Negro" of 1967, and speculate on where that and subsequent cohorts of middle-aged and older blacks might be in the 21st century. This perspective highlights the importance of life span continuity in the black experience in the United States, reflected in cumulative individual and social deficits, the strength of birth cohort experiences for an oppressed minority, and the important effects that aging and period events may have in shaping the future of existing cohorts of black American adults (J. S. Jackson, in press).

The findings from the first Nationwide Conference on the Health Status of the "Negro" in 1967 at Howard University are still applicable today and succinctly make the point of this chapter. During the conference, Cornely (1968) reported on the widening health gap between blacks and whites, pointing specifically to fetal death rates, life expectancy, childhood health risks, and disease-specific causes of death, all indicating significant increased risks in the "Negro" population. Since this notable conference and report there have been both improvements in black health status over the early and middle

From *Aging in Black America*, James Jackson, et al., eds. (Thousand Oaks, CA: Sage Publications, 1993.) Reprinted by permission of Sage Publications, Inc.

stages of the life course and continued discrepancies from that of the general population. The realization that today's African-American elders were the middle-aged "Negroes" of 1967 when this report was written, starkly highlights the importance of a life span framework in interpreting and understanding the life circumstances of African Americans at every position in the life-cycle, but most importantly in older adulthood.

At many points in this chapter we will refer the reader to Table 29.1. This table provides a brief examination of change and stability among middle-aged and older cohorts over the period 1979–1980 to 1987 in several life domains. These data are based upon the NSBA respondents and a second wave of data collection on the original sample, the Panel Survey of Black Americans (J. S. Jackson & Wolford, 1992). This table provides a summary of gross changes in several life domains as the middle-aged and older black cohorts aged from 1979–1980 to 1987. These data are based upon the 915 respondents for whom we have complete responses from both points in time and are weighted to reflect the distribution of the original NSBA sample. These percentages indicate whether individuals in a given cohort show decreases, stability, or increases on a particular indicator as they age over the 7–8 year period. Thus, Column 1 shows the changes or stability in life satisfaction and indicates the proportions of individuals who showed increases, decreases, or remained the same in reported life satisfaction from 1980 to 1987 as they aged from 35–44 to 43–52, 45–54 to 53–62, and so on, through those who were 75 and over in 1979–1980 and over 83 years of age in 1987. Other domains include the amount and frequency of help gained from church members, amount of health satisfaction, the degree of health disability, whether the amount of informal support changed, whether the respondents were more or less likely to vote in presidential and local elections, the degree of race group identity, and whether different age cohorts were more or less likely to show a change in work status.

POPULATION COMPOSITION TRENDS: THE AGING OF BLACK AMERICA

This chapter highlights the importance of the demographic changes in the older total and black populations. The transformation of the age structure will have important effects on the work and retirement experiences, health, and functioning of older blacks and the availability of informal and formal supports. Based upon the middle projection series of the U.S. Census Bureau (1.9 ultimate lifetime births per woman, mortality life expectancy of 79.6

Table 29.1 Change from 1980 to 1987 in the Proportion of People Showing Increases, Stability, or Decreases in Life Satisfaction, Help from the Church, Frequency of Help from Church, Health Satisfaction, Health Disability, Amount of Informal Help, Voting in Last Presidential Election, Voting in Last Local Election, Racial Identification, and Employment Status (in percentages)

Life domain age change in years 1980–1987	Type of change 1980–1987	Life satisfaction	Church help	Often church help	Health satisfaction	Health disability	Help receipt	Vote president	Vote local	Race identity	Employment status
35–44 to 45–52	Increases	31	16	33	17	29	31	16	19	15	13
	Stability	51	54	32	59	54	42	82	74	64	73
	Decreases	18	30	25	24	17	27	2	7	21	14
45–52 to 53–62	Increases	26	15	22	20	35	33	19	14	18	6
	Stability	50	51	38	53	55	37	75	72	66	79
	Decreases	24	34	40	27	10	30	6	4	16	15
55–64 to 63–72	Increases	25	27	32	19	24	14	13	22	17	2
	Stability	53	42	29	58	59	32	85	71	74	76
	Decreases	22	31	39	23	17	54	2	7	9	22
65–74 to 73–82	Increases	22	15	44	17	25	16	11	22	12	2
	Stability	63	50	32	56	57	40	75	64	75	62
	Decreases	15	35	24	27	18	44	14	14	13	36
75+ to 83+	Increases	12	13	24	26	3	0	5	9	20	0
	Stability	53	74	48	35	62	69	92	83	70	13
	Decreases	35	13	28	39	35	31	3	8	10	87

years in 2050, and annual net immigration of 450,000), it is projected that sustained growth will occur in the over age 65 group until the year 2010. From 2010 through 2030 the postwar baby boom cohorts will increase the over age 65 group from 39 to 65 million. By the year 2030, every fifth American will be over the age of 65 (Siegel & Taeuber, 1986).

Of those individuals over the age of 65, one of the most rapidly growing demographic groups are persons over the age of 85 (Suzman & Riley, 1985). The baby boom cohorts will continue to have a major impact on the societal age structure and will swell the ranks of the over age 85 group from an expected 9 million in 2030 to 16 million by 2050. These projections also suggest comparable effects on estimates for other age groupings, 75 years and older, for example, in the elderly population. As pointed out by several authors, however, reductions in current mortality rates would lead to even greater increases in these projected numbers (Siegel & Davidson, 1984; Siegel & Taeuber, 1986; Suzman & Riley, 1985).

The projected changes in the age structure of the population have resulted in much speculation regarding the social and policy implications of an aging society (Neugarten & Neugarten, 1986; Palmer & Gould, 1986), the rise in the total dependency ratio (Siegel & Taeuber, 1986), individual health, health service delivery, and rising health costs in a population with a large proportion of longevous members (Davis 1986; Gibson, 1986; Manton & Soldo, 1985; Soldo, 1980). Morbidity and mortality will continue to increase within the older population as an outcome of the increasing numbers of individuals living to older ages (Davis, 1986; Siegel & Davidson, 1984).

Racial and ethnic minorities are also contributing to the aging of the United States at a slightly higher rate than in the general population (J. S. Jackson, Burns & Gibson, 1992; Siegel & Davidson, 1984). Demographic trends over the last four decades and projections over the next four indicate a significant upward shift in the mean age of the black population and greater concentrations of blacks in all age ranges over 45, with the largest *percentage* shift to occur in blacks 85 years of age and older. Most projections (Siegel & Davidson, 1984) suggest rather large increases in both blacks and whites over the age of 65, particularly for the oldest old, with commensurate larger proportionate increases among the black elderly. These latter increases undoubtedly reflect the greater environmental advantages of these recent black older cohorts in comparison to previous cohorts. Because blacks show greater morbidity at each point in the life span prior to age 65, the relative meaning of increasing proportions and numbers of older blacks in the population must be examined.

LIFE COURSE OF AFRICAN AMERICANS

Although little theory exists regarding life span continuity and discontinuity of racial and ethnic group members (J. J. Jackson, 1985; J. S. Jackson, in press; J. S. Jackson, Burns & Gibson, 1992), it is clear that life circumstances during younger ages have significant influences upon the quality of life in the latter stages of the life course. From a social problems perspective, some have marked this as the multiple jeopardy hypothesis (Dowd & Bengtson, 1978; J. J. Jackson, 1980, 1985). This hypothesis holds that negative environmental, social, and economic conditions early in the life course of blacks have deleterious effects on later social, psychological, and biological growth (J. J. Jackson, 1981). These accumulate over the individual life span and when combined with the negative consequences of old age itself, eventuate in higher levels of morbidity and mortality at earlier years in old age than is the case for whites.

At almost every point of the life span blacks have greater disability and morbidity (J. J. Jackson, 1981). In infancy this is marked by higher mortality figures as well as accident and disease rates. Adolescence, young adulthood, and even older ages of blacks are characterized by comparatively higher homicide deaths than whites. Middle age and early old age show increased disability, early retirement, and ultimately higher death rates in the black as compared to the general population. It is only after the age of 75 to 80 that blacks tend to show increased longevity in comparison to whites (J. S. Jackson, Burns & Gibson, 1992; Manton, 1982; Manton, Poss & Wing, 1979; Markides, 1983).

It has been suggested that this racial crossover phenomenon in the oldest old black and white populations is an artifact of age misreporting in older cohorts, particularly the tendency of older blacks to inflate their ages. Others have argued strongly that this is a consistent finding with cross-national support in other cultures (J. J. Jackson, 1985; J. S. Jackson, Antonucci & Gibson, 1990a; Manton, 1982; Omran, 1977). In support of the substance of this observed crossover it has been suggested that genetic and environmental factors act in tandem on a heterogeneous black population to produce hardier older blacks (Gibson & Jackson, 1987, 1992; Manton, Poss & Wing, 1979). One direct implication of this explanation is the existence of differential aging processes within black and white populations (Manton, 1982). As noted by J. J. Jackson (1985), however, no research findings yet support this latter claim. This issue is still under investigation, prompted by recent research showing positive outcomes in aging and effective functioning in the black oldest old (Gibson & Jackson, 1987, 1992).

Many older blacks continue to work in very productive formal employment roles. Coleman's (1993) analyses support a traditional finding in the literature that good health is positively related to employment in older ages. She then speculates on what this employment may mean, given that blacks have a long history of secondary labor market involvement. Marital roles and need also appear to play a role in accounting for who is working or not. She concludes that work for older blacks, as in the younger populations, serves a variety of functional and need-reduction roles and that there is no inevitable decline with age that necessarily drives older black workers from the labor force. At the same time, Gibson (1993) shows that traditional definitions of retirement are misapplied in this cohort of older blacks. Though one can find the traditionally retired individual, many older African Americans defy easy description and seem to fall into underemployed worker, disabled workers, and people whose retired status is not clearly ascertained (''unretired-retired''). As shown in Table 29.1, different age cohorts show stability of initial work patterns through the 65–74 years of age cohort (73%, 79%, 76%, and 62%). It is only as the 75 and older cohort ages over the 7-year period that work shows a decided decrease (87% indicating a decrease in working). Interestingly, each of the five age cohorts examined shows a significant decline in work status and a significant increase in reported health disability. Issues of choice, a lifetime of labor force participation in secondary sector jobs, and structural impediments to mobility all could contribute to the wide diversity of work and retirement roles discussed in Coleman (1993) and Gibson (1993), and supported by the patterns over the 7-year period shown in Table 29.1.

There is a general tendency in the United States to view African Americans in simplistic and undifferentiated ways, assuming a large degree of homogeneity in values, motives, social and psychological statuses, and behaviors (J. S. Jackson, in press; Jaynes & Williams, 1989). Although racially based categorical treatment results in some extent of group uniformity in attitudes and behaviors, it has always been true that there exists a rich heterogeneity among blacks (J. S. Jackson, in press). Research demonstrates that African Americans span the same spectrum of structural circumstances, psychological statuses, and social beliefs as the millions of other Americans of different ethnic and cultural backgrounds (J. S. Jackson, in press; Stanford, 1990). But a unique history and the nature of their group and individual developmental and aging experiences, all serve to place vast numbers of Americans of African descent in the United States from cradle to grave at disproportionate risk for physical, social, and psychological harm.

In the face of these harsh realities of life, our research findings show older African Americans to be a diverse and heterogenous population, possessing a wide array of group and personal resources at every point in the age span (J. S. Jackson, 1991; Stanford, 1990). For example, R. J. Smith and M. C. Thornton (1993) point to the continuing importance of group solidarity among older blacks. Their results indicate that this solidarity is related in very complex ways to socioeconomic factors and defies simple characterization. These results point to the importance of group consciousness and group interests as a continuing potential resource in older ages among blacks. Table 29.1 indicates a great deal of stability in race group identity among the different age cohorts as they age. These data also point to the possibility that this race group identity may be linked to age, as both stability and increases over time are more prevalent in the older cohorts. Brown and Barnes-Nacoste (1993) demonstrate the power and efficacy of this solidarity as it relates to political empowerment and participation. Their findings clearly implicate group solidarity as a mediator of racial socialization in the voting process among this older cohort of blacks. As shown in Table 29.1, remarkable stability and increased political participation (presidential and local voting)is found across all age cohorts with some increments in the original older age cohorts. Like most of the chapters in this volume, the data in Table 29.1 and the results in Smith and Thornton (1993) and Brown and Barnes-Nacoste (1993) document the continuing potency and significance of group interest and racial solidarity in today's older black cohorts.

Brown and Barnes-Nacoste (1993) notably develop a conceptual model that attempts to place region of early socialization experiences in a causal chain of group interest and ultimate political behavior. Taylor and Thornton (1993) further examine the correlates of voting, suggesting that organized religious involvement is important in the voting behavior of older blacks. These findings suggest that both group interests, as expressed in group identity and consciousness, and organizational memberships have important, independent influences on political behavior. It may be that the organizational aspects of attachment, whether to the group or to a social and political structure like the church, provide the underlying mediating factor.

The changing age structure will have important influences on the health and effective functioning of older blacks (Gibson, 1986; Richardson, 1991). Because older black Americans of the year 2047 have already been born, the continuing imbalanced sex ratio, segregated geographic distribution, and pro-portion in poverty, among other structural factors, will have profound influ-ences upon family structure, health status, and the well-being of older blacks over the next 50–60 years (J. S. Jackson, in press). A life span framework is needed to explore how environmental stressors influence and interact with group and personal resources (e.g., Smith & Thornton, 1993; Brown & Barnes-Nacoste, 1993) to impede or facilitate the quality of life of successive cohorts of African Americans (Baltes, 1987; Barresi, 1987).

Notable improvements in the life situations of blacks (Farley, 1987), par-ticularly health, have occurred over the last 40 years (J. J. Jackson, 1981; J. S. Jackson, Antonucci & Gibson, 1990a). Recent literature (e.g, Farley, 1987; Gibson, 1986; Jaynes & Williams, 1989), however, points to significant remaining structural barriers, particularly for poor blacks. These problems include the difficulties of single-parent households, high infant mortality and morbidity, childhood diseases, poor diets, lack of preventive health care, de-teriorating neighborhoods, poverty, adolescent violence, un-and underem-ployment, teen pregnancy, drug and alcohol abuse, and broken marriages. Although the causal relationships are not known (Williams, 1990), it is clear that these are predisposing factors for high morbidity and mortality across the life span (Dressler, 1991; Haan & Kaplan, 1985; Hamburg, Elliott & Parron, 1982).

Concurrent with changes in the age composition of the population, trends in poverty status and family structure among black Americans have important consequences for future cohorts of older persons. In the past 30 years, the structure of U.S. families has undergone substantial changes. During this period, both white and black families have witnessed higher divorce rates, increases in female-headed households, a higher proportion of births to un-married mothers, larger percentages of children living in female-headed households, and a higher percentage of children living in poverty. Although these demographic changes have been experienced by both blacks and whites, black families have disproportionately suffered their impact (Jaynes & Wil-liams, 1989; Taylor et al., 1990).

One of the major causes of these changes in poverty status and family structure among blacks is the declining rate of marriage. Over the past 30 years, larger proportions of black adults have either postponed marriage or have declined to marry at all. Although most black women will marry at some point in their lives, the overall proportion who ever marry could range as low as 70% or 80% (Rodgers & Thornton, 1985). In contrast, 94% of black women born in the 1930s eventually married. Currently, these women make up the cohort of older black women 53–62 years of age. Recent trends suggest that as a result of later marriages; higher rates of separation, divorce, and widowhood; and more time spent in separated, divorced, and widowed statuses, black females as a whole will spend a greater part of their lives unmarried (Taylor et al., 1990).

The decrease in length of time in marriage is an important contributing factor in the substantial increases in nonmarital births, childhood poverty, and female-headed households. Presently, about 6 of 10 black births are to unmarried mothers, half of all black children live in poverty, half of all black children live with their mothers but not their fathers, and over one in four black households is headed by a single female. All of these trends have increased over the past two decades and coincide with the reduced length of time spent in marriage by black Americans (Taylor et al., 1990).

Although the impact of the decrease in the length of time in marriage has definite consequences for the status of black children and young adults, additional effects can be predicted for later portions of the life span. In particular, fewer years in marriage would likely act to intensify rates of being unmarried among older women. We can expect that, distinct from past cohorts, older women who are widowed would make up a smaller proportion of the group of older unmarried women. Further, the trend toward a decline in marriage suggests that the proportion of never-married older women will increase in future cohorts of black elderly. Older black women will spend more time without marital partners, a trend that would seemingly exacerbate the present economic and social problems facing this group.

In particular, the companionship of a spouse, wider informal support relationships within families, living arrangements, and income adequacy will all be affected. These factors have been identified in the literature as having particular and significant impacts on the quality of life among older adults. Spouses are consistently noted as important sources of instrumental and socioemotional assistance and as central figures in informal support networks (Chatters, Taylor & Jackson, 1985). Further, married status has been associated with enhanced perceptions of well-being among older black adults (Chatters, 1988). Although the specific life course patterns of support will vary across marital status designations, overall family resources to these women may be unavailable or truncated. Family support networks are particularly crucial in the areas of health status, formal health resource use, and self-care activities (e.g., medication use, diet, therapies) of older persons. As shown in Table 29.1, one of the most volatile domains of life is the amount of informal help received over the 7-year period. For the two younger cohorts, increased age is almost equally likely to result in reports of both increased and decreased assistance from family and friends. In the three older cohorts, reports of decreased support are from 30% to 40% greater than indications of increased assistance. The changes in spousal and friend networks discussed here could account for this observed diminishment in informal assistance over time.

With regard to living arrangements for older black women, in 1940, 9.4% lived alone as compared to 31.4% of older black women in 1980. As living alone is an important predictor of nursing home utilization, it is anticipated that the increased tendency to live alone may lead to greater institutionalization for this group (Shapiro & Ross, 1989). But although older black women are less likely to be married than their white counterparts, about equal percentages share households with others (Sweet & Bumpass, 1987). Consequently, the existence of extended family households may, in part, mitigate this situation. Similarly, older never-married, divorced, and widowed black women will have fewer economic resources than their married counterparts. Although older blacks generally experience high rates of poverty, married couples have higher incomes and a lower incidence of poverty than do their non-married counterparts (Taylor & Chatters, 1988).

We have been attempting to develop a coherent life span framework within which the nature of the economic, social, and psychological lives of black Americans can be understood and explained in the context of historical and current structural disadvantage and blocked mobility opportunities (J. S. Jackson, 1991; J. S. Jackson, in press; J. S. Jackson, Antonucci & Gibson, 1990a, 1990b; J. S. Jackson, Taylor & Chatters, 1993). In general, our data collections have been designed to explore scientifically the nature of African Americans' reactions to their unequal status in the United States. Specifically, the research reported in this volume has addressed the question of how structural disadvantages in the environment are translated at different points in the individual and group life cycle into physical, social, and psychological aspects of group and self.

This work has focused on such things as neighborhood and family integration, self-esteem, personal efficacy, closeness of personal and social relationships, physical and mental health, group solidarity and political participation, and work and retirement. Thus, McAdoo (1993) notes the deterioration in urban neighborhoods and the resultant victimization, stress, and perceptions of vulnerability among older African Americans. His findings indicate that black older adults may have very effective mechanisms for handling the stress and strains caused by environmental stressors. The findings of Jayakody (1993) provide one possible mechanism by which this positive adjustment may occur. Her findings suggest the overall importance of the neighborhood and neighbors in providing a psychologically supportive environment as well as a tangible source of resource potential for older blacks. Notably, her findings point to some peculiar cultural and historical legacies, that is, the fact that older African Americans living in the South are more likely to report neighborhood integration, even controlling for urbanicity. Even though as we point out, deteriorating neighborhoods provide an increasingly "dry" source of support for this generation of older blacks, neighbors are a continuing source of psychological, social, and tangible support. At the same time, the data in Table 29.1 indicate low stability in reported life satisfaction and a decrease over the 7-year period.

Taylor, Keith, and Tucker (1993) point out the complicated role relationships that exist among older men and women and the potential changes over the individual life course in the assumption of helper roles. Chatters and Taylor (1993) make a similar point indicating the importance of adult children in providing tangible and intangible support to older blacks. Finally, Engram and Lockery (1993) remind us of the intimacies and close relationships that exist among older African-American partners and the importance of love, companionship, and support in the well-being and effective functioning of older black adults. These findings stand in marked contrast to the almost total avoidance in the literature of the investigation of close personal relationships among older African Americans. As might be expected, these relationships are important, and when combined with the findings on neighboring, family, and friend relationships paint a picture of older black Americans in more variegated and contexualized manner. This richer perspective counters the sterile and sexless portrait of older blacks that has dominated historical and contemporary mass media and research presentations. Because historical trends and projections continue to herald unbalanced sex ratios in older ages, the root causes of widowhood and single status among older blacks must be examined.

Both Taylor (1993) and J. M. Smith (1993) point to complex and important roles of organized religion in the lives of older blacks. Importantly, both these chapters provide debunking information to simplistic notions of religious belief among blacks. Taylor's findings point to the heterogeneity among blacks in religious affiliations and the multidimensional nature of religious involvement that exists. His findings suggest that older blacks perceive the role of the church in this broad sense and seek succor from the church and religion in both a spiritual and tangible sense. J. M. Smith provides some support for the structural analysis of Taylor and attempts to model the potential dynamic interplay of structural position, family processes, and church involvement. Her findings belie previous work that has ascribed a simple relationship between social structural position and religious involvement. Historically, many writers have viewed the church in simplistic terms of salvation, denying its fundamental position in the secular life of African Americans. J. M. Smith's work suggests that in the presence of controls for primary and secondary group integration as well as frequency of service and urbanicity, clear relationships among achieved socioeconomic status and religious involvement are not present. Rather than denying the importance of achieved socioeconomic statuses in religious involvement, these results suggest that a much more complicated set of causal relationships may exist among these statuses, neighborhood, and family and friend integration. Somewhat disturbing are the trends suggested in Table 29.1, indicating that African Americans of all age cohorts were more likely to report decreased support from church sources over the 7-year period of 1980 to 1987. When combined with the previous deterioration in informal family and friend support, this paints a possibly bleak picture for future cohorts in what has been historically an important source of sustenance for black elders.

We have oriented our studies to examine how the age cohort into which blacks are born; the social, political, and economic events that occur to blacks born together; and the individual aging process at different points in a person's life course influence the adaptation and quality of life of individuals, families, and larger groups of African Americans. For example, we recognize that blacks born before the 1940s faced very different environmental constraints and have experienced a very different set of life tasks, events, opportunities, and disappointments than those born in the 1970s (Baker, 1987). In addition to significant changes in the legal structure, health care advances, family changes, urban migration, and macroeconomic influences all differed dramatically for these very different birth cohorts, as they will for future cohorts of blacks (J. S. Jackson, in press; Richardson, 1991).

How these different birth cohorts, historical and current environmental events, and individual differences in aging processes interact with one another forms the overall context of this research. Although one focus is on the scientific aspects of phenomena such as political behavior, mental disorder, or service provision, the overarching framework is one that contextualizes these individual and group experiences by birth cohort, period events, and individual aging processes.

A set of fairly firm conclusions can be drawn from a review of the material on health, mortality, morbidity, and risk factors. It appears that the examination of black status and functioning, at least that of aging adults, has been conducted in a relative vacuum. Although several authors have indicated the necessity of considering life course models (e.g., Barresi, 1987; Manton & Soldo, 1985), and history, cohort, and period effects in the nature of black statuses and functioning, few have actually collected the type of data or conducted the types of analyses that would shed any light on this process. This has been the fault as much of a lack of good conceptual models of older black adults as a lack of quality data over time on sizable numbers of representative samples of black Americans.

Blacks arrive at older ages with significant amounts of previous disease and ill health. The available cohort data for cause specific mortality and morbidity across the life course over the last few decades indicates that there are accumulated deficits that perhaps place black older people at greater risk than comparably aged whites (J. S. Jackson, 1991). Similarly, the fact that blacks actually outlive their white counterparts in the very older ages suggests possible selection factors at work that may result in hardier oldest old blacks (Gibson & Jackson, 1987, 1992). Cohort experiences of blacks play a major role in the nature of their health experiences over the life course in terms of the quality of health care from birth, exposure to risk factors, and the presence of exogenous noxious environmental factors. Additionally, and with possible differences due to birth cohort and period, prejudice and discrimination as a source of stress and blocked opportunities are pervasive across the life span (Baker, 1987; Dressler, 1991).

Edmonds (1993) provides graphic illustration of the self-reported health conditions of African-American elderly. Her findings show that self-reported diseases and health satisfaction do not bear simple linear relationships to age among elderly African Americans (Gibson & Jackson, 1987). Similarly, Chatters (1993) notes the complexity of understanding health disability and concomitant stress and perceived strain. Chatters suggests that health disability may serve to debilitate coping resources that themselves play important roles in militating the stress-distress relationship. Edmonds notes that structural position and location (rural and Southern) can have negative influences on health outcomes and perceptions of individual satisfaction. Gibson (1993, table 16.1) shows significant percentage decreases in health satisfaction and increased reports of health disability over all age cohorts during the 7-year period.

Somewhat disturbingly, Greene, Jackson, and Neighbors (1993) find that for stressful problems, oldest old black Americans may experience the lowest levels of formal and informal assistance, and that this relationship may hold across socioeconomic and gender groups. This finding is made even more worrisome by the previously reported trends in decreased informal support shown in Gibson (1993). We believe that Edmonds (1993), Chatters (1993), and Greene, Jackson, and Neighbors (1993) provide a clear example of the role of health as both a resource for older blacks as well as a stressor that has influences in other domains of life. In the presence of good physical and mental health, older blacks report active and effective lives. In the absence of such good health and in the presence of significant disability, older blacks report poor functioning and concomitant stress and strains. These data also show that informal and professional help is not always readily available, even though informal supports play an important role among older blacks in preventing and alleviating deleterious environmental problems.

CONCLUSIONS AND IMPLICATIONS

We have argued that previous and contemporary cohorts of blacks have been and are at considerable risk. Blacks have in the past spent and are most likely in the future to spend the majority of their childhood in low-income, single-parent, female-headed households and to be exposed to inadequate educational opportunities. Their job prospects early in life have been poor and will be perhaps even poorer in future cohorts. And a large proportion have suffered and will continue to suffer chronic disease prior to reaching middle adulthood.

None of these structural and health deficits strikes at the psychological and social-psychological phenomena of life among black Americans—lack of perceived control, discouragement, and other effects of discrimination that impede the development of motivating aspirations and expectations of a successful life. When these social and psychological reactions are combined with substantial structural barriers to educational and occupational mobility and high probability of exposure to environmental risk factors, the success of blacks in achieving older ages is remarkable (Jaynes & Williams, 1989).

The results of reviews and empirical analyses, however, clearly indicate that older age among blacks is not a time of inevitable decline (J. S. Jackson, in press; J. S. Jackson, Antonucci & Gibson, 1990a; Rowe, 1985). The evidence points to the fact that real changes in life-style, environmental risk reduction, and medical interventions can have positive influences on the quantity and quality of late life among older black adults, even given negative life course experiences. Some data (e.g., Gibson & Jackson, 1987, 1992) show that many older blacks are free from functional disability (Edmonds, 1993; Chatters, 1993) and limitations of activity due to chronic illness and disease. In fact, after the age of 65, blacks and whites, within sex groups, differ very little in years of expected remaining life. Health care has improved significantly for older black adults and consecutive cohorts have been better educated and better able to take advantage of available opportunities.

At the same time, without extensive environmental interventions, it is highly likely that a significant, and we suggest growing, proportion of older black adults of the year 2047—those being born in 1992—are at severe risk for impoverished conditions and poor social, physical, and psychological health in old age. This is particularly true compared to the middle-aged cohort of 1967—the elderly of today with whom we began this chapter. This gloomy prediction is not predicated on biological dimensions of racial differences, but instead is based upon the physical, social, psychological, and environmental risk factors intimately correlated with racial and ethnic group membership in U.S. society and the inevitable poor prognosis of the life experience paths into older ages of so many African Americans (J. S. Jackson, in press).

REFERENCES

Anderson, N. B., & Shumaker, S. A. (1989). Race, reactivity, and blood pressure regulation. Health Psychology, 8, 483–486.

Baker, F. M. (1987). The Afro-American life cycle: Success, failure, and mental health. Journal of the National Medical Association, 7, 625–633.

Baltes, P. B. (1987). Theoretical propositions of life-span developmental psychology: On the dynamics between growth and decline. Developmental Psychology, 23, 616–626.

Barresi, C. M. (1987). Ethnic aging and the life course. In D. E. Gelfand and C. M. Barresi (Eds.), Ethnic dimensions of aging (pp. 18–34). New York: Springer.

Brown, R. E., & Barnes-Nacoste, R. W. (1993). Group consciousness and political behavior. In James S. Jackson, Linda M. Chatters, & Robert Joseph Taylor (Eds.), Aging in Black America (pp. 217–232). Thousand Oaks, CA: Sage.

Chatters, L. M. (1988). Subjective well-being evaluations among older black Americans. Psychology and Aging, 3, 184–190.

Chatters, L. M. (1993). Health disability and its consequences for subjective stress. In James S. Jackson, Linda M. Chatters, & Robert Joseph Taylor (Eds.), Aging in Black America (pp. 167–183). Thousand Oaks, CA: Sage.

Chatters, L. M., & Taylor, R. J. (1993). Intergenerational support: The provision of assistance to parents by adult children. In James S. Jackson, Linda M. Chatters, & Robert Joseph Taylor (Eds.), Aging in Black America (pp. 69–83). Thousand Oaks, CA: Sage.

Chatters, L. M., Taylor, R. J., & Jackson, J. S. (1985). Size and composition of the informal helper network of elderly blacks. Journal of Gerontology, 40, 605–614.

Coleman, L. M. (1993). The black Americans who keep working. In James S. Jackson, Linda M. Chatters, & Robert Joseph Taylor (Eds.), Aging in Black America (pp. 253–276). Thousand Oaks, CA: Sage.

Cornely, P. B. (1968). The health status of the negro today and in the future. American Journal of Public Health, 58 (4), 647–654.

Davis, K. (1986). Aging and the health-care system: Economic and structural issues. Daedalus, 115, 227–246.

Dowd, J. J., & Bengtson, V. L. (1978). Aging in minority populations: An examination of the double jeopardy hypothesis.

Dressler, W. W. (1991). Social class, skin color, and arterial blood pressure in two societies. Ethnicity and Disease, 1, 60–77.

Edmonds, M. M. (1993). Physical health. In James S. Jackson, Linda M. Chatters, & Robert Joseph Taylor (Eds.), Aging in Black America (pp. 151–166). Thousand Oaks, CA: Sage.

Engram, E., & Lockery, S. A. (1993). Intimate partnerships. In James S. Jackson, Linda M. Chatters, & Robert Joseph Taylor (Eds.), Aging in Black America (pp. 84–97). Thousand Oaks, CA: Sage.

Farley, R. (1987). Who are black Americans?: The quality of life for black Americans twenty years after the civil rights revolution. Milbank Memorial Fund Quarterly, 65 (Supp), 9–34.

Gibson, R. C. (1986). Blacks in an aging society. Daedalus, 115 (1), 349–371.

Gibson, R. C. (1993). The black American retirement experience. In James S. Jackson, Linda M. Chatters, & Robert Joseph Taylor (Eds.), Aging in Black America (pp. 277–297). Thousand Oaks, CA: Sage.

Gibson, R. C., & Jackson, J. S. (1987). Health, physical functioning, and informal supports of the black elderly. Milbank Quarterly, 65 (Suppl. 1), 1–34.

Gibson, R. C., & Jackson, J. S. (1992). The black oldest old: Health, functioning, and informal support. In R. M. Suzman, D. P. Willis, & K. G. Manton (Eds.), The oldest old (pp. 506–515). New York: Oxford University Press.

Greene, R. L., Jackson, J. S., & Neighbors, H. W. (1993). Mental health and health-seeking behavior. In James S. Jackson, Linda M. Chatters, & Robert Joseph Taylor (Eds.), Aging in Black America (pp. 185–200). Thousand Oaks, CA: Sage.

Haan, M. N., & Kaplan, G. A. (1985). The contribution of socioeconomic position to minority health. Report of the Secretary's Task Force on Black and Minority Health: Vol. 2. Crosscutting issues in minority health. Washington, DC: U.S. Department of Health and Human Services.

Hamburg, D. A., Elliott, G. R., & Parron, D. L. (1982). Health and behavior: Frontiers of research in the biobehavioral sciences. Washington, DC: National Academy Press.

Jackson, J. J. (1980). Minorities and Aging. Belmont, CA: Wadsworth.

Jackson, J. J. (1981). Urban black Americans. In A. Harwood (Ed.), Ethnicity and health care (pp. 37–129). Cambridge, MA: Harvard University Press.

Jackson, J. J. (1985). Race, national origin, ethnicity, and aging. In R. H. Binstock

& E. Shanas (Eds.), Handbook of aging and the social sciences (pp. 264–303). New York: Van Nostrand Reinhold.

Jackson, J. S. (Ed.). (1991). Life in black America. Newbury Park, CA: Sage.

Jackson, J. S. (in press). Racial influences on adult development and aging. In R. Kastenbaum (Ed.), The encyclopedia of adult development. Phoenix, AZ: Oryx.

Jackson, J. S., Antonucci, T. C., & Gibson, R. C. (1990a). Cultural, racial, and ethnic minority influences on aging. In J. E. Birren & K. W. Schaie (Eds.), Handbook of the psychology of aging (3rd ed., pp. 102–123). New York: Academic Press.

Jackson, J. S., Antonucci, T. C., & Gibson, R. C. (1990b). Social relations, productive activities, and coping with stress in late life. In M. A. P. Stephens, J. H. Crowther, S. E. Hobfoll, & D. L. Tennenbaum (Eds.), Stress and coping in later life families (pp. 193–212). Washington, DC: Hemisphere.

Jackson, J. S., Burns, C. J., & Gibson, R. C., (1992). An overview of geriatric care in ethnic and racial minority groups. In E. Calkins, A. B. Ford, & P. R. Katz (Eds.), Practice of geriatrics (2nd ed., pp. 57–64). Philadelphia: W. B. Saunders.

Jackson, J. S., Taylor, R. J., & Chatters, L. M. (1993). Roles and resources of the black elderly. In James S. Jackson, Linda M. Chatters, & Robert Joseph Taylor (Eds.), Aging in Black America (pp. 1–18). Thousand Oaks, CA: Sage.

Jackson, J. S., & Wolford, M. L. (1992). Changes from 1980 to 1987 in the mental health status of African Americans. Journal of Geriatric Psychiatry, 25 (1), 15–67.

Jayakody, R. (1993). Neighborhoods and neighbor relations. In James S. Jackson, Linda M. Chatters, & Robert Joseph Taylor (Eds.), Aging in Black America (pp. 21–27). Thousand Oaks, CA: Sage.

Jaynes, G. D., & Williams, R. M., Jr. (Eds.). (1989). A common destiny: Blacks and American society. Washington, DC: National Academy Press.

Manton, K. (1982). Differential life expectancy: Possible explanations during the later years. In R. C. Manuel (Ed.), Minority aging: Sociological and social psychological issues (pp. 63–70). Westport, CT: Greenwood Press.

Manton, K. G., & Soldo, B. J. (1985). Dynamics of health changes in the oldest old: New perspectives and evidence. Milbank Memorial Fund Quarterly, 63, 206–285.

Manton, K., Poss, S. S., & Wing, S. (1979). The black/white mortality crossover: Investigation from the perspective of the components of aging. The Gerontologist, 19, 291–300.

Markides, K. S. (1983). Mortality among minority populations: A review of recent patterns and trends. Public Health Reports.

McAdoo, J. L. (1993). Crime stress, self-esteem, and life satisfaction. In James S. Jackson, Linda M. Chatters, & Robert Joseph Taylor (Eds.), Aging in Black America (pp. 38–48). Thousand Oaks, CA: Sage.

Neugarten, B. L., & Neugarten, D. A. (1986). Age in the aging society. Daedalus, 115, B1–49.

Omran, A. R. (1977). Epidemiologic transition in the U.S. The Population Bulletin, 32, 3–42.

Palmer, J. L., & Gould, S. G. (1986). The economic consequences of an aging society. Daedalus, 115, 295–324.

Richardson, J. (1991). Aging and health: Black elders. *(Stanford Geriatric Education Center Working Paper Series, No. 4: Ethnogeriatric Reviews). Stanford, CA: Stanford University, Geriatric Education Center, Division of Family & Community Medicine.*

Rodgers, W. L., & Thornton, A. (1985). *Changing patterns of first marriage in the United States.* Demography, 22, 265–279.

Rowe, J. W. (1985). *Health care of the elderly.* New England Journal of Medicine, 312, *827–835.*

Shapiro, E., & Ross, N. (1989). *Predictors and patterns of nursing home and home care use. In M. Peterson, & D. White (Eds.),* Health care of the elderly: An information sourcebook. *Newbury Park, CA: Sage.*

Siegel, J. S., & Davidson, M. (1984). Demographic and socioeconomic aspects of aging in the United States. *Current Population Reports, Series P-23, No. 138. Washington, DC: Government Printing Office.*

Siegel, J. S., & Taeuber, C. M. (1986). *Demographic perspectives on the long-lived society.* Daedalus, 115, *77–118.*

Smith, J. M. (1993). *Function and supportive roles of church and religion. In James S. Jackson, Linda M. Chatters, & Robert Joseph Taylor (Eds.),* Aging in Black America *(pp. 124–147). Thousand Oaks, CA: Sage.*

Smith, R. J., & Thornton, M. C. (1993). *Identity and consciousness: Group Solidarity. In James S. Jackson, Linda M. Chatters, & Robert Joseph Taylor (Eds.),* Aging in Black America *(pp. 203–216). Thousand Oaks, CA: Sage.*

Soldo, B. (1980). *America's elderly in the 1980s.* Population Bulletin, 35, *3–47.*

Stanford, E. P. (1990). *Diverse black aged. In Z. Harel, E. A. McKinney, & M. Williams (Eds.),* Black aged: Understanding diversity and service needs *(pp. 33–49). Newbury Park, CA: Sage.*

Suzman, R., & Riley, M. W. (1985). *Introducing the "oldest old." In R. Suzman, and M. W. Riley (Eds.),* The oldest old. Milbank Memorial Fund Quarterly, 63, *177–186.*

Sweet, J. A., & Bumpass, L. L. (1987). American families and households. *New York: Russell Sage Foundation.*

Taylor, R. J. (1993). *Religion and religious observances. In James S. Jackson, Linda M. Chatters, & Robert Joseph Taylor (Eds.),* Aging in Black America *(pp. 101–123). Thousand Oaks, CA: Sage.*

Taylor, R. J., & Chatters, L. M. (1988). *Church members as a source of informal social support,* Review of Religious Research, 30, *193–203.*

Taylor, R. J., Chatters, L. M., Tucker, M. B., & Lewis, E. (1990). *Developments in research on black families: A decade review.* Journal of Marriage and the Family, 52, *933–1014.*

Taylor, R. J., Keith, V. M., & Tucker M. B. (1993). *Gender, marital, financial and friendship roles. In James S. Jackson, Linda M. Chatters, & Robert Joseph Taylor (Eds.),* Aging in Black America *(pp. 49–68). Thousand Oaks, CA: Sage.*

Taylor, R. J., & Thornton, M. C. (1993). *Demographic and religious correlates of voting behavior. In James S. Jackson, Linda M. Chatters, & Robert Joseph Taylor (Eds.),* Aging in Black America *(pp. 233–249). Thousand Oaks, CA: Sage.*

Wilkinson, D. T., & King, G. (1987). *Conceptual and methodological issues in the use of race as a variable: Policy implications.* Milbank Memorial Fund Quarterly, 65 *(Suppl, 1), 56–71.*

Williams, D. R. (1990). Socioeconomic differentials in health: A review and redirection. Social Psychology Quarterly, 53, *81–99.*

PART 4

Clinical and Applied Issues

Introduction

M. Powell Lawton

From the beginning, psychological studies of aging have been concerned with problems facing older people and with means for ameliorating them. The chapters in this part deal with psychological well-being, memory and learning, caregiving and its strains, housing, institutions, bereavement, and death.

Morale (Kutner, Fanshel, Togo & Langner, 1956) and life satisfaction were early representations of what is more broadly thought of as psychological well-being. The Life Satisfaction Index (LSI) of Bernice L. Neugarten, Robert J. Havighurst, and Sheldon S. Tobin remains one of the most carefully constructed such measures and is still in wide use. Their chapter, which chronicles the derivation of the construct and its conversion into a usable empirical measure, illustrates the effective combination of the clinical and psychometric perspectives. Since the LSI's publication in 1961, scores of investigators have sought to augment the construct and improve the measurement of psychological well-being. A relatively recent contribution in this area, for which there was no space in this volume, was an attempt by Carol Ryff (1989) to account for both positive and negative aspects of mental health rather than pathology.

Planned housing for older people, an important national program that accounts for perhaps two million elders, has also provided a setting in which to study normal patterns of aging. The classic research in housing for the elderly was Frances Carp's *A Future for the Aged* (1966). Carp's chapter here summarizes some of the most important findings from that book and adds the very meaningful long-term followup evaluation. The research of Carp and many others has generally provided highly affirmative conclusions about the psychological and social outcomes of moving into such age-segregated housing. M. Powell Lawton and Bonnie Simon's chapter reports on research performed in a similar setting. They found that less-healthy tenants were more locally dependent for friends (i.e., chose people on the same floor) than healthier tenants. They therefore were more deprived, if one thinks of people's choices of friends as being most fulfilling when a larger pool of potential choices is available. This finding, in turn, is what led to the generalization that vulnerable people are more subject to the influence (whether good or bad) of environment; this "environmental docility hypothesis" has been utilized widely by environmental designers in search of higher-quality environments for elders.

The clinical psychology of later life was slow to develop as a subspecialty. Only now, with reimbursement for clinical psychological services available through Medicare, has a critical mass of clinicians devoted to this work become established. One of the pioneers in this effort was Robert L. Kahn, whose article with several of his students from the University of Chicago is included here. Kahn and Alvin Goldfarb's Mental Status Questionnaire (Kahn, Goldfarb, Pollack & Peck, 1960) was an early and still-utilized brief reassessment device for cognitive decline. In the chapter included here, Kahn and his associates probe more deeply the relationships between memory dysfunction and depression. Their very interesting conclusion is that within a psychiatric population, memory complaints are not related to measured cognitive functioning, but rather to depression, regardless of cognitive functioning level.

A more recent direction taken by both clinicians and researchers is to test the extent to which cognitive training (sometimes delivered in the setting of a "memory clinic") can compensate for the age disadvantage usually found in comparing younger and older subjects cross-sectionally. In their chapter, K. Warner Schaie and Sherry L. Willis demonstrate, first, that training focused on the primary ability underlying a specific test could produce improvement on that test in older people tested a number of years earlier. In addition, improvement was demonstrated both among those who had declined over time and those whose performance had remained stable.

Several chapters in this book deal with the social aspects of aging. Caregiving research has consumed a great deal of journal space in the past decade. The selection by Janice Kiecolt-Glaser and her colleagues was chosen particularly because it made a new contribution to what had become an old research area. There is general consensus that caregiving stress is associated with depression and other indicators of psychological distress. Kiecolt-Glaser and her colleagues report that psychoimmunological functions also show signs of stress-related response in caregivers as compared to noncaregivers.

The life stresses consequent to bereavement have received much research attention. Larry W. Thompson, Dolores Gallagher-Thompson, and their colleagues mapped the courses of psychological distress and grief over thirty months following spousal bereavement. Although the norm was clearly for psychological recovery over this period of time, some widowed people continued to show disturbance. The difference between psychological distress and grief was clearly indicated, however, by the persistence of grief after the more general distress had dissipated. Another illuminating and prospective study of bereavement may be found in Stanley Murrell and Samuel Himmelfarb (1989).

Not surprisingly, gerontological research has been directed to clearly problematic contexts as well as to those more widely experienced by all. Institutions have been a favorite locus for such research. A classic study, whose conclusions continue to be relevant today, was the longitudinal study of applicants to a nursing home, followed through their admission and early period of residence, conducted by Morton A. Lieberman and Sheldon S. Tobin. Their chapter, with Valencia N. Prock, demonstrates with quantitative analysis of rich clinical data the stress experienced by the applicant group as compared to community residents and veteran residents, the last of whom had already adapted to institutional life. Another picture of the negative aspects of institutional life was contributed by a continuing program of research led by Margret M. Baltes. One of the first publications from this study was the article by Baltes and her colleagues included in this volume. These authors demonstrate how staff systematically reinforce residents' dependent behavior and ignore their independent behavior. An integrative treatment of a broader view of personal control is seen in P. B. Baltes and M. M. Baltes (1986).

Death has also been a favorite topic for gerontological research, if not for psychology in general or our society at large. The work of Robert Kastenbaum has led the way for thirty years. The article included here is one of the first that sought to document empirically what occurs at the end of life among hospitalized geriatric patients, studied through the staff-conducted "psychological autopsy" (Kastenbaum & Weisman, 1972). These retrospective views by staff indicated that the majority of patients were cognitively aware during the period before death and were not identifiably fearful about death. Nonetheless, they tended to be seen as "invisible," perhaps betraying a societal bias toward denial of death and the process of dying.

REFERENCES

Baltes, P. B. & Baltes, M. M. (Eds.) (1986). The psychology of control and aging. Hillsdale, NJ: Lawrence Erlbaum Associates.

Carp, F. M. (1966). A future for the aged. Austin: University of Texas Press.

Kahn, R. L., Goldfarb, A. I., Pollack, M. & Peck, A. (1960). Brief objective measures for the determination of mental status in the aged. American Journal of Psychiatry, 117, 326–328.

Kastenbaum, R. & Weisman, A. D. (1972). The psychological autopsy as a research procedure in gerontology. In D. P. Kent, R. Kastenbaum & S. Sherwood (Eds.) Research, planning and action for the elderly (pp. 210–244). New York: Behavioral Publications.

Kutner, B., Fanshel, D., Togo, A. & Langner, T. S. (1956). Five hundred over sixty. New York: Russell Sage Foundation.

Murrell, S. A. & Himmelfarb, S. (1989). Effects of attachment bereavement and pre-event conditions on subsequent depressive symptoms in older adults. Psychology and Aging, 4, 166–172.

Ryff, C. D. (1989). Happiness is everything, or is it? Explorations on the meaning of psychological well-being. Journal of Personality and Social Psychology, 57, 1069–1081.

30. The Measurement of Life Satisfaction

Bernice L. Neugarten, Robert J. Havighurst, and Sheldon S. Tobin

THERE HAVE BEEN various attempts to define and to measure the psychological well-being of older people, usually with the goal of using such a measure as an operational definition of ''successful'' aging. Different terms have been used in approaching this problem (terms such as adjustment, competence, morale, or happiness); and different criteria, as well as different techniques of measurement, have been employed. A number of cogent criticisms have been made of these attempts at definition and measurement, largely because they are inextricably involved with value judgments. (e.g., Rosow, in press).

In many researches on aging, however, it becomes necessary to establish some measure of success or well-being in relation to which other social and psychological variables can be studied. In such research undertakings, therefore, rather than forego a measure of psychological well-being, it becomes the goal instead to construct as refined and as valid a measure as possible. Once the investigator makes his value judgments explicit by the choice of his terms and his criteria, furthermore, the actual construction and validation of such a measure can go forward in relatively straightforward and value-free manner.

In earlier approaches to this problem, there have been two general points of view. One focuses upon the overt behavior of the individual and utilizes social criteria of success or competence. Studies that fall within this category tend to be ones in which level and range of activities and extent of social participation are the variables to be measured; and in which the assumption is made, implicitly or explicitly, that the greater the extent of social participation, and the less the individual varies from the pattern of activity that characterized him in middle age, the greater is his well-being.

The other point of view focuses upon the individual's internal frame of reference, with only secondary attention given to his level of social partici-

From *The Journal of Gerontology* 16 (1961): 134–43. Reprinted with permission of the Gerontological Society of America.

pation. Here the variables to be measured have been the individual's own evaluations of his present or past life, his satisfaction, or his happiness. The assumptions are, whether or not explicitly stated, that the individual himself is the only proper judge of his well-being; that the value judgments of the investigator can thus be minimized; and, perhaps most important, that it is not appropriate to measure well-being in old age by the same standards that apply to middle age, namely, standards based upon activity or social involvement.

As an example of the first point of view, Havighurst and Albrecht (1953), using public opinion as the criterion, developed a scale for measuring the social acceptability of the older person's behavior. Another example is the activity score on the schedule, "Your Activities and Attitudes" (Cavan et al., 1949; Havighurst & Albrecht, 1953); a score which sums up a person's participation in a number of different activities.

Most of the measuring instruments used in previous studies do, in fact, combine elements from both general approaches. For instance, in the Chicago Attitude Inventory (Cavan et al., 1949; Havighurst & Albrecht, 1953; Havighurst, 1957) a person is asked about his economic situation, work, family, friends, health, and so on, and about his happiness and feelings of usefulness. While the emphasis is upon feelings of satisfaction, a high score depends indirectly upon a high level of activity.

A second such measure is the Cavan Adjustment Rating Scale (Cavan et al., 1949; Havighurst, 1957). This is a rating based on interview data which takes into account not only the person's associations with family, friends, and formal and informal groups, but also his feelings of importance and satisfaction and his emotional stability.

Another measure that combines elements of both approaches is the social role performance measure used by Havighurst (1957). Here competence in the social roles of worker, parent, spouse, homemaker, citizen, friend, association member and church member is rated from interview data; with the ratings based not only upon extent of reported activity, but also upon the individual's investment in and satisfaction with his performance in each role.

As part of a larger study of psychological and social factors involved in aging, the Kansas City Study of Adult Life, the present investigators sought to develop a measure of the second general type—one that would use the individual's own evaluations as the point of reference; and one that would be relatively independent of level of activity or social participation. There have been other attempts to devise a measure with these general characteristics. For example, a few investigators (Kuhlen, 1948; Lebo, 1953; Rose,

1955; Pollak, 1948) have used direct self-reports of happiness. Although they are extremely vulnerable to conscious and unconscious psychological defenses, such self-reports have not usually been checked for validity against a more objective criterion.

Another example is Kutner's Morale Scale (Kutner et al., 1956), which is based upon responses to seven items such as, "On the whole, how satisfied would you say you are with your way of life today?" This instrument was not regarded as satisfactory for our purposes for several reasons: (1) It has not been validated against an outside criterion; (2) it is based upon the assumption that psychological well-being is a unidimensional phenomenon, for the scale has been constructed to form a scale of the Guttman type; (3) there have been scaling difficulties when the items have been used with populations other than the one originally studied. Thus, one of the seven items had to be scored differently for a New York City population than for an Elmira population (Kutner et al., 1956, p. 303); and an even greater effect of this type was seen when the scale was adapted for use with rural residents of South Dakota (Morrison & Kristjanson, 1958). In short, the items which are successful in producing a Guttman scale for one population are not altogether the same for another population.

Most recently, a Morale Index was developed by our collaborators on the Kansas City Study of Adult Life (Cumming, Dean, & Newell 1958) consisting of four questions of which one was, "Do you wish you could see more of your relatives than you do now? Less? Your neighbors? Your friends?" (R is scored positively if he answers "Things are all right as they are.").

At the time the present investigators began work on this problem, that Index seemed unsatisfactory for several reasons.[1] It was based on so few items that scores might prove highly unreliable; the Index had been validated against only a small sample of cases; and, most important, it appeared to be a unidimensional measure reflecting, for the most part, resignation or conformity to the status quo. The Index seemed, therefore, not to reflect our own concepts of psychological well-being.

The research reported here had two purposes, each requiring a somewhat different set of procedures. The first, as already indicated, was to devise a measure of successful aging for use in the Kansas City Studies, a measure that would be derived relatively independently from various other psychological and social variables. The second purpose was to devise a short, easily-administered instrument that could be used in other studies and to validate that instrument against Kansas City data.

After a description of the study population, the report that follows deals with the derivation and validation of the Life Satisfaction Ratings (LSR) and the scales upon which the ratings are based; then with the derivation and validation of two short self-administered instruments, the Life Satisfaction Index A (LSIA) and the Life Satisfaction Index B (LSIB).

THE STUDY POPULATION

Table 30.1 shows the distribution of the study population by age, sex, and social class. In brief, the upper-middle class represents business and professional levels; lower-middle, white-collar occupational levels; and the upper-lower represents blue-collar levels.

This population was composed of members of two groups. The first, referred to as the panel group, were persons aged 50 to 70 at the time of the first interview in 1956. The panel represents a stratified probability sample of middle and working class white persons of this age range residing in the metropolitan area of Kansas City. Excluded were the chronically ill and the

Table 30.1. The Study Population: By Age at First Interview, Sex, and Social Class.

	Age group					
Social class	50–56	57–63	64–70	71–79	80–89	Total
Upper-middle:						
Men	6	7	5	2	2	22
Women	7	6	6	6	3	28
Lower-middle:						
Men	4	4	7	7	6	28
Women	6	3	5	7	6	27
Upper-lower:						
Men	8	7	4	17	5	41
Women	5	7	6	10	3	31
Total	36	34	33	49	25	177

NOTE: Social class placements for panel members (the first three age groups in the table) were based upon an Index of Social Characteristics in which occupation (or former occupation), level of education, and area of residence were the three main factors. For the quasi-panel (the last two age groups in the table) this Index is less useful, since, with advancing age of R, neither educational level nor former occupation can be assumed to have the same social-class values as for the group who are presently middle-aged. (For example, the semi-skilled worker today generally occupies a lower position in the social system than 40 years ago). We are indebted to Dr. Wayne Wheeler, Field Director of the Kansas City Study, for his assistance in analyzing the social data available on these older persons and in arriving at their class placements. Because this whole problem of social-class placements for aged persons remains a difficult one, however, we may still have placed a disproportionate number into the upper-lower class.

physically impaired. The method by which the panel was selected resulted in a group that is biased toward middle class—in other words, that is better educated, wealthier, and of higher occupational and residential prestige than the universe of 50 to 70-year-olds.

The second group, referred to as the quasi-panel, were persons aged 70–90 who joined the Kansas City Study two years after field work had begun. This older group was built up on the basis of quota sampling rather than probability sampling. The group consists of middle- and working-class persons, none of them financially deprived and none of them bed-ridden or senile.

While the panel probably has a greater middle-class bias than the quasi-panel, it is likely that the older members of the study population are less representative of their universe than is true of the panel members. Not only are these older persons better off financially, but they are in better health than most 70 to 90-year-olds, and thus represent an advantaged rather than a typical group.

Of the original panel, 74 per cent remained as cooperating respondents by the end of the fourth round of interviews, at which time the Life Satisfaction Ratings described below were made. Of the original quasi-panel, 83 per cent remained at the same point in time, after two rounds of interviews. Thus, in addition to the various biases operating in the original selection of the two groups (for instance, 16 percent of those contacted refused to join the panel), there is an unmeasurable effect on the present study due to sample attrition. Of the attrition, 15 per cent was due to deaths; 10 per cent, to geographical moves; and the rest, to refusals to be interviewed the second, third, or fourth time. There is evidence also that persons who were relatively socially isolated constituted a disproportionate number of the drop-outs.

All these factors should be kept in mind in considering the range of Life Satisfaction Ratings obtained for this study population and in considering the generalizations that emerged regarding age differences.

The Data

The data consisted of lengthy and repeated interviews covering many aspects of the respondent's life pattern, his attitudes, and his values. Included was information on the daily round and the usual week-end round of activity; other household members; relatives, friends, and neighbors; income and work; religion; voluntary organizations; estimates of the amount of social interaction as compared with the amount at age 45; attitudes toward old age, illness, death, and immortality; questions about loneliness, boredom, anger; and questions regarding the respondent's role models and his self-image. The first interview for the quasi-panel was a special schedule combining questions from the first three panel interviews. Both groups had the same fourth-round interview.

THE LIFE SATISFACTION RATINGS

The first problem was to analyze our concept of psychological well-being into a sufficient number of components to represent its complexity, and then to find ways of measuring these components from interview data. Working with a group of graduate students in a research seminar, the investigators began by examining the measures of adjustment and morale that had been used in previous studies, and by defining distinguishable components. Definitions were tried out against case material; independent judgments of the cases were compared; the concepts were redefined; and so on.[2] Finally operational definitions of the following components were obtained: Zest (vs. apathy); Resolution and fortitude; Congruence between desired and achieved goals; Positive self-concept; and Mood tone. More detailed definitions appear in the scales reproduced below, but in brief, an individual was regarded as being at the positive end of the continuum of psychological well-being to the extent that he: (A) takes pleasure from the round of activities that constitutes his everyday life; (B) regards his life as meaningful and accepts resolutely that which life has been; (C) feels he has succeeded in achieving his major goals; (D) holds a positive image of self; and (E) maintains happy and optimistic attitudes and mood.

Each of these five components was rated on a five-point scale (with 5, high); and the ratings were summed to obtain an overall rating with a possible range from 5 to 25.[3]

We then sought a suitable term by which to refer to this overall rating; or, in other words, the best name for the five scales. The term "adjustment" is unsuitable because it carries the implication that conformity is the most desirable pattern of behavior. "Psychological well-being" is, if nothing else, an awkward phrase. "Morale," in many ways, captures best the qualities here being described, but there was the practical problem that there are already in use in gerontological research two different scales entitled Morale. The term Life Satisfaction was finally adopted on grounds that, although it is not altogether adequate, it comes close to representing the five components.

In making the Life Satisfaction Ratings, all the interview data on each respondent were utilized. Thus the ratings are based, not on R's direct self report of satisfaction (although some questions of this type were included in the interviews), but on the inferences drawn by the raters from all the information available on R, including his interpersonal relationships and how others reacted toward him.

The four rounds of interviewing had been spaced over approximately two and one-half years. In those few cases where marked changes had occurred in R's life situation within that interval of time, and where psychological well-being seemed to have changed accordingly, the rating represented the situation at the most recent point in time, at Interview 4.

LIFE SATISFACTION RATING SCALES

A. *Zest vs. apathy*. To be rated here are enthusiasm of response and degree of ego-involvement—in any of various activities, persons, or ideas, whether or not these are activities which involve R with other people, are "good" or "socially approved" or "status-giving." Thus, R who "just loves to sit home and knit" rates as high as R who "loves to get out and meet people." Although a low rating is given for listlessness and apathy, physical energy *per se* is not to be involved in this rating. Low ratings are given for being "bored with most things"; for "I have to force myself to do things"; and also for meaningless (and unenjoyed) hyper-activity.

5. Speaks of several activities and relationships with enthusiasm. Feels that "now" is the best time of life. Loves to do things, even sitting at home. Takes up new activities; makes new friends readily, seeks self-improvement. Shows zest in several areas of life.

4. Shows zest, but it is limited to one or two special interests, or limited to certain periods of time. May show disappointment or anger when things go wrong, if they keep him from active enjoyment of life. Plans ahead, even though in small time units.

3. Has a bland approach to life. Does not seem to get much pleasure out of the things he does. Seeks relaxation and a limited degree of involvement. May be quite detached (aloof) from many activities, things, or people.

2. Thinks life is monotonous for the most part. May complain of fatigue. Feels bored with many things. If active, finds little meaning or enjoyment in the activity.

1. Lives on the basis of routine. Doesn't think anything worth doing.

B. *Resolution and fortitude*. The extent to which R accepts personal responsibility for his life; the opposite of feeling resigned, or of merely condoning or passively accepting that which life has brought him. The extent to which R accepts his life as meaningful and inevitable, and is relatively unafraid of death. Erikson's "integrity." Not to be confused with "autonomy" or the extent to which R's life has been self-propelled or characterized by initiative. R may not have been a person of high initiative, but yet he may accept resolutely and relatively positively that which life has been for him. R may feel life was a series of hard knocks, but that he has stood up under them (this would be a high rating).

There are two types of low ratings; the highly intropunitive, where R blames himself overly much; and the extrapunitive, where R blames others or the world in general for whatever failures or disappointments he has experienced.

5. Try and try again attitude. Bloody but unbowed. Fights back; withstanding, not giving up. Active personal responsibility—take the bad and the good and make the most of it. Wouldn't change the past.

4. Can take life as it comes. "I have no complaint on the way life has treated me." Assumes responsibility readily. "If you look for the good side of life, you'll find it." Does not mind talking about difficulties in life, but does not dwell on them either. "You have to give up some things."

3. Says, "I've had my ups and downs; sometimes on top, sometimes on the bottom." Shows a trace of extrapunitiveness or intropunitiveness concerning his difficulties in life.

2. Feels he hasn't done better because he hasn't gotten the breaks. Feels great difference in life now as compared to age 45; the change has been for the worse. "I've worked hard but never got anywhere."

1. Talks of hard knocks which he has not mastered (extrapunitive). Feels helpless. Blames self a great deal (intropunitive). Overwhelmed by life.

C. *Congruence between desired and achieved goals*. The extent to which R feels he has achieved his goals in life, whatever those goals might be; feels he has succeeded in accomplishing what *he* regards as important. High ratings go, for instance, to R who says, "I've managed to keep out of jail" just as to R who says, "I managed to send all *my* kids through college." Low ratings go to R who feels he's missed most of his opportunities, or who says, "I've never been suited to my work," or "I always wanted to be a doctor, but never could get there.'' Also to *R* who wants most to be "loved," but instead feels merely "approved." (Expressions of regret for lack of education are not counted because they are stereotyped responses among all but the group of highest social status.)

5. Feels he has accomplished what he wanted to do. He has achieved or is achieving his own personal goals.

4. Regrets somewhat the chances missed during life. "Maybe I could have made more of certain opportunities." Nevertheless, feels that he has been fairly successful in accomplishing what he wanted to do in life.

3. Has a fifty-fifty record of opportunities taken and opportunities missed. Would have done some things differently, if he had his life to live over. Might have gotten more education.

2. Has regrets about major opportunities missed but feels good about accomplishment in one area (may be his avocation).

1. Feels he has missed most opportunities in life.

D. *Self-concept.* *R*'s concept of self—physical as well as psychological and social attributes. High ratings go to *R* who is concerned with grooming and appearance; who thinks of himself as wise, mellow (and thus is comfortable in giving advice to others); who feels proud of his accomplishments; who feels he deserves whatever good breaks he has had; who feels he is important to someone else. Low ratings are given to *R* who feels "old," weak, sick, incompetent; who feels himself a burden to others; who speaks disparagingly of self or of old people.

5. Feels at his best. "I do better work now than ever before." "There was never any better time." Thinks of self as wise, mellow; physically able or attractive; feels important to others. Feels he has the right to indulge himself.

4. Feels more fortunate than the average. Is sure that he can meet the exigencies of life. "When I retire, I'll just substitute other activities." Compensates well for any difficulty of health. Feels worthy of being indulged. "Things I want to do, I can do, but I'll not overexert myself." Feels in control of self in relation to the situation.

3. Sees self as competent in at least one area, e.g., work; but has doubts about self in other areas. Acknowledges loss of youthful vigor, but accepts it in a realistic way. Feels relatively unimportant, but doesn't mind. Feels he takes, but also gives. Senses a general, but not extreme, loss of status as he grows older. Reports health better than average.

2. Feels that other people look down on him. Tends to speak disparagingly of older people. Is defensive about what the years are doing to him.

1. Feels old. Feels in the way, or worthless. Makes self-disparaging remarks. "I'm endured by others."

E. *Mood tone.* High ratings for *R* who expresses happy, optimistic attitudes and mood; who uses spontaneous, positively-toned effective terms for people and things; who takes pleasure from life and expresses it. Low ratings for depression, "feel blue and lonely"; for feelings of bitterness; for frequent irritability and anger. (Here we consider not only *R*'s verbalized attitudes in the interview; but make inferences from all we know of his interpersonal relationships, how others react toward him.)

5. "This is the best time of my life." Is nearly always cheerful, optimistic. Cheerfulness may seem unrealistic to an observer, but *R* shows no sign of "putting up a bold front."

4. Gets pleasure out of life, knows it and shows it. There is enough restraint to seem appropriate to a younger person. Usually feels positive affect. Optimistic.

3. Seems to move along on an even temperamental keel. Any depressions are neutralized by positive mood swings. Generally neutral-to-positive affect. May show some irritability.

2. Wants things quiet and peaceful. General neutral-to-negative affect. Some depression.

1. Pessimistic, complaining, bitter. Complains of being lonely. Feels "blue" a good deal of the time. May get angry when in contact with people.[3]

Reliability of Ratings

Ratings were made on every case by two judges working independently. The judges were members of a student-faculty research seminar. A system was followed by which judges and groups of cases were systematically varied. In all, 14 judges rated the 177 cases, and all but one judge maintained a high level of agreement with the others with whom he was paired. The coefficient of correlation between two LSR ratings for the 177 cases was .78. (Since, in all subsequent steps, the average of the two ratings was used, the Spearman-Brown coefficient of attenuation can be employed to raise the coefficient to .87.) Of 885 paired judgments, 94 per cent showed exact agreement or agreement within one step on the 5-step scale. (On the same basis, inter-judge agreement varied only slightly from one component to the next. It was 97 per cent for Zest; 96 per cent for Resolution; 92 per cent for Congruence; 96 per cent for Self-concept; and 92 per cent for Mood tone.)

For the 177 cases, LSR scores ranged from 8 to 25, with the mean, 17.8, and the standard deviation, 4.6.

Intercorrelations between Components

Table 30.2 shows the intercorrelations between the five components of Life Satisfaction. While positively interrelated, they nevertheless show a fair degree of independence, supporting the assumption that more than one dimension are involved in the scales. Without submitting these coefficients to a factor analysis, it appears that Zest, Mood tone, and possibly Self-concept involve one factor, with the probability of one or two other factors operating in the matrix.

Characteristics of the LSR

For this sample of 177 cases there was no correlation between Life Satisfaction and age (r was $-.07$). (It is likely that, with a less advantaged group of people, there will be a negative relationship between the two variables.)

Using an Index of Social Characteristics (ISC) based on three factors, level of education, area of residence, and occupation (or former occupation), the correlation between LSR and ISC was .39. Thus, there is a positive, but not marked relationship between Life Satisfaction and socioeconomic status.

There was no significant sex difference on LSR scores. The mean for the women was 17.9 (S. D., 3.58); and for the men, 17.5 (S. D., 4.04).

With regard to marital status, the non-married (the single, divorced, separated, and widowed) had significantly lower LSR scores. This relationship held true for both sexes, and for both younger and older subgroups in the study population.

Table 30.2. Intercorrelations of the Components of Life Satisfaction (N = 177).

	Resolution	Congruence	Self-concept	Mood tone
Zest	.67	.56	.79	.84
Resolution		.70	.83	.48
Congruence			.73	.57
Self-concept				.82

Validity of the Ratings

The LSR depended on scoring by judges who had read all the recorded interview material, but who had not themselves interviewed the respondent. In seeking to establish an outside criterion by which these ratings could be validated, the investigators thought it desirable to have an experienced clinical psychologist interview the respondents and then make his own ratings of Life Satisfaction.

For various practical reasons, it was not until some 18 to 22 months had elapsed after Interview 4 that these clinical interviews were begun.[4] By this time, a fifth and sixth wave of interviewing had intervened, and there had been further attrition of the study population due not only to deaths and geographic moves, but also to refusals. Nevertheless, over a three-month period, 80 respondents were interviewed at length by the clinical psychologist; and it is his ratings (LSR-C1) that constitute a validity check on the LSR. These interviews and ratings were made by the clinician without any prior knowledge of the respondent—that is, without reading any of the earlier interviews and without discussion of the case with other members of the research staff.

The 80 cases were representative of the 177 as regards sex, age, and social class. They had, however, a slightly higher mean score on the LSR. (Mean LSR for the 177 cases was 17.8; for the 80 cases seen by the clinician, it was 18.9. Twenty-five per cent of the total 177, but only 15 per cent of the 80 cases, were persons with LSR scores of 14.5 or less.) In other words, a disproportionate number of drop-outs in the 18 to 24-month interval were persons who were low on Life Satisfaction.

Using the average of the two judges' ratings for the LSR score, the correlation between LSR and LSR-C1 for the 80 cases was .64. Of 400 paired judgments, 76 per cent represented exact agreement or agreement within one step on the 5-step scale. (On the same basis, agreement between LSR and LSR-C1 varied somewhat from one component to the next. It was 86 per cent for Zest; 76 per cent for Resolution; 73 per cent for Congruence; 78 per cent for Self-concept; and 69 per cent for Mood tone).

Further study was made of several cases for whom there was marked disagreement between the LSR and the LSR-C1. As anticipated, these cases were of two types: (1) There were a few who had been rated higher on LSR, and where it seemed a reasonable explanation that the clinical psychologist had succeeded in probing beneath the respondent's defenses and had obtained a truer picture of his feelings.

Mrs. B, for instance, was a woman whose façade was successful throughout the first four interviews in convincing the judges reading the interviews that she was a person who had achieved all her major goals; that she was resolute, competent, happy, even in the face of repeated physical illnesses. In the more intensive interview, however, she broke down and wept, and said she felt life had been unjust and that she had been an unlucky person. It was the clinician's interpretation that she had long been depressed, and that the somatic illnesses had been a defense against the depression. She was a woman with a strong moral code and with tremendous pride; who went through life feeling that at no time must she reveal her disappointments.

(2) There were a few cases where the respondent's life situation had changed drastically in the interval of time between the LSR and the LSR-C1 ratings. The respondent had suffered severe illness, or had been widowed, and the crisis had brought on a depression. In a few instances, however, the change had been for the better, as reflected in a higher LSR-C1 rating.

One man, at the time of Interview 4, had just been widowed. A year earlier he had been retired from his job as a salesman, and he was worried about money as well as being depressed over the death of his wife. When seen by the clinical psychologist, however, he freely discussed the fact that two years earlier he had experienced a depression, but that now he was recovered. He had found a new job selling, door to door, and he enjoyed what he called his "contacts with the public." He was living in a small apartment near his daughter's family, and he described with enthusiasm his grandchildren and the outings he had with them on weekends.

In general, the correlation of .64 between LSR and LSR-C1 was interpreted by the investigators as providing a satisfactory degree of validation for the LSR, given the various factors already mentioned: (1) the lapse of time between the two ratings; (2) the fact that a number of persons low on Life Satisfaction had dropped out of the study, thus narrowing the range of LSR scores for the 80 cases—a fact that, in turn, tended to lower the coefficient of correlation; (3) the fact that the LSR was based only on recorded interview data; the LSR-C1, on face-to-face interaction; (4) the greater depth of the clinical psychologist's interviews.

It is of some interest in this connection that the correlation between LSR and LSR-C1 was higher for the older members of the sample. For 30 cases aged 70 and over, r was .70; for the 50 cases aged 69 and below, r was .53. It may be that the aged individual has less of a tendency to give conforming or "normative" responses in the regular interview situation than does the younger individual; thus providing fewer instances in which the clinical psychologist's depth questions revealed a different level of functioning than shown by replies to the more structured interviews. It might be, on the other hand, that in some manner of which the investigators were unaware, they devised interview questions and rating scales for Life Satisfaction that are more appropriate for the very old respondent than for the somewhat younger respondent and that, as a result, different judges were more likely to agree in their evaluations of persons over 70.[5] Whatever the explanation, age differences such as these should be explored further in future studies.

THE LIFE SATISFACTION INDEXES

While the LSR is likely to prove useful in other studies where the amount of information about a respondent is less extensive than in the Kansas City Study, the LSR will require at least one long interview with the respondent. It may therefore be too cumbersome to be used on a large scale. Consequently, using the LSR as the validating criterion, the investigators attempted to devise a self-report instrument which would take only a few minutes to administer. Two such instruments were devised, to be used separately or together.

The Derivation of the Indexes

From the larger group on whom LSR scores were available, a sample of 60 cases were selected that represented the full range of age, sex, and social class. Of these 60 cases, the high scorers and the low scorers on LSR were used as criterion groups. A long list of items and open-ended questions from Interviews 1 through 4 were then studied to select those that differentiated these two groups. (Some of these items had originally been taken from Kutner's Morale Scale.) In addition to this item analysis, certain new items were written which reflected each of the five components of Life Satisfaction.

Two preliminary instruments then emerged. The first, called the Life Satisfaction Index A (LSIA) consisted of 25 attitude items for which only an "agree" or "disagree" response is required. The second, the Life Satisfaction Index B (LSIB) consisted of 17 open-ended questions and check-list items, to be scored on a three-point scale.

These two instruments were then administered to 92 respondents along with Interview 6. (A number of respondents had already been interviewed in this sixth wave of field work by the time these instruments were ready. Because 92 seemed a large enough N for our purposes, no attempt was made to return and administer these instruments to those who had already been interviewed.)

When 60 of the 92 cases were in, preliminary computations were made.

Scores on LSIA correlated .52 with LSR; scores on LSIB correlated .59 with LSR. These results seemed to warrant further efforts at refining and trimming the instruments. When all 92 cases were in, therefore, an item analysis was undertaken whereby each item of the Indexes was studied for the extent to which it differentiated the high and low LSR groups among the 92. (Top and bottom quartiles on LSR were used as criterion groups.)

As a result of this analysis, five items of LSIA and seven items of LSIB were discarded. In their final form, these Indexes are given below, together with their scoring keys.[6]

Life Satisfaction Index A

Here are some statements about life in general that people feel differently about. Would you read each statement on the list, and if you agree with it, put a check mark in the space under "AGREE." If you do not agree with a statement, put a check mark in the space under "DISAGREE." If you are not sure one way of the other, put a check mark in the space under "?." PLEASE BE SURE TO ANSWER EVERY QUESTION ON THE LIST.

(Key: score 1 point for each response marked X.)

	AGREE	DISAGREE	?
1. As I grow older, things seem better than I thought they would be.	x		
2. I have gotten more of the breaks in life than most of the people I know.	x		
3. This is the dreariest time of my life.		x	
4. I am just as happy as when I was younger.	x		
5. My life could be happier than it is now.		x	
6. These are the best years of my life.	x		
7. Most of the things I do are boring or monotonous.		x	
8. I expect some interesting and pleasant things to happen to me in the future.	x		
9. The things I do are as interesting to me as they ever were.	x		
10. I feel old and somewhat tired.		x	
11. I feel my age, but it does not bother me.	x		
12. As I look back on my life, I am fairly well satisfied.	x		
13. I would not change my past life even if I could.	x		
14. Compared to other people my age, I've made a lot of foolish decisions in my life.		x	
15. Compared to other people my age, I make a good appearance.	x		
16. I have made plans for things I'll be doing a month or a year from now.	x		

	AGREE	DISAGREE	?
17. When I think back over my life, I didn't get most of the important things I wanted.	_____	___x___	_____
18. Compared to other people, I get down in the dumps too often.	_____	___x___	_____
19. I've gotten pretty much what I expected out of life.	___x___	_____	_____
20. In spite of what people say, the lot of the average man is getting worse, not better.	_____	___x___	_____

Life Satisfaction Index B (with scoring key)

Would you please comment freely in answer to the following questions?

1. What are the best things about being the age you are now?
   1. a positive answer
   0. nothing good about it
2. What do you think you will be doing five years from now? How do you expect things will be different from the way they are now, in your life?
   2. better, or no change
   1. contingent—"It depends"
   0. worse
3. What is the most important thing in your life right now?
   2. anything outside of self, or pleasant interpretation of future
   1. "Hanging on"; keeping health, or job
   0. getting out of present difficulty, or "nothing now," or reference to the past
4. How happy would you say you are right now, compared with the earlier periods in your life?
   2. this is the happiest time; all have been happy; or, hard to make a choice
   1. some decrease in recent years
   0. earlier periods were better, this is a bad time
5. Do you ever worry about your ability to do what people expect of you— to meet demands that people make on you?
   2. no
   1. qualified yes or no
   0. yes

6. If you could do anything you pleased, in what part of——would you most like to live?

   2. present location

   0. any other location

7. How often do you find yourself feeling lonely?

   2. never; hardly ever

   1. sometimes

   0. fairly often; very often

8. How often do you feel there is no point in living?

   2. never; hardly ever

   1. sometimes

   0. fairly often; very often

9. Do you wish you could see more of your close friends than you do, or would you like more time to yourself?

   2. O.K. as is

   0. wish could see more of friends

   0. wish more time to self

10. How much unhappiness would you say you find in your life today?

    2. almost none

    1. some

    0. a great deal

11. As you get older, would you say things seem to be better or worse than you thought they would be?

    2. better

    1. about as expected

    0. worse

12. How satisfied would you say you are with your way of life?

    2. very satisfied

    1. fairly satisfied

    0. not very satisfied

As shown in Table 30.3, the coefficient of correlation between the final form of LSIA and LSR was .55. The mean score on LSIA was 12.4, and the standard deviation, 4.4). The correlation between the final form of LSIB and LSR was .58. (The mean score for LSIB was 15.1, the standard deviation, 4.7). For combined scores on the two Indexes, the correlation with LSR was .61. (The mean for the combined scores was 27.6; the standard deviation, 6.7).

Table 30.3. Coefficients of Correlation for Various Measures of Life Satisfaction

	1	2	3	4	5	6
(1) LSR	—	.64 (80)	.55 (89)	.58 (89)	.39 (177)	−.07 (177)
(2) LSR-C1		—	.39 (51)	.47 (52)	.21 (80)	.09 (80)
(3) LSIA			—	.73 (91)	.36 (79)	−.10 (86)
(4) LSIB				—	.41 (80)	−.07 (86)
(5) Socioeconomic status					—	—[a]
(6) Age						—

NOTE:—The number of cases on which the correlation is based is shown in parentheses.

[a] This relationship is zero by definition, since the sample was deliberately selected to control for age and socioeconomic status.

Validity of the Indexes

As just described, the derivation and validation of the Indexes proceeded as a single set of operations; and the LSR cannot be regarded as an outside criterion. It is noteworthy, despite this fact, that the correlations between Index scores and LSR are only moderate in size.

It is true that the sixth wave of interviewing began about 14 months after the fourth wave, so that the interval of time between LSR and the two Index scores for the same respondent was, in some instances, as much as 18 to 20 months. This lapse of time probably operated to lower somewhat the congruence between the measures.

Nevertheless, the more important point is undoubtedly that direct self-reports, even though carefully measured, can be expected to agree only partially with the evaluations of life satisfaction made by an outside observer (in this case, the judges who made the LSR ratings.)

Certain additional steps were carried out in respect to validation. Scores on the two Indexes, for instance, were compared with LSR-C1 (the ratings made by the clinical psychologist). Of the 80 cases on whom LSR-C1 scores were available, only 51 had LSIA scores; 52, LSIB. For this relatively small number of cases, the correlations with LSR-C1 were .39 and .47 respectively. These correlations were probably lowered by the fact, already mentioned, that the respondents interviewed by the clinical psychologist constituted a superior group with regard to Life Satisfaction, thus providing a narrow range of scores on which to assess these correlations.

The question was also raised regarding the extent to which LSIA and LSIB were more reflective of Mood Tone alone than of the other components of

LSR. Scores on each of the two Indexes correlated no higher, however, with ratings on Mood Tone alone than with LSR ratings.

Age Differences

We have already commented on the fact that, in rating Life Satisfaction (LSR and LSR-C1), agreement between the clinical psychologist and the other raters was greater for the older respondents than for the younger. A parallel phenomenon was true with regard to scores on the two Indexes. For persons under 65, LSR-C1 correlated .05 with LSIA, and .32 with LSIB. For persons over 65, the correlations were .55 and .59 respectively. While the *Ns* on which these correlations are based are small, the finding parallels the earlier one with regard to greater consistency between measures for respondents of advanced age.

The question once more arises as to whether this greater consistency is an artifact of the measures themselves, or whether it reflects an increasing consistency in psychological behavior in aged persons.

Whatever the explanation, a review of all the relationships here reported between LSR, LSR-C1, LSIA and LSIB seems to warrant the conclusion that the Indexes are more successful instruments for persons over 65 than for younger persons.

SUMMARY

This paper reports the derivation of a set of scales for rating Life Satisfaction, using data on 177 men and women aged 50 to 90. The ratings were based on lengthy interview material, and were validated against the judgments of a clinical psychologist who re-interviewed and rated 80 cases. The scales appear to be relatively satisfactory and may prove useful to other investigators interested in a measure of the psychological well-being of older people.

In addition, two short self-report Indexes of Life Satisfaction were devised and validated against the Life Satisfaction Ratings. While considerable effort was expended in refining these instruments, the effort was only moderately successful. If used with caution, the Indexes will perhaps be useful for certain group measurements of persons over 65.

The rating scales and the two Indexes are reproduced here.

NOTES

1. The Morale Index, in its most recent form, is described by Cumming and Henry (in press).

2. The investigators were aided by Dr. Lois Dean, who was then Field Director of the Kansas City Study. Dr. Dean had interviewed certain of the respondents at great length, and had made an analysis of morale in the aged. Several of the components later incorporated into the LSR stemmed from her analysis.

3. Other investigators may use the Scales and Indexes reproduced in this report without permission from either the present investigators or the *Journal of Gerontology*.

4. We are indebted to Mr. William Crotty for obtaining these 80 interviews and making the LSR-C1 ratings.

5. In this connection, it is not uncommon for psychiatrists to remark that a half-hour interview is sufficient to evaluate the adjustment or mental health of an old person; but that it takes considerably more time to make a similar evaluation for a younger person.

6. See note 3 above.

REFERENCES

Cavan, Ruth S., Burgess, E. W., Havighurst, R. J. & Goldhamer, H. Personal adjustment in old age. *Chicago: Science Research Associates, 1949.*

Cumming, Elaine, Dean, Lois R. & Newell, D. S. What is "morale"? A case history of a validity problem. Hum. Organization, *1958, 17 (2), 3–8.*

Cumming, Elaine & Henry, W. E. Growing old. *New York: Basic Books, in press.*

Havighurst, R. J. The social competence of middle-aged people. Genet. Psychol. Monogr., *1957, 56, 297–375.*

Havighurst, R. J. & Albrecht, Ruth. Older people. *New York: Longmans, Green, 1953.*

Kuhlen, R. G. Age trends in adjustment during the adult years as reflected in happiness ratings. Amer. J. Psychol., *1948, 3, 307. (Abstract)*

Kutner, B., Fanshel, D., Togo, Alice M. & Langner, T. S. Five hundred over sixty. *New York: Russell Sage Found., 1956.*

Lebo, D. Some factors said to make for happiness in old age. J. clin. Psychol., *1953, 9, 385–390.*

Morrison, D. & Kristjanson, G. A. Personal adjustment among older persons. *Agricultural Experiment Station Technical Bulletin No. 21. Brookings: South Dakota State College, 1958.*

Pollak, O. Social adjustment in old age. *New York: Social Science Research Council, 1948.*

Rose, A. M. Factors associated with life satisfaction of middle-class, middle-aged persons. Marriage & Family Living, *1955, 17, 15–19.*

Rosow, I. Adjustment of the normal aged: concept and measurement. Paper given at the International Research Seminar on the Social and Psychological Aspects of Aging, Berkeley, August, 1960; in R. H. Williams, J. E. Birren, Wilma Donahue & C. Tibbitts (Eds.), Psychological and social processes of aging: an international seminar, in press.

31. Short-Term and Long-Term Prediction of Adjustment to a New Environment

Frances M. Carp

ANY SIGNIFICANT change in a person or his situation may cause a disturbance in his adaptive equilibrium (Klein & Lindemann, 1961). Old techniques for dealing with the world may be inadequate; new ones may be needed. Depending upon the individual's adaptive resources in relation to the problems posed, the outcome may lie anywhere from total disorganization and destruction of adaptive capacity to increased sense of mastery and improvement in adaptive resources (Eisdorfer, 1968; Erikson, 1959; Hartmann, 1958; Lazarus, 1966; Selye & Prioreschi, 1960).

STUDIES OF GROUP TRENDS

This range of outcomes has been observed in old organisms as they respond to environmental change. For example, change in residence can have deleterious effects on old persons, including rise in death rate (Aldrich & Mendkoff, 1963; Lieberman, 1961, 1966; Miller & Liebermann, 1965), or it can have generally favorable results (Carp, 1966; Donahue, 1966, Hamovitch, 1968). What accounts for the difference in outcomes? Obviously the results are always determined by the interaction of personal and situational factors (Carp, 1968; Vale & Vale, 1969).

Studies in group trends are valuable in coming to understand the nature of the environment-person interaction which determines the outcome of various types of change in residence for various types of older people. For example, it is useful, though not surprising, to know that transfer from one nursing home to another has different consequences for a group of frail old people than does a self-initiated move from sub-standard housing to a new apartment for a group of old people capable of independent living. It is additionally informative to know that community-resident elderly people, in

From *The Journal of Gerontology* 29, no. 4 (1974): 444–53. Reprinted with permission of the Gerontological Society of America.

general, seem to benefit following a move from substandard and socially isolating housing to a new, specially designed apartment building which includes a senior center.

Analysis of Differences within Groups

However, adjustment to a new situation is not necessarily uniform among residents (Carp, 1966). Attention to individual differences in adaptation to the situation may provide additional insights into the nature of the person-environment function. When the new environment is "held constant," what characteristics of persons are associated with level or quality of adaptation? Within a group of old persons subjected to a particular environmental modification, which ones adapt most successfully? Answers to these questions will provide information regarding the nature of person-situation congruence and the demands of adapting to a new situation. They have obvious implications for the design of living arrangements for old people and for the selection of environments appropriate to individuals.

Short-Run and Long-Range Prediction

Another consideration for research design is the time required to achieve adaptive equilibrium in a new environment and the question of whether determinants of early adaptation persist, fade or are reversed in the determination of adjustments in the long run. To date, efforts to account for differences in adaptation following a move have focused on relatively short-term consequences. Behaviors and attitudes during a "honeymoon" or "shake-down cruise" phase of community development may not be those when the situation stabilizes and the community is established. Due to "sleeper" effects (Kagan & Moss, 1960) the order of importance, or even the nature of variables which determine adjustment, may be different over the short run and the long. It is important, therefore, to validate short-run findings over longer time periods.

DESIGN OF THE STUDY

This study is concerned with some determinants of adjustment to a new living situation within a group of community resident old people all of whom moved simultaneously to the same new living situation. The research design was prediction through time, as the most incisive test. Predictions were made before the old people moved and were tested at two subsequent points in time, at intervals of 18 months and 8 years.

LONG-RUN AND SHORT-RUN ADAPTATION

Predictions over the 18-months period looked rather useful (Carp, 1966). However, in view of the unknown latency of adaptive equilibrium, the earlier results were reported as tentative only, and the study was continued. An interval of 8 years was considered sufficiently long to allow for the dissipation of Hawthorne, honeymoon, and sleeper effects, and to provide adequate test of a predictive battery. The present report is on the testing, over the 8-year interval, of a regression equation which was developed at the end of the 18-months interval. The present study is concerned with whether correlates of adjustment over the shorter time are useful as predictors of relative adjustment over the longer interval among members of the original in-moving group who remained in the situation.

THE CHANGE IN LIVING SITUATION

When the initial data were collected, most subjects lived in substandard housing. The typical dwelling was one room in an old two-or three-story house which had once been a single family dwelling. Bathroom and kitchen facilities were often shared with other people and sometimes were on different floors. There was little privacy and little companionship. Nearly all subjects reported suffering from social isolation as well as from the physical inadequacies of their housing. A minority lived (usually with children) in housing which was physically standard but which involved over-crowding and interpersonal friction.

Following the first data collection, subjects moved into apartments in a newly completed nine-story building designed for older people (Victoria Plaza). Over 200 age peers lived under the same roof. Each apartment had its own kitchen (no meal service was available). There was no medical care unit, though there was a clinic facility staffed by visiting nurses. The senior center for the county was located on the ground floor of the building, as were the offices of Senior Center and Housing Authority staffs. Generally staff emphasis was upon activity and sociability (Wacker, 1960).

THE CRITERIA OF ADJUSTMENT

Establishment of criteria for adjustment, particularly in regard to older persons, poses difficult problems (Kuhlen 1959; Rosow, 1963). For this report, three varieties of adjustment, components of adjustment, or viewpoints on adjustment were selected.

The Resident's Happiness

Surely the person's own satisfaction in the new situation should be considered. One indicator of an unresolved adjustment problem, lack of equilibrium, or stress is a feeling of being upset or unhappy (Caplan, 1964). The measure used in the data-analysis reported here was the happiness section of the Havighurst, Burgess, and Cavan attitude survey (1948).

Perception by Peers

Another aspect of adaptation to group living is relationships with other tenants. A second criterion was subject's score on a sociometric instrument (Carp, 1966) administered to all residents.

Administration Judgments

In some sense, the most definitive evaluation of adjustment in any such setting is the opinion of staff. A third criterion was the averaged ratings of the two top administrators, the director of the residence and the director of the senior center, on a 7-point scale of adjustment to the situation. The raters worked independently of each other and without knowledge of research data.

Relationships among Criteria

On an a priori basis it seemed unlikely that the three criterion measures would be in perfect agreement. The fact that a person is happy does not negate the possibility that he bothers his neighbors. The administrator, charged with making a success of a new service in the community, may give low marks to a resident who, with great joy, withdraws into his own apartment and revels in this opportunity for privacy, or one who pursues an active and sociable life-style, but elsewhere. Investigation of the relationships among criterion measures when the 18-month data became available supported the view that combination into a unitary or composite criterion measure was not justified (Carp, 1969a). Therefore, each was maintained as a separate index.

THE PREDICTORS OF ADJUSTMENT

The goal was to identify characteristics of applicants which would predict their success in adapting to the new living situation, as indicated by their own satisfaction and their acceptance by the peer group as well as in the judgment of the staff. The living situation was a "given"; the degree of congruence would be determined by the "fit" of the individual to the circumstance. Capacity for independent living was a requisite for admission. Despite the safety features and the limitation to older tenants, the design of the building, inclusion of a senior community center, and attitudes surrounding plans for the Plaza all pointed to an active, interested, sociable clientele (Wacker, 1960).

Search was therefore made for indicators of capacity for independent living and for adaptation to an environment with provision for formal and informal activity, in close proximity to over 200 other elderly people, and in a milieu with expectations of high rates of activity and social involvement. Predictor items were identified prior to any data collection. To the extent possible, they were selected from among the items for which data were to be collected from applicants. In the case of five variables, it was necessary to use data to be collected at a later time. In the case of these items, efforts were undertaken simultaneously to develop measures appropriate for use with applicants, if the variables proved useful.

Capability for Independent Living

A person's resources for independent living are of various sorts. Some might be called *situational*:

Income. Money was limited among members of this group, but there was an income range, and it was expected that relatively good financial resources would be conducive to adjustment in the new situation. One predictor item, therefore, was income.

Marital status. Moving as a member of a couple, rather than alone, should facilitate adjustment to a new situation. Marital status was included, comparing those who were married and living with the spouse to all others, whether single, widowed, divorced, or separated.

Other resources for independent living are more in the nature of *personal descriptors*:

Chronological age. Within the limited age range eligible for admission, advanced years may be detrimental to adaptation to a new situation. Therefore chronological age at the last birthday was included among the predictors.

Education. Education should facilitate independent living and use of the resources in Victoria Plaza. The index was the highest school grade attended.

Job level. The type of work of previous years may also be associated with ability to adapt and to make use of new environmental resources. The job level of the work done by the man (or the husband of the woman) applicant during most of his working years was used.

Self-concept. Favorable self-concept is one aspect of ego strength and therefore should be conducive to independent living and good adjustment. The index was the average of scores on three of the Attitude Scales of Cavan, Burgess, Havighurst, and Goldhamer (1949), those on health, ability to work, and usefulness.

Physical, mental and emotional *impairments* will tend to reduce the capacity for independent living:

Physical disability. Though the building had special design features to make it safe and convenient for older people, it was intended for those capable of carrying out the normal routines of life on their own. Sensory-motor impairments might interfere with normal activities of self-care as well as with interpersonal relationships in the Plaza. The index was a composite of signs of disability (such as defective vision, deafness, or crippling) which tended to interfere with the interview procedures, on the assumption that they would similarly interfere with day-to-day activities.

Confusion. Memory loss should be detrimental to adaptation in a situation oriented to independent living. Interviewers rated applicants on 5-point scales with regard to confusion in remembering dates, places and names; the index used in the prediction equation was the average of the three.

Senility. Though the Plaza was designed for older citizens, it was not planned for the senile, and signs of senility in an applicant should contraindicate successful adjustment there. At the close of interviewing and testing each applicant, the interviewer completed the Senility Index of Cavan et al. (1949) and it was scored in the usual way.[1]

Neurotic-type complaints. Neuroticism is generally detrimental to adaptation. The health checklist used in the interview included sleeplessness, bad dreams, tiring too easily, food not tasting good, feeling blue, nervousness, disliking noise, worrying, and forgetfulness. The predictor score was the number of these items the applicant reported to "bother" him. with opportunities for and expectations of high

Activity and Involvement

In addition to the requirement for independent living, Victoria Plaza's physical design and staff orientation pointed to an environment activity levels and involvement among the residents. Person-situation congruence in regard to activity and involvement should characterize the more successful residents.

Desire for organized activity. Considering the staff plans, and inclusion of the senior center within the building, it seemed likely that person-situation congruence would be closest for individuals who sought participation in formal associations or clubs rather than those aversive to such organized activities. Present memberships were highly constrained by the life circumstances of the applicants and therefore might not be predictive of future behavior in the new setting. Therefore the applicants were asked to name groups or organizations they would like to join, if circumstances permitted. For purposes of prediction, no attention was paid to the type of desired affiliation, but only to whether the applicant named one or more organizations.

Desire for informal activities. Moving into the Plaza would open up to residents a variety of leisure-time activities which did not entail formal organizations. If he were to get the most out of the new situation, to become a member of the resident community and to do what seemed desirable in the view of the planners, the resident should be favorably inclined to take part in these informal activities. The score used in prediction was the number of activities (regardless of type) an applicant mentioned when asked what things he would like to do if he had the opportunity.

Attendance at religious services. Current behavior may be a better predictor of future action than is a verbal report regarding desires or intentions, so it seemed advisable to include some index of pre-move activity, but one which was not too much determined by situational factors. One activity which seems to be relatively unconstrained by the circumstances in which older people live is church attendance. This may be due to the distribution of religious institutions in local neighborhoods, while other types of community facilities tend to be more centralized (Carp, in press).

Disengagement. Because the Plaza was planned for active life-styles among its residents, tendencies to disengage were expected to contraindicate adjustment there. An index was devised for this purpose, on which the interviewer rated each applicant (Carp, 1966, 1968).

Age identification. Victoria Plaza was expected to provide an environment more suitable to those who perceived themselves as "middle aged" rather than as old, elderly, or aged, regardless of calendar age. The interview asked for the age group in which the respondent felt he belonged, and responses were dichotomized to provide the index.

Feelings about the future. Anxiety about the future and fear of death were expected to be detrimental to development of the busy, active life-style anticipated in the Plaza. In addition, the design of the building necessitated the delivery of medical care and the removal of the dead by means of an elevator located in the middle of the senior center. This design feature might exacerbate apprehensions among persons prone to them. Applicants were asked what they felt about the future and about the end of life. Answers were categorized into those which indicated secure acceptance as against those which showed avoidance or apprehension and were combined for the two questions.

Sociability

Sociability was an obvious goal in the building design and the management plans. The predictors include indexes of inclination toward sociability and those of social stimulus value.

Active social pastimes. One predictor combined activity and sociability. The expectation was that the more sociable and the more active pastimes the applicant currently pursued despite the situational constraints, the more likely he was to achieve successful adjustment to the new situation with its richer opportunity for active, social life-styles. Respondents' enumeration of their leisure activities was the basis for the score. One point was added for each activity the respondent said he usually did with other people, and one point was added for each which had been pre-coded as active.

Number of close friends. It seemed likely that the person with few or no friends would be less likely to take advantage of the new opportunity for personal interaction which the Plaza would afford and that the person who named a very large number of people as "close friends" might be distorting reality. Therefore, the number of persons named as close friends was squared to allow for the curvilinearity of relationship between this variable and the indexes of adjustment, and in view of the prediction that applicants who reported about the average number of close friends would be more successful as residents of the Plaza than would applicants who named very few or very many.

Number of friends in youth. As with activities, the number of applicants' friends at present was arbitrarily determined, to a considerable degree, by physical and social conditions of their lives. Readiness to make friends may be more important than present number in predicting social success in the new situation. Assuming that inclination toward sociability remains fairly constant through life, an index based on the past might better predict future behavior in the new situation which would afford richer opportunity for friendship development. The interview included questions on the number of friends of the same sex and of the opposite sex when the respondent was in his early teens. Answers were tabulated in terms of recollections of having more, fewer, or about the same number as most contemporaries. The score was the average of responses to the two questions.

Relationships with parents in youth. Relationships with parents are generally accepted as important determinants of character and personality, and particularly of subsequent relationships with other people. The teen years were selected for scrutiny because during this period inter-generational conflict is most likely. People who recall strong and healthy relationships with their parents at that time probably grew up incorporating few conflictive tendencies and enjoying pleasant interpersonal associations. For the attempt to predict adjustment to Victoria Plaza, an average was taken of the scores (on 5-point scales) representing recollection of relationship with father and with mother. There was no assumption that people's responses tally with realities of the time they were growing up, but only that they may reflect interest in sociability and confidence in their own competence in this area, perhaps better than similar questions about the current time, when most were living in socially constraining situations.

Attitude toward current others. Better adjustment to Plaza life was expected for applicants who had favorable attitudes toward other people who were meaningful in their lives at present. The index used was the average of the Cavan et al. Attitude Scales for friends and for family.

Certain personality-behavior traits relevant to *social stimulus* value should be predictive of adjustment in the new living situation which was so clearly oriented to sociability. Initial data on applicants did not include measures of these traits. In view of their possible importance, it seemed worthwhile to use estimates collected at a later time. While this has negative connotations for a study based on prediction over time, it seemed preferable to omitting them altogether. The results of the 18-month "concurrent prediction" with these variables indicated that the variables were relevant to short-run adjustment. The 8-year study tests their predictive value across a period of 6 ½ years. Therefore, included in the predictor set were five items for which data were collected after the first year of operation in Victoria Plaza.

Scores on the following five items were the averages of 7-point ratings made by 11 raters: the Manager of the Plaza; the Director of the Senior Center; the latter's secretary; the Public Health nurse, the city recreation worker, and the public librarian assigned to the building; the man in charge of maintenance; his assistant; the night watchman; and two data collectors.[2]

Snobbishness. It was anticipated that people who did not appear to consider themselves "better" than their neighbors would adjust better to the close living in the Plaza, while a supercilious attitude would be an obstacle to adjustment in the community of Victoria Plaza. This characteristic was rated on a scale which ran from "superior and above others (in the sense of snobbishness)" to "congenial with other people."

Nosiness and the tendency to gossip. Undue interest in the affairs of others was likely to be a handicap to adjustment in the Plaza, especially in the view of other residents. Clearly, the almost congregate style of living and certain features of the building itself would provide opportunity for inquisitiveness into the lives of others and for gossip.

Nervousness. Another personality-behavior trait probably relevant to adjustment to community living is the tendency to worry, to be easily upset, to become overwrought, and to be overly sensitive *versus* the capacity to maintain equilibrium and to remain calm.

Fastidiousness and good taste. As concerned as the applicants generally were with the ugliness and unavoidable dirtiness of their living situations, it seemed obvious that they would tend to reject and dislike anyone who did not keep his apartment and himself clean and attractive. Surely these tendencies would also be objectionable to staff. To provide an index, two items on which residents were rated by the 11 persons were combined. One dealt with tidiness and orderliness *versus* carelessness, and the other dealt with artistic and esthetic sensitivity.

General likability. An important element of capacity to adjust to such an environment as Victoria Plaza, at least in the view of peer and staff, is over-all likability, regardless of the specific traits comprising this social-stimulus value. The 11 raters assessed each resident on a scale which ran from "From a purely personal point of view, I like this person," to "From a purely personal point of view, I dislike this person."

Over-all Person-Situation Congruence

Before they collected the baseline data from applicants, the interviewers were well informed about the physical design of the building and about plans for its management. At the end of some 6 hours of individual interviewing and testing, they were fairly familiar with each applicant assigned to them. In the summary regarding each applicant, the interviewer gave his over-all evaluation of the person as a prospective resident in the new community. These statements were translated into scores on a 5-point scale and included among the predictors.

SUBJECTS

For the study on the impact of Victoria Plaza, data were collected on 352 legally qualified applicants. Of them, 204 moved into the new facility when it opened. At the time of final data collection, 133 members of the original inmoving group remained as Plaza residents. Thirty-six had died and 30 had been put in nursing homes. Another 16 had moved out, several of them (6) to be with children, though 4 were asked to move. For purposes of the present analysis, data were available on all 133 for two of the criterion variables—staff judgments and peer evaluations. Six residents refused to be interviewed, or were ill or on trips, so self-evaluations of happiness were available on only 127.

The group was homogeneous from the start. Subjects were predominantly Anglo-Saxon in background and native-born. Average education was eighth grade, typical for persons in this age group (von Mering & Weniger, 1959). During working years the men and the husbands of the women had been in middle-range jobs and income brackets. Currently they were poor, though no more so than typical persons in the same age range. At the time of first data collection, the average income ($94.40 per mo.) was similar to that of persons 65 and older who were receiving Social Security benefits (U.S. Bureau of Census, 1958). At first contact, they ranged in age from 52 to 92, with a mean of 72.24. Screening for public housing eligibility tended to eliminate the poorly informed, the passive, the less intelligent, and the physically handicapped.

DATA ANALYSIS

Using criterion data collected on the 204 inmovers at the end of the first year of operation of Victoria Plaza, stepwise multiple regression analysis (following Bottenberg & Ward, 1963) was used to establish a prediction equation with the 27 predictors, for each of the three adjustment criteria. In the case of 22 predictor items, data were collected 18 months prior to criterion data; in the case of 5, predictor data were collected at approximately the same time as were criterion data.

The regression weights and constants developed in this analysis were used to predict criterion scores based on data which were collected after the 8-year interval for the survivors. In this second analysis, prediction was across time for all variables, though it was across only 6 ½ years for 5 items.

The analyses reported here test the predictive efficiency, over an 8-year period, of one set of variables and their weights which were demonstrated to be useful in accounting for individual differences in adjustment at the end of the first year of residence in a new living situation. This study is a ''cross-validation over time'' of three prediction equations and is concerned specifically with the long-term validity of a prediction system which accounted rather well for differences in short-run adjustment.

Only the original inmovers were considered eligible for these analyses. From a theoretical point of view, replacements must be excluded because of cohort variation and on grounds that the living situation, at least from a social-psychological viewpoint, may be different for them. From a practical standpoint, baseline data are available only on the original group.

Further, these analyses are concerned only with those members of the first in-moving group who remained in the situation and therefore adapted to at least a minimal degree. Remaining in the situation versus leaving it is an important and objective index of adjustment. In this case most attrition was due to death or illness rather than to voluntary or administrative separation, which provides an even more clear-cut and noncontroversial criterion of adaptation. Determination of the predictors of these important indexes is essential, is the subject of other analyses, and will be the subject of other reports. However, it also seems important to understand the sources of variation in adjustment among persons who remained in the situation. At the moment, no method presents itself for scaling death and other sources of attrition together with the other indexes of adjustment into a unitary criterion variable. It is possible that viewing the results of the present analyses, together with those in which death and separation are criteria, will suggest such a procedure for future studies.

A separate report will be made in regard to those who left the Plaza, most of them in death. Still another report will discuss the original in-movers within the context of the total population, including replacements. Limitation of consideration to the relatively successful movers puts stringent requirements on any prediction system. The correlation coefficients would be increased if it were possible to use one criterion which extended from death to optimal adjustment. However, there were individual differences in satisfaction with the new environment, in acceptability to its other residents, and in the judgment of staff members, and it seems useful to learn about the determinants of these differences and to test their persistence through time.

RESULTS

Efficiency of Prediction

Table 31.1 summarizes results over both time intervals, for the 22 predictors for which data were collected at baseline, the 5 for which data were collected simultaneously with the 18-month criterion data, and for the whole set of 27. The 18-month coefficients are not corrected for shrinkage (Wiggins, 1973). In the validation analysis across the 8-year interval as well as in the original analysis over an 18-month period, the systems account for appreciable amounts of the variance in all indexes of adjustment. The equations which accounted for variance in early adjustment scores also predicted relative 8-year status rather well.

Though the correlation coefficients are not extremely large, they are of respectable size for predicting behavior in a different environment, over extended time periods. Furthermore, the size of the coefficients must be interpreted in view of the fact that the equations were developed on a group of subjects which had already undergone preselection according to the admis-

Table 31.1. Efficiency of Predicting Adjustment over 18 Months and over 8 Years

Criterion	Predictors		
	22 Items	5 Items	27 Items
(a) Self	R	R	R
18 mo.	.55*	.24*	.56*
8 yrs.	.48*	.13	.51*
(b) Peers			
18 mo.	.45*	.50*	.53*
8 yrs.	.23*	.54*	.55*
(c) Administrators			
18 mo.	.51*	.75*	.78*
8 yrs.	.36*	.52*	.55*

N for 18 mo. = 204. N for 8 years = 127 (a); 133 (b,c).
* Significant at the .01 level.

sions standards of the Housing Authority and which therefore was homogeneous in many ways; and that the validation analysis used data from a sub-group of respondents made even more homogeneous by loss of the residents who, by some standards, were least well adapted to the situation. Coefficients might well be larger with unselected subjects.

The results suggest that the quality of an older person's adaptation to a new environment depends to a considerable extent upon circumstances, habits, and attitudes which can be assessed prior to involvement in the new environment and that long-range adjustment shares determinants with short-range adjustment.

Predictors of Adjustment

The findings cast some light upon the nature of determinants of adaptation to a new and different environment on the part of old, relatively intact people. The specific correlates depend somewhat upon the definition of adjustment. Tables 31.2, 31.3, and 31.4 show the stepwise multiple correlation between each of the three criteria and the primary predictor variables.

Happiness. To predict an applicant's happiness in the new living situation, one important piece of information about him was that he had a favorable view of himself, his usefulness and ability (Table 31.2). Another important predictor was a composite score based upon an optimistic attitude toward the future plus a secure rather than fearfully avoiding one toward death. Identi-

Table 31.2. Primary Predictors of Happiness

Predictors	Multiple correlation
Self-attitude	.300
+ Feeling about future	.383
+ Age-group identification	.424
+ Attitude toward parents during teens	.435
+ Attitude toward family and friends	.440
+ Number of activities wanted	.445
+ Interest in joining some group	.452

fication with the middle-aged rather than the old, aged, or elderly was predictive of happiness, as were recollections of strong and warm relationships with one's parents during the teen years and present satisfaction with family and friends. The number of activities an applicant would like to take part in and his desire to join one or more organizations were less important but also augured well for his subsequent happiness as a resident.

Acceptance among peers. With scores from sociometric ratings by the other residents as the criterion for adjustment, determinants were almost completely different from those for happiness (Table 31.3). The best predictors of favorable peer judgments were the tendency to be congenial rather than snobbish, tidy and artistically sensitive rather than careless and esthetically insensitive, to mind one's own business rather than being nosey and a gossip, to be married and living with the spouse rather than in any other marital status, to remain calm rather than to be easily upset, to be young within the age range, to have a large amount of education relative to the group, and to have above average income compared to the other residents.

Table 31.3. Primary Predictors of Popularity

Predictors	Multiple correlation
Snobbishness (reversed)	.364
+ Tidiness	.430
+ Tendency to gossip (reversed)	.482
+ Marital status	.501
+ Nervousness (reversed)	.506
+ Age (reversed)	.527
+ Education	.531
+ Income	.534

Table 31.4. Primary Predictors of Administrators'
Evaluations

Predictors	Multiple correlation
Nosiness	.527
+ Snobbishness (reversed)	.697
+ Participation in activities	.728
+ Confusion in initial interview (reversed)	.742
+ Nervousness (reversed)	.750
+ Church attendance	.760
+ Tidiness	.772

Administrator ratings. The strongest determinant of adjustment as rated by administrators was contrary to one of the primary predictors of peer judgments. The strongest correlate with administrator ratings of adjustment was the tendency to be nosey and to gossip (Table 31.4).

This correlation does not mean that administrators consider gossipy people best adjusted. In the context of other correlates of administrator ratings, it seems clear that administrators perceived adaptation to the situation almost exclusively in terms of organized activity and sociability within it. This view is confirmed by relationships with variables not in the prediction equation. For example, frequency of using the Senior Center was almost identical with administrator ratings on adjustment to the new residential situation ($r = .92$), and other variables strongly correlated with administrator judgments of adaptation were talkativeness, participation in organized activities, and tendency to welcome outsiders to the Senior Center.

SUMMARY AND IMPLICATIONS

The results of this study support the role of person-situation congruence in determining adjustment and indicate the feasibility of identifying characteristics of community-resident old persons which are predictive of their subsequent adjustment in a particular, different environment. Furthermore, they suggest that determinants of short-run and long-term adjustment to a living situation have much in common. Predictor variables selected to measure characteristics of persons relevant to their congruence with the new situation provided statistically significant and usefully large correlation coefficients at 18 months and again at 8 years with each of three criteria, subjective happiness, acceptance among resident peers, and staff ratings of adjustment to the residential setting. The nature and importance of predictor items vary according to the definition of adjustment.

This paper deals only with the predictive efficiency, over an 8-year period, of one set of variables and weights which were useful in accounting for individual differences at the end of the first year of residence. It is possible that long-range adjustment to the new living situation can be more accurately predicted using a different system of weights or different predictor variables and by the use of more cogent criterion measures. These possibilities are being pursued in additional analyses of the data, and future reports will present other equations which account for more of the variance over the 8-year interval, for the criteria used in these analyses and for others which became available for the final stages of the study. The present analysis is concerned solely with the long-term validity of a system which accounted rather well for variations in three measures of short-run adjustment to the new situation.

Cross-validation of the prediction equation in the more usual sense, that is, with a different group of subjects and a similar but separate residential setting, also remains to be done. Baseline data on applicants to a second facility (Villa Tranchese) and data on residents at the end of the first year have been collected for this purpose.

NOTES

1. Subsequent work (Carp, 1969b) suggests that the index measures ordinary maladjustment rather than age-specific senility, but the role in predicting adjustment remains the same.

2. Self-report instruments which could be used with applicants have now been validated against the ratings and will be reported elsewhere.

REFERENCES

Aldrich, D. K., & Mendkoff, E. Relocation of the aged and disabled: A mortality study. In Journal of the American Geriatrics Society, 1963, 11, 185–194.

Bottenberg, R. A., & Ward, J. H., Jr. Applied multiple linear regression. Technical Documentary Report PRL-TDR-63-6 March, 1963, 6570th Personnel Research Laboratory Aerospace Medical Division, Air Force Systems Command, Lackland AFB, Texas, Project 7719, Task 771901.

Caplan, G. Principles of preventive psychiatry. Basic Books, New York, 1964.

Carp, F. M. A future for the aged: The residents of Victoria Plaza, University of Texas Press, Austin, 1966.

Carp, F. M. Person-situation congruence in engagement. Gerontologist, 1968, 8, 184–188.

Carp, F. M. Compound criteria in gerontological research. Journal of Gerontology, *1969, 24, 341–347. (a)*

Carp, F. M. Senility or garden-variety maladjustment? Journal of Gerontology, *1969, 24, 203–208. (b)*

Carp, F. M. Some environmental effects upon the mobility of older people. (in press)

Cavan, R. S., Burgess, E. W., Havighurst, R. J. & Goldhamer, H. Personal adjustment in old age. *Science Research Assoc., Inc., Chicago, 1949.*

Donahue, W. Impact of living arrangements on ego development in the elderly. In F. M. Carp (Ed.), Patterns of living and housing of middle-aged and older people. *USGPO, Washington, 1966.*

Eisdorfer, C. Discussion. In F. M. Carp (Ed.), The retirement process. *PHS-Pub. No. 1778, USGPO, Washington, 1968.*

Erikson, E. H. The problem of ego identity. Psychological Issues, *1959, 1, 101–164.*

Hamovitch, M. B. Social and psychological factors in adjustment in a retirement village. In F. M. Carp (Ed.), The retirement process, *PHS-Pub. No. 1778, USGPO, Washington, 1968.*

Hartmann, H. Ego psychology and the problem of adaptation. *David Rapaport (Trans.), International Universities Press, New York, 1958.*

Havighurst, R. J., Burgess E. & Cavan, R. Your activities and attitudes. *Science Research Assoc., Chicago, 1948.*

Kagan, J. & Moss, H. A. The stability of passive and dependent behavior from childhood through adulthood. Child Development, *1960, 31, 313–321.*

Klein, D. C. & Lindemann, E. Preventive intervention in individual and family crisis situations. In G. Caplan (Ed.), Prevention of mental disorders in children: Initial exploration. *Basic Books, New York, 1961.*

Kuhlen, R. G. Aging and life adjustment. In J. E. Birren (Ed.), Handbook-of aging and the individual. *University of Chicago Press, Chicago, 1959.*

Lazarus, R. S. Psychological stress and the coping process. *McGraw-Hill, New York, 1966.*

Lieberman, M. A. Relationship of mortality rates to entrance to a home for the aged. Geriatrics, *1961, 16, 515–519.*

Lieberman, M. A. Factors in environmental change. In F. M. Carp (Ed.), Patterns of living and housing of middle-aged and older people. *USGPO, Washington, 1966.*

Miller, D. & Lieberman, M. A. The relationship of affect state: Adaptive capacity or reactions to stress. Journal of Gerontology. *1965, 20, 492–497.*

Rosow, I. Adjustment of the normal aged. In R. H. Williams, C. Tibbitts & W. Donahue (Eds.), Processes of aging, *Vol. 2. Atherton Press, New York, 1963.*

Selye, H. & Prioreschi, P. Stress theory of aging. In N W. Shock (Ed.), Aging: Social and biological aspects. *American Assoc. for the Advancement of Science, 1960.*

U.S. Bureau of Census, 1958.

Vale, J. R. & Vale, C. A. Individual differences and general laws in psychology: A reconciliation. American Psychologist, *1969, 24, 1092–1108.*

von Mering, O. & Weniger, F. Social-cultural background of the aging individual.

In J. E. Birren (Ed.), Handbook of aging and the individual. *Univ. of Chicago Press, Chicago, 1959.*

Wacker, M. (Ed.), Victoria Plaza Apartments. *Clegg Publishing, San Antonio, 1960.*

Wiggins, J. S. Personality and prediction principles of personality assessment. *Addison-Wesley, Reading, MA, 1973.*

32. The Ecology of Social Relationships in Housing for the Elderly

M. Powell Lawton and Bonnie Simon

A PERSON MAY structure space and the objects within space in an active manner, altering the environment in the service of his needs, or, conversely, he may vary his behavior as a function of the space and objects in it, adapting to a relatively fixed environment. While the active and passive use of the physical environment by man have long been the concern of the architect, designer, planner, and ecologist, systematic attempts to link these sciences with behavioral science are relatively recent in origin. Barker (1965) has defined the field of ecological psychology, linking physical environment and behavior in the concept of the "behavior setting." Sommer in a series of studies has investigated the way people manipulate space and objects, and how their behavior varies as a function of the physical setting (Sommer 1965, 1966; Sommer & Ross, 1958). Hall (1966) has incorporated "proxemics"— the science of how man spaces himself with reference to others—into a general theory of communication (Hall, 1959). Ittelson and associates (Ittelson, 1960, 1964) have investigated attitudes and perception as they relate to use of space and objects. Social ecology, or environmental psychology— depending on whether one wishes to emphasize the individual or the group— is an emergent science which promises to help solve some major problems of the present and future.

We propose the general hypothesis that there is a relationship between the state of the organism and its docility in the face of environmental restrictions. That is, the more competent the organism—in terms of health, intelligence, ego strength, social role performance, or cultural evolution—the less will be the proportion of variance in behavior attributable to physical objects or conditions around him; let us call this the "environmental docility hypothesis." With high degrees of competence, he will, in common parlance, rise above his environment. However, reduction in competence, or "deprived status," heightens his behavioral dependence on external conditions.

From *The Gerontologist* 8 (1967): 108–15. Reprinted with permission of the Gerontological Society of America.

Gerontology offers the opportunity to test hypotheses about environment and behavior and to study both the older person manipulating his environment in the service of his needs and his behavior as a function of a relatively fixed environmental field. The older person may suffer impaired health, cognition, and personal and social adjustment, and thus become subject to directives from environmental objects which in earlier life he would have minimized. This greater susceptibility of older people to the environmental effect enhances the possibility of testing hypotheses about the person-environment interface. Specifically, the planning of communities, buildings, and institutions for the elderly offers an opportunity to observe people of reduced competence dealing with new physical environments.

BACKGROUND OF THE PRESENT STUDY

＊Old age, or its physical limitations, reduces the range of activities available to the individual, so that his instrumental behavior may become less satisfactory in attaining appropriate goals, such as housing, proper food, and social contact. Thus, physical distance between S and goal object may assume heightened importance where competence is low. Proximity to age peers and increased opportunity for social relationships are major advantages of planned congregate housing.

Previous work with younger populations indicates that proximity is a prime factor in the determination of friendship formation. As Newcomb (1964) and others have found, the importance of proximity diminishes with time and the establishment of contacts outside the proximal situation. Thus, proximity may be a factor in friendship formation that is replaced by other common bases for friendship where the freedom to interact is not restricted by the confinement of the individual to his immediate environment. In the elderly, advanced age, poor physical health, widowhood, and other limiting factors may enhance the effects of proximity and reduce the range of possibilities for relationships based on the satisfaction of mutual needs.

In younger populations, it has been further shown that a residential location which is central to the hub of activity increases the number of casual contacts a person is likely to have during a typical day, and consequently facilitates the friendship formation process. Festinger and his associates (1950) found that younger married couples easily converted such casual opportunities into occasions for forming friendships. We need to determine whether older people also do.

Proximity to a social goal object has been examined from several points of view in a longitudinal study of housing for the elderly now under way at the Philadelphia Geriatric Center:

Physical distance from the S's apartment to his chosen friend's apartment, expressed most easily as the dichotomy of own-floor vs. other-floor sociometric choice. To have as a friend a person who lives at a greater physical distance may require the S to exert more effort to maintain the friendship than he would if the friend lived on his own floor. The person who limits his choices to people on his own floor will be called "floor-bound."

Deliberate traversal of space in order to have social contact vs. dependence on chance encounters in common-space behavior settings. Operationally, this variable distinguishes the person who has recently visited or has been visited by his first-chosen friend from the one who usually sees his friend elsewhere in the building.

Combining these two variables in a 2 × 2 combination results in four subgroups, which may be ordered in a continuum of degrees to which environmental inertia is overcome in the service of social interaction. Most inertia is overcome by the S whose friend is on another floor and who exchanges visits with that friend; least inertia is overcome by the person whose friend is on the same floor and who does not visit; the person who visits a same-floor friend or who does not visit his friend on another floor lies between the extremes of this continuum of inertia counteracted.

Manipulation of the physical environment to serve social needs. Psychological distance from one's neighbor may be expressed through maintaining a closed apartment door compared to an open one. One of several possible reasons for keeping a door open is a social reason: it may be an invitation for a neighbor to drop in, or a means of participation in social activity through direct verbal and motoric interaction.

Locus of social interaction. An active effort to minimize the spacing between himself and others is exerted by the S who visits with his friend, or who goes to a space where the probability of meeting another person is high. Thus, the population of common spaces in an environment may have an important effect on the opportunity the individual has for social interaction.

The susceptibility of an older person to the effect of proximity on friendship formation should, according to the environmental docility hypothesis, vary with certain aspects of competence: physical health, independence, social integration, social status, to name a few. Theoretically, more competent people should be freer to search beyond their immediate environs for friends with common interests, backgrounds, or personalities, and would therefore show less floor-boundedness than those people limited in various ways.

The above four dimensions, each related to the distance between the S and his friend, may be investigated (1) by comparisons among Ss or (2) among housing sites with respect to spatial behaviors and other characteristics.

The present study will present information from both of these points of view, as well as some purely descriptive ecological data. The comparisons among sites must be considered basically as a "clinical" study. Although the total sample consists of almost 1,000 Ss, the number of environments that can be compared at this point is 2, 3, 4 or 5, not a respectable N by any standard. Therefore, some selected findings will be presented in order to illustrate the manner in which older Ss use space, and to show some consistencies of social space usage within the environments studied.

Materials and Methods

Subjects. This study of adjustment to housing has involved interviewing a large number of Ss in different types of housing. All Ss or their spouses were 62 or over and all were residents of age-segregated, semicongregate, high-rise housing built under public housing or federally-aided housing programs for lower-middle incomes (Section 202 or Section 231). Table 32.1 shows the locale, the income level of the occupants, the total population, and the number of Ss seen in the surveys described below.

Table 32.1. Characteristics of Samples

Site	Locale	Income level	Total population	Sociometric survey N			Long interview N
				3 Mo.	1 Yr.	5 Yr.	
A	Small city	lower middle	279	—	231	—	140
B	Small city	low	160	137	148	—	120
C	Large metropolitan area	low	209	—	162	—	120
D	Large city	middle	251	246	233	—	84
E	Large city	middle	264	—	—	197	—
Total			1,163	383	774	197	464

Procedure. The study design involved seeing tenants at one or more of the following time periods with respect to their occupancy of the apartment building: (a) during the month prior to occupancy: (b) three months following occupancy; (c) one year following occupancy; and (d) five years after the building was occupied. The size of the sample was determined by attempting to interview either a prechosen proportion of the entire population (e.g., one half of site A and one-third of site D) or, as we later decided, a minimum of 120, which would be likely to yield a follow-up sample of about 100 after one year of occupancy. The number of *S*s in the "long interview" column of Table 32.1 indicates the number seen prior to occupancy in the different sites. With the exception of Site E, most Ss in a given building occupied the building at the same time. An effort was made to do a complete sociometric survey of each building, but refusals and people whom we could not reach diminished the actual number of people seen in each site at post-occupancy time as shown in the "sociometric survey N" column of Table 32.1. The total completion rate was 84%.

The long preoccupancy interview consisted of questions regarding social background, attitudes to housing, recent life history, social interaction with friends and relatives, formal associations, health, and morale. Interviewing time averaged about 75 minutes, and most of the interviews were done in the respondent's domicile.

The later sociometric surveys consisted of the request to name one's best friends in the congregate housing site. All names given were accepted, but if less than three were named the respondent was urged to name others. This survey was done three months after occupancy in sites B and D, one year after occupancy in sites A, B, C, and D, and five years after site E opened.

At the time of the 12-month or 5-year sociometric survey, a series of behavioral observations was done in the halls and common spaces of the buildings. A minimum of two observations each were done at 9 A.M., 11 A.M., 1 P.M., 4 P.M., and 8 P.M. at each site. Observations were made in summer and fall, and only on days when weather permitted sitting outdoors. The observed behaviors of interest in the present study were:

(a) Incidence of open apartment doors.
(b) Number of tenants observable in halls, common spaces, and immediately adjacent outdoor areas.

Incidence as of the moment was the unit of measurement. That is, the observer walked through all spaces of the building tallying number of people, their behavior, and which doors were open as he passed them on his rounds. A complete tour took 20 to 35 minutes.

RESULTS

Spatial Aspects of Social Interaction

The effect of proximity. Proximity was found to be a very potent determinant of sociometric choice at every time and location. Table 32.2 shows the number of people choosing none, one, two, and three friends on their own floors, with only the first three sociometric choices considered. The times of the survey with respect to the opening of the building are shown in the first column. For each site taken separately χ^2 tests of goodness of fit between observed distribution of choices and the distribution to be expected if there were no tendency to choose friends on one's own floor showed very highly significant effects of proximity ($P < 0.001$ in all instances). For site D, this effect of proximity was tested on a smaller scale within individual floors. The relationship between units of distance from one apartment to another on the same floor and sociometric choice made was again highly significant ($P < 0.001$). These findings are in general agreement with those reported by Carp (1966) in public housing for the elderly and by Friedman (1966) in a home for aged.

Changes in the effect of proximity over time. Sites B and D were surveyed shortly after occupancy and again after a year. In neither site was there any significant change over this period of time in the degree of floorboundedness (for site B, $\chi^2 = 2.5$, and for site D, $\chi^2 = 2.1$, both with 3 d.f., $p > 0.005$). Site E was surveyed five years after its opening. The distribution of own-

Table 32.2. Number of Own-Floor Choices (out of First Three)

Site	Time	0	1	2	3	Total making any choices
B	3-mo.	18	22	37	43	120
D	3-mo.	85	65	32	20	202
A	12-mo.	91	51	30	21	193
B	12-mo.	26	21	33	56	136
C	12-mo.	65	38	29	13	145
D	12-mo.	89	56	28	17	190
E	5 yr.	87	54	28	7	176

floor choices when related to the individual S's length of residence showed no relationship between floor-boundedness and time in the building ($\chi^2 =$ 11.31, 10 d.f., $p > 0.05$). Further, floorboundedness was no less characteristic of Site E after five years than of Sites A, C, and D after one year, or site D after three months. These results corroborate Friedman's (1966) finding showing no change in floorboundedness over time among residents of an old age home. They are at variance, however, with other studies demonstrating a decreased effect of proximity on friendship formation in college students (Newcomb, 1964).

Other variables as mediators between proximity and friendship choice. The environmental docility hypothesis predicts that limitations on the competence of older people (i.e., "deprived" status) would tend to make them more subject to the effect of proximity and less likely to choose friends on the basis of common statuses and shared experiences. In sites B and C the effect of proximity was studied as a function of the following attributes:

(a) Physical health (rated following physical examination on a 6-point scale of functional capacity in Site D; self-reported in Site B)
(b) Nativity (Eastern European vs. other)
(c) Marital status (currently married versus not married)
(d) Age
(e) Sex
(f) Income

Three months following occupancy, there was a tendency for the less healthy of the 202 Ss making any choice in Site D to be more floorbound in their choices ($\chi^2 = 3.97$, 1 d.f., $P < 0.05$), as were those born in Eastern Europe ($\chi^2 = 8.38$, 1 d.f., $P < 0.01$). The presently married showed a marginal tendency to be less floorbound ($\chi^2 = 3.63$, 1 d.f., $P < 0.10$). The other factors investigated did not affect the degree to which proximity determined choices.

In Site B, self-reported physical health was not associated with floorboundedness three months following occupancy. There were too few foreign-born for an adequate test of the association between place of birth and floorboundedness. Men were less floorbound than women ($\chi^2 = 5.02$, 1 d.f., $P < 0.05$), but marital status was not associated with floorboundedness.

After one year, none of these factors were related to floorboundedness in Site D, while in Site B the following relationships were found: men were less floorbound than women ($\chi^2 = 10.29$, 1 d.f., $p < 0.01$); the married were less floorbound than the not married; and those with higher income were less floorbound than those with lower income ($\chi^2 = 7.09$, 1 d.f., $p < 0.01$).

Thus, while every "deprived" status, except greater chronological age, at one time or another mediates the effect of proximity on choices, these relationships do not appear to be stable over time. Indeed, in Site B, their effects as mediators increase over time, while in Site D their effects disappear. We shall discuss later this contrast among the sites.

Traversal of space for social interaction. Proximity as a factor in visiting behavior was investigated during the 12-month follow-up long interviews with Ss in sites A, B, and D. When the first-named friend in the sociometric lived on the same floor that the S did, he was more likely to have visited or been visited by that friend during the past week (χ^2 for the three sites were, respectively, 4.23, 4.67, and 6.75, 1 d.f.).

The variable representing the overcoming of environmental inertia was based on the four cell-types of same floor—other floor friend vs. visited—did not visit. The S's choice of first-named friend was characterized as follows:

SV—same floor friend, visited recently
SN—same floor friend, did not visit recently
OV—other floor friend, visited recently
ON—other floor friend, did not visit recently

The relationship between overcoming inertia and a number of variables relating to the chooser's well-being was tested with Site B and Site D separately. Some of these variables were sets of rational indices constructed by the grouping of interview items which bore some face relationship to the variables in question; each item was given a unit score based on the dichotomization of its distribution. Table 32.3 shows the names given to these indices. While there was an index of the same name for the two sites, the interview schedules used at the two sites differed. The indices are not comparable and the means shown in Table 32.3 are not to be compared between sites, but only within rows for each site singly.

The administrative staff of each site also performed ratings after a year on the four characteristics shown at the bottom of Table 32.3: happiness, independence, social activity, and quality of relationships with peers.

One-way analyses of variance between the four "inertia" groups revealed significantly different mean ratings in the indices marked with "b" in Table

Table 32.3. Mean Scores on Indices and Ratings for Location—Visiting Status Groups in Two Sites

Index	No. items in index	Site B Location — visiting status[a]				No. items in index	Site D Location — visiting status[a]			
		SN	SV	ON	OV		SN	SV	ON	OV
Disengagement	10	3.85	3.90	4.44	4.35	4	1.67	1.58	1.91	2.09
Acceptance of status quo	20	10.28	13.35	14.55	13.70[b]	14	8.08	8.84	9.36	10.39
Evaluation of site	15	7.42	8.78	9.55	8.41[b]	16	8.08	8.05	8.85	9.48
Contact with friends	8	2.05	4.04	3.66	3.82	7	2.75	3.05	3.39	3.30
Alienation	11	2.85	1.53	1.77	1.41[b]	11	3.25	3.00	2.94	2.78
On-site activities	4	.67	1.31	1.44	2.06	3	1.50	1.63	1.76	1.70
Enriching activities	11	3.50	3.70	5.66	5.00[b]	6	1.83	2.16	2.21	2.65
Contact with children	4	1.60	1.65	2.44	2.05[b]	4	1.58	2.05	1.85	2.04
Mobility	8	3.30	3.94	4.22	5.23[b]	5	2.08	2.63	2.36	2.91
Wish for services	10	2.14	2.96	2.90	2.64	7	2.00	2.68	2.67	2.00[b]
Rosow health scale	6	2.50	2.96	2.65	3.00	6	2.33	2.74	2.54	3.04
Happiness	1–4	2.28	2.09	2.00	2.11	3–12	7.30	6.83	6.18	5.77
Independence	1–5	3.57	3.84	3.77	4.11	3–12	7.75	8.95	9.25	9.61[b]
Social activity	1–4	2.00	2.18	2.33	2.81	3–9	5.00	5.41	5.89	6.22
Relations with peers	1–3	2.25	2.00	2.11	1.88	3–9	4.00	4.00	3.85	3.48
N		12	19	33	23		9	17	34	23
Sums of ranks of means		59	41	31	29		59	46.5	35	19.5

[a]SN = same floor—no visit; SV = same floor visit; ON = other floor—no visit; OV = other floor—visit.

[b]Differences among index means within site significant at .05 level or better.

32.3. However, inasmuch as a direction was predicted for the means of the indices for the inertia groups, the march of means across rows without regard to their significance appeared to follow a definite pattern: the mean representing greater well-being usually occurred for the other floor—no visiting (SN) group. Therefore, for each site separately, the Friedman analysis of variance by ranks (χ^2_r, Siegel, 1956) was performed. The bottom row of Table 32.3 shows rank sums obtained for this test. These result in a χ^2_r, of 21.12 for Site B and 31.82 for Site D, each significant beyond the .001 level for 3 d.f. In both sites, those whose first-named friend was on the same floor tended to be slightly lower in most of the indices of well-being than those whose friend was on another floor. In Site D, those whose friend was on another floor and had recently visited were clearly higher on measures of well-being. In Site B, however, this group was indistinguishable from the group which chose friends on other floors and did not visit.

Thus, while the actual differences are small, the fact that the same pattern is repeated over a variety of indices, over two sources of data (interview question and staff ratings), and in two sites, gives some substance to the assertion that floorbound choice, visiting pattern, and their combination reflect some basic personal characteristics of older people.

Manipulation of the Physical Environment

An open apartment door in an urban high-rise building is a relatively infrequent occurrence. Its frequency in Site B (a mean of 29.8 open doors per observation period) was great enough to lead us to investigate its meaning. Wide variations in summer temperature and humidity occurred during the observations, but these were not related to number of open doors, even though the building was not air-conditioned. Doors were equipped with chains, and a door on chain was not counted as open.

We hypothesized that the open door was literally an invitation to social interaction. Confirmation of this notion was found in the highly significant relationship between the total number of occasions an individual's door was open and the number of friends he named ($\chi^2 = 12.1$, $p < 0.001$).

The open, inviting door should exert a particular pull on those living in proximity to it. Using only the first three choices given, a strong tendency to have an open door was seen among those giving more sociometric choices to people on their own floor ($\chi^2 = 11.0$, 1 d.f., $p < 0.01$). The open door appeared to be solely a social phenomenon, however, as there was no relationship between number of open doors and health, activity, mobility, or energy expenditure. While there are undoubtedly other reasons for keeping one's door open, or not open, the invitation to socialize appears to be outstanding.

Physical and Social Characteristics of the Sites

Table 32.4 shows selected characteristics of Sites A, B, C, and D. Analysis of these characteristics on a "clinical" basis demonstrates consistencies among the physical environment, the social behavior of the occupants, and the manner in which the occupants use space and objects. Although the number of observation tours completed varies among the sites, the distributions over times of day and days of the week are similar among sites. In addition to the number of observation tours, Table 32.4 shows the following:

Open doors. The mean number of open doors per tour was calculated, and then expressed as a percentage of the total number of apartments in each site.

Population in common spaces. The number of people observed in halls, common spaces, and adjacent outdoor areas was counted. The mean count per tour was then expressed as a percentage of the total number of occupants in each site.

Friends recently visited. Using the total number of sociometric choices made by all people in a given site as denominator, the percentage of all friendships which involved visiting within the past week was calculated for each site.

   Site A is located in a resort area, and its occupants are active people. Their high rate of visiting suggests that the small proportion of the total population observed in a single observation tour probably is due to people being out of

Table 32.4. Environmental Characteristics of Four Sites

Site	On-site services	Extent of common space	Floor boundedness	Number observations	Mean % apt. doors open	Mean % pop. in common spaces	% Friends visited
A	None	Moderate	Average	23	1.3	5.3	74
B	None	Low	High	25	20.6	10.6	72
C	None	Low	Average	14	8.0	9.3	54
D	Medical, meals, housekeeping	High	Average	10	5.5[a] 20.3[b]	14.7	59

[a] Apartment (n = 219).
[b] Medical care area (n = 31).

the building rather than isolated in their apartments. There is no lack of common space, but the center of summer life is the boardwalk. The very low number of open doors is probably an index of the relatively small number of people in their apartments at a given time. Thus, the location of Site A fosters an out-of-building focus of activity and tends to expand the radius of social relationships within the building—the friends one encounters on the beach or the boardwalk are not necessarily residents of one's own floor.

Site B contrasts markedly with Site A—all the indices listed mark Site B as a socially in-centered environment. That is, friends are found primarily within a very small radius. Within this radius is a high rate of visiting and a high incidence of open doors. Even though the extent of common space is small, a relatively high proportion of the total population is seen in it. Those who do not interact in the nearby apartment of a friend do not leave the building as often as those in Site A do. Site B is thus socially restricted in range, but internally cohesive.

The tenants of Site B were the most socially restricted prior to occupancy, also. One possibility to explain the increase in the degree to which "deprived" status affected floorbound sociometric choice after a year might be: all tenants at first might be equally restricted in their range of behavior in the new environment, in line with their lifelong habits. As time goes on, the "non-deprived" exercise their greater freedom, and the "deprived" fall back into greater dependence on local friendships. This possibility is being tested with further data analysis.

Site C, similar in socioeconomic level to Site B, shows a similar use of common space to Site B, but restricted on-site social behavior. That is, the rate of visiting is relatively low, and friendship choices are floorbound to an average degree. Site C appears to be the least cohesive of the four environments.

Site D differs radically from the other sites in a number of ways, two of which are the existence of a common dining room as well as a 31-room floor on which full medical and nursing services are provided. More of the population of Site D is visible at a given time than at any other site, while visiting rate is relatively low, and open door incidence outside the medical care area is moderate. Restriction of social radius in this site is only partly a matter of floorboundedness. If one considers sociometric choice given to a tablemate as another type of restriction, then the radius of social interaction in Site D is as low as in Site B. Thus, social relationships in Site D seem in-centered, but casual, depending on random contacts in common spaces and nearby apartments. This relatively superficial level of interaction appears consistent with the lesser physical independence of the tenants of Site D. The existence of the common dining room where tenants gather before and after meals and the waiting room for the doctor's office insure a large number of casual contacts. We suggest that the disappearance of "deprived" statuses as mediators of floorboundedness after a year is due to the relatively high probability of physical encounter between any two people in Site D.

DISCUSSION

Proximity did turn out to be of great importance in the creation of a social structure: the role of the apartment house floor as the focus of interaction emerged immediately. These findings, similar to those reported by Carp (1966) and Friedman (1966), underline the importance of casual contacts which lead to exploratory conversations as the basis for viable friendships.

We thought that in a new community the immediate need to create a social structure out of the chaos and alienation may have strengthened proximity as a determinant of friendship formation. The results show, however, that proximity endures as a facilitator of friendship and is not a product of a special situation such as existed in the early days of occupancy. There was no difference in the number of proximate choices made by tenants of Site E when they were differentiated on the basis of length of residence in the building. Thus, tenants who moved into a community with a social structure already formed still tended to pick friends on the basis of proximity in the same way that earlier occupants had done, and the original tenants persisted in using this basis for choice.

This persistence of proximity as a determinant of sociometric choice contrasts with other findings, such as those reported in studies of college dormitory occupancy, which point out the relatively temporary nature of proximity as a determinant. The explorations leading to the discovery of similar interests and statuses that generally typify the social processes of college students require mobility and the investment of effort on the part of the friendship seeker. It seems reasonable to suppose that the elderly are less mobile and energetic and, perhaps, less in need of friendships formed on the basis of finely differentiated similarities. Indeed, there may be a greater risk of incurring future debts or threats to one's self-esteem if one makes similarity-based friendships; as Gillespie (1967) suggests, those formed through chance encounter may be less "risky." Friedman (1966) suggests that common statuses were a much weaker determinant of choice in his home for aged than was proximity. Exploration of this issue in the present sites is in process.

The investigation of "deprived" status as a mediating characteristic in proximity-bound friendships suggests that even within the confines of a single building, friendship formation and spatial behavior may be sensitive to these differences. However, the effects appear to differ in different locations, at different times, and with different statuses.

When the attempt was made to develop indices of competence, well-being, and activity, these factors did appear to affect the spatial pattern of friendship choice after a year of residence. The inconsistent manner in which competence mediates between choice of friend and the location of the friend may reflect the relative weakness of the relationship, and the restricted range of competence sampled in our S population: that is, our Ss were relatively healthy and independent. Among his community residents Rosow (1967) analyzed the effect of social class, role loss, age, sex, marital status, employment, and health on the tendency to respond to the age density of the neighborhood in friendships. He found that working-class, role-deprived, older, female, not presently married, and, to a lesser extent, unemployed and less healthy people, were more likely to respond to high concentrations of older neighbors by heightened dependence on local friendships. His larger number of Ss, wider range of competence represented, and the more gross scale of proximity (in-neighborhood vs. out-of-neighborhood, rather than own-floor vs. other-floor) undoubtedly combine to highlight this mediating effect of competence.

Thus, the limitation of friendships to those formed on the basis of proximity may be regarded from two points of view. First, such a limitation may be seen as an indicator, other things being equal, of possible reduced status or competence. Alternatively, making friends where one finds them represents the adaptive capacity to take advantage of a presented opportunity. Hence, Rosow's clear demonstration that people of varying competence show differential sensitivity to age concentrations is a strong argument in favor of planned manipulation of age density. Those who make neither local friends nor distant friends are either voluntarily isolated or socially deprived.

The door represents one of the few components of an apartment which can be manipulated to alter space in service of other needs. The wide variation among sites and among individuals within sites in frequency of door-opening, plus the correlation of open doors with other social variables, demonstrates that this alteration of structure is not random. There are, of course, other reasons for opening a door—creating a crossdraft, anticipating the arrival of a visitor, or curiosity about who can be seen in the hall, to name a few. Similarly, the most obvious reason for a door being closed most of the time is that the occupant is usually not at home, perhaps working or busy in off-site activity. Alternatively, front-door security may be a problem, as was possibly true in Site A, which had fewest open doors. Separating out the *Ss* who respond to these influences could only intensify the relationship of the open door to social behavior among the remainder of the *Ss*, however.

Thus, within the area of gerontology, it is profitable to look at the manner in which older people use the given part of the environment and at a small way in which they attempt to alter it. Longer looks at the behavioral ecology of older people should provide useful ideas for the planning of buildings and programs.

CONCLUSIONS

Tenants in housing for the elderly use space in ways consistent with their social styles.

Tenants in housing for the elderly modify their physical environments in accord with their social needs.

There are consistencies among the characteristics of the environment, the characteristics of the people in it, and the manner in which the people and the environment interact.

Supportive evidence in favor of the environmental docility hypothesis to occupancy to be the most floorbound in the new community. Further, in two sites, the social behavior of the least competent on a variety of indices was maximally docile to the physical restrictions of distance.

REFERENCES

Barker, R. G. Explorations in ecological psychology. Amer. Psychol., 20 *(1): 1–14, 1965.*

Carp, F. A future for the aged. *University of Texas Press, Austin, 1966.*

Festinger, L., S. Schachter & K. Back. Social pressures in informal groups: A study of human factors in housing. *Harper, New York, 1950.*

Friedman, E. P. Spatial proximity and social interaction in a home for the aged. J. Geront., *21:556–570, 1966.*

Gillespie, M. W. The neighborhood integration of the aged: a reconsideration and test of the disengagement hypothesis. Gerontologist, 7: 32 (pt. II), *1967 (abstract).*

Hall, E. T. The silent language. *Doubleday, New York, 1959.*

Hall, E. T. The hidden dimension. *Doubleday, New York, 1966.*

Ittelson, W. Some factors influencing the design and function of psychiatric facilities. *Mimeo report. Brooklyn College Psychology Dept., 1960.*

Ittelson, W. Environmental psychology and architectural planning. Paper presented at American Hospital Association conference on hospital planning. *New York, December 1964.*

Newcomb, T. M. The acquaintance process. *Holt, Rinehart & Winston, New York, 1964.*

Rosow, I. Social integration of the aged. *Free Press, New York, 1967.*

Siegel, S. Nonparametric statistics for the behavioral sciences. *McGraw-Hill, New York, 1956.*

Sommer, R. Further studies of small group ecology. Sociometry, *28:337–348, 1965.*

Sommer, R. Man's proximate environment. J. Soc. Issues, *22:59–70, 1966.*

Sommer, R., & H. Ross: Social interaction on a geriatric ward. Int. J. Soc. Psychiat., *4:128–133, 1958.*

33. Memory Complaint and Impairment in the Aged

The Effect of Depression and Altered Brain Function

Robert L. Kahn, Steven H. Zarit, Nancy M. Hilbert, and George Niederehe

THE CLINICAL evaluation of memory impairment as a psychiatric symptom in the elderly presents many difficulties. Although this stems, in part, from such problems as differentiating the relative effects of depression and altered brain function,[1] it may not even be clear to the clinician as to whether pathologic or "normal" cognitive change has occurred. One of the major confounding factors in the formulation of accurate clinical appraisal is the existence of negative stereotypes of aging, of which the expectation of intellectual decline is one of the most widespread. Evidence of memory impairment with advancing age in particular is a common observation, whether reported impressionistically[2] or in numerous empirical studies.[3] In addition to the general stereotype, there are specific corollary stereotypes, such as those embodied in the convention that recent memory is expected to be more impaired than remote memory. These stereotypes have been increasingly questioned in recent years, with the apparent decline in cognitive function attributed to extraneous factors such as anxiety[4] or the methodologic problems, such as confounding age differences with cohort differences in educational and cultural backgrounds.[5] Longitudinal studies have minimized the cognitive decline with age[6] and indicate that deterioration, when it occurs, is related to mortality.[7,8]

Undoubtedly, one of the major contributory reasons for the commonly shared stereotype of cognitive decline is that older persons do, in fact, complain more about their memory.[9] There is some indication, however, that complaint about memory is not congruent with actual functioning. In studying a normal community population of aged, Perlin and Butler[10] observed a discrepancy between the clinical impression of memory loss and test data, with

Reprinted by permission from the *Archives of General Psychiatry 32* (1975): 1569–73. Copyright © 1975 by the American Medical Association.

subjects performing better than had been anticipated after hearing their self-reports of increasing loss of memory. In a study of community and psychiatric populations, Lowenthal et al.[9] found that complaints about age stereotypes, including memory difficulty, increased with age and were greater in psychiatric patients than community subjects. However, the reports of memory impairment in their study tended to fluctuate over time and were not corroborated by brief formal testing.

Affective status may be the critical factor related to this apparent discrepancy between complaint and functioning. Complaints about memory have previously been reported as common among depressed patients,[11,12] but there is disagreement concerning the concomitant amount of cognitive change. Some studies emphasize that these changes are extensive.[13,14] Using psychiatrist's ratings, Grinker and co-workers[15] found impaired recent memory in 21% and poor remote memory in 14% of persons with depressive disorders. Kiloh[16] has reported that some depressed persons manifest behavior that resembles an organic mental syndrome, complaining about poor intellectual performance and scoring relatively lower on a battery of psychometric tests. In contrast, Friedman[17] has reported only minimal evidence of intellectual impairment in depressed subjects on a large battery of standardized procedures, even though his patients considered themselves as helpless and reported difficulties in performing the tests.

The purpose of the present study is to further clarify the status of memory impairment in older persons by determining the relationship of complaints about memory to actual functioning, and the relative effects of the major psychopathological disorders of the aged—depression and altered brain function.

SUBJECTS AND METHODS

This series consisted of 153 persons evaluated in the Gerontology Clinic in the outpatient unit of the University of Chicago Department of Psychiatry. The subjects were limited to persons 50-years-old and older, and included 82 patients referred from the psychiatric outpatient unit, 31 of whom were psychiatric inpatients and 40 subjects who participated as collaterals of the patient group. Among the latter were 25 spouses, six siblings, four children, two parents, two nieces, and one sister-in-law. Informed consent was obtained from all subjects after the nature of the procedures had been fully explained. The age range was 50 to 91 with a mean of 65.1 years, and included 53 men and 100 women. The mean educational background was 10.0 years. Since a number of persons designated as collaterals manifested noticeable degrees of depression and brain dysfunction, subjects were classed operationally according to their clinical functioning rather than their administrative status.

Each subject was given a clinical interview. The presence and severity of a complaint about memory was determined from spontaneous comments and from response to the global question, ''Do you have any trouble with your memory?'' The complaint was rated on a five-point scale of increasing severity. Subjects who complained about their memory were asked to provide illustrative examples. All subjects were also asked to rate the relative quality of their memory for recent and remote events, stating whether there was any superiority of one or the other, and whether either was as good as it used to be. If, after all this questioning, there was still no complaint, the subject was asked, ''Has there been *any change* in your memory since you were younger?''

Determinations of affective condition were made by means of the Hamilton Rating Scale for Depression,[18] in which the symptoms are rated by the examiner on the basis of the interview behavior and responses, and a 14-item self-rated Adjective Mood Checklist derived from McNair and Lorr.[19] Neither of these scales included questions on memory function. Scores on the Hamilton ranged from 0 to 30, with a median of 10.5. On the basis of criteria for this scale provided by Mowbray,[20] our sample would consist largely of mild to moderate severities of depression. The median score was about the same for both normal and altered brain function groups.

Two procedures were used to evaluate brain function—the Face-Hand Test and the Mental Status Questionnaire.[21] The Face-Hand Test determines a subject's ability to perceive double simultaneous stimulation applied to the cheeks and backs of the hands in varying asymmetric combinations, with a judgment of altered brain function being made if errors persist after the fourth trial. The most common errors are misperceptions of the stimulus applied to the hand, either extinction, in which no stimulus is reported, or displacement, in which the stimulus to the hand is reported as being felt on the cheek. The Mental Status Questionnaire consists of ten orientation and information questions and was rated positive for altered brain function if there were three or more incorrect responses. Since the Mental Status Questionnaire includes some questions involving memory, there is some circularity in using it as an independent variable to study differences in memory function. For this reason, both measures of brain function were analyzed separately. Forty-eight subjects were rated as having altered brain function on at least one of these measures, with 38 being positive on the Face-Hand Test and 28 on the Mental Status Questionnaire.

The memory tests employed were varied to cover all types of memory, namely, primary, secondary, and tertiary.[22] They included Digit Span forward and backward, the Babcock Story Recall Test[23] (involving recall of a paragraph immediately after presentation and after a ten-minute interval), and a paired-associates learning task,[24] in which the subject is asked to learn word pairs with unfamiliar associations, such as "knife" with "chimney," until the criterion of three successive correct responses to each pair is reached. In addition, four scales of ten questions each were developed to measure recent and remote memory respectively for personal life-events and for general occurrences. Recent personal items included the patient's doctor's name, the name of the neighborhood and the street one block away from where the person lives, and children's current ages. Remote personal events were such things as the names of schools attended, year married, and children's birth-dates. Recent general items tapped contemporary events such as the season of the year, a current, prominent news story, and the name of the mayor of the city. Remote general memory was assessed with questions about prominent historical events or personages, including names of past presidents, and the date of the bombing of Pearl Harbor.

RESULTS

Of the 153 subjects, only 36 (24%) had no complaint about memory. In 75 subjects (approximately half the sample), the complaint was more than minimal. Complaint about memory was found to have little correlation with actual memory function. As demonstrated in Table 33.1, the correlations between complaint and function for the total sample were all low and nonsignificant. The correlations increase when the subjects are differentiated according to the various criteria of altered brain function, but in an inconsistent pattern. Among persons negative for altered brain function as determined by either the Face-Hand Test or the Mental Status Questionnaire there are a few low, but significant correlations between complaint and the measures of recent and remote memory. However, among those positive on the Mental Status Questionnaire, the correlations tended to be the highest of all, but with negative correlations, in which high complaint is related to better performance on the tests, reaching significance on Digits Backward. Only on the Babcock

Table 33.1. Correlation (r Values) of Global Memory Complaint to Actual Functioning on Memory Tests

Memory tests	Total sample	Combined organic		Face-hand		Mental status questionnaire	
		Negative, 105 patients	Positive, 48 patients	Negative, 115 patients	Positive, 38 patients	Negative, 125 patients	Positive, 28 patients
Digits forward	−.07	−.09	−.09	−.10	.09	−.03	−.20
Digits backward	−.04	−.05	−.14	−.11	−.05	−.06	−.33*
Babcock immediate	.05	−.01	.06	.11	.06	.08	.14
Babcock delayed	.05	.05	.12	.09	.05	.02	.39*
Paired associates	.07	.02	.02	.09	.10	.12	.18
Recent personal	.07	.14	−.08	.13	.07	.19†	−.20
Recent general	−.06	−.05	−.24	.01	−.08	.04	−.32
Remote personal	.08	.02	.02	.18†	.19	.19†	.03
Remote general	.04	.05	−.12	.13†	.03	.12	−.15

NOTE: Positive correlations signify that the greater the complaint, the greater the impairment of performance.
$*p = .05.$
$†p < .10.$

delayed story recall is there a significant correlation of complaint and poor performance.

In contrast to the poor relation of complaint and function, there are very significant correlations between memory complaint and depression, as shown in Table 33.2. The correlations are consistently high among the persons with normal brain function, whether using the combined criteria or the Face-Hand Test or Mental Status Questionnaire alone. Among those positive for altered brain function the correlations are much lower, and attain significance only among those positive on the Face-Hand Test.

The association among the measures of complaint, memory function, depression and altered brain function is illustrated in Figure 33.1. The sample was divided at the median score on the Hamilton scale into low and high depression groups for both those with normal and altered brain function as determined by the combined criteria. Standard scores above and below the mean have been graphed for the global complaint about memory and for a combined measure of memory function calculated by averaging the percentage correct on each of the memory tests. It is clear that although the level of memory function is much poorer in the organic groups, there is marked variation in the complaint according to the level of depression. Among those

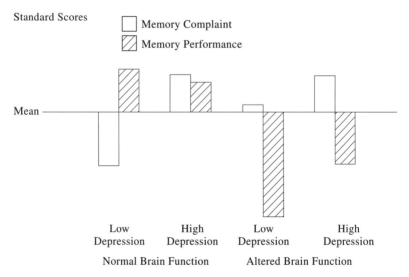

Figure 33.1. Relation of memory complaint and memory performance (combined performance on memory tests) according to level of depression (Hamilton Scale) and presence of altered brain function (combining Face-Hand Test and Mental Status Questionnaire).

Table 33.2. Correlations (r Values) of Complaints about Memory with Levels of Depression

Depression scale	Total sample	Combined organic		Face-hand		Mental status questionnaire	
		Negative, 105 patients	Positve, 48 patients	Negative, 115 patients	Positve, 38 patients	Negative, 125 patients	Positive, 38 patients
Hamilton rating	.29*	.33*	.20	.32*	.27†	.38*	−.07
Adjective checklist	.35*	.44*	.16	.40*	.27†	.45*	−.05

*P < .001.
†P < .05.

with normal brain function, performance did not differ appreciably between those with high and low depression (t test $= 1.31$, $P =$ not significant [ns]), but those who were depressed complained significantly more about memory ($t = 3.29$, $P < .001$). In the altered brain function group, those who were more depressed had greater complaints about memory ($t = .05$, $P =$ ns) but actually did significantly better on the tests ($t = 4.42$, $P < .001$). Among those with high depression, persons with normal brain function complained about memory as much as those with altered brain function ($t = .05$, $P =$ ns), even though the latter had a far greater difficulty on the memory procedures ($t = 6.45$, $P < .001$).

The incongruity between complaints and performance was sometimes strikingly demonstrated in the clinical situation among married couples. In four instances during the intake process, one spouse was designated as the patient and the other as the collateral, with both spouses complaining of the patient's memory impairment; on examination, however, the collateral spouse was found to perform more poorly than the patient.

In fifty-nine instances, more than one third of the total sample, it was subjectively reported that recent memory was poorer than remote memory. Almost all persons in the sample, however, had objectively higher scores on the two scales of recent events than on the tests for long-term memory, with those who complained specifically about recent memory performing as well as those without this complaint. On the other hand, a two-way analysis of variance shows that this complaint is significantly related to depression (Table 33.3).

No significant relationship was found between memory complaint and age

Table 33.3. Relation of Complaints about Recent and Remote Memory to Depression

Complaint	Normal brain function, 103 patients*	Altered brain function, 48 patients
Both equal	10.21	10.82
No. of patients	47	17
Remote memory poorer	11.06	9.60
No. of patients	18	10
Recent memory poorer	14.08	12.00
No. of patients	38	21

NOTE: Hamilton Rating Scale for Depression. A 2×3 analysis of variance on the Hamilton ratings with two levels of brain function and the three types of complaint as factors indicates a significant effect only for complaint ($F = 3.08$, $P < .05$).

*Information about recent and remote memory was obtained from a total of 151 subjects.

or education. Although both these variables are related to performance, partialing out the effects of education did not materially alter the pattern or magnitude of intercorrelations between complaint and performance as reported above. The relationship of age to performance is a reflection of the distribution of altered brain function. Among those with normal brain function, 76% were in their 50s or 60s, while among those with altered brain function, only 39% were this young.

COMMENT

This study indicated that there is a marked incongruity between complaint about memory and actual memory performance in a sample of older psychiatric patients and patient collaterals. Complaints can occur with or without an actual deficit in memory. Impairment on memory tests was, as would be expected, strongly associated with evidence of organic brain dysfunction, but complaints about memory, rather than reflecting cognitive condition, were found to be a manifestation of depression. In some instances, persons who complained about memory actually functioned better than those who did not.

The relation of memory complaint to depression rather than actual performance is consistent with the discrepancies in self-assessment of performance that have been previously reported in depressive. Beck[25] observed that depressed patients were more pessimistic in predicting or judging the quality of their work on a card-sorting task than controls, although actual performance was the same in both groups. Depressed persons have been reported as showing discrepancies in describing themselves on the self-rating of symptoms when compared to an observer's ratings[26] and to present a greater difference between their real and ideal self-images on a semantic differential.[12] Colbert and Harrow[27] studied a group of hospitalized depressed patients and found a discrepancy in the symptom of psychomotor retardation, with the patients and their families reporting a more severe condition than observed directly in clinical and test situations. In the present study, those who complained about their memory gave such illustrations as forgetting to buy something in the store or misplacing one's glasses or keys. These are commonplace incidents of forgetfulness that would be ignored by younger or less depressed persons, but they were perceived by depressed older persons as indicating a marked decline in mental functioning.

Although the discrepancy between complaint and performance may be regarded in itself as the operational manifestation of depression as Beck[25] suggests, it must also be considered that exaggeration of symptoms, complaints, or negative perceptions may reflect an underlying personality structure. Monroe[28] studied nonpsychiatric community subjects with complaints of poor sleeping. While physiologic differences from noncomplainers were actually observed, such as lower total rapid eye movement time in poor sleepers, they slept ''much better'' than could have been expected on the basis of their original subjective description of sleep patterns. In a study of neurotic depressives admitted to an inpatient unit, Schless et al.[29] had their patients do their own rating of the stress value of life events reported in the scale developed by Holmes and Rahe.[30] They found that while preserving the same ranking as normal groups, the depressed patients viewed life events as uniformly more stressful. The ascribed weights were independent of the severity of depression and whether the event had been personally experienced or not, and remained constant from beginning to end of hospitalization although there had been considerable symptomatic improvement.

In addition to exaggeration of symptoms and stresses, the pattern of memory complaint in depression is apparently associated with a greater tendency to stereotyped thinking. Previous studies of social attitudes and of the use of language in depressed persons have shown stereotyped attitudes and marked use of clichés.[31,32] In this study, the expression of the cliché about remote memory being better than recent memory was unrelated to actual functioning and was associated with higher depression scores. Apart from its importance for aging depressives, this aging stereotype seems to be of questionable utility for clinical evaluation. Based on the Ribot law of regression, according to which memory is lost in the reverse order of which it was acquired, the stereotype is, at best, of doubtful value because of such methodologic complexities as task equivalence,[3] and at worst, is not substantiated by systematic observation.[33]

Just as memory impairment is exaggerated in persons with normal brain function who are depressed, so memory impairment is minimized in persons with altered brain function who are not depressed. It is striking that among those with demonstrable memory impairment, the degree of complaint is still associated with affective status. In part, it may be that older depressed persons will complain about their memory regardless of whether their functioning is good or actually impaired. It is also likely that the difference between low and high depression in the organic patients is related to the severity of altered brain function, as the low depressed organics did noticeably better on the memory test. With a minimal amount of altered brain function there may be a depressive reaction, while those with more severe altered brain dysfunction will show denial. The relationship between severity of brain dysfunction in older persons and depression and denial has been previously demonstrated in a study of older persons suffering from strokes.[34] Compared to younger persons, aged patients with minimal brain damage were more severely depressed, while those with increasing severity of brain impairment tended to deny difficulties in areas such as walking and the use of the affected arm. This view of the relation of depression to severity of brain dysfunction is supported by the study of Kay et al.[35] who found that the prognosis for recovery from organic brain syndrome in elderly patients was much better when "functional" symptoms were part of the clinical picture than when they were not.

CONCLUSION

Contrary to the prevailing stereotype on the inevitability of memory decline with age, memory impairment as a clinical psychopathologic symptom in older persons is a complex phenomenon in which complaint must be differentiated from performance. The pattern of memory complaint and function depends on the interaction of the two major psychopathologic disorders of the aged—depression and altered brain function. Altered brain function is associated with poor performance and depression with high complaint. Congruence is shown by persons with low depression and normal brain function who do well on memory tests and have no complaints, and at the opposite extreme, by those with altered brain function and high depression who both do poorly on memory tests and have high complaint. Among those with normal brain function, severe depression will lead to exaggeration of the complaint; in those with altered brain function and low depression, the complaint will be minimized. Exaggerated memory complaint is considered one manifestation of a general pattern of discrepant reporting of symptoms by depressed persons, and may be related to an underlying personality factor characterized by general exaggeration of stress and the use of stereotypes in communication. The conviction that recent memory is more impaired than remote memory is not substantiated empirically, but is considered part of the stereotyped thinking related to depression and the associated personality factors. Minimization of memory complaint appears to be part of the denial adaptation characteristic of severely altered brain function.

REFERENCES

1. Whitehead A. *Verbal learning and memory in elderly depressives.* Br J Psychiatry 123:203–208, 1973.

2. *Wechsler D. Intelligence, memory and the aging process, in Hoch PH, Zubin J (eds):* Psychopathology of Aging. *New York, Grune & Stratton, 1961, pp. 152–159.*

3. *Botwinick J.* Cognitive Processes in Maturity and Old Age. *New York, Springer, 1967.*

4. *Eisdorfer C. Verbal learning and response time in the aged.* J Genet Psychol *107:15–22, 1965.*

5. *Baltes PB, Labouvie GV. Adult development of intellectual performance: Description, explanation, and modification, in Eisdorfer C, Lawton MP (eds):* The Psychology of Adult Development and Aging. *Washington, DC, American Psychological Association, 1973, pp. 157–219.*

6. *Schaie KW. Translations in gerontology—from lab to life: Intellectual functioning.* Am Psychol *29:802–807, 1974.*

7. *Jarvik LF, Falek A. Intellectual stability and survival in the aged.* J Gerontology *18:173–176, 1963.*

8. *Blum J, Clark ET, Jarvik LF. The New York State Psychiatric Institute study of aging twins, in Jarvik LF, Eisdorfer C, Blum J (eds):* Intellectual Functioning in Adults. *New York, Springer, 1973, pp. 13–20.*

9. *Lowenthal MF, Berkman PL, et al.* Aging and Mental Disorder in San Francisco. *San Francisco, Jossey-Bass, 1967.*

10. *Perlin S, Butler RN. Psychiatric aspects of adaptation to the aging experience, in Birren JE, Butler RN, Greenhouse SW, et al. (eds).* Human Aging: A Biological and Behavioral Study. *U.S. Government Printing Office, 1963, pp. 159–213.*

11. *Ianzito BM, Cadoret RJ, Pugh DD. Thought disorder in depression.* Am J Psychiatry *131:703–707, 1974.*

12. *Marsella AJ, Walker BA, Johnson F. Personality correlates of depressive disorders in female college students of different ethnic groups.* Int J Soc Psychiatry *19:77–83, 1973.*

13. *Allison RS. Changes in behavior and impairment of memory and intellect in later life.* Geriatrics *10:306–311, 1955.*

14. *Williams WS, Jaco EG. An evaluation of functional psychoses in old age.* Am J Psychiatry *114:910–916, 1958.*

15. *Grinker RR, Miller J, Sabshin M, et al.* The Phenomena of Depression. *New York, Paul B Hoeber, 1961.*

16. *Kiloh LG. Pseudo-dementia.* Acta Psychiatr Scand *37:336–351, 1961.*

17. *Friedman AS. Minimal effects of severe depression on cognitive functioning.* J Abnorm Soc Psychol *69:237–243, 1964.*

18. *Hamilton M. Development of a rating scale for primary depressive illness.* Br J Soc Clin Psychiatry *6:278–296, 1967.*

19. *McNair DM, Lorr M. An analysis of mood in neurotics.* J Abnorm Soc Psychol *69:620–627, 1964.*

20. *Mowbray RM. The Hamilton Rating Scale for depression: A factor analysis.* Psychol Med *2:272–280, 1972.*

21. *Kahn RL, Goldfarb AI, Pollack M. et al. Brief objective measures for the determination of mental status in the aged.* Am J Psychiatry *117:326–328, 1960.*

22. *Fozard JL, Thomas JC Jr. Psychology of aging, in Howells JG (ed),* Modern

Perspectives in the Psychiatry of Old Age. *New York, Brunner/Mazel, 1975, pp. 170–187.*

23. Babcock H. *An experiment in the measurement of mental deterioration.* Arch Psychol *117:105, 1930.*

24. Inglis J. *A paired-associate learning test for use with elderly psychiatric patients.* J Ment Dis *105:440–443, 1959.*

25. Beck AT. Depression: Clinical, Experimental and Theoretical Aspects. *New York, Paul B. Hoeber, 1971.*

26. Prusoff BA, Klerman GL, Paykel ES. *Concordance between clinical assessments and patients' self-report in depression.* Arch Gen Psychiatry *26: 546–552, 1972.*

27. Colbert J, Harrow M. *Psychomotor retardation in depressive syndromes.* J Nerv Ment Dis *145:405–417, 1967.*

28. Monroe LJ. *Psychological and physiological differences between good and poor sleepers.* J Abnorm Psychol *72:255–264, 1967.*

29. Schless AP, Schwartz L, Goetz C, et al. *How depressive view the significance of life events.* Br J Psychiatry *125:406–410, 1974.*

30. Holmes T, Rahe R. *The social readjustment rating scale.* J Psychosom Res *2: 213–217, 1967.*

31. Kahn RL, Pollack M, Fink M. *Social attitude (California F Scale) and convulsive therapy.* J Nerv Ment Dis *130:187–192, 1960.*

32. Kahn RL, Fink M. *Changes in language during electro-shock therapy, in Hoch PH, Zubin J (eds),* Psychopathology of Communication. *New York, Grune & Stratton, 1958.*

33. Shapiro MB, Post F, Lofving B, et al. *"Memory function" in psychiatric patients over sixty: Some methodological and diagnostic implications.* J Ment Sci *102: 223–246, 1956.*

34. Zarit SH, Kahn RL. *Aging and adaptation to illness.* J Gerontol *30:67–72, 1975.*

35. Kay DW, Norris V, Post F. *Prognosis in psychiatric disorders of the elderly: An attempt to define indicators of early death and early recovery.* J Ment Sci *102: 129–140, 1956.*

34. Can Decline in Adult Intellectual Functioning Be Reversed?

K. Warner Shaie and Sherry L. Willis

A LONGITUDINAL sequential research program that has now extended over nearly 3 decades has permitted the collection of substantial descriptive data on the adult life course of some of the principal dimensions of intelligence as identified from a psychometric perspective (Schaie, 1983). This data base informs us that the onset and rate of normative decline differs by ability. Statistically significant decline can be observed for some abilities in individuals in their mid-50s; effect sizes for such decline, however, remain small until the 60s are reached (Schaie & Hertzog, 1983). Thereafter, age-related decline reaches substantial magnitudes, and the proportion of individuals who show reliable decline increases markedly for every 7-year age interval beyond age 60. Nevertheless, it needs to be stressed that there are wide individual differences in the onset of cognitive decline, with many older individuals demonstrating stable levels of intellectual performance into the 70s and some few not showing any decline until the early eighties (Schaie, 1984).

Given the substantial individual differences in decline, we next began to examine possible sources that might help explain these differences. Persons with cardiovascular disease were found to be at excess risk with respect to ability decline. However, it soon became apparent that cardiovascular disease may only be a mediator of decline. That is, adverse life styles that contribute to the incidence of disease may also directly contribute to the occurrence of mental decline (cf. Hertzog, Schaie & Gribbin, 1978). Detailed analyses of personal characteristics of our study participants have shown that life styles that include the pursuit of high levels of environmental stimulation, particularly those that include continuing formal and informal education, tend to be related to the maintenance of high levels of intellectual functioning (Gribbin, Schaie & Parham, 1980; Schaie, 1984).

The relationship between intellectually stimulating pursuits and main-

Reprinted by permission from *Developmental Psychology* 22, no. 2 (1986): 223–32. Copyright © 1986 by the American Psychological Association.

tenance of abilities thus far has been shown to be reciprocal rather than causal (Stone, 1980). On the one hand, persons who maintain their ability levels into old age may be more likely to seek out experiences of an educational nature. Alternately, exposure to educational experiences in adulthood may be instrumental in maintaining stable levels of intellectual functioning into old age. The question of the causality of naturalistic phenomena can rarely be tested directly in the laboratory. Nevertheless, it may be possible to demonstrate under controlled conditions that intellectual performance in later adulthood can be successfully improved by means of educational training procedures. An adequate answer to this question, however, must take into account the fact that the nature of performance improvement associated with training is far more complicated in later adulthood than at earlier life stages. In childhood, for example, performance improvement associated with training represents a higher level of functioning than previously demonstrated by the child; hence training gains imply the acquisition of new skills or knowledge (Detterman & Sternberg, 1982). Improvement through training in later adulthood, however, could reflect either remediation of performance decrements from prior levels of functioning or the acquisition of new levels of performance not previously demonstrated.

During the past decade and a half there has been an increased focus in the study of adult intelligence on examining the modifiability of intellectual performance in later adulthood through cognitive training procedures (Giambra & Arenberg, 1980; Willis & Baltes, 1980). There is recurrent interest in the question of whether and how well ''old dogs can be taught new tricks.'' From the point of view of both developmental theory and societal benefit, however, it is even more important to ask the question whether such intervention can result in the remediation of reliable age-related decline. The theoretical importance of this question lies in the fact that if it can be shown that reliably demonstrated decline can indeed be reversed then grave doubts would arise as to the universality of irreversible decrement models that assume normative patterns of intellectual decline. These models, of course, also imply that the observed behavioral deficit should be isomorphic with adverse physiological age changes (cf. Botwinick, 1977; Salthouse, 1982). Instead, support would be offered to the greater plausibility of behavioral deficit being occasioned by specific patterns of disuse that are amenable to remediation for at least some individuals and would strengthen contentions as to the plasticity of behavior throughout life (cf. Baltes & Willis, 1977). In addition, findings of successful remediation efforts at the ability level would have important implications for the development of educational intervention programs that might be helpful in restoring the intellectual competence of many older individuals to levels that would maintain or at least prolong their ability to function independently.

Previous cognitive training research has strongly suggested the modifiability of older adults' performance on a number of intelligence dimensions (e.g., memory span, inductive reasoning, cognitive problem solving, spatial egocentrism; for reviews see Denney, 1982; Poon, Walsh-Sweeney & Fozard, 1980; Sterns & Sanders, 1980; Willis, 1985). Training effects have been shown to transfer to multiple measures of the ability trained, and performance improvement has been maintained at 6-month post-tests (Baltes & Willis, 1982). However, to our knowledge, all of the previous training studies in later adulthood have been conducted within a cross-sectional design, and thus it was not possible to determine whether training improvement represented remediation of prior cognitive decline or the acquisition of new performance levels for subjects suffering no decline. Examination of this question requires a longitudinal subject population, such that training improvement can be compared with subjects' prior level of functioning. This article represents a first report of a study that focuses on the above question.

METHOD

Subjects

Subjects were 229 older adults (male = 97; female = 132) from the Seattle metropolitan area, who had been participants in the Seattle Longitudinal Study (SLS) since 1970 or earlier (Schaie, 1983). All subjects are, or had been, members of the Group Health Cooperative of Puget Sound, a health maintenance organization. Mean age of the total sample was 72.8 years (range = 64–95; SD = 6.41). Mean educational level was 13.9 years (range = 6–20; SD = 2.98). There were no sex differences in age or educational level. Mean income level was $19,879 (range = $1,000–$33,000; SD = $8,520). All subjects were community dwelling. Most of the subjects were Caucasian. Prior to initiation of the study, each subject's physician was contacted and asked to indicate whether the subject suffered any known physical or mental disabilities that would interfere with participation in the study; subjects so identified were not included in the study.

Design and Procedure

Classification of participants. Subjects' test performances on the Thurstone (1948) Primary Mental Ability (PMA) Reasoning and Spatial Orientation measures were classified as having remained stable or having declined over the prior 14-year interval (1970–1984). Subjects entered the study at different points in time (from 1956 through 1970); thus, performance in 1970 was used as a common baseline in order to have a uniform criterion for all subjects. The statistical criterion for the definition of decline was 1 standard error (SE) of measurement or greater (Reasoning = 4 raw score points; Space = 6 raw score points). Subjects were first classified by placing a 1 SE confidence interval about their observed 1970 score (cf. Dudek, 1979). If their 1977 score fell below this interval they were provisionally considered to have declined, otherwise to be stable. Next their 1984 pretest score was considered. Decline subjects who in 1984 returned to within the confidence interval about their 1970 score were then reclassified as stables. Stable subjects whose 1984 score dropped below a 1 SE interval about their 1970 score were reclassified as decliners. Thus, any subject whose score had cumulatively declined by more than 1 SE below the 1970 base was considered to have declined significantly.

There were 107 subjects (46.7% of sample) classified as having remained stable on both ability measures; 35 subjects (15%) had declined on Reasoning but not on Space; 37 subjects (16%) had declined on Space but not on Reasoning; and 50 subjects (21.8%) had declined on both measures. As would be expected, stable subjects (M = 70.9 years; SD = 5.35) were somewhat younger than decline subjects (M = 74.4 years; SD = 6.84), $p < .001$). Although the mean age differed, it should be noted that a wide range occurred for both stables (range = 64–85 years) and decliners (64–95 years). Decline and stable subjects did not differ significantly on educational level or income.

Effects of regression on classification. In 1970, prior to the onset of decline, there was no significant difference between subjects who were classified as stables or decliners on Space performance; the decline subjects, at the time, however, performed significantly better ($p < .02$) than the stable subjects on the Reasoning measure in 1970. The possibility then arises that statistical regression effects could have led to the erroneous classification of 1970 high scorers to the decline group and of low scores to the stable group. Several lines of evidence argue against this possibility. First of all, both tests used have fairly high reliabilities. Although the split-half coefficients in the .90s reported by Thurstone (1948) may be overstated due to the slightly speeded nature of the tests, our own data on long-term stability have consistently run to .70 or higher for Space and .80 or higher for Reasoning (Schaie, 1983, 1985). As an independent check on the plausibility of regression effects, however, we conducted a time-reversed control analysis (cf. Baltes, et al., 1972; Campbell & Stanley, 1966).

In a time-reversed control analysis one partitions scores at the point of origin (1970 in our case) into the highest, middle, and lowest thirds, and computes means for these levels at both origin and final measurement point (1984 pretest in our case). The traces from the first to the second time of measurement are then examined to see whether they are parallel or show apparent regression effects. In the latter case the mean score for the highest third should have decreased, whereas the mean for the lowest third should have increased. The same strategy is then used to partition scores at the final point (1984 pretest in our case) into three ability levels and to compute means

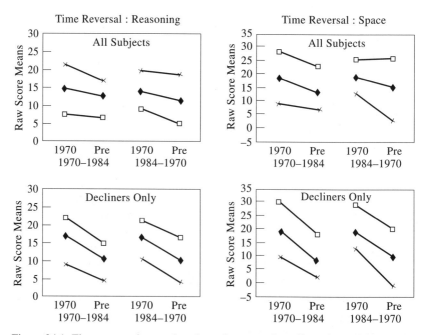

Figure 34.1. Time-reversed control analyses for regression effects from 1970 to 1984 for the Primary Mental Ability Space and Reasoning tests for all subjects and for decline subjects only.

for these ability groupings at the point of origin. If regression effects have occurred, then the traces for the "backward" (1984–1970) analyses should actually be the mirror images of the traces for the "forward" (1970–1984) analyses. Figure 34.1 shows the results of the time-reversed control analyses for Space and Reasoning both for the total group and separately for the decliners. The traces shown in this figure are clearly incompatible with the presence of substantial regression effect. We can conclude, then, that our classification error rate (as specified by our confidence limits) has not been significantly increased by regression effects.

Assignment of subjects. Subjects were assigned to either Reasoning or Space training programs based on their performance status. Subjects who had declined on Reasoning, but not on Space, or vice versa were assigned to the training program for the ability exhibiting decline. Subjects who had remained stable on both abilities or had shown decline on both abilities were randomly assigned to one of the training programs. Space training subjects included 51 stables (male = 23; female = 28) and 67 decliners (male = 29; female = 38). Reasoning training subjects included 56 stables (male = 25; female = 31) and 55 decliners (male = 20; female = 35). Stable subjects in Space training were significantly younger ($p < .03$) and better educated ($p < .05$) than decliners. Stable subjects in Reasoning training were also significantly younger ($p < .001$) than decliners, but decliners were significantly better educated ($p < .01$) than stables. There was no difference in income for either program.

Procedure. The study involved a pretest-treatment-posttest control group design. The Reasoning training group served as a treatment control for the Space training group and vice versa. All subjects had previously participated in the SLS and were informed via a series of letters that a new phase of the study was beginning. Subjects indicating an interest in participation were visited in their homes by a staff member. The purpose of the home visit was to discuss details of the study and to answer questions, to assess sensory handicaps that might interfere with participation, and to determine whether the home was a suitable place for conducting the training sessions. Subjects were administered a broad psychometric ability battery in two pretest sessions (2½ hours per session). Based on their prior longitudinal performance plus their pretest scores, subjects were assigned to either the Reasoning or Space training program. Training involved five 1-hour individually conducted training sessions. The majority of subjects were trained in their homes. Two middle-aged trainers, with prior educational experience in working with adults, served as trainers. Subjects were randomly assigned to the trainers within pragmatic constraints, such that each trainer trained approximately equal numbers of stable and decline subjects in each training program. Following training, subjects were assessed on a posttest battery involving the same measures administered at pretest. Subjects were paid $100 for participation in the study.

Measures

The pretest–posttest battery involved psychometric measures representing five primary mental abilities, including the Thurstone PMA measures (Thurstone, 1948) administered at previous SLS assessments. Each ability was represented by two to four marker measures. The data to be presented focus on the measures representing the Spatial Orientation and Reasoning abilities; these abilities were the target of training.

Spatial Orientation was assessed by four measures. Three of the tests (PMA Space, Object Rotation, Alphanumeric Rotation) are multiple-response measures of two-dimensional mental rotation ability. The subject is shown a model line drawing and asked to identify which of six choices shows the model drawn in different spatial orientations. There are two or three correct responses possible for each test item. The Object Rotation test (Schaie, 1985) and the Alphanumeric test were constructed such that the angle of rotation in each answer choice is identical with the angle used in the PMA Spatial Orientation test (Thurstone, 1948). The three tests vary in item content. Stimuli for the PMA test are abstract figures; the Object Rotation test involves drawings of familiar objects; and the Alphanumeric test contains letters and numbers. The fourth test, Cube Comparisons (Ekstrom et al., 1976), assesses mental rotation in three-dimensional space.

Reasoning ability was assessed by four measures. The PMA Reasoning measure (Thurstone, 1948) assesses inductive reasoning ability via letter series problems. The subject is shown a series of letters and must select the next letter in the series from five letter choices. The ADEPT Letter Series test (Blieszner, Willis, & Baltes, 1981) also contains letter series problems; however, some of the problems involve pattern description rules other than those found on the PMA measure. The Word Series test (Schaie, 1985) parallels the PMA measure in that the same pattern description rule is used for each item; however, the test stimuli are days of the week or months of the year, rather than letters. The Number Series test (Ekstrom et al., 1976) involves series of numbers rather than letters and involves different types of pattern description rules involving mathematical computations. The PMA Spatial Orientation and Reasoning tests were administered at previous SLS measurement points and thus provide the most direct assessment of training improvement and remediation.

Training Programs

The focus of the training was on facilitating the subject's use of effective cognitive strategies identified in previous research on the respective abilities. A content task analysis was conducted on the two PMA measures.

Reasoning. For each item of the Reasoning test, the pattern description rule(s) used in problem solution were identified. Four major types of pattern description rules (identity, next, skips, and backward next) were identified, similar to those discussed previously in the literature (Holzman, Pellegrino & Glaser, 1982; Kotovsky & Simon, 1973). Practice problems and exercises were developed, based on these pattern description rules. Practice problems often involved content other than letters, so that the applicability of these rules to other content areas could be explored. For example, patterns of musical notes and travel schedules were devised based on these rules, and subjects were to identify the next note or destination in the series. No training problems were identical in content to test items. Subjects were taught through modeling, feedback, and practice procedures to identify these pattern description rules. These multiple procedures were employed in order to optimize training effects, rather than to assess their differential effectiveness. Three strategies for identifying the patterns were emphasized in training: visual scanning of the series, saying the series aloud in order to hear the letter pattern, and underlining repeated letters occurring throughout the series. Once a hypothesis regarding the pattern type was generated, subjects were then taught to mark repetitions of the pattern within the series, and thus to determine the next letter required to fit the pattern rule.

Space. A content task analysis of the PMA Spatial Orientation test was conducted to identify the angle of rotation for each answer choice. Practice problems were developed to represent the angle rotations identified in the task analysis (45°, 90°, 135°, 180°). Cognitive strategies to facilitate mental rotation that were focused on in training included: (a) development of concrete terms for various angles; (b) practice with manual rotation of figures prior to mental rotation; (c) practice with rotation of drawings of concrete, familiar objects prior to introduction of abstract figures; (d) subject-generated names for abstract figures; and (e) having the subject focus on two or more features of the figure during rotation. These cognitive strategies had been identified in prior descriptive research on mental rotation ability (Cooper & Shepard, 1973; Egan, 1981; Kail, Pellegrino & Carter, 1980).

RESULTS

Results of the study are reported in three parts. First, analyses are provided for training improvement at the level of ability factor scores. Second, analyses of training effects at the level of raw scores are reported for the PMA Reasoning and Space tests because these are the measures for which longitudinal data are available. Finally, the proportion of subjects demonstrating remediation of decline is reported.

Analyses of Factor Scores

The factor structure of the pretest ability battery was examined via confirmatory factor analyses. An acceptable five-factor model χ^2 (243, $N = 1,401$) $= 463.17$, $p < .001$, representing the hypothesized primary mental ability factors (Reasoning, Verbal, Space, Number, and Perceptual Speed), was obtained. Marker measures of the Reasoning and Space abilities had significant loadings, as predicted, on their respective factors. Factor regression weights for tests loading on the Reasoning factor were: PMA Reasoning = .378; ADEPT Letter Series = .213; Word Series = .298; Number Series = .111. Factor weights of tests loading on the Space factor were: PMA Space = .260; Object Rotation = .393; Alphanumeric = .287; Cube Comparison = .060. Although Number Series and Cube Comparison contribute relatively little variance to their respective factors, they were retained because they helped obtain better definition of the factors within the broader ability space in which they were embedded. Factor scores were computed for the Reasoning and Space abilities by standardizing ($M = 50$; $SD = 10$) the raw scores to the pretest base and then multiplying the standardized scores by their respective regression weights.

To examine training effects at the factor level, two Training (Reasoning, Space) × Status (stable, decline) × Sex × Occasion (pretest, posttest) analyses of variance (ANOVAS) with repeated measures were performed separately on the Reasoning and Space factor scores (Table 34.1). For Reasoning, there were significant main effects for status ($p < .001$), sex ($p < .03$), and occasion ($p < .001$). The status and sex main effects reflected the lower scores

Table 34.1. Summary of Analyses of Variance: Factor Scores

Source	MS	dfs	F
	Reasoning		
Training	336.58	1	2.18
Status	3038.35	1	19.66***
Training × Status	25.71	1	0.17
Sex	733.10	1	4.74*
Training × Sex	362.67	1	2.35
Status × Sex	30.31	1	0.20
Training × Status × Sex	0.08	1	0.00
Error	154.59	221	
Occasion	1649.15	1	303.15***
Training × Occasion	205.99	1	37.86***
Status × Occasion	1.76	1	0.34
Training × Status × Occasion	7.76	1	1.43
Sex × Occasion	0.58	1	0.11
Training × Sex × Occasion	1.18	1	0.22
Status × Sex × Occasion	0.07	1	0.01
Training × Status × Sex × Occasion	1.08	1	0.20
Error	5.44	221	
	Space		
Training	84.19	1	0.56
Status	3884.11	1	30.10***
Training × Status	26.33	1	0.20
Sex	852.04	1	6.60**
Training × Sex	521.31	1	4.04*
Status × Sex	423.18	1	3.28
Training × Status × Sex	79.17	1	0.61
Error	129.06	221	
Occasion	1556.41	1	195.48***
Training × Occasion	41.82	1	5.25*
Status × Occasion	9.49	1	1.19
Training × Status × Occasion	18.14	1	2.28
Sex × Occasion	4.14	1	0.52
Training × Sex × Occasion	16.27	1	2.04
Status × Sex × Occasion	0.75	1	0.09
Training × Status × Sex × Occasion	4.83	1	0.61
Error	7.96	221	

*$p < .05$. **$p < .01$. ***$p < .001$.

of decliners and men, respectively. The occasion main effect represents retest effects occurring for both groups. More importantly with regard to training effects, there was a significant Training × Occasion interaction ($p < .001$), indicating a training effect at posttest. No status, sex, or sex × status comparisons within the Reasoning training group were significant; thus, the training effect was general and not specific to status and/or sex. Figure 34.2 shows the pretest–posttest gain computed from the standardized factor scores for

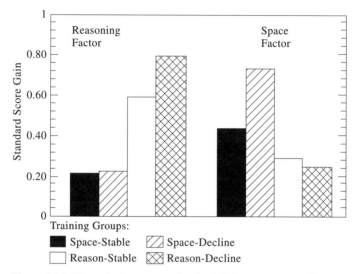

Figure 34.2. Mean factor score gains by training program and status (in standard score units).

the Reasoning and Space abilities for four training subgroups (stable/decline on Reasoning, stable/decline on Space). Each set of four bars in Figure 34.2 compares the two subgroups trained on Reasoning with the two trained on Space (see legend for Figure 34.2). That is, each training group serves as a control for the other training condition.

For Space, there were significant main effects for status ($p < .001$), sex ($p < .01$), and occasion ($p < .001$; Table 1). The status and sex main effects reflect the lower scores of the decliners and women, respectively, across occasions. The occasion main effect indicates retest effects occurring for both Reasoning and Space groups. There were significant interactions for Training × Occasion ($p < .02$) and Training × Sex ($p < .04$). The Training × Occasion interaction indicated a significant training effect at posttest. The Training × Sex interaction indicates that the overall performance on Space was higher for the target training group than for the controls for women but not for men.

Raw Score Analyses: PMA Reasoning and Space

To examine training effects for the two measures with longitudinal data, two Training (Reasoning, Space) × Status × Sex × Occasion ANOVAS with repeated measures were performed separately for the PMA Reasoning and

Table 34.2. Summary of Analyses of Variance: Primary Mental Ability Raw Scores

Source	MS	dfs	F
	Reasoning		
Training	41.03	1	0.61
Status	1471.25	1	21.89***
Training × Status	1.34	1	0.02
Sex	483.58	1	7.20**
Training × Sex	113.37	1	1.69
Status × Sex	54.51	1	0.81
Training × Status × Sex	5.77	1	0.09
Error	67.20	221	
Occasion	857.75	1	150.24***
Training × Occasion	231.02	1	40.47***
Status × Occasion	12.24	1	2.14
Training × Status × Occasion	12.71	1	2.23
Sex × Occasion	2.77	1	0.48
Training × Sex × Occasion	0.75	1	0.13
Status × Sex × Occasion	7.24	1	1.27
Training × Status × Sex × Occasion	16.16	1	2.83
Error	5.71	221	
	Space		
Training	470.12	1	2.91
Status	4228.33	1	26.14***
Training × Status	177.70	1	1.10
Sex	922.39	1	5.70*
Training × Sex	359.65	1	2.22
Status × Sex	388.56	1	2.40
Training × Status × Sex	0.66	1	0.00
Error	161.74	221	
Occasion	2044.16	1	90.68***
Training × Occasion	301.64	1	13.38***
Status × Occasion	49.23	1	2.18
Training × Status × Occasion	106.56	1	4.73*
Sex × Occasion	85.12	1	3.78*
Training × Sex × Occasion	55.47	1	2.46
Status × Sex × Occasion	46.55	1	2.06
Training × Status × Sex × Occasion	0.53	1	0.02
Error	22.54	221	

*$p < .05$. **$p < .01$. ***$p < .001$.

Space tests (Table 34.2). For PMA Reasoning, there were significant main effects for status ($p < .001$), sex ($p < .01$), and occasion ($p < .001$). The status and sex main effects again reflect the lower scores on the target measure for decliners and men, respectively. The occasion main effect represents retest effects occurring for both groups. With respect to training effects of central concern, there was a significant Training × Occasion interaction ($p < .001$), indicating higher performance of those trained on Reasoning at posttest. There was a trend toward a significant fourfold interaction ($p < .09$). Post hoc test on PMA Reasoning gain scores indicated that decliners showed greater gain than did stables. Sex and Sex × Status effects were not significant. When the Reasoning and Space training groups were compared, there were significant Reasoning training effects for stables ($p < .001$), decliners ($p < .001$), stable women ($p < .002$), and male and female decliners ($p < .001$).

For PMA Space, there were significant main effects for status ($p < .001$), sex ($p < .02$), and occasion ($p < .001$; Table 34.2). The status and sex main effects reflect the lower scores of the decliners and women, respectively, across occasions. The occasion main effect indicates retest effects occurring for both the Reasoning and Space training groups. As for the crucial results with respect to the training paradigm, there were significant interactions for Training × Occasion ($p < .004$) and Training × Status × Occasion ($p < .05$). The Training × Occasion interaction indicated a significantly higher performance for the Space training group at posttest. The triple interaction with Status reflects greater training gain for the decliners at posttest. A significant Sex × Occasion interaction ($p < .05$) suggests the occurrence of larger retest effects for women. Post hoc tests on PMA Space gain scores indicated that there were significantly greater ($p < .01$) gains for decliners than for stables.

Distinguishing between Regression and Training Effects

In order to exclude the possibility that regression effects might confound the results of the training study, we first of all examined the stability of our instruments over the interval between pretest and posttest by administering the measures over the same interval to a group 172 subjects of comparable age and socioeconomic status who did not receive any training. Stability coefficients obtained in this study were found to be .917 for the Space factor score and .939 for the Reasoning factor score. Stabilities for the two PMA measures were found to be .838 for Space and .886 for Reasoning. These estimates were next used to compute regressed deviation scores for our experimental subjects (cf. Nunnally, 1978). The ANOVAS described above were then repeated on the adjusted scores. As would be expected in light of the high stabilities, resulting F ratios differed only trivially, and none of the previously reported findings was significantly affected.

Effects of Age, Education, and Income

Because of slight differences between subgroups in terms of demographic characteristics, we also repeated the ANOVAS covarying on age, education, and income. Again, effects of the covariance adjustments were trivial, and none of the findings reported above was changed significantly.

Pretest–Posttest Training Improvement: Proportion of Subjects

The proportion of subjects showing statistically reliable pretest–posttest training improvement on the PMA Reasoning or Space measure was computed. The statistical criterion for significant improvement was defined as a gain $\geq$ 1 SE from pretest to posttest. The proportion of subjects at the individual level with reliable training gain is shown in Table 34.3. Approximately one half of the subjects in each training group showed significant pretest–posttest improvement. Although there was a trend for a greater proportion of decline subjects to show improvement in both training conditions, the difference between proportions is statistically significant only for the Space group ($p <$ .01).

Remediation of Decline

The final set of analyses examined the percentage of decline subjects whose posttest scores were equivalent to their 1970 performance. That is, we asked for what percentage of subjects did training result in a 14-year remediation to their 1970 performance level? Because longitudinal data are available only for the PMA tests, remediation was assessed with regard to the PMA Rea-

Table 34.3. Proportion of Subjects Achieving Significant Pretest to Posttest Training Gain

Status	Reasoning			Space		
	Men	Women	Total	Men	Women	Total
Stable	52.0	54.8	53.6	34.8	42.9	39.2
Decline	60.0	60.0	60.0	51.7	57.9	55.2
Total	55.6	57.6	56.8	44.2	51.5	48.3

NOTE: Significant training improvement was defined as a pretest–posttest gain of $\geq$ 1 standard error of measurement on the Primary Mental Ability Reasoning or Space test.

Table 34.4. Remediation of Ability Decline: Proportion of Subjects

	Reasoning		Space		
Criterion	Men ($n = 20$)	Women ($n = 35$)	Men ($n = 29$)	Women ($n = 38$)	Grand total
1 SEM[a]	55.0	65.7	55.2	68.4	62.3
To 1970 score[b]	50.0	40.0	31.0	42.1	40.2

[a] Proportion of decline subjects whose 1970 Primary Mental Ability (PMA) scores and 1984 PMA posttest scores differed by ≤ 1 standard error of measurement.
[b] Proportion of decline subjects whose 1984 PMA posttest score was ≥ their 1970 PMA score.

soning and Space measures. Two criterion levels were used to define remediation. The first level defined remediation as having occurred when the difference between the subjects' PMA posttest score and their 1970 score was ≤ 1 SE. This criterion employed the same statistical definition (1 SE) as that used in classifying subjects with regard to 1970–1984 decline. The second criterion level was even more conservative and defined remediation as the attainment of a PMA posttest score that was equal to or greater than the 1970 score. Table 34.4 and Figure 34.3 present the proportion of decline subjects reaching these remediation criteria. Sixty-two percent of the decline subjects were remediated to their predecline level if the 1 SE criterion is used. In both training groups more women were returned to their 1970 score level than were men. Using the more conservative criterion of return to the 1970 base level, 40% of the decline subjects' posttest scores were equal to or greater than their 1970 score. By this more stringent criterion, more women than men were returned to base level for Space, whereas more men than women were returned to their base level for Reasoning.

DISCUSSION

Differential Ability Decline

This experimental study is the most recent phase of a descriptive, longitudinal program of research that has examined intellectual change in adulthood over the past 28 years. In this study we focused on the modifiability of change occurring from late midlife into old age. A major finding of the Seattle Longitudinal Study has been the observation of wide individual differences in the onset and magnitude of intellectual decline. The initial phase of this study, which involved the classification of individuals with regard to decline status

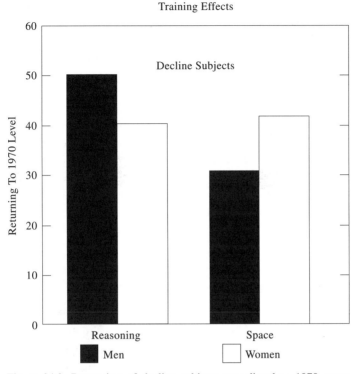

Figure 34.3. Proportion of decline subjects remediated to 1970 score level.

on two primary abilities, provides further support for the variability of cognitive functioning in later adulthood. Almost one half (46%) of the subjects exhibited no statistically reliable decline on either of the primary abilities studied over the previous 14-year period. The finding that less than one quarter of the subjects showed decline on both Space and Reasoning argues further that the onset of decline varies significantly across various abilities. For most individuals the pattern of decline appears to be selective, perhaps even ability specific, rather than global and catastrophic. The considerable stability in intellectual functioning is noteworthy, given that both of the abilities studied (Inductive Reasoning, Spatial Orientation) involve abstract reasoning on speeded measures and would thus be expected to exhibit normative patterns of decline if one were to extrapolate from the widely accepted classical pattern of cognitive aging (Botwinick, 1977).

Some might argue, however, that regression effects could mask decline in the less able or exaggerate decline for those at the top ability levels. This issue has been previously examined (Baltes et al., 1972) and it was shown that such effects are likely only when measures of low reliability are used. That is not the case here, and we demonstrated further by means of a time-reversed control analysis that our decline criterion appears reasonably linked to ontogenetic effects that generalize across ability groupings and are minimally impacted by statistical regression.

Whereas subjects showing no decline were on average 2 years younger than those having declined, there is a wide age range (64–85 years) for those classified as stable, suggesting that for some individuals cognitive decline may be a condition of old-old age, rather than occurring in middle or young-old age. We do not construe these data to imply that there is no cognitive decline in old age, although some have in the past accused us of this position (Donaldson, 1981; Horn & Donaldson, 1976). Rather, we believe these data to argue for large individual differences in the onset and pattern of intellectual aging.

Training Effects at the Factorial Level

Significant training effects were demonstrated for both Reasoning and Space abilities. These effects were demonstrated at the ability factor level as well as at the individual measure level. The observation of significant effects at the factorial level is important in that it extends the findings of prior cross-sectional training research, which has examined training improvement at the level of individual measures. Some (Birren, Cunningham & Yamamoto, 1982; Donaldson, 1981) have questioned the breadth of training effects when assessed with respect to individual measures. The current data indicate that the effects of training are not restricted to performance on one specific test but rather reflect training improvement at the level of the primary ability.

Decline Status and Training Effects

Two major questions were addressed in this study. The first question focused on the differential effectiveness of training for remediating cognitive decline versus the development of new performance levels in the elderly showing no previous decline. The second question asks for how large a proportion of subjects exhibiting decline can there be remediation through training to a previously observed (1970) level of performance. Longitudinal data are required to address these questions because the prior intellectual history of the subjects must be known in order to examine the differential effects of training (remediation vs. new learning) and to determine the extent to which remediation has occurred. Prior training studies have been cross-sectional in design, and whereas many have found significant treatment effects, the nature of the observed training gain could not be specified.

With regard to the first question, no statistically significant interaction effects involving decline status were found at the ability level. However, decliners did improve significantly more than did the stable subjects on the PMA Space test (see Table 34.2). The greater effectiveness of training for decliners is further supported by an examination of the proportion of subjects attaining significant training gain from pretest to posttest. Fifty-five percent ($n = 37$) of the decliners in the Space training group achieved significant pretest–posttest training improvement, compared with 39% ($n = 20$) of the stables; the difference in the proportion of decline versus stable subjects showing improvement was statistically significant ($p < .01$). This difference is less pronounced in Reasoning training where 60% ($n = 33$) of the decliners showed significant pretest–posttest training gains, compared with 53.6% ($n = 30$) of the stables. Although age, education, and income are associated with ability decline, covarying on these demographic variables does not significantly alter any of our findings.

Whereas a greater proportion of decliners showed pretest–posttest training improvement, it is impressive to note that marked improvement was also seen for the stable subjects. More than half of the stables in the Reasoning training showed significant pretest-posttest gain, as did approximately 40% of the stables in Space training (Table 34.3). Many elderly persons who remain at stable levels of functioning are still disadvantaged by limited early educational and experiential opportunities. Intervention techniques such as those used in this study may therefore have utility in improving specific cognitive skills in these otherwise well-functioning persons.

Remediation of Ability Decline

The second major question focused on the extent to which training is effective in remediating decline to a previous performance level. Remediation of decline was examined over a 14-year period (1970–1984). For most of the subjects in the study the 1970 basepoint represents a performance level prior to the onset of statistically reliable decline. Most subjects in 1970 had not reached the age at which normative patterns of statistically significant decline have been noted for their cohorts (Schaie, 1983). Remediation of decline was defined as occurring when a subject's 1984 posttest score was equivalent to his or her 1970 score on the relevant PMA measure. Forty percent of subjects exhibited remediation of decline on the ability trained, when the more conservative estimate of remediation was used, and 62% when a more lenient (confidence interval) criterion was employed (Table 34.4). There was no significant difference in the proportion of subjects for whom remediation occurred for Reasoning versus Space training. Thus, the data suggest that decline on both Space and Reasoning ability is responsive to training efforts.

The finding that observed cognitive decline can be remediated for large proportions of subjects as the result of the application of quite modest experiential intervention procedures suggests strongly that at least a portion of the previously observed decline may be attributable to disuse. What our intervention procedures seem to accomplish is to reactivate behaviors and skills that have remained in the subjects' behavioral repertoire but that have not been actively employed (Bearison, 1974; Overton & Newman, 1982).

Training and Sex

The sex main effects (Tables 34.1 and 34.2) indicate sex differences for both abilities, but in the opposite direction. There is a significant difference in favor of women on Inductive Reasoning and in favor of men on Space. These patterns of sex difference have been noted in previous research (Maccoby & Jacklin, 1974; Schaie, 1983). A number of trends in the data suggest that the training may have been particularly effective for women. Sex effects are most salient for Space training. Across both training programs, 67% of the women decliners were remediated within 1 SE of their 1970 performance level, compared with 55% of the male decliners (Table 34.4).

Conclusions

The major objectives of this study were to examine whether or not cognitive decline that had been reliably demonstrated over a substantial period of time could be reversed by educational training techniques, and whether stable performance in old age could be significantly improved. In order to answer these questions it was necessary to classify older members of a long-term longitudinal study into those who had declined and those who had remained stable and to develop a paradigm that would provide appropriate controls by training both decliners and stables on two different target abilities.

The results of the study clearly show that: (a) Cognitive training techniques can reverse reliably documented decline over a 14-year period in a substantial number of older adults; (b) such reversal can be documented for at least two abilities; (c) training procedures enhance the performance of those older persons who have remained stable; and (d) magnitudes of training effects are unrelated to age, education, and income.

Highly significant retest effects were found for all subgroups and can be attributed in part to the extensive test batteries that provided practice on several measures of each target ability. The training paradigm employing two training programs, however, provides the necessary controls to permit the conclusion that training results are specific to the objectives of each training program and that subjects trained in each program on average show significantly greater gains than do the controls receiving the alternate training program.

It should be kept in mind that all our subjects were community dwelling adults in fair to excellent health condition who lived in reasonably supportive environments. We consequently would not wish to claim that we have discovered methods that are likely to reverse cognitive changes of a neuropathological nature that are found in some of the elderly. Our approaches, however, are directly applicable to the remediation of the cognitive decline seen in many older adults without psychopathology that may be the result of experiential changes commonly occurring in the later stages of life.

Although the improvement and reversal of decline demonstrated in this study are impressive, it should be understood that such results may be a rather conservative estimate of what could be achieved by more extensive programs of this kind. The training procedures employed in this study were relatively brief (five 1-hour sessions), compared with the massive educational interventions common earlier in the lifespan, and the breadth of remediation possible with more extensive training efforts has yet to be examined.

Most importantly, our findings lend support to contentions regarding the plasticity of behavior into late adulthood. They suggest that for at least a substantial proportion of the community dwelling elderly, observed cognitive decline is not irreversible, is likely to be attributable to disuse, and can be subjected to environmental manipulations involving relatively simple and inexpensive educational training techniques.

REFERENCES

Baltes, P. B., Nesselroade, J. R., Schaie, K. W. & Labouvie, E. W. (1972). On the dilemma of regression effects in examining ability-level-related differentials in ontogenetic patterns of intelligence. Developmental Psychology, 6, 78–84.

Baltes, P. B. & Willis, S. L. (1977). Toward psychological theories of aging and development. In J. E. Birren & K. W. Schaie (Eds.), Handbook of the psychology of aging (pp. 128–154). New York: Van Nostrand Reinhold.

Baltes, P. B. & Willis, S. L. (1982). Enhancement (plasticity) of intellectual functioning in old age: Penn State's Adult Development and Enrichment Project (ADEPT). In F. I. M. Craik & S. E. Trehub (Eds.), Aging and cognitive processes (pp. 353–389). New York: Plenum Press.

Bearison, D. (1974). The construct of regression: A Piagetian approach. Merrill-Palmer Quarterly, 20, 21–30.

Birren, J. E., Cunningham, W. R. & Yamamoto, K. (1982). Psychology of adult development and aging. Annual Review of Psychology, 34, 543–575.

Blieszner, R., Willis, S. L. & Baltes, P. B. (1981). Training research in aging on the fluid ability of inductive reasoning. Journal of Applied Developmental Psychology, 2, 247–265.

Botwinick, J. (1977). Intellectual abilities. In J. E. Birren & K. W. Schaie (Eds.), Handbook of the psychology of aging (pp. 580–605). New York: Van Nostrand Reinhold.

Campbell, D. T. & Stanley, J. C. (1966). Experimental and quasi-experimental designs for research. Chicago: Rand McNally.

Cooper, L. B., & Shepard, R. N. (1973). Chronometric studies of rotation of mental images. In W. G. Chase (Ed.), Visual information processing (pp. 75–96). New York: Academic Press.

Denney, N. W. (1982). Aging and cognitive changes. In B. B. Wolman (Ed.), Handbook of developmental psychology (pp. 807–827). Englewood Cliffs, NJ: Prentice-Hall.

Detterman, D. K. & Sternberg, R. J. (Eds.). (1982). How much can intelligence be increased? Norwood, NJ: Ablex.

Donaldson, G. (1981). Letter to the editor. Journal of Gerontology, 36, 634–636.

Dudek, F. J. (1979). The continuing misinterpretation of the standard error of measurement. Psychological Bulletin, 86, 335–337.

Egan, D. E. (1981). An analysis of spatial orientation test performance. Intelligence, 5, 85–100.

Ekstrom, R. B., French, J. W., Harman, H. & Derman, D. (1976). Kit of factor-referenced cognitive tests (Rev. ed.). Princeton, NJ: Educational Testing Service.

Giambra, L. M., & Arenberg, D. (1980). Problem solving, concept learning, and aging. In L. W. Poon (Ed.), Aging in the 1980s (pp. 253–259). Washington, DC: American Psychological Association.

Gribbin, K., Schaie, K. W. & Parham, I. A. (1980). Complexity of life style and maintenance of intellectual abilities. Journal of Social Issues, 21, 47–61.

Hertzog, C. K., Schaie, K. W. & Gribbin, K. (1978). Cardiovascular disease and changes in intellectual functioning from middle to old age. Journal of Gerontology, 33, 872–883.

Holzman, T. G., Pellegrino, J. W. & Glaser, R. (1982). Cognitive dimensions of numerical rule induction. Journal of Educational Psychology, 74, 360–373.

Horn, J. L. & Donaldson, G. (1976). On the myth of intellectual decline in adulthood. American Psychologist, 31, 701–719.

Kail, R., Pellegrino, J. & Carter, P. (1980). Developmental changes in mental rotation. Journal of Experimental Child Psychology, 39, *102–116.*

Kotovsky, K. & Simon, H. A. (1973). Empirical tests of a theory of human acquisition of concepts for sequential patterns. Cognitive Psychology, 4, *399–424.*

Maccoby, E. & Jacklin, C. (1974). The psychology of sex differences. *Stanford, CA: Stanford University Press.*

Nunnally, J. C. (1978). Psychometric theory *(2nd Ed.). New York: McGraw-Hill.*

Overton, W. F. & Newman, J. L. (1982). Cognitive development: A competence-activation/utilization approach. In T. Field, A. Huston, H. Quay, L. Troll & G. Finlay (Eds.), Review of human development *(pp. 217–241). New York: Wiley.*

Poon, L. W., Walsh-Sweeney, L. & Fozard, J. L. (1980). Memory training for the elderly. In L. W. Poon, J. L. Fozard, L. S. Cermak, D. Arenberg & L. W. Thompson (Eds.), New directions in memory and aging *(pp. 461–484). Hillsdale, NJ: Erlbaum.*

Salthouse, T. A. (1982). Adult cognition. *New York: Springer-Verlag.*

Schaie, K. W. (1983). The Seattle Longitudinal Study: A 21-year exploration of psychometric intelligence in adulthood. In K. W. Schaie (Ed.), Longitudinal studies of adult psychological development *(pp. 64–135). New York: Guilford.*

Schaie, K. W. (1984). Midlife influences upon intellectual functioning in old age. International Journal of Behavioral Development, 7, *463–478.*

Schaie, K. W. (1985). Manual for the Schaie-Thurstone Adult Mental Abilities Test (STAMAT). *Palo Alto, CA: Consulting Psychologists Press.*

Schaie, K. W. & Hertzog, C. (1983). Fourteen-year cohort-sequential studies of adult intelligence. Developmental Psychology, 19, *531–543.*

Sterns, H. L. & Sanders, R. E. (1980). Training and education in the elderly. In R. E. Turner & H. W. Reese (Eds.), Life-span developmental psychology: Intervention *(pp. 307–330). New York: Academic Press.*

Stone, V. (1980). Structural modeling of the relations among environmental variables, health status and intelligence in adulthood. *Unpublished doctoral dissertation, University of Southern California, Los Angeles. CA.*

Thurstone, L. L. (1948). Primary mental abilities. *Chicago: University of Chicago Press.*

Willis, S. L. (1985). Towards an educational psychology of the adult learner: Cognitive and intellectual bases. In J. E. Birren & K. W. Schaie (Eds.), Handbook of the psychology of aging *(2nd ed.; pp. 818–847). New York: Van Nostrand Reinhold.*

Willis, S. L. & Baltes, P. B. (1980). Intelligence in adulthood and aging: Contemporary issues. In L. W. Poon (Ed.), Aging in the 1980s *(pp. 260–272). Washington, DC: American Psychological Association.*

35. Chronic Stress and Immunity in Family Caregivers of Alzheimer's Disease Victims

Janice K. Kiecolt-Glaser, Ronald Glaser,
Edwin C. Shuttleworth, Carol S. Dyer,
Paula Ogrocki, and Carl E. Speicher

THERE IS GOOD EVIDENCE that acute stressful events are associated with adverse immunologic changes in humans (1, 2). Even relatively common-place events like academic examinations have been linked to transient changes in immunity; data from blood samples taken during examinations show poorer cellular immunity than those taken 1 month to 6 weeks earlier, when students were less distressed (3–7). In addition, individuals undergoing major novel stressful life changes such as marital separation and divorce have a poorer proliferative response than well-matched comparison subjects (8); bereaved spouses show poorer mitogen responsiveness after the death of a spouse than before (9).

There is some evidence from rodent studies suggesting that the chronicity of the stressor mediates both immunologic responses and tumor development. Data from one rodent study by Monjan and Collector (10) suggested that chronic stress might lead to an enhancement of immune function. Using daily high-intensity intermittent noise, they found that the acute or short-term consequence of the auditory stressor was immunosuppression, while more chronic stress appeared to result in enhanced mitogen responsiveness. Similarly, Sklar and Anisman (11) found that tumor size and survival were adversely affected by a single session of inescapable shock in mice injected with a tumor. However, mice that underwent ten daily shock sessions had tumor areas that were significantly less than those of controls, and survival times approximated those of the controls.

Although these data suggest that there may be adaptation or even enhancement of immunity in response to a more chronic stressor, there are problems in extrapolating from research with rodents to humans. In particular, adaptation may be different because the nature of the stressor is quite different;

Reprinted by permission from *Psychosomatic Medicine* 49 (1987): 523–35. Copyright © 1987 by Williams and Wilkins.

physical stressors like intermittent loud noise, rotational stress, or electric shock are used in rodent research, and adaptation to physical stressors could be quite different than adjustment to the cognitive stressors that are of primary interest in research with humans. Use of family caregivers for Alzheimer's disease (AD) victims provides an opportunity to examine the immunologic and psychologic consequences of a more chronic psycho-social stressor.

AD affects two million older adults in this country. The progressive cognitive impairments that are characteristic of AD lead to increasing needs for supportive care of afflicted individuals. Although mild memory impairments may be the only obvious problem in the early stages, the irreversible deterioration of brain tissue eventually culminates in profound cognitive and behavioral changes, including disorientation, incontinence, and an inability to provide any self-care (12, 13). Since the modal survival time after onset is approximately 8 years (14), long-term care of these patients by family members may be conceptualized as a chronic stressor (15). The majority of AD patients live in the community, under the care of their relatives (13).

Cross-sectional data from several laboratories suggest that the stresses of AD caregiving leave family members at high risk for depression (16, 17). Moreover, there may be some progressive deterioration in caregivers' well-being over time related to the increasing impairment in the AD family member. George and Gwyther (18) found substantial deterioration in caregivers' well-being when measures were taken at one-year intervals, including perceived decrements in health, decreased satisfaction with the amount of time available for social participation, decreased life satisfaction, and increased levels of stress-related psychiatric symptoms. These changes were particularly noteworthy because the baseline (time one) levels of well-being in these caregivers were already quite low in absolute terms.

Although limited evidence suggests that caregiving responsibilities may be associated with self-reported health impairments (19, 20), the health of AD caregivers has not been studied using objective physiologic measures. The relatively high incidence of depression among caregivers could have implications for their health, particularly in regard to immune function. Convergent data have linked depression with impaired immune function (9, 21, 22).

In order to better understand the health-related consequences of caregiving, we obtained psychologic data and blood samples for immunologic and nutritional analyses from AD caregivers and socio-demographically matched comparison subjects. We expected that caregivers would be more depressed and would have poorer immune status than comparison subjects. Moreover, greater impairment in AD patients was expected to be correlated with greater dysfunction in caregivers.

METHODS

The subjects were 34 caregivers and 34 matched comparison subjects. All subjects were interviewed and completed questionnaires at the time blood was drawn for the immunologic assays. All blood samples were drawn at the same time of day to control for diurnal variation.

The caregivers were recruited from the practices of an Ohio State neurologist and an internist (n = 20), and from local support groups affiliated with the Alzheimer's Disease and Related Disorders Association (n = 14). The comparison subjects were recruited from newspaper advertisements, notes placed on community bulletin boards, and personal contacts.

In our laboratory's behavioral immunology research with younger populations we normally limit participation to those individuals who are not taking any medication and who have no health problems with possible immunologic components. However, caregivers are primarily middle-aged or older, and the majority of older adults are likely to be taking some medications. Limiting the sample to those who are unmedicated would probably result in biased data, because only the very healthiest of the population would be eligible (23). An alternative strategy that we used successfully in other research with older adults (24) involved selecting as subjects those individuals who were not taking any immunosuppressive medication, and whose health problems did not have an immunologic component (e.g., excluding those individuals with cancer, recent surgeries, strokes, hormonal disorders, etc.). There is evidence that this approach results in reliable data: Goodwin and coworkers (25) examined various immunologic parameters in 279 healthy and 24 chronically ill individuals over 65, and in young controls. Although there were the expected differences between the young and old subjects on certain aspects of immune function, there were not differences between the two groups of older adults. They noted that the data supported age-related relationships in immune function, rather than age-associated diseases.

In addition, we matched subjects on the presence of absence of two kinds of medication—use of beta blockers for hypertension and estrogen supplements. Beta blockers are widely prescribed among the elderly, and data from in vitro studies suggest that they may have some consequences for blastogenesis (26). Although we are unaware of any comparable immunologic data for estrogen, there is good evidence for interactions between the immune system and the endocrine system (2). Rather than exclude all caregivers who might use these medications, we selectively recruited matched comparison subjects (described below) who were similarly medicated.

Subjects were also matched on three sociodemographic dimensions: age, sex, and education. Education was used as the socioeconomic status variable for matching purposes because occupation is of limited value in a sample that includes significant numbers of older women who may or may not have worked outside the home (27).

Self-Report Data

Depression, social contact, loneliness, self-reported physical health, and financial resources were assessed. The self-report measures we used have been used previously in studies with older adults.

Demographic and health data. Information on age, sex, years of education, current or former occupation, and household income were obtained. Health status data included medication usage, caffeine intake, and recent alcohol intake. Subjects were asked how many hours they had slept in the last 3 days compared to their usual needs, and whether they had experienced any recent weight changes, particularly during the previous week. Data on recent illnesses included the number of physician visits during the previous 6 months, and the number of days the subject was ill enough to be in bed during the same time period.

Depression. The short form of the Beck Depression Inventory (BDI) (28) was used because it appears to be more sensitive to mild to moderate levels of depression than other scales that are more biologically based (29); in addition, it has fewer somatically based items that may be characteristic of older non-depressed individuals. It has been used extensively in research, including several studies with caregivers (15). Population norms provide cutoffs for varying levels of depression.

Social contact. We collected social contact information using selected questions from the Older Americans' Resources and Services Multidimensional Functional Assessment Questionnaire (OARS), since there are good normative data for older adults, and its reliability and validity have been well-documented (30). The questions included information on the number of persons the subject knew well enough to visit in their homes, the number of times the subject talked to someone else in the past week, and the number of times they spent time with someone who did not live with them (and who was not their AD relative). They were also asked how often they find themselves feeling lonely.

AD patient history and current functioning. Information on the estimated duration of the illness was provided by the family caregiver, as well as the time since a physician had made a tentative diagnosis of AD. Caregivers were also asked to estimate the amount of time they spent in caregiving activities during the previous week.

The ratings of family members can provide one source of reliable data on level of AD patient function (31). Family members responded to the Memory and Behavior Problem Checklist (MBPC) (32) by providing ratings of the frequency of relevant behaviors associated with AD, as well as separate reaction ratings for the degree of associated bother or upset. The sum of the cross products of these two ratings provides a measure of the impact of the behaviors (33).

Immunologic Assays

The five immunologic assays included assessment of the percentages of total T lymphocytes, helper T lymphocytes, suppressor T lymphocytes, and natural killer (NK) cells. We also measured antibody titers to the latent herpesvirus Epstein–Barr virus (EBV), the etiologic agent for infectious mononucleosis.

Monoclonal antibodies were used to provide data on certain quantitative aspects of immune function. Natural killer cell percentages were assessed because NK cells are thought to be an important antiviral and antitumor defense. Distress-related changes in NK cell percentages have been found previously in medical students (7). Reliable stress-related changes in a functional NK measure, NK cell lysis, have been shown with two different target cells (3, 4, 7).

Data on the relative percentages of helper and suppressor T lymphocytes were also collected. Helper T cells stimulate important immunologic activities, including the production of antibody by B lymphocytes, an important defense against bacterial infections. Suppressor T cells act to shut off the activity of helper cells when sufficient antibody has been produced. Low helper-to-suppressor cell ratios are associated with immunodeficiency (34). Alterations in the percentages of helper and suppressor cells have been associated with examination stress (4, 5).

We measured antibody to EBV because antibody titers to latent herpes-viruses appear to provide an indirect measure of cellular immune system competency (6). For example, patients on immunosuppressive therapies like chemotherapy or patients with immunosuppressive diseases (e.g., AIDS) have characteristic elevated herpesvirus antibody titers; cessation of an immuno-suppressive drug therapy is ultimately followed by a drop in antibody titers to latent herpes-viruses. The increased herpesvirus antibody production in immunosuppressive conditions is thought to reflect the humoral immune sys-tem's response to an increased load of viral antigens. We have previously shown large and reliable stress-related changes in antibody titers to EBV and herpes simplex virus using a type 1 antigen (HSV-1) in medical students (6) as well as decrements in HSV-1 antibody titers in elderly adults following a relaxation intervention (24).

It should be noted that there is some evidence for the genetic transmission of early-onset AD (35), and there is some suggestion that AD may have an etiology related to immune function. The early-onset form of AD probably accounts for a relatively small proportion of AD patients, and the types of immunologic assays we used have not been related to the presence or absence of AD in previous studies (36). Therefore, although we used offspring car-egivers, we did not expect that their immunologic data would be different from other subjects without a family history of AD.

NK, T lymphocyte, and T lymphocyte subset assays. The percentages of total T lymphocytes helper-to-inducer T cells, and suppressor-to-cytotoxic T cells were determined using the monoclonal antibodies OKT-3, OKT-4, and OKT-8, respectively (Ortho), as previously described (5). The Leu-11 monoclonal antibody (Becton-Dickerson) was used to measure the percentage of NK cells.

Briefly, lymphocytes isolated on Hypaque–Ficoll gradients were washed with trypsin diluent and then resuspended in complete RPMI 1640 medium supplemented with 20% fetal bovine serum. Monocytes were removed by placing the cell suspensions in plastic tissue culture flasks and incubating at 37°C in a CO_2 incubator for 2 hours. The nonadherent cells were washed off and used to determine percentage of T-cell subsets. Lymphocytes (10^6) were incubated in 0.01 ml of Leu-11. OKT-3, OKT-4, or OKT-8 monoclonal an-tibody for 30 minutes on ice. Cells were washed with cold RPMI 1640/PBS (1:1), resuspended in goat antimouse IgG conjugated to fluorescein isothio-cyanate (Cappel Laboratories), and incubated for an additional 30 minutes on ice. The cells were washed and assayed, using an Ortho System 50 flu-orescence activated cell sorter (FACS).

Immunofluorescence assay. The indirect immunofluorescence (IF) assay was used to measure antibodies to EBV virus capsid antigen (VCA) (6). Antibody titers were assayed using smears of HR-1 cells. Cells were fixed in acetone at room temperature for 10 minutes, adsorbed with twofold dilutions of plasma prepared in phosphate-buffered saline (PBS), pH 7.4, for 30 minutes at 37°C. The cells were washed with PBS and readsorbed with goat antihuman IgG conjugated to fluorescein isothiocyanate (FITC) for 30 minutes at 37°C. The cells were washed with PBS, counterstained with Evans blue, mounted in Protex, and examined with a Zeiss UV microscope. A background control for the FITC-labeled antibody was performed. Antibody titers were determined by the highest dilution of plasma still able to demonstrate IF positive cells. All slides were read blind coded.

Nutritional Assays

Albumin and transferrin, two nutritional assays with relatively shorter and longer half-lives, were included to provide objective information on the nutritional status of subjects. There are well documented impairments in various aspects of immune function in undernourished individuals, and moderate to severe protein-caloric malnutrition is associated with increased frequency and severity of infection (37).

Protein assays provide better information on global nutritional status than those for carbohydrates and fats, since the former have varied nutritional building blocks, as well as very complex synthetic pathways. Different protein markers were used because of the differences in their half-lives; the half-life of albumin is 2–3 weeks, in comparison to 8 days for transferrin.

The procedure used to measure albumin is an adaptation of the bromcresol green dye-binding method of Rodkey (38), later modified by Doumas (39). This procedure is recognized as a particularly good procedure as compared to other dye-binding techniques because of its specificity and freedom from interference.

Transferrin is an iron-transporting protein. Concentration in plasma is affected by dietary intake of iron. Nutritionally deficient but calorie-rich diets are generally lacking in iron, and, as a result, plasma iron levels tend to be low and transferrin levels high. It has been shown that estimation of transferrin levels may be used to assess the effectiveness of total parenteral nutrition (40).

A rate nephelometry procedure using a Beckman human immunoglobulin reagent kit and a Beckman immunochemistry analyzer system was used to analyze transferrin levels. Antibody to human transferrin was used in the assay, in which the peak rate signal caused by the antigen–antibody complex is proportional to the increase in light scatter that is read by the instrument (41).

RESULTS

Sociodemographic Data

Sociodemographic data are shown in Table 35.1. Subjects ranged in age from 34 to 82. There were no reliable differences between caregivers and comparison subjects on the matching variables of age or education, or in subjects' total family income, $Fs < 1$. Six of the matched pairs were taking beta blocking medication, and five of the women in each cohort were taking an estrogen supplement.

The majority of the caregivers were spouses ($n = 20$), 13 were adult children, and 1 was an in-law. Half of the caregivers lived with their impaired relative ($n = 17$), 10 AD patients were in nursing homes, and 7 of the AD

Table 35.1. Subjects' Sociodemographic Characteristics

	AD caregivers	Comparison subjects
Sex		
Males	11	11
Females	23	23
Age	59.32 (12.98)	60.29 (13.27)
Marital status		
Married	32	29
Separated/divorced	1	4
Widowed	1	1
Number of children	2.90 (1.84)	2.44 (1.46)
Education		
Partial high school	1	—
High school graduate	5	7
Post high school business or trade school	2	4
1–3 years college	7	6
College graduate	11	7
Postgraduate college	8	10
Annual family income		
10,000–14,999	2	3
15,000–19,999	6	5
20,000–29,999	4	6
30,000–39,999	9	4
40,000 or more	11	15
Unanswered	2	1

victims lived alone or with another relative but had additional care provided by our interviewees. The length of time reported since the caregiver reported that he or she had first noticed any AD symptoms ranged from 9 months to 16 years, with a mean of 5.45 years (SD = 3.82). The time that had elapsed since the initial physician's diagnosis of probable AD ranged from a new diagnosis to 11 years, with a mean and median of 2.83 years and 2.04 years, respectively.

Initial analyses of variance (ANOVAs) that included sex of subject revealed no differential sex effects for the major immunologic and self-report variables. Therefore, data were combined for subsequent analyses using ANOVAs with one variable, group membership.

Self-Report Data

Psychologic data are shown in Table 35.2. Caregivers had significantly higher scores on the short form of the BDI than comparison subjects, $F(1,66) = 4.02$, $p < 0.05$. Similarly, caregivers reported significantly lower general life satisfaction than comparison subjects, $F(1,66) = 5.34$, $p < 0.05$. Caregivers also rated their mental health as poorer than did comparison subjects on the OARS item, $F(1,66) = 8.11$, $p < 0.01$. Caregivers were significantly more

Table 35.2. Means (SDs) for Psychologic Data from the BDI and the OARS

	AD caregivers	Comparison subjects
Beck Depression Inventory short form[a]	4.88 (6.18)	2.48 (2.58)
Current life satisfaction[a] (0 = poor, 2 = good)	1.62 (0.66)	1.91 (0.29)
Self-rated current mental health[b]	1.84 (0.87)	2.38 (0.65)
Self-rated mental health, compared to 5 years ago (0 = worse, 3 = better)[a]	1.57 (1.07)	2.03 (0.75)
Number of people known well enough to visit in their homes (0 = none, 3 = 5 or more)	2.90 (0.38)	2.85 (0.43)
Frequency of phone conversations with friends, relatives, or others in the past week (0 = none, 3 = daily or more)	2.42 (0.66)	2.35 (0.59)
Frequency of visits with someone not living with subject in the past week (0 = none, 3 = daily or more)	2.12 (0.74)	1.88 (0.84)
Feelings of loneliness (0 = quite often, 2 = almost never)	1.48 (0.61)	1.64 (0.59)

[a] $p < 0.05$.
[b] $p < 0.01$.

Table 35.3. Correlations among Impaired Indices for the AD Victim and Depression and Social Contacts in Caregivers

	1.	2.	3.	4.	5.	6.	7.
1. MBPC frequency	1.00						
2. MBPC upset	0.62[a]	1.00					
3. MBPC cross-product of frequency and upset	0.61[a]	0.93[a]	1.00				
4. BDI depression score	0.28[b]	0.48[c]	0.60[a]	1.00			
5. Number of people known well enough to visit in their home	−0.25	−0.66[a]	−0.63[a]	−0.45[c]	1.00		
6. Frequency of phone conversations, past week	0.10	0.09	0.07	0.16	0.19	1.00	
7. Frequency of visits, past week	−0.23	−0.43[c]	−0.42[c]	−0.51[a]	0.48[a]	0.15	1.00
8. Feelings of loneliness	−0.44[c]	−0.41[c]	−0.46[c]	−0.50[a]	0.32[b]	0.02	0.35[b]

[a] $p < 0.001$.
[b] $p < 0.05$.
[c] $p < 0.01$.

likely than comparison subjects to say that there was a negative change in their mental health compared to 5 years ago, $F(1,66) = 4.79$, $p < 0.05$.

There were no significant differences between caregivers and comparison subjects on social support and loneliness questions from the OARS, as shown in Table 35.2. However, the pattern of correlations among AD impairment indices and social contact items shown in Table 35.3 suggests that caregivers with more impaired relatives had fewer social contacts with others and were lonelier. In addition, the significant correlations between BDI scores and the three indices of impairment from the Memory and Behavior Problems Checklist suggest that greater impairment in the AD patient may be associated with greater distress in the caregiver.

Immunologic Data

Comparisons of immunologic data showed differences in the predicted direction, as seen in Table 35.4. The AD caregivers had significantly higher antibody titers to EBV VCA than comparison subjects, $F(1,65) = 4.65$, $p < 0.05$, presumably reflecting poorer cellular immune system control of herpes virus latency in the former. Caregivers had significantly lower percentages of both total T lymphocytes, $F(1,62) = 4.87$, $p < 0.01$, and helper T lymphocytes than comparison subjects, $F(1,62) = 18.49$, $p < 0.0001$. Although the two groups did not differ in the relative percentages of suppressor T cells, $F(1,62) = 1.12$, there were significant differences in the helper-to-

Table 35.4. Means [SDs] for Immunologic and Nutritional Data

	AD caregivers	Comparison subjects
Immunologic Assays		
EBV VAC[a,b]	640.70 (570.01)	376.72 (446.39)
Percentage of total T lymphocytes[b]	48.72 (13.97)	56.53 (14.15)
Percentage of helper T lymphocytes[c]	33.51 (10.86)	45.94 (12.05)
Percentage of suppressor T lymphocytes	18.30 (10.50)	21.02 (9.86)
Helper–suppressor ratio[d]	1.90 (0.97)	2.80 (1.86)
Percentage of NK cells	12.88 (6.92)	15.35 (9.53)
Nutritional Assays		
Albumin	4.23 (0.33)	4.14 (0.25)
Transferrin	296.78 (48.14)	284.79 (59.21)

[a] Higher antibody titers to a latent herpesvirus are thought to reflect *poorer* cellular immune system control over virus latency.
[b] $p < 0.05$.
[c] $p < 0.0001$.
[d] $p < 0.01$.

suppressor ratio, $F_{(1,62)} = 5.77$, $p < 0.05$. There were no significant differences in the percentages of NK cells, $F_{(1,56)} = 1.27$.

Nutritional Data

We used two nutritional markers, plasma albumin and transferrin levels, to assess the nutritional status of the subjects, since inadequate nutrition is associated with impairments in immunity. All subjects were within normal; range for both markers. The two groups did not show even marginal differences on either albumin, $F_{(1,66)} = 1.81$, or transferrin, $F < 1$. Thus, there is no evidence that the immunologic differences simply reflect underlying differences in nutrition.

Health-Related Data

The two groups did not differ reliably in the number of physician visits during the previous 6 months, or in the number of days they were ill in the same time period, $Fs < 1$. Similarly, there were not reliable differences in self-ratings of current health, or health as of 1 year ago, $Fs < 1$.

The two groups did not show differences in behavior that might have immunologic or other health-related consequences, including the number of smokers in the two groups, the number of packs smoked per week, the amount of alcohol consumed in the previous week, the average number of drinks normally consumed in a week, or in caffeine use, $Fs < 1$. There were no differences between the groups in recent weight change, $F(1,66) = 2.12$. There was a significant difference between the two groups in the amount of sleep subjects reported within the previous 3 days, $F(1,66) = 4.60, p < 0.05$, but the differences were not large. Caregivers reported an average of 23.07 (SD = 1.98) hours, whereas comparison subjects reported a mean of 24.32 hours (SD = 2.83).

In order to help evaluate the possibility that any psychologic and immunologic differences between the two groups simply reflected differences in the amount of sleep, correlations were computed between sleep and the immunologic parameters in caregivers. All of the correlations were negative, but none was significant. Sleep correlated -0.10 with BDI scores, whereas correlations between sleep and the immunologic measures ranged from -0.01 to -0.23.

Residence of AD Victim and Functioning of Caregiver

In order to evaluate possible differences among caregiver functioning as consequence of where their AD relative lived (with them, in an institution, or elsewhere), we compared demographic, self-report, immunologic, and nutritional data. The caregivers whose relative lived elsewhere were younger (mean age of 45.57, SD = 9.62) than those whose relative lived with them (mean = 62.06, SD = 10.00) or those whose relative was institutionalized (mean = 65.80, SD = 12.87), $F(2.31) = 2.42, P < 0.01$. There were no differences in the total time spent each day in caregiving activities, $F(2,31) = 2.20$, in part as a function of the very wide variability within each of the three groups: those living with their impaired relative reported spending an average of 9.87 hours a day (SD = 9.99), those whose relative was institutionalized reported a mean of 3.1 hours each day (SD = 2.33), and those whose relative lived elsewhere reported an average of 6.42 hours per day (SD = 7.93). Those caregivers whose relatives were institutionalized reported a significantly longer duration of illness, $F(2,31) = 12.18, p < 0.0001$. The two groups did not differ reliably on any of the three memory and behavior indices, $Fs < 1$.

There were no reliable differences on BDI scores, life satisfaction, or self-rated mental or physical health. There were significant immunologic differences only for percentages of NK cells, $F(2,27) = 6.49, p < 0.01$, with those whose relative was institutionalized having the highest values, with a mean of 19.26 (SD = 9.24), compared to those who lived with their AD relative (mean = 10.17, SD = 4.07), and those whose relative lived elsewhere (mean = 11.40, SD = 4.25). Nutritional comparisons showed no significant differences among these three groups.

Differences in AD Caregivers As a Function of Support Group Attendance

We compared the 14 caregivers who attended a support group with the 20 who did not. The two groups did not differ reliably on age, education, or family income. Support group members had been caregiving for substantially longer periods of time, $F(1,31) = 7.66$, $p < 0.01$. Support group members rated themselves as significantly less lonely, $F(1,31) = 6.11$, $p < 0.05$, and had significantly higher percentages of NK cells than nonmembers, $F(1,29 = 7.10$, $p < 0.01$. The differences on other psychologic or immunologic parameters were not significant.

DISCUSSION

Taken together, these data support the primary hypothesis of the investigation: caregivers appear more distressed and have poorer immune function than their well-matched age peers. We found no evidence that the observed differences were a function of nutrition, alcohol use, or caffeine intake. Although the caregivers reported less sleep than comparison subjects, as would be expected from other studies (42), the amount of sleep was not reliably correlated with immune function or mood in caregivers.

The differences in immunity between the caregiving and comparison subject groups are particularly noteworthy, because these caregivers are less distressed than other caregiver samples described in the literature (15–17). These differences may be related to the fact that our caregivers were relatively well-educated, and income data suggest that they have more financial resources than described in other similar samples (33, 43). Given these relative advantages, it is reasonable to suggest that these data represent a ''best case scenario'' (44). The persistence of significant psychologic and physiologic differences between our two cohorts in spite of these relative advantages strongly supports the hypothesized negative impact of caregiving responsibilities.

In contrast to other studies (43, 45), we did not find that caregivers were more likely than individuals without comparable responsibilities to become isolated from their usual companions and social activities because of the time demands. However, we did find correlation evidence within the caregiver cohort that linked greater impairment in the AD victim with fewer social contacts and greater depression and loneliness. If caregivers experience increased social isolation as their relative's condition deteriorates, it could have important consequences; research with both older and younger adults suggests that social support may moderate stress-related depression or dysphoria and may also be related to morbidity and mortality (46, 47).

The immunologic data provide evidence of persistent alterations in cellular immunity associated with a chronic psychosocial stressor, in contrast to the longer-term adaptation or enhancement of immunity found in some studies with rodents (10, 11). Related evidence consistent with possible longer-term immunologic alterations in humans was provided in research on immune function, marital quality, and marital disruption (8); however, immunologic changes in these individuals were more closely tied to their adaptation to an acute stressor, marital disruption.

Although we did not find health differences between the two cohorts, the observed immunologic differences are consistent with the kinds of changes (though of a much lesser magnitude) that are observed in immune-suppressed patients. For example, transplant patients and AIDS patients are good examples of immune suppression, although resulting from different processes; within both groups it is known that reactivation of latent virus occurs, including reactivation of EBV with associated increases in EBV antibody titers (49). There are higher EBV antibody titers among elderly than among younger adults (50), consistent with evidence that the former have relative deficits compared to their younger counterparts on some functional or qualitative immunologic assays (25, 51).

Data from other studies suggest there may be a number of other stress-related immunologic changes associated with acute stress, and such changes may have health consequences. For example, medical students followed over an academic year showed higher EBV antibody titers concomitant with a decrease in specific cell killing of EBV-infected cells during examination, compared with samples taken between examination periods (52). Other concurrent immunologic changes included markedly lower production of γ interferon by lymphocytes stimulated with Con A associated with examination stress. The activity of a lymphokine, leukocyte migration-inhibition factor, normally suppressed during recrudescence of herpes simplex virus type 2 infections, was altered during examination periods, and an increase in both plasma and intracellular levels of cyclic AMP was associated with examination stress as well. The medical students also reported more illness during examination periods.

Chronic distress-related immunosuppression may have its most important health consequences in groups with other, preexisting immunologic impairments, such as older adults with age-related decrements in immune function (48). Indirect evidence consistent with this premise is provided by the remarkably high mortality rates for elderly psychiatric patients from pneumonia: within the first year after psychiatric admission, there are fifty times more deaths from this infectious disease than found among age-matched general population counterparts. The ratio drops to twenty times that of their age-matched counterparts by the second year of institutionalization, suggesting that the hospital environment per se may be a less critical factor in mortality than the transition (53). In this context it should be noted that depression is the leading reason for psychiatric hospitalization in the elderly (54).

Since the modal age of onset for AD is 65–69 years (14), AD caregivers are themselves most often middle-aged or elderly (55). The significant functional immunologic decrements that accompany aging (25) are thought to be associated with the increased morbidity and mortality of infectious disease in the elderly (49, 52). Longitudinal studies with chronically stressed at-risk groups like caregivers may provide valuable information on the contribution of psychosocial variables to morbidity and mortality.

REFERENCES

1. Solomon GF, Amkraut AA. *Psychoneuroendocrinological effects on the immune response.* Annu Rev Microbiol *35:155–184, 1981.*
2. Ader R (ed). Psychoneuroimmunology. *New York, Academic, 1981.*
3. Kiecolt-Glaser JK, Garner W, Speicher CE, Penn G, Glaser R. *Psychosocial modifiers of immunocompetence in medical students.* Psychosom Med *46:7–14, 1984.*
4. Kiecolt-Glaser JK, Glaser R, Strain E, Stout J, Tarr K, Holliday J, Speicher C. *Modulation of cellular immunity in medical students.* J Behav Med *9:5–21, 1986.*
5. Glaser R, Kiecolt-Glaser JK, Stout JC, Tarr KL, Holliday JE. *Stress-related impairments in cellular immunity.* Psychiatry Res *16:233–239, 1985.*
6. Glaser R, Kiecolt-Glaser JK, Speicher CE, Holliday JE. *Stress, loneliness, and changes in herpesvirus latency.* J Behav Med *8:249–260, 1985.*
7. Glaser R, Rice J, Speicher CE, Stout JC, Kiecolt-Glaser JK. *Stress depresses interferon production by leukocytes concomitant with a decrease in natural killer cell activity.* Behav Neurosci, *100:675–678, 1986.*
8. Kiecolt-Glaser JK, Fisher LD, Ogrocki P. Stout JC, Speicher CE, Glaser R.

Marital quality, marital disruption, and immune function. Psychosom Med *49: 13–34, 1987.*

9. *Stein M, Keller SE, Schleifer SJ. Stress and immunomodulation: The role of depression and neuroendocrine function.* J Immunol *135:827s–833s, 1985.*

10. *Monjan AA, Collector MI. Stress-induced modulation of the immune response.* Science *196:307–308, 1977.*

11. *Sklar LS, Anisman H. Stress and coping factors influence tumor growth.* Science *205:513–515, 1979.*

12. *Reisberg B (ed).* Alzheimer's Disease: The Standard Reference. *New York, Free Press, 1983.*

13. *Heckler MM. The fight against Alzheimer's Disease.* Am Psychol *40:1240–1244, 1985.*

14. *Heston LL, Mastri AR, Anderson VE, White G. Dementia of the Alzheimer type.* Arch Gen Psychiatry *38:1085–1091, 1981.*

15. *Fiore J, Becker J, Coppel DB. Social network interactions: A buffer or a stress?* Am J Community Psychol *11:423–439, 1983.*

16. *Crook TH, Miller NE. The challenge of Alzheimer's Disease.* Am Psychol *40: 1245–1250, 1985.*

17. *Eisdorfer C, Kennedy G, Wisnieski W, Cohen D. Depression and attributional style in families coping with the stress of caring for a relative with Alzheimer's Disease.* Gerontologist *23:115–116, 1983.*

18. *George LK, Gwyther LP. The dynamics of caregiver burden: Changes in caregiver well-being over time. Paper presented at the annual meeting of the Gerontological Society of America, San Antonio, November 1984.*

19. *Brocklehurst JC, Morris P, Andrews K, Richards B, Laycock P. Social effects of stroke.* Soc Sci Med *15A:35–39, 1981.*

20. *Sainsbury P, Grad de Alarcon J. The psychiatrist and the geriatric patient: The effects of community care on the family of the geriatric patient.* J Geriatr Psychiatry *4:23–41, 1970.*

21. *Schleifer SJ, Keller SE, Meyerson AT, Raskin MJ, Davis KL, Stein M. Lymphocyte function in major depressive disorder.* Arch Gen Psychiatry *41:484–486, 1984.*

22. *Kiecolt-Glaser JK, Stephens RE, Lipetz PD, Speicher CE, Glaser R. Distress and DNA repair in human lymphocytes.* J Behav Med *8:311–320, 1985.*

23. *Krauss IK. Between-and within-group comparisons in aging research. In Poon LA (ed),* Aging in the 1980s: Psychological Issues. *Washington, DC, 1980, pp. 542–551.*

24. *Kiecolt-Glaser JK, Glaser R, Williger D, Stout J, Messick G, Sheppard S, Ricker D, Romisher SC, Briner W, Bonnell G, Donnerberg R. Psychosocial enhancement of immunocompetence in a geriatric population.* Health Psychol *4: 25–41, 1985.*

25. *Goodwin JS, Searles RP, Tung KSK. Immunological responses of a healthy elderly population.* Clin Exp Immunol *48:403–410, 1982.*

26. *Goodwin JS, Messner RP, Williams RC, Inhibitors of T-cell mitogenesis: Effects of mitogen dosage.* Cell Immunol *45:303–308, 1979.*

27. *Rook KS. The negative side of social interaction: Impact on psychological well-being.* J Pers Soc Psychol *46:1097–1108, 1984.*

28. *Beck AT.* Depression: Clinical, Experimental, and Theoretical Aspects. *New York, Harper and Row, 1967.*

29. *Hammen CL. Assessment: A clinical cognitive emphasis. In Rehm LP (ed),* Behavioral Therapy for Depression: Present Status and Future Directions. *New York, Academic, 1981*

30. *Fillenbaum GG, Smyer MA. The development, validity, and reliability of the OARS Multidimensional Functional Assessment Questionnaire.* J Gerontol *36: 428–434, 1981.*

31. *Reifler BV, Eisdorfer C. A clinic for the impaired elderly and their families.* Am J Psychiatry *137:1399–1403, 1980.*

32. *Zarit SH, Orr NK, Zarit JM.* The Hidden Victims of Alzheimer's Disease: Families Under Stress. *New York, New York University Press, 1985.*

33. *Zarit SH, Todd PA, Zarit JM. Subjective burden of husbands and wives as caregivers: A longitudinal study.* Gerontologist *26:260–266, 1986.*

34. *Reinherz EL, Schlossmen SF. Regulation of immune response—Inducer and suppressor T-lymphocyte subsets in human beings.* N Engl J Med *303:370–373, 1980.*

35. *Heston LL. Genetic relationships in early-onset Alzheimer's dementia, pp 566–568. In Cutler NR, moderator, Alzheimer's disease and Down's syndrome: New insights.* Ann Inter Med *103:566–578, 1985.*

36. *Leffell MS, Lumsden L, Steiger WA. An analysis of T lymphocyte subpopulations in patients with Alzheimer's Disease.* J Am Geriatr Soc *33:4–8, 1985.*

37. *Chandra RK, Newberne PM.* Nutrition, Immunity and Infection: Mechanisms of Interactions. *New York, Plenum, 1977.*

38. *Rodkey FL. Direct spectrophotometric determination of albumin in human serum.* Clin Chem *11:478–487, 1985.*

39. *Doumas BT, Watson WA, Biggs HG. Albumin and the measurement of serum albumin with bromcresol green.* Clin Chim Acta *31:87–96, 1971.*

40. *Keyser JW.* Human Plasma Proteins. *New York, Wiley, 1979.*

41. *Buffone GJ.* Transferrin, ICS-14. *Fullerton CA, Beckman Instruments, 1980.*

42. *Rabins PV, Mace HL, Lucas MJ. The impact of dementia on the family.* JAMA *248:333–335, 1982.*

43. *George LK, Gwyther LP. Caregiver well-being: A multidimensional examination of family caregivers of demented adults.* Gerontologist *26:253–259, 1986.*

44. *Gwyther LP, George LK. Caregivers for dementia patients: Complex determinants of well-being and burden.* Gerontologist *26:245–247, 1986.*

45. *Johnson CL, Catalano DJ. A longitudinal study of family supports to impaired elderly.* Gerontologist *23:612–618, 1983.*

46. *Blazer D. Social support and mortality in an elderly community population.* Am J Epidemiol *115:684–694, 1982.*

47. *Cohen CI, Teresi J, Holmes D. Social networks, stress, and physical health: A longitudinal study of an inner-city elderly population.* J Gerontol *40:478–486, 1985.*

48. *Kiecolt-Glaser JK, Glaser R. Interpersonal relationships and immune function. In Carstensen L, Neale J (eds),* Mechanisms of Physiological Influence on Health. *New York, Wiley, in press.*

49. *Glaser R, Gottlieb-Stematsky T (eds).* Human Herpesvirus Infections: Clinical Aspects. *New York, Marcel Dekker, 1982.*

50. *Glaser R, Strain EC, Tarr K, Holliday JE, Donnerberg RL, Kiecolt-Glaser JK. Changes in Epstein-Barr virus antibody titers associated with aging.* Proc Soc Exp Biol Med *179:253–355, 1985.*

51. *Roberts-Thomson IC, Whittingham S, Youngchaiyud U, MacKay IR. Aging, immune response, and mortality.* Lancet *2:368–370, 1974.*

52. *Glaser R, Rice J, Sheridan J, Fertel R, Stout J, Speicher CE, Pinsky D, Kotur M, Post A, Beck M, Kiecolt-Glaser JK. Stress-related immune suppression: Health implications.* Brain Behav Immun, *in press.*

53. *Craig TJ, Lin SP. Mortality among elderly psychiatric patients: Basis for preventive intervention.* J Am Geriatr Soc *29:181–185, 1981.*

54. *Solomon K. The depressed patient: Social antecedents psychopathologic changes in the elderly.* J Am Geriatr Soc *29:14–18, 1981.*

55. *Zarit SH, Reever KE, Bach-Peterson J. Relatives of the impaired elderly: Correlates of feelings of burden.* Gerontologist *20:649–655, 1980.*

36. The Effects of Late-Life Spousal Bereavement over a Thirty-Month Interval

Larry W. Thompson, Dolores Gallagher-Thompson,
Andrew Futterman, Michael J. Gilewski,
and James Peterson

IT IS WELL documented that both younger and older bereaved individuals typically show many symptoms characteristic of depression (Breckenridge et al., 1986; Gallagher, Breckenridge, Thompson & Peterson, 1983; Lund, Caserta & Dimond, 1986; Murrell & Himmelfarb, 1989; Pearlin, 1982; Reich, Zautra & Guarnaccia, 1989; W. Stroebe, M. Stroebe & Domittner, 1985; Zisook & Schuchter, 1986) and report more physical complaints than nonbereaved individuals (Maddison & Viola, 1968; Thompson et al., 1984) in the months immediately following a loss. This negative impact of bereavement on mental and physical health has been called the *loss effect* (W. Stroebe & M. Stroebe, 1987). Although physical health changes have received considerable attention as a consequence of bereavement, we focus on measures of psychological distress in this chapter.

Gender may influence the response to loss and the magnitude of the loss effect, though the extent and nature of this influence is controversial. One set of studies suggests that women demonstrate more emotional distress than men in bereavement (e.g., Gallagher, Breckenridge, Thompson, Peterson 1983). This finding is in keeping with more generally observed sex differences in depressive symptomatology (see Nolen-Hoeksema, 1987, for review). Another set of studies suggests that although widows may report more distress, it is the widowers who actually suffer more (M. Stroebe & W. Stroebe, 1983). Yet other studies point to broad similarities in the bereavement response of men and women (Lund, Caserta & Dimond, 1986; Van Zandt, Mou & Abbott, 1989).

The duration of time following loss and the method of mental and physical

Reprinted by permission from *Psychology and Aging* 6, no. 3 (1991): 1–8. Copyright © 1991 by the American Psychological Association.

health assessment are two additional important determinants of the degree of loss effect (W. Stroebe & M. Stroebe, 1987). Although the bereaved may report poorer physical health and more depressive symptomatology at two to four months following loss (Gallagher, Breckenridge, Thompson & Peterson, 1983; Parkes & Weiss, 1983; Thompson et al., 1984), by 2 years post-loss most studies suggest that bereaved and nonbereaved persons are comparable on indexes of depression (Lund, Caserta & Dimond, 1989; W. Stroebe & M. Stroebe, 1987).

When asked about their adjustment to loss in more specific terms, however, as opposed to describing their general mood (e.g., on a depression inventory), studies present a different picture (see Wortman & Silver, 1989, for a review). Even 2 to 4 years after loss, bereaved individuals still frequently report difficulties adapting to the loss (Lund et al., 1985; Parkes & Weiss, 1983; Zisook & Schuchter, 1986). Such findings, coupled with reported differences between the symptomatology of grief and depression on depression scales (Breckenridge et al., 1986; Gallagher, Breckenridge, Thompson, Dessonville & Amaral, 1982), point to the importance of assessing the bereavement response by using specific measures of grief and adaptation to loss in addition to general measures of psychological distress, especially later in bereavement. Few studies have reported on changes in both grief and other measures of distress.

Although several studies have evaluated bereavement effects longitudinally (Falleti et al., 1989; Heyman & Gianturco, 1973; Lund, Caserta & Dimond, 1986, 1989; Maddison & Viola, 1968; Parkes & Weiss, 1983; W. Stroebe 1985; Van Zandt, Mou & Abbott, 1989; Zisook & Schuchter, 1986), only a few studies have compared an older sample of widows and widowers with an appropriate comparison sample (e.g., Faletti et al., 1989; Lund, Caserta & Dimond, 1989; Van Zandt, Mou & Abbott, 1989).

Our study reports the effects of spousal bereavement on psychological distress over a 2½ year period in a community sample of older men and women (over 55 years of age). In this study we used standardized measures of grief, depression, and psychopathology, permitting an examination of different dimensions of psychological distress. We used a comparison community sample of elderly men and women who were not currently undergoing spousal bereavement, but who had recently experienced death of a close friend or family member, thus permitting an evaluation of bereavement effects on psychological distress independent of normal aging effects.

Three hypotheses were proposed:

1. The first hypothesis predicted that elders who have suffered the loss of

their spouse would report higher levels of distress at 2, 12, and 30 months than would elders who have not suffered a similar loss. More specifically, we hypothesized that measures of grief would show greater differences between bereaved individuals and controls than would measures of depression and general psychopathology. This is in keeping with findings reported previously (Gallagher, Breckenridge, Thompson, & Peterson, 1983) and studies indicating long-term difficulties in resolving grief and issues of loss (Lund, Caserta & Dimond, 1985; Parkes & Weiss, 1983; Wortman & Silver, 1989; Zisook & Schuchter, 1986).

2. The second hypothesis predicted that the bereaved individuals and controls would demonstrate differential change in measures of psychological distress over time. It was anticipated that bereaved elders would report less distress at 12 and 30 months following loss than they had at 2 months. Similar measures among comparison controls, however, were not expected to change.

3. The third hypothesis predicted that women would report greater psychological distress than men at 2, 12, and 30 months, regardless of bereavement status. This is in keeping with previously reported findings of gender differences in mental health (Gallagher, Breckenridge, Thompson & Peterson, 1983). More generally, it is also in keeping with gender differences in depressive symptomatology reported by Nolen-Hoeksema (1987).

METHOD

Subjects

Two hundred and twelve bereaved elders (99 men and 113 women) and a comparison control sample of 162 elders (84 men and 78 women) participated in this study. Details of the sampling procedure and group demographics have been described in earlier studies (Gallagher, Breckenridge, Thompson & Peterson, 1983; Thompson et al., 1984). Briefly, to obtain participants for the bereaved sample, death certificates at the Los Angeles County Health Department were searched periodically, and all spouses of persons over 55 who had died within the preceding 2 to 4 weeks were mailed a description of the project and a stamped postcard with which willingness to be interviewed could be indicated. Mailings were sent to 2,450 persons. Of the 735 who responded (30%), 212 met the age criteria and also resided within a reasonable distance from the research center to permit home interviews. Participants for the comparison sample were recruited from senior centers, residential facilities for elders, and the Emeriti Center mailing list of the University of

Southern California. These were adults over age 55, who either were currently married or, if currently single, had not lost a spouse through death or divorce within the past 5 years. However, to be eligible for participation in the study, each control respondent had to have experienced the death of either another family member or a close friend within the past 5 years. Both bereaved and comparison samples can be characterized as Caucasian, well educated (80% had some high school), and of moderate socioeconomic status (most had income between $10,000 and $30,000). The age range of all subjects was 55–83 years. The two groups were roughly comparable in age: Means for bereaved and comparison samples were 68.20 years ($SD = 7.84$ years) and 70.11 years ($SD = 7.65$ years), respectively. Subjects in both groups had been married for many years: the mean number of years married for the bereaved group was 38.68 years ($SD = 13.08$), and the mean for the comparison sample (including those who were no longer married or were living alone) was 37.43 years ($SD = 14.02$).

Procedure

Structured interviews were conducted at three times following the loss of spouse, at approximately 2 months, 12 months, and 30 months. Interviews and measures were completed in the subjects' homes unless they requested to come to the research center. In the interviews the following were reviewed: demographic characteristics, religious beliefs and practices, coping strategies used in response to spousal loss, prior stressful life events, utilization of social supports, upheaval in routines of daily living, judgments of subjects' marital relationship, and self-ratings of psychological and physical health status. Comparable interviews were conducted at identical intervals with the comparison subjects. (Copies of all measures are available on request.)

Four self-report measures of psychological distress obtained at all times of measurement were considered in our analyses, as follows: (a) the *Beck Depression* Inventory (BDI; Beck et al., 1961); (b) the Global Severity Scale of mental health symptoms on the *Brief Symptom* Inventory (BSI; Derogatis, 1977; Derogatis & Spencer, 1982) (c) rating of current grief on the Texas Inventory of Grief–Revised (TIGCUR: Faschingbauer, 1981; Faschingbauer, Devaul & Zisook, 1977), and (d) rating of past grief on the Texas Inventory of Grief–Revised (TIGPAST; Faschingbauer, 1981; Faschingbauer, Devaul & Zisook, 1977).

The BDI is a multiple-choice symptom scale developed to assess the severity of depression. Twenty-one items tap aspects of depressive features, such as sleep and appetite problems, sadness, guilt and self-reproach, suicidal ideation, and loss of interest in everyday activities. Reliability and concurrent validity (with psychiatric diagnoses) have been demonstrated in older adult samples (Gallagher, Breckenridge, Steinmetz, & Thompson, 1983; Gallagher, Nies & Thompson, 1982).

The BSI is a 53-item version of the Hopkins Symptom Checklist (HSCL-90; Derogatis, 1977) developed by Derogatis and Spencer (1982). The BSI yields scores on nine dimensions of psychopathology (e.g., psychoticism, anxiety, phobic reaction). In our report, the Global Severity Index, an average of the nine scales, was used (BSISEV). Adequate psychometric properties of this instrument and index have been demonstrated in several populations and are reviewed in Derogatis and Spencer (1982). Norms for this measure with the elderly are reported in Hale, Cochran, and Hedgepeth (1984).

The TIG is a self-report measure of both past disruption due to loss and current feelings of grief. Ratings of agreement with descriptive statements (e.g., "I was unusually irritable after the person died," "I miss this person terribly") are made on Likert-type scales (1 = entirely false, 5 = entirely true). Eight items comprise the past disruption scale. (TIGPAST) with scores potentially ranging from 0 to 40;13 items comprise the current grief scale (TIGCUR), with scores ranging on this scale from 0 to 65. Reliabilities from .70 to .90 have been reported for the two TIG subscales; these and other psychometric properties are reviewed in Faschingbauer (1981) and Faschingbauer, Devaul, and Zisook (1977). Bereaved subjects were instructed to fill out the form with their spouse in mind. Control subjects were asked to think of a recent death of a significant person in their life, identify that person by relationship (e.g., sister, brother, mother, father, in-law, close friend, etc.), indicate how many months ago the death occurred, and complete the measure with that death in mind. Higher scores on all measures are indicative of greater psychological distress.

Design

To test hypotheses relating to group and gender differences and to change across time in distress following the loss of spouse, a $2 \times 2 \times 3$ multivariate profile analysis of repeated measures (Morrison, 1976) was used. In this design, group (bereaved vs. controls) and gender (male vs. female) were the between-subjects, independent variables; the four indexes of psychological distress were within-subject, dependent variables measured at 2, 12, and 30 months. This design is doubly multivariate (Bock, 1975): First, there are multiple dependent variables that are analyzed through multivariate analysis of variance (MANOVA); second, each variable is measured more than once in a repeated-measures fashion. Taken together, each of these repeated-measures are treated as a multivariate profile and analyzed through a MANOVA. Analyses involved ordinary least squares estimation and associate listwise-deletion procedures (Wilkinson, 1989). In all analyses, multivariate tests were conducted first, by using the F approximation of the Wilks's lambda likelihood ratio (Rao, 1973). When multivariate tests were significant, univariate tests were then examined by using the Bonferroni procedure to maintain Type I error at nominal levels (Bray & Maxwell, 1985).

We completed two sets of analyses to test the hypotheses: The first compared the bereaved group and the *total* control group across the 30-month period, but included only the BDI and the BSISEV scores. These analyses permitted us to evaluate bereavement and gender effects and their interaction with time on measures of depression and general psychopathology.

The second set of analyses included the two grief measures as well, but a restricted sample of the controls was used in the comparison with the bereaved samples. This was done because legitimate concerns could be raised as to whether spousal loss is distinctly different from the grief experienced because of other losses, and therefore comparisons between the two might be inappropriate. This issue has received attention indirectly (e.g., Wortman & Silver, 1989), but there have been few empirical studies comparing the impact of spousal loss with the loss of other family members. Bass, Noelker, Townsend, and Deimling (1990) reported that conjugal compared with parental loss results in lower well-being and reported health changes along with increased difficulty in adjustment, but acknowledged some controversy in the literature even about this and suggested that "whether and how the relationship between survivors and deceased relatives may influence the bereavement experience" (1990, p. 33) should be a useful point of departure for subsequent studies.

For purposes of this article, we considered that grief in general can be viewed on a continuum, regardless of the source of loss. Note that the TIG was designed to measure the level of grief, irrespective of the nature of the relationship between the bereaved and the deceased. To our knowledge, prior research comparing intensity of grief following loss of spouse as opposed to other relatives has not been assessed by using a measure designed specifically to report levels of the grief experience. However, because there may be some concern on the part of the readers regarding this comparison, we decided to include only those control subjects who were reporting a loss that presumably would be most similar to the loss of a spouse. Therefore, in our sample we felt the comparison controls for the grief measures should be restricted to subjects who were reporting their level of grief for the loss of another immediate family member.

RESULTS

Of the 374 subjects (212 bereaved, 162 controls) who began the study, 224 (60%; 123 bereaved, 101 controls) completed all of the self-report measures at all three times. This level of subject attrition is similar to that of other bereavement studies involving elders; for example, Lund, Caserta, and Dimond (1986) had a 34% attrition rate at the end of 2 years.

Table 36.1 shows the means and standard deviations of each distress measure at 2, 12, and 30 months for those subjects who remained in the study. Inspection of the means for the BDI indicates that all four groups were within

Table 36.1. Means and Standard Deviations for Self-Report Measures of Depression, General Psychopathology, and Grief Obtained from Elderly Widows, Widowers, and Control Subjects

	Bereaved				Controls			
	Men (*n* = 42)		Women (*n* = 81)		Men (*n* = 51)		Women (*n* = 50)	
Time point	*M*	*SD*	*M*	*SD*	*M*	*SD*	*M*	*SD*
2 months postloss								
BDI	7.66	6.26	10.65	8.23	4.34	4.21	7.78	6.76
BSISEV	.51	.51	.62	.54	.38	.44	.49	.42
TIGCUR	43.97	10.36	44.66	12.10	27.08	11.15	30.59	13.60
TIGPAST	18.57	6.73	19.73	6.89	11.49	5.57	13.71	8.89
12 months postloss								
BDI	6.50	9.43	8.10	7.18	5.65	5.41	6.56	6.41
BSISEV	.38	.33	.47	.40	.36	.35	.42	.42
TIGCUR	38.87	13.40	39.07	11.20	24.64	11.02	29.66	12.60
TIGPAST	18.85	12.02	19.33	6.59	11.40	5.30	14.02	6.85
30 months postloss								
BDI	5.28	5.28	7.22	6.31	6.24	6.88	6.62	5.83
BSISEV	.36	.45	.49	.52	.41	.46	.41	.42
TIGCUR	36.12	10.12	35.98	11.46	26.24	11.55	30.09	11.43
TIGPAST	17.64	7.36	17.67	7.37	12.00	5.02	13.14	7.47

NOTE: Grief measures are included here for the total control group, although analyses of grief measures reported in the text were completed by using the restricted comparison control group reported in Table 36.2. BDI = Beck Depression Inventory. BSISEV = Global severity rating of the Brief Symptom Inventory. TIGCUR = Rating of current grief on the Texas Inventory of Grief–Revised. TIGPAST = Rating of grief at the time of the loss on the Texas Inventory of Grief–Revised.

normal ranges at each time of measurement, with the exception of the bereaved women at 2 months following the loss of the spouse. Bereaved women then had a mean BDI score of 10.65, which is in the mild depression range clinically (Gallagher, Breckenridge, Steinmetz & Thompson, 1983). The BSI-SEV scores were very similar to means for normal community samples in this age range at all time points (Hale, Cochran & Hedgepeth, 1984). The level of current grief (TIGCUR) reported by bereaved elders at 2 months (M = 43.39 for men and women combined) appeared to be somewhat higher than that reported for two younger adult samples (Faschingbauer, 1981). However, TIGCUR means at 12 and 30 months (Ms = 37.97 and 35.80, respectively, for men and women combined) were more similar to those reported by Faschingbauer (1981) for the time period covering the 1st year of bereavement (M = 37.10) and the period from 1 to 5 years following spousal loss (M = 34.28). Comparisons between the two samples also appeared to be similar on the measure reflecting the level of disruption at the time of the loss (TIGPAST). Unfortunately, more specific age and time comparisons could not be made with the data presented by Faschingbauer because finer grained breakdowns of his data (by age and time since loss) were not available.

Overall Severity of Distress among Bereaved and Control Elders

Hypothesis 1 predicted that scores on measures of psychological distress would be greater in the bereaved compared with the control group. In particular, this hypothesis predicted that this effect would be more evident in measures of grief rather than measures of symptoms of depression or general psychopathology. To test this hypothesis, we considered results from both sets of analyses. In the first set of analyses the MANOVA completed on the entire sample, using only the BDI and BSISEV scores, yielded an overall main effect for group that was not significant, $F(2, 233) = 0.76$. The interaction of Group $\times$ Time for these two measures was highly significant, but this is reported later. In contrast, when the grief measures were included, while using the restricted comparison sample, the main effect of bereavement summed across all three measurement times was highly significant, $F(4, 116) = 19.95$, $p < .001$. A closer look at the univariate analyses indicated that this was due primarily to the measures of current grief, $F(1, 169) = 63.90$, $p < .001$, and past grief, $F(1, 169) = 38.17$, $p < .001$, rather than the measures of depression, $F(1, 169) = 1.48$, and general psychopathology, $F(1, 169) = 2.273$. Table 36.2 provides the means and standard deviations for the

Table 36.2. Measures of Depression, General Psychopathology, and Grief for Elderly Widows and Widowers Compared with Control Subjects Who Had Lost an Immediate Family Member

	Bereaved				Controls			
	Men ($n = 42$)		Women ($n = 81$)		Men ($n = 24$)		Women ($n = 50$)	
Time point	M	SD	M	SD	M	SD	M	SD
2 months postloss								
BDI	7.66	6.26	10.65	8.23	4.38	4.91	7.04	6.59
BSISEV	.51	.51	.62	.54	.27	.34	.40	.43
TIGCUR	43.97	10.36	44.66	12.10	25.00	10.25	28.11	12.70
TIGPAST	18.57	6.73	19.73	6.89	10.55	4.84	11.77	6.47
12 months postloss								
BDI	6.50	9.43	8.10	7.18	5.75	6.16	7.19	6.85
BSISEV	.38	.33	.47	.40	.35	.38	.36	.44
TIGCUR	38.87	13.40	39.07	11.20	24.29	10.17	26.88	11.10
TIGPAST	18.85	12.02	19.33	6.59	12.62	5.31	13.19	7.12
30 months postloss								
BDI	5.28	5.28	7.22	6.31	5.08	6.24	5.96	5.84
BSISEV	.36	.45	.49	.52	.33	.49	.40	.41
TIGCUR	36.12	10.12	35.98	11.46	24.25	9.02	29.19	10.87
TIGPAST	17.64	7.36	17.67	7.37	11.37	5.30	12.79	6.72

NOTE: BDI = Beck Depression Inventory. BSISEV = Global severity rating of the Brief Symptom Inventory. TIGCUR = Rating of current grief on the Texas Inventory of Grief–Revised. TIGPAST = Rating of grief at the time of the loss of the Texas Inventory of Grief–Revised.

spousally bereaved and their control counterparts who reported grief due to the death of an immediate family member. As can be seen in both Tables 36.1 and 36.2, the TIGCUR and TIGPAST were higher for the spousally bereaved than for the two comparison groups throughout the 30-month period, whereas the BDI and the BSISEV measures were elevated for the bereaved group only during the early portion of the bereavement period. Thus, Hypothesis 1 is generally supported. However, Group $\times$ Time analyses revealed significant differences between groups on the depression and general psychopathology measures at specific time points, as well.

Differential Change in Psychological Distress of Bereaved and Control Elders

Hypothesis 2 predicted a decrease in psychological distress over a 30-month period among bereaved elders, whereas little change was expected among members of the comparison group. The test of this hypothesis was the Bereavement Status × Time of Measurement interaction effect in the MANOVA. Both sets of analyses yielded highly significant interactions, $F(4, 231)$ = 2.90, $p < .05$, and $F(8, 162) = 4.64$, $p < .001$, for the first and second sets, respectively). In the first set a significant linear, $F(1, 234) = 5.641$, $p < .02$, and quadratic, $F(1, 234) = 4.671$, $p < .05$, trend was observed for the BDI, as well as significant quadratic trend for the BSISEV, $F(1, 234)$ = 4.891, $p < .05$. Inspection of Table 36.1 indicates that the bereaved showed a greater decline in measures of psychological distress over the 2½ year period of the study than did the controls. In the second set of analyses, univariate tests of the linear and quadratic trends (i.e., orthogonal polynomials) demonstrated that the multivariate Group × Time effect was attributable primarily to a significant Group × Quadratic Trend in BDI, $F(1, 169)$ = 5.58, $p < .02$, and a Group × Linear Trend in TIGCUR, $F(1, 169)$ = 25.39, $p < .001$.

A comparison of adjacent times of measurement in the first set of analyses (i.e., 2 vs. 12 months, and 12 vs. 30 months) showed a group effect on change in the BDI from 2 to 12 months, $F(1, 234) = 7.78$, $p < .01$, but no effect thereafter from 12 to 30 months, $F(1, 234) = 1.20$. An inspection of Table 36.1 shows that the BDI scores for the bereaved subjects were higher initially but, as will be seen in subsequent analyses, by the end of 1 year there was no difference between bereaved and control subjects. A similar pattern was evident for the BSISEV. There was a significant decline from 2 to 12 months, $F(1, 234) = 4.44$, $p < .05$, but no effect from 12 to 30 months, $F(1, 234)$ = 0.10. This picture was still apparent for the BDI and BSISEV in the reduced sample that included the two grief measures (Table 36.2).

Simple effects of time within each group further illustrates the nature of this interaction. For the bereaved group, there was a highly significant decline from 2 to 12 months on both the BDI, $F(1, 121) = 12.34$, $p < .005$, and the BSISEV, $F(1, 121) = 7.27$, $p < .01$, as expected, with no significant decline from 12 to 30 months on either measure, $F(1, 121) = 0.17$, $F(1, 121)$ = 0.11, for the BDI and the BSISEV, respectively. Control subjects, on the other hand, showed no significant changes on any of these comparisons. In contrast, the TIGCUR was highly significant for the period from 12 to 30 months, $F(1, 169) = 4.55$, $p < .05$, as well as from 2 to 12 months, $F(1, 169) = 7.50$, $p < .01$. As expected, the control subjects showed no change across time for TIGCUR. There was no significant change across time for TIGPAST for the control group. Turning now to a comparison of groups at each time of measurement, the effect of bereavement status on overall psychological distress was significant at all three times: at 2 months, $F(4, 166)$ = 25.18, $p < .001$; at 12 months, $F(4, 166)$ = 13.39, $p < .001$; and at 30 months, $F(4, 166)$ = 8.95, $p < .001$. Once again, univariate tests highlighted a different pattern for the symptoms of depression and general psychopathology than for the measures of grief. Significant differences in grief between bereaved and control subjects were apparent throughout: at 2 months: TIGCUR, $F(1, 220)$ = 91.83, $p < .001$; TIGPAST, $F(1, 220)$ = 46.97, $p < .001$; at 12 months: TIGCUR, $F(1, 220)$ = 65.09, $p < .001$; TIGPAST, $F(1, 220)$ = 36.87, $p < .001$; and at 30 months: TIGCUR, $F(1, 220)$ = 32.52, $p < .001$; TIGPAST, $F(1, 220)$ = 30.33, $p < .001$. As Table 36.1 illustrates, the bereaved sample reported higher levels of both current and past grief than the controls at 2, 12, and 30 months following loss. It is noteworthy that although there was a steady decline in TIGCUR throughout the study, the spousally bereaved were still showing significantly higher current and past grief at 30 months than were their control counterparts who were grieving the death of a nonspouse family member.

The effect of bereavement on symptoms of depression and general psychopathology, on the other hand, was significant only at 2 months following loss: BDI, $F(1, 169)$ = 5.20, $p < .05$; BSISEV, $F(1, 169)$ = 5.04, $p < .05$. Bereaved subjects reported more severe depression and more severe psychopathology. At both 12 and 30 months following loss, the univariate values were nonsignificant: BDI, $F(1, 169)$ = 0.05, at 12 months; BDI, $F(1, 169)$ = 0.89, at 30 months; BSISEV, $F(1, 169)$ = 0.66, at 12 months; and BSISEV, $F(1, 169)$ = 1.04, at 30 months. This pattern was identical for the larger sample in which only the BDI and BSISEV scores were included for analyses.

Thus, Hypothesis 2 is supported. Bereaved subjects showed greater declines across time than did the controls for measures of current grief, depression, and general psychopathology, and the only change in the measure of past grief was a slight increase for the control group. By the end of 1 year, depression and psychopathology had decreased to a point near the control group levels and showed minimal declines thereafter. The level of current grief, on the other hand, continued to decrease significantly throughout the 30-month period but was still higher than the levels for the control group at the end of 2½ years. The measure of past grief was also higher for the bereaved than for the controls, at all times of measurement.

Gender Differences in Psychological Distress

In the first set of analyses, the MANOVA indicated that the overall main effect of gender was significant, $F(2, 233) = 3.67$, $p < .05$. Univariate analyses showed that both the BDI, $F(1, 234) = 7.32$, $p < .01$, and the BSISEV, $F(1, 234) = 4.15$, $p < .05$, were significantly higher in women than in men. Gender was also assessed at 2, 12, and 30 months separately in the MANOVA. Women reported greater depression at 2 months, $F(1, 234) = 9.95$, $p < .01$, and 12 months, $F(1, 234) = 7.84$, $p < .01$, but not at 30 months, $F(1, 234) = 0.85$. The BSISEV was higher for women at 2 months, $F(1, 234) = 9.07$, $p < .01$; but not at 12 months, $F(1, 234) = 2.45$; or 30 months, $F(1, 234) = 1.08$. The interaction between gender and bereavement status was not significant, $F(2, 233) = 0.66$.

In contrast, the second set of analyses, which included the grief measures, did not yield a significant overall main effect of gender, $F(4, 166) = 1.43$. In view of the gender effects seen earlier, and the fact that sex differences are frequently reported on depression measures, it seemed reasonable to evaluate the four measures separately for these two groups. As noted previously, univariate analysis showed a significant gender effect for the BDI, $F(1, 169) = 5.73$, $p < .02$, and the BSISEV, $F(1, 169) = 4.70$, $p < .05$, at 2 months, but this effect was not apparent for TIGCUR, $F(1, 169) = 0.33$, or TIGPAST $F(1, 169) = 2.56$. There was no evidence of a Gender × Time, Gender × Group, or third order interaction for any of the four measures. At 12 months the effect of gender on the BDI was still significant, $F(1, 169) = 5.16$, $p < .05$, but there was no difference for the BSISEV, $F(1, 169) = 0.83$, TIGCUR, $F(1, 169) = 0.07$, or TIGPAST, $F(1, 169) = 0.62$. As with the analyses at 2 months, none of the interactions were significant. By 30 months there was no gender effect on any of the measures.

Looking within the spousally bereaved group only, at 2 months the overall effect of gender in the MANOVA was significant, $F(4, 118) = 2.45$, $p < .05$. Once again, this was due to the difference for the BDI, $F(1, 121) = 4.63$, $p < .05$, and the BSISEV, $F(1, 121) = 4.84$, $p < .05$. There was no significant effect of gender for the TIGCUR, $F(1, 121) = 8.23$, and the TIGPAST, $F(1, 121) = 2.23$. At 12 months the MANOVA for gender was again significant, $F(4, 118) = 2.64$, $p < .05$. Univariate analyses showed a significant effect for the BDI, $F(1, 121) = 8.474$, $p < .005$, but not for the BSISEV, $F(1, 121) = 2.15$, the TIGCUR, $F(1, 121 = 0.06$, or the TIGPAST, $F(1,121) = 0.18$. There was no significant gender effect at 30 months. The Gender × Bereavement Status interaction effect on psychological distress was nonsignificant at all three times of measurement: at 2 months, $F(4, 166)$ = 0.52; at 12 months, $F(4, 166)$ = 0.44; and at 30 months, $F(4, 166)$ = 1.08.

Thus, in general these data suggest that women report more symptoms of depression and overall psychopathology than men, particularly in the 1st year of bereavement, but do not report more grief following loss. In fact, as Tables 36.1 and 36.2 show, the level of grief among widowers and widows at 2, 12, and 30 months was approximately equal.

DISCUSSION

Results indicate that significant differences in psychological distress were found on several standardized measures at 2, 12, and 30 months following death of the spouse between bereaved and comparison subjects who also reported grief due to the loss of an immediate family member. Although severity of depression and psychopathology in older spousally bereaved men and women returned to the level of the comparison sample by 12 months, differences in the severity of self-reported current and past grief between these two groups remained for 30 months post-loss.

These findings highlight important differences between grief and depression over the bereavement course, especially as time goes on and 2 to 3 years have passed. These data are consistent with other reports pointing out that although depression or psychopathology may subside over the first 12 months, distress over issues relating to the loss itself is likely to persist for a number of years (Parkes & Weiss, 1983).

Women, regardless of bereavement status, reported more depression and symptoms of psychopathology than men, but gender differences were minimal in the expression of grief. A possible explanation for this might be that behavioral expressions of grief, such as weeping for the lost spouse, yearning for their presence, remembering the spouse fondly, and so on, are consistent with both male and female gender roles, but expressions of depression are not. This explanation finds support in two recent studies and in a recent review of the depression literature: Futterman, Gallagher, Thompson, Lovett, and Gilewski (1990) found that both widowers and widows similarly exaggerate the positive attributes of their lost spouse and marriage. Cornelius (1984), in a study of implicit rules or "scripts" that constrain emotional expression, found that men and women use similar scripts in determining the appropriateness and meaningfulness of weeping. Taken together, these findings suggest that both men and women express longing for their lost spouse in similar ways.

Nolen-Hoeksema (1987), on the other hand, presented a comprehensive review of the gender differences in depression literature and described a clear pattern of results: Women report more depressive symptoms than men. She provides a potential explanation for this consistent finding: Women ruminate over depressive thoughts and overreport depression, whereas men deny such thoughts and underreport depression. Different gender-related behavioral styles such as these are compatible with findings of gender differences in depression, regardless of bereavement status. Following loss or any other stressor, men and women will exhibit different tendencies to express depressive symptomatology.

Clinically, these results are instructive for a number of reasons. First, they emphasize the need for a broader based assessment of the grieving person. In addition to the evaluation of more general mood and psychopathological symptomatology, this should include a more direct assessment of symptoms of grief and loss, reflecting the intensity of yearning for the person who died and how this might have an impact on various facets of current social adjustment.

Second, these findings may have implications for the development of models of normal grieving (c.f. Wortman & Silver, 1989, for a detailed evaluation of current theories of coping with loss). Thus, although a sizeable proportion of elderly persons undergoing bereavement can be expected to report minimal symptoms of general distress within the 1st year, it appears that adaptation to the loss of a spouse, if measured specifically in terms of grief resolution, may take much longer than 2 or 3 years, if it ever occurs. That is, contrary to theories suggesting stages of grief culminating in grief-resolution, it may be that thoroughly working through the pain relating to the loss of a spouse of 20 to 30 years is not something to be expected. As Wortman and Silver (1989) suggested, complete grief-resolution simply may not occur. On the contrary, perhaps, the normal grief response may involve living with grief long after the loss occurs and learning to mentally "compartmentalize" distress associated with the loss and recognize appropriate times to express it.

These results also have implications for the bereavement researcher. W. Stroebe and M. Stroebe (1987) suggested that when evaluating bereavement-specific aspects of loss (e.g., yearning for the deceased) it is not essential to have a comparison sample. When assessing bereavement response among elders, however, this suggestion may not be valid. More often than not, elders have had to deal with losses of significant others prior to the loss of their spouse (Heyman & Gianturco, 1973). It is not surprising, therefore, that the control subjects in our sample reported some grief on current and past grief inventories. Although their level of grief was not equal to that found in the spousally bereaved sample, it was not insignificant (either then or at 12 and 30 months), suggesting that other losses clearly have their own long-term impact.

There are several limitations to be noted regarding this study. The first concerns generalizability of findings because this sample consisted of a well-educated Caucasian group who volunteered to participate in longitudinal research. We do not know the extent to which their experience is similar to that of other social or ethnic groups, or to the less socially advantaged. Second, it would be desirable to have followed these subjects longer, to determine if subjective grief remains high for an even greater number of years and thus empirically test whether or not spousal grief ever really ends. Finally, careful longitudinal research is needed to investigate the long-term effects of other types of major losses, such as death of one's adult child, which may cause even more profound grief than loss of a spouse.

REFERENCES

Bass, D. M., Noelker, L. S., Townsend, A. L. & Deimling, G. T. (1990). Losing an aged relative: Perceptual differences between spouses and adult children. Omega, 21, 21–40.

Beck, A. T., Ward, C. H., Mendelson, M., Mock, J. E. & Erbaugh, J. (1961). An inventory for measuring depression. Archives of General Psychiatry, 4, 561–571.

Bock, R. D. (1975). Multivariate statistical methods in behavioral research. New York: McGraw-Hill.

Bray, J. H. & Maxwell, S. E. (1985). Multivariate analysis of variance. Beverly Hills, CA: Sage.

Breckenridge, J. N., Gallagher, D., Thompson, L. W. & Peterson, J. (1986). Characteristic depressive symptoms of bereaved elders. Journal of Gerontology, 41, 163–168.

Cornelius, R. (1984). A role model of adult emotional expression. In C. Z. Malatesta & C. E. Izard (Eds.), Emotion in adult development (pp. 213–235). Beverly Hills, CA: Sage.

Derogatis, L. (1977). SCL-90: Administration, scoring, and procedures manual—1. Baltimore, MD: Johns Hopkins University School of Medicine.

Derogatis, L. & Spencer, P. (1982). The Brief Symptom Inventory (BSI) administration, scoring and procedures manual. Baltimore, MD: Johns Hopkins University School of Medicine.

Falleti, M. V., Gibbs, J. M., Clark, M. C., Pruchno, R. A. & Berman, E. C. (1989).

Longitudinal course of bereavement in older adults. In D. A. Lund (Ed.), Older bereaved spouses: Research with practical applications *(pp. 37–51). New York: Hemisphere.*

Faschingbauer, T. R. *(1981).* Texas Inventory of Grief–Revised manual. *Houston, TX: Honeycomb.*

Faschingbauer, T. R., Devaul, R. D. & Zisook, S. *(1977). Development of the Texas Inventory of Grief.* American Journal of Psychiatry, 134, *696–698.*

Futterman, A., Gallagher, D., Thompson, L. W., Lovett, S. & Gilewski, M. *(1990). Retrospective assessment of marital adjustment and depression during the first two years of spousal bereavement.* Psychology and Aging, 5, *277–283.*

Gallagher, D., Breckenridge, J. N., Steinmetz, J. & Thompson, L. W. *(1983). The Beck Depression Inventory and the Research Diagnostic Criteria.* Journal of Consulting and Clinical Psychology, 51, *945–946.*

Gallagher, D., Breckenridge, J. N., Thompson, L. W. Dessonville, C. & Amaral, P. *(1982). Similarities and differences between normal grief and depression in older adults.* Essence, 5, *127–140.*

Gallagher, D., Breckenridge, J., Thompson, L. W. & Peterson, J. A. *(1983). Effects of bereavement on indicators of mental health in elderly widows and widowers.* Journal of Gerontology, 38, *565–571.*

Gallagher, D., Nies, G. & Thompson, L. W. *(1982). Reliability of the Beck Depression Inventory with older adults.* Journal of Consulting and Clinical Psychology, 50, *152–153.*

Hale, W. D., Cochran, C. D. & Hedgepeth, B. *(1984). Norms for the elderly in the Brief Symptom Inventory.* Journal of Consulting and Clinical Psychology, 52, *321–322.*

Heyman, D. K. & Gianturco, D. T. *(1973). Long-term adaptation by the elderly to bereavement.* Journal of Gerontology, 28, *359–362.*

Lund, D. A., Caserta, M. S. & Dimond, M. F. *(1986). Gender differences through two years of bereavement among the elderly.* The Gerontologist, 26, *314–320.*

Lund, D. A., Caserta, M. S. & Dimond, M. F. *(1989). Impact of spousal bereavement on subjective well-being of older adults. In D. A. Lund (Ed.),* Older bereaved spouses: Research with practical applications *(pp. 3–15). New York: Hemisphere.*

Lund, D. A., Dimond, M. F., Caserta, M. S., Johnson, R. J., Poulton, J. L. & Connelly, J. R. *(1985). Identifying elderly with coping difficulties after two years of bereavement.* Omega, 16, *213–224.*

Maddison, D. C. & Viola, A. *(1968). The health of widows in the year following bereavement.* Journal of Psychosomatic Research, 12, *297–306.*

Morrison, D. F. *(1976).* Multivariate methods in statistics. *New York: McGraw-Hill.*

Murrell, S. A. & Himmelfarb, S. *(1989). Effects of attachment bereavement and pre-event conditions on subsequent depressive symptoms in older adults.* Psychology and Aging, 4, *166–172.*

Nolen-Hoeksema, S. *(1987). Sex differences in unipolar depression: Evidence and theory.* Psychological Bulletin, 101, *259–282.*

Parkes, C. M. & Weiss, R. S. *(1983).* Recovery from bereavement. *New York: Basic Books.*

Pearlin, L. *(1982). Discontinuities in the study of aging. In T. K. Hareven & K. J.*

Adams (Eds), Aging and life course transitions (pp. 55–74). New York: Guilford Press.

Rao, C. R. (1973). Linear statistical inference and its applications (2nd ed.). New York: Wiley.

Reich, J. W., Zautra, A. J. & Guarnaccia, C.-A1 (1989). Effects of disability and bereavement on the mental health and recovery of older adults. Psychology and Aging, 4, 57–65.

Stroebe, M. S. & Stroebe, W. (1983). Who suffers more? Sex differences in health risks of the widowed. Psychological Bulletin, 93, 279–301.

Stroebe, M. S. & Stroebe, W. (1989). Who participates in bereavement research?: A review and empirical study. Omega, 20, 1–29.

Stroebe, W. & Stroebe, M. S. (1987). Bereavement and health: The psychological and physical consequences of partner loss. Cambridge, England: Cambridge University Press.

Stroebe, W., Stroebe, M. S. & Domittner, G. (1985). The impact of recent bereavement on the mental and physical health of young widows and widowers. Tübingen, Germany: Psychological Institute, Tübingen University.

Thompson, L. W., Breckenridge, J. N., Gallagher, D. & Peterson, J. A. (1984). Effects of bereavement on self-perceptions of physical health in elderly widows and widowers. Journal of Gerontology, 39, 309–314.

Van Zandt, S., Mou, R. & Abbott, R. (1989). Mental and physical health of rural bereaved and nonbereaved elders: A longitudinal study. In D. A. Lund (Ed.), Older bereaved spouses: Research with practical applications (pp. 25–35). New York: Hemisphere.

Wilkinson, L. (1989). Systat: Version 4. Evanston, IL: Systat.

Wortman, C. B. & Silver, R. C. (1989). The myths of coping with loss. Journal of Consulting and Clinical Psychology, 57, 349–357.

Zisook, S. & Schuchter, S. R. (1986). The first four years of widow-hood. Psychiatric Annals, 15, 288–294.

37. Psychological Effects of Institutionalization

Morton A. Lieberman, Valencia N. Prock, and Sheldon S. Tobin

THE PRESENT STUDY—the first in a series examining the psychological effects of institutionalization on ambulatory aged—was designed to differentiate the effects of awaiting institutionalization from those living in an institution. Three groups were compared cross-sectionally: institutionalized aged, older persons living in the community, and older persons on institutional waiting lists. The assumption underlying this comparison was that differences between the community and waiting list samples would reflect effects of pre-institutional disruptions, whereas differences between the waiting list and institutional samples would reflect the effects of institutionalization.

The evidence accumulated over the past 15 years leaves little doubt that institutionalized populations exhibit many differences from non-institutionalized populations. Studies of the psychological effects of institutionalization have usually attributed differences to the adverse effects of living in institutions—be they orphanages, boarding schools, hospitals, cloisters, army barracks, old age homes, internment and concentration camps, or prisons. No matter what the particular characteristics of the population or the unique qualities of the total institution, the general thrust of empirical evidence emerging from many studies suggests that living in an institutional environment may have noxious physical and psychological effects upon the individual, whether young or old.

A variety of terms, usually negative in connotation, have been used to describe the different socio-psychological effects of living in institutions, such as "mortification and curtailment of the self" (Goffman, 1961), "institutional dependency" (Coser, 1956; Straus, 1951), "hospitalism" (Spitz, 1945), "depersonalization" (Townsend, 1962), "institutionalism" (Martin, 1955), "regressive pattern to infantile reactions" (Laverty, 1950), and "apathy" reaction including severe withdrawal (Bettelheim, 1943; Cohen, 1953;

From *The Journal of Gerontology* 23 (1968): 343–53. Reprinted with permission of the Gerontological Society of America.

Frankl, 1963; Nardini, 1952; Strassman, Thaler & Schein, 1956; Tas, 1951), and "psychological institutionalism" (Bettelheim & Sylvester, 1948).

Observational studies of infants in institutions have suggested that the lack of an adequate object relationship may threaten the infant's life, may cause serious and even irreversible changes in such areas of maturation as motor and language development, and may create psychosomatic disturbances (Bakwin, 1949; Bowlby 1952; Brodbeck & Irwin, 1946; Freud, 1943; Freud & Burlingham, 1944; Goldfarb, 1945; Provence & Ritvo, 1961; Ribble, 1943; Spitz & Wolf, 1946).

Cross-sectional studies that have compared institutionalized elderly persons to those living in the community have generally shown the institutionalized groups to have an impaired level of overall adjustment, a reduced capacity for independent thought and action, depressive mood tone, low self-esteem, and other negative attributes (Ames, Learned, Metraux & Walker, 1954; Chalfen, 1956; Davidson & Kruglov, 1952; Davol, 1958; Fink, Green, & Bender, 1952; Lakin, 1960; Laverty, 1950; Lieberman & Lakin, 1963; Mason, 1954; Pan, 1948; Pollack, Karp, Kahn & Goldfarb, 1962; Scott, 1955; Townsend, 1962; Tuckman & Lorge, 1952; Webb, 1959).

Good evidence that can explain these effects and attribute them to specific aspects of institutional life has been harder to develop, however. Many investigators (Bettelheim, 1950; Freud & Burlingham, 1944; Goffman, 1961; Goldfarb, 1943; Greenblatt, Levinson & Williams, 1957; Spitz, 1945; Stanton & Schwartz, 1954; Szurek, 1951; Townsend, 1962) have related these adverse psychological effects to the structure of the institution. Others have attributed them to population differences (Davol, 1958; Fogel, Swepston, Zintek, Vernier, Fitzgerald, Marnocha & Weschler, 1956; Webb, 1959; Wolfe & Davis, 1964).

Although the number of studies interpreting institutional effects on aged populations is large, the answers to two questions in particular have remained ambiguous: (1) the effects of prolonged institutionalization, and (2) the parameters of institutional life associated with psychological changes. Much of the ambiguity is attributable to inadequate sample control or comparison, or error owing to selective attrition within the institutional populations.

Many control samples have been inadequate for isolating the effects of institutionalization because they have been matched to the institutional population on demographic and physical variables only. Where the decision for institutionalization has been unrelated to a disruption in everyday living, it is reasonable to assume that certain psychological variables are associated with the selection of institutional life and consequently that control samples must be matched for psychological as well as demographic and physical characteristics. Otherwise phenomena may be reported as institutional effects that may actually result from comparing a psychologically selective sample with a more psychologically heterogeneous control population. On the other hand, if personal disruptions have brought about the institutionalization, the control sample must have undergone the same sorts of disruption, so that reactions to the disruption may be distinguished from reactions to the institutionalization per se.

Selective attrition within institutional populations, stemming from selective discharge or mortality, has been a further source of error. Investigators who have studied institutionalized aged (Aldrich & Mendkoff, 1963; Camargo & Preston, 1945; Kay, Norris & Post, 1956; Miller & Lieberman, 1965; Roth, 1955; Whittier & Williams, 1956) have suggested that mortality and morbidity are not random, and that long-term institutionalized older persons are a select group of survivors. Indeed, a sample of long-term institutionalized aged may differ little from a demographically matched community sample because those aged most affected by institutionalization are unrepresented among long-term institutional aged.

Another source of error has been the restricted range of psychological dimensions used to assess the effects of institutionalization. The usual tactic has been to assess reactions to institutionalization, under-sampling for levels and types of psychological functioning associated with institutional living. The present study was designed to circumvent these barriers to differentiating effects associated with becoming an institutionalized person from effects associated with living in an institution by employing a wide array of psychological variables to compare three samples: a community sample of aged persons who would be likely to seek care in the homes for the aged if disruptions occurred; a waiting list sample who had experienced disruptions that led them to seek institutionalization actively; and aged persons who had been institutionalized from one to three years.

MATERIALS AND METHODS

The Samples

A total of 99 Ss comprised the three samples; 34 Ss who had lived from one to three years in either of two homes for the aged (INST) affiliated with the

Jewish Federation of Chicago; 25 *S*s on the waiting list (WL) for the same institutions; and 40 community (COM) residents. The WL sample was the criterion group to which the other two samples were matched.

The WL sample of 25 *S*s was selected from a pool of 35 *S*s who were on the waiting list. The criteria for inclusion were that the WL *S* must be residing in the community during the time of waiting, without spouse, over 65 years of age, and able to complete an extensive battery of tests and interviews. Of the 35 people on the WL, 6 were not included because they were living in nursing homes, 1 person was married, another was under 65, and 2 could not complete the battery of interviews and tests.

The INST sample was drawn from a pool of 141 *S*s who had lived in either of the two institutions from one to three years. Residents who had lived in the institutions for less than one year were excluded to control for initial effects of institutionalization. (It was assumed that post-institutionalization acute reactions to environmental change would have ceased after a year, and that *S*s would be integrated into their new environment and would manifest psychological effects associated with this new adaptation.) By selecting residents who had lived in the institution at least one year, the bias was toward selecting the more adequate residents; the less adequate residents would have died or become moribund within the first year. The upper limit of three years post-institutionalization was chosen to increase the comparability of the age range for the three samples. Of the 141 *S*s residing in the institutions for one to three years, 65 *S*s did not meet three criteria for selection: 35 of these 65 *S*s were non-ambulatory; 20 were unable to speak English well enough to take part in the interview; and 10 were deteriorated compared to their levels at admission. The remaining 76 *S*s were currently admissible by the criteria of the two institutions. From this pool of 76 *S*s, 34 *S*s were randomly selected. In turn, 10 of the 34 *S*s were excluded on the basis of objective indices of impairment (more than three errors on the Mental Status Questionnaire and more than six points on the Self-Care Index). The final 24 *S*s, therefore, represented a sampling from the more mentally alert and physically healthy residents in the two institutions (38% of the total population).

The COM sample presented a more difficult selection problem. An attempt to use a snow-balling procedure for gathering names from the waiting lists *S*s proved unworkable; the intake records of the WL and INST group, however, revealed that the majority of the female *S*s had been members of a variety of neighborhood organizations prior to institutionalization. The female COM sample was built by approaching these neighborhood organizations.

Since no similar pattern of pre-institutional organizational affiliation existed for males in the INST group, the male COM Ss were located through sampling those residential concentrations where the male Ss had lived prior to institutionalization. Of 57 community aged who volunteered in response to verbal and written invitations to participate, 17 were excluded from this sample: 9 did not meet the criteria of age or marital status, 1 lived in an institutional setting, and 7 would not complete the interview. The remaining 40 Ss comprised the COM sample.

Although clearly a complicated and somewhat cumbersome method of sample selection, it represented as homogeneous a group as seemed feasible to gather. The three samples were similarly distributed with respect to sex, ethnicity, marital status, years of widowhood, country of birth, age of entry into the United States, occupation of head of household, occupation of father, number of living children, number of living siblings, household living arrangements (prior to admission for the institutional group), neighborhood and self-report on the number of diseases and number of symptoms (all were ambulatory). All Ss were Jewish and were 68 to 92 years old. They differed slightly in educational level[1] but not in mental status.

Thus, the total of 99 Ss was composed of (1) a waiting list (WL) sample of 25 Ss drawn from a random population of aged who had been accepted to two homes for the aged; (2) a community (COM) sample of 40 Ss that matched the waiting list sample on specific demographic variables (and thus a sample biased toward comparability to the WL group); and (3) an institutional (INST) sample of 24 Ss that represented undeteriorated survivors (and in this sense a sample systematically biased toward survivorship and absence of major physical or mental changes).

Measures

The choice of variables to be measured was based on two criteria: (a) to sample a wide range of behaviors, and (b) to include variables that had been discussed by other investigators who have studied differences between aged living in the community and residents of old age homes. In all, 21 variables were assessed. They may be conveniently categorized into seven areas: (1) cognitive functioning; (2) body orientation; (3) personality traits; (4) self-image; (5) time perspective; (6) affect states; and (7) relations with people. An attempt was made to use at least two different measurement techniques for each of these seven dimensions or areas, as shown in Table 37.1.

The data were gathered in a series of three or more interviews, ranging

Table 37.1. Description of Measures

Dimension	Measure	Description
		Realm I. Cognitive Functioning
D 1. Impairment	1a. Mental Status	Test, Mental Status Questionnaire (Kahn, Pollack, & Goldfarb, 1961) 10 questions regarding orientation in time and space. Scored for number of errors, $R = 0$–10, St.,[a] $r = .91$.
	1b. Learning-Retention	Test, Inglis (1959), Paired-Word Associates Learning, three unrelated word-pairs. Scored for number of trials to criteria of three corrections. $R = 0$–30, St. $= .39$.
D 2. Perceptual Organization	2a. Perceptual Adequacy	Five Thematic Apperception Test (TAT) cards of Murray (1943) series (1, 2, 6BM, 7BM, 17BM) scored by Dana (1955) system for perceptual organization (PO) and range (PR). Special instructional set developed includes presentation of sample TAT card IJ-R[b] for PO, rho $= .65$; for PR $= .72$, St. for total score (PO + PR), $r = .60$.
	2b. Visual-Motor Organization	Adequacy of copying Designs 1, 3, 8 from a series of 9 designs developed by Bender (1938); Bender-Gestalt Test (BGT). The 3 designs account for 89% of total variance when scored by Pascal and Suttell (1951) system for deviations from actual designs. I-JR, rho $= .97$, St., $r = .66$.
D 3. Complexity	3. Ego Energy	The 5 Murray TAT cards scored by Rosen (1960) ego energy system for (1) introduction of non-pictured characters, (2) introduction of conflict, (3) activity-energy level and (4) affect intensity. I-JR, rho $= .91$.

Realm II. Body Orientation

D 4. Health Anxiety	4. Fac. H.A.	Factor analysis (principal component, varimax rotation) of inter-correlation matrix of 10 measures related to body orientation revealed 3 distinct factors. The 10 measures included ratings of responses to projective tasks (Sentence Completion Test [SCT] and Reitman Stick Figure Test [Reitman & Robertson, 1950] for quantity and quality of preoccupation as well as positive-negative evaluation of body-image; self evaluation of health and functional self-care (New York Health Information Foundation, 1961; and self-report on specific diseases and symptoms. Each of the 3 Factors had loadings on measures using projective and self-descriptive data. Loadings reported by Prock (1965).
D 5. Body Preoccupation	5. Fac. B.P.	
D 6. Health Needs	6. Fac. H.N.	

Realm III. Affects

D 7. Anxiety	7. Cattell Anxiety	Factor-Analysis (principal component, varimax solution) of 21 affect measures revealed 4 factors. The 21 measures included projective tasks (SCT, TAT & Reitman); structural tasks, size of BGT & Time Estimate; self report tasks, Cattell 16PF (Cattell, 1962 & see D16); Srole Anomie Scale (Srole, 1956) and the Osgood Semantic Differential (Osgood, Suci & Tannenbaum, 1957); and interview items for judgments of (1) Mood in the Earliest Memory (Tobin, 1966), (2) Life Satisfaction (Neugarten, Havighurst & Tobin, 1961), (3) Mood tone (Prock, 1965), and (4) Depression (Eaton, 1965). *First Factor*—D8a, Mood composed of loadings on 4 judgments of interview items, Osgood, Cattell Factor F, and a rating of Mood using the TAT: used the weightings for the Mood Fac. Score. *Second Factor*—D7, Cattell Anxiety. *Third Factor*—D10, Emotional Reactivity included (1) Cattell Factor I and (2) Number of positive affects in Reitman Stick Figure Test. *Fourth Factor*—D9, Acceptance of Life included (1) Quantity of positive affect to Park Bench TAT Card (Lieberman & Lakin, 1963), (2) Acceptance of death in completion of SCT stem "To me, death is . . .," and (3) Positive attitude toward past life in completion of SCT stem "My past life . . ." Srole Anomie scale did not appear on Factors and is used as a separate score, D8b.
D 8. Need	8a. Mood Fac. Score	
D 9. Acceptance of Life	8b. Anomie	
D10. Emotional Reactivity.	9. Fac. Acc. Life	
	10. Fac. Emot. React.	

Table 37.1. (Continued) Description of Measures

Dimension	Measure	Description
		Realm IV. Time Perspective
D11. Futurity	11a. Extensionality	Completion of 3 SCT items scored for extension of self into future: (1) "I look forward to . . . ," (2) "An hour is . . . ," and (3) "Time is . . ." IJ-R, 93% exact agreement on 3-point and 4-point scales.
	11b. Stated Futurity	Responses to 3 interview items (meaning of time, planning ahead and meaning of future) scored for extensionality. IJ-R, 88% exact agreement on 3-point and 4-point scales.
	11c. Heterosexual Futurity	Responses to Park Bench TAT card scored for quality and extent of long-term involvement in heterosexual relations on 4-point scale, R 0–3, final score is sum of 2 independent judgments, R = 0–6. IJ-R, 78% exact and 98% within one-step agreement.
	11d. Future Events	Frequency of future events responses to 5 Murray TAT cards. IJ-R, rho = .65, St. = .60.
		Realm V. Relations with People
D12. Attitudes	12a. Dependency	Rating of interview data on 6-point scale, R 1–6; where low score for open dependency in which there are needs to be cared for which are perceived as unmet, where mid-range scores for acceptance of such needs that are perceived as met, and high scores for denial of needs for support from others. Inter-rater reliability, rho = .81 for 10 cases.
	12b. Meaning of Others	Responses to Park Bench TAT card scored for (1) extent and quality of expectations, (2) amount of interpersonal investment, and (3) quality of investment. Two independent judgments were summed for score. For 3 scales, 78%–82% exact agreement, at least 98% within one-step disagreement.
	12c. Social Relations	From factor-analysis of 32 measures of relations with people, 5 measures formed first factor. Loadings used for weighting of 5 measures: rating of quantity of social and family interaction, quality of social and family interaction and social role quantity.

D13. Style 13a. IP Dominance 13b. IP Submissive 13c. IP Friendly 13d. IP Unfriendly 13e. IP No. of Styles 13f. IP Effectiveness	Response to inter-personal Role Playing Task (IRPT). Nine dyadic role-playing situations involves inter-personal problems, scored for major style (dominant, submissive, friendly, unfriendly toward other). R = 1–9. For outcome, judgment of effectiveness for each situation scored on 0–4 scale, R 0–36. Inter-judge reliability on Styles was 86% exact agreement, and reliability for outcome was rho = .95 for 10 cases.
D14. Orientation 14a. Cattell Introversion	See D16. Cattell 16PF Global Introversion-Extraversion Factor, is a second order Factor summing 5 primary factors.
14b. Object Cathexis	Responses to 6 SCT stems, each which have a clear object focus, are each rated on a 6-point scale (0–2.5) for object investment (Watson, 1965). R 0–15, IJ-R, r = .66.

Realm VI. Self-Image

D15. Content 15. OCT AP Power-Success OCT BC Narcissistic-Expl. OCT DE Hostility OCT FG Unconv. Activity OCT HI Masochism- Weakness OCT JK Conformity-Trust OCT LM Collabor.- Pure Love OCT NO Tenderness- Generous Global Score:Love Global Score: Dominance	S selects those items that describe self from a pool of 48 items. Sets of 3 items, which are Guttman scaled, are based upon the Leary (1957) inter-personal category system. Categories collapsed to form 8 Octants, where 6 items can be selected for each. R 0–6 per each of the 8 Octants. Global scores are computed from Octant scores. St. of item choice, 83%.

Realm VII. Personality Traits

D16. Cattell Traits 16. 15 Factor Scores	The Cattell (1962) 16 Personality Factor Test (16PF) Test was used where S is asked to agree or disagree with 6 items for each factor. Factor 13, intelligence, was not appropriate for this sample. Thus, S was asked to respond to 90 items in all, where R = 0–6 for each of the 15 Factors used. Each of Cattell's 90 items in Form C of 16PF was modified after pre-test with present population.

[a] St. = Stability. Stability computed for N of at least 20, using Community aged who were tested at a 1-year interval.

in length from 8 to 12 hours. Ten psychological tests were included in the interview: the Cattell (1962) Personality Test (Form C), a 32-item Sentence Completion Test, 5 bipolar self-evaluation items from Osgood, Suci, and Tannenbaum, Scale (1957), the Srole (1956) Anomie Scale, a Word Learning Test (Inglis, 1959), the Mental Status Questionnaire (Kahn, Pollack & Goldfarb, 1961), the Reitman Stick Figure Test, (Reitman & Robertson, 1950), a Self-Sort Task (a series of phrases which best describe the S as he is now), an Interpersonal Role-Playing Task (nine dyadic stories to which S is required to provide an appropriate ending), and six cards (#1, #2, #6BM, #7BM, #10, #17BM) from the Murray (1943) TAT series as well as six cards from the Institutional TAT series (Lieberman & Lakin, 1963). Nine interview schedules included S's self-report on health and personal care (Q2), current living situation (Q1), daily round of activity (Q3), relations with people (Q10), life history data on main stresses (Q6), feelings about self and growing old (Q5), evaluation of life attitudes toward activities (Q8), and affects (Q9). In addition, the interviewers completed six schedules which included a rating of life satisfaction, test-taking behavior, feelings toward the S, and an evaluation of the S.[2]

RESULTS

Similarities among the COM, INST and WL Samples

Means and standard deviations were computed for the three samples on each measure as shown in Column A of Table 37.2, t tests were used for specific comparisons. Column C1 indicates those variables in which no statistically significant differences were found in any of the comparisons between the INST, the COM, and WL, or the COM and WL groups. Similarities among the three samples were concentrated in three realms—Relationships with People (V), Self-Image (VI), and Personality Traits (VII). Similarities occurred on variables assessing Interpersonal Style (13), Orientation to People (14), Self-Concept (15), and Personality Traits on a standard personality test (16). One would not expect these types of variables to be as sensitive to an environmental influence such as institutionalization as such variables as Anxiety, Depression, and the like. Table 37.2, column B, which shows the mean and standard deviations for each of the variables, indicates that the three samples were heterogeneous on these measures.

Total Effects of Institutionalization

Column C2, Table 37.2, compares the COM and INST groups. This comparison between an institutional and a community control group fails to differentiate the possible effects of applying to a home from those of living in an institutional environment. Such a comparison, however, is useful in showing the articulation of this study with other studies of institutional effects on the aged. The data presented in Column C2 reflect the findings that typically have been reported in studies of institutional aged. Column C2 shows numerous differences, indicating the poorer psychological status of the INST group compared to the COM controls. Indeed, the only dimensions not showing such differences are those relating to Self-Imagery (Realm VI) and Personality Traits (Realm VII).

Effects of Pre-institutional Period—Comparison of COM and WL Samples

Column C3, Table 37.2, shows those variables on which the COM and WL significantly differ from each other. The pattern of differences between these two groups resembles the pattern of differences shown between the COM group and the INST group (Table 37.1, C2). It is noteworthy that the WL group resembled the INST group more than the community controls in several ways that articulate closely to aspects cited in the literature as effects of institutional living. The WL group had a significantly lower degree of future perspective than the COM group (11a, b, c, d), a characteristic frequently attributed to the effects of institutional living. Interpersonal attitudes of unconflicted dependency (D12), low emotional involvement in people (D12b) and low involvement in interpersonal relations (D12c) were also characteristics of the WL group that have been cited as effects of institutional living. The affect pattern, excluding anxiety (which would be characteristic of the WL but not the INST group), resembled what has been described in the literature as an institutional pattern. Some noteworthy differences however, show up between the data in C2 and C3. These differences are explored in detail in the following analyses.

Effects of Living in an Institutional Environment—Comparison of WL and INST Samples

Column C4 shows the measures in which statistically significant differences were found between the WL and INST groups. Column C4a indicates those

Table 37.2. t-Test Comparisons among the Three Samples

A. Dimensions, Variables and Measures	B. Group Means and SDs						C. Comparisons among Com, WL, and Inst Samples					
	Community group (C)		Waiting list (WL)		Institutionalized (I)		1. Equality	2. Total effect	3. WL effect	4. Institutional Effect		
										a Amel	b Adverse	c Stable
	Mn	SD	Mn	SD	Mn	SD	C=WL=I[a]	I<C	WL<C	I>WL	I<WL	I=WL
I. Cognitive Functioning												
1a. Mental Status[a]	0.5	1.2	0.8	1.3	1.7	2.4		X[b]			X[b]	
1b. Learning-Retention[a]	7.6	8.7	11.5	10.6	16.2	10.5		X			X	
2a. Adequacy	27.5	5.1	19.3	5.5	22.0	5.3		X	X[b]	X[b]		
2b. Visual-Motor[a]	26.6	13.9	32.4	15.5	33.0	16.4		X				0[c]
3. Ego Energy	17.5	5.7	14.9	6.0	15.9	6.4			X			0
II. Body Orientation												
4. Fac. Health Anxiety[a]	.23	0.8	.20	1.0	−.41	1.0		X		X		
5. Fac. Body Preoccup.[a]	−.13	1.2	−.20	1.0	.23	0.8		X			X	
6. Fac. Health Need[a]	−.14	0.8	.08	1.1	.29	1.2						0
III. Affects												
7. Cattell Anxiety[a]	24.8	6.2	29.5	6.8	26.0	7.6			X	X		
8a. Mood	2.0	3.9	−2.2	4.7	−0.2	4.5			X	X		
8b. Anomie[a]	14.4	4.6	15.2	4.9	16.0	3.9	0[c]					
9. Fac. Accept. of Life	1.0	1.8	−0.6	2.1	−0.4	1.6		X	X			
10. Fac. Emot. Reactivity	0.0	1.4	0.8	1.8	−0.4	1.5		X			X	
IV. Time Perspective												
11a. Extensionality	8.2	1.6	6.8	1.4	6.9	2.0		X	X			0
11b. Stated Futurity	7.7	2.1	6.2	1.8	5.6	2.4		X	X			0
11c. Heterosexual	5.0	1.5	3.2	1.7	3.6	1.6		X	X			0
11d. Future Events	1.2	1.3	0.4	6.7	0.7	0.9		X	X			0

V. Relations with People

							I	II	III	IV
12a. Dependency	4.3	1.8	2.6	1.8	3.5	1.6		X	X	
12b. Meaning of others	1.3	2.3	−1.3	2.3	−0.2	2.6	X	X	X	
12c. Social relations	4.8	6.5	−2.7	8.8	−2.8	8.2	X	X	X	0
13a. Dominance	2.7	1.4	2.3	1.6	2.8	1.7	0			
13b. Submissive	1.6	1.3	1.4	1.2	1.7	2.2	0			
13c. Friendly	2.4	1.0	1.6	1.4	1.2	1.1		X		0
13d. Unfriendly	2.3	1.0	2.8	1.7	2.4	1.2	0			
13e. No. of styles	4.6	1.2	3.7	1.1	3.5	1.0	X	X		0
13f. Effectiveness	21.7	5.8	20.8	7.2	19.5	6.9	0			
14a. Cattell Introver.	20.5	4.7	22.2	6.3	21.3	5.1	0			
14b. Object Cathexis	7.9	2.3	8.0	2.1	8.0	2.0	0			

VI. Self-Image

							I	II	III	IV
15. Oct. AP-Power	10.8	4.6	9.6	3.6	9.5	3.9	0			0
BC-Narcissism	14.1	2.7	12.4	4.4	13.6	3.7		X		
DE-Hostility	10.5	3.4	11.1	5.5	11.4	4.6	0			
FG-Unc. Activity	11.9	3.8	11.7	5.3	12.1	6.5	0			
HI-Masochism	12.6	3.6	14.0	5.6	13.3	4.2	0			
JK-Conformity	10.8	2.9	12.6	4.6	9.4	3.2		X	X	
LM-Collaborative	14.9	3.2	16.3	4.7	14.9	4.3	0		X	
NO-Tenderness	14.2	3.8	12.3	4.5	15.7	4.3		X	X	
Global: Love	52.4	8.6	46.5	14.8	52.1	10.5	0	X	X	
Global: Dominance	53.6	9.6	55.8	11.7	53.1	12.5			X	X

VII. Personality Traits

		I
16. Cattell Factor Scores		0

(Of 15 scores, 2 are included in other measures:
(F) Glum, with Mood Factor, (I) Emotional Reactivity Factor.
Of the remaining 13, 10 did not show any significant differences.)

---

[a] Tests or Factors scored for errors or negativity, so that higher scores are "worse than" lower scores. Significance level used for *t*-test differences was the .10 level, one–tailed test of hypotheses.

[b] X = Significant *t* test.

[c] 0 = No significant difference.

[d] C = Community sample, WL = Waiting sample, I = Institutional sample.

measures on which the institutional group had a better score than the waiting list; C4b shows those measures on which the Ss on the waiting list had better scores than the institutional group; and C4c shows where no statistically significant differences were found. Again, assuming the homogeneity of the three samples, the findings shown in Column 4 indicate three general effects:

"Amelioration." In several areas of psychological functioning the surviving INST group was at a better level than the WL group. This was particularly true in Realm III (Affects) and Realm V (Interpersonal Relations). The level of depression and anxiety was considerably lower in the INST group, and on the attitudinal indicators of interpersonal relations the INST group showed consistently better scores indicating more meaningful involvements than the WL group.

   These differences between the INST and WL groups suggest that living in the institution may have ameliorated some of the crisis-related reactions to the waiting list period.

"Negative effects" of institutional living. Column C4b indicates that those survivors living in the institution had (a) lower scores in the impairment area of cognitive functioning; (b) showed more preoccupation with body and focus around issues of the body; and (c) were less emotionally responsive or reactive than the WL group. Thus, living in a home for the aged appears to have had some negative effects, even on survivors.

Similarities between INST and WL groups. Column 4c shows those measures where the INST and WL groups resemble one another. The factors that appear to affect those awaiting entrance into an institution seem to continue their influence after institutionalization. Thus, certain negative characteristics that are most appropriately ascribed to the process of becoming an institutionalized person, rather than to institutionalized life, are unaffected by the person's changed living pattern. This was particularly true of Realm IV (Time Perspective).

DISCUSSION

In finding that certain psychological qualities were more affected among aged awaiting institutionalization than among long-term institutional residents, the present study suggests a conclusion at variance with much of the existing literature. Effects that have been frequently ascribed to institutional living (lower future time perspective, increased psychological distance from others, and increased feelings of despair) are here reported as aspects of the waiting period, implying that these psychological qualities may articulate more to the symbolic meanings and fantasies surrounding institutionalization than to the actual experience of institutional life. Crises about separation, loss, and rejection have been observed during the waiting period (Lieberman & Lakin, 1963), and these concerns may induce changes that have heretofore been considered effects of living in institutions.

The strength of this conclusion depends, of course, on the particular variables assessed. The present study measured certain cognitive functions, the affective life of the individual, conceptions of self and body, attitudes toward and perceptions of others, as well as issues of time perspective and styles of interpersonal relationship that appear more affected in the waiting list group than in the institutionalized group. Institutionalization seems far more critical than the waiting period, however, with respect to such an extreme reaction as death (Lieberman, 1961).

In a previous study of an aged population (Lieberman, 1961) the death rate following institutionalization was two and a half times greater than in the waiting period. In the present study, 50% of the potentially available institutional population could not be studied because they died or became morbid. Moreover, some of the most adverse psychological effects (again, effects not considered in this study) have been observed in the first months of institutional life (Lieberman, 1966). Clearly, institutionalization has profound effects, and the conclusion that the waiting period has greater psychological impact is valid only in comparing the WL group to the survivors of the first year of institutional life.

The specific psychological qualities distinguishing the waiting list sample from the institutional and community groups are more reasonably attributed to situational determinants of the waiting period than to a hypothesis of personality types. The similarities of the three samples on such dimensions as interpersonal style, interpersonal orientation, self-image, and personality traits support a conclusion that, for the two institutions studied, a wide range of "personality types" can be found entering old age homes.

Within the confines of the sampling procedure used in this study, it seems clear that controlling for personality type is relatively unimportant in studying institutional effects on the very aged. This suggestion is consistent with the findings of other investigators who have studied institutionalization in the very aged. For example, Brody (1966) and Lowenthal (1964) suggested that any aged person may become an institutionalized aged individual if precipitating changes occur in social supports or physical status. A follow-up of the COM sample further supported the conclusion that personality character-istics were less important than situational determinants of institutionalization. Of the 40 Ss originally in the COM sample, 4 applied to the institution with 32 months after being interviewed.

Although most of the variance in the data occurred in the waiting list group, some important effects of long-term living in an institutional environ-ment are suggested, if the homogeneity of the sample is assumed. The insti-tutional environment appears to affect survivors adversely with respect to disorientation to time and space, increased preoccupation with body, and lowered emotional responsivity—taken together, these three dimensions sug-gest increased insulation from the environment. The cross-sectional design of this study makes it impossible to determine whether or not these are char-acteristics actually shaped by the environment.

The data have suggested that living in an institution may have ameliora-tive, as well as adverse, effects. The decision to enter the institution, awaiting the consequent separation, etc., appears to set off affective reactions and a view of people which are somewhat muted and perhaps corrected by living in the institution. For individuals directed toward institutional settings by social circumstances, some of the psychological effects of the transition pe-riod are diminished by life in the institution.

This cross-sectional comparison suggests that institutionalization may best be viewed as a complex process beginning from the point when an aged person seriously considers institutionalization, through a critical phase preceding and perhaps immediately following actual entrance to the institution, to a period of long-term residence in the institution. Thus, reactions to institutionalization must be examined at at least three points in time—before, immediately after, and over a long period following the initial phase—if lawful relationships be-tween psychological effects and institutional attributes are to be derived.

The profound psychological effects of the waiting period make the prob-lem of studying the therapeutics of institutionalization exceedingly complex. The power usually inherent in a Time 1, Time 2 study of therapeutics is complicated in this set of circumstances because of the effects of the waiting period on the aged. Changes may simply reflect modification or amelioration from the depressed baseline state of the person on the waiting list, rather than what is more usually thought of as therapeutic benefit.

One final implication seems worthy of note. Although the problems that are inherent should be apparent in a cross-sectional study where survivorship characteristics are present, the findings on the psychological effects of the waiting period are less open to such methodological problems. They raise the question of the appropriate deployment of resources in benefiting the aged in need of protective settings. There is sufficient empirical data on the negative implications of placing the elderly in institutional settings. Considerable effort has been invested in attempting to correct gross and subtle deficiencies in institutional environments as an antidote to the maladaptive reactions of the residents. The data presented here point to the question of whether such resources might be effectively expended in working with the aged client in the critical six months to a year before he is institutionalized. It is far beyond the data available in this study to suggest the economics of these two strategies. The institutions studied are both high quality environments, so that additional benefits might be gained in these particular institutions by attention to the pre-institutional period. Whether changes are warranted in structures of less well endowed institutions is an open question. Nor can we, at this time, speak about the non-survivors, for whom structural changes in the institutional setting might have been ameliorative. The effects of the waiting period are clearly destructive for most of the individuals studied.

SUMMARY

The effects of awaiting institutionalization were differentiated from the effects of living in an institution. Cross-section comparisons were made of institutionalized ($N = 34$), community ($N = 40$), and waiting list ($N = 25$), aged Ss on 21 psychological dimensions grouped into seven areas of functioning: (1) Cognitive Functioning, (2) Body Orientation, (3) Personality Traits, (4) Self-Image, (5) Time Perspective, (6) Affect States, and (7) Relations with People. The pattern of similarities and differences among these groups on the measures indicated: (a) psychological effects (low time perspective, psychological distance from others, and feelings of despair) that have usually been associated with living in an institution were characteristic of the waiting period, (b) specific personality traits were not associated with entrance into old age homes, (c) living in an institutional environment had both ameliorative effects (on the depressed affect level of the waiting list group) as well as adverse effects (time orientation, body focus, and lowered emotional reactivity).

NOTES

1. The COM group had a higher level of grade school education than the other two groups. The frequency count revealed, however, that the averages were pushed up by a small, but higher, proportion of community Ss (4) who had completed college.

2. Copies of the Interview Schedules and unpublished tests are available on request from the Principal Investigator.

REFERENCES

Aldrich, C. K. & E. Mendkoff. Relocation of the aged and disabled: a mortality study. J. Amer. Geriat. Soc., 11, *185–194, 1963.*

Ames, L. B., J. Learned, R. Metraux & R. Walker. Rorschach responses in old age. *Hoeber-Harper, New York, 1954.*

Bakwin, H. Emotional deprivation in infants. J. Pediat., 35, *512–521, 1949.*

Bender, L. A visual motor gestalt test and its clinical use. *American Orthopsychiatry Assn., New York, Res. Monogr. No. 3, 1938, 176 pp.*

Bettelheim, B. Individual and mass behavior in extreme situations. J. Abnorm. (Soc.) Psychol., 38, *417–452, 1943.*

Bettelheim, B. Love is not enough. *Free Press, Glencoe, Ill., 1950.*

Bettelheim, B. & E. Sylvester: A therapeutic milieu. Amer. J. Orthopsychiat., 18, *191–206, 1948.*

Bowlby, J. Maternal care and mental health. *World Health Organization, Geneva, 1952.*

Brodbeck, A. J. & O. C. Irwin. The speech behavior of infants without families. Child Develop., 17, *146–156, 1946.*

Brody, E. M. The aging family. Gerontologist, 6, *4–13, 1966.*

Camargo, O. & G. H. Preston: What happens to patients who are hospitalized for the first time when over sixty-five? Amer. J. Psychiat., 102, *168–173, 1945.*

Cattell, R. B. Handbook supplement for Form C of the Sixteen Personality Factor Test. *Institute for Personality and Ability Testing, Champaign, Ill., 2nd Ed., 1962.*

Chalfen, L. Leisure-time adjustment of the aged. II. Activities and interests and some factors influencing choice. J. genet. Psychol., 88, *261–276, 1956.*

Cohen, E. A. Human behavior in the concentration camp. *W. W. Norton, New York, 1953.*

Coser, R. L. A home away from home. Soc. Probl., 4, *3–17, 1956.*

Dana, R. H. Clinical diagnosis and objective TAT scoring. J. Abnorm. (Soc.) Psychol., 50, *19–25, 1955.*

Davidson, H. H. & L. Kruglov. Personality characteristics of the institutionalized aged. J. Consult. Psychol., 16, *5–12, 1952.*

Davol, S. H. Some determinants of sociometric relationships and group structure in a veteran's administration domiciliary. Unpublished doctoral dissertation, University of Rochester, 1958.

Eaton, A. M. The phenomenon of depression in the aged. Unpublished Master's paper, Committee on Human Development, University of Chicago, 1965.

Fink, M., M. A. Green & M. B. Bender. The face-hand test as a diagnostic sign of organic mental syndrome. Neurology, 2, *48–56, 1952.*

Fogel, E. J., E. R. Swepston, S. S. Zintek, C. M. Vernier, J. F. Fitzgerald, R. S. Marnocha & C. H. Weschler. Problems of the aging; conclusions derived from two years of interdisciplinary study of domiciliary members in a veterans administration center. Amer. J. Psychiat., 112, *724–730, 1956.*

Frankl, V. E. Man's search for meaning. *Washington Square Press, New York, 1963.*

Freud, A. War and children. *International University Press, New York, 1943.*

Freud, A. Observations on child development. Psychoanal. Stud. Child, 6, *18–30, 1951.*

Freud, A. & D. T. Burlingham. Infants without families. *International University Press, New York, 1944.*

Goffman, E. Asylums; essays on the social situation of mental patients and other inmates. *Doubleday, Garden City, N.Y., 1961.*

Goldfarb, W. The effects of early institutional care on adolescent personality. J. Exp. Educ., 12, *106–129, 1943.*

Goldfarb, W. Effects of psychological deprivation in infancy and subsequent stimulation. Amer. J. Psychiat., 102, *18–43, 1945.*

Greenblatt, M., D. J. Levinson & R. H. Williams. The patient and the mental hospital. *Free Press, Glencoe, Ill., 1957.*

Inglis, J. A paired-associate learning test for use with elderly psychiatric patients. J. Ment. Sci., 105, *440–443, 1959.*

Kahn, R. L., M. Pollack & A. I. Goldfarb. Factors related to individual differences in mental status of institutionalized aged. Chap. 5 in P. H. Hoch & J. Zubin (Eds.), Psychopathology of Aging. *Grune & Stratton, New York, 1961, pp. 104–113.*

Kay, D., V. Norris & F. Post. Prognosis in psychiatric disorders of the elderly. J. Ment. Sci., 102, *129–140, 1956.*

Lakin, M. Formal characteristics of human figure drawings by institutionalized and non-institutionalized aged. J. Geront., 15, *76–78, 1960.*

Laverty, R. Nonresident aid—community versus institutional care for older people. J. Geront., 5, *370–374, 1950.*

Leary, T. Interpersonal diagnosis of personality. *Ronald Press, New York, 1957.*

Lieberman, M. A. Relationship of mortality rates to entrance to a home for the aged. Geriatrics, 16, *515–519, 1961.*

Lieberman, M. A. Factors in environmental change. Chap. 10 in F. M. Carp and W. M. Burnett (Eds.) Patterns of Living and Housing of Middle-Aged and Older People. *Publ. Health Service, U.S. Department Health Education & Wellfair 1966, PHS Publ. No. 1496, pp. 117–125.*

Lieberman, M. A. & M. Lakin. On becoming an institutionalized person. In R. H. Williams, C. Tibbitts, & W. Donahue (Eds.), Processes of Aging Vol. I. Social and Psychological Perspectives. *Atherton Press, New York, 1963, pp. 475–503.*

Lowenthal, M. F. Lives in distress: The paths of the elderly to the psychiatric ward. *Basic Books, New York, 1964.*

Martin, D. Institutionalisation. Lancet, 269, *1188–1190, 1955.*

Mason, E. P. Some correlates of self-judgments of the aged. J. Geront., 9, *324–337, 1954.*

Miller, D. & M. A. Lieberman. The relationship of affect state adaptive capacity to reactions to stress. J. Geront., 20, *492–497, 1965.*

Murray, H. A. Manual of Thematic Apperception Test. *Harvard University Press, Cambridge, Mass., 1943.*

Nardini, J. E. Survival factors in American prisoners of war of the Japanese. Amer. J. Psychiat., 109, *241–248, 1952.*

Neugarten, B., R. Havighurst, & S. S. Tobin. The measurement of life satisfaction. J. Geront., 16, *134–143, 1961.*

New York Health Information Foundation (by Ethel Shanas). Family relationships of older people—living arrangements, health status, and family ties of those aged 65 and over, as reported by the aged, the persons to whom they would turn in a health crisis, and the general public. *New York, 1961, Res. Series 20.*

Osgood, C., G. Suci & P. H. Tannenbaum. The measurement of meaning. *University of Illinois Press, Urbana, 1957.*

Pan, J. A study of the influence of institutionalization on the social adjustment of old people. J. Geront., 3, *276–280, 1948.*

Pascal, G. R. & B. J. Suttell. The Bender-Gestalt Test: Quantification and validity for adults. *Grune & Stratton, New York, 1951.*

Pollack, M., E. Karp., R. L. Kahn A. I. Goldfarb. Perception of self in institutionalized aged subjects. I. Response patterns to mirror reflection. J. Geront., 17, *405–408, 1962.*

Prock, V. N. Effects of institutionalization—a comparison of community, waiting list, and institutionalized aged persons. Unpublished doctoral dissertation, Committee on Human Development, University of Chicago, 1965.

Provence, S. & S. Ritvo. Effects of deprivation on institutionalized infants: Disturbances in development of relationship to inanimate objects. Psychoanal. Stud. Child, 16, *189–205, 1961.*

Reitman, F. & J. P. Robertson. Reitman's Pin-Man Test: A means of disclosing impaired conceptual thinking. J. Nerv. Ment. Dis., 112, *498–510, 1950.*

Ribble, M. The rights of infants: Early psychological needs and their satisfaction. *Columbia University Press, New York, 1943.*

Rosen, J. L. Ego functions in the middle and later years, a thematic apperception study. Unpublished doctoral dissertation, Committee on Human Development, University of Chicago, 1960.

Roth, M. The natural history of mental disorders in old age. J. Ment. Sci., 101, *281–301, 1955.*

Scott, F. G. Factors in the personal adjustment of institutionalized and non-institutionalized aged. Amer. Sociol. Rev., 20, *538–546, 1955.*

Spitz, R. A. Hospitalism—an inquiry into the genesis of psychiatric conditions in early childhood. Psychoanal. Stud. Child, 1, *53–74, 1945.*

Spitz, R. A. & K. M. Wolf. Anaclitic depression: an inquiry into the genesis of psychiatric conditions in early childhood. Psychoanal. Stud. Child, 2, *313–342, 1946.*

Srole, L. Social integration and certain corollaries: An exploratory study. Amer. Sociol. Rev., 21, *709–716, 1956.*

Stanton, A. H. & M. S. Schwartz. The mental hospital. *Basic Books, New York, 1954.*

Strassman, H. D., M. B. Thaler & E. H. Schein. A prisoner of war syndrome: Apathy as a reaction to severe stress. Amer. J. Psychiat., 112, *998–1003, 1956.*

Straus, R. Nonadditive pathological drinking patterns of homeless men. Quart. J. Stud. Alcohol., 12, *601–611, 1951.*

Szurek, S. A. The family and the staff in hospital psychiatric therapy of children. Amer. J. Ortho-psychiat., 21, *597–611, 1951.*

Tas, J. Psychical disorders among inmates of concentration camps and repatriates. Psychiatric Quart., 25, *679–690, 1951.*

Tobin, S. S. Childhood reminiscence and institutionalization in the aged. Proceedings of the Seventh International Congress of Gerontology, Vienna, Austria, June 26–July 2, 1966, Vol. 6. *Wien. Med. Akad., Wien, 1966, pp. 215–216.*

Townsend, P. The last refuge—a survey of residential institutions and homes for the aged in England and Wales. *Routledge and Kegan Paul, London, 1962.*

Tuckman, J. & I. Lorge: The effect of institutionalization on attitudes towards old people. J. Abnorm. (Soc.) Psychol., 47, *337–344, 1952.*

Watson, A. Objects and objectivity: A study of the relationship between narcissim and intellectual subjectivity. Unpublished doctoral dissertation, University of Chicago, 1965.

Webb, M. A. Longitudinal sociopsychologic study of a randomly selected group of institutionalized veterans. J. Amer. Geriat. Soc., 7, *730–740, 1959.*

Whittier, J. R. & D. Williams. The coincidence of constancy of mortality figures for aged psychotic patients admitted to state hospitals. J. Nerv. Ment. Dis., 124, *618–620, 1956.*

Wolfe, R. N. & J. A. Davis, Intelligence and central life interests in two groups of older men. Psychol. Rep., 14, *847–852, 1964.*

38. On the Social Ecology of Dependence and Independence in Elderly Nursing Home Residents

A Replication and Extension

Margret M. Baltes, Sara Honn, Elisabeth M. Barton, MaryJo Orzech, and Dan Lago

DEPENDENCE IS NOT only a "conspicuous feature of early childhood" (Maccoby & Masters, 1970, p. 72) but also a feature of old age (Exton-Smith & Evans, 1977; Kalish, 1969; Lehr, 1977). Recently, efforts have been made to examine the *conditions under which* dependence occurs or does not occur. Such process-oriented research includes efforts to consider cognitive personality-related mechanisms (i.e., Langer & Rodin, 1976; Rodin & Langer, 1977; Seligman, 1975) and the role of social interactions for the understanding of dependence (Baltes et al., 1980; Barton et al., 1980; Lester & Baltes, 1978; Stephens & Willems, 1979).

To analyze dependence as the outcome of an interaction between the organism and the social environment, we have utilized the operant learning model as a conceptual framework and direct observation as the main methodology (Baltes, 1982). Our operant-observational findings on the social ecology surrounding dependent and independent behaviors in nursing homes so far are two-fold. First, for dependent behaviors of elderly nursing home residents, we find dependence-supportive behavior by staff as the most likely behavior consequence. In contrast, for dependent independent behavior on the part of the elderly resident, we see either no response at all by staff or staff behavior that is incongruent with the preceding behavior of the elderly resident. Based on these operant-observational findings, it appears that the two kinds of behaviors (dependence vs. independence) are associated with different social ecologies.

The present study continues this line of work and has two main objectives

---

From *The Journal of Gerontology* 38 (1973): 556–64. Reprinted with permission of the Gerontological Society of America.

involving replication and extension. Past work is replicated in the same setting (a nonproprietary nursing home), but the study covers a wider range of conditions. First, time was extended to involve the entire daytime for observations and three longitudinal occasions of measurement covering a 6-month period. Second, elderly nursing home residents were stratified by length of institutionalization. Third, the observation code was extended to include independent and dependent behavior on the part of residents not only as they relate to self-care but also to all other prosocial as well as asocial activities occurring throughout the day. Finally, an attempt was made to tap other social contingencies beyond those involving the nursing home staff. The behaviors of every social agent, including staff, visitors, volunteer workers, and fellow residents, were considered.

METHOD

Setting and Participants

The setting of the present study was a nonproprietary nursing home located in rural central Pennsylvania. The three-story building (one story had been used in one of our previous studies) has a capacity of about 250 beds for intermediate and skilled nursing care. As to the social ecology of the elderly nursing home residents, visitors, volunteer workers, fellow residents, and staff were considered potential social agents. Practically all visitors, volunteer workers, fellow residents, and staff who were asked to participate volunteered (e.g., 57 out of about 60 staff members).

Elderly residents representing the targets of our study came from the entire nursing home. The total resident population of the nursing home was first classified by length of institutionalization into four possible groups; group 1, 2 to 12 months; group 2, 12 to 36 months; group 3, 48 to 60 months; and group 4, more than 84 months. Of the volunteering residents, 12 were selected randomly from each group. The initial sample of elderly residents comprised 48 elderly persons, 22 men and 26 women. A total of eight residents dropped out of the study, four because they withdrew informed consent, three because of death, one because of insufficient observations.

The 40 remaining residents, ranging in age from 57 to 96 ($M = 81.2$ years) consisted of 20 men and 20 women. The 40 residents varied in their medical problems; those reported most frequently in the medical charts were arteriosclerosis, cerebral arteriosclerosis, and cardiovascular diseases. In terms of care, 18 residents received skilled nursing care, 22 intermediate nursing care. The four groups did not differ in these demographic and medical data.

Behavior Categories

A total of 10 behavior categories comprised the observation code. Five of these involved behaviors of elderly residents, and five referred to the behavior of their social partners. In contrast with our past work, the categories of residents' behavior were extended to include not only independent and dependent behaviors related to self-care (i.e., dressing, toileting, eating) but also other activities judged to be relevant to dependence and independence. Accordingly, we differentiated between dependent behaviors in the context of self-care and nonengagement. In addition to independent behaviors related to self-care, we coded prosocial or constructively engaged and obstructively engaged behaviors separately. There were six categories of social partners' behaviors: supportive of independent self-care behaviors (any encouragement of independent or discouragement of dependent behaviors); supportive of dependent behaviors (any encouragement of dependent or discouragement of independent behaviors); supportive of engaged behavior; supportive of nonengaged behavior; no response; and leaving. Behavior supportive of nonengaged behaviors showed a total of 20 behaviors only and was deleted from the data analysis. All behaviors were defined as and restricted to observable acts only. For a more detailed definition of the behavior categories as well as for the observer training manual, contact the first author.

Apparatus

The Datamyte 904, a portable battery-powered system, was used (Electro General Corporation, Minnetonka, MN) to perform data collection, storage, and computer interface functions. The second, fourth, and fifth author plus one graduate student were trained to record observations using the behavior code and the Datamyte.

Design and Procedure

The 40 residents were observed on three occasions: July, September, and December. Each occasion of measurement consisted of daily observations over a 14-day period. Residents were observed randomly each day with the restriction that each resident was observed during each hour of the day between 7 A.M. and 7 P.M. at least once during the 14 days.

Observations of a resident commenced when the selected resident was encountered by the observer. Observations were made for 3 minutes, during which the resident's behavior and interactions with others were recorded continuously in the sequence in which they occurred. When a behavior of a resident continued for longer than 10 seconds, it was re-recorded. Thus, each behavior unit recorded was 10 seconds in length unless a new behavior occured in a faster pace.

For purposes of reliability assessment, the two observers of the day performed simultaneous observations on two randomly selected residents either at the beginning or the end of a daily circuit. Interobserver reliability was computed in two ways. First, Spearman rho correlations were calculated between two observers per occasion per resident behavior category. Averaged across the three occasions, these intercorrelations were .71 for constructively engaged, .76 for obstructively engaged, .74 for nonengaged, .91 for independent personal maintenance, and .90 for dependent personal maintenance behavior (for occasion 1 the five correlations are significant at the .005 level, for occasion 2 at the .05, and for occasion 3 at the .01 level).

Second, because such data are the focus of our research, interobserver reliability was computed not only at the level of single behavior frequency but on the level of behavior sequences. Thus, conditional probabilities were determined for all immediately subsequent behaviors (lag 1; for explanation of sequential lag analysis see the Results section) for each resident behavior and each occasion as well as across occasions. These behavior sequence profiles were compared for observers A and B via product-moment correlations separately for each of the five resident behaviors as criterion or antecedent behaviors. The correlations range in the .90s, indicating high interobserver reliability for interactional sequences (rather than single behavior frequencies) as well. Note that in both reliability computations we analyze separately for each behavior thus differentiating between low and high frequency behaviors.

RESULTS

The results will be described in three steps. First, we shall look at the frequencies of elderly residents' behaviors, second at the frequencies of the social partners' behaviors, and third at the interactional behavior patterns involving elderly residents and their social partners.

Resident Behavior

The observed frequencies of the five residents' behaviors show only small and nonsignificant differences between occasions within each group. Temporal stability on the level of interindividual differences is generally high also. Of the 10 correlations between occasion 1 and 2 and 2 and 3, eight are significant ($p < .002$). Based on these findings we decided to collapse the data across the three occasions of measurement for each group (see Table 38.1). In terms of absolute frequencies across occasions and groups, a total

Table 38.1. Frequencies and Percentages of Resident and Social Partners Behaviors

Behaviors	Length of institutionalization (months)				
	2–12	12–36	48–60	84+	Total
	Resident				
Independent Personal Maintenance	1,673	1,088	1,218	1,252	5,231
	6.04	3.92	4.40	4.52	18.87
Dependent Personal Maintenance	254	249	169	162	834
	.92	.90	.61	.58	3.01
Nonengaged	3,201	3,861	3,987	3,342	14,391
	11.55	13.93	14.38	12.06	51.91
Constructively Engaged	1,692	1,720	1,789	1,203	6,404
	6.10	6.20	6.45	4.34	23.10
Obstructively Engaged	17	169	200	475	861
	.06	.61	.72	1.71	3.11
Total	6,837	7,087	7,363	6,434	27,721
	24.66	25.27	26.56	23.21	100.00
	Social Partners				
Supportive of Independence	44	60	42	26	172
	.89	1.21	.85	.53	3.48
Supportive of Dependence	212	216	165	157	750
	4.29	4.37	3.34	3.18	15.18
Supportive of Engagement	677	559	391	214	1,841
	13.70	11.31	7.91	4.33	37.25
No Response	488	500	462	376	1,826
	9.87	10.12	9.85	7.61	36.95
Leaving	78	94	101	81	354
	1.58	1.90	2.04	1.64	7.16
Total	1,499	1,429	1,161	854	4,943
	30.33	28.91	23.49	17.29	100.00

NOTE: Sequential lag analyses consider only those resident behaviors that occur in the presence of social partners.

of 27,721 behavioral instances of residents' behaviors is recorded. Of this total behavior pool 5,231 (19%) represent independent personal maintenance and 834 (3%) involve dependent personal maintenance behaviors; 6,404 (23%) are constructively engaged; 861 (3%) are obstructively engaged behaviors; 14,391 (52%) represent nonengaged behaviors.

To test these data for statistical significance, a four by five factorial analysis of variance was used with length of institutionalization and behavior category as independent factors. The results show a main effect for behavior category, $F (4, 124) = 79.34, p < .001; \omega^2 = .64$; no main effect for length of institutionalization, $F (3, 31) = 1.21, p = .324$; and no interaction effect, $F (12, 124) = .64, p = .802$. Using a posteriori t tests, we find nonengaged behavior to be significantly more frequent than all the other four behaviors; constructively engaged behavior and independent personal maintenance were significantly more frequent than the remaining two, obstructively engaged and dependent personal maintenance behaviors. When the data were subjected to a nonparametric analysis (Kruskal-Wallis), the same results were obtained.

Behaviors of Social Partners

A total of 4,943 behaviors of social partners were recorded across all three occasions and 40 residents. Of these observations, approximately 50% refer to staff and approximately 35% to fellow residents interacting with a focal resident; about 10% of the observations refer to resident-visitor or resident-volunteer worker interactions; the remaining 5% refer to resident-group interactions.

Table 38.1 shows the frequency of behaviors of social partners per group and behavior category. Here, too, a four by five analysis of variance was performed. The results show a significant main effect for behavior category, $F (4, 124) = 27.62, p = .001, \omega^2 = .37$; no main effect for length of institutionalization, $F (3, 31) = 1.96, p = .141$; and no interaction effect, $F (12, 124) = 1.12, p = .350$. A posteriori t test results show no response and engagement-supportive behaviors as significantly more frequent than the remaining three behaviors of the social partners; in addition, behavior supportive of dependent personal maintenance was significantly more frequent than the remaining two behaviors (i.e., leaving and supportive of independent personal maintenance behavior).

Interactional Sequences of Behavior Patterns

The next step in the analysis involved the examination of social interactions by means of computation of sequential conditional probabilities linking the behavior of elderly residents to their social partners. The analysis is sequential because it deals with the temporal order of residents-and partner-related events. It is conditional because it specifies the preceding events as the "if" condition for which the probability of differing subsequent events is examined. The target events in this study are all elderly residents' behaviors since we want to ascertain the social contingencies succeeding their occurrence. For these target or criterion events statistically significant deviations of the conditional probability from the base probability of a consequent event are identified. The conditional probabilities are computed for behavioral events removed one, two, three, etc., units (lags) from the criterion behavior. Such computation of lags provides a representation of the time-extended order of events following the criterion behavior. (For a more detailed description of the statistical procedure see Barton et al., 1980.) The statistical program LAGS (Sackett, 1977; Sackett et al., 1979) served as the data-analytical framework. Significance testing has been corrected in the computer program according to Allison and Liker's (1982) suggestion.

Sequential lag analyses were computed per group, per occasion, per group across occasions, and across groups and occasions. Sequential behavior patterns looked nearly identical. We will, therefore, restrict our discussion to the overall sequential lag analyses (lag 1 and lag 2 data are shown in Table 38.2; the reader who is interested in the entire sequential data should contact the first author). Graphical representations of sequential patterns are given only when the criterion resident behavior shows a significant effect on behaviors of the social partner.

Criterion: Residents' Dependent Personal
Maintenance Behavior

Residents' dependent behavior in the presence of social partners has a base probability of .03. Note first that this base rate is quite low. It is, for example, lower than that for resident's independent personal maintenance behavior (.16).

Two consequent events depart from their base probability (with $p < .05$): dependence-supportive behavior by social partners and residents' dependent

Table 38.2. Base and Conditional Probabilities for All Consequent Behaviors at Lag 1 and Lag 2 Separately for Each Resident Behavior as Criterion Behavior

Consequent behaviors	Criterion behaviors					
	Construc-tively engaged	Indepen-dent personal mainte-nance	Depen-dent personal mainte-nance	Non-engaged	Obstruc-tively engaged	Base probabili-ties
			LAG 1			
Resident						
Constructively Engaged	.50[a]	.12	.08	.03	.05	.19
Independent Personal Maintenance	.07	.63[a]	.02	.02	.04	.16
Dependent Personal Maintenance	.00	.00	.11[a]	.00	.01	.03
Nonengaged	.06	.06	.02	.84[a]	.21	.44
Obstructively Engaged	.01	.01	.02	.01	.57[a]	.03
Social Partners						
Supportive of Engagement	.23[a]	.05	.10[a]	.01	.03	.06
Supportive of Dependent Personal Maintenance	.02	.02	.48[a]	.01	.02	.03
No Response	.09	.08	.08	.07	.07	.06
			LAG 2			
Resident						
Constructively Engaged	.64[a]	.15	.13	.04	.06	.19
Independent Personal Maintenance	.10	.62[a]	.06	.03	.05	.16
Dependent Personal Maintenance	.02	.02	.39[a]	.01	.02	.03
Nonengaged	.10	.10	.09	.86[a]	.21	.44
Obstructively Engaged	.01	.01	.01	.01	.59[a]	.03
Social Partners						
Supportive of Engagement	.07	.05	.08	.01	.02	.06
Supportive of Dependent Personal Maintenance	.01	.01	.12[a]	.01	.02	.03
No Response	.04	.03	.07	.03	.03	.06

NOTE: Two behaviors of social partners (supportive of independent personal maintenance and leaving) are not included; their conditional probability never exceeded .03. Statistical significance is indicated only for those conditional probabilities exceeding .10. [a] $p \leq .05$

Criterion Behavior: Constructively Engaged

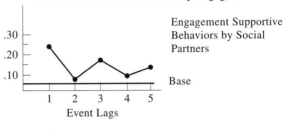

Criterion Behavior: Dependent Personal Maintenance

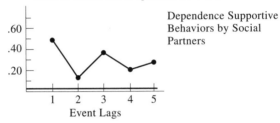

Figure 38.1. Lagged conditional probabilities (lag 1 to 5) for two consequent behaviors (engagement supportive behaviors by social partners and dependence supportive behaviors by social partners) given resident behaviors as antecedent event (constructively engaged behavior and dependent personal maintenance behavior respectively). Straight lines represent base probabilities of each of the consequent events.

personal maintenance behavior. Thus, the occurrence of dependent personal maintenance behaviors by residents has an effect on what behaviors social partners display. This effect is particularly obvious at lag 1, when the conditional probability for the social partners' dependence-supportive behavior is .48 compared with its base rate of .02. There continues to be a statistically significant elevation in dependence-supportive behavior at all lags, with conditional probabilities ranging from .12 to .34 (see Figure 38.1, lower part). The criterion behavior itself, dependent personal maintenance behavior, is elevated also in the temporal flow subsequent to its occurrence, namely at lags 2 and 4 (.40 and .32).

Criterion: Residents' Independent Personal Maintenance Behavior

Residents' independent personal maintenance behavior in the presence of others has a base probability of .16. The most frequent consequent event (p <.05) is a continuation of the residents' independent personal maintenance behaviors, showing conditional probabilities in the .50s and .60s. Independence-supportive behavior by social partners (base probability = .01) is in no way affected by the antecedent criterion behavior of resident's independence. Even the consequent probability of a diverging social behavior (i.e., dependence-supportive behavior) is neither reduced nor enhanced when elderly residents exhibit independent personal maintenance.

Criterion: Residents' Constructively Engaged Behavior

For this criterion behavior, there are again two significantly increased behavior consequences: the behavior itself and engagement-supportive behavior by the social partner. For all five lags the conditional probabilities for residents' constructively engaged behavior following a previous instance of itself are significantly (p <.05) increased and range from .50 at lag 1 to .64 at lag 2 and remain in the .50s for the subsequent three lags. Engagement-supportive behavior by others (base probability = .06) shows conditional probabilities (p <.05) following resident constructively engaged behaviors ranging from a high of .23 at lag 1 to a low of .07 at lag 2. This outcome is another case for a convergence between the residents' and their social partners' action sequence (see Figure 38.1, upper part).

Criterion: Residents' Obstructively Engaged Behavior

Note first that such behavior has a very low base probability (.03). The consequent behavior flow shows the behavior itself (i.e., obstructively engaged behavior) to be the most frequent (p <.05) follow-up behavior for all lags, accounting for 60% of all behavioral consequences. Non-engaged behavior is the second most likely consequence at all lags, despite the fact that the conditional probabilities which range in the .20s, are lower than the base probability of .44. As to social consequences or behaviors of the social partners, the criterion behavior does not appear to affect the action of social partners.

Criterion: Residents' Nonengaged Behavior

Here again only one consequent behavior shows an increase beyond its base probability. Nonengaged behavior itself is the most frequent ($p < .05$), almost exclusive event following an instance of residents' nonengaged behavior. Residents' nonengaged behavior in the presence of others has a base probability of .44. Its conditional probability following a previous instance of itself rises above .80 for all five lags. Nonengaged behaviors by elderly residents, then, do not lead to a particular set of actions or reactions of social partners.

Additional Interactional Analyses

Three additional lag analyses were performed. First, event lags were determined under the condition that the criterion behavior could not be followed by itself at lag 1; that is, only behavior offsets were identified as criterion behaviors. The interaction patterns of (a) continuous external support for dependent, (b) intermittent external support for constructively engaged, and (c) no external support for independent personal maintenance, obstructively engaged, and nonengaged behavior remain the same as for the analyses reported above.

Second and third, when attempting to identify possible effects of organismic variables such as sex and care status of residents, we find quantitative differences in level of behavior but only minor differences in interactional patterns. These differences, however, are based on relatively small samples and tentative statistical methodology and are less than impressive. The central finding is one of similarity in interactional patterns.

DISCUSSION

The focus of the present study is on sequential behavior interactions between elderly nursing home residents and their social environment. A more complete picture of both residents' as well as their social partners' behaviors in the nursing home context has been gained by the extension of the behavior code and of observations across all times of the day and social partners other than staff. In general, relevant findings are in agreement with previous observations (Baltes et al., 1980; Barton et al., 1980; Lester & Baltes, 1978), although they suggest further specification.

Behavior Frequencies

In terms of behavior frequencies, the first major finding of this replication and extension study is one of much similarity and robustness. Additional times of day, varying length of institutionalization, increased numbers of behavior categories, as well as occasions of measurement and types of social partners did not alter the basic picture gained in previous studies. We still find a relatively independent elderly resident (18% independent personal maintenance plus 24% constructively engaged behaviors) who, however, is frequently nonengaged (52%). We still find a social ecology, even though extended beyond staff, that shows more supportive behaviors of dependent personal maintenance (15%) than of independent personal maintenance (4 %) and a fair amount of no response (37%). In addition, though, we find evidence for independence support by social partners namely in form of behaviors supportive of constructive engagement (37%).

As to occasion of measurement, we find no significant differences between occasions in the four groups. Furthermore, the longitudinal stability of residents' behaviors appears to be high across the 6-months interval. This fact might be due to the time interval being too short to demonstrate behavior changes. Nevertheless, such an effect would have been expected in group 1, given the frequent statement in the literature that major changes in residents take place during the first half year after institutionalization. Considering, however, that the four groups did not differ in mean age, range of age, nor health status, the lack of institutionalization effect becomes more understandable. The variation in length of institutionalization was cross-sectional. Thus, the samples may very well have been affected by selective survival or selective mortality. Only long-term longitudinal follow-ups can provide adequate information on the effect of institutionalization. Until then, we are impressed with the robustness of the present findings.

Elderly Resident–Social Partner Interactions

When looking at the interaction patterns between elderly residents and their social partners it is important to note that here, too, the extension features did not alter the basic outcome but helped to differentiate the basic interaction patterns found in our previous studies. Independent personal maintenance behaviors of residents continue to find no reactions from the social ecology, even if social partners other than staff are considered. A newly defined category of independence, constructively engaged behavior, does receive inter-mittent support from social partners. A resident who is involved in prosocial behaviors not only continues to be so but intermittently experiences positive attention from social partners for such behavior. This discrepant finding for the two independence-related behaviors suggests that they function differently in terms of setting the stage (stimulus control) for social interaction. It appears important to maintain such a differentiation in the observational code in fu-ture work.

Dependent personal maintenance behavior is followed consistently by de-pendence-supportive behaviors from social partners. Dependent behaviors ob-viously act as prompts for social partners to behave in a congruent fashion, namely supportive of dependence. In contrast, when residents exhibit nonen-gaged behaviors there is no reaction (supportive or disruptive) from the social ecology. For whatever reasons, nonengaged behaviors appear to possess no direct information for action by others. As is true for the case of independ-ence, it appears necessary to differentiate between these two types of de-pendence-related behaviors (i.e., dependent personal maintenance and nonengagement); they exhibit different social interaction patterns that need explication in future work.

In summary, the present findings corroborate earlier data on the discrepant social ecologies for independent and dependent behavior of the elderly resi-dent. The extension of the social ecology to include social partners other than staff did not alter the interactional patterns. A congruent interaction pattern for dependent behavior remains. For independent personal maintenance be-haviors, contingencies from social partners can still not be observed. Our data show, however, that these independent behaviors are clustered in chains. Chaining (an operant term) as a vehicle to maintain independent personal maintenance behaviors seems most plausible. Unfortunately, our data do not allow us to discern different events within the same behavior category a posteriori. We do not know whether a clustering means a continuation of the same independent behavior or whether the cluster consists of a chain of dif-ferent independent acts.

The extension of two types of categories of dependence-and independence-related behaviors proved useful. The present findings show that neither do-main is a single homogeneous class. With respect to independence, the present findings allow us to differentiate interactional patterns related to in-dependent personal maintenance from constructively and obstructively en-gaged behaviors. The difference between the positive social contingencies (for independent-constructive behaviors) and zero contingency (for independent personal maintenance behaviors) is important from an ecological viewpoint. This differential social reaction seems to speak to expected role-behavior congruencies of residents and staff in institutions (Goffman, 1960). With respect to dependence, a differentiation between patterns related to dependent and nonengaged behaviors seems necessary.

In addition to the general need for differentiation, the present findings on the interactional patterns surrounding dependent personal maintenance behaviors by residents suggest the need to differentiate between dependency (as defined here) and learned helplessness as described by Seligman (1975). Learned helplessness is the product of objective or subjective noncontingency. The regularity of specific and systematic social consequences upon dependent behaviors and the lack thereof upon independent behaviors seen in the present nursing home study determine a situation contrary to that apt to produce learned helplessness. The finding is one of contingency, not one of noncontingency.

Our description of dependency is also different from Rodin and Langer's (1977) discussion of lack of control. Rodin and Langer (1977) and Langer (1979), using a cognitive approach, have argued that real or expected experiences of physical deficiencies and of social prejudices lead the elderly person to perceive lack of control over his/her environment which, in turn, leads to dependency in the sense of learned helplessness. We would argue that our data suggest that dependent behaviors, even if resulting from loss of control, can be instrumental. If dependency is followed by a systematic contingency, a person engaging in dependent behavior will set the occasion for that contingency to occur and, therefore, will control the environment. It appears necessary to gain a clearer understanding of the differences between types of dependent and independent behaviors and their consequences, before we label a dependent elderly person as helpless or out of control (Baltes & Skinner, 1983).

REFERENCES

Allison, P. D. & Liker, J. K. Analyzing sequential categorical data on dyadic interaction: A comment on Gottman. Psychological Bulletin, 1982, 91, 393–403.

Baltes, M. M. Environmental factors in dependency among nursing home residents: A social ecology analysis. In T. A. Wills (Ed.), Basic processes in helping relationships. Academic Press, New York, 1982.

Baltes, M. M., Burgess, R. L. & Stewart, R. B. Independence and dependence in self-care behaviors in nursing home residents: An operant observational study. International Journal of Behavioral Development, 1980, 3, 489–500.

Baltes, M. M. & Skinner, E. H. *Cognitive performance deficits and hospitalization: Learned helplessness, instrumental passivity, or what?* Journal of Personality and Social Psychology, *1983.*

Barton, E. M., Baltes, M. M. & Orzech, M. J. *On the etiology of dependence in older nursing home residents during morning care: The role of staff behavior.* Journal of Personality and Social Psychology, *1980, 38, 423–431.*

Exton-Smith, A. N. & Evans, J. G. (Eds.) Care of the elderly: Meeting the challenge of dependency. *Academic Press, New York, 1977.*

Goffman, E. *Characteristics of total institutions. In M. R. Stein, A. J. Violich & D. M. White (Eds.),* Identity and anxiety: Survival of the person in mass society. *Free Press, Glencoe, IL, 1960.*

Kalish, R. A. (Ed.). The dependencies of old people. *Institute of Gerontology, University of Michigan, Ann Arbor, MI, 1969.*

Langer, E. J. *The illusion of incompetence. In L. C. Perlmuter & R. A. Monty (Eds.),* Choice and perceived control. *Erlbaum, Hillsdale, NJ, 1979.*

Langer, E. J. & Rodin, J. *The effects of choice and enhanced personal responsibility for the aged: A field experiment in an institutional setting.* Journal of Personality and Social Psychology, *1976, 34, 191–198.*

Lehr, U. Psychologie des Alterns. *Quelle & Meyer, Heidelberg, Germany, 1977.*

Lester, P. B. & Baltes, M. M. *Functional interdependence of the social environment and the behavior of the institutionalized aged.* Journal of Gerontological Nursing, *1978, 4, 23–32.*

Maccoby, E. E. & Masters, J. C. *Attachment and dependence. In P. H. Mussen (Ed.),* Carmichael's manual of child psychology *(Vol. 2). Wiley, New York, 1970.*

Rodin, J. & Langer, E. F. *Long-term effects of a control-relevant intervention with the institutionalized aged.* Journal of Personality and Social Psychology, *1977, 35, 897–902.*

Sackett, G. T. *The lag sequential analysis of contingency and cyclicity in behavioral interaction research. In J. Osofski (ED.),* Handbook of infant development. *Wiley, New York, 1977.*

Sackett, G. T., Holm, R., Crowley, C. & Henkins, A. *Computer technology: A Fortran program for lag sequential analysis of contingency and cyclicity in behavioral interaction data.* Behavior Research Methods and Instrumentation, *1979, 11, 366–378.*

Seligman, M. W. P. *Helplessness: On depression, development and death. Freeman, San Francisco, CA, 1975.*

Stephens, M. A. P. & Willems, E. P. *Everyday behavior of older persons in institutional housing: Some implications for design. In A. D. Seidel & S. Danford (Eds.),* Environmental design: Research, theory, and application. *Buffalo, NY, 1979.*

39. The Mental Life of Dying Geriatric Patients

Robert Kastenbaum

Not much is known about the psychological aspects of the dying process in aged men and women. We lack systematic descriptions of even the most obvious aspects of the process, nor have we been favored with an abundance of adequate research strategies and conceptualizations. Absence of satisfactory data, methodology, and concepts severely limits the ability of the social sciences to contribute to the welfare of those who are aged and dying and, of course, it also severely limits our ability to construct general theoretical models of the individual from birth to death.

This brief paper considers a few aspects of the mental life of dying geriatric patients. The basic aim is to help prepare the way for investigations whose methods and concepts will do more justice to the significance of the subject matter.

BACKGROUND

As part of a research and training project, efforts are being made to investigate the psychosocial aspects of dying and death in hospitalized geriatric patients. The project is affiliated with Cushing Hospital, Framingham, Massachusetts. This accredited hospital, operated by the Commonwealth of Massachusetts, is devoted exclusively to the care of men and women over the age of 65. The average census in recent years has been 640 patients. The age of the population has gradually increased to its present level, which is a mean age of 83 years. All patients are voluntary admissions.

Medical, nursing, and dental services are supplemented by departments of occupational therapy, psychology, and social service. The hospital has many aspects of a self-contained community, operating its own food, laundry, recreational, library, fire, and police services. Nevertheless, Cushing Hospital pursues an active "open door" policy, encouraging many levels of interchange with the surrounding communities.

From *The Gerontologist* 7, no. 2 (June 1967): 97–100. Reprinted with permission of the Gerontological Society of America.

EXPERIMENTAL PROBLEM

This portion of the total study attempts to describe the mental life of dying geriatric patients as perceived by the staff members who were in most intimate contact with them. Attention is limited to three general variables: mental status, explicit death references, and social visibility. By "social visibility" is meant the degree to which a patient became well-known to hospital personnel.

It is sometimes assumed that aged and dying patients are usually in poor mental contact prior to death. There seems to be more difference of opinion concerning the aged dying person's orientation toward his own death, particularly as to the presence or absence of strong negative affect (Kastenbaum & Aisenberg, in press). Since these opinions obviously have implications for treatment of the dying, it seems important to gather empirical information. As we are concerned here with the mental life of dying geriatric patients perceived through the eyes of staff members, it seemed relevant to inquire also into the nature of the relationship between staff and patients, thus the inclusion of a "social visibility" variable. It is important to emphasize that the investigation reported here is still in progress and that it is just one of several approaches being employed in an attempt to gain an adequate picture of human behavior and experience in the later years of life with special reference to dying and death.

PROCEDURE: THE PSYCHOLOGICAL AUTOPSY

The material reported here derives from the first 61 cases in the psychological autopsy series. Each week a multi-disciplinary team gives detailed consideration to the case of a recently deceased patient. These sessions are intended to provide clues for more specific research projects, practical suggestions that might be used for the benefit of present and future patients, and an opportunity for the sharing of experiences and ideas by personnel who otherwise function within the bounds of their respective disciplines. Preliminary gathering of information and supplementary interviews are carried out by project personnel. Participants include psychologists, physicians, nursing personnel, social workers, chaplains, occupational therapists, and other persons who may have something to contribute on a particular case. Proceedings are tape-recorded and abstracted. A psychiatric consultant (Avery D. Weisman, M.D.) comments upon each case and prepares his independent summary. More detailed information on the psychological autopsy procedure has been presented elsewhere (Kastenbaum & Weisman, 1966).

SUBJECTS

The present sample includes 31 men with a mean age at death of 82.8 years and 30 women with a mean age at death of 81.7 years. Most patients had been married (men: 87%; women: 83%), but those whose spouses were still alive at the time of their death were in the minority (men: 29%; women 3%). Only one woman was survived by her husband, while nine men were survived by their wives. The median length of stay at Cushing Hospital was 25 months for the men and 26 months for the women.

RESULTS

Mental Status

The mental status of each patient was classified into one of four categories after consideration of all available information:

     I. Consistently in clear contact until death.
    II. Fluctuating between clear contact and confusion.
   III. Consistently in partial contact.
   IV. Consistently our of contact.

While these categories represent the patient's mental status in the last months, weeks, and days of his life, it was not uncommon for a person to lapse into a brief comatose period immediately before death. In the case of two men it was considered that we did not have sufficient information available to categorize mental status.

The results suggest that almost all the dying geriatric patients in this sample had retained some ability to observe and interpret their situation (Table 39.1). Approximately half of the total sample (49%) was rated as having been consistently in clear contact, with the other half almost equally divided between those who were in and out of contact (26%) and those who were consistently in partial contact (22%). Only two patients were consistently out of contact during the last days of life. These findings obviously lend no credence to the assumption that massive cognitive impairment is the typical status of the aged dying person.

Table 39.1. Mental Status

	Alert consistently	Alert/confused fluctuations	Partial contact	Confused consistently	N
Men	15	6	7	1	29[a]
Women	14	9	6	1	30
Total	29	15	13	2	59[a]

[a] Insufficient information for rating of two men.

The age-span encompassed by this sample was from 69 to 96 years. Thus there seemed to be a large enough range to indicate whether or not increasing age within the geriatric category is associated with deceased mental status. No such relationship was found in this study.

References to Death

Having established that most dying patients were perceived as retaining some degree of mental alertness, we then reviewed all reports of references to death that they had made. It should be kept in mind that "false negatives" are much more likely to occur than are "false positives." We cannot establish that a patient never referred to death, nor can we establish that we have learned all that he did say on the subject. Only a complete transcript of every patient's every utterance would permit definitive conclusions to be drawn. Even here we have limited the present analysis merely to direct statements concerning death, recognizing that many other statements refer indirectly to death.

Explicit death references were made by 57% of the patients, according to available reports (Table 39.2). There was a slight tendency for women to speak more frequently of death, but this difference was not significant.

Accepting attitudes toward one's own death were heard more frequently

Table 39.2. Death References

	No. patients for whom death references were reported			
	Positive	Negative	Neutral	Total
Men	7	1	7	15
Women	14	2	4	20
Total	21	3	11	35

than negative or rejecting attitudes. Only three patients expressed fear, alarm, or other negative affects. The other 21 patients expressed attitudes ranging from a calm waiting for death to a strong wish for an end to their suffering.

Within the limits of the present data, then, it would seem that relatively few dying geriatric patients express direct negative statements concerning their own death, in comparison with those who express an attitude of acceptance. Yet the fact remains that approximately three-fifths of the total sample either did not converse on the subject, or their comments were not reported by staff members.

No relationship was found between the age of the patient at death and either the probability of his making an explicit statement concerning death or the type of statement made. Furthermore, there was no relationship between death statements and the length of time the patient had been a resident of Cushing Hospital.

Social Visibility

An attempt was made to determine the "social visibility" of each patient prior to his terminal phase. "Social visibility" does not seem to be a personal characteristic of the patient in the same sense as his mental status or death verbalizations; rather, it is the result of his transactions with those around him. Within the limits of the available information we cannot say how much of a patient's "social visibility" was based upon his own behavior, and how much upon the perceptions of hospital personnel, but it is upon these perceptions that the ratings were made. It should be noted that even mental status and death verbalizations are known to us only through the perceptions and recollections of staff members; thus, all the variables are best regarded as interpersonal constructions rather than entities that reside strictly within the patient or the staff member.

Based upon all available information, each patient was rated as either relatively well known or relatively unknown to the hospital staff. Doubtful cases were credited as "socially visible"; only a gross lack of information and affect concerning the patient provided the basis for classification as relatively unknown. Evidence of a strong relationship with even one staff member was sufficient to classify the patient as socially visible.

Slightly less than half the patients were classified as "socially visible" (44%), with no appreciable sex difference in this respect (Table 39.3). There was also no systematic relationship to chronological age.

An additional rating was made for those patients who seemed to be so-

Table 39.3. Social Visibility

	Not well known	Socially liked	Visibly disliked	Patients neutral	Mixed	Total visible
Men	16	9	0	4	2	15
Women	18	6	1	2	3	12
Total	34	15	1	6	5	27

cially visible. The quality of staff attitudes was categorized by content analysis of all statements made by personnel either during the psychological autopsies proper, or in supplementary interviews. Patients were classified as being either liked, disliked, liked by some and disliked by others, or eliciting only indifferent or neutral comments. The findings may be biased by the taboo against disliking any patient, and the belief that one not only should treat all patients alike but should have no differential feelings. Slightly more than half the "visible" patients seemed to be well liked by the staff members who knew them (57%), while only one patient was generally disliked. The remaining patients were almost equally divided between those about whom the staff had no emotionally tinged statements to make or had divided opinions.

Interrelationships

As already noted, mental status, death references, and social visibility were not related systematically to age or length of residence in Cushing Hospital. Except for a slight, nonsignificant tendency for women to speak more frequently of death, no sex differences were found for this set of variables.

Among the three major variables only one clear relationship emerged. Patients who were consistently alert proved to be more socially visible than patients who had any degree of mental impairment ($p=0.01$, χ^2 8.36 with 1 d.f.).

There was the hint of another relationship although the number of cases involved is too small for meaningful statistical analysis. There were five patients in the total sample toward whom the staff had mixed attitudes—some personnel liking and some disliking the patient. All these patients gave positive references to death, and all were in consistently good mental contact. Thus, patients toward whom the staff had mixed feelings constituted only

8% of the total sample, but 24% of those who gave positive references to the prospect of their own death.

DISCUSSION

It is sometimes assumed that most aged patients are in poor mental contact as they are dying. The present findings do not support this assumption. There have been conflicting opinions as to whether or not aged persons, dying persons, or persons both aged and dying have strong fears of death. Relatively few negative statements about one's personal death were heard from this sample of dying aged persons; in fact, there was a 7:1 ratio in favor of positive statements.

The most obvious criticism of these findings is that they lack true objectivity. The information presented here was derived in large part from reports of staff members who were performing direct services to the patients and not engaged in the systematic collection of research data. This criticism appears to be supported by the relationship obtained between mental status and social visibility, although no strong relationship was found between death references and social visibility.

However, the focus of this study is upon dying as an interpersonal phenomenon. Certainly it is important to establish as best we can the level and content of the dying person's mental life from an objective standpoint. But the treatment the patient receives is associated more directly with how his mental life is perceived by those charged with his care. The very fact that staff members are not disinterested observers and are not making aloof scientific ratings gives a particular kind of significance to their reports. They do not solicit death statements, nor have they any vested interest in theories of aging and death. Eventually we hope to supplement information gathered by these means with more standardized or "objective" techniques—but there is no compelling reason to believe that the "truth" resides in either of these approaches taken separately. Theoretically, we would expect that an integration of material gathered from a more or less detached perspective and from an engrossment in daily care would provide the most useful picture (Kastenbaum, 1966).

One of the most direct implications of the present findings is that more attention should be given to the psychosocial care of dying geriatric patients. The fact that almost all patients were perceived as retaining a fairly high quality of mental functioning argues against treatment programs designed solely to meet physical needs. This is not the place to offer detailed suggestions, but one might simply mention the desirability of reconsidering the usual scheduling of duties for ward personnel to provide more opportunity to converse with patients, of providing training experiences to ward personnel with special reference to the interpersonal aspects of dying, and to establishing a ward milieu that is not wholly medical in character.

Among the unsolved questions in this study one might call particular attention to the almost complete absence of negative comments concerning personal death. Taking the results at face value, we would have to say that geriatric patients seldom are worried or depressed about the prospect of their own death per se (which is quite different than their attitudes toward the progressive discomfort and debility of dying). But it is also possible that negative feelings were experienced but not expressed, perhaps because of an interpersonal atmosphere that discourages death verbalizations (e.g., Kastenbaum, 1964; in press). Or it could be the case that negative statements were made, but selectively forgotten by the staff members. Subsequent research should help us to determine which of these alternatives has the most factual support.

SUMMARY

Analysis of psychological autopsy findings for 61 geriatric patients failed to support the assumption that most aged persons are in poor mental contact as they are dying. Positive (accepting or longing-for) references to one's own death were heard much more frequently than negative (fear, depression) references. Those patients who were in the best mental contact also tended to be most "socially visible" to hospital personnel. Implications of the study were briefly discussed.

REFERENCES

Kastenbaum, R. The interpersonal context of death in a geriatric institution. *Presented at 17th annual meeting, the Gerontological Society, Minneapolis, 1964.*

Kastenbaum, R. Developmental-field theory and the aged person's inner experience. Gerontologist, *6: 10–13, 1966.*

Kastenbaum, R. Multiple perspectives on a geriatric "Death Valley." Comm. Mental Health J., *in press.*

Kastenbaum, R. & R. B. Aisenberg. The psychology of death. *Springer, N.Y., in press.*

Kastenbaum, R. & A. D. Weisman. The psychological autopsy as a research method in gerontology. *Presented at 19th annual meeting, the Gerontological Society, New York, 1966. To be published in D. P. Kent, R. Kastenbaum, & S. Sherwood (Ed.),* Research, planning and social action for the elderly: The power and potential of the social sciences. *Columbia University Press, N.Y., in press.*

Index

Page numbers followed by *f* refer to figures; page numbers followed by *t* refer to tabular material.

Absurdities, detection of, age and, 140
Accuracy, signal-to-noise ratio and, 345–346
Acquiescence, on Older Persons' Scale, 545–546
Activation hypothesis, 20
Active ego style, 76, 77t
Activities, organized, and adjustment to residential change, 640–641
Activity level
  and affect, 82–84
  high, and role re-engagement, 59–60
  in nursing home visits study, 563–564, 564t
Activity theory, 68, 511
  engagement in, 72
Adaptation, social engagement and, 450t–452t, 450–453
ADEPT Letter Series Test, 688
Adjective Mood Checklist, 671
Adolescent development, historical events and, 106
Affect
  and activity level, 82–84
  anticipated, in social partners study, 520, 523, 533
  disengagement and, 82–84
  in institutionalized elders, 745t, 750t
  positive *vs.* negative, personality correlates of, 466
  regarding role activity, 79, 80t, 81, 81t
Affect Balance Scale, 464
  temperamental traits and, 469–470, 470t–471t
African-American elderly
  demographic trends among, 589, 590t, 591, 601
  employment among, 593
  environmental stressors among, 597–598
  health status of, 595, 600–602
  heterogeneity of, 593–594
  longevity of, 592

  multiple jeopardy hypothesis and, 592
  political behavior of, 590t, 594
  racial group identity among, 590t, 594
  social supports of, 590t, 598–599
African-Americans
  family structure among, 595–596
  health status of, 595, 600–602
  infant mortality among, 592
  living arrangements among, 597
Age. *See also under* specific variables
  corrections for, on memory test scores, 145–148, 146t–147t
  differences in, and developmental change, 32–33, 42–46
Age identification, and adjustment to residential change, 641
Aging
  ambivalence toward, and responses on Older Persons' Scale, 545–546
  gain-loss dynamic in, 96–101, 98f, 99t
  "hardware" *vs.* "software" changes in, 354–355
  and loss of control, 550
Aging men, ego states of, 431
Albumin, in Alzheimer's patients' caregivers, 710–711
Algebra, maintenance of knowledge in, 304t–312t, 304–313, 306f-313f. *See also* Mathematics, knowledge maintenance of
Alloplastic mastery, 431
Alpha intelligence test. *See* Army Alpha intelligence test
Alphanumeric Rotation measure, 688
Alzheimer's disease, natural history of, 705
Alzheimer's patients' caregivers
  demographic data in, 711t, 711–712
  immunity in, 704–718
    assays of, 708–710
    health status and, 714–715
    residence of patient and, 715–716